Gelitten Gestorben Auferstanden

Passions- und Ostertraditionen im antiken Christentum

Herausgegeben von

Tobias Nicklas, Andreas Merkt und Joseph Verheyden

Mohr Siebeck

Tobias Nicklas ist Ordinarius für Exegese und Hermeneutik des Neuen Testaments an der Universität Regensburg.

Andreas Merkt ist Ordinarius für Historische Theologie (Alte Kirchengeschichte und Patristik) an der Universität Regensburg.

Joseph Verheyden ist Professor für Neues Testament an der Katholischen Universität Leuven, Belgien.

ISBN 978-3-16-150233-0
ISSN 0340-9570 (Wissenschaftliche Untersuchungen zum Neuen Testament, 2. Reihe)

Die Deutsche Nationalbibliothek verzeichnet diese Publikation in der Deutschen Nationalbibliographie; detaillierte bibliographische Daten sind im Internet über *http://dnb.d-nb.de* abrufbar.

Das Buch wurde von Gulde-Druck in Tübingen auf alterungsbeständiges Werkdruckpapier gedruckt und von der Buchbinderei Held in Rottenburg gebunden.

Wissenschaftliche Untersuchungen zum Neuen Testament · 2. Reihe

Herausgeber / Editor
Jörg Frey (München)

Mitherausgeber / Associate Editors
Friedrich Avemarie (Marburg)
Markus Bockmuehl (Oxford)
Hans-Josef Klauck (Chicago, IL)

273

Vorwort

Passion und Auferstehung Jesu von Nazaret dürfen in keinem christlichen Glaubensbekenntnis fehlen. Die ältesten Zeugnisse, die wir darüber besitzen, finden sich im Neuen Testament: Nicht nur die Evangelien erzählen ausführlich von Jesu Leiden, seiner Kreuzigung und Auferstehung bzw. Himmelfahrt, auch Paulus beschreibt Christus immer als den Gekreuzigten und Auferweckten und entwickelt von diesem Zentrum aus entscheidende Linien seiner Theologie.

Der vorliegende Band aber stellt nicht die übliche Frage nach den Wurzeln des christlichen Bekenntnisses zum gekreuzigten und auferweckten Jesus von Nazaret, der als Christus und Sohn Gottes verstanden wird, sondern interessiert sich für die unterschiedlichen Richtungen, in die sich dieser Glaube und die damit verbundenen Textwelten, Vorstellungen und Ideen weiterentwickelt haben.

Die hier gesammelten Beiträge gehen in ihrem Kern auf zwei Tagungen zurück: ein Seminar der Arbeitsgruppe „Christian Apocrypha" auf der Jahrestagung der *Society of Biblical Literatur*e (SBL) in San Diego, Kalifornien, im November 2007 und ein Treffen der Projektgruppe des „Novum Testamentum Patristicum" (NTP) auf der „International Conference on Patristic Studies" im August 2007 in Oxford. Für die Veröffentlichung und zur Abrundung des Bandes wurden weitere Autoren angefragt.

Als Herausgeber sind wir allen beteiligten Autoren für ihre Mitarbeit, aber auch ihre Geduld bis zur Entstehung des Bandes zu Dank verpflichtet. Zu erwähnen ist auch das Organisationskommittee der SBL-„Christian Apocrypha Group", allen voran Prof. Dr. Francois Bovon und Prof. Dr. Ann Graham Brock, die das erste der beiden Treffen, in dem apokryphe Texte im Vordergrund standen, möglich gemacht haben.

Wir danken Prof. Dr. Jörg Frey für die Aufnahme dieser Sammlung in die renommierte Reihe „Wissenschaftliche Untersuchungen zum Neuen Testament" sowie den Mitarbeiterinnen und Mitarbeitern des Verlags Mohr Siebeck, vor allem natürlich Herrn Dr. Henning Ziebritzki, für die freundliche und unkomplizierte Weise der Zusammenarbeit.

Ohne Frau Dr. Michaela Hallermayer, wissenschaftliche Mitarbeiterin am Lehrstuhl für Historische Theologie (Alte Kirchengeschichte und Patrologie) der Universität Regensburg, die für alle Formatierungen und die Hauptarbeit bei der Erstellung des Registers verantwortlich zeichnete, wäre die Herausgabe dieses Bandes sicherlich nicht möglich gewesen. Ihr gilt unser herzlicher Dank!

Als Herausgeber des *Novum Testamentum Patristicum* (NTP) denken wir hier auch an zwei Gründerväter dieses Projekts. Am 8. August 2007 ist Gerhard May im Alter von 66 Jahren verstorben. Seine früh einsetzende Krankheit hinderte ihn an der Verwirklichung vieler Pläne, darunter auch die Erstellung des NTP-Bandes zum Epheserbrief. Die Mitglieder der NTP-Gruppe schätzten vor allem seine kommunikative, ruhige und freundliche Art, die er mit einem breitem Fachwissen verband. Keine neun Monate später, am 25. April 2008, ist auch Basil Studer OSB, kurz vor seinem 83. Geburtstag, verstorben. Er hat die patristische Welt und insbesondere die Autoren des NTP durch seine profunden Kenntnisse bereichert. Trotz seines nimmermüden Arbeitseifers konnte er den NTP-Band zu den Johannesbriefen nicht mehr vollenden. Die Herausgeber wie auch die Autoren und Autorinnen des NTP werden beiden ein ehrendes und dankbares Andenken bewahren.

Regensburg und Leuven im Oktober 2009

Tobias Nicklas, Andreas Merkt und Joseph Verheyden

Inhaltsverzeichnis

Passion and Martyrdom Traditions in the Apocryphal Acts of the Apostles

István Czachesz

Only few of the Apocryphal Acts of the Apostles contain an extended report of the passion and resurrection of Jesus. Whereas the texts imply knowledge of the death and resurrection of Jesus by the reader, most of them provide only summaries of these traditions, or references to them – apart from the passion narrative in the *Gospel of the Acts of John*.[1] In this article I will argue that, notwithstanding the scarcity of reports about Jesus' passion and resurrection in the Apocryphal Acts of the Apostles, these books contain a wealth of relevant material that helps us in the study of passion and resurrection traditions. I will particularly elaborate on the hypothesis, suggested in a former publication,[2] that the passion and resurrection narratives as well as the martyrdom of the apostles (in the Apocryphal Acts) derive from the same narrative tradition and should be regarded as variants of the same basic story. (1) In the first part of the article, I will describe a cognitive psychological model that provides the methodological scenario against which we will interpret our sources. (2) In the second part of my contribution, I will provide arguments for the hypothesis that the passion and resurrection narratives about Jesus, on the one hand, and the martyrdom narratives about the apostles, on the other hand, originate from a common martyrdom script, rather than the martyrdom stories imitating Jesus' death and resurrection. (3) In the third part, I will briefly examine the death of the martyrs in the *Gospel of Mark* and the major Apocryphal Acts of the Apostles from the perspective of the proposed theory.

---

[1] *Acts of John* 87–105. For the interpretation of this section as a gospel, see I. Czachesz, "The Gospel of Peter and the Apocryphal Acts of the Apostles: Using Cognitive Science to Reconstruct Gospel Traditions," in *Das Evangelium nach Petrus* (ed. T. Nicklas and Th.J. Kraus; TU 158; Berlin and New York 2007), 245–261 at 245–247; id., *Commission Narratives: A Comparative Study of the Canonical and Apocryphal Acts* (Studies in Early Christian Apocrypha; Leuven and Dudley 2007), 102–106; id., "The *Gospel of the Acts of John*: Its Relation to the Fourth Gospel," in *Legacy of John: Second Century Reception of the Fourth Gospel* (ed. T. Rasimus; Leiden and Boston 2009), in press.

[2] I. Czachesz, "Gospel of Peter," (n. 1) 261.

1. The transmission of stories: a cognitive psychological model

The model of narrative transmission that we will be using in this article has been outlined in some former publications.[3] In the transmission of early Christian traditions, memory has played a significant role. This has been recognized first by form criticism, and more recently by authors embracing orality studies.[4] It would be a mistake, however, to regard early Christianity as a purely oral culture,[5] or to reduce the examination of the role of memory to oral transmission alone.[6] The nature of ancient literacy was such that memory played a significant role in all aspects of it. Ancients habitually read aloud, had texts read to them by slaves, or listened to public readings.[7] Owning books had the significant function of signalling social and intellectual status, and reading was mostly a social activity: typically, books were read and discussed in bookstores or at dinners and symposia held in private homes.[8] When listening to a text and subsequently discussing it with a group of peers, people encountered literature as an oral/aural rather than as a visual event. In a Jewish context, in addition to bookstores and private homes, synagogues and study-houses (*bātê-midrash*) provided

---

[3] I. Czachesz, "The Gospels and Cognitive Science," in *Learned Antiquity: Scholarship and Society in the Near East, the Greco-Roman World, and the Early Medieval West* (ed. A.A. MacDonald et al.; Groningen Studies in Cultural Change 5; Leuven 2003), 25–36; id., "The Transmission of Early Christian Thought: Toward a Cognitive Psychological Model," *SR* 36 (2007), 65-84; id., "Rewriting and Textual Fluidity in Antiquity: Exploring the Sociocultural and Psychological Context of Earliest Christian Literacy," in *Myths, Martyrs, and Modernity: Studies in the History of Religions in Honour of Jan N. Bremmer* (ed. J.H.F. Dijkstra et al.; Leiden and Boston 2009), in press.

[4] E.g. W.H. Kelber, *The Oral and the Written Gospel: Hermeneutics of Speaking and Writing in the Synoptic Tradition, Mark, Paul and Q* (Philadelphia 1983); J.D.G. Dunn, *Jesus Remembered* (Grand Rapids and Cambridge 2003); J.A. Draper (ed.), *Orality, Literacy, and Colonialism in Antiquity* (Leiden and Boston 2004); R.K. McIver and M. Carroll, "Distinguishing Characteristics of Orally Transmitted Material when Compared to Material Transmitted by Literary Means," *Applied Cognitive Psychology* 18 (2004), 1251–1269; A. Kirk and T. Thatcher, *Memory, Tradition, and Text: Uses of the Past in Early Christianity* (Atlanta 2005); R.A. Horsley et al. (ed.), *Performing the Gospel: Orality, Memory, and Mark. Essays Dedicated to Werner Kelber* (Minneapolis 2006).

[5] R. Uro, "Thomas and Oral Tradition," in *Thomas at the Crossroads* (ed. id.; Edinburgh et al. 1998), 8–32; R. Uro, *Thomas: Seeking the Historical Context of the Gospel of Thomas* (London and New York 2003), 106–133; Czachesz, "Transmission" (n. 3), 67.

[6] Czachesz, "Rewriting" (n. 3).

[7] W.A. Johnson, "Toward a Sociology of Reading in Classical Antiquity," *The American Journal of Philology* 121 (2000), 593–627; R.J. Starr, "The Circulation of Literary Texts in the Roman World," *The Classical Quarterly* 37 (1987), 213–223.

[8] E. Rawson, *Intellectual Life in the Late Roman Republic* (London 1985), 52; Starr, "Circulation" (n. 7), 223; Johnson, "Sociology of Reading " (n. 7), 612–615.

opportunities for intellectual exchange about religious literature.[9] When people discuss about texts in our days, participants often have printed copies or photocopies before them. In antiquity, participants in such discussions had to maintain a memory of the text to be able to talk about it, as well as they had to cite other relevant literature by heart rather than looking them up in their Bibles, for example. Authoring texts also involved memory to a great extent. The use of written sources was constrained in several ways. First, books were written continuously (*scriptio continua*), without punctuation or word division, thus providing no visual aids that would aid the eye in finding particular passages. Second, the scroll format was less then optimal for jumping across different parts of a book to find a passage or compare different passages. Third, ancients did not use desks on which they could have laid out scrolls (or later codices), which would have enabled them to use multiple sources critically (in a modern sense) when writing a new text.[10] Again, relying on memory or having slaves to read out sources aloud (which again involved the use of memory) could provide solutions to overcome such difficulties. For the study of the transmission of early Christian traditions it is therefore imperative to understand how we retain texts in memory and how we retrieve them when we want to retell them or use them in a discussion or while writing a book.

Most studies that considered the use of memory in ancient culture so far have concentrated on techniques to expand the limitations of memory. Both rhetoricians and rabbis had special ways to increase the span and accuracy of their memories.[11] Yet this is by far not the only way we can look at memory in the context of literary transmission. Only a minority of the literate members of ancient society (and of people involved in textual transmission in general) were rhetoricians or rabbis. Moreover, how memory works relies largely on cognitive structures that influence remembering in experts and laypersons, modern and ancient alike. In this contribution I will only deal with the transmission of narrative materials, which is particularly relevant to the study of passion, resurrection, and martyrdom narratives.

In Frederic Bartlett's famous experiment, Cambridge students had to recall a North American folktale, the "War of the Ghosts."[12] These experiments, and similar others, led Bartlett to the idea that our memory makes

---

[9] C. Hezser, *Jewish Literacy in Roman Palestine* (TSAJ; Tübingen 2001), 101–103.

[10] F.G. Downing, "A Paradigm Perplex: Luke, Matthew and Mark," *NTS* 38 (1992), 15–36.

[11] E.g. Quintilian, *Institutio oratoria* 11.2; J. Bowker, *The Targums and Rabbinic Literature: An Introduction to Jewish Interpretations of Scripture* (Cambridge 1969), 40–90.

[12] F. Bartlett, *Remembering: A Study in Experimental & Social Psychology* (Cambridge 1932).

use of mental *schemas*; he defined "schema" as "an active organization of past reactions, or of past experiences."[13] New information that does not fit into our mental schemas, will be either changed so that it matches them, or will be forgotten. The story of the "War of the Ghosts" underwent substantial changes both when the same subjects had to recall it at various time intervals, as well as in the experiment in which the story was transmitted from one subject to another in a chain-like fashion. In the latter case, however, the changes were such that the resulting stories "would hardly ever be connected with the original by any person who had no access to some intermediate version."[14] More importantly, however, the alterations in the texts showed regularities, to which we will immediately return.

A model of how narrative schemas function in remembering has been suggested by Roger C. Schank and Robert P. Abelson.[15] Their primary focus was on understanding how we accumulate knowledge in everyday life. "Some episodes," they argued, "are reminiscent of others. As an economy measure in the storage of episodes, when enough of them are alike they are remembered in terms of a standardized generalized episode which we call a script."[16] A *script* functions then as "a set of expectations about what will happen next in a well-understood situation."[17] When we receive sufficient amount of information that is related to a given script, the script is evoked (instantiated).[18] Scripts make clear what is going to happen in a given situation and what acts of various participants indicate.[19] They provide a memory structure, serving as a storehouse of old experiences in terms of which new experience can be encoded into memory; thinking means finding the most appropriate script to use. Finally, new information can modify the script.[20] A famous example is the restaurant script: 1) *actor* goes to *restaurant*; 2) *actor* is seated; 3) *actor* orders *meal* from *waiter*; 4) *waiter* brings *meal* to *actor*; 5) *actor* eats *meal*; 6) *actor* gives money to *waiter*; 7) *actor* leaves *restaurant*. Entering a restaurant, but also other information that contains a reference to an element of a restaurant visit, evokes the script; we will then have no difficulty, for example, finding out how to get

---

[13] Ibid., 201.

[14] Ibid., 171.

[15] R.C. Schank and R.P. Abelson, *Scripts, Plans, Goals, and Understanding: An Inquiry into Human Knowledge Structures* (Hillsdale, N.J., and New York 1977); id., "Knowledge and Memory: The Real Story," in *Knowledge and Memory: The Real Story* (ed. R.S. Wyer et al; Advances in Social Cognition 8; Hillsdale, N.J. 1995), 1–85.

[16] Schank and Abelson, *Scripts, Plans, Goals* (n. 15), 10, 16–19.

[17] Schank and Abelson, "Knowledge and Memory" (n. 15), 5.

[18] Schank and Abelson, *Scripts, Plans, Goals* (n. 15), 46–50, describe very precise rules for the application of scripts.

[19] Schank and Abelson, "Knowledge and Memory" (n. 15), 5.

[20] Ibid., 6.

food from the waiter or understanding why someone paid in the end. We prefer to avoid having to revise our scripts, because even minor changes in our memories might require us to reconfigure many other parts of our knowledge, involving "effortful cognitive operations."[21] As a consequence, we tend to preserve our scripts and accommodate new information to them, rather than the other way around, which falls in line nicely with Bartlett's empirical observations about the function of schemas in remembering.

Schank and Abelson also recognize the significance of storytelling as the context of remembering.[22] We recall memories as stories, which we usually tell in a particular social setting.[23] While telling and retelling a story, however, we always adapt it to cultural norms, in order to create a coherent narrative. Since nothing in life occurs as a culturally coherent story, in practice we always "lie" when we recall past events. Bartlett as well as Schank and Abelson pay attention to the social context of remembering. Whereas they observe that stories tend to get more and more condensed during subsequent repetitions, they also recognize that this is not necessarily true in all settings.[24] Bartlett particularly refers to the social stimulus that is underlying oral performance,[25] a factor that has been frequently referred to in orality studies.[26] Schank and Abelson write about "embellishments" that consist of fictional details added to the story as it is performed repeatedly.[27] That is, whereas the original details of the event tend to be compressed or forgotten, new details are being added. One has to remark that there is a difference between the "War of the Ghosts" and some other material used by Bartlett, on the one hand, and the events (such as a restaurant visit) that are in the focus of Schank and Abelson's interest. The former type of material had been selected for its unfamiliar (Native American) cultural character and became adapted in transmission to mental schemas related to another (British) culture: the process that took place here was transformation from one schema to another. The latter type of material (a restaurant script) comes from first-hand experience and is stored immediately as culturally familiar or relevant information in memory.

How memories are stored was the main interest of Bartlett as well as of Schank and Abelson. David Rubin, in turn, proposed a new explanation

---

21 Ibid., 17.

22 Ibid., 33–34.

23 Ibid., 41–49.

24 Bartlett, *Remembering* (n. 12), 175; Schank and Abelson, "Knowledge and Memory" (n. 15), 36–37.

25 Bartlett, *Remembering* (n. 12), 174.

26 A.B. Lord, *The Singer of Tales* (Cambridge, MA 1960); M. and A. Parry, *The Making of Homeric Verse: The Collected Papers of Milman Parry* (Oxford 1971).

27 Schank and Abelson, "Knowledge and Memory" (n. 15), 35–36.

regarding the cognitive mechanisms that underlie the *recall* of oral tradition.[28] Rubin's theory takes its departure from the observation that the structure of oral tradition is sequential, that is, in an oral composition "[o]ne word follows another as the physical effects of the first word are lost."[29] Unlike the reader of a text, the singer and listeners of an oral composition do not have simultaneous access to words or phrases in a text, except when they follow each other immediately. Oral traditions are therefore "recalled serially, from beginning to end," in a process that Rubin calls *serial recall*.[30] The mechanism by which this occurs is *cuing*. The cues that make serial recall possible consist of various constraints, by which a word or phrase limits the choice of the next word or phrase in such a way that results in a sufficiently close reproduction of the text (cue-item discriminability). Constraints include imagery, theme, rhyme, alliteration, rhythm, and music. At the beginning of the song, genre-specific constraints provide initial cues. The "singer" starts out with an initial word or phrase, rhythm, or melody, and follows the various constraints, often implicit and subconscious ones, to produce the next word, phrase, or line, until the end of the text is reached. Rubin puts particular emphasis on the local nature of cuing, as opposed to relying on an overall schema or theme. He quotes interesting examples of how particular details of a text are accessible even to experts only after a "running start." For example, an exorcist on Sri Lanka, when asked to give information on a particular demon, suggested the following procedure: "I will sing it and you tell me when the demon you want has his name mentioned. Then I will go slow so that you can put it onto tape recorder."[31]

The mechanism of serial recall seems to be at odds with the various schema models, which explain memory with reference to global rather than local organizing principles. The contradiction, however, disappears if we think about the different settings that are presupposed by these models. As mentioned before, memories usually tend to become more and more concise and adapt to existing mental schemas. However, when a social setting of oral performance is presupposed, texts tend to become increasingly longer, by performers adding new details and embellishments to them. In the course of repeated performances, or as the text is learned and performed by other singers, the development of the tradition will heavily depend, in addition to script-like schemas, on the constraints that make serial recall possible. The best way to understand the transmission of narratives is there-

[28] D.C. Rubin, *Memory in Oral Traditions: The Cognitive Psychology of Epic, Ballads, and Counting-Out Rhymes* (New York 1995).

[29] Ibid., 175.

[30] Ibid., 175–179.

[31] Ibid., 190.

fore to regard them as scripts that are fleshed out with the help of serial recall. Identifying scripts and themes in classical texts has a long tradition in the so-called formulaic school of Homeric studies,[32] as well as in the form-critical approach to biblical texts. Finally, as Rubin observes, there is a group of texts, which he calls "sacred texts," that are supposed to be recalled verbatim.[33] When recalling the Preamble of the American Constitution or *Psalm* 23, for example, the use of synonyms, substitute words, or embellishments is not acceptable. One has to remark, however, that "sacred texts" are often recited with typical errors, which go unnoticed by the performer, and sometimes even by the listeners, probably because they fulfil the various constraints – even if they change the *meaning* of the text.

Schemas (scripts), cuing mechanisms, and the social setting of recall can be thought of as constraints, which provide us with criteria to understand (and predict) in which ways memories and traditions change over time. Some of these factors are culturally shaped and determined; others, such as scripts for interpreting personal experience, can be influenced by individual differences. There is yet another group of constraints that is especially relevant for understanding the formation of repeatedly transmitted texts, ideas, and beliefs, undergoing a process of repeated reproduction.

Experimental work conducted since the 1970s has demonstrated that humans cross-culturally share a number of ontological categories to make sense of their environment, including the categories of HUMAN, ANIMAL, PLANT, ARTIFACT, and (natural) OBJECT.[34] In this case, by ontological categories we do not mean an articulated, let alone philosophical, categorization of the world. Ontological categories are implicit, intuitive notions about "clusters of properties that unambiguously and uniquely belong to all members of a given category at that level." For example, "[a]ll animals are alive, have offspring, and grow in ways that only animals do."[35] In other words, people have particular expectations toward things belonging to a particular category. Based on Keil's works on ontological

---

[32] Ibid., 210–220; E. Minchin, *Homer and the Resources of Memory: Some Applications of Cognitive Theory to the Iliad and the Odyssey* (Oxford and New York 2001).

[33] Rubin, *Memory in Oral Traditions* (n. 28), 181.

[34] F.C. Keil, *Semantic and Conceptual Development: An Ontological Perspective* (Cambridge, MA 1979), 48; S. Atran, "Basic Conceptual Domains," *Mind & Language* 4 (1989), 7–16; idem, *In Gods we Trust: The Evolutionary Landscape of Religion* (Oxford and New York 2002), 98; P. Boyer, "Cognitive Constraints on Cultural Representations: Natural Ontologies and Religious Ideas," in *Mapping the Mind: Domain Specificity in Cognition and Culture* (ed. L.A. Hirschfeld and S.A. Gelman; Cambridge 1994), 400–401; id., *Religion Explained: The Evolutionary Origins of Religious Thought* (New York 2001), 90.

[35] F.C. Keil, *Concepts, Kinds, and Cognitive Development* (Cambridge, MA 1989), 214.

categories, anthropologist Pascal Boyer developed a theory of *minimal counterintuitiveness*. He proposed that ideas violating intuitive expectations about ordinary events and states, that is, ones that "combine certain schematic assumptions provided by intuitive ontologies with nonschematic ones provided by explicit cultural transmission," have a better chance to be remembered in cultural transmission than ideas not containing such violations.[36] Violations of ontological expectations, however, cannot be excessive: such concepts are difficult to remember and will not be transmitted. Boyer has particularly suggested that religious ideas are minimally counterintuitive.[37] The idea of a ghost that can go through walls, for example, is based on the ontological category of human beings, but violates our expectations about intuitive physics that should otherwise apply to humans.

Involuntary response to emotionally salient motifs in textual traditions is another factor that contributes to their selective transmission.[38] Children spontaneously imitate facial expressions and other bodily movements at a very early age, indeed, right after birth.[39] A significant contribution to understanding imitation has been the discovery of so-called *mirror neurons* in monkeys in the late 1990s.[40] These neurons are activated when monkeys observe an action in another monkey as well as when animals themselves act in such a way. In humans, as well, the observation of actions performed by others activates brain areas that are also responsible for the movement of different parts of the body.[41] There are similar findings about emotion: the same brain parts that are involved in the feeling of disgust and pain are

---

[36] P. Boyer, *The Naturalness of Religious Ideas: A Cognitive Theory of Religion* (Berkeley 1994), 48, 121, and passim.

[37] Boyer, *Religion Explained* (n. 34), 58–106; I. Pyysiäinen, *How Religion Works: Towards a New Cognitive Science of Religion* (Leiden and Boston 2001), 9–23.

[38] I. Czachesz, *The Grotesque Body in Early Christian Literature: Hell, Scatology, and Metamorphosis* (unpublished Habilitationsschrift Heidelberg 2007), 202–207; id., "Metamorphosis and Mind: Cognitive Explorations of the Grotesque in Early Christian Literature," in *Metamorphoses: Resurrection, Body and Transformative Practices in Early Christianity* (ed. T. Karlsen Seim and J. Økland; Berlin and New York 2009), 219–243.

[39] A.N. Meltzoff, "Elements of a Developmental Theory of Imitation," in *The Imitative Mind: Development, Evolution, and Brain Bases* (ed. id. and W. Prinz; Cambridge Studies in Cognitive Perceptual Development; Cambridge, U.K. and New York 2002), 19–41; S. Hurley and N. Chater, "Introduction: The Importance of Imitation," in *Perspectives on Imitation: From Neuroscience to Social Science. Volume 2. Imitation, Human Development, and Culture* (ed. S. Hurley and N. Chater; Cambridge and London 2005), 1–52.

[40] G. Rizzolatti and L. Craighero, "The Mirror-Neuron System," *Annual Review of Neuroscience* 27 (2004), 169–192.

[41] G. Rizzolatti, et al, "The Mirror System in Humans," in *Mirror Neurons and the Evolution of Brain and Language* (ed. M.I. Stamenov, et al; Amsterdam 2002), 37–59.

also activated when we empathize with such emotions.[42] Not only do we not actually have to carry out actions or be exposed to pain in order to empathize with them, but also a limited amount of information is sufficient to activate the relevant brain areas and to elicit empathy.[43] Recent experimental findings support the hypothesis that emotionally arousing details in stories enhance the memorability of the gist and details (both central and peripheral) of the narrative.[44] In sum, we can identify at least two constraints that enhance the memory of certain types of details in stories: minimal counterintuitiveness and emotional salience.

If we now put together the pieces, we arrive at the following cognitive psychological model of the transmission of narratives. When hearing a narrative, or a detail of it, an appropriate script will be activated in our minds. The story will be remembered as an instance of the respective script. Details that do not fit in with the script will be eliminated or adapted to the script. Typical tendencies that Bartlett observed during the repeated reproduction of stories include omission, abbreviation, rationalization, fluidity of proper names and titles (of stories), bias toward the concrete (at the cost of arguments or reasoning), and a loss of individual characteristics (in favour of commonplace characterizations and epithets).[45] All being equal, however, minimally counterintuitive details and emotionally salient details will stick to memory better than other details, and the latter will also create a halo of enhanced memorization for the gist of story as well as for other details. When the story is recalled, either for oral performance or for written citation, a number of cues will be used to reproduce the text based on the appropriate script. The cuing mechanisms will serve as constraints that determine what and how will be recalled and performed. Depending on the social context of communication, the story will be tailored and embellishments will be added. When the recipients hear or read the story, the constraints of memorization will come to play once again, resulting in a cycle that can be repeated at will. Bartlett also remarks that whereas texts usually change gradually in the course of repeated reproduction, in almost every series an individual version comes in at some point that results in a sudden break away from the original text. We can hypothesize that such idiosyncratic versions contribute to the homogenization of different tradi-

---

[42] C. Keysers and D.I. Perrett, "Demystifying Social Cognition: A Hebbian Perspective," *Trends in Cognitive Sciences* 8 (2004), 501–507; T. Singer et al., "Empathy for Pain Involves the Affective but Not Sensory Components of Pain," *Science* 303 (2004), 1157–1162.

[43] V. Gallese et al., "A Unifying View of the Basis of Social Cognition," *Trends in Cognitive Sciences* 8 (2004), 396–403.

[44] C. Laney et al., "Memory for Thematically Arousing Events," *Memory & Cognition* 32 (2004), 1149–1159.

[45] Bartlett, *Remembering* (n. 12), 124–129, 141–146.

tions, since they make subsequent versions less dependent on the original text and more dependent on the cognitive psychological regularities of memory and transmission.

2. Passion and Martyrdom: Common Origins?

There are evident similarities between the passion narratives of the canonical and apocryphal gospels, on the one hand, and the martyrdom narratives of the Apocryphal Acts of the Apostles, on the other hand. In most of the Apocryphal Acts, the apostle is arrested, interrogated, imprisoned, mocked, and executed, much in the same way as Jesus in the passion narratives. The apostle can even appear after his death, similarly as Jesus does in the post-resurrection episodes. How can we account for these similarities? This is the question that I try to answer in the rest of my article. According to a famous passage of the *Martyrdom of Polycarp*, the martyrs were loved "as disciples and imitators of the Lord" (ὡς μαθητὰς καὶ μιμητὰς τοῦ κυρίου).[46] Based on this and other remarks of the *Martyrdom of Polycarp*,[47] as well as other references in early Christian literature,[48] it has been frequently argued that the martyrs imitated Christ.[49] In a similar vein, the martyrdom of Stephen in the Acts of the Apostles has been interpreted as an imitation of the passion narrative.[50] What does this imply for the interpretation of the similarities between the passion narratives and the martyrdom of the apostles in the Apocryphal Acts? Were the latter written so that the apostles' martyrdom would imitate Christ's passion?

To give an answer to these questions is not as easy as it might seem. Without being able to undertake an exhausting survey of imitation in context of early Christian literature, let us only recognize some of the most relevant aspects of the subject that are helpful in examining the connection between the passion narratives and the martyrdom of the apostles. 1) First, as already A.D. Nock has noticed, the idea that the "unique attractiveness

---

[46] *M.Pol.* 17.3.

[47] *M.Pol.* 1.2.

[48] E.g. *Heb* 12.2; *Rev* 1.5, 2.13, 11,3, 17.6; *The Martyrs of Lyons* (Eusebius, *h.e.* 5.2.2).

[49] E.g. G. Constable, *Three Studies in Medieval Religious and Social Thought* (Cambridge and New York 1995), 143–248; L.L. Thompson, *The Book of Revelation: Apocalypse and Empire* (New York 1990), 189; E.S. Bolman and P. Godeau, *Monastic Visions: Wall Paintings in the Monastery of St. Antony at the Red Sea* (New Haven 2002), 54; H. Rhee, *Early Christian Literature: Christ and Culture in the Second and Third Centuries* (New York 2005), 92–96.

[50] L.T. Johnson and D.J. Harrington, *The Acts of the Apostles* (Collegeville, Minn. 1992), 110–113, 142–144.

of the central figure of Christianity" was a key to the success of the Church is an anachronistic one, guided by nineteenth century idealism and humanitarianism. In the early Christian tradition, the emphasis was on Christ's superhuman qualities: for the early Church, he was a divine saviour rather than a human being setting a pattern for a better way of life.[51] We cannot simply take it for granted, as a general rule, that the Acts of the Martyrs (or the Acts of the Apostles) put an emphasis on the "imitation of the life and death of Jesus."[52] 2) Second, the notion of "imitation" was frequently employed in antiquity in the sense of living up to certain ideals. An important function of Greek biographies was to provide models for coming generations to follow.[53] This concept is also found in Jewish literature, especially in apocryphal sources and Philo,[54] and includes the "imitation" of biblical heroes, martyrs,[55] and even the "imitation" of God.[56] In the New Testament, Paul frequently calls his readers to imitate him as well as Jesus.[57] In all of these references, the point is to take an example from an outstanding figure in living up to some standard or ideal. For instance, the example of the martyrs in *4 Maccabees* teaches the reader how passions can be controlled to endure extreme sufferings. 3) Third, commentators of the New Testament have particularly drawn on the philosophers' advice about how a disciple can learn from his master by co-habiting with him or by imitating his words and deeds.[58] Whereas such a scenario could certainly be envisaged by the authors of the Gospels in connection with Jesus and his closest circle, it is a less likely one in the context of Paul and his congregations, not to mention Paul's relation to Jesus, or the relation of the martyrs (such as Stephen or Polycarp in our examples) to Jesus. Stoic advices about assuming a philosopher's life cannot be taken as a decisive argument

---

[51] A.D. Nock, *Conversion* (New York 1933), 210.

[52] W.T. Cavanaugh, *Torture and Eucharist: Theology, Politics, and the Body of Christ* (Oxford 1998), 62.

[53] A. Dihle, *Studien zur griechischen Biographie* (Göttingen 1970), 20.

[54] Wisd 4.2; *TestXIIPatr* 12.3.1, 12.4.1 and below; cf. W. Michaelis, "Mimeomai," in *ThWNT* (ed. G. Kittel et al.; Stuttgart etc. 1942), 661–678.

[55] *4 Macc* 9.23, 13.9.

[56] *TestXIIPatr* 10.4.3, μιμεῖται κύριον.

[57] 1Cor 4.16; 11.1; Phil 3.17; 1 Thess 1.6; 2 Thess 3.7,9; cf. W.P. De Boer, *The Imitation of Paul: An Exegetical Study* (Kampen 1962); V.A. Copan, *Saint Paul as Spiritual Director: An Analysis of the Imitation of Paul with Implications and Applications to the Practice of Spiritual Direction* (Milton Keynes and Colorado Springs 2007); C. Gieschen, "Christian Identity in a Pagan Thessalonica: The Imitation of Paul's Cruciform Life," *Concordia Theological Quarterly* 72 (2008), 3–18.

[58] Seneca, *ep.* 6.5–6; Dio Chrysostom 55.4–5; cf. C.H. Talbert, *Literary Patterns, Theological Themes, and the Genre of Luke-Acts* (Missoula, Mont. 1974), 89–110; A.J. Malherbe, *Paul and the Thessalonians: The Philosophic Tradition of Pastoral Care* (Philadelphia 1987), 52–53.

about the meaning of "imitation" in our texts. 4) Fourth, the occurrence of the themes of learning by imitation or living up to ideals by imitation in a text does now allow any direct conclusion about the imitation of sources by the author, such as the biography of the imitated hero.

A quick look at some of the martyrdom narratives of the Apocryphal Acts gives further support to these observations. In *Acts of Peter* 35, in the famous *quo vadis* episode, Jesus explicitly tells Peter, "Yes, Peter, again I shall be crucified (πάλιν σταυροῦμαι)." After seeing Jesus ascending to heaven, Peter returns to Rome "rejoicing and praising the Lord because he said, 'I am being crucified'." The conclusion of the episode emphasizes once again: "This was to happen to Peter." Thus the reader of the *Acts of Peter* is explicitly instructed to understand Peter's martyrdom as an imitation of Jesus' death. In his address to the cross (ch. 37), Peter contemplates the "mystery" of the cross, on which Christ suffered. The overall design of the martyrdom narrative is similar to the plot of the passion narratives (to which we will return immediately), yet the details of the story do not imitate the passion narratives. For example, Peter wants to be crucified head downwards, does not actually suffer,[59] and delivers a lengthy sermon from the cross – however, without repeating any of Jesus' words on Golgotha. It is the fact of martyrdom through crucifixion that serves as the point of comparison, and no attempt is made to a step-by-step imitation of the passion narrative. The point will be clear if we take a look at the *Martyrdom of Polycarp*, where we can see a different narrative strategy: emphasizing imitative details. In this martyrdom text, we read comments such as "they who betrayed [Polycarp] might undergo the punishment of Judas himself" (6.2); Polycarp being carried to the city on an ass, the day being "the great Sabbath" (8.1); when he was bound he was like a "distinguished ram" (14.1); and the Jews guarded (ἐτήρησαν) the spot as Christians wanted to collect Polycarp's body, lest they would start to worship him instead of Christ (17.2; cf. *Matthew* 27.62–66; *Gospel of Peter* 29–33). To summarize our observations: whereas the *Acts of Peter* tells a story with an overall design similar to Jesus' passion, but without emphasizing imitative details, the *Martyrdom of Polycarp* employs explicit references to emphasize the imitative details in its narrative, the overall design of which is not particularly similar to the passion narratives.

A detailed analysis of all martyrdom narratives, comparing them with the passion narratives, cannot be undertaken in this article, even if we restricted the investigation to the major Apocryphal Acts. We will have to limit ourselves to examining a couple of passages in the next section. In

[59] M. Pesthy, "Cross and Death in the Apocryphal Acts of the Apostles," in *Apocryphal Acts of Peter* (ed. J.N. Bremmer; Louvain and Ithaca, NY 1998), 123–133 at 124–126.

order to gain a broad overview, however, we can first turn the results of a previous comparative study of the Apocryphal Acts and the *Gospel of Peter*.[60] This comparison revealed that besides the agreements between the martyrdom narratives of the Apocryphal Acts with the canonical passion narratives, there are a number of agreements among one or more of the Apocryphal Acts, the *Gospel of Peter*, and occasionally other sources, that are, however, not found in any of the canonical gospels. For example, Jesus and the apostles are actually *ordered* to be crucified (*Gospel of Peter* 2; *Acts of Peter* 36; *Martyrdom of Paul* 3; *Acts of Andrew* 51; *Acts of Thomas* 106), they are being "dragged" (σύρω) by the soldiers (*Gospel of Peter* 6; *Acts of Andrew* 52; *Acts of Thomas* 106; Justin, *1 Apology* 35.6), and the cross speaks or is personified (*Gospel of Peter* 41–42; *Acts of John* 98–101; *Acts of Peter* 37; *Acts of Andrew* 54; *Gospel of the Savior* in Pap. Berol. 22220; *Ethiopic Apocalypse of Peter* 1). In many other instances, one or two of the Apocryphal Acts contain parallels with the *Gospel of Peter*, whereas the others agree with another gospel narrative or with none.[61] It can be further observed that the same martyrdom narrative can sometimes agree with the *Gospel of Peter*, yet at other times with one or more of the canonical gospels. The report of the apostle's death in the *Acts of Peter* 40 and *Acts of Andrew* 63 ("handed over his spirit"), for example, agrees with the canonical gospels against the *Gospel of Peter*.

The problem with which we are faced resembles the synoptic question, but it is much more complicated, due to the involvement of the greater number of parallel texts. In the study of the synoptics, scribal transmission has been the ruling metaphor. The intertextual relations among the texts have been explained by positing authors who selectively copied, merged, and modified their sources. We have seen that such a compositional process is unlikely to have taken place under the circumstances of ancient literacy.[62] Adding the technical improbability of what we can call the "editing model" to our previous observations about the phenomenon of imitation, we can conclude that such a complex range of agreements and differences among the sources can hardly be explained with reference to the compositional technique of literary imitation. Instead, we suggest that the matrix of similarities and variations in our sources originated, to a large extent, from a different process, that is, from the effects of memorization and recall on the oral and scribal composition and transmission of the martyrdom and passion narratives.

---

[60] Czachesz, "Gospel of Peter" (n. 1).

[61] Ibid., 253–254. Add *Acts of Peter* 41 to the one but last row of the table.

[62] See also Downing, "A Paradigm Perplex" (n. 10), 15–36; McIver and Carroll, "Distinguishing Characteristics of Orally Transmitted Material" (n. 4), 1251–1269.

How did a martyrdom script emerge in early Christianity? Stories of martyrdom were well-known in both Greek and Jewish traditions. We have already mentioned that epitomizing outstanding heroes as examples for coming generations was a major motivation behind the emergence of the biographical tradition in ancient Athens. The first known representative of the genre, Plato's *Apology of Socrates*,[63] powerfully introduces its hero through narrating his martyrdom. Half a millennium later, Socrates' example decisively shaped Christian images of martyrdom.[64] In Jewish literature, at the same time, biographies mainly followed idealized patterns rather than portraying individual personalities.[65] And the ideal, it seems, was peaceful death rather than martyrdom. Even the martyrdom of a suffering prophet like Jeremiah is missing from the earliest tradition. In the Hellenistic period this situation changed. Paradoxically, it was probably under the influence of the Greek ideal that the story of the Maccabees, the emblematic figures of Jewish national pride, was coloured by the martyrdom narratives of Eleazar and the mother with seven sons.[66] The martyrdom narratives preserved in the books of the Maccabees contributed an important element to the martyrdom script, that is, oriental interest in gruesome details.[67] At the time when Christianity was emerging, the ideal of martyrdom became increasingly valued in the Roman world. Beginning with the early principate, Stoic contempt of death was famous, and accounts of Stoic martyrs circulated.[68] A particularly remarkable group of martyrdom texts is preserved in the so-called *Acta Alexandrinorum*, containing records of the processes of Alexandrian noblemen, written proba-

---

[63] Dihle, *Studien* (n. 53), 18, 19, 35, 36, etc.; P.C. Miller, *Biography in Late Antiquity: A Quest for the Holy Man* (Berkeley 1983), 7.

[64] As various scholars suggested, Acts 17 probably alludes to Socrates; see, for example, J.C. O'Neill, *The Theology of Acts in its Historical Setting* (London 1970), 160–171. Lucian, *Passing of Peregrinus* 12, reports that Christians called Peregrinus, when he was in prison, "the new Socrates." For the second and third century Fathers, see K. Döring, *Exemplum Socratis: Studien zur Sokratesnachwirkung in der kynisch-stoischen Popularphilosophie der frühen Kaiserzeit und im frühen Christentum* (Wiesbaden 1979), 143–161. For Eusebius' *Life of Origen* 6.3.7, see Miller, *Biography* (n. 63), 87.

[65] K. Baltzer, *Die Biographie der Propheten* (Neukirchen-Vluyn 1975).

[66] 2Macc 6–7; 4 Macc 5–12. Explicit references to those passages are found in *Martyrdom of Marian and James* 13.1 and *Martyrdom of Montanus and Lucius* 16.4; cf. A. Hilhorst, "Fourth Maccabees in Christian Martyrdom Texts," in *Ultima Aetas: Time, Tense, and Transience in the Ancient World. Studies in Honour of Jan den Boeft* (ed. C. Kroon and D. den Hengst; Amsterdam 2000), 107–122.

[67] For the sources of torture in early Christian imagination, see I. Czachesz, "Torture in Hell and Reality: The *Visio Pauli*," in *The Visio Pauli and the Gnostic Apocalypse of Paul* (ed. J.N. Bremmer and I. Czachesz; Studies in Early Christian Apocrypha; Leuven and Dudley, MA 2007), 130–143; Czachesz, *Grotesque Body* (n. 38), 11–34.

[68] H. Musurillo, *Acta Alexandrinorum (Acts of the Pagan Martyrs)* (Oxford 1954), 239–242.

bly between the middle of the first to end of the second century AD.[69] Whereas the Socratic, stoic, and cynic martyr ideal probably inspired formative Christianity, a direct influence of the *Acta Alexandrinorum* on the earliest Christian martyrdom narratives is unlikely.[70] In sum, the Christian martyrdom script united elements from two different traditions. On the one hand, it incorporated the Greek emphasis on Socratic wisdom during the trial, including a testimony or farewell speech; on the other hand, it inherited from the Maccabean tradition a detailed description of ordeals and death.

In the earliest Christian martyrdom narratives, particularly in Jesus' passion and the martyrdom of the apostles, we can identify the following *martyrdom script*: 1. arrest; 2. imprisonment and tortures; 3. reaction of the martyr's companions; 4. significant words of the martyr; 5. conviction; 6. way to the place of execution; 7. last words of the martyr; 8. death; 9. miraculous signs; 10. reaction of friends and enemies; 11. resurrection; 12. appearances. Although this presentation of the martyrdom script resembles the way form criticism describes the "forms" of tradition that belong to particular situations of life (*Sitze im Leben*), or the way "themes" are presented in the oral formulaic school, a script should be understood not so much as a standard set of motifs but rather as a bundle of cultural expectations that are learned by exposure to different kinds of texts, experiences, and social exchange. For example, we can think about the restaurant script as a convenient parallel: it is derived from a large number of bits and pieces, including restaurant visits of all sorts as well as novels, movies scenes, anecdotes, etc. Although we cannot pursue this issue in more detail in this contribution, we remark that the task of locating the origins of the Christian martyrdom script will have to involve the analysis of social locations where Greek (Socratic, stoic, cynic) and Jewish (Maccabean, prophetic) martyrdom traditions could merge, such as in Jewish elite circles with Greek literate education.[71]

The last two elements of the script, resurrection and appearances, deserve special attention. In a cognitive psychological study of early Christian ideas about Jesus' resurrection,[72] I have argued that passion stories containing accounts of the resurrected Jesus have been more successful in the transmission than passion stories without such episodes, due to their minimally counterintuitive details (see above). This seems to contradict the suggestion that resurrection and appearances after death were parts of a

---

[69] Ibid., 83–232.

[70] Cf. ibid. v, 244, 262; K. Berger, "Hellenistische Gattungen im Neuen Testament," in *ANRW II* 25, 2 (1984), 1031–1432, 1250–1251.

[71] Cf. Czachesz, "Rewriting" (n. 3).

[72] Id., "Early Christian Views on Jesus' Resurrection: Toward a Cognitive Psychological Interpretation," *NedThT* 61 (2007), 47–59.

standard Christian martyrdom script. One can solve this contradiction in two ways. First, resurrection and appearances after death could develop in each narrative individually, due to their minimally counterintuitive features. Second, we can alternatively hypothesize that due to their memorable features, these elements became integrated in the martyrdom script at an early stage, and it was this longer martyrdom script that served as a template for the transmission of the passion of Jesus and the martyrdom of the apostles.

Instead of using the concept of imitation, we can now rely on the martyrdom script as a key factor in explaining the relation of the martyrdom narratives of the Apocryphal Acts to the passion narratives. According to this alternative explanation, a narrative script of martyrdom, derived from Jewish and Greek tradition, determined how earliest Christianity transmitted the passion narratives and the martyrdom traditions about the apostles. This (rather than the concept of imitation) explains the similarities in the overall design of the narratives. During the early phase of transmission, which was probably dominated by orality, the tradition was shaped by the memory constrains that have been outlined in the previous section, changing the stories over time and producing different versions. Influences among different stories developed gradually, especially after the texts had been disseminated in a broader social and geographical circle. This accounts for the (verbatim) agreements in minor details. A quick look at the historical timeframe supports the viability of such a solution. Since the first written gospels cannot be dated much earlier than 70 CE,[73] the circulation of narratives about the death of Paul (and Peter), traditionally set under Nero, could predate the written gospels.[74] Other early martyrdom traditions include the Stephen story (in *Acts* 6.8–8.1) and the death of James (brother of John, in *Acts* 12.1–3). Even after written gospels existed, it took time until they started to circulate broadly, and martyrdom traditions could develop without direct contact with them. Also some Apocryphal Acts (particularly the *Acts of Paul*) could very well be written before

[73] Attempts at establishing substantially earlier dates, such as by J.G. Crossley, *The Date of Mark's Gospel: Insight from the Law in Earliest Christianity* (London and New York 2004), remain highly controversial. For a balanced overview, see F. Horn, "Einleitung in das Neue Testament: Tendenzen und Entwicklungen. I," *ThR* 68 (2003), 45–79; F. Horn, "Einleitung in das Neue Testament: Tendenzen und Entwicklungen. II," *ThR* 68 (2003), 129–150.

[74] The martyrdom of Peter and Paul is reported first in 1 Clem 5. Cf. H. Löhr, "Zur Paulus-Notiz in 1 Clem 5,5–7," in *Das Ende des Paulus* (ed. F.W. Horn et al., BZNW 112; Berlin and New York 2001), 212–213; U. Schnelle, *Paulus: Leben und Denken* (Berlin and New York 2003), 425–431.

some of the (canonical) gospels.[75] Finally, as we have seen, the memory effects continued to influence transmission significantly in the phase of written transmission and secondary orality.

3. The Death of the Martyr

In the last section of my contribution I will make a few observations about an important part of the martyrdom script, that is, the death of the martyr and the events immediately surrounding it: 7. last words of the martyr; 8. death; 9. miraculous signs; 10. reaction of friends and enemies.[76] The texts with which I will deal include the relevant section of the *Gospel of Mark* (15.33–39) and four of the major Apocryphal Acts: *Martyrdom of Paul* 5; *Acts of Peter* 38–40; *Acts of Andrew* 54–64; and *Acts of Thomas* 167–168 (in the *Acts of John* the apostle dies a peaceful death). A quick look at the five passages reveals that they substantially differ with regard to their length and details. The most concise and straightforward account is found in Paul's *Martyrdom*:

> 7 And turning toward the east, Paul lifted up his hands to heaven and prayed at length; and after having conversed in Hebrew with the fathers during prayer 8 he bent his neck, without speaking any more. When the executioner cut off his head 9 milk splashed on the tunic of the soldier. 10 And the soldier and all who stood near by were astonished at this sight and glorified God who had thus honoured Paul. And they went away and reported everything to Caesar (trans. J.K. Elliott).

The narrative as it stands is probably the result of a chain of repeated reproduction, which favours brevity and concreteness. For example, the conciseness of the report about the last words of Paul becomes obvious if we compare it with Andrew's last words (*Acts of Andrew* 63) or Thomas' prayer (*Acts of Thomas* 167), which include a great number of mythological and theological details. Andrew's last words are also preceded by a long sermon told from the cross for "three days and three nights" (ch. 59), and Peter speaks at length, as well, while hanging head downwards (*Acts of Peter* 38–39). These long sermons are almost certainly written compositions that at some point were combined with the oral sources.

The text of the *Gospel of Mark* contains verbatim quotations of Jesus' last words, yet it does not include a lengthy address that would indicate the inclusion of a written composition. Jesus' words "why have you forsaken me" add an emotional detail to the story and suggest true suffering, con-

---

[75] See e.g. A. Hilhorst, "Tertullian on the Acts of Paul," in *The Apocryphal Acts of Paul and Thecla* (ed. J.N. Bremmer; Studies on the Apocryphal Acts of the Apostles; Kampen 1996), 150–163 for an early dating of the *Acts of Paul*.

[76] I retain the numbering of the elements of the martyrdom script (see above).

trary to the martyrdom of the apostles, from which any reference to the human experience of suffering is absent.[77] Above we have seen that such emotionally laden details are important tools for the memorization of narratives, enhancing the memorability of both the particular motif as well as the memorability of the whole narrative and its details. Other emotionally laden details of the execution of Jesus, such as the mocking by the soldiers, probably had similar effects on the course of oral transmission and contributed to the richness of details in this part of the gospel narratives. As a consequence, the whole episode of Jesus' death probably retained the characteristics of the oral tradition.

Miraculous signs at the death of the martyr are found in some of our texts (*Mark*, *Acts of Paul*), but not in all of them. In the passion narrative, the death of Jesus is introduced by the three-hour darkness on "the whole land" (or on "the whole earth") and immediately followed by the tearing apart of the curtain of the temple. In the *Martyrdom of Paul*, milk splashes out of the neck of the apostle after he is beheaded. No miraculous signs are reported at the death of Peter, Andrew, and Thomas – if we do not count the miracle that Andrew was talking for three days and nights from the cross. Such details are attention grabbing and therefore unlikely to disappear from the narrative once they had been introduced.[78] This prompts the question of whether miraculous signs at the martyr's death are parts of the martyrdom script or were only included occasionally in the narratives. To formulate the question differently, we are asking whether such miracles formed part of the cultural expectations in terms of which the first Christians remembered Jesus and the martyrs or only gradually developed in transmission, due to their memorable features. The gradual accumulation of miraculous details can be observed in other martyrdom stories, such as in different versions of the martyrdom of Justin.[79] Stephen's martyrdom provides an interesting case: here the martyr sees "the heavens opened and the Son of Man standing at the right hand of God" (*Acts* 7.56), which is, however, not a sign in the sense of being a divine vindication of the hero in front of his executors – as it is not seen by anyone else than Stephen, in contrast to the signs at Jesus' and Paul's deaths. It is also difficult to decide about the counterintuitive nature of some of these signs. We can call them counterintuitive in a technical sense only if they violate cross-culturally held expectations about ontological categories. Complete darkness during the day is arguable contrary to very basic intuitions about the cycle of nature. However, the splitting of a drapery and the simultaneous

---

[77] M. Pesthy, "Cross and Death" (n. 59), 124–126.

[78] This might also provide an argument against the dependence of the Lukan passion on the Markan narrative.

[79] Cf. A. Hilhorst, "The Apocryphal Acts as Martyrdom Texts: The Case of the Acts of Andrew," in *Apocryphal Acts of John* (Kampen and Ithaca, NY 1995), 1–14.

occurrence of such an event with Jesus' death is unexpected, yet not strictly speaking counterintuitive. Milk flowing forth from a human's blood vessels is probably counterintuitive, since we have deeply rooted intuitions about the human body, to which the appearance of blood certainly belongs. In addition to the counterintuitive nature of the signs, also their context determines how stable they are in transmission. This might explain that in some contexts (for example when an event is interpreted as a sign) even surprising motifs that are not technically speaking counterintuitive can be consistently retained.[80]

Finally, let us consider an example of how stylistic constrains serving as cues for serial recall can be identified in texts. We can observe that the death of the martyr in the gospels, the Apocryphal Acts, and the Acts of the Martyrs is usually expressed by phrases meaning "gave up his spirit," such as ἐξέπνευσεν, ἀπέπνευσεν, ἀφῆκεν / παρέδωκεν / ἀπέδωκεν τὸ πνεῦμα).[81] When the speaker arrives at this detail, he knows that a phrase with "spirit" is appropriate in this context, but the actual formulation is influenced by a number of other cues, including the rhythmic structure of the preceding words. For example, *Mark* 15.37 contains an almost perfect Iambic trimeter:

(ὁ δὲ 'Ιησοῦς) ἀφεὶς φωνὴν μεγάλην ἐξέπνευσεν.
- - v - | - - v v - | v - - -

Furthermore, Mark cannot use ἀφίημι in connection with "spirit", as does *Matthew* 27.50, because he has already used it in the phrase ἀφεὶς φωνήν. The parallel text of *John* 19.30 has alliteration at this place: κλίνας τὴν κεφαλὴν παρέδωκεν τὸ πνεῦμα ("Then he bowed his head and gave up his spirit").

4. Conclusion

In this article I have put forward the hypothesis that passion and martyrdom narratives in early Christian tradition made use of a common narrative schema, called the *martyrdom script*, which stemmed from both Jewish and Greek cultural traditions. We have shown that the concept of imitation is not sufficient to explain the kinds of similarities and differences that exist among the passion and martyrdom traditions. The use of a common

[80] It has to be noted that the theory of counterintuitiveness predicts that such ideas enjoy an advantage in transmission *all else being equal* – therefore the contextual effects mentioned do not influence the validity of the theory itself.

[81] E.g. *Martyrdom of Saint Carpus* 47; *Martyrdom of Pionius* 21.9; *Martyrdom of St. Conon* 6.5. For comparing the Apocryphal Acts with the Acts of the Martyrs, see Hilhorst, "The Apocryphal Acts as Martyrdom Texts" (n. 79).

script, in contrast, explains the similarities in the overall structure of the narratives. The stories received their present form due to the memory effects constraining repeated reproduction and serial recall, as well as to the salience of concepts with counterintuitive and emotionally laden features. Whereas oral transmission is especially responsible for the shaping of the texts by these mechanisms, the memory effects continued to influence transmission significantly in the phase of written transmission and secondary orality. Observations about the death of Jesus and the apostles illustrated how various features of the texts can be understood against this scenario.

Dream Magic: The Dream of Pilate's Wife and the Accusation of Magic in the *Acts of Pilate*[1]

DEREK S. DODSON

Among the canonical Gospels, only the Gospel of Matthew makes reference to Pilate's wife. In the context of the Matthean passion narrative, the reference reads: "While [Pilate] was sitting on the judgment seat, his wife sent [word] to him saying, '[Let there be] nothing between you and that innocent man, for today I have suffered greatly in a dream on account of him' (καθημένου δὲ αὐτοῦ ἐπὶ τοῦ βήματος ἀπέστειλεν πρὸς αὐτὸν ἡ γυνὴ αὐτοῦ λέγουσα· μηδὲν σοὶ καὶ τῷ δικαίῳ ἐκείνῳ πολλὰ γὰρ ἔπαθον σήμερον κατ' ὄναρ δι' αὐτόν – 27:29)." This comment about Pilate's wife and her dream introduces a certain interpretive ambiguity. Neither the dream itself, nor its meaning are narrated.[2] The dream of Pilate's wife is mentioned as part of her message to Pilate, which is given in direct discourse and simply contains her response to or experience of the dream. The reader is only given the perspective and understanding of Pilate's wife; there is no comment or explanation from an omniscient narrator as to the meaning or purpose of the dream. Questions, then, arise as to the nature or content of her dream, and what is being emphasized.[3] This ambiguity is

---

[1] This essay originated from a paper presented at the Society of Biblical Literature annual meeting in San Diego, California, Nov. 19, 2007, for the Christian Apocrypha group.

[2] In regard to this interpretative ambiguity of Pilate's wife's dream, the dreams of Matt 1–2 (1:18b–25; 2:12, 13–15, 19–21, 22) are quite different. Either the dreams are narrated (1:18b–25; 2:13–15, 19–21), and thus their meaning is "self-evident", or the significance of the dreams are noted by the narrator (2:12, 22).

[3] This interpretative ambiguity is exhibited by the different interpretations offered by modern commentators. W.D. Davies and D.C. Allison, *The Gospel According to Matthew 3* (ICC; Edinburgh 1997), 587, suggests that she suffers because of some concern that an innocent man might be found guilty. J. Nolland, *The Gospel of Matthew* (NIGTC; Grand Rapids 2005), 1172, and J. Gnilka, *Das Matthäusevangelium* 2 (HTKNT 1; Freiburg i. Br. [2]1992), 456, suggest that her suffering is related, not to the execution of an innocent man, but to some sense of self-interest. M. Frenschkowski, "Traum und Traumdeutung im Matthäusevangelium: Einige Beobachtungen," *JAC* 41 (1998), 34, interprets the dream as a nightmare, portending some catastrophe or revealing the displeasure of the divine. W. Carter, *Pontius Pilate: Portraits of a Roman Governor* (Collegeville, Minn.

reflected in the reception of Matthew's Gospel, which variously attributes the origin of Pilate's wife's dream either to God or to the devil.[4] For example, John Chrysostom interprets the dream as a sign from God intended to dissuade Pilate against executing Jesus.[5] On the other hand, pseudo-Ignatius credits Pilate's wife's dream to the devil in order to thwart the event of the cross and thus his own destruction.[6] But in the *Acts of Pilate*, the Jewish leaders attribute the source of Pilate's wife's dream to none other than Jesus. My primary purpose in this essay is to explicate the ancient context that connects the Jewish leaders' allegation that Jesus is responsible for the dream of Pilate's wife with their accusation that Jesus is a magician. A corollary purpose is to consider the rhetoric of magic and its role in the characterization of the Jewish leaders.

1. The Accusation of Magic

The *Acts of Pilate* exhibits several apologetic concerns that early Christianity found itself having to address.[7] One of these concerns is the accusation that Jesus practiced magic, a charge that came from both pagan and Jewish opponents. For example, Justin Martyr suggests that Jewish charges of magic were present during the ministry of Jesus: "But though they saw such works [i.e., miracles], they asserted it was magical art. For they dared to call [Jesus] a magician (μάγον) and a deceiver of the people (λαοπλάνον)."[8] In his apology to Celsus, Origen has to respond to the allegation that Jesus' miracles were performed "by help of magic," which Jesus supposedly learned during his childhood in Egypt.[9]

The tradition of this polemic is reflected in the *Acts of Pilate*. In an effort to fill out the canonical narratives, the *Acts of Pilate* elaborates the false accusations brought against Jesus by the high priest and Jewish leaders. In chapter 1, paragraph 1, the Jewish leaders appear before Pilate and level several charges against Jesus. First, they infer that Jesus was born of an illegitimate union between Joseph and Mary, an inference that is later

2003), 94, has the unusual interpretation that the message of Pilate's wife actually "functions as encouragement to Pilate to remove Jesus quickly."

[4] For references, see U. Luz, *Matthew 21 – 28* (trans. J.E. Crouch; Hermeneia; Minneapolis 2005), 499 n. 60 and 61.

[5] John Chrysostom, *Hom. Matt.* 86.

[6] Pseudo-Ignatius, *Ad Phil.* 4.

[7] M. Starowieyski, "Éléments apologétiques dans les Apocryphes", in *Les apologistes chrétiens et la culture grecque* (ed. B. Pouderon and J. Doré; ThH 105; Paris 1998), 193–197.

[8] Justin Martyr, *dial.* 69.7 (ANF 1:233).

[9] Origen, *Cels.* 1.38 (ANF 4:413).

addressed in the narrative (chap. 2.3). Second, they accuse Jesus of defiling the Sabbath and destroying the Jewish law by healing on the Sabbath, activities that the Jewish leaders say stem from Jesus' "evil practices" (ἀπὸ κακῶν πραξέων).[10] When Pilate inquires as to the nature of these "evil practices," the Jewish leaders respond, "He is a sorcerer (γόης), and by Beelzebub, the ruler of the demons, he casts out demons, and all [of them] are subject to him" (1.1). Thus, Jesus is charged with being a sorcerer whose healing activities stem from magical practices.

As the narrative unfolds, Jesus is brought to appear before Pilate, where he is miraculously greeted by the Roman standards that bore the image of the emperor. As Jesus enters, the Roman standards bow and revere him (1.5–6), despite the standard-bearers' attempt to hold them upright. In turn, Pilate becomes fearful and seeks to leave the judgment seat. At this point, the Matthean reference to Pilate's wife and her dream is introduced. It reads, "While he was still thinking of getting up, his wife sent [word] to him saying '[Let there be] nothing between you and this innocent man, for I have suffered greatly in the night on account of him'" (ἔτι δὲ αὐτοῦ ἐνθυμουμένου ἀναστῆναι, ἡ γυνὴ αὐτοῦ ἔπεμψεν πρὸς αὐτὸν λέγουσα· μηδὲν σοὶ καὶ τῷ ἀνθρώπῳ τῷ δικαίῳ τούτῳ· πολλὰ γὰρ ἔπαθον δι' αὐτὸν νυκτός – 2.1). In addition to informing the Jewish leaders of this message, Pilate also reminds them that his wife is a God-fearer (θεοσεβής) and observes the Jewish traditions. The Jewish leaders then respond, "Did we not tell you that he is a sorcerer (γόης)? Behold, he sent a dream (ὀνειροπόλημα ἔπεμψε) to your wife" (2.1). The connection between sorcery and dreams would not be lost on an ancient audience, for among the larger practice of magic in antiquity was the practice of dream magic.

2. The Accusation in Context of Ancient Dream Magic[11]

The association between ancient magic and dreams is exhibited most clearly in the Greek Magical Papyri. The collection of Greek Magical Papyri contains two types of dream rituals or spells: (1) the dream-request ritual (ὀνειραιτητά) and (2) the dream-sending ritual (ὀνειροπομπός, ὀνειροπομπία). In the dream-request ritual, the practitioner conjures revelatory dreams for him or herself; in the dream-sending ritual, the practitioner invokes dreams to appear to another person for some specified task. Though

[10] Translations of the *Acts of Pilate* are mine. I follow the 'A' text form of C. Tischendorf, *Evangelia Apocrypha* (Leipzig 1853).

[11] For this section, I have used material from my monograph *Reading Dreams: An Audience-Critical Approach to the Dreams in the Gospel of Matthew* (LNTS 397; London: T & T Clark International 2009), 18–28.

a few magical rituals are general spells and claim the ability to do both,[12] dream rituals are for the most part specifically designed for either requesting a dream or sending a dream. The primary purpose of dream-request rituals is the revelation of some knowledge, information, or advice. Consider the following example:

Request for a dream oracle (ὀνειραιτητά), a request which is always used. Formula to be spoken to the day lamp: "NAIENCHRĒ NAIENCHRĒ, mother of fire and water, you are the one who rises before, ARCHENTECHTHA; reveal to me concerning the NN matter. If yes, show me a plant and water, but if not, fire and iron, immediately, immediately."[13]

The practitioner of this magical ritual presumably would need advice or information that is easily answered by "yes" or "no."[14] Most of the dream-request rituals are much more elaborate and do not restrict the requested information to a simple "yes" or "no" but leave it open-ended with the formulaic "reveal to me concerning the NN matter."[15] The magical ritual entitled "Dream-Request from Besas" is a case in point.[16] The ritual first calls for the practitioner to draw a picture of the god Besa, which is found "in the beginning of the book."[17] The figure is to be drawn presumably on the hand[18] with ink made from the "blood of a white dove, likewise of a crow, also sap of the mulberry, juice of single-stemmed wormwood, cinnabar, and rainwater".[19] After the drawing of Besa, the practitioner then wraps his or her hand with a black cloth of Isis. The prayer-formula, which is quite

---

[12] For example, PGM IV. 2441–2621: "It inflicts sickness excellently and destroys powerfully, sends dreams beautifully, accomplishes dream revelations marvellously and in its many demonstrations has been marvelled at for having no failure in these matters" (lines 2443–6 [Betz, 82–83]). See also, PGM IV. 2006–2125, esp. lines 2076–81. Note: all translations of the Greek Magical Papyri are from H.D. Betz (ed.), *The Greek Magical Papyri in Translation, Including the Demotic Spells* (Chicago ²1992).

[13] PGM VII. 250–254 (Betz, 123).

[14] Cf. also PGM XXIIb. 27–31 (Betz, 261): "[If] the petition I have made is appropriate, [show] me water and a grove; if otherwise, show me water and a stone"; and XXIIb. 32–35 (Betz, 261): "If this matter has been granted to me, show me a courtesan; otherwise, a soldier."

[15] See PGM IV. 2501–2505; IV. 3172–3208 (line 3207); VII. 222–249 (line 247); VII. 359–369 (line 369); VII. 478–490 (line 479); VII. 703–726 (line 714); VII. 740–755 (line 744); VII. 795–854 (line 36; cf. 841); VII. 1009–1016 (line 1015); XII. 144–152 (line 152).

[16] PGM VII. 222–249 (Betz, 122–123). Cf. the parallel dream-request ritual VIII. 64–110.

[17] The picture is missing from the papyri, but the parallel spell VIII. 64–110 provides a description and illustration of the Besa figure to be drawn: "A naked man, standing, having a diadem on his head, and in his right hand a sword that by means of a bent [arm] rests on his neck, and in the left hand a wand" (lines 105–109 [Betz, 147–148]).

[18] Once again, based on PGM VIII. 64–110.

[19] PGM VII. 222–249, lines 223–5 (Betz, 122).

lengthy, is to be spoken to a lamp and ends with a petition, where the specific request is to be inserted: "Come, Lord, reveal to me concerning the NN matter, without deceit, without treachery, immediately, immediately; quickly, quickly."[20]

Whereas the purpose of dream-request rituals is limited to revelation, the functions of dream-sending rituals can be grouped under three types. The first type of dream-sending ritual is for the purpose of erotic attraction.[21] For example, one love-attracting ritual includes as an addendum the procedure for using an Eros doll that will serve as an "assistant and supporter and sender of dreams."[22] The Eros doll will send dreams that will accomplish the plan of the practitioner: "Turn the 'soul' of her NN to me NN, so that she may love me, so that she may feel passion for me, so that she may give me what is in her power."[23] The following is the procedure:

> Go late at night to the house [of the woman] you want, knock on her door with the Eros and say: "Lo, she NN resides here; wherefore stand beside her and, after assuming the likeness of the god or daimon whom she worships, say what I propose." And go to your home, set the table, spread a pure linen cloth, and seasonal flowers, and set the figure upon it. Then make a burnt offering to it and continuously say the spell of invocation. And send him, and he will act without fail. And whenever you bend her to your will with the stone, on that night it sends dreams, for on a different night it is busy with different matters.[24]

The second type of dream-sending ritual is for revelation. This type of ritual differs from the dream-request ritual in that the revelation requested through a dream is for a third party, not the one who performs the magical spell. The following is such a magical ritual, which has the title "Zminis of Tentyra's spell for sending dreams":

> Take a clean cloth, and (according to Ostanes) with myrrh ink draw a figure on it which is humanlike in appearance but has four wings, having the left arm outstretched along with two left wings, and having the other arm bent with the fist clinched. Then upon the head [draw] a royal headdress and a cloak over its arm, with two spirals on the cloak. Atop the head [draw] bull horns and to the buttocks a bird's tail. Have his right hand held near his stomach and clinched, and on either ankle have a sword extended.
>
> Also write on the strip the following names of the god and whatever you want him, [NN], to see and how: "CHALAMANDRIOPH IDEARZO THREDAPHNIO ERTHIBELNIN RYTHADNIKO PSAMOMERICH, to all of you I speak, also to you, () very powerful daimon: go into the house of this person and tell him such-and-such."
>
> Next take a lamp neither coloured red nor inscribed, and after you put a wick in it, fill it with cedar oil, and light it. Invoke the following names of the god, three [times]: "CHA-

[20] PGM VII. 222–249, lines 247–8 (Betz, 123).

[21] PGM IV. 1716–1870; VII. 407–410; VII. 862–918.

[22] PGM IV.1716–1870, line 1850 (Betz, 71). Cf. the dream-request ritual PGM VII. 478–490, where Eros is called upon for general revelation.

[23] PGM IV.1716–1870, lines 1807–9 (Betz, 70).

[24] PGM IV. 1716–1870, lines 1841–70 (Betz, 71).

LAMANDRIOPH IDEARZO THREDAPHNIO ERTHIBELNIN RYTHADNIKO PSAMOMERICH, O sacred names of the god, listen to me – you also, O Good Daimon, whose might is very great among the gods, listen to me: go to him, NN, into his house, where he sleeps, into his bedroom, and stand beside him, causing fear, trembling, by using the great and mighty names of the god. And tell him such-and-such. I conjure you [by] your power, [by] the great god, SEITH, [by] the hour in which you were begotten a great god, [by] the god revealing it now (?), [by] the 365 names of the great god, to go to him, NN, this very night, and to tell him in a dream such-and-such."[25]

The third type of dream-sending ritual can be called an imprecatory dream, which is intended to cause harm or injury to another person whether physically or psychologically. In the *Greek Magical Papyri*, there is not a dream-magic ritual that is specifically designed for imprecatory purposes, but dream-sending is sometimes listed as one means by which someone could bring harm or injury to another. For example, one imprecatory ritual has the following spell:

Let all the darkness of clouds be dispersed for me, and let the goddess AKTIŌPHIS shine for me, and let her hear my holy voice. For I come announcing the slander of NN, a defiled and unholy woman, for she has slanderously brought your holy mysteries to the knowledge of men. She, NN, is the one, [not] I, who says, "I have seen the greatest goddess, after leaving the heavenly vault, on earth without sandals, sword in hand, and [speaking] a foul name." It is she, NN, who said, "I saw [the goddess] drinking blood." She, NN, said it, not I, AKTIŌPHIS ERESCHIGAL NEBOUTOSOUALĒTH PHORPHORBA SATRAPAMMŌN CHOIRIXIĒ, flesh eater. Go to her NN and take away her sleep and put a burning heat in her soul, punishment and frenzied passion in her thoughts, and banish her from every place and from every house, and attract her here to me, NN.[26]

The ritual provides specific ways by which this harm can be effected, and one way is sending a dream.[27] Interestingly, another imprecatory ritual, which includes sending dreams, provides a protective charm for the practitioner, so that he or she will be guarded "from every daimon of the air on the earth and under the earth, and from every angel and phantom and ghostly visitation and enchantment."[28] Thus, this protective charm ironically guards against the very kind of imprecatory magic being administered by the spell.

Lest we think that the belief and practice of dream-magic in the Greco-Roman world is confined to the Greek Magical Papyri, consider the following Jewish and Christian references to dream magic.[29]

---

[25] PGM XII. 121–143 (Betz, 157–158).

[26] PGM IV.2441–2621, lines 2474–2490 (Betz, 83).

[27] PGM IV.2441–2621, line 2500.

[28] PGM IV.2622–2707, lines 2699–2701 (Betz, 88).

[29] Despite the strong objection to magic in the biblical tradition and patristic literature, Jewish and Christian religious practices included elements that are considered magical. For helpful discussions and bibliographies, see P.S. Alexander, "Incantations and Books of Magic", in *The History of the Jewish People in the Age of Jesus Christ* by

The Dead Sea Scroll 4Q560 should be mentioned, though it is badly fragmented and its significance for dream magic is based on emendation.[30] The text is an incantation formula intended to ward off various demons or evil spirits, particularly in relation to childbirth, sickness, sleep, and possibly the security of possessions. The line associated with dream magic is as follows: ". . . and forbidden to disturb by night in dreams or by da]y in sleep, the male Shrine-spirit and the female Shrine-spirit, breacher-demons of. . ."[31] Though the term "sleep" is intact, Penney and Wise emend the text to include dreams. Their emendation is convincingly based on third to sixth century Aramaic (Babylonian) incantation bowls and amulets that contain parallels to 4Q560 including charms against the visitation of demons in dreams. The emendation also is informed by the widespread belief, both Ancient Near Eastern and Greco-Roman, that dreams were a means of demonic harm.[32] As Penney and Wise state, "4Q560 is therefore an important witness to the development of magical traditions in the Greco-Roman world generally, and among Second Temple Jews specifically."[33]

The widespread practice of dream magic in the Greco-Roman world is also attested, and sharply criticized, in Christian apologetics and polemics. As a part of his argument for the immortality of the soul and resurrection, Justin Martyr asks his pagan readers to consider the various practices of divination including "sent-dreams and [daemon]-attendants (ὀνειροπομποὶ

Emil Schürer (rev. and eds. G. Vermes, F. Millar, and M. Goodman; vol. 3; Edinburgh 1986), 342–79; and D.E. Aune, "Magic in Early Christianity," *ANRW* 2.23.1 (1980), 1507–1557. Unlike scholarship in the nineteenth and early twentieth century, modern scholarship has come to recognize that magic in its ancient context is not antithetical to religion but represents one end of a spectrum of religious practices. See N. Janowitz, *Magic in the Roman World: Pagans, Jews and Christians* (London 2001), 1–8; M. Meyer and R. Smith (eds.), *Ancient Christian Magic: Coptic Texts of Ritual Power* (San Francisco 1994), 1–9; H.-J. Klauck, *The Religious Context of Early Christianity: A Guide to Graeco-Roman Religions* (trans. B. McNeil; Edinburgh 2000), 215–18; H.D. Betz, "Magic and Mystery in the Greek Magical Papyri," in *Magika Hiera: Ancient Greek Magic and Religion* (ed. C.A. Faraone and D. Obbink; Oxford 1991), 244–259; R.L. Fowler, "Greek Magic, Greek Religion", in *Oxford Readings in Greek Religion* (ed. R. Buxton; New York 2000), 317–343; Aune, "Magic in Early Christianity" (cf. above paragraph), 1510–1516.

[30] This discussion of 4Q560 is based on D.L. Penney and M.O. Wise, "By the Power of Beelzebub: An Aramaic Incantation Formula from Qumran (4Q560)", *JBL* 113 (1994), 627–650.

[31] 4Q560 I, 5 as cited in Penney and Wise, "By the Power of Beelzebub" (n. 30), 632.

[32] See above discussion of PGM IV. 2622–2707. See also references listed in Penney and Wise, "By the Power of Beelzebub" (n. 30), 642 fn. 65 and 67.

[33] Ibid., 649.

καὶ πάρεδροι) that are summoned by the *magoi*".[34] Tertullian characterizes pagan diviners as magicians who practice necromancy, perform deceptive miracles, and "put dreams into people's minds by the power of the angels and demons whose aid they have invited."[35] Irenaeus describes the practices of certain heresies in terms of magic. The followers of Simon Magus are said to practice the magical arts of exorcisms, incantations, love-charms, spells, attendants (*paredri*), and sent-dreams (*oniropompi*).[36] The Carpocrates are described in similar terms; they perform incantations, love-charms, attendants (*paredri*), and sent-dreams (*oniropompi*).[37]

These comments directed at opponents in a polemical setting, of course, are reminiscent of the accusations levelled against Jesus in the *Acts of Pilate* and perhaps reveal a kind of rhetoric of magic. The accusation of magic was typical of ancient polemic and often included stereotypical language.[38] As a matter of fact, the *Acts of Pilate* participates in an ancient literary strategy for countering charges of magic: an adversarial or accusatory setting in which allegations of magic are defended against and yet the miraculous powers of the accused individual are affirmed.[39] An ancient audience of the *Acts of Pilate* would recognize this rhetoric of magic, particularly the accusation of dream-magic, for what it is: an empty, baseless accusation. Moreover, within the narrative of the *Acts of Pilate*, the accusation of magic brought against Jesus becomes consequently less about Jesus and more about the characterization of the Jewish leaders as slanderous and corrupt.

3. Reading *Acts of Pilate* 2.1 in Light of Ancient Dream Magic

At this point, let us return to the *Acts of Pilate* to consider the charge of magic in light of the previous discussion. At the beginning of this essay, I suggested that the Matthean reference to Pilate's wife's dream introduces an interpretive ambiguity about its content and exact meaning. What we

---

[34] Justin, *1 Apol.* 18.3. For the role of daemon-attendants in dream magic, see S. Eitrem, "Dreams and Divination in Magical Ritual", in *Magika Hiera: Ancient Greek Magic and Religion* (ed. C.A. Faraone and D. Obbink; New York 1991), 180–181.

[35] Tertullian, *Apol.* 23 (ANF 3:37).

[36] Irenaeus, *Haer.* 1.23.4.

[37] Irenaeus, *Haer.* 1.25.3.

[38] See Janowitz, *Magic in the Roman World* (n. 29), 9–26; and M. Choi, "Christianity, Magic, and Difference: Name-Calling and Resistance between the Lines in Contra Celsum," *Sem.* 79 (1997), 75–92.

[39] A. Bingham Kolenkow, "A Problem of Power: How Miracle Doers Counter Charges of Magic in the Hellenistic World", in *SBL 1976 Seminar Papers* (ed. G. MacRae; Missoula, Mont. 1976), 105–110.

are told, however, is that she suffered (πάσχω). This response to the dream most certainly permitted an interpretation that Pilate's wife experienced a dream as a result of magic. Our review of dream magic, especially for the revelatory and imprecatory purposes, included a feature of terror and fright. To facilitate this interpretation of Pilate's wife's dream and in turn to set up the accusation of dream magic, we should note a couple of slight modifications of the Matthean quotation. In Matthew's Gospel, Pilate's wife says that she "suffered greatly today in a dream on account of him" (27:19). We should first note that the *Acts of Pilate* changes the temporal reference from "today" to "night." The dream-magic rituals reveal a consistent orientation to the time of night. By altering the dream experience to an explicitly night setting, which certainly contributes to an experience of dread and anxiety, the *Acts of Pilate* creates a narrative more conducive to an accusation of dream magic.

The second modification of the Matthean reference is the omission of the term "dream" from Pilate's wife's message; the text simply reads, "I suffered greatly in the night on account of him." It is the Jewish leaders who mention a dream, not Pilate's wife. The Jewish leaders allege that Pilate's wife has suffered because of a sent-dream by the sorcerer Jesus. Matthew uses the customary dream term ὄναρ in the message of Pilate's wife. In the *Acts of Pilate*, however, the Jewish leaders use a possibly more prejudiced term, ὀνειροπόλημα. The term is quite uncommon in Greek literature, and it is not listed in Liddell, Scott, and Jones's *Greek-English Lexicon*. Though the term may simply be a synonym for ὄνειρος ("dream"), it seems to have the connotation of "warring-dream," "destructive-dream," or perhaps even a "haunting-dream."[40] Within the narrative of the *Acts of Pilate*, these modifications allow the portrayal of the Jewish leaders as using the rhetoric of magic to become more apparent. By having the Jewish leaders allege a sent-dream and employ the term ὀνειροπόλημα, the accusation of dream magic by the Jewish leaders is presented in a manner that highlights the polemic of magic on their part, and so characterizes them as ones participating in slander and false testimony.

[40] A search in the Thesaurus Linguae Graecae database resulted in two instances of the term ὀνειροπόλημα: (1) Clement of Alexandria, *Quis div.* 25.4.3, who speaks of an individual's soul being internally harassed by "impious desires, various pleasures, worthless hopes, and destructive dreams (φθαρτ<ικ>ῶν ὀνειροπολημάτων)"; and (2) Nicolaus of Damascus, *FGH* Frag. 101, who uses the term for the dreams of Julius Caesar's wife concerning his death.

4. Conclusion

In the *Acts of Pilate*, Jesus is accused of being a sorcerer by the Jewish leaders, a charge that is made in relation to the dream of Pilate's wife; they allege that Jesus sent the dream. The context for such an allegation is the belief and practice of dream magic, a form of divination that was known in the ancient Mediterranean world. Drawing primarily upon the Greek Magical Papyri, this essay has explicated the belief and practice of dream magic in order to understand more sufficiently the correlation between the accusation of magic and the assertion that Jesus is responsible for the dream of Pilate's wife. It was consequently noted that this accusation of dream magic ironically functions in the narrative to characterize the Jewish leaders as libellous and deceitful.

Passionsdarstellungen in der frühchristlichen Kunst

JUTTA DRESKEN-WEILAND

Einleitung

In frühchristlicher Zeit sind figürliche Darstellungen der Kreuzigung Christi selten. Dieser Beitrag fragt danach, welche Bilder der Kreuzigung Christi sich erhalten haben, warum es nur so wenige Kreuzigungsdarstellungen gibt und welche Szenen aus der Passion im Bild erscheinen.

1. Erhaltene Darstellungen der Kreuzigung Christi in der Kunst

Figürliche Darstellungen des gekreuzigten Christus finden sich in der frühchristlichen Kunst erst seit dem frühen 5. Jh. Ihnen geht das in Papyri bereits um 200 belegte Staurogramm, das wohl als eine abstrakte Darstellung des am Kreuz hängenden Christus zu verstehen ist, und die im Folgenden behandelte, etwa gleichzeitige magische Gemme voran[1]. Bei den beiden Denkmälern aus dem 5. Jh. handelt es sich um ein Elfenbeinkästchen in London und die Holztür von S. Sabina. Das Elfenbeinkästchen in London[2] wird in der Forschung einhellig in die 20er Jahre des 5. Jhs. datiert. Diese Datierung beruht auf der Grundlage von Stilvergleichen, doch ist von den verglichenen Denkmälern keines sicher datiert, so dass es angemessener er-

---

[1] Dieser Beitrag ist hervorgegangen aus dem DFG-Projekt „Bilder und Inschriften als Spiegel für Jenseitsvorstellungen der frühen Christen“, das am Lehrstuhl von Prof. Dr. Andreas Merkt, Alte Kirchengeschichte und Patrologie, an der Universität Regensburg angesiedelt ist. Zum Thema zuletzt, allerdings ohne weiterführende Aspekte und auf der Grundlage überholter Publikationen F. HARLEY, The Narration of Christ's Passion in Early Christian Art, in: Byzantine Narrative. Papers in Honour of Roger Scott, Melbourne 2006, 220–232. – Zum Staurogramm s. L.W. HURTADO, The Staurogram in Early Christian Manuscripts: The Earliest Visual Reference to the Crucified Jesus, in: TH.J. KRAUS/T. NICKLAS (Hg.), New Testament Manuscripts. Their Texts and Their World, TENT 2, Leiden/Boston 2006, 207–226; DERS., The Earliest Christian Artifacts. Manuscripts and Christian Origin, Grand Rapids, Mich. 2008, 135–154.

[2] W.F. VOLBACH, Elfenbeinarbeiten der Spätantike und des frühen Mittelalters, Mainz 1976, Nr. 116; s. eine farbige Abbildung in: Dalla terra alle genti. La diffusione del cristianesimo nei primi secoli, Mailand 1996, 239 Nr. 108.

scheint, von einer Datierung in die erste Hälfte des 5. Jhs. zu sprechen. Mit einiger Sicherheit lässt sich sagen, dass es wohl in Rom hergestellt worden ist, da zu den stilistisch nahe stehenden Stücken stadtrömische[3] gehören.

Die Holztür von S. Sabina ist sicherer datiert, denn sie wurde von dem Presbyter Petrus aus Dalmatien zur Zeit des Pontifikates Coelestins (422–432) gestiftet, wohl aber erst unter seinem Nachfolger Sixtus III. (432–440) vollendet[4], da die Weihe der Kirche vom Liber Pontificalis in seinem Pontifikat erwähnt wird. Gisela Jeremias, die der Holztür eine Monographie gewidmet hat, nimmt die Entstehung der Tür in den Jahren zwischen 431 und 433 an. Sehr wahrscheinlich wurde sie in Rom von einem stadtrömischen Künstler hergestellt[5].

Das Londoner Passionskästchen und die Holztür von S. Sabina weisen folgende Gemeinsamkeiten auf: die weit geöffneten Augen des Gekreuzigten, der nackte Körper mit dem Subligaculum um die Hüften, die angenagelten Hände und die frei stehenden (London) bzw. schwebenden Füße (Rom). Den Gemeinsamkeiten stehen Unterschiede gegenüber: ein vollständig dargestelltes Kreuz mit Titulus in London, und ein nur angedeutetes Kreuz in Rom, der deutlich erhöht und der knapp über dem Erdboden schwebende, fast den Boden berührende Christus; seine waagrecht ausgestreckten und seine angewinkelten Arme; der jugendliche, mit einem Nimbus versehene und der bärtige Kopf; Maria und Johannes zur Rechten und ein Soldat zur Linken Christi sowie die beiden Schächer zur Rechten und zur Linken Jesu[6].

Für die Interpretation dieser beiden Kreuzigungsdarstellungen ist wichtig, dass Christus mit offenen Augen und vor dem Kreuz stehend dargestellt ist. Dass diese Ikonographie mit Absicht gewählt wurde, lässt sich zum Beispiel auf dem Londoner Kästchen erkennen, wo der erhängte Judas in schlaffer Körperhaltung mit geschlossenen Augen als tot gekennzeichnet ist[7]. Das Stehen Jesu vor dem Kreuz und seine geöffneten Augen werden als Hinweis auf seine Göttlichkeit bzw. auf die Überwindung des Todes durch die Auferstehung gedeutet[8], sind also ein mit theologischem Inhalt gefülltes Bildelement. Der Verzicht auf die Wiedergabe der unvorstellbaren Qualen einer Kreuzigung steht dabei in der Tradition antiker

---

[3] Das Diptychon der Lampadier: VOLBACH (s. Anm. 2), Nr. 54.

[4] H. BRANDENBURG, Die frühchristlichen Kirchen Roms vom 4. bis zum 7. Jh., Regensburg 2004, 167.

[5] G. JEREMIAS, Die Holztür der Basilika S. Sabina in Rom, Tübingen 1980, 107.

[6] Ebd., 61.

[7] Darauf weist M. MRASS, Art. Kreuzigung Christi, in: RBK V (1995), 287 hin.

[8] C. BARBER, Figure and Likeness. On the Limits of Representation in Byzantine Iconoclasm, Princeton 2002, 49 zur Darstellung Jesu mit geöffneten Augen am Triumphbogen von S. Maria Antiqua; BRANDENBURG (s. Anm. 4), 176.

Ikonographie, die Wunden, Leid und Schmerzen mit Ausnahme einiger weniger Bildthemen (die Schindung des Marsyas) nicht darstellt.

2. Magische Darstellungen der Kreuzigung Christi

Die älteren Bilder des gekreuzigten Christus sind dagegen realistischer. Hier ist vor allem eine Darstellung der Kreuzigung Christi auf einer sogenannten magischen Gemme zu nennen, die in London aufbewahrt wird. Die magischen Gemmen sind Edel- und Schmucksteine mit eingeschnittenen Bildern und Inschriften, die in der Antike als Amulette dienten und deren Bildmotive und Inschriften eng mit den in magischen Texten und Papyri geäußerten Vorstellungen korrespondieren. Sie stammen wohl ursprünglich aus dem römischen Ägypten, da die Ikonographie der ägyptischen Götter eine große Rolle spielt, und waren vor allem im 2. und 3. Jh. im gesamten Römischen Reich verbreitet, sind allerdings auch noch später anzutreffen[9]. Da die Gattung inzwischen vor allem von Simone Michel eingehend und gründlich bearbeitet worden ist und das betreffende, in London aufbewahrte Stück in Größe, Material und Bearbeitung dem in der Gattung Üblichen entspricht, ist an seiner Echtheit nicht zu zweifeln, zumal auch andere christliche Bilder und Zeichen auf den Gemmen vorkommen[10]. Die Gemmen mit Kreuzigungsdarstellungen gehören zu den Amuletten, die auf „Regeneration und göttlichen Schutz" zielen[11], wobei letzterer sich auf das Weiterleben nach dem Tod beziehen soll. Von wem diese Gemmen benutzt wurden, ist unbekannt; dass Christen zu ihnen gehörten, ist nicht unwahrscheinlich.

Der Amulettcharakter des grün-braunen Jaspis im Britischen Museum (Abb. 1) geht aus der Inschrift hervor, die die Kreuzigung rahmt. Sie nennt Jesus Christus ([ΚΥΡ]ΙΕ ΠΑΤΗΡ ΙΗΣΟΥ ΧΡΙΣΤΕ), aber auch typische Zauberworte wie „Somamnôamôa", die aus der Wiederholung dreier ähnlich klingender Silben bestehen, sowie Anagramme, in denen die Wörter „Iaô"[12] und „Jesus" verschlüsselt sind[13]. Auf der Rückseite enthält die Inschrift Varianten des Namens „Jesus", „Emmanuel", sowie die beiden mehrfach belegten, in ihrem Sinn jedoch unbekannten Zauberwörter

---

[9] S. MICHEL, Die magischen Gemmen, Berlin 2004, XIII.

[10] S. MICHEL, Die magischen Gemmen im Britischen Museum, London 2001, 269–291; DIES. (s. Anm. 9), 113–145; zuletzt J. SPIER, Late Antique and Early Christian Gems, Wiesbaden 2007, 73 Nr. 443, 74f.; F. HARLEY/J. SPIER in: Picturing the Bible. The Earliest Christian Art, Kimbell Art Museum 2007, 228f.

[11] MICHEL (s. Anm. 9), 113.

[12] Dies ist der auf den Gemmen am häufigsten gebrauchte Namen für den Sonnengott; S. MICHEL, Bunte Steine – dunkle Bilder: „Magische Gemmen". Ausst.-Kat. 2001, 123.

[13] MICHEL (s. Anm. 10), 283 Nr. 457 Farbtaf. VI; DIES. (Anm. 9), 124.

„ΒΑΔΗΤΟΦWΘ“[14] und „CATPAΠΕΡΚΜΗΦ“(„Satraperkmêph“; letzterer ist möglicherweise eine Bezeichnung für den ägyptischen Schöpfergott Amun)[15].

Im Gemmenbild ist Christus an das Kreuz, das hier eine T-Form hat, gefesselt, und seine Hände hängen kraftlos nach unten. Er ist nackt; sein bärtiger Kopf ist nach links gewandt, und die leicht angewinkelt abgespreizten Beine unterstützen den Eindruck des Hängens. Die Darstellung der Gemme entspricht, was Simone Michel unbekannt war, tatsächlich einer antiken Methode der Kreuzigung, wie sie vor einigen Jahren anhand eines Skelettfundes des 1. Jhs. aus einem Ossuarium in Jerusalem rekonstruiert werden konnte[16]. Wie die von einem 17 bis 18 cm langen Nagel durchbohrte Ferse erkennen ließ, hatte man den verurteilten Jehohanan (der Name ist als Inschrift auf dem Ossuarium zu lesen) durch einen seitlich durch die Ferse gehauenen Nagel ans Kreuz geschlagen. Die Anbringung der Beine am Kreuz kann aufgrund des Befundes durch die aufeinander gelegten oder durch die in gespreizter Haltung zur Deckung gebrachten Fersen erreicht worden sein; letzteres erklärt die seltsam breite Haltung der Beine auf der Gemme[17] (Abb. 2). Die medizinische Untersuchung der Arme ließ als Möglichkeit außerdem annehmen, dass der Verurteilte ans Kreuz gebunden und nicht genagelt wurde[18]. Auch bei der Gemme im Britischen Museum sind herabhängende Hände zu erkennen. Neben dieser sind auch andere Varianten der Kreuzigung möglich und wurden wohl auch durchgeführt: Das Anbinden der Arme half im holzarmen Nahen Osten, den kostbaren Rohstoff Holz zu sparen, da das Querholz wieder verwendet werden konnte. Medizinhistoriker weisen darauf hin, dass die Art und Weise der Befestigung der Arme über die Dauer des Todeskampfes entschied[19]. Der Willkür und Grausamkeit der die Kreuzigung Durchführenden waren kaum Grenzen gesetzt[20].

---

[14] SPIER (s. Anm. 10), 75 referiert die in Zauberpapyri geläufige Deutung „Gott der zweiten Stunde“.

[15] MICHEL, (s. Anm. 10), 284 Nr. 457; dies. (Anm. 9), 124. Weitere Möglichkeiten bei SPIER (s. Anm. 10), 75.

[16] J. ZIAS in: Dalla terra alle genti. La diffusione del cristianesimo nei primi secoli, Mailand 1996, 169 Nr.5.

[17] S. die Rekonstruktionszeichnung von ZIAS (s. Anm. 16), 46 mit gespreizten Beinen; die seitlich aufeinander gelegten Beine bei W. BÖSEN, Der letzte Tag des Jesus von Nazaret, Freiburg i.Br. [3]1994, 278; verschiedene anhand des Befundes mögliche Rekonstruktionen bei F.T. ZUGIBE, The Cross and the Shroud. A Medical Inquiry into the Crucifixion, New York 1988, 74.

[18] ZIAS (s. Anm. 16), 48.

[19] Ebd., 47.

[20] Eine Skizze mit verschiedenen Möglichkeiten bei BÖSEN (s. Anm.17), 280.

Verschiedene Quellen weisen darauf hin, dass der Verurteilte tatsächlich nackt, wie auf der Gemme dargestellt, an das Kreuz gehängt wurde[21], um die Demütigung und die Schande der Kreuzigung noch zu erhöhen[22].

Auf den gewaltsamen Tod Jesu nimmt das Bild somit deutlich Bezug. Da gewaltsam ums Leben gekommenen Menschen eine besondere Macht zugeschrieben wurde, wie aus den magischen Papyri hervorgeht, die zum Beispiel den großen ägyptischen Gott Osiris sehr häufig erwähnen, verwundert nicht, dass man für die Gemmen die Kreuzigung Christi als Bild für einen wirksamen göttlichen Schutz auswählte[23], und dass man die Todesart auch deutlich erkennbar ins Bild setzte, um diesen Schutz zu erhalten. Interessanterweise ist diese Gemme aus einem grünen (grün-braunen) Jaspis gearbeitet, der neben dem Heliotrop bevorzugt für Osirismotive oder generell für Darstellungen benutzt wurde, die auf ein Leben nach dem Tod zielen. Die Gemme ist also auch unter diesem Aspekt stimmig[24]. Aufgrund des Schnittes und der Politur wird die Gemme von Michel „in das möglicherweise späte 2., sicherlich aber frühe 3. Jh." datiert[25]; Jeffrey Spier weist darauf hin, dass Stil, Material und Inschriften typisch für magische Gemmen des 2. und 3. Jhs. sind[26].

Im Britischen Museum befindet sich noch eine weitere Gemme mit einer Kreuzigungsdarstellung, die grob gearbeitet und erst im 4./5. Jh. entstanden ist. Über dem Kopf Christi befindet sich die aramäische Inschrift „Jesus M(essias)", während auf der Rückseite eine nicht transkribierbare Inschrift und magische Zeichen angebracht sind[27]. Auf die Wiedergabe des Kreuzes wird verzichtet; Jesu Kopf umgibt ein Nimbus[28]. Den Gekreuzigten rahmen zwei deutlich kleiner dargestellte Figuren, die wohl kniend dar-

---

[21] Vgl. Mk 15,24; Joh 19,23f. A. ZESTERMANN, Die Kreuzigung bei den Alten, Brüssel 1868, 47 verweist auf Artemidor Onirocrit 2,53; die ausdrückliche Erwähnung einer Kreuzigung in kostbarer Kleidung bei Justin, apol. 18,7 und Tacit. h. 4,3 lässt seiner Meinung nach annehmen, dass genau das Gegenteil der Fall war.

[22] Ebd. 48.

[23] MICHEL (s. Anm. 9), 125.

[24] Ebd., 126.

[25] Ebd., 126.

[26] SPIER (s. Anm. 10), 75.

[27] MICHEL (s. Anm. 10), 284f. Nr. 458. Zu den beiden Gemmen im Britischen Museum und zu weiteren, späteren Beispielen auf Gemmen s. F. HARLEY, Invocations and Immolation: The Supplicatory Use of Christ's Name on Crucifixion Amulets of the Early Christian Period, in: P. ALLEN/W. MAYER/L. CROSS (Hg.), Prayer and Spirituality in the Early Church II, Brisbane 1999, 245–257; SPIER (s. o. Anm. 10), 73f.

[28] Dieser ist nicht ein Zeichen für eine spätere Entstehung der Gemme, wie MICHEL (s. Anm. 9), 126 meint, da der Nimbus bereits in der paganen Kunst bei Göttern erscheint.

gestellt sind und die Hände zum Gebet erhoben haben. Für eine Benennung dieser Gestalten fehlen Anhaltspunkte[29].

3. Ein antichristliches Bild

Ein Beispiel für ein Kreuzigungsbild in antichristlichem Kontext ist das Spottkruzifix vom Palatin, eine Ritzdarstellung, die einen Gekreuzigten mit eselähnlichem Hals und Kopf zeigt. Der Graffito stammt aus dem so genannten Pädagogium auf dem Palatin, das aufgrund der erhaltenen Inschriften und Ritzzeichnungen wohl von Sklaven und Freigelassenen frequentiert wurde. Die genaue Funktion des Raumes lässt sich nicht sicher bestimmen[30]. Die in diesem Raum gefundenen Graffiti gehören meist dem späten 2. und dem 3. Jh. an, so dass das Spottkruzifix ebenfalls in diese Zeit datiert wird[31].

Das Bild zeigt den Gekreuzigten vor einem Tau-Kreuz. Seine Füße stehen auf einem Querbalken, und er ist mit einem kurzen Gewand bekleidet. Ihm wendet sich ein links stehender Mann zu, ebenfalls in kurzem Gewand, und erhebt die rechte Hand anbetend. Die Beischrift verdeutlicht die karikierende Absicht des Graffito: ΑΛΕ/ΧΑΜΕΝΟϹ/ ϹΕΒΕΤΕ ΘΕΟΝ. Offensichtlich sollte der Christ Alexamenos mit diesem Bild verspottet werden. Ob der Spott auf das auch in zeitgenössischen schriftlichen Quellen bekannte Gerücht zielt, die Juden und Christen verehrten einen eselsköpfigen Gott[32], oder ob die den Eseln zugeschriebene Dummheit und Widerborstigkeit im Vordergrund steht, muss hier offen bleiben. Die Kreuzi-

---

[29] MICHEL (s. Anm. 9), 126 schlägt Johannes und Maria vor. Leider lässt sich an den Gestalten nicht einmal feststellen, ob sie männlich oder weiblich sind. – Christusbilder lassen sich auch in späteren Zeiten noch auf magischen Gemmen finden und verweisen auf die Wirkung seines Bildes in anderen Bereichen der spätantiken Magie: Als Beispiel soll hier lediglich ein im 6. oder 7. Jh. entstandener Hämatith im Metropolitan Museum genannt werden, dessen Darstellung der Heilung der Blutflüssigen offensichtlich die Genesung von Frauenleiden bewirken sollte, s. MICHEL 127. Gute Abbildung in: D. STUTZINGER, Spätantike und frühes Christentum. Ausst.-Kat. Frankfurt 1982, 560 Nr. 165.

[30] E. PAPI in: LTUR 4, Rom 1999, 7f.

[31] G. SACCO, Il graffito blasfemo del Paedagogium nella Domus Augustana del Palatino, in: I. DI STEFANO MANZELLA (Hg.), Le iscrizioni dei cristiani in Vaticano. Materiali e contributi scientifici per una mostra epigrafica, Città del Vaticano 1997, 193f. S. zuletzt A. MERKT, „Eine Religion von törichten Weibern und ungebildeten Handwerkern." Ideologie und Realität eines Klischees zum frühen Christentum, in: F.R. PROSTMEIER (Hg.), Frühchristentum und Kultur, Freiburg i.Br. 2007, 296f.

[32] SACCO (s. Anm. 31), 193 mit Hinweis auf Tertullian, ad nationes I 11,1–5, 14,1–2; Apologeticum 16,12–14; Min. Felix, Octavius 9,3; 29,7.

gung als entehrendste aller Todesstrafen[33] durfte in einer verspottenden Darstellung aus heidnischer Sicht natürlich nicht fehlen. In ihren Details ist die Darstellung wohl nicht besonders ernst zu nehmen, da sie ja schnell und mit wenigen Strichen angefertigt wurde. So wurde der Gekreuzigte wie auch der verehrende Alexamenos mit einem kurzen, von der arbeitenden Bevölkerung getragenen Gewand bekleidet, beide Gestalten also quasi im „Einheits-Look“ der am Kaiserhof in dienenden Positionen Beschäftigten wiedergegeben.

4. Kreuzigung als Todesstrafe und ihre Auswirkung auf die frühchristliche Kunst

Für Christen war die Kreuzigung in den Anfängen christlicher Kunst kein Thema für figürliche Darstellungen, zumal die Kreuzigung im 4. Jh. wohl noch praktiziert wurde. Die in der Literatur in der Regel zu lesende Behauptung, die Kreuzigung sei von Constantin abgeschafft worden, welche auf einer Textstelle bei Aurelius Viktor in seiner 361 verfassten Schrift „De Caesaribus“ (41,4) beruht[34], trifft wohl nicht zu, zumal kein Gesetz angeführt wird. Andere Quellen erwähnen die Kreuzigung noch bis in das späte 4. Jh. als Hinrichtungsart[35]. Daher verwundert es nicht, dass Bilder bzw. eine Anspielung auf die Kreuzigung nicht-öffentlichen Orten wie den

[33] Quellen zu der Kreuzigung als höchster und härtester Strafe bei ZESTERMANN (s. Anm. 21), 20–28.

[34] MRASS (s. Anm. 7), 293 mit Hinweis darauf, dass Constantin zwischen 319 und 323 die Kreuzigung als Strafe noch einmal einsetzt. In der entsprechenden Passage bei Aurelius Victor geht es um eine Gegenüberstellung von Constantin und Licinius, in der darauf hingewiesen wird, dass Constantin seine Feinde ohne Beeinträchtigung an ihrem Leben und ihren Gütern weiterleben lässt und die Kreuzigungsstrafe mit dem Brechen der Beine nicht mehr durchführt; Licinius dagegen verhält sich weniger vorbildlich. S. dazu auch den Kommentar von H.W. BIRD (Hg.), Aurelius Victor, De Caesaribus, Liverpool 1994, 189f. Anm. 4. Für K. GROSS-ALBENHAUSEN und M. FUHRMANN (Hg.), Aurelius Victor. Die römischen Kaiser. Liber de Caesaribus, Zürich 2002, 276 handelt es sich bei dem „supplicium patibulorum“ um einen Halsblock aus zwei Hälften, die um den Hals des Verurteilten gelegt und an die seine Hände gebunden oder genagelt wurden. Der Verurteilte wurde an diesem Block an einem Pfahl hinaufgezogen, so dass das „patibulum“ die Querstange eines Kreuzes bildete.

[35] ZESTERMANN (s. Anm. 21), 19 verweist auf eine 337–340 geschriebene Stelle bei Firmicus Maternus, Math. 8, die die Kreuzigung als Strafe erwähnt. Sie wird auch noch von anderen Schriftstellern des 4. Jh. erwähnt, zuletzt von Pacatus, s. ZESTERMANN 19 mit Nachweisen. S. auch RBK V (1995), 22f. (E. DINKLER/E. DINKLER VON SCHUBERT), wo darauf hingewiesen wird, dass die Abschaffung der Kreuzigungsstrafe durch Constantin nicht durch ein Gesetz zu belegen ist; möglicherweise kam sie durch Gewohnheitsrecht außer Gebrauch.

bereits erwähnten Papyri oder einer verborgen in den Gewändern getragenen Gemme vorbehalten bleiben[36].

Darstellungen der Kreuzigung Christi werden in schriftlichen Quellen erst um 400 erwähnt; so beschreibt einer der Tituli im Dittochaeum des Prudentius, das 24 Bilder aus dem Alten und 24 aus dem Neuen Testament kommentiert, die Kreuzigung Christi[37]. In der zwischen 441 und 445 erbauten Kathedrale von Narbonne soll sich nach einem Bericht des Gregor von Tours ein Bild des gekreuzigten Christus befunden haben[38]. Im Osten stammt die älteste Nachricht aus dem frühen 6. Jh., als Chorikios von Gaza die Ausstattung der Sergioskirche von Gaza beschreibt, in der ein Gemäldezyklus das Leben Christi von der Verkündigung bis zur Himmelfahrt schilderte[39].

Häufiger werden folgende Bilder aus dem Kontext der Passion dargestellt: die „Hahnszene", das Tropaion, der Einzug in Jerusalem und Christus vor Pilatus.

5. Die „Petrus-Christus-Hahn-Szene"

Die „Petrus-Christus-Hahn-Szene" wird in den Katakomben nur zweimal[40], aber auf den Sarkophagen recht häufig dargestellt. Petrus führt in der Mehrzahl der Darstellungen seine rechte Hand in einem erschrocken oder nachdenklich wirkenden Gestus zum Kinn bzw. Mund[41], während Christus mit der Rechten stets einen Redegestus ausführt und in der Linken oft eine Buchrolle hält. Zwischen den beiden befindet sich ein Hahn, der meist auf

---

[36] Zu den Staurogrammen in den Papyri s.o. Anm. 1. MRASS (s. Anm.7) 290 nimmt Darstellungen der Kreuzigung Christi „im Gefolge der konstantinischen Wende" an; die Auffindung des Kreuzes Christi, die in konstantinische Zeit datiert wird, S. Heid, Die gute Absicht im Schweigen Eusebs über die Kreuzauffindung, in: RQ 96 (2001) 37–56, hier 41, und das Einsetzen der Verehrung des Kreuzes Christi haben mit der Darstellung der Kreuzigung nichts zu tun.

[37] MRASS (s. Anm. 7), 289f.

[38] Ebd., 289. Zur Geschichte der Kirche s. X. BARAL I ALTET/P.-A. FEVRIER, Province ecclesiastique de Narbonne (Narbonensis prima). (= Topographie chrétienne de la Gaule des origines au millieu du VIIIe siècle 7), Paris 1989, 20f.

[39] MRASS (s. Anm. 7), 294 mit Hinweis auf or. I 75. Eine englische Übersetzung bei C. MANGO, The Art of the Byzantine Empire, New Jersey 1972, 64–68.

[40] In der Ciriaca-Katakombe: J. WILPERT, Die Malereien der Katakomben Roms, Freiburg i.Br. 1903, Taf. 242,1 (4. Jh.), und in der Commodilla-Katakombe: J.G. DECKERS/G. MIETKE/A. WEILAND, Die Katakombe „Commodilla". Repertorium der Malereien, Münster/Città del Vaticano 1994, Nr. 5–4 Farbtaf. 27b (spät- bis nachdamasianische Zeit).

[41] Zu den Interpretationen dieser Geste s. P.G. POST, De Haanscène in de vroegchristelijke Kunst. Een iconografische en iconologische analyse, Heerlen 1984, 145.

dem Boden steht[42]. Das Tier weist darauf hin, dass das Geschehen mit der Verleugnung Christi durch Petrus zu tun hat, welche alle vier Evangelien schildern[43]. Diese drei Bildelemente vereinen wohl zwei Erzählungen des Neuen Testamentes im Kontext der Passion Christi, und zwar die Ansage der Verleugnung und die Beauftragung des Petrus[44], wobei nicht ausgeschlossen werden kann, dass noch auf ein drittes Moment angespielt wird, und zwar auf die Trauer und Bestürzung Petri nach der erfolgten Verleugnung[45].

Eine eingehendere Untersuchung der Szene zeigt, dass in ihr verschiedene Bedeutungsebenen verschränkt sind. Die Aussage der frühchristlichen Predigten und Kommentare, die sich mit der Verleugnung beschäftigen, legt den Schwerpunkt der Interpretation auf Barmherzigkeit und Sündenvergebung[46]; das Bild des Petrus bestimmen trotz seines Versagens Würde und Autorität[47].

Bei einer Betrachtung der einzelnen Darstellungen fällt auf, dass die Szene nicht nur eine Petrus-, sondern genauso eine Christusszene ist[48], denn seine Gestalt verdeckt auf einigen Sarkophagen die des Petrus[49]. Der Redegestus Christi und die von Petrus ausgeführte Bewegung finden ihre Parallelen in der Ikonographie des philosophischen Gesprächs. Unter den im 3. Jh. und noch im frühen 4. Jh. beliebten sogenannten Musen-Philosophen-Sarkophagen findet sich der Redegestus auf fast allen Sarkophagen. Die Haltung des Petrus, der mit dem Greifen ans Kinn seine Aufmerksamkeit, sein Zuhören und Nachdenken und wohl auch seine Betroffenheit über das Gehörte zum Ausdruck bringen kann, lässt sich ebenfalls in dieser

---

[42] Zum Hahn auf der Säule s. POST (s. Anm. 41), 152, 156f. Auf einem Sarkophag in Saint-Maximin, B. CHRISTERN-BRIESENICK, Repertorium der christlich-antiken Sarkophage III, Mainz 2003, Nr. 499, steht der Hahn auf einem Kasten.

[43] Mt 26,69–75; Mk 14,66–72; Lk 22,53–62; Joh 18,15–25.

[44] Diese Benennung bei CHRISTERN-BRIESENICK (s. Anm. 42), 300.

[45] Allerdings entspricht die Szene nicht dem biblischen Geschehen, da Christus während der Verleugnung gefesselt ist und sich in einiger Entfernung von Petrus aufhält.

[46] Zum Beispiel Johannes Chrysostomus, hom. 83, PG 59, 447–453, Übersetzung Knors 709–723; Augustinus, Io. ev. tr. 123,5, ed. R. Willems, CCL 36, 679f. (Turnhout 1954), 679f.

[47] POST (s. Anm. 41), 141f.

[48] Ebd.

[49] H. BRANDENBURG, Repertorium der christlich-antiken Sarkophage I, Wiesbaden 1968, Nr. 241 in San Sebastiano, Nr. 771 im Museo Nazionale Romano, CHRISTERN-BRIESENICK (s. Anm. 42), Nr. 222 in Clermont-Ferrand, Nr. 297 in Marseille, Nr. 364 in Narbonne, M. SOTOMAYOR, Sarcofagos romano-cristianos de España, Granada 1975, 26 Taf. 5,2 in Erustes; Taf. 5,3 in Martos. Auf einer Glasschale in Desenzano aus der 2. Hälfte des 4. Jhs. werden nur Christus und der Hahn dargestellt: F. PAOLUCCI, *I vetri incisi dall' Italia settentrionale e dalla Rezia nel periodo medio e tardo imperiale*, Firenze 1997, 150f.

Sarkophaggruppe auf Stücken des 3. und frühen 4. Jhs. nachweisen[50]. Die Petrus-Christus-Hahn-Szene präsentiert sich somit als Fortführung der philosophischen Lehrszene in christlichem Kontext; sie zeigt Christus als Lehrer der wahren Philosophie, die vom Hörer mit Aufmerksamkeit und persönlicher Betroffenheit aufgenommen wird.

Der Gestus der zum Gesicht geführten Hand begegnet in christlichem Kontext ebenfalls als Reaktion auf eine Theophanie[51], allerdings nicht besonders häufig. Aus dem 4. Jh. ist die Darstellung der Himmelfahrt des Elias in einem Arkosol der Domitilla-Katakombe zu nennen, wo Elisäus mit erhobenem und zum Kopf geführtem Arm dem Geschehen zuschaut[52]. Auch für Petrus ist der erhobene Arm nachzuweisen[53]. Deutet man die Hahnszene in diesem Sinn als Theophanie, bringt der Gestus Erstaunen und Ehrerbietung in Bezug auf Christus zum Ausdruck[54].

Die Interpretation des Gestus Petri enthält somit Aspekte, die über die Wiedergabe der neutestamentlichen Szenen der Verleugnungsansage und der Beauftragung mit dem Hirtenamt hinaus und auf Christus als den wahren Philosophen und den wahren Gott hinweisen.

Zur Erschließung des Inhalts der Szene ist auch die Bedeutung des Hahns einzubeziehen, die dieser in den frühchristlichen Texten und in der Liturgie hat. Bereits in der aus dem 3. Jh. stammenden Traditio Apostolica[55] wird die Stunde des Hahnenschreis als Gebetszeit und Gedenken an und Hoffnung auf die Auferstehung erwähnt[56]. Der Hahn kommt ebenfalls in dem Hymnus „Aeterne rerum conditor“ des Ambrosius vor, der wohl für das täglich von der Pfarrgemeinde gesungene Morgenoffizium geschaffen wurde[57], und in dem von Prudentius verfassten Hymnus „Ad galli cantum“, der zu dessen „Cathemerinon liber“ mit zwölf literarischen Hymnen zu

[50] B. Ewald, Der Philosoph als Leitbild. Ikonographische Untersuchungen an römischen Sarkophagreliefs, Mainz 1999, Kat. A 28 Taf. 16,2 in S. Lorenzo (3. Jh.); D 4 Taf. 41 im Palazzo Balestra (ausgehendes 3. Jh.); D 9 Taf. 46,5 im Museo Nazionale Romano (Anfang 4. Jh.); G 17 Taf. 90 in den Musei Vaticani (275–280); I 16 Taf. 104,5 im Palazzo Merolli (2. H. 3. Jh.); I 18 Taf. 104,5 in San Severino Marche (2. H. 3. Jh.).

[51] Post (s. Anm. 41), 148. Die Beispiele, die Post nennt, entstammen meist dem 5. Jh. oder sind noch später entstanden.

[52] Wilpert (s. Anm.40), Taf. 230,2.

[53] Brandenburg (s. Anm. 49), 9 Nr. 39 (seitlich erhobener Arm); Nr. 624a.

[54] Post (s. Anm. 41), 149.

[55] W. Geerlings (Hg.), Traditio Apostolica, FC 1, Freiburg i.Br. 1999, 149 weist darauf hin, dass die Traditio Apostolica nicht mit Sicherheit Hippolyt zugewiesen werden kann.

[56] Trad. Apost. 41, ed. W. Geerlings, FC 1, Freiburg 1991, 306–309.

[57] A. Franz, Tageslauf und Heilsgeschichte. Untersuchungen zum literarischen Text und liturgischen Kontext der Tagzeitenhymnen des Ambrosius von Mailand, St. Ottilien 1994, 360.

wichtigen Abschnitten des Tages und des Jahres gehört[58]. Der Hahn besitzt in diesen und anderen patristischen Texten drei Bedeutungsebenen[59], die nebeneinander existieren und inhaltlich nicht voneinander zu trennen sind: Zunächst einmal gilt er als Zeuge Christi. Hier enthält ein koptisches Apokryphon, das aus dem griechischen Bartholomäus-Evangelium stammen könnte[60], ein besonders anschauliches Zeugnis: Der Text berichtet von einem gebratenen Hahn, der durch Christus beim letzten Abendmahl zum Leben erweckt wird, um auf seine eigene Auferstehung hinzuweisen:

> „Jesus berührte den Hahn und sagte zu ihm: „Ich sage dir, Hahn, lebe, wie du es tatest. Dass du mit den Flügeln schlagen und dich in die Lüfte erheben kannst, um den Tag anzukündigen, an dem ich überliefert werde." Da erhebt sich der Hahn von dem Teller. Er springt davon. Jesus sagt zu Matthias: „Da siehst du den Vogel, den du geschlachtet hast; er ist nach drei Stunden auferstanden. Mich wird man kreuzigen; und mein Blut wird das Heil der Völker; und ich werde am dritten Tag auferstehen."[61]

Auf einer zweiten Bedeutungsebene erscheint der Hahn als Zeichen der Erlösung, und auf einer dritten als Sinnbild Christi[62]. Es soll hier darauf verzichtet werden, weitere Texte anzuführen; die Durchsicht der frühchristlichen Texte, die den Hahn erwähnen, zeigt eindeutig, dass dieser als Sinnbild Christi eine wichtige Rolle in Bezug auf Auferstehung und Parusie einnimmt. Die mit dem Hahn verbundenen Bedeutungen veranschaulichen, was bereits im Kontext der ikonographischen Analyse anklang: Dass nämlich der Schwerpunkt des Bildinhaltes auf Christus liegt[63], und dass von ihm Heil und Erlösung erwartet wird.

Die einzelnen Aspekte der Bedeutung der Petrus-Christus-Hahn-Szene fasse ich noch einmal zusammen:

1. Die Ikonographie der Szene auf den frühchristlichen Sarkophagen meint die Ansage der Verleugnung, den Moment nach der Verleugnung und die Beauftragung Petri.
2. Frühchristliche Texte interpretieren Verleugnung und Beauftragung Petri als Bilder für Sündenvergebung, Gnade und Barmherzigkeit Christi.
3. Die Ikonographie der von Christus und Petrus ausgeführten Gesten hat ihre Parallele im philosophischen Lehrgespräch („Christus als der wahre Philosoph").

---

[58] LACL[3] (2002), 599 (S. DÖPP).

[59] FRANZ (s. Anm. 57), 174.

[60] NTApo[6] (1990), 438.

[61] FRANZ (s. Anm. 57), 168.

[62] Ebd., 174; s. auch C. NAUERTH, Art. Hahn, in: RAC 13 (1986), 364.

[63] Vgl. z.B. E. DASSMANN, Die Szene Christus-Petrus mit dem Hahn. Zum Verhältnis von Komposition und Interpretation auf christlichen Sarkophagen, in: Pietas. Festschrift für B. Kötting (= JbAChr-Erg.-Bd 8), Münster 1980, 526; darauf weist auch POST (s. Anm. 41), 133 hin.

4. Der Hahn ist in frühchristlichen Texten Sinnbild Christi, wobei Auferstehung und Erlösung deutlich im Vordergrund stehen. Die Einbeziehung des Hahnes macht deutlich, dass der inhaltliche Schwerpunkt der Szene auf Christus und nicht auf Petrus liegt.

Um zu erwägen, welche Bedeutungsebenen auf den Grabmälern Relevanz besaßen, lohnt ein Blick auf die frühchristlichen Grabinschriften aus Rom, die – über das häufige „in pace" hinausgehend – Aussagen zum Leben nach dem Tod machen. Bei einer Zusammenstellung von solchen Texten aus dem Zeitraum von 200 bis zum im Jahre 355 beginnenden Pontifikat des Damasus ergibt sich, dass Aussagen zur Gemeinschaft mit Gott die zahlreichste Gruppe sind. Der Aspekt der Sündenvergebung wird in den Inschriften nicht erwähnt[64], was darauf hinweist, dass dieser auch für die das Grab schmückenden Bilder eher im Hintergrund stand, zumal Buße zu Lebzeiten abgeleistet werden sollte[65]. Möglicherweise besaß die Interpretation der Hahnszene als Bild für die Sündenvergebung auf Gegenständen des Alltagslebens Relevanz.

Neben der Gemeinschaft mit Gott und, in der Häufigkeit darauf folgend, sind die Wünsche für die Verstorbenen, die auf deren Wohlergehen im Jenseits zielen, die wichtigsten Anliegen der stadtrömischen Inschriften, die sich zum Leben nach dem Tod äußern. Zu diesen gehören auch Aussagen zum Refrigerium, das ein Zustand bzw. ein Ort ist, der vom ewigen Leben und der Auferstehung unterschieden ist, in dem aber ein Kontakt mit Gott besteht[66].

Die aus Texten und Bildern gewonnenen Aussagen lassen sich ohne Schwierigkeiten mit den epigraphischen Texten in Einklang bringen: Die Hahnszene als Christusbild bzw. der in ihr zum Ausdruck kommende Aus-

---

[64] S. die Graphik bei J. DRESKEN-WEILAND, Vorstellungen von Tod und Jenseits in den frühchristlichen Grabinschriften des 3.–6. Jhs. in Rom, Italien und Afrika, in: RQ 101 (2006), 289–312, hier 292f.

[65] G. STUHLFAUTH, Die apokryphen Petrusgeschichten in der altchristlichen Kunst, Berlin/Leipzig 1925, 19 erklärt Beliebtheit und Bedeutung der Petrus-Hahn-Szene wie folgt: „Nicht um den Apostel zu erniedrigen, hat die altchristliche Kunst dieses Motiv geschaffen und so häufig wiedergeben, sondern weil sein, des Apostels Ansehen aufs höchste gestiegen war, wurde dieses und wurden andere Petrusmotive im 4. Jahrhundert dem Bilderkreis einverleibt und um in dem Motiv der Verleugnungsansage insbesondere dem Gläubigen eine neue Gewähr seiner eigenen Errettung ungeachtet aller Schuld und Sünde vor Augen zu führen."

[66] Der Kontakt mit Gott ist als wesentliches Element des Refrigeriums der Interpretation von A.M. STUIBER, Refrigerium interim. Die Vorstellungen vom Zwischenzustand und die frühchristliche Grabeskunst, Bonn 1957, 105–120 hinzuzufügen. Die Arbeit Stuibers beruht in Bezug auf die frühchristlichen Inschriften auf A.M. SCHNEIDER, Refrigerium I. Nach literarischen Quellen und Inschriften, Freiburg i.Br. 1928, 19–25, also auf einer viel schmaleren Materialbasis.

druck der Gnade und Barmherzigkeit Gottes passen gut zu der Gemeinschaft mit Gott, die sich die Verstorbenen erhoffen. Der Hahn als Sinnbild Christi bzw. der Erlösung und der Auferstehung entspricht der in den Inschriften geäußerten Erwartung eines positiven jenseitigen Zustandes und dessen Beendigung am Jüngsten Tag.

Eines wird aus der Vielzahl der Bedeutungsebenen, die in Bildern und Texten zur Hahnszene übereinander liegen, deutlich: die Passion Christi ist eine unter mehreren Möglichkeiten. Es sei noch einmal betont, dass die Hahnszene zu den wichtigen Bildthemen auf Sarkophagen des 4. Jhs. gehört, die während der gesamten Periode zu finden sind. Im späten 4. Jh., als auf den Sarkophagfronten deutlich weniger Themen und erzählende Szenen dargestellt werden, scheint dem Thema eine besondere Bedeutung zuzukommen, zumal es mehrfach unmittelbar neben der die Mitte der Front einnehmenden repräsentativen Christusszene steht[67].

6. Das Tropaion

Die Passion Christi wird in der frühchristlichen Kunst stets von ihrem Ergebnis her, der Überwindung des Todes, betrachtet, wie sie seit dem 2. Viertel des 4. Jhs. entstandene Säulensarkophage zeigen. Ein Sarkophag in den Vatikanischen Museen (Rep. I 49), der um die Mitte des 4. Jh. entstanden ist, zeigt in der Mitte der Front einen Lorbeerkranz, der von Bändern umwunden ist und in den ein Christusmonogramm eingeschrieben ist; unter dem Christogramm befindet sich ein kreuzartiges Gestell, auf dessen Querarmen zwei Tauben sitzen. Dieses Gestell ist das Tropaion, das Siegeszeichen eines hellenistischen und römischen Heerführers, an dem die Waffen der besiegten Herrscher aufgehängt wurden. Das Tropaion wurde stets mit dem Namen des siegreichen Feldherren bezeichnet – hier mit dem Namen Christi. Die unter dem Tropaion sitzenden Soldaten gehören zur bildlichen Tradition, da bei seiner Errichtung und Einweihung Soldaten des gegnerischen Heeres, deren körperliche Verfassung, Kleidung und Haltung die Niederlage bezeugten, neben das Tropaion gruppiert wurden. Die Soldaten, die auf unserem Sarkophag unter dem Tropaion sitzen, verfügen noch über ihre Waffen, und der Linke von ihnen schläft auf seinen Schild gelehnt: Es sind wohl die Soldaten gemeint, die das Grab Christi bewach-

[67] BRANDENBURG (s. Anm. 49), Nr. 676 (neben dominus legem dat); Nr. 755 (neben Christus und der Samariterin); J. DRESKEN-WEILAND, Repertorium der christlich-antiken Sarkophage II, Mainz 1998, Nr. 108 (auf Riefelsarkophag im oberen rechten Eckfeld); Nr. 138 (mit der Heilung der Bluflüssigen verschmolzen zur Mittelszene); CHRISTERN-BRIESENICK (s. Anm. 42), Nr. 497 (rechts des Tropaion); Nr. 499 (links des dominus legem dat).

ten – vor dem Hintergrund der antiken Bildtradition, die an dieser Stelle Unterlegene darstellte. Im ersten Bildfeld links ist Simon von Cyrene in Arbeitskleidung dargestellt, der das Kreuz trägt und von einem Soldaten begleitet wird. Das nächste Feld zeigt Christus, dem ein Soldat in Vorwegnahme seiner Auferstehung als Sieger einen Lorbeerkranz über den Kopf hält. Im Bildfeld rechts der Mitte ist Christus, begleitet von einem Soldaten, zu sehen; außen der sitzende Pilatus, der seine linke Hand in einem Gestus der Betrübnis an das Kinn führt, neben ihm ein Soldat oder ein Beamter, vor ihm ein Diener, der ihm eine Schale und eine Kanne zum Händewaschen hinhält. Ein vierter auf Christi Sieg über den Tod verweisender Lorbeerkranz ist hier im Giebel aufgehängt. Der Triumph Christi steht also klar im Vordergrund.

Die Mittelnische wird oben durch die beiden Büsten von Sol und Luna eingerahmt und die Erlösungstat Christi somit in kosmische Dimensionen eingeordnet. Hier ist wie in der frühchristlichen Kunst allgemein eine Vielschichtigkeit der Aussagen zu beobachten, die es nicht erlaubt, die Aussage eines Bildes auf einen Aspekt zu beschränken, sondern unterschiedliche Bedeutungen und Bedeutungsebenen berücksichtigen muss: bei diesem Sarkophag Leiden und Sterben Christi, sein Triumph und seine überzeitliche Herrschaft über die Welt. Nur dieser Sarkophag beschränkt sich auf Szenen, die der Passion entnommen sind; das Tropaion wird auf anderen Sarkophagen am häufigsten mit akklamierenden Aposteln kombiniert, die den Aspekt der Huldigung Christi ins Bild bringen[68].

7. Der Einzug in Jerusalem und Christus vor Pilatus

Mit diesen beiden Bildthemen, die zu den häufiger dargestellten Passionsszenen gehören, sind wiederum Elemente ausgewählt, die sich zur Gestaltung repräsentativer Bilder eignen. Der Einzug Christi in Jerusalem, der bereits zu Beginn des 4. Jhs. auf den Sarkophagen zu finden ist, lehnt sich ikonographisch an den Adventus des Kaisers an und kennzeichnet Christus als Herrscher.

„Christus vor Pilatus“ umfasst in der Regel zwei Szenen: Christus, von Soldaten begleitet, steht wie ein Würdenträger vor Pilatus, der von Dienern umgeben auf einer *sella* thront und in das Nachdenken über das Geschehende versunken scheint; ein Diener hält Geräte für die Handwaschung bereit. Diese Ikonographie findet sich seit dem 2. Viertel oder 2. Drittel des 4. Jhs. auf christlichen Sarkophagen. Sie entspricht einer auch schon in

---

[68] BRANDENBURG (s. Anm. 49), Nr. 59 (und 209); 62, 65, 175, 224, 667, 933; DRESKEN-WEILAND (s. Anm. 49), Nr. 143, 146; CHRISTERN-BRIESENICK (s. Anm. 42), Nr. 49, 67, 282, 294, 503, 504.

anderen Bildern bereits im frühen 4. Jh. festzustellenden Tendenz[69], Christus seinem herrscherlichen Rang entsprechend abzubilden, wie dies auch in einer Darstellung Christi vor Pilatus auf einem Sarkophag in Arles zum Ausdruck kommt[70].

In frühchristlicher Zeit werden Kreuzigungsdarstellungen nie häufig, wahrscheinlich deswegen, weil sich das mit der Kreuzigung verbundene Schändliche und Entehrende kaum vollständig in den Hintergrund drängen ließ[71]. Zudem hat sich in der Spätantike anders als im Hochmittelalter keine besondere Passionsfrömmigkeit herausgebildet, entsprechend gehören auch andere Darstellungen, die sich auf die Passion beziehen, nicht zu den beliebten Bildthemen. Welche Bilder den Christen des 3. und vor allem des 4. Jhs. wichtig waren, lässt sich nur innerhalb der Grabkunst und der Gattungen der Katakombenmalerei und der Sarkophage sagen. Dort sind es interessanterweise die Brotvermehrung und die Auferweckung des Lazarus, die die Hoffnung der Christen auf ein Leben bei Gott zum Ausdruck bringen.

Abb. 1: London, Britisches Museum, Gemme mit Kreuzigungsdarstellung

[69] Auf den Sarkophagen in Rom, BRANDENBURG (s. Anm. 49), Nr. 241 (Mittelbild im oberen Fries), in Florenz, DRESKEN-WEILAND (s. Anm. 49), Nr. 10 und in Arles, CHRISTERN-BRIESENICK (s. Anm. 42), Nr. 32.

[70] CHRISTERN-BRIESENICK (s. Anm. 42), Nr. 53: Christus wird von einem Soldaten nicht wie ein Gefangener vorgeführt, sondern wie ein empfohlener Gast eingeführt.

[71] Vgl. MRASS (s. Anm. 7), 293. S. hierzu auch S. HEID, Frühe Kritik am Gekreuzigten und das Ringen um eine christliche Antwort, in: TThZ 101 (2001), 85–114.

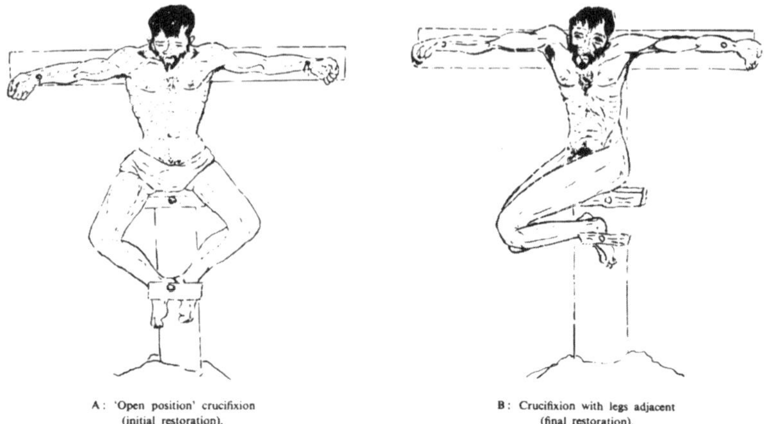

A: 'Open position' crucifixion
(initial restoration).
B: Crucifixion with legs adjacent
(final restoration).

Figure 7-20

Reconstructions of an A.D. 7 crucified man.
Reconstructions (initial and final) of the position on the cross established from the Giv'at ha Mivtar excavations.
(Courtesy of Israel Exploration Society and Mrs. Nicu Haas).

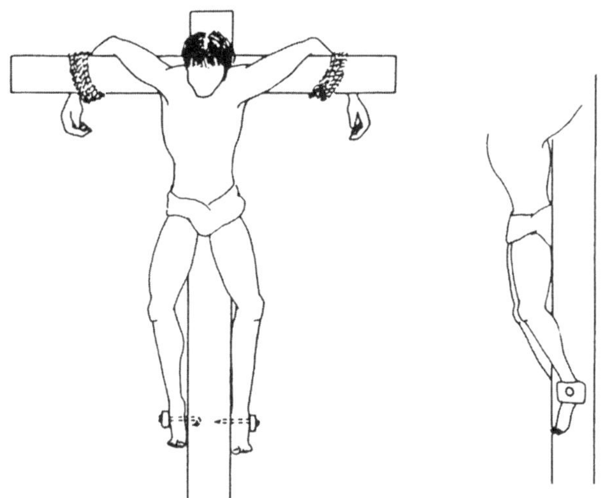

Figure 7-21

Reconstruction of A.D. 7 crucified man.
(Courtesy of Drs. Zia and Sekeles).

Abb. 2: Möglichkeiten der Kreuzigung,
Rekonstruktion auf Basis eines Knochenfundes aus dem Jahr 7 n. Chr., nach Zugibe (Anm.7).

Passion Traditions in the *Gospel of Peter*

PAUL FOSTER

1. Introduction

From beginning to end, what survives of the *Gospel of Peter* can accurately be classed as passion and resurrection traditions. The *editio princeps* described this text, which was excavated from an ancient Christian grave at Akhmîm during the winter season dig of 1886/87, as "un récit de la Passion du Christ."[1] Others supported this self-evident judgment with Swete stating that the *Gospel of Peter* was the "longest history of the Passion" and in an attempt to quantify its length in relation to the canonical accounts Swete stated that "the Petrine account is considerably the longest of the five, and exceeds by about one fourth the average length of the four canonical narratives."[2] Such lengthening could theoretically be achieved in a number of ways: (i) redactional expansion; (ii) conflation of parallel accounts from canonical sources; and (iii) incorporation of traditions not found previously in the canonical accounts. As the individual Passion traditions in the *Gospel of Peter* are considered, these alternatives will be examined to ascertain whether they account for the form of tradition present. It does need to be acknowledged from the outset that the actual extent of the Passion traditions in the *Gospel of Peter* remains unknown. The extant portion of text begins mid-sentence, with a trial scene presumably having been described in further detail. However, the starting point of this narrative remains unknown. Whether the text was only a Passion account, or whether it commenced at an earlier point of the life of Jesus, such as during his ministry phase or even with an infancy account, cannot be determined with any degree of certainty.[3]

---

[1] U. Bouriant, "Fragments du texte grec du livre d'Énoch et de quelques écrits attribués à saint Pierre", in *Mémoires publiés par les membres de la Mission archéologique française au Caire* (t. IX, fasc. 1; Paris 1892), 137.

[2] H.B. Swete, *The Akhmîm Fragment of the Apocryphal Gospel of St Peter* (London 1893), xiii.

[3] In his description of a text known as *The Gospel of Peter* Origen makes the following comment "But some say the brothers of Jesus are, from a tradition based upon the Gospel according to Peter, as it is entitled, or the Book of James, sons of Joseph from a former wife, who was married to him before Mary." (Origen, *comm. in Mt* X 17). It has

An important introductory issue is the definition of what precisely constitutes a "Passion tradition". Nickelsburg offers the following definition: "This term usually designates the sections of the canonical gospels that recount the suffering and death of Jesus of Nazareth: Matt 26–27; Mark 14–15; Luke 22:23 [*sic*, 22–23]; and John 12–19."[4] Here resurrection or empty tomb traditions are considered to be beyond the boundary of what is classified as Passion traditions. Although not as explicitly stated, in discussing the Markan Passion narrative, Best sees the pre-Markan form of the Passion commencing at 14:1 and ending at 15:39 with the centurion's confession. Again empty tomb traditions are not considered to be part of the Passion narrative. Rather the material in Mark 16:1–8 is seen as "the necessary completion to the story of the Cross: necessary because in the Markan predictions of the Cross the Resurrection has always been mentioned."[5] Therefore, according to Best, while the material in Mark 16:1–8 is integral to the Markan gospel, it was not original to the pre-Markan Passion narrative. By contrast, discussing the Lukan form of the Passion, Taylor includes resurrection traditions as part of the Passion narrative. Initially, in passing, he refers to "the Passion narrative of Lk. xxii–xxiv", and then defines a pre-existing unit slightly more narrowly stating "a special source lies behind Lk. xxii. 14 – xxiv."[6] Although there is a difference of opinion as to whether or not empty tomb and resurrection traditions constitute part of the wider category of Passion traditions, the scholarly consensus appears to have more consistently viewed the Passion ending at the point of Jesus' death (along with immediately related events). By contrast, the traditions surrounding the first Easter morning have been viewed as originally developed and circulating separately from accounts of the death. This categorization can be seen in numerous recent studies on the Passion. Raymond Brown's *Death of the Messiah* is representative of this trend, with his treatment concluding with the death of Jesus and immediately fol-

---

been suggested that this may either be a tradition in an infancy account or a parallel to the type of tradition in Mk 6:3. If either suggestion were the case, then the extent of the *Gospel of Peter* would be considerably greater than the fragment preserved. However, such suggestions remain speculative and it is probably safest not to build any conclusions on such hypotheses.

[4] G.W.E. Nickelsburg, "Passion Narratives", in D.N. Freedman (ed.), *Anchor Bible Dictionary* (vol. 5; New York 1992), 172.

[5] E. Best, *The Temptation and the Passion: The Markan Soteriology* (SNTSMS 2; Cambridge 1965), 90, 102.

[6] V. Taylor, *The Passion Narrative of St Luke: A Critical and Historical Investigation* (SNTSMS 19; Cambridge 1972), 3, 17.

lowing events of the interment of the body coupled with the stationing of the guard at the sepulchre (Matt 27:62–66; Luke 23:56b).[7]

If similar boundaries are adopted for the extant traditions contained in the Akhmîm copy of the *Gospel of Peter*, then the first half of the text should be considered as Passion narrative (*Gos. Pet.* 1.1–8.33). However, the second half of the text would be classified as empty tomb and resurrection traditions (*Gos. Pet.* 9.34–14.60). Thus, the extant Passion traditions contained in the *Gospel of Peter* commence with the notice of "Jews", "Herod" and "his judges" refusing to wash their hands (*Gos. Pet.* 1.1), and extends as far as the description of the sealing of the tomb after the crucifixion (*Gos. Pet.* 8.33). While such a separation of Passion and resurrection traditions may have made good sense for the canonical accounts, where as Best argued the presence of a literary seam may be detected between these two blocks of material,[8] it needs to be noted that no such literary seam exists at a similar point in the *Gospel of Peter*. In fact quite the opposite is the case. The guard at the tomb story unifies both "categories" of traditions, and *Gos. Pet.* 9.34 follows directly on from the preceding verse without any literary seam or change in setting. Nonetheless, in line with the widely accepted understanding of the term "Passion narrative" and so as not to confuse generally accepted categories, the principal focus will be on those traditions concerning the trial, suffering and crucifixion of Jesus (*Gos. Pet.* 1.1–8.33). However, material will be considered in this discussion from the resurrection section (*Gos. Pet.* 9.34–14.60), when it is relevant to traditions in the Passion narrative section.

2. The Relationship of the *Gospel of Peter* to the Canonical Gospels

There is an established divide between those scholars who view the *Gospel of Peter* as independent of the canonical gospels and those who see it as dependent: consciously reshaping traditions probably drawn from all four gospels. One scholar who exemplifies these different possibilities was Harnack, who famously oscillated between the two positions in various publications.[9] While the consensus appeared to favour the case for dependence upon the canonical gospels, the theory of independence was strongly ar-

---

[7] R.E. Brown, *The Death of the Messiah: From Gethsemane to Grave* (vol. 2; ABRL; New York 1994), esp. 1284–1313.

[8] Best, *Temptation* (n. 5).

[9] For a description of this change of viewpoint see Semeria, "L'Évangile de Pierre", *RB* (1894), 541–542.

ticulated by Gardner-Smith in 1926.[10] However, the arguments he mounted had little impact on the prevailing scholarly view, namely that the *Gospel of Peter* was dependent on canonical accounts. Nearly sixty years later the issue was re-opened by Crossan, who developed a more nuanced explanation.[11] Crossan acknowledges that in its final form the *Gospel of Peter* is dependent upon the canonical accounts. He states,

> "I agree, of course, our present Gospel of Peter is dependent on the canonical gospels. That has always been my position. I have never been very clear, and still am not very clear, on what exact processes were involved in that dependency. I have never argued that such dependency had to be (since it clearly is not) on the model of direct and observable scribal copying."[12]

However, such a statement only represents the "tip of the iceberg" of Crossan's overall theory. He advocates that the final form of the *Gospel of Peter* preserves an extensive and recoverable pre-canonical source, which is independent of the canonical gospels. This source is named by Crossan as 'the *Cross Gospel*'. Separating later canonical material and redactional linking material, results in the following classification of the various parts of the *Gospel of Peter*.

TABLE 1: Crossan's Redactional Layers in *The Gospel of Peter*

Independent Tradition	Redactional Preparation	Dependent Tradition
GP 1 (1.1–6.22)	with 2.3–5a for	*GP* 2 (6.23–24)
GP 3 (7.25–9.34)	with 7.26–27 for	*GP* 6 (14.58–60)
GP 4 (9.35–11.49)	with 9.37 and 11.43–44 for	*GP* 5 (12.50–13.57)

It is never entirely clear how Crossan views the "redactional preparation". It appears that this is material that was part of the "Cross Gospel" that the author of the *Gospel of Peter* "retouched" to aid the integration of the "dependent tradition" material, rather than being material created *de novo*. Either way what the totality of the theory allows, is for Crossan to acknowledge the presence of traditions that derive from canonical accounts, but to set these aside, and instead to focus on the bulk of the narrative (some forty-seven out of sixty verses) which are deemed to represent an earlier form of passion traditions. In fact, Crossan takes his theory a stage further

---

[10] P. Gardner-Smith, "The Gospel of Peter", *JTS* 27 (1926), 255–271 and "The Date of the Gospel of Peter", *JTS* 27 (1926), 401–407.

[11] J.D. Crossan, *Four Other Gospels* (Minneapolis 1985), 125–181; the debate was perhaps re-opened by the earlier article of H. Koester, "Apocryphal and Canonical Gospels", *HTR* 73, 105–130, but Crossan's theories have dominated the case for independence.

[12] J.D. Crossan, "The Gospel of Peter and the Canonical Gospels", *Forum* n.s. 1.1 (1998), 7–51, here 31.

and argues that it is the putative "Cross Gospel" which is the source for the canonical accounts rather than *vice versa*.[13]

Reactions to Crossan's theory have been varied. Some have largely adopted his ideas, either with various modifications,[14] or by suggesting alternative redactional processes.[15] Others have failed to be persuaded by the existence of a "Cross Gospel" source.[16] Since the purpose of this discussion is not to note all the variants positions that have arisen in the aftermath of Crossan's theory, nor to provide a detailed rebuttal of his arguments, only a few brief statements will be made as to why the treatment of the Passion traditions in the *Gospel of Peter* offered here will work from the basis that the *Gospel of Peter* is dependent on the canonical accounts and does not preserve a large-scale independent pre-canonical gospel source.

Primarily there are three reasons for holding to the theory that the *Gospel of Peter* is literarily dependent on the canonical gospels.[17] First, even if one allows Crossan to strip away the material in his "dependent tradition" layer, there is still material in his putative "Cross Gospel" that appears to be dependent upon canonical forms of the tradition. An example of this, which will be discussed more fully below, is the account of the thief on the cross (*Gos. Pet.* 4.13–14). This narrative shows clear signs of being familiar with, and developing from canonical forms of the tradition. Secondly, the basis for separating out the "dependent tradition" appears dubious. There are no obvious literary seams or differences in vocabulary to justify

---

[13] J.D. Crossan, *The Cross that Spoke: The Origins of the Passion Narrative* (San Francisco 1988), esp. 16–30.

[14] Mirecki appears to weaken Crossan's argument by removing his more sophisticated argument that the *Gospel of Peter* in its final form was dependent on the canonical accounts. Thus Mirecki makes even more radical claims than those advanced by Crossan. He states, "The *Gospel of Peter* (=*Gos. Pet.*) was a narrative gospel of the synoptic type which circulated in the mid-1st century under the authority of the name Peter. An earlier form of the gospel probably served as one of the major sources for the canonical gospels." Thus, for Mirecki, the final version of the *Gospel of Peter* appears to have been in circulation by the middle of the first century, presumably prior to the composition of any of the canonical accounts. Yet, there was also an earlier literary stage which the evangelists drew upon in composing their own narratives. It is uncertain when this primitive form was composed, but according to Mirecki's outline this must have been earlier than 50 C.E. P.A. Mirecki, "Peter, Gospel of", in D.N. Freedman (ed.), *The Anchor Bible Dictionary* (vol. 5; New York 1992), 278–281.

[15] Dewey discerns a layer of tradition that is even earlier than Crossan's "Cross Gospel". See A.J. Dewey, "The Passion Narrative of the Gospel of Peter", *Forum*, n.s. 1.1 (1998), 53–69.

[16] Brown, *Death of the Messiah* (n. 7), 1317–1349.

[17] For further discussion of these points see P. Foster, "The Gospel of Peter", in P. Foster (ed.), *The Non-Canonical Gospels* (London 2008), 30–42, esp. 38–40.

this. Instead it appears to be demanded in order to make Crossan's theory work, rather than being suggested by close analysis of the text. Thirdly, the theological perspectives of the *Gospel of Peter*, such as the heightening of miraculous elements, exculpating Pilate, and the increased anti-Jewish attitudes all seem to reflect a document composed in the second century. Therefore, both in terms of the specific details within the text and at the general level of the overall theological trajectory being promoted in the *Gospel of Peter*, the theory that the text is dependent on canonical gospels best explains the evidence. The *Gospel of Peter* does contain elements that are not part of the canonical tradition, but these are best understood as either later pious developments, or as reflecting the theological concerns of the author.

3. The Passion Traditions Contained in the *Gospel of Peter*

In this section the individual passion traditions that occur in *Gos. Pet.* 1.1–8.33 will be considered in sequence. The purpose of each treatment will be to describe new elements that are added to the tradition, to consider how existing traditions drawn from the canonical accounts have been preserved or modified, and to analyze how such a retelling of the Passion narrative serves the author's overall theological purpose. In many ways the last goal involves an interpretative spiral, since it is only by considering modifications to the tradition that it is possible to build up an overall theory of authorial purpose, and then this picture is used to inform the investigation of how the author reshaped the received tradition. Obviously, there is a potential for a certain degree of circularity in such a process, but by being aware of this danger and by constantly checking suggestions of authorial purpose against the actual text, it is to be hoped that the danger of importing and imposing false hermeneutical grids upon the text can be avoided.

3.1 Hand-washing, Pilate's Protest, and Herod's Authority (Gos. Pet. 1.1–2)

The surviving fragment of the *Gospel of Peter* opens with a scene that does not occur in the canonical account, but which does appear to assume knowledge of a tradition unique to Matthew's gospel – that of Pilate symbolically washing his hands to declare his innocence (Matt 27:24).[18] Although caution should be exhibited in discussing what may have been contained in the now no longer extant section of the text, it does appear highly plausible

[18] This is assumed to be the case by various commentators on the text. For instance, see L. Vaganay, *L'Évangile de Pierre* (ÉtB, 2nd ed., Paris 1930), 202.

that a report of Pilate's hand-washing was present, and that the author of the *Gospel of Peter* created the scene in *Gos. Pet.* 1.1–2 to juxtapose the innocence of Pilate with the guilt of those who refuse to wash their hands. The tradition of Pilate washing his hands was of ongoing interest to Christian writers in antiquity. Consequently, it is unsurprising that it should be subject to retelling in various accounts. In addition to the *Gospel of Peter* this is also exemplified in the *Acts of Pilate*.

καὶ λαβὼν ὕδωρ ὁ Πιλᾶτος ἀπενίψατο τὰς χεῖρας αὐτοῦ ἀπέναντι τοῦ ἡλίου λέγων· ʼΑθῷός εἰμι ἀπὸ τοῦ αἵματος τοῦ δικαίου τούτου· ὑμεῖς ὄψεσθε. πάλιν κράζουσιν οἱ ʼΙουδαῖοι ὅτι τὸ αἷμα αὐτοῦ ἐφ' ἡμᾶς καὶ ἐπὶ τὰ τέκνα ἡμῶν. (Act. Pil. 9.4b)[19]

Here the tradition contained in the *Acts of Pilate* appears to be dependent upon Matthew's account, but shows no knowledge of the opening scene from the surviving portion of the *Gospel of Peter*. Thus, while it shows continuing interest in Pilate's actions of hand washing, it does not witness the form of the tradition preserved in the *Gospel of Peter*.

In contrast to the role of Pilate in the canonical accounts where he oversees the execution of Jesus, in the *Gospel of Peter* his authority is made subservient to that of Herod Antipas and he becomes a figure of protest against the injustice of the trial, albeit without power to right the wrongs he observes. As the surviving portion of the text commences, it shifts the blame for the trial onto a combination of three groups who willingly accept the responsibility for the actions which follow.

τ[ῶν] δὲ ʼΙουδαίων οὐδεὶς ἐνίψατο τὰς χεῖρας, οὐδὲ ʽΗρῴδης οὐδὲ τις ṭῶν κριτῶν αὐτοῦ. καὶ μ̣ὴ̣ βουληθέντων νίψασθαι ἀνέστη Πειλᾶτος. (*Gos. Pet.* 1.1)

In effect the refusal of "Jews", "Herod" and "his judges" to wash their hands implicates representative Jewish figures in the death of Jesus, while simultaneously portraying Pilate as a figure of honour who is caught up in the evil machinations of others.[20]

The character of Herod Antipas takes on an enlarged significance in this version of the Passion story, beyond that attributed to him in the synoptic gospels. It is only in the Lukan account that Antipas is depicted as having any involvement with the events of Jesus' trial (Luke 23:7–15). In what is almost a total reversal of roles, in comparison with the *Gospel of Peter*, in Luke's account it is Antipas who plays the subservient role. Moreover, although Antipas hears the accusations of the chief priests and the scribes (Luke 23:9), he disregards their charges as baseless (Luke 23:10). Furthermore, instead of the trial causing tension between Pilate and Antipas,

---

[19] Tischendorf, *Evangelia Apocrypha*, 230.

[20] Brown notes both an "intensification" of the symbolism of hand-washing in the *Gospel of Peter* and also that "[t]he interpretation in *GPet* has clearly developed beyond that in Matt." Brown, *Death of the Messiah* 1 (n. 7), 834.

according to Luke the incident reconciles the two figures (Luke 23:12). Even more strikingly, Antipas declares Jesus' innocence (Luke 23:15), rather than condemning him to death. It would appear that the *Gospel of Peter* is aware of the tradition of Herod Antipas' involvement in the trial (presumably through knowledge of the third gospel), but nonetheless radically rewrites this tradition to advance the author's own theological agenda. Among other concerns, this agenda involves an exercise in "blame-shifting". This is achieved by having Herod take control of the execution (*Gos. Pet.* 1.2) after Pilate has made his futile protest and withdrawal from the unjust trial (*Gos. Pet.* 1.1).

3.2 The Figure of Joseph (Gos. Pet. 2.3–5)

In the four canonical versions of the Passion narrative a character called Joseph, associated with the town of Arimathea (Matt 27:57; Mark 15:43; Luke 23:50; John 19:38), makes request to Pilate for the body of Jesus after the crucifixion. Although the same incident is narrated in the *Gospel of Peter* the details are recast with significant variation. First, the request for the body comes before the crucifixion (*Gos. Pet.* 2.3). This appears to reflect a wider concern in the text that preparations are not reactive, but rather they anticipate the usual events surrounding an execution. This allows for the resurrection scenes to be portrayed as having even greater impact since followers such as Joseph assume the finality of the crucifixion. Secondly, although the request is made to Pilate he functions as no more than an intermediary brokering the agreement of Antipas (*Gos. Pet.* 2.4). Again this casts Pilate in a positive light while simultaneously absolving him of blame since he is powerless to stop the events taking place. A third difference is the use of a scriptural citation which Antipas offers as the reason why, speaking cohortatively, ἡμεῖς αὐτὸν ἐθάπτομεν, he can do nothing other than comply with the correct treatment of the corpse as required by Torah (*Gos. Pet.* 2.5). Such a response serves both to identify Antipas as a representative and leader of Jewish figures in the text,[21] and more pointedly the citation of Deut 21:23 is intended to illustrate the punctilious law observance in the face of gross breaches of justice.[22]

One further feature that should be noted in the reformulation of this tradition in the *Gospel of Peter* is the comment that Joseph and Pilate were personally acquainted. The description of Joseph as "a friend of Pilate" is a striking new detail, unevidenced in the canonical accounts. However, this

[21] Swete, *Akhmîm Fragment* (n. 2), 2.

[22] It is likely that the author is drawing on Septuagintal form of the text: οὐκ ἐπικοιμηθήσεται τὸ σῶμα αὐτοῦ ἐπὶ τοῦ ξύλου ἀλλὰ ταφῇ θάψετε αὐτὸν ἐν τῇ ἡμέρᾳ ἐκείνῃ (Deut 21:23 LXX), although it should be noted that this is an accurate rending of the MT form of the text: לֹא־תָלִין נִבְלָתוֹ עַל־הָעֵץ כִּי־קָבוֹר תִּקְבְּרֶנּוּ בַּיּוֹם הַהוּא.

may represent a radical rewriting of the brief comment about the friendship that developed between Pilate and Antipas (Luke 23:12). If this is the case, then the intention would be to subvert the Lukan description of a friendly relationship between Pilate and Antipas. Presumably this is required within the narrative world of the *Gospel of Peter* since the existence of such a friendship would undermine the ideological orientation of the *Gospel of Peter*, which presents Pilate and Antipas as opposing each other in relation to the trial and condemnation of Jesus.

3.3 Scourging and Mocking of Jesus (Gos. Pet. 3.6–9)

This scene is highly compressed, involves a different set of characters, and is an act of crowd violence rather than the regularized preliminary to a Roman crucifixion. The emphasis moves this description in the direction of characterizing the Passion as being the spontaneous action of a rapidly formed mob, rather than the verdict of a Roman trial. Thus the irregularity and illegality of the process are highlighted in order to portray Jesus as a victim of petty religious jealousies.

Instead of the carrying his cross to the place of execution either himself (John 19:16b–17a) or by Simon (Matt 27:31b–32//Mark 15:20b–21//Luke 23:26–32), Jesus is pushed and dragged along by the fast moving mob.[23] Preparations are not made in advance, instead the mockery is due to what are presented as the instant actions by groups or individual members of the crowd. Notwithstanding this, the actual torments they inflict draw heavily upon the traditions of mockery and scourging in the canonical accounts. The first act, intended to mock Jesus' kingly pretensions, is dressing him in a purple robe (*Gos. Pet.* 3.7). According to three of the canonical accounts the girding of Jesus in a robe is undertaken by Roman soldiers as part of their mockery (Matt 27:28; Mark 15:17; John 19:2). However, Luke attributes this to the soldiers of Herod Antipas (Luke 23:11),[24] but in that context it is the prelude to the declaration of Jesus' innocence. While Matthew and Luke may both play down the kingly associations of the purple robe mentioned by Mark, the *Gospel of Peter* not only recognizes this theme, but develops it further. This is achieved through the *Gospel of Peter* retaining the description of the garment as purple, but even more ex-

---

[23] In some ways the representation of the treatment of Jesus at the hands of a mob aligns more closely with the description of Stephen's death (Acts 7:57b–58a) or the attempt to stone Paul (Acts 14:19).

[24] According to Fitzmyer "[t]here is no suggestion in this Lucan episode that this gorgeous robe has anything to do with Jesus' alleged kingship. That is to read a Markan nuance into it. It is chosen to mock his guiltlessness." J.A. Fitzmyer, *The Gospel According to Luke X–XXIV* (AncB; New York 1985), 1482.

plicitly through the description of Jesus being mocked as "King of Israel".[25]

The act of seating Jesus on the judgment seat (*Gos. Pet.* 3.7) appears to understand the somewhat ambiguous tradition of John 19:13 as referring to Jesus being made to sit on the *bema*. Justin Martyr appears to have taken this tradition from the fourth gospel as a reference to Jesus himself being sat on the judgment seat (*1 Apol.* 35.6).[26] The *Gospel of Peter*, however, rewrites this tradition by both changing the terminology used for the seat from βήματος to καθέδραν κρίσεως, and by replacing Pilate as Jesus' interlocutor, with a Jewish mob who shout insults rather than seek answers. Again the author appears to have a desire to modify known Passion traditions and to recast them for the purpose of presenting Jewish figures as those who instigated Jesus' unjust death.

The catalogue of abuses that follows is assembled from canonical traditions. However, for narrative impact, the abuses are arranged as a rapid sequence of events as individuals step forward to inflict pain on Jesus. The description is one of thoroughgoing cruelty that is presented as being divorced from legitimate justice.

> And one of them brought a thorn crown and placed it on the head of the Lord. And others who stood by were spitting in his face, and others struck his cheeks, others were piercing him with a reed and some were scourging him saying, "With this honour let us honour the son of God." (*Gos. Pet.* 3.8–9)

This staccato sequence ignores practical problems such as the manufacture of a crown of thorns (apparently one was simply to hand). Instead the emphasis is on the unrelenting sequence of torture and mockery. Brown suggests that the "crown of thorns" mentioned in the canonical accounts was not intended as an implement of torture, but that "the crown is part of the royal mockery, like the robe and sceptre."[27] While it is not impossible that this remains part of the emphasis in the *Gospel of Peter*, yet given the sequence of physical abuse that follows it is not unlikely that the "thorn crown" was also meant to be understood as inflicting pain. A number of the elements are drawn from the sequence of the abuse contained in the Markan and Matthean accounts of the Roman mockery: dressing in a robe, weaving and placing of crown of thorns on Jesus' head, hailing as "King of the Jews", striking with reed, spitting, bending the knee in mock worship (Mark 15:16–20a//Matt 27:27–31a). The *Gospel of Peter* recounts the use of a robe, the placement of a thorn crown on his head, spitting, slapping, the use of a reed to inflict pain, and a general comment that they scourged

[25] See M.G. Mara, *Évangile de Pierre: Introduction, Texte Critique, Traduction, Commentaire et Index* (SC 201; Paris 1973), 94.

[26] Swete, *Akhmîm Fragment* (n. 2), 4.

[27] Brown, *The Death of the Messiah* 1 (n. 7), 866.

him – as though the last element was separate from the preceding abuses. The mock homage comes last, with Jesus not hailed as "King of the Jews", but described as "Son of God". While the latter title may have resonated more with Roman readers, the primary motivation for this change would appear to be a desire to distance Jesus from association with Judaism. Similar to the use of the Christological title βασιλεῦ τοῦ 'Ισραήλ at the end of *Gos. Pet.* 3.7, the appellation τὸν υἱὸν τοῦ θεοῦ is used scornfully by this fourth group of tormentors, who fail to perceive that what they are saying in jest represents a reality beyond their present perception.

The title ὁ υἱὸς τοῦ θεοῦ has also been used previously in this section in *Gos. Pet.* 3.6 where the recalcitrant mob expressed their unified desire to drag Jesus to the place of execution. The title is used on two further occasions in the Akhmîm text, but the significance is markedly different. The first occurs in *Gos. Pet.* 11.45, when the centurion and his company use this title to recount the miraculous events that have transpired. In this context, as a group they make the confession, ἀληθῶς υἱὸς ἦν θεοῦ. This is followed by Pilate addressing the Jews and declaring his own innocence, referring to Jesus as ὁ υἱὸς τοῦ θεοῦ. In both these cases Roman characters accept the title as an accurate description without qualification or any sense of mocking.[28] Thus, the author of the Akhmîm text shows a degree of sophistication in the way Christological titles are deployed, having multi-valence depending on which characters articulate the title, and also reflecting the circumstance in which the title is used.

3.4 Crucifixion between Two Criminals (Gos. Pet. 4.10–14)

The purpose of the recasting of this tradition appears to be twofold. First, an incident with negative overtones is softened, and secondly, a heightened Christological affirmation is introduced into the new form of this pericope. Thus the *Gospel of Peter* further develops a tradition that already shows signs of evolution within the synoptic accounts.

Matthew and Mark (Matt 27:44//Mark 15:32b) describe the two other men who are being crucified with Jesus as joining with the onlookers in reviling Jesus. The Lukan handling of this tradition plausibly provided the impetus for the author of the *Gospel of Peter* to further modify this tradition. Luke creates two different responses from the co-crucified. Whereas Mark, followed by Matthew, editorially notes that the both thieves replicated the mockery of the onlookers, neither reports the direct speech of either character, Luke gives voice to both. The first to speak does not so much revile Jesus, but issues a plaintive challenge to Jesus to prove his

[28] As Mara comments, "Pilate accepte non seulement le rapport de la commission, mais encore la conclusion qui en dérive et que la commission a explicitement affirmé: υἱὸς ἦν θεοῦ." Mara, *Évangile de Pierre* (n. 25), 194.

status and in the process to benefit all three being crucified: οὐχὶ σὺ εἶ ὁ χριστός; σῶσον σεαυτὸν καὶ ἡμᾶς (Luke 23:39).[29] The second thief, however, rebukes his fellow victim for a lack of reverence, affirms that Jesus is being punished unjustly, and implores Jesus saying, Ἰησοῦ, μνήσθητί μου ὅταν ἔλθῃς εἰς τὴν βασιλείαν σου (Lk 23:41).

This radical reworking of the tradition by Luke, prepares for an even more creative recasting of the incident in the *Gospel of Peter*. First, for the *Gospel of Peter* there is no record of either thief speaking against Jesus. Such a negative response is totally deleted from the narrative. In fact, even the onlookers do not cast insults at Jesus. Rather, one thief alone is given a voice. He rebukes those who are crucifying Jesus by challenging them to declare the grounds for the punishment. In the process he describes Jesus by using the elevated Christological description 'the saviour of men'.

Εἷς δέ τις τῶν κακούργων ἐκείνων ὠνείδησεν αὐτοὺς λέγων· Ἡμεις διὰ τὰ κακὰ ἃ ἐποιήσαμεν οὕτω πεπόνθαμεν, οὗτος δὲ σωτὴρ γενόμενος τῶν ἀνθρώπων τί ἠδίκησεν ὑμᾶς; (*Gos. Pet.* 4.13)

This section concludes by introducing a further radical revision. In the Fourth Gospel the Jewish leaders ask for the legs of the victims to be broken in order to hasten their deaths (John 19:31–33). As the Johannine narrative makes clear, this is not an act of mercy, but emerges from a religious desire to remove the bodies prior to the Sabbath.[30] This request for leg-breaking, which could be construed as a partial act of mercy on the part of the Jews in the Fourth Gospel, is taken up by the author of the *Gospel of Peter*. Instead of seeking to break the legs of this suffering criminal to speed death, the leaders of the mob single him out for heightened torment, supposing that such an act will deny him even the relief that might be afforded by a swift death. Obviously, the author is unfamiliar with the mechanics of crucifixion and misunderstands the effect of leg-breaking for the victim.

Although Crossan sees the material in *Gos. Pet.* 4.10–14 as part of his early "Cross Gospel" source, dating to the mid first century and being used by the synoptic evangelists, this seems to stretch plausibility beyond breaking point.[31] It is difficult to imagine any explanation of tradition history that originated with an account of one thief who utters a declaration of the

---

[29] Although the actual words spoken by the thief are a challenge to prove status, Luke describes the speech of the first thief using the verb βλασφημέω, which is not a neutral term but carries negative connotations.

[30] On the practice of breaking the legs of those being crucified see N. Haas, "Anthropological Observations on the Skeletal Remains from Giv'at ha-Mivtar," *IEJ* 20 (1970), 38–59. Haas reports the case of a skeleton of a crucified man discovered with one fractured leg and the other smashed to pieces.

[31] Crossan, *The Cross that Spoke* (n. 13), 16, 160–174.

injustice of Jesus' crucifixion coupled with an elevated Christological declaration, and this is undone by later evangelists in various ways. This would require Mark to delete all positive aspects of this tradition and transform it into a thoroughgoing scene of abuse. Matthew, supposedly with Mark and the "Cross Gospel" before him, shows preference for the less developed Markan form. Also Luke supposedly conflates the Markan version with the "Cross Gospel" by retaining one reviling thief, but to partially solve the theological difficulty takes over some aspects of the account from the second source. If this had been a Lukan concern it would have been more natural to adopt the complete form of the tradition from the "Cross Gospel". Moreover, the Christological title of the putative "Cross Gospel", which names Jesus as "the saviour of men", appears to align with the theological outlook of Luke-Acts so well that it is difficult to see why the third evangelist would delete this element from his source. Lastly, Crossan's theory requires that all three synoptic accounts deleted the incidental reference to "leg-breaking", but John who neglects the main thrust of "Cross Gospel" 4:10–14 transforms the "leg-breaking" into the significant retained detail in his narrative.[32]

If one assumes, however, that the author of the *Gospel of Peter* received the forms of the Passion tradition from all four canonical gospels a much more plausible account can be proposed. All references to problematic reviling fellow victims of crucifixion are deleted, the elevated Christological perspectives of later generations surface in the narrative, and a Johannine tradition is conflated with a pericope that originates in the synoptic tradition.

One further significant modification of the Passion narrative which occurs in this pericope should be noted. The wording of the *titulus* is changed, although the form of wording is not totally stable in the canonical accounts:

Matt 27:37	οὗτός ἐστιν Ἰησοῦς ὁ βασιλεὺς τῶν Ἰουδαίων.
Mark 15:26	ὁ βασιλεὺς τῶν Ἰουδαίων.[33]
Luke 23:38	ὁ βασιλεὺς τῶν Ἰουδαίων οὗτος.
John 19:19	Ἰησοῦς ὁ Ναζωραῖος ὁ βασιλεὺς τῶν Ἰουδαίων.
Gos. Pet. 4.11	οὗτός ἐστιν ὁ βασιλεὺς τοῦ Ἰσραήλ.

The use of the demonstrative pronoun followed by the third person singular form ἐστιν suggests that the author of the *Gospel of Peter* is most closely following the Matthean form of the tradition at this point. If this is the case then there are two changes that can easily be explained on the basis of the author's theological preferences. Nowhere in the extant portion

[32] See Foster, "The Gospel of Peter" (n. 17), 39–40.
[33] Cf. *The Acts of Pilate* 10.1.

of the text is the name Ἰησοῦς used, instead Christological titles, especially ὁ κύριος, constitute the common form of reference. Thus deleting the name Ἰησοῦς is unsurprising. Secondly, the genitive plural τῶν Ἰουδαίων is replaced by the singular form τοῦ Ἰσραήλ. This is obviously part of the author's wider anti-Jewish perspective.[34] While contemporary Judaism is viewed as recalcitrant and responsible for the death of Jesus, historic Israel is viewed as a different, and, perhaps in the mind of the author, an unrelated entity. Therefore, to distance Jesus from any Jewish association, the consistent description that occurs in all four canonical accounts ὁ βασιλεὺς τῶν Ἰουδαίων is altered to ὁ βασιλεὺς τοῦ Ἰσραήλ. This suits the theological perspective of the text.

3.5 The Death-Cry (Gos. Pet. 5.15–20)

Again a theologically challenging synoptic tradition is modified by the author of the *Gospel of Peter*. The Markan cry of dereliction (Mark 15:34), replicated in a slightly modified form by Matthew (Matt 27:46), is totally recast in the *Gospel of Peter*. Although Luke creates his own version of this tradition (Luke 23:46) on this occasion it appears that the author of the *Gospel of Peter* has not been directly influenced by the Lukan form, but rather has created an independent solution to replace the cry of abandonment.

Within the extant Passion narrative preserved in the *Gospel of Peter* the cry from the cross is the single utterance given to Jesus. The form of words reported is: ἡ δύναμίς μου ἡ δύναμις κατέλειψάς με (*Gos. Pet.* 5.19). There are some structural affinities with the Markan and Matthean versions of this tradition.

ἡ δύναμίς μου ἡ δύναμις κατέλειψάς με	(*Gos. Pet.* 5.19b)
Θεέ μου θεέ μου, ἱνατί με ἐγκατέλιπες;	(Matt 27:46)
ὁ θεός μου ὁ θεός μου, εἰς τί ἐγκατέλιπές με;	(Mark 15:34)

The repetition of the address to the subject is present in all three cases, and different forms of compounds of the simplex verb λείπω all reveal some type of relationship between these three versions. Apart from these points of contact, the form in the *Gospel of Peter* shows great freedom in handling this tradition. The utterance is transformed from a despairing question into a statement of self-observed fact.

From the earliest stage of research on the *Gospel of Peter*, it was suggested that this form of the cry provided the strongest evidence that the text had a docetic orientation.[35] Such an understanding has been challenged

[34] Vaganay , *L'Évangile de Pierre* (n. 18), 238.

[35] Swete lists this cry as one of the "unorthodox additions". Swete, *Akhmîm Fragment* (n. 2), xxxviii.

in recent scholarship.[36] The problem with this docetic reading is that Jesus is not protected from physical suffering, since he declares the moment of his power leaving him only after he has endured the torments of scourging and crucifixion. Rather, the recast version of this tradition seeks to obviate the theological difficulties of the Markan text, which in bleak terms presents a Jesus who declares his God-forsakenness at the point of his death.[37] In place of this theological conundrum, the *Gospel of Peter* provides an emotive cry. However, this is a statement of recognition about life-force leaving the crucified Jesus, rather than a desperate question concerning the presence of God. The purpose in rewriting this tradition is to replace a theologically problematic dominical cry with a domesticated description of self-awareness.

A further development in this pericope in the *Gospel of Peter* is the emphasis upon the miraculous darkness and the perplexed response of the onlookers.[38] In the synoptic accounts the reference to darkness is notable, but brief (Matt 27:45; Mark 15:33; Luke 23:44). This element of the tradition is significantly expanded here (*Gos. Pet.* 5.15, 18). The author initially presents a description of the darkness combined with another report of punctilious concern about Torah observance in the face of gross injustice (*Gos. Pet.* 5.15). The halakhic concern is again whether the body has been left suspended after sunset (cf. *Gos. Pet.* 2.5). In the same pericope the author returns to the theme of darkness noting the physical effect on those present who had to carry lamps and were stumbling in this unnatural darkness.

The author also makes an explicit editorial comment about the guilt of those complicit in the crucifixion. He states καὶ ἐπλήρωσαν πάντα καὶ ἐτελείωσαν κατὰ τῆς κεφαλῆς αὐτῶν τὰ ἁμαρτήματα. (*Gos. Pet.* 5.17). Here the themes of scriptural fulfillment and judgment coalesce. This may reflect second century disputes over whether Jewish or Christian interpretations of scripture were correct, and of greatest importance for the latter group whether the scriptures foretold and supported claims of Jesus' suffering messiahship.

---

[36] J.W. McCant, "The Gospel of Peter: Docetism Reconsidered", *NTS* 30 (1984), 258–273.

[37] M.D. Hooker, *The Gospel according to Mark* (BNTC; London 1991), 375–376.

[38] There may be a further anti-Jewish element in this description of the darkness. Whereas the synoptic authors present the all encompassing reference ἐφ' ὅλην τὴν γῆν the author of the *Gospel of Peter* may wish to demonstrate that this darkness was a judgment on the inhabitants of Judaea alone, and not on the whole earth be giving the description σκότος κατέσχε πᾶσαν τὴν Ἰουδαίαν. See Vaganay, *L'Évangile de Pierre* (n. 18), 249.

3.6 Removal of the Body from the Cross and Burial (Gos. Pet. 6.21–24)

In terms of the actual mechanics of taking the body down from the cross, the canonical accounts are silent. Here the *Gospel of Peter* engages in an exercise of narrative gap-filling. However the purpose is not simply to create a fuller account, for the additional details are loaded with theological freight. The text supplies the following tradition:

καὶ τότε ἀπέσπασαν τοὺς ἥλους ἀπὸ τῶν χειρῶν τοῦ κυρίου καὶ ἔθηκαν αὐτὸν ἐπὶ τῆς γῆς· καὶ ἡ γῆ πᾶσα ἐσείσθη καὶ φόβος μέγας ἐγένετο. (*Gos. Pet.* 6.21).

Reference to nails, ἥλοι, is a relatively late element in the Passion tradition. Perhaps the origin of this detail stems from the post-resurrection scene where Thomas demands to see the nail marks in Jesus' body (John 20:25). Regardless of origin, such a detail soon became a fixed element in references to the crucifixion. Thus Ignatius states:

ἀληθῶς ἐπὶ Ποντίου Πιλάτου καὶ Ἡρώδου τετράρχου καθηλωμένον ὑπὲρ ἡμῶν ἐν σαρκί (*I.Smyr.* 1.2)

Truly, in the time of Pontius Pilate and Herod the Tetrarch, he was nailed on our behalf in the flesh.

Similarly, the author of the *Epistle of Barnabas*, citing Ps 22:20 as prophecy, makes the following reference to 'nailing':

λέγει γὰρ ὁ προφητεύων ἐπ' αὐτῷ· Φεῖσαί μου τῆς ψυχῆς ἀπὸ 'Ρομφαίας, καὶ Καθήλωσόν μου τὰς σάρκας, ὅτι πονηρευομένων συναγωγὴ ἐπανέστησάν μοι (*Barn.* 5.13)

For the one who prophesied about him said, 'Spare my life from the sword' and 'Nail my flesh, because an assembly of evildoers has risen up against me.'

Both these authors in common employ a compound verbal form, whereas John and the *Gospel of Peter* share a nominal reference to the nails, rather than to the act of nailing. Commentators have noted that the extraction of the nails as further evidence that the account is not docetic in nature.[39]

Further support can be adduced for rejecting a docetic interpretation from the geophysical phenomenon that accompanies the act of placing the body on the ground. The *Gospel of Peter* signals to readers that the apparently lifeless corpse is still to be regarded as sacred, for even the earth itself trembles when it comes into contact with the holy body. There is no theology of an insignificant outer shell here, which functioned as nothing more than a container for the true divine being. In many ways the quest to discover docetic elements in the text in order to demonstrate that it aligned with Serapion's description, had the effect of obscuring some early schol-

[39] See Semeria, "L'Évangile de Pierre" (n. 9), see in particular the discussion on 534–539; and as Mara states, "L'épisode de l'extraction des clous des mains du Seigneur est, de toute évidence, un passage qui n'est pas docète." Mara, *Évangile de Pierre* (n. 25), 142.

ars from seeing those elements in the text that would be highly problematic for a docetic Christology.[40]

Two storylines are resumed in this pericope. The author returns to the concern that the body may have been left on the cross after sunset, and also take up briefly a description of the actions of Joseph. In the canonical versions of the Passion narrative these subplots form single undivided units. In the synoptic accounts the darkness is simply narrated as lasting from the sixth to ninth hour with little elaboration (Matt 27:45; Mark 15:33; Luke 23:44–45a).[41] It is in the Fourth Gospel that the concern over the body remaining on the cross is mentioned (John 19:31). In the *Gospel of Peter* these traditions are brought together and surface in the narrative three times (*Gos. Pet.* 2.5; 5.15, 18; 6.22–23a). Likewise, in the four canonical accounts, the story of Joseph of Arimathea occurs as a single continuous pericope (Matt 27:57–60; Mark 15:43–46; Luke 23:50–53; John 19:38–40). By splitting these previously unified incidents, the author creates a heightened sense of tension within the narrative. While there are definitely stylistic motives for such a retelling of the Passion narrative, these are not divorced from theological concerns. In particular, Jewish Torah observance is caricatured as concern for minutiae while overlooking gross injustice.[42]

3.7 Reactions of Jewish Groups and Companions (Gos. Pet. 7.25–27)

Providing psychological insights into the states of mind of characters in the narrative is another way in which canonical traditions are adapted.[43] This pericope is a combination of two novelistic created scenes. The first is the meeting of Jewish figures, Jews, elders and priests, who begin a lament, recognize their sins, and acknowledge coming judgment on Jerusalem

---

[40] Typical of this older perspective is the comment of Harris, "one thing is clear: he [the author of the *Gospel of Peter*] is a Docetist." J.R. Harris, *The Newly-Recovered Gospel of St. Peter* (London 1893), 35.

[41] Luke adds to brief expansion "the sun being darkened" (Lk 23:45a) to the Markan and Matthean statement that there was darkness over all the land from the sixth to the ninth hour.

[42] Although in these two instances the author of the *Gospel of Peter* splits previously unified storylines, with the description of the guard at the tomb it appears that he unifies source material from Matthew that had been presented in separate scenes. While Brown has argued that there was a unified pre-Matthean "guard at the tomb" source which Matthew split and the *Gospel of Peter* preserved as a unified source (R.E. Brown, "The Gospel of Peter and Canonical Gospel Priority", *NTS* 33 (1987), 321–343) the novelistic details in the version in the *Gospel of Peter* make it more likely that the source was the Matthean account and the author demonstrates his adroitness in either unifying or dividing canonical source material.

[43] See Vaganay, *L'Évangile de Pierre* (n. 18), 268.

(*Gos. Pet.* 7.25). By contrast, the clandestine meeting of disciples presents this group as paralyzed with fear. Although not developed in the narrative, the implication appears to be that they are incapable of stealing the body. Thus the characterization of disciples in this scene may act as a prelude to the guard at the tomb story, which functions apologetically to rebut the charge that the resurrection was in fact a case of body snatching.[44]

The lament of the Jewish leaders may initially be seen as a softening of their negative portrayal. However, the author does not relinquish his aim of shifting the blame for the crucifixion onto Jewish figures so easily. Later in the narrative it becomes apparent that the Jewish leaders are only concerned about self-preservation, rather than showing any remorse over their own actions (*Gos. Pet.* 11.48).[45]

The second part of this pericope is a further example of the author's technique of expanding minor details that occur in the canonical accounts. The Fourth Gospel records a fearful post-resurrection meeting of the disciples (John 20:19). If this is the basis of the scene in *Gos. Pet.* 7.26–27, then it must be acknowledged that the author has exercised great freedom in rewriting it. The timing is changed so it occurs immediately post-crucifixion, rather than post-resurrection. Because of this temporal alteration, it is no longer possible to record an appearance of the risen Jesus in this context. Instead, it forms part of the author's larger sequence of reporting events that occurred between the crucifixion and Easter morning.

3.8 Securing the Sepulchre (Gos. Pet. 8.28–33)

This section commences the lengthy story of the incidents at the tomb, but it also concludes what would normally be classified as Passion traditions with the body being safely deposited in the tomb. An interesting division of Jewish attitudes is set up at the commencement of this pericope. The populace, ὁ λαὸς ἅπας, show signs of genuine repentance after witnessing the signs that accompanied Jesus' death. From the pre-modern perspective of the author, heightened miraculous portents function to enable belief. This becomes even more obvious in the resurrection narratives that follow. The description of the crowds returning home beating their chests is drawn from Luke 23:48, καὶ πάντες οἱ συμπαραγενόμενοι ὄχλοι ἐπὶ τὴν θεωρίαν ταύτην, θεωρήσαντες τὰ γενόμενα, τύπτοντες τὰ στήθη ὑπέστρεφον. From a non-Passion context the author of the *Gospel of Peter* appears to have

[44] In relation to the Matthean version Davies and Allison note that "this tale is apologetics and polemic at the same time". W.D. Davies and D.C. Allison, *The Gospel according to Saint Matthew* (vol. 3; ICC; Edinburgh 1997), 652. The same twin purposes are present in the *Gospel of Peter*.

[45] Brown distinguishes between this group and the "*repentant* Jews" of (8.28b). See Brown, *The Death of the Messiah* (vol. 2) (n. 7), 1190.

been influenced by the reference to the Pharisees hearing the crowds whispering about Jesus in John 7:32, ἤκουσαν οἱ Φαρισαῖοι τοῦ ὄχλου γογγύζοντος περὶ αὐτοῦ ταῦτα. Although the term ὄχλος, shared by the canonical accounts in these passages, is replaced by λαός, the author's more favoured term,[46] nonetheless the neutral or even slightly positive nuance is carried over, replacing the negative depiction of λαός in *Gos. Pet.* 2.5.

The response of the Jewish leadership is the means by which the author maintains the negative portrayal of that group. Rather than join with the crowd in an expression of repentance, out of fear they approach Pilate to secure the tomb. In the Matthean account the response of Pilate is somewhat ambivalent: ἔφη αὐτοῖς ὁ Πιλᾶτος· ἔχετε κουστωδίαν· ὑπάγετε ἀσφαλίσασθε ὡς οἴδατε (Matt 27:65). However, here the narrative leaves no doubt that Pilate provides Roman soldiers to secure the tomb. The centurion in charge is named as Petronius (*Gos. Pet.* 8.31), and the invention of this detail not only supplies colour, but more importantly is intended to give the narrative a sense of evidential authenticity.[47] Further apologetically motivated details are added to this strand of the Passion narrative. The stone is of such size and weight that requires all who are present, the Roman contingents and the Jewish elders and scribes, to move it into place. The generalized act of sealing the tomb, σφραγίσαντες τὸν λίθον, described in Matt 27:66 is replaced by a more exact process of setting seven seals ἐπέχρεισαν ἑπτὰ σφραγῖδας (*Gos. Pet.* 8.33), and the Romans pitch a tent on site to accommodate the soldiers. For the author of the *Gospel of Peter*, possible objections to the resurrection tradition are anticipated at the beginning of that narrative by setting up such a network of security measures around the tomb that the suggestion that the disciples took the body becomes an impossibility.[48] With the body laid to rest and the tomb secured and guarded the Passion narrative of the *Gospel of Peter* comes to an end and the text moves into its next phase, that of describing the miraculous happenings of the resurrection.

---

[46] The author of the Akhmîm text uses the term λαός on four occasions (*Gos. Pet.* 2.5; 8.28, 30; 11.47. By comparison ὄχλος occurs only once (*Gos. Pet.* 9.34).

[47] Bauckham notes the naming of Petronius as an exception to his general theory that "named characters were eyewitnesses who not only originated the traditions to which their names were attached but also continued to tell these stories as authoritative guarantors of their traditions." R. Bauckham, *Jesus and the Eyewitnesses: The Gospels as Eyewitness Testimony* (Grand Rapids, Mich. 2006), 39, 43. However, perhaps rather than taking the case of Petronius as a notable exception to this overall theory, it may be the case that the theory does not gain support from the full range of textual data.

[48] A similar argument is found in the writings of Chrysostom. Responding to those who would oppose Christian claims about the resurrection he states "So then, because of your preventive measures the proof of his resurrection is incontrovertible. Since it [the tomb] was sealed there was no deception." Chrysostom 89.1 = *PG* 59.781.

4. Motivations behind the *Gospel of Peter's* Passion Narrative

It needs to be recalled that as the text is preserved it only provides a fragmentary account of the Passion narrative. It appears to commence the story at some point after Pilate's washing of hands, which in the canonical gospels is narrated only in Matt 27:24. Taking the Matthean narrative as the basis of comparison the following preliminary comments should be borne in mind.[49] Following Nickelsberg's reasonably self-evident claim that the Matthean Passion narrative includes the material in chapters 26–27,[50] it can be noted that this covers one hundred and forty-one verses of text. The parallel material in the *Gospel of Peter* starts no earlier than the conclusion of the scene with Jesus before Pilate (Matt 27:26). Therefore, employing a generous estimate, it may be stated the Passion narrative in the *Gospel of Peter* parallels the final forty verses of Matthew's one hundred and forty-one verse Passion account. If it is assumed that the *Gospel of Peter* did contain a complete text of these traditions (and that is admittedly an unprovable assumption without further manuscript discoveries or more decisive patristic testimony) then what remains is about 28.4% of the Passion narrative.[51] This means that the conclusions that are suggested here concerning the author's recasting of Passion traditions must be seen as tentative, since they may be based on approximately only one quarter of the complete Passion narrative. Notwithstanding this limitation some clear tendencies appear to emerge.

There are at least seven factors that appear to account for the way in which the author of the *Gospel of Peter* has rewritten the canonical Passion traditions. These are not always achieved through discrete changes, rather sometimes a single modification to the tradition can function to achieve more than one of the author's purposes. The following are the authorial aims that have been detected as the basis for the various redactional changes in the form of the Passion narrative preserved in the *Gospel of Peter*:

1. Shifting blame for the crucifixion from Roman authorities to Jewish figures.
2. Producing a Christology that aligns with the author's elevated understanding of Jesus.

---

[49] Given the wide usage of the Gospel of Matthew in the early church in general, and its obvious importance as a source for the *Gospel of Peter*, it is appropriate to make the following comparisons using Matthew as a representative of the shape of the Passion narrative known to the author of the *Gospel of Peter*.

[50] Nickelsburg, "Passion Narratives" (n. 4), 172.

[51] This is not to claim that there are direct parallels in the *Gospel of Peter* to all the traditions contained in Matt 27:27–66. Rather, it simply allows for a broad estimate of the approximate percentage of the Passion narrative that be preserved in the *Gospel of Peter* if the assumption is correct that it did contain a full account of the events surrounding the death of Jesus.

3. Heightening miraculous elements as a means of commending belief.
4. Resolving theologically problematic features in the canonical form of the Passion narratives.
5. Creating a form of the tradition that is more robust for apologetic purposes.
6. Filling gaps in the narrative to satisfy the curiosity of the pious.
7. Producing a stylistically more developed text with greater points of narrative tension.

The first of these features is recurring and frequent. Such changes seek to remove the stigma of Jesus being condemned by what may be viewed in Gentile eyes as legitimate Roman jurisdiction.[52] Instead, blame for the death of Jesus is shifted on to what may be a relatively soft target, especially if the *Gospel of Peter* was composed after the Jewish Revolt of 66–70 C.E., the Trajanic rebellion of diaspora Jews 115–117 C.E,[53] and maybe even in the aftermath of the Bar Kochba revolt of 132–135 C.E.[54] The most obvious places in the text where this exercise in "blame-shifting" occurs is with Herod Antipas taking control of the brief pronouncement of condemnation in the face of Pilate's protest, and by having a brutal Jewish mob carry out the execution of Jesus. – The Christological perspective of the author is presented in a number of ways. These include the repeated use of the term κύριος, changing the record of the inscription on the *titulus* to "king of Israel" to distance Jesus from association with Jews, and by not using the name Jesus. Miraculous elements become more prominent in the resurrection narrative in the second part of this text. However, already in the Passion account the darkening of the sky and the quaking of the ground when the body is laid on the earth are intended as portents of divine status and power. There are two most notable theological problems that are resolved in this form of the Passion tradition. The first is the decision not to give a voice to either or both of the fellow victims of crucifixion as revilers of Jesus. Instead, only one speaks and he reviles those involved in the crucifixion of Jesus. The second theological problem that is resolved is that of the Markan and Matthean form of the cry of dereliction. Instead of a despairing question about divine abandonment, this is transformed into an emotive moment of recognition when Jesus' life-force leaves him. Both these changes resolve potentially negative statements about how others

[52] On this aspect of the text see J. Verheyden, "The Purpose of the Gospel of Peter", in *Das Evangelium nach Petrus: Text, Kontexte, Intertexte* (ed. Th.J. Kraus and T. Nicklas; TU 158; Berlin 2007), 281–301, esp. 290–298; and T. Nicklas, "Die 'Juden' im Petrusevangelium (PCair. 10759). Ein Testfall", *NTS* 47 (2001), 206–221.

[53] See the discussion in P. Foster, "The Apology of Quadratus," in *The Writings of the Apostolic Fathers* (ed. P. Foster, London 2007), 52–62, see esp. 54–55.

[54] For details of the ramifications of the Bar Kochba revolt on the perception of Jews by Rome see H. Eshel, "The Bar Kochba Revolt", in *The Cambridge History of Judaism* (vol. IV: The Late Roman-Rabbinic Period; ed. S.T. Katz; Cambridge 2006), 105–127.

perceived Jesus, or how he perceived himself at the moment of his death.[55] – The main area in which the author introduces changes that make the text more robust for apologetic reasons is in the description of the securing of the tomb by Roman soldiers. Not only do they provide stringent security measures, but their assumed independence serves to verify the claim made in the narrative world of this text that stories of the disciples stealing the body were nothing more than rumours circulated by self-interested Jewish leaders. Gap filling in non-canonical texts is a well known phenomenon and is perhaps most clearly seen in infancy accounts, such as the *Infancy Gospel of Thomas* or the *Protevangelium of James*. Within the Passion narrative of the *Gospel of Peter* a similar tendency can be detected at a number of points. The description of removing the corpse from the cross is unparalleled in the synoptic accounts. This is not in itself of great theological importance, although it does create the possibility of describing the quaking earth when the body is removed from the cross.[56] Finally, some changes appear to be introduced partially for stylistic or narratival reasons. Thus, the repeated refrain about concern over the body remaining on the cross after sunset creates a tension in the storyline, although it simultaneously presents Jewish Torah observance in a negative way. The story of Joseph is told in two scenes, rather than the single scene of the canonical accounts. This may be both a stylistic development, but also shows that the followers of Jesus were not thinking in terms of resurrection prior to the event. – The *Gospel of Peter* is at times a very free rewriting of the canonical Passion narrative.[57] However, this does not mean the canonical gospels have been ignored – in fact quite the opposite. The author has quarried those traditions to serve his own theological purposes, but his retelling of the death of Jesus is not totally constrained by pre-existing forms of the tradition. The author's multifaceted motivations for changing the text are at times highly transparent, while in other places it is hard to detect the underlying motive. What is fully apparent is that this text is a deeply theological reflection on the Passion narratives that occur in the canonical gospels, it retells the story to reinforce certain theological presuppositions, but it achieves those ideological goals by telling a racy and riveting account of the Passion and resurrection for second-century Christians.

---

[55] Foster, "The Gospel of Peter" (n. 17), 35.

[56] Vaganay, *L'Évangile de Pierre* (n. 18), 259–260.

[57] On the application of social-memory theory to account for such variation see A. Kirk, "Tradition and memory in the *Gospel of Peter*," in *Das Evangelium nach Petrus: Text, Kontexte, Intertexte* (ed. Th.J. Kraus and T. Nicklas; TU 158; Berlin 2007), 135–158.

La Passion dans les *Acta Pilati*

CHRISTIANE FURRER

L'objet de cet article sur la réception des traditions évangéliques concernant la Passion dans le texte des Actes de Pilate (AP) consiste à traiter un certain nombre de questions qui permettent d'entrer au cœur des préoccupations d'ordre théologique de leur auteur. Dans un premier temps nous exposerons en quoi consistent les AP, quelles sont les sources auxquelles l'auteur a puisé, quelle forme et quel cadre il a donné à son texte. Dans un deuxième temps, nous chercherons quelle est la portée des certains témoignages exprimés lors du procès de Jésus et celle du vocabulaire johannique utilisé dans les interrogatoires de Pilate, puis nous verrons, d'après la scène de la sentence, à qui incombe la responsabilité de la condamnation de Jésus. Finalement nous étudierons comment l'auteur exploite et réactualise les scènes originales de la crucifixion (Luc) et de la résurrection (Matthieu) et comment il rend compte de la mission universelle (Marc) et de l'ascension du Christ. L'étude de ces questions permet de mettre au jour les intentions évangélisatrices de l'auteur de cet écrit apocryphe du IVe siècle.

Les Actes de Pilate et leurs sources

Nous disposons actuellement de deux recensions grecques des *Actes de Pilate* (AP) ou *Actes faits sous Ponce Pilate*[1], dont la première (A), la plus ancienne et la plus courte, compte seize chapitres[2]. Cette première recension, basée sur l'étude de seize manuscrits se compose d'un titre et d'un prologue (certains manuscrits y ajoutent une préface). Le titre est le sui-

[1] Nous ne retenons pas l'hypothèse de Pilate auteur du texte, même si nous savons qu'il aurait été l'auteur de lettres et de rapports qu'il destinait à Tibère entre autres. La correspondance de Pilate avec ses supérieurs ne peut guère être mise en doute, par contre, on ne voit guère Pilate composer un drame dont il est acteur et reste en fin de compte celui qui conditionne irrémédiablement les événements.

[2] La deuxième recension (contenant 27 chapitres) dénommée B par K.v.Tischendorf et que l'on retrouve dans une forme latine dite A, est citée par les médiévistes sous le nom d'*Évangile de Nicodème*, version la plus répandue au Moyen-Âge ; elle complète le texte avec la narration de la Descente du Christ aux Enfers.

vant : « Mémoire relatif à notre Seigneur Jésus Christ établi sous Ponce Pilate ». Le texte contient en fait le récit de la Passion, de la Résurrection et de l'Ascension du Seigneur. Dans le prologue[3], le texte est présenté comme la traduction *d'Actes rédigés d'abord en langue hébraïque par des Juifs, au temps de notre Seigneur Jésus-Christ.* La traduction aurait été faite par « Ananias, présenté comme garde du corps, de rang prétorien et jusrisconsulte… (au temps de l'empereur) Flavius Théodose, an XVII de son règne et an V de celui de Flavius Valentin, en la neuvième indiction », c'est-à-dire en 440–441. Aujourd'hui, nous retenons comme date plausible de rédaction des AP, la seconde décennie du IVe siècle. La préface présente Nicodème comme auteur et rédacteur du récit ; en fait Nicodème n'est présent, dans le texte, que comme témoin des actions de Joseph d'Arimathée et comme un Juif presque disciple de Jésus ; l'auteur du travail de compilation et de traduction du récit doit plutôt être un narrateur extérieur et discret, qui non seulement a un plan défini en tête mais qui connaît fort bien les sources bibliques.

Où commence la Passion et où finit-elle ? Dans les AP, le texte commence avec le procès romain, faisant l'impasse sur Gethsémani et le procès juif. Par contre, le récit se développe au-delà de l'ensevelissement, se poursuit avec une recherche de témoignages menée par les Juifs pour retrouver Jésus et Joseph d'Arimathée et se termine par une reconnaissance générale par le peuple des faits concernant l'événement dans son entier.

L'ensemble du récit, d'une composition assez libre, s'inspire largement des textes évangéliques auxquels il ajoute des scènes qui tiennent du miracle[4]. L'auteur des AP a puisé, touchant au thème de la Passion seulement, une septantaine de références[5] chez Matthieu, une trentaine chez Luc, une trentaine chez Jean, et une dizaine chez Marc. Toujours sur le même thème de la Passion, les deux tiers de l'ensemble de la tradition évangélique n'ont pas été retenus ; cela s'explique en partie par l'absence de l'intervention des personnages qui ne sont pas directement concernés par le procès ou qui sortent du thème traité[6]. Certains des passages repris sont communs à trois

---

[3] Le prologue revêt un caractère fictif, son but étant sans doute de donner au texte qu'il présente plus d'impact et de crédibilité.

[4] Nous nous basons ici sur le texte des évangiles canoniques et non pas sur leurs propres sources communes ou indépendantes. Pour cette étude nous renvoyons à *La Mort du Messie. De Gethsémani au tombeau : Encyclopédie de la Passion du Christ*, éd. Bayard, Paris, 2005, de Raymond E. Brown. Le miracle des enseignes ou celui de la libération de Joseph d'Arimathée font partie des scènes miraculeuses des AP.

[5] Les références sont constituées de reprises plus ou moins longues, allant d'un mot à la longueur d'un verset et pouvant reproduire une scène entière. Elles se répartissent sur l'ensemble des seize chapitres des AP.

[6] Judas, Hérode, Marie, Pierre, Marie de Magdala, les disciples, Thomas, Simon-Pierre n'apparaissent pas dans notre texte.

ou quatre évangiles, d'autres propres à un seul, et ces derniers avec une assez grande fidélité[7] : le vocabulaire est le même, la structure des phrases est respectée, même si l'ordre de certains éléments est parfois différent (Jn 18, 28–38). Dans la seconde partie qui suit la mort du Christ, les rapports avec la trame biblique s'estompent et ne subsistent que des reprises ponctuelles et disparates de l'Ancien et du Nouveau Testament[8]. Les sources sont souvent implicites (allusion aux paroles de Goliath : 1 S 17,44), parfois explicites (ch.15,1 : « comme l'enseigne la Sainte Ecriture) »(2 R 2) et parfois sous forme de citations précises[9].

A travers les événements de la Passion et de la Résurrection du Sauveur, l'auteur des AP s'intéresse tout particulièrement à l'attitude des chefs juifs, soit au cours de la Passion, soit dans leurs réactions après la Résurrection. Plusieurs de leurs interventions sont qualifiées de mauvaise foi[10]. Pilate, dans un mouvement d'impatience face à leur comportement, évoquera l'histoire de leur peuple ingrat qui ne devrait avoir que de la reconnaissance et non pas de la haine à l'égard de leur Dieu et de ses bienfaits. Ce rappel fait allusion au caractère séditieux de ce peuple et l'on sait à quel point Pilate était soucieux de la bonne marche de son état et craignait les révoltes en tout genre. L'auteur, par ailleurs, mettra plus de poids dans son récit sur certains personnages comme Pilate, Jésus, Anne et Caïphe ou Joseph d'Arimathée. Les douze Juifs dévots et les trois Galiléens recevront une place privilégiée dans les débats et les témoins, comme le messager ou la femme de Pilate, Véronique, les deux larrons (Gestas et Dymas), le centurion, les gardes du tombeau ; Lévi et son père joueront un rôle prépondérant par rapport à la portée du message apologétique de l'auteur des AP.

---

[7] Nous retenons ici de Jean : le dialogue entre Jésus et Pilate. De Luc : la crucifixion, la mort et l'ensevelissement de Jésus. De Matthieu : la proclamation de l'innocence de Pilate et la séquence du lavement des mains, puis la garde du tombeau et les soldats soudoyés. De l'appendice de Marc: la mission universelle.

[8] On trouve des extraits dans la Genèse, l'Exode, le Deutéronome, Josué, Rois, Samuel et quelques parallèles sont tirés des Actes des Apôtres et de l'épître aux Romains.

[9] Les paroles de Syméon, en Luc 2,28–32 ou la parole divine en Dt 2,35 cité en Rm 12,19.

[10] Ils n'acceptent pas le miracle des enseignes, ils tentent de discréditer les défenseurs de Jésus. Le témoignage de la femme de Pilate serait dû à la magie, les miracles ne devraient pas se faire pendant le sabbat, une femme n'aurait pas le droit de témoigner, etc. Ils expliquent les ténèbres lors de la mort de Jésus par une éclipse de soleil, ils tentent de corrompre les gardes du tombeau et chassent les trois témoins des entretiens de Jésus avec ses disiples au moment de son ascension.

Forme et genre littéraire : le drame liturgique

Au-delà d'un récit correspondant à la fin des évangiles, les AP se rapprochent de la forme d'une pièce dramatique constituée de dialogues et de scènes théâtrales, teintée d'éléments de type liturgique[11] et clairement connotée d'une intention apologétique. Par ailleurs, la première et la plus grande partie du texte (ch. 1–11) est ancrée dans le cadre d'un procès fait d'interrogatoires et de témoignages, à caractère polémique et didactique[12] ; la seconde partie (ch. 12–16) est reprise sous forme d'une enquête qui se clôt par un hymne exprimant une reconnaissance des faits, correspondant à un acte de foi unanime.

Imaginons la naissance d'une dramatisation (liturgique) à Jérusalem autour de l'événement du procès au IVe s.[13] Les AP seraient à considérer comme une pièce de théâtre en deux parties, constituée d'actes, de scènes et de dialogues et faisant agir et parler des personnages, des acteurs, comme les protagonistes (Pilate, Jésus), ou encore des groupes de personnes, comme les Juifs ou la foule. Le drame du procès et de la crucifixion du Christ se déroule au palais de Pilate et sur la colline de Golgotha au cours d'une seule journée. Le drame de l'enquête et de la recherche des preuves, où interviennent les témoignages des trois Galiléens et les prières des chefs de la synagogue ou de leurs envoyés, se déroule, lui, sur une période de quarante jours[14], tantôt à Jérusalem, tantôt en Galilée, tantôt à la synagogue, lors de l'assemblée du sanhédrin, tantôt dans la maison de Joseph d'Arimathée et celle de Nicodème. Le mouvement de reconnaissance manifesté par les Juifs puis par la foule, face aux événements et à l'accomplissement des paroles de Jésus, progresse d'une manière proportionnelle à

---

[11] Les prières, les repas, l'onction de Joseph, les citations vétérotestamentaires, les formules, l'hymne final, les nombreuses répétitions tripartites (les 3 motifs d'accusation (x3), les 3 entretiens avec Jésus, les 3 phrases de Pilate, les 3 témoins devant la croix, les 3 phrases de Jésus sur la croix, les 3 Galiléens, les 3 hommes fournis pour l'enquête, les 3 jours de recherche), les occurrences des chiffres 7 (les 7 miracles, les 7 hommes à la recherche de Jésus, les 7 témoignages juifs) et 12 (les 12 hommes forts, les 12 Juifs bienveillants), sont des manifestations et des signes de type liturgique caractéristiques de pratiques rituelles et sacramentelles.

[12] Il s'y insère, en particulier dans le débat sur les motifs d'accusation avancés par les Juifs, des éléments d'ordre polémique qui font ressortir des préoccupations virulentes de l'époque et laissent discrètement entendre et voir l'état et le reflet de querelles provenant de différents milieux juifs par rapport à la condamnation du Christ.

[13] Ce type de dramatisation sur un thème pascal n'est pas totalement inconnu à cette époque : nous faisons allusion au drame liturgique des *Femmes saintes au tombeau du Christ* et nous pourrions renvoyer le lecteur à la tragédie chrétienne du *Christus patiens* attribué à Grégoire de Nazianze.

[14] Période qui correspond à l'absence de Joseph d'Arimathée (parallèle à celle de Jésus).

la montée de la colère et du désarroi des Juifs. Et ce processus d'ordre psychologique aboutit, comme par un coup de théâtre, à un « happy end » ou un heureux dénouement, la pièce se terminant avec un hymne final où le peuple tout entier confesse sa foi et rentre, heureux, chez lui. Les scènes descriptives et les visions ou les miracles s'intègrent particulièrement bien dans une pièce de théâtre (θέατρον – θεάομαι) comme, par exemple les enseignes qui, par deux fois, se penchent, malgré toutes les précautions prises pour éviter un subterfuge, la libération de Joseph (par le Christ) d'une maison sans porte ni fenêtres ou encore les événements pendant la résurrection (Mt) où les phénomènes surnaturels ou inexplicables interviennent (le voile se déchire ou l'ange apparaît tel un éclair blanc). La scène au pied de la croix revêt elle aussi un caractère très théâtral et spectaculaire: non seulement le vocabulaire utilisé par l'auteur met l'accent sur le visuel[15], mais le mouvement des foules et de la communauté en tant que simple témoin oculaire rehausse le caractère dramatique et tragique de la scène. Ils font peut-être le lien avec l'imagerie propre au christianisme populaire appréciée par des lecteurs sensibles au spectaculaire. Des constatations, des réactions ou des leçons de morale, souvent inspirées de sources vétérotestamentaires, venant soit de Pilate[16] lui-même, soit de Joseph[17], soit des Juifs[18] ou de Nicodème[19], recherché par les Juifs[20], soit encore de Lévi[21],

---

[15] Le verbe *assister* (συμπαραγίνομαι), le nom *spectacle* (θεωρία), le verbe *voir* répété 2 fois (θεωρέω).

[16] « Votre peuple est toujours en état de révolte et il s'oppose à ses bienfaiteurs » AP 7,2.

[17] Joseph reprochera aux Juifs leurs mauvaises actions et les menacera, à l'aide de références à l'AT, de la colère imminente du Seigneur : « ce propos (la menace des Juifs : « nous donnerons ta chair aux oiseaux du ciel et aux bêtes sauvages de la terre » cf. 1 S 17,44) vient de l'orgueilleux Goliath qui a blâmé le Dieu vivant et le saint David » (AP 12,2) ; Dieu a dit : « à moi le jugement (la vengeance), c'est moi qui rétribuerai » (Dt. 32,35, cité en Rm. 12,19 ; He. 10,30).

[18] Les Juifs feront part de leurs doutes, de leurs craintes et de leur douleur (AP 14,3) : « Pourquoi un tel signe en Israël ? pourquoi notre âme est-elle abattue ? Peut-on croire le récit des soldats ? et de surcroît de la part d'incirconcis (ce n'est pas possible) ? Que dire du fait qu'ils ont été achetés ? » Ce passage montre bien la situation de malaise dans laquelle se trouvent, à ce stade, les autorités juives. Plus loin encore : « quelle est cette colère qui nous arrive ? »

[19] Nicodème va demander des éclaircissements à propos de l'élévation de Jésus au ciel. Le rappel du récit (AP 15,1 ; cf. Mc 16,15–19 ; 2 R 2,14–17) que fait Nicodème concernant Elie et Elisée et l'élévation mystérieuse d'Elie sous l'effet d'un souffle sur une montagne ou dans les cieux, a suffi pour convaincre les autorités. C'est aussi chez Nicodème que les Juifs interrogeront Joseph sur tout ce qui s'est passé depuis son arrestation, en le conjurant, à la manière d'Achar devant le prophète (cf. Jos 7,19) de tout révéler sans cacher un seul mot de l'histoire (AP 15,5).

[20] Nicodème est intervenu auprès des autorités juives à la manière de Gamaliel dans les Actes des Apôtres, dénonçant l'acharnement des autorités à l'égard des témoins de

ou des trois Galiléens[22] permettent à l'auteur des AP de tisser des liens logiques dans le récit et de prendre un peu de recul et de distance par rapport au récit. Elles viennent également à l'appui d'un enseignement d'ordre théologique et apologétique, soutenues par des manifestations comme la prière, les formules de grâce et de paix et l'hymne final[23]. Dans une volonté de vraisemblance et une recherche d'authenticité, l'auteur a eu le souci, dans sa pièce de théâtre, de nommer un certain nombre de personnes jusqu'à identifier même les membres du sanhédrin[24].

Le personnage de Nicodème mérite un aparté, d'une part parce qu'il entre dans un des titres de notre texte, d'autre part parce qu'il représente à lui seul le peuple juif à convertir, figure emblématique d'une nouvelle naissance[25]. Si la pièce va bel et bien dans le sens d'une conversion progressive de tout un peuple, elle peut bien rappeler le cheminement long et difficile que Nicodème a vécu depuis sa première rencontre de nuit avec Jésus jusqu'à prendre courageusement le parti de Jésus, jusqu'à recevoir son corps même. En effet, Mme C. Renouard, dans son article sur le personnage de Nicodème, analyse le cheminement spirituel de Nicodème dans les chapitres 3, 7 et 19 de l'Evangile de Jean. Jésus répond à Nicodème qui vient de l'aborder (Jn 3,3): « en vérité, en vérité, je te le dis, à moins de

Jésus (Ac 5,38–40). Il n'hésite pas à prendre la défense de Jésus en présence du gouverneur.

[21] Les paroles de Syméon rapportées par Lévi (AP 16,1,2) : « Car mes yeux ont vu ton salut que tu as préparé face à tous les peuples : lumière pour la révélation aux païens et gloire d'Israël ton peuple ».

[22] « Il disait à ses disciples : allez dans le monde entier et prêchez l'évangile à toute la création... » AP 14,1.

[23] « Béni soit le Seigneur qui a donné le repos au peuple d'Israël, conformément à tout ce qu'il a dit ! Pas une seule parole proférée à Moïse et à son serviteur, parmi toutes ses paroles de bonté, n'est tombée. Puisse le seigneur notre Dieu être avec nous, comme il l'était avec nos pères ! Puisse-t-il ne pas nous perdre, pour que notre cœur soit près de lui, pour que nous marchions dans ses voies, pour que nous sauvegardions ses commandements ainsi que les instructions qu'il avait remis à nos pères ! C'est alors que le Seigneur sera instauré roi sur toute la terre, ce jour-là. Il sera seul Seigneur et son nom sera unique. Seigneur, notre roi ! Notre Sauveur ! Il n'en est pas de semblable à toi, Seigneur ! Tu es grand, Seigneur, et grand est ton nom par ta puissance ! Guéris-nous, Seigneur, et nous serons guéris ! Sauve-nous, Seigneur et nous serons sauvés ! Car nous sommes ta part, nous sommes ton héritage, et le Seigneur n'abandonnera pas son peuple, à cause de son grand nom. Car le Seigneur a commencé de faire de nous son peuple » AP 16,4.

[24] A côté d'Anne et de Caïphe, nous avons en AP 1,1 : Soumné, Dothaï, Gamaliel, Juda, Lévis, Nephtalim, Alexandre et Jaïr. Les témoins seront également mentionnés en AP 2,4: Lazare, Astérios, Antonios, Jacobos, Esaïe, Anne, Samuel, Isaac, Phinès, Krispos, Agrippas et Juda.

[25] Christine Renouard : « Le personnage de Nicodème comme figure de nouvelle naissance » in : EThR 79 (2004), 563–573.

naître de nouveau, nul ne peut voir le royaume de Dieu ». La transformation doit être si totale qu'elle peut s'exprimer en termes de naissance. C'est bien le renoncement à ce qui l'a défini jusqu'à maintenant qui est présenté comme indispensable à Nicodème (un homme d'entre les Pharisiens). De même cette réponse peut s'adresser au peuple incrédule (des Pharisiens ou des autres Juifs) qui veut le condamner. Mais le peuple, comme Nicodème, ne comprend pas ce langage et en restera au premier degré de la rationalité pure. Au chapitre 7, Nicodème se démarque de sa première position. Il dit aux Pharisiens qui cherchaient à arrêter Jésus (Jn 7,51): « Notre Loi condamnerait-elle un homme sans l'avoir entendu et sans savoir ce qu'il fait ? ». Ce que réclame Nicodème, c'est d'abord d'entendre celui qu'on accuse : il met ainsi en défaut les Pharisiens sur leur propre terrain, en leur rappelant les exigences de la loi[26]. Ce que nous avons là correspond bien à une demande de la part de Nicodème d'instruire un procès en bonne et due forme comprenant l'audition de l'accusé ainsi que celle de ses témoins. Et cela correspond parfaitement au contenu de notre texte apocryphe dans sa première partie. Au chapitre 19, 40 Nicodème, avec Joseph d'Arimathée, prend le corps de Jésus. Mme C. Renouard y voit là « une haute portée symbolique de l'acte effectué par les deux hommes. La mort de Jésus est accueillie, acceptée dans sa réalité concrète et humaine, dont témoigne ce corps à ensevelir, et en même temps déjà dépassée, réinterprétée par les caractéristiques de l'ensevelissement qui affirment, avant même la résurrection, la messianité de Jésus »[27]. Ainsi le parcours se reconnaît dans différents cas à mettre en parallèle : le Prologue de Jean décrit en effet, face au mouvement répété du logos ou de la lumière en direction du monde, un refus du monde de l'accueillir[28], comme Nicodème, qui ne pouvait d'abord que manifester son incrédulité face à l'annonce de la nouvelle naissance, comme le peuple juif qui reste enfermé dans la lecture unilatérale de ses lois. Mais l'ouverture de l'homme à cette extériorité radicale est cependant affirmée comme possible[29] et c'est ce que comprend finalement Nicodème : « naître de nouveau, d'en haut », c'est s'ouvrir à une réalité qui n'est pas celle des hommes, transcender sa réalité propre, s'ouvrir à l'altérité. C'est accepter d'être institué du dehors, comme le développe Jn 1,13[30]. Et c'est aussi ce que semblent comprendre finalement les membres

[26] Cf. Dt 1,16 : « vous entendrez les causes de vos frères, et vous trancherez avec justice ».

[27] Cf. art. cité dans la note 25, p. 570.

[28] Cf. Jn 1 : « la ténèbre ne l'a pas saisie » (v. 5), « le monde ne l'a pas reconnu » (v. 10), « les siens ne l'ont pas accueilli » (v. 11).

[29] Cf. Jn 1,12 : « mais à ceux qui l'ont reçu (le Verbe, le Logos, la lumière), à ceux qui croient en son nom, il a donné le pouvoir de devenir enfants de Dieu ».

[30] Jn 1,13 : « Ceux-là ne sont pas nés du sang, ni d'un vouloir de chair, ni d'un vouloir d'homme, mais de Dieu ».

du sanhédrin (paroles des prêtres et des Lévites en 16, 3, 2: « sachez qu'il règne pour l'éternité et qu'il a suscité un peuple nouveau ») et le peuple juif, dans ses prières et son hymne final.

Nous avons donc en Nicodème un personnage crucial, très johannique, inconnu des synoptiques, qui donne à la pièce son symbolisme théologique. C'est un disciple relativement insignifiant, mais qui a eu une importance insigne à l'intérieur de la tradition johannique où sa proximité durable avec Jésus fut perçue comme le modèle du comportement de la communauté.

Alors que la veillée pascale et l'annonce de la résurrection marquent le sommet de la vie sacramentelle de la communauté des croyants, on pourrait admettre que la condamnation et le jugement du Christ n'ont pas leur place dans ce contexte de renouveau. Situation tragique, voire honteuse pour le chrétien, ces événements pénibles, longuement décrits et parfois répétitifs ne méritaient certainement pas d'être à ce point mis en avant. Et pourtant tous les éléments semblent être réunis pour en faire une histoire scénique qui, au-delà du mouvement dramatique apporté aux données textuelles, leur confère une dimension à caractère apologétique : l'objectif mis en valeur par la dramatisation veut voir, pendant le procès, l'impasse totale dans laquelle Pilate se retrouve acculé et à la fin des AP, la conversion des Juifs et des hésitants ; c'est la dynamique même de l'enchaînement des scènes qui nous le démontre.

Au IIe et au IIIe s., nous rappelle Pierre Jounel[31], la veillée pascale de la communauté consistait en une lecture de la parole de Dieu et en prières, au terme d'un jeûne intégral de deux jours, dans l'attente du retour du Christ. Au IVe s. la Nuit pascale devient la grande nuit sacramentelle au cours de laquelle les nouveaux chrétiens étaient appelés à mourir et à ressusciter avec le Christ par leur initiation aux mystères. A Rome, Constantinople, Alexandrie ou Antioche, c'est par milliers que, certaines années, les catéchumènes descendaient dans les eaux sanctifiées, recevaient l'imposition des mains et l'onction chrismale, puis communiaient au corps et au sang du Christ dans l'assemblée des frères. C'est en fonction de cette nuit baptismale que les rites de la veillée pascale devaient recevoir la structure et les formulaires qu'ils ont conservés en Occident jusqu'à ce jour : bénédiction solennelle de la lumière, qui va brûler dans la nuit jusqu'à ce que paraisse l'étoile du matin, amples lectures de l'Ancien Testament séparées par des cantiques et des prières, célébration du baptême et de la confirmation, puis de l'Eucharistie pascale. La « pièce de théâtre » pourrait bien s'accomplir au sein d'une célébration chrétienne, dans ce contexte de la période pascale. Nous verrons que tous les ingrédients sont rassemblés

---

[31] P. Jounel, préface, in *Le drame liturgique de Pâques du Xe au XIIIe s.*, Liturgie et théâtre, par Blandine-Dominique Berger , Théologie historique 37 , Paris 1976.

pour constituer ce qui aurait pu être *un drame liturgique*[32], même si nous ne disposons pas d'indications ou de notes écrites à ce propos. Selon Mme B.-D. Berger[33], la dramatisation liturgique avait commencé au IVe s. à Jérusalem, d'une façon originale et spécifique, sur les lieux même où se déroulèrent les événements évangéliques. Notre texte, daté du IVe siècle, pourrait y avoir sa place. Pâques est pour les chrétiens la fête des fêtes ; elle est le centre de la Révélation et le sommet de l'Histoire du salut. Dans la semaine sainte, qui s'étend du dimanche des Rameaux à celui de Pâques, trois jours sont particulièrement vénérés : ceux du *sacratissimum triduum crucifixi, sepulti, suscitati*, comme le dira saint Augustin[34], qui vont du jeudi soir au dimanche soir ou de la dernière Cène au soir de la Résurrection, selon les récits évangéliques.

Or, dans le récit des AP, les douze premiers chapitres concernent les événements du vendredi seulement. Tout commence par l'accusation de Jésus par les Juifs qui se sont rendus auprès de Pilate le vendredi matin jusqu'au chapitre 12.3 où ils enferment Joseph d'Arimathée et qu'interviennent les témoins de la mort du Christ. Le chapitre 13 recouvre les journées du samedi et du dimanche, avec la disparition de Joseph d'Arimathée ainsi que celle du Christ. Il reste 3 chapitres (14 à 16) pour parler de la résurrection de Jésus, de son apparition et de son ascension avec tous les témoignages qui l'accompagnent jusqu'à l'hymne final. Cette seconde partie se déroule sur une période de 40 jours, jusqu'au dimanche de l'Ascension. Deux bons tiers des AP traitent donc des événements centraux de la fête de Pâques et tout particulièrement du premier jour du triduum. Dans un ouvrage portant le titre d'Actes, il était attendu que l'on traitât essentiellement des faits et gestes du Christ sous Ponce Pilate. Dans la seconde partie, toute l'histoire de Joseph d'Arimathée, vivant après la mort de Jésus, est construite comme en parallèle avec celle de Jésus[35] : il est arrêté et condamné à mourir, il ressort miraculeusement grâce à Jésus de sa prison, se retire quarante jours et finira par entrer dans Jérusalem sur un âne (comme Jésus), acclamé puis reconnu unanimement comme porteur d'un message qui réactualise la vérité de l'éternité de Jésus. Ainsi non seulement le caractère dynamique et animé de la pièce, mais l'apport didactique émanant des scènes descriptives et des constats, ainsi que l'accent mis sur le triduum pascal et les éléments de type liturgique permettront de vivre un

[32] Cet adjectif « liturgique » est mentionné avec prudence, le premier drame dit « liturgique » n'étant pas mentionné avant le Xe siècle.

[33] P. 49 de l'ouvrage cité dans la note 31.

[34] Augustin, *Epist.* 55,24 ; PL 33, col. 215.

[35] Le procédé de la *syncrisis* permettra à l'auteur des AP relancer l'enquête en rapportant cette fois les faits et les gestes de Joseph après la mort du Christ.

drame se jouant pendant la période pascale et apportant son message de foi et d'espérance.

Le cadre d'un procès

Les neuf premiers chapitres des AP décrivent et représentent le déroulement d'un procès de l'accusation des Juifs à la sentence finale, comprenant dans les démarches attendues de la justice, la défense du parti de l'accusé représenté par les douze Juifs pieux, les témoignages divers entrant dans la vie de l'accusé, ainsi que les débats entre juge, accusé, accusateurs et défenseurs. Les échanges ont lieu tantôt en public tantôt en privé. Les interrogatoires meublent pour la plus grande partie cette phase de l'histoire et se démarquent sur ce point des évangiles synoptiques.

Le procès commence par une mise en accusation[36] par les Juifs (les accusateurs) de Jésus devant Pilate (le juge) auquel ils viennent demander de faire comparaître Jésus (l'accusé) devant un tribunal[37] dans l'intention de le faire condamner à mort. Cela, seul le gouverneur pouvait l'accomplir[38]. Par rapport à la procédure judiciaire, nous savons que l'exécution de la peine capitale était sous le contrôle du préfet ou procurateur romain, et non des autorités du sanhédrin. Nous ne disposons ni de documents ni de rapports du procès, mais nous savons qu'il y a volonté ici de dramatiser la signification religieuse de la condamnation de Jésus. La pièce se poursuit par une mise en place d'un tribunal[39], au prétoire, avec interrogations successives de la part de Pilate, ponctuées d'allées et de venues, d'entrées et de sorties du prétoire ou du palais, des mises à l'écart et même un tirer de

[36] Ils l'accusent de nombreux agissements (κατηγορέω, πράξει).

[37] « Ἀχθήτω ἀκουσθῆναι ».

[38] Cf. J.-P. Lémonon, *Ponce Pilate*, Paris, 2007, 82–83 : « le gouverneur de Judée, détenteur de l'*imperium*, avait seul le pouvoir de permettre l'exécution d'une sentence capitale, si bien qu'un procès juif qui aboutissait à une décision de peine capitale n'avait de sens que dans la mesure où le gouverneur acceptait la condamnation et l'exécution ».

[39] « Παρίστημι βήματι » (estrade ou tribunal). Au Ier siècle, le site du procès est en principe le prétoire, c'est-à-dire la résidence du gouverneur, centre administratif, mais pas un lieu où se rend la justice, celle-ci s'exerçant dans une basilique, un forum, une place ou une cour publique avec un podium ou une tribune. C'est Césarée qui était le centre de l'administration romaine de Judée et le préfet y avait sa résidence. Il ne montait à Jérusalem qu'en certaines occasions, notamment lors de fêtes juives. Les interrogatoires privés se font à l'intérieur du prétoire. Dans les AP, trois siècles plus tard, la mise en scène cherche vraisemblablement à asseoir une autorité juridique et à donner un cadre officiel au procès.

rideau[40] au moment de la sentence de Pilate qui annoncera deux actes : la flagellation et la crucifixion.

L'auteur des AP, en développant largement le dialogue entre Jésus et Pilate, nous aide sans doute à compléter les minutes du procès, mais ne donne pas vraiment de valeur au procès historique. Par contre, la conversation entre Jésus et Pilate reflète des questions capitales pour comprendre le message du texte : Jésus est venu en ce monde pour témoigner de la vérité, et Pilate doit affronter ce débat puisqu'il se tient devant *la vérité*. Pilate connaît la charge contre Jésus : il se prétend le roi des Juifs. Selon la loi romaine, cela pouvait passer pour une sédition et les auteurs de sédition, ceux qui soulèvent le peuple, sont passibles de la crucifixion[41]. L'auteur des AP relève que Jésus, en se posant lui-même comme roi (donc rival aux yeux d'un païen) peut passer pour l'auteur d'un crime de lèse-majesté contre l'empereur et le peuple romain[42]. On sait bien qu'aucun de ses propos ne suggère une intention d'établir une royauté politique ici-bas. Cependant il faut le juger et en fonction de quelle loi ? A défaut d'une loi spécifique, il faudra admettre que c'est un principe général de maintien de l'ordre dans une province soumise qui peut avoir gouverné le traitement d'un non-citoyen comme Jésus. Dans le cas de Jésus qui ne plaide pas coupable, mais n'affirme pas non plus son innocence et ne conteste pas les accusations portées contre lui, on peut se demander s'il est légal de le juger coupable. Quant aux cris de la foule contre Jésus, ils font pression sur le préfet et ils pourraient, dans le contexte du procès, représenter la voix d'un jury reconnu. Mais Pilate souhaite s'assurer par lui-même de la culpabilité de Jésus. Il soupçonne que le vrai problème est une affaire intérieure juive, religieuse plutôt que politique[43]. Il ne veut pas que l'affaire explose en une émeute à Jérusalem, surtout dans le contexte de la Pâque.

La première intervention introduit le procès avec une présentation du personnage accusé (il est fils de Joseph, né de Marie), forme d'identification, suivie d'une première énumération de trois accusations : il se dit fils de Dieu et roi, il viole le sabbat[44] et il veut détruire la loi de « nos pères ».

---

[40] Chap. 9 : « Pilate ordonna qu'on tirât le voile de l'estrade sur laquelle il était assis ».

[41] Cf. R.E. Brown, cité dans la note 4, p. 800 sqq.

[42] Voire les commentaires plus tardifs de la *lex Iulia de majestatis* (DJ 4, 48, 4, 3–4) chez Marcien et surtout chez Scaevola qui parle d'un roi d'une nation étrangère refusant par intention délictueuse de se soumettre au peuple romain ; cf. Brown, cité dans la note 4, note 104, p.801.

[43] Par trois fois dans les AP, Pilate demandera aux instances juives de le juger ellesmêmes, car il ne voit pas sur quel grief ou quel motif d'accusation il pourrait le condamner.

[44] Les Juifs diront plus loin : « nous avons une loi : ne guérir personne le jour du sabbat ». Le grief (dicté par la loi juive) en tant que tel ne sera pas retenu, mais Pilate le re-

L'identification de Jésus se trouve dans la tradition évangélique lors de la visite de Jésus à Nazareth[45]. La première des trois accusations se compose d'un extrait de Luc (Christ, roi) et d'un extrait de Matthieu (sur la croix : il a dit, je suis fils de Dieu) et de Jean 19,7 qui met en avant l'autorité de la Loi juive[46]. La deuxième accusation trouve son équivalent dans Jn 5, 9–18 (AP 6,1) au moment du témoignage d'un des miraculés; quant à la troisième, Mt (5,17) y fait allusion, en la présentant sous forme négative : « ne croyez pas que je suis venu abolir la loi ou les prophètes, je ne suis pas venu abolir, mais accomplir ». On constate dans le cadre du procès le déroulement attendu qui est de savoir *qui est le coupable,* puis *ce qu'on lui reproche.* Or le juge Pilate attend des actes portant sur des actes concrets : « *quels sont ses agissements* (τίνα ἃ πράττει) ? Et plus loin : « *quelles sortes de mauvais agissements* ? » Les Juifs font alors allusion à des actes de sorcellerie[47]. Or ces actes, en tant que tels sont des guérisons qui ne correspondent nullement à des actes répréhensibles. Les raisons invoquées et les manifestations extérieures n'ayant aux yeux de Pilate aucune valeur juridique, les motifs d'accusation ne sont pas retenus comme tels et les Juifs en présentent trois nouveaux: Jésus est né de la débauche, sa naissance a correspondu à un enlèvement d'enfants, ses parents ont fui en Egypte par manque de confiance[48]. Nous connaissons une partie des faits par les références bibliques de Matthieu[49]. Les douze Juifs défenseurs de Jésus[50] vont réfuter le premier motif en attestant[51] la véracité des fiançailles de Joseph et de Marie[52]. La vaine répétition des motifs comme celui de la débauche, de la sorcellerie ou de la prétention à être fils de Dieu et roi, motifs entachés d'un malentendu au niveau du sens et de la portée des

---

prendra plus tard et mettra l'accent sur l'acte de guérison, qui lui n'est pas un acte répréhensible.

[45] C'est un exemple d'insertion dans le procès d'un élément connu dans un contexte et dans un cadre différent.

[46] « Nous avons une Loi, et selon la Loi il doit mourir, parce qu'il s'est fait Fils de Dieu », Jn 19,7 : υἱὸν θεοῦ ἑαυτὸν ἐποίησεν.

[47] « C'est un sorcier ; il chasse les démons par Béelzéboul, le chef des démons, et tout lui est soumis ». L'allusion porte vraisemblablement sur la capacité de Jésus à accomplir des miracles sous forme de guérisons.

[48] Motifs qui ne seront pas retenus par Pilate, ne correspondant pas à des actes directs de l'accusé.

[49] Cf. Mt 2,13–16.

[50] Ceux-ci seront traités de « prosélytes » par les Juifs qui tenteront de mettre leurs paroles en doute.

[51] Mais, lorsque le juge Pilate leur demande de le reconnaître, ils ne voudront pas jurer au nom de leur loi : cf. Mt 5,34 : « or moi je vous dis de ne pas jurer du tout ».

[52] La mauvaise foi des Juifs se manifestera une fois de plus : Anne et Caïphe mettront la parole des douze Juifs face à celle de la foule, comme si le nombre devait donner foi à leur parti contre les autres.

mots, va pousser Pilate à aller au-delà de la question de Jean 18,29[53] en demandant les raisons pour lesquelles les Juifs veulent le tuer (AP 2,6). Ni l'explication d'ordre psychologique, à savoir la jalousie, ni le qualificatif de *malfaiteur* ne justifieront une condamnation pour Pilate. Trois fois il répondra : « je ne trouve aucun motif d'accusation contre lui »[54], et dira : « Prenez-le, vous, et jugez-le selon votre loi »[55], comme un leitmotiv, une manière de scander le texte, échelons nouveaux de la dramatisation. Voyant leur dernière tentative échouer[56], les Juifs changent de registre et reviennent à l'attaque avec des arguments plus familiers à Pilate, concernant l'autorité et le pouvoir de Rome (AP 4,2) : Jésus se prétend fils de Dieu et roi des Juifs. C'est un blasphème contre Dieu. Or le blasphème contre César mérite la mort, qu'en est-il donc du blasphème contre Dieu ? Il y a là provocation de la part des Juifs qui mettent en parallèle une loi politique humaine applicable aux mœurs romaines et une loi propre aux Juifs. Pilate se rend bien compte que la justice juive ne correspond pas à celle du pouvoir qu'il représente. La loi juive condamnerait Jésus à la lapidation, mais les Juifs réclament la crucifixion[57], qui tient des Romains, cependant l'homme que l'on prétend coupable, selon Pilate, ne la mérite pas ! Alors que chez Matthieu[58], la discussion n'aboutit à rien et que le tumulte menace, dans les AP, c'est avec une autre menace, celle d'une forme d'autorité que les Juifs vont exciter la susceptibilité de Pilate en rappelant insidieusement l'épisode des mages et d'Hérode qui en voulait à ce nouveau roi. Cet élément précis et d'ordre politique fait peur à Pilate et ce sera le point culminant atteint par l'accusation. Devant une autorité romaine, Pilate n'insiste plus : il rend son verdict sous forme de sentence[59]. Le mo-

---

[53] « Quelle accusation portez-vous contre cet homme ? »

[54] AP 3,1 ; 4,1 ; 7 1.

[55] AP 3,1 ; 4,3 ; 4,4.

[56] Il s'agit de l'élément qui ressortait de l'échange préliminaire devant le sanhédrin et qui avait été qualifié de faux témoignage chez Marc (14,57) : « je peux détruire ce temple et en trois jours le relever » (AP 4,1) et il ajoutait : « j'en bâtirai un autre non fait de main d'homme » (Marc 14,58).

[57] Cf. R.E. Brown, cité dans la note 4, p.833 : il y aurait ironie de la part de Pilate face aux Juifs qui n'auraient pas le pouvoir de crucifier ou pas de raison suffisante. « Les Juifs de Judée n'étaient », en effet, « pas autorisés à exécuter ».

[58] Cf. Mt 27,24–25.

[59] Cette dernière revêt un caractère particulier dans le texte des AP (chap.9) ; elle est mise en évidence sous la forme d'un sous-titre dans un manuscrit (le Lavra 117) : ἀπόφασις κατὰ τοῦ Ἰησοῦ, c'est-à-dire « sentence contre Jésus » et elle correspond à une déclaration de Pilate : « Ta propre nation s'est moquée de toi en tant que roi ; à cause de cela je déclare qu'en premier lieu tu sois flagellé en raison des lois sacrées des pieux rois et ensuite qu'on te suspende à la croix dans le jardin où on t'a arrêté avec les deux brigands saisis avec toi ».

ment est d'autant plus solennel qu'il se traduit par une déclamation, de caractère on ne peut plus théâtral.

Le débat se déroule sur deux plans. Il démarre sur des accusations d'ordre religieux : on accuse au nom d'une loi juive. Mais Pilate, lui, réagit en homme essentiellement guidé par sa conscience d'homme politique, cherchant vainement à comprendre le bien-fondé des arguments de l'accusation. Et ce sont finalement les arguments d'ordre politique liés à l'autorité du roi[60] qui mèneront l'action et déclencheront la décision finale. Le caractère juridique du procès doublé par les débats politisés ont le mérite d'apporter au lecteur ou au public présent une autorité indéniable au texte.

Portée des témoignages et du vocabulaire

Une des originalités qui fait l'intérêt des AP réside dans le choix des témoins qui se succèderont au fil de l'histoire, témoins d'origines diverses[61] et allant tous progressivement dans le sens d'une reconnaissance de l'autorité de Jésus et d'une conversion à la foi chrétienne. La scène de l'introduction de Jésus par le messager de Pilate est à ce point de vue spectaculaire, d'autant plus qu'elle sera soulignée par une action miraculeuse ; c'est sous forme visuelle et scénique que la première démonstration de reconnaissance devant Jésus aura lieu. Dès le début du procès, le messager de Pilate se prosterne, prend une étoffe et l'étend sur le sol devant Jésus en guise d'accueil et d'invitation à entrer. La deuxième forme de reconnaissance se fera par le dialogue : les Juifs reconnaîtront Jésus comme roi à son entrée à Jérusalem et témoigneront de la journée des Rameaux en reprenant l'expression « Hosanna ». Le messager n'est alors qu'un témoin d'une manifestation bien reconnue par les Juifs. A la suite de la double reconnaissance par le messager et par les Juifs de l'événement des Rameaux, intervient un troisième phénomène : les images impériales des étendards romains rendent hommage à Jésus en se prosternant devant lui. C'est là un témoignage inattendu de l'autorité de Jésus, autorité qui agit donc ici sur le pouvoir romain ! La royauté de Jésus, refusée par les Juifs dans le procès, est ainsi non seulement reconnue par le courrier, mais également par les enseignes, étrangers tous deux au milieu chrétien.

L'obstacle principal qui va figer la discussion et conduire irrémédiablement au verdict connu est bien mis en évidence dans les AP par le décalage notoire entre le sens de certains mots et leur portée significative, pro-

[60] Jésus se disant roi des Juifs ; blasphème contre César, le roi ; Hérode à la recherche du roi de Bethléem.

[61] Des personnes d'origine juive ou romaine, païenne ou chrétienne, de rang social divers, provenant de la garde romaine, de la foule ou de la famille de Pilate.

pre à l'usage de chacun des interlocuteurs. Dans un premier temps, on remarque un décalage entre les motifs d'accusation d'ordre religieux (destinés à être jugés par un procès juif) et le verdict qui doit être appliqué et qui ne peut l'être, politiquement parlant, que par la justice romaine. Autrement dit, décalage entre les critères de *la justice juive* et ceux de *la justice romaine*. Dans la loi en rapport avec le jour du sabbat, Pilate ne voit rien de mal à la guérison en soi et y relèvera au contraire une action positive. Il a déplacé l'objet de l'accusation : il ignore la loi juive du sabbat qui n'entre pas dans la juridiction romaine. On observe la même ignorance, plus loin, de nouveau à propos du sabbat, avec la réponse des douze Juifs[62]. Dans l'accusation de sorcellerie « c'est un sorcier[63], il chasse les démons par Béelzéboul (AP 1,1)[64] », Pilate verra une guérison et refusera d'admettre qu'une bonne action puisse être commise par un démon, Béelzéboul, et remplacera ce dernier par Asclépios, seul véritable guérisseur. L'insistance de Pilate est d'ailleurs significative : à trois reprises il dit son incompréhension et son refus de poursuivre le jugement. Cette insistance est particulièrement significative d'une volonté de l'auteur de souligner à quel point l'objet du procès est déplacé : il s'agit d'un problème d'ordre religieux et pas politique. Donc ce n'est pas le problème de Pilate ! Or on sait que les Juifs vont lui fournir un argument qui remettra le terme de l'accusation dans le domaine politique pour condamner Jésus comme danger contre le pouvoir romain.

Il y a décalage dans un deuxième temps entre le sens que revêtent les propos de Jésus et qui appartient au monde *divin* et celui des propos de Pilate, l'homme représentant les instances politiques et juridiques du monde *humain*. Dans les AP, trois interrogatoires de Pilate avec Jésus interviennent en alternance avec ceux des Juifs et des douze Juifs pieux : un premier sur un jeu de mot sur le pouvoir (cf. Jn 19,10–11. AP 2,2). Un deuxième entretien sur la royauté[65] et la vérité : Jn 18, 33–38 ; AP 3,2. Un troisième entretien sur la décision finale que doit prendre Pilate, dictée par

---

[62] « Ils sont jaloux parce qu'il guérit le jour du sabbat » AP 2,6.

[63] Le sorcier tient du magicien et du faiseur de magie ; les miracles ou actes magiques auraient-ils une connotation négative aux yeux des Juifs ? Oui, s'ils signifiaient qu'ils sont actes de charlatan ou d'imposteur, ce qui reste à prouver aux yeux de Pilate. Le mot « magoi » utilisé par ailleurs ne représente que les observateurs et les astrologues venus d'Orient suivre l'étoile exceptionnelle.

[64] Accusation présente dans les quatre évangiles (Mt 9,34 et 12,24, Mc 3,22 et Lc 11,15 dans un autre contexte, et où Luc ajoute en 10,17 : « même les démons nous sont soumis en ton nom» : τὰ δαιμόνια ὑποτάσσεται.

[65] La notion de temple (celui que Jésus prétend détruire et reconstruire en trois jours) entre dans le même genre d'observation (AP 4,3). Là encore, on constate une incompréhension, un décalage dans la portée du discours, une impossibilité de correspondre et de progresser dans la discussion.

les Ecritures (AP 4,3). Dans les trois cas, la discussion ne peut aboutir, chacun des partis en présence ayant sa propre vue des choses absolument incompatible avec l'autre ! Pilate qui ne pouvait entrer dans la conception de la loi juive ne peut, là non plus, entrer dans cette nouvelle dimension de la vérité, celle des chrétiens.

La notion de pouvoir[66] (ἐξουσία) recouvre plusieurs sens. Il s'agit à première vue du pouvoir qu'a Pilate (dans Jean) ou qu'ont les Juifs (dans les AP) d'intervenir[67] en tant qu'autorité institutionnelle, politique et/ou juridique. Or dans la bouche de Jésus, le même mot « pouvoir » en grec prend une autre connotation[68] : chacun a la liberté et la faculté de s'exprimer en tant qu'individu, il a un pouvoir *personnel* qui lui est propre, une éthique, un sens du bien et du mal, dicté par son milieu d'éducation et de formation. Les deux notions sont presque opposées, la liberté de parole pouvant défier le pouvoir politique ! Par ailleurs l'origine de cette autorité est divine chez Jésus, elle a un caractère tout humain chez les Juifs comme chez Pilate : nous voyons là un glissement d'un monde dans un autre, un double langage et la communication ne se fait pas sinon en passant à deux niveaux différents. Ce décalage de la portée du sens va faire progresser la tension dramatique : ce n'est plus la forme (la non-réponse) mais le fond de la question qui est posé dans le débat. Et c'est également l'occasion de mettre en avant le pouvoir qui vient de Dieu, pouvoir non encore reconnu, ni par Pilate, ni par les Juifs.

Le deuxième entretien de Jésus avec Pilate, inspiré du texte de Jean, dans une suite presque ininterrompue de 18, 29–38b (AP 2,6–4,1) mais dans un ordre légèrement différent, traite du thème du roi[69], du royaume ou de la royauté, et de la vérité. Ce dialogue est important dans le cours du procès, car il permet de mettre en avant deux éléments capitaux pour comprendre l'accusé : son royaume qui n'est pas de ce monde[70] et la vérité qui émane du ciel[71]. L'accusé aura ainsi été entendu en personne et le lecteur aura bénéficié d'un échange un peu plus étoffé que celui donné par les au-

---

[66] « S'ils n'avaient pas de pouvoir, ils ne diraient rien » : εἰ μὴ εἶχον ἐξουσίαν ... AP 2,2.

[67] Jn 19,10 : « Ne sais-tu pas que j'ai pouvoir de te relâcher et que j'ai pouvoir de te crucifier ? Jésus répondit : tu n'aurais aucun pouvoir contre moi s'il ne t'avait été donné d'en haut.... »

[68] « Chacun est maître de ses propos, chacun a le pouvoir de dire le bien ou le mal » AP 2,2.

[69] Le thème sera repris sous la forme de « Jésus roi » en Jn 19, 12/15/19–20 (AP chap. 7–9).

[70] Jn 18,36 et AP 3,2 : « Jésus répondit : mon royaume n'est pas de ce monde. Si ma royauté était de ce monde, mes gardes auraient combattu pour que je ne sois pas livré aux Juifs ».

[71] Complément apporté par l'auteur des AP.

tres évangélistes. Non seulement cet ajout complète les données du procès mais il apporte un élément d'ordre didactique.

L'interrogatoire est centré en général, dans les évangiles, sur une seule et même question : « es-tu le roi des Juifs ? » et une seule et même réponse : « Tu le dis. ». Or ce titre n'a jamais été revendiqué par Jésus avant et il n'y a pas de relation avec les questions du procès juif qui précède. Il a dû exister un noyau historique du procès romain : Pilate a condamné Jésus accusé d'être le « roi des Juifs », à mourir sur la croix. Selon N. A. Dahl[72], « le roi des Juifs » est un très ancien motif qui aurait été spiritualisé par Jean. Cette question-réponse, dont la formulation est la même dans les quatre évangiles, faisait tellement partie intégrante de la tradition qu'elle devait être conservée, même par Jean, qui y inséra une interprétation développée, ainsi que les AP qui reprennent Jean en grande partie ici[73]. On ignore si Pilate savait vraiment tout des accusations des Juifs contre Jésus. Mais ce que les lecteurs ou auditeurs peuvent croire, c'est que cette unique question sur la royauté de Jésus intéresse vraiment les Romains. Les sujets de préoccupation pour les autorités juives étaient religieuses ; la question romaine a une tonalité politique. Cependant la réponse de Jésus devient éclairante dans son interprétation qui rend le texte dramatiquement explicite[74]. A la question « es-tu le roi des Juifs ? », Jésus répond mais complète comme s'il voulait souligner l'origine et la provenance de ces mots. En tout cas ce développement remet en évidence la responsabilité et l'origine des accusations, à savoir la nation juive et les grands prêtres.

Jésus répètera trois fois : « mon royaume n'est pas de ce monde ». Le royaume de Jésus ainsi que les dons de Jésus ne sont pas de ce monde ; ce qui les rend vrais ou réels est qu'ils viennent de Dieu. Ils sont entrés avec lui dans le monde, mais comme lui, ils ne sont pas de ce monde (Jn 17,16). Jésus est donc roi, mais avec la nuance non négligeable : « tu dis que je suis roi ». La responsabilité est reportée sur Pilate et laisse entendre subtilement que le sens du mot roi n'est sans doute pas le même dans la bouche de Jésus que dans celle de Pilate. L'auteur doit avoir en tête le texte complet du verset : je suis né et je suis venu (d'en haut) dans le monde pour cela, c'est à dire pour porter témoignage à la vérité[75], afin que tout homme qui émane de la vérité écoute ma voix (comme celle d'un roi). Pilate ne pourra pas comprendre un royaume qui n'est pas établi par l'effort humain mais par Dieu, non seulement parce qu'il est représentant d'une puissance terrestre, mais parce qu'il n'émane pas de cette même vérité. Il ne pourra pas non plus comprendre que ce royaume qui n'est pas de ce monde ne

---

[72] Cf. R.E. Brown cité dans la note 4, 809.

[73] Cf. Jn 18,33 et 18,37b ; AP 3,1 et 3,2.

[74] Jn 18,36–37 et AP 3,2.

[75] Jn 18,37.

peut pas menacer le pouvoir de César. Et la phrase : « quiconque est de la vérité entend ma voix » est un test pour Pilate ; le juge est jugé ! Les gardes qui auraient lutté pour Jésus sont les brebis qui émanent de la vérité eux aussi et qui entendent sa voix. La question de Pilate : « qu'est-ce que la vérité ? » montre son incapacité à reconnaître la vérité et à entendre la voix de Jésus et que lui-même n'appartient par conséquent pas à Dieu. Les AP explicitent remarquablement bien le contexte : Jésus ne garde pas le silence, mais répond : « la vérité émane du ciel ». Une dernière tentative de Pilate pour comprendre : « sur la terre, il n'y a pas de vérité ? » et Jésus de constater (avec l'auteur qui souligne ainsi le décalage irrémédiable entre le langage et le monde de Jésus avec celui du monde terrestre) : « vois ceux qui disent la vérité, comment ils sont jugés par ceux qui ont le pouvoir sur terre ! ». Autrement dit, il y a peut-être une vérité sur terre, mais combien elle diffère de la vérité du ciel, puisqu'elle condamne ceux qui ont la vérité du ciel et le pouvoir du ciel.

Si le procès romain johannique est presque trois fois plus long que celui de Marc, celui des AP, quand il reprend les données de Jean, ajoute encore des éléments au profit de la dramatisation des faits[76]. Le troisième entretien de Pilate avec Jésus donne une note finale à la condition inévitable et indétournable de l'histoire : « que vais-je faire de toi ? » dit Pilate et Jésus de répondre : « comme il t'a été donné de faire... »[77]. C'est ainsi donc, rappelle Jésus dans le texte des AP, que l'histoire doit s'accomplir, conformément aux Ecritures.

Ces exemples montrent d'une part que les Juifs accusent avec leur conception propre de la loi, d'autre part que Jésus parle de sa vision du monde divin, de son royaume et de sa vérité et finalement que ces événements obéissent à l'autorité des Ecritures. L'échange aura mis sous les yeux du lecteur – du spectateur – non seulement tout ce que le message de Jésus apporte de nouveau dans son explicitation, mais aussi le fait que l'impossibilité pour Pilate et ceux qui ne comprennent pas, d'entrer dans cette démarche, conduira irrémédiablement à la condamnation à mort (par ailleurs prévue par les Ecritures).

---

[76] E. Haenchen, « Jesus vor Pilatus (Jn 18,28–19,15) », *TLZ* 85 (1960), col. 93–102, Jn 2, p.185 : « La version johannique de la scène avec Pilate est de loin supérieure à celles de Matthieu et de Luc » ; R.E. Brown cité dans la note 4, 845 : « Jean nous a donné le chef-d'œuvre du drame chrétien primitif, en déployant avec perspicacité la confrontation du divin et de l'humain ».

[77] C'est-à-dire comme « Moïse et les prophètes ont d'avance prêché à propos de cette mort et de la résurrection » (AP 4,3).

A qui donc la responsabilité de la condamnation ?

Dès le début de la scène du lavement des mains, on voit, tant du côté de Matthieu que de celui de l'auteur des AP, une atmosphère d'alarme pour les Romains, inquiets de possibles troubles à Jérusalem, en particulier en période de fête. Mais dans les AP, il en faut plus pour faire agir Pilate. C'est la nouvelle que l'accusé correspond au roi qu'Hérode avait cherché à tuer qui pousse Pilate à prendre une décision. Mais avant, il s'efforce de se libérer de la faute de mettre à mort un innocent : il prit de l'eau, se lava les mains en face du soleil[78] disant : « je suis innocent du sang de ce juste[79]. A vous de voir ! »[80]. Pilate, en disant « ce juste » , resserre la proximité avec le message de sa femme (27,19) : « qu'il n'y ait rien entre toi et ce juste ». Peut-être cherchait-il là à accomplir le vœu de sa femme. L'expression « à vous de voir » ou « vous verrez », renvoie la responsabilité sur les foules qui ont exigé la crucifixion ; mais ce sera tout de même à lui, finalement, de décider. Alors que Matthieu utilise le mot « foule » qui doit être un des éléments constituants de « tout le peuple »[81], dans les AP, l'expression reste : « les Juifs ». Les autorités du sanhédrin ont condamné Jésus à mort pour blasphème, les foules se sont laissées convaincre par ces autorités de devenir l'instrument principal, en poussant Pilate à livrer Jésus à la crucifixion. Toute la communauté a donc participé au jugement du blasphème et cela rend « tout le peuple » responsable du sang innocent. Dans l'usage de l'AT, le peuple c'est Israël, le peuple de Dieu et ici, c'est le peuple juif, au sens ethnique. On sait que les chrétiens de l'église de Matthieu étaient en lutte, au Ier siècle, contre la synagogue et estimaient avoir été persécutés par les autorités juives. On peut toujours voir, trois siècles plus tard, dans cette expression des AP, une certaine hostilité envers les synagogues et une façon de faire retomber la responsabilité du sang de Jésus sur « nous », « nos enfants » et « tout le peuple » et nous devons y sentir une puissance dramatique. La réflexion sur la responsabilité créée par le sang de Jésus n'a pas commencé avec Matthieu. La formule « son sang sur nous et sur nos enfants » est une formule de la Loi israélite au sujet de la responsabilité de la mort[82] et ce contexte vétéro-testamentaire éclaire le passage en question. Pilate se prépare à condamner à la crucifixion un homme qu'il

[78] « En présence de la foule », dans Mt 27,24. L'allusion au soleil, dans les AP, dénote une manifestation païenne, où Pilate semble prendre à témoin le Dieu soleil.

[79] L'allusion au « juste » apparaît deux autres fois dans les AP : lors du récit du songe par la femme de Pilate et lors de la constatation du garde au pied de la croix.

[80] Les psaumes 26,6 et 73,13 illustrent ce lavement des mains en signe d'innocence.

[81] En Lv. 24, 10–16, il est dit qu'un blasphémateur doit être mis à mort par « toute la communauté ».

[82] Cf. R.E. Brown cité dans la note 4, 929 qui donne nombre d'exemples de l'AT usant de cette formule.

considère juste ou innocent, et il se lave les mains pour démontrer son refus de porter la responsabilité de l'effusion de sang de cet homme. Par l'expression « son sang sur nous et sur nos enfants », la foule parlant au nom de tout le peuple accepte la responsabilité. Ce ne sont pas des gens ivres de sang ou cruels ; ils sont persuadés que Jésus est un blasphémateur, comme le sanhédrin l'a jugé. Mais dans la perspective matthéenne, ironiquement, ce sont eux qui ont finalement accepté la responsabilité alors que tous les autres tentaient de l'éviter. Jésus est innocent ; cela signifie que Dieu a puni ou punira pour son sang tous ceux qui sont impliqués et cela inclut certainement « tout le peuple » qui a accepté cette responsabilité.

Pour en venir à la responsabilité de Pilate, alors que chez Jean, en 19,7, les Juifs disaient, après la réaction de Pilate qui veut leur remettre la responsabilité du procès : « nous avons une Loi, et selon la Loi il doit mourir, parce qu'il s'est fait Fils de Dieu», dans les AP, à deux reprises, nous avons : « il se dit fils de Dieu et roi » (I,1 et IV,5). Pilate semble surtout se préoccuper de la menace liée à la royauté de Jésus. Deux interventions le montrent :

a) En Jn 19,12b, et surtout dans les AP 7,1[83] : les Juifs menacent Pilate des conséquences d'une libération de « cet individu ». Le texte montre bien pourquoi Pilate a accédé à l'exigence de la populace : s'il ne fait pas ce qu'ils attendent de lui, ils le dénonceront comme déloyal envers l'empereur. Dans un usage romain plus tardif, « ami de César » était un titre honorifique conféré en reconnaissance d'un service rendu. Si Pilate portait ce titre, les Juifs l'accusent de ne pas lui être fidèle.

b) Avec la deuxième allusion au roi évoquée par l'épisode d'Hérode, on voit que la charge initiale du procès, « le roi des juifs » revient et domine dans l'intervention finale.

Le sens des mots, une fois de plus, prend une valeur propre, qu'il appartienne au royaume divin incarné dans le Jésus johannique ou au royaume terrestre incarné dans le gouverneur romain. Jésus est en conflit avec le prince de ce monde ; dans la mesure où les maîtres de la terre sont les instruments de ce prince, le pouvoir et le royaume de Jésus sont en conflit avec eux. Quant aux passages repris de Matthieu, dans ses exemples concrets, ils manifestent une tendance à souligner les responsabilités de chacun dans le procès. Le choix de ces deux tendances semble en fin de compte tendre à disculper Pilate (dans le premier cas, Pilate ne peut pas comprendre, il n'est pas du monde de Jésus, dans le second cas, il manifeste concrètement son retrait de la responsabilité de la condamnation) et à

[83] Jn et AP : « si tu relâches cet homme, tu n'es pas ami de César ». Puis Jn : « Quiconque se fait roi s'oppose à César » et Ap : « parce qu'il se dit Fils de Dieu et roi ; tu veux donc que celui-ci soit roi et pas César ? ».

reporter sur les Juifs la plus grande responsabilité dans la crucifixion de Jésus.

La crucifixion avec Luc : les paroles de Jésus et le bon larron

Avec l'épisode de la crucifixion dans les AP, nous quittons le monde politique et juridique d'ici-bas pour vivre une sorte de moment charnière, ouvrant des perspectives nouvelles sur un monde nouveau. C'est essentiellement la structure du récit de Luc qui prévaut dans les AP. Bien des éléments de Luc font écho à des thèmes communs à Luc–Actes : le pardon, la paix avec Dieu, la foule sympathisante opposée aux dirigeants et c'est ce même contenu qui intéresse l'auteur des AP. Les éléments[84] qu'il reprend à Luc seul manifestent une théologie bienveillante, à la fois quant au rôle des participants et quant à l'exercice de la miséricorde de Jésus, une théologie qui est au fondement de cette adaptation (imaginative ou pas) que fait Luc de son matériel de travail. Son développement dramatique du rôle du malfaiteur sympathisant se rapproche de la technique de Jean qui choisit quelques incidents de la crucifixion et met en lumière leurs virtualités. L'épisode de la croix ne comprend, sur le modèle de Luc, que trois paroles de Jésus sur sept, toutes trois reflétant la théologie positive de Luc et écartant les interventions qui laisseraient un goût amer à des événements que les Ecritures rendaient incontournables. Ce sont :

– « Père, pardonne-leur, car ils ne savent pas ce qu'ils font » (Lc 23, 34a ; AP 10,1) : le sentiment qu'exprime cette phrase est devenu l'essence même de l'attitude chrétienne face à l'hostilité. Et c'est sans aucun doute un reflet de l'attitude de l'auteur du IVe s. ou de celle qu'il veut proposer à ses auditeurs.

– « Amen, je te le dis, ce jour avec moi, tu seras au paradis » (Luc 23,43 ; AP 10,2) : deuxième exemple du pardon qui guérit et prolongation du schéma de miséricorde exprimé précédemment.

– « Père, en tes mains je remets mon esprit » (Luc 23,46 ; AP 11,1) troisième témoignage de l'indulgence et de l'humilité de Jésus.

Cet homme juste meurt de la mort des injustes et permet ainsi la conversion des pécheurs. Par ailleurs, il apprend indirectement à ses disciples à renoncer à la puissance des hommes pour triompher par le seul

---

[84] Eléments communs aux AP et à Luc : la prière de Jésus au Père pour le pardon, la miséricorde de Jésus, les spectateurs qui observent sans hostilité, le malfaiteur blasphémant et celui qui sympathise et qui est récompensé, les deux réactions qui adoucissent l'impact négatif de la scène, le phénomène des ténèbres et de la déchirure du voile, le cri de Jésus, le centurion qui loue Dieu, les foules qui se frappent la poitrine (Mc et Mt), les gens et les femmes qui observent.

moyen efficace, le saint-Esprit. Avant la scène des malfaiteurs sur la croix, l'auteur des AP glisse, sur le modèle structurel de Luc, l'épisode de l'inscription et de l'accusation chez Jean : il développe l'inscription en un épisode important et en modifie la portée. C'est Pilate qui rédige le titre. Même si on peut l'imaginer aussi dans les autres évangiles, ici, l'immédiateté de l'attribution à Pilate permet à Jean et à l'auteur des AP de faire de la scène au pied de la croix une rencontre personnelle, prolongeant le débat du procès. Alors que les grands prêtres avaient forcé Pilate à condamner Jésus, qu'il savait innocent, maintenant avec ironie Pilate renvoie la balle à ses interlocuteurs juifs en proclamant qu'il s'en tient à l'accusation qu'ils ont formulée. L'usage délibéré que fait Pilate de l'accusation juive est implicite dans les AP : « après la sentence, Pilate ordonna que la charge contre lui soit rédigée comme un titre, en grec, en latin et en hébreu, exactement comme les Juifs l'avaient dit : « il est le roi des Juifs ». Dans cette dramatisation, le gouverneur romain a retrouvé son autorité. La solennité du titre est encore accrue par l'indication que le titre était trilingue. Les trois langues ont une force symbolique. L'hébreu est la langue sacrée des Ecritures d'Israël, le latin est la langue du conquérant romain, le grec est la langue dans laquelle le message sur Jésus est proclamé et rédigé. Ayant rencontré la vérité (Jésus), Pilate est conduit à faire une proclamation impériale prophétiquement vraie dans sa formulation.

Autour de la scène des brigands, chez Luc comme dans les AP, le groupe neutre du peuple en train d'observer avertit les lecteurs que le tableau du Golgotha n'est pas totalement négatif. Les deux auteurs concluent la scène par un épisode centré sur un personnage qui n'est pas vraiment neutre, « l'autre » malfaiteur qui va témoigner de l'innocence de Jésus. Les AP reprennent mot pour mot le passage de Jésus sur la croix, du dialogue des deux larrons et de la foule devant la croix en Luc 23, 34–37/ 39–49[85] et 50 (AP chap. 10 et 11). La mention des deux larrons crucifiés qui injurient Jésus se trouve chez Matthieu et Marc, mais seul Luc développe le dialogue entre les deux larrons et Jésus. L'effet dramatique de la scène est spectaculaire : il est souligné d'une part par le mouvement positif et inattendu du bon larron et d'autre part par la prise de conscience d'une réalité bien peu reconnue jusque-là et de surcroît, au moment le plus désespéré. Le bon larron est le premier témoin à reconnaître sa faute et c'est le premier témoin qui montre sa foi dans le royaume de Dieu[86]. De plus cet épisode donne à Jésus l'occasion de prononcer sur la croix les derniers mots de sa vie adressés à des êtres humains. La mise en forme d'une énonciation est une manière de plus de faire parler un acteur et de donner l'accent drama-

[85] Notons un passage important mais placé ailleurs dans l'Evangile : Lc 2,22–35 : la rencontre à Jérusalem de Jésus et de ses parents avec Syméon, AP chap. 16,1,2.

[86] Lc 23,42 : « Jésus, souviens-toi de moi quand tu viendras dans ton royaume ».

tique voulu. L'intervention du centurion, deuxième témoin, est rapportée par la plupart, mais l'ajout de Luc est significatif : « il glorifiait Dieu » (AP 11,1). Luc a adapté ce passage à son objectif théologique et à sa vision sotériologique de la croix qui conduit à la résurrection, ce qui s'intègre parfaitement à la visée de l'auteur des AP. Chez Luc et dans les AP, le sarcasme et le blasphème répété de l'un des malfaiteurs reçoivent une réponse directe de son compagnon. Il y a opposition entre les deux personnages. Les trois condamnés ont connu la même expérience judiciaire, deux à juste titre, un injustement[87]. On remarque que le malfaiteur a une fonction assez comparable à celle de la femme de Pilate : cette judaïsante qui n'avait encore jamais vu Jésus, pouvait affirmer que c'était un « juste ». Elle savait cela par révélation divine lors d'un songe. Pour elle comme pour le bon larron ou le centurion, l'innocence de Jésus s'impose dès la première fois qu'ils le voient. Seuls ceux qui sont aveuglés par l'ignorance ne le reconnaissent pas (Ac 3,17). Les paroles du bon larron laissent entendre que Jésus va monter de la croix dans le Royaume et il s'attend à ce que Jésus soit vengé et gagne son Royaume ; il demande qu'on se souvienne de lui à ce moment-là. C'est sans doute dans la réponse de Jésus qu'apparaît toute la portée du message intéressant l'auteur des AP. En effet, ces mots de Jésus manifestent la miséricorde divine au-delà de toute attente. L'expression « en ce jour » a une tonalité eschatologique et pourrait faire allusion à une période de salut inaugurée par la mort de Jésus. Jour chronologique qui est aussi un moment eschatologique de salut. Pour Luc et l'auteur des AP, être avec le Christ renvoie à une destinée d'après la mort. Pour les partisans du paradis comme le plus haut des cieux ou le bonheur ultime d'être avec le Christ dans la présence plénière de Dieu, et pour un larron qui représenterait un gentil, la pointe du récit pourrait être la conversion des gentils au dernier jour du monde : c'est exactement ce que nous vivons dans le 16ème chapitre des AP. Cette histoire enseigne en tout cas la miséricorde gratuite de Dieu exercée par et en Jésus. On sait que le Jésus lucanien durant son ministère pardonnait les péchés (5,20 ; 7,48) et apportait le salut (19,9). Le fait que Jésus puisse parler avec une telle autorité du sort du larron crucifié montre qu'il a le pouvoir du jugement de Dieu, pouvoir qu'il exerce miséricordieusement. Une fois de plus on a là une vision sotériologique de la croix parfaitement à sa place dans le contexte des AP.

Avant que Jésus ne meure, Luc et les AP ont associé l'obscurité sur toute la terre à la déchirure du voile du Sanctuaire : ainsi les deux interventions divines menaçantes constituent un tableau auquel Jésus réagit par un acte de confiance en l'amour de Dieu (Lc 23,46 ; AP 11,1). Ainsi Luc et

---

[87] Cf. dans la bouche du centurion (AP 11,1) : « cet homme était juste » ; dans celle du bon larron (AP 10,2) : « nous recevons ce que nos actes ont mérité » ; dans celle de Pilate (4,2): « dans ce qu'il a fait, il n'y a rien qui mérite la mort ».

les AP possèdent tous les éléments pour rendre positif le scénario qui suit la mort de Jésus, avec le trio du centurion, des foules et des femmes de Galilée favorables à Jésus. D'abondants indices gréco-romains prouvent que l'on envisageait communément des signes extraordinaires pour accompagner la mort de grands hommes. Le signe des ténèbres et de la déchirure du voile du Sanctuaire devaient être pris dans cet esprit-là ; quoi qu'il en soit la scène est spectaculaire et entre dans les messages à retenir du drame apocryphe. Quant au cri d'agonie, Luc et les AP l'ont gardé sans retenir le cri désespéré d'abandon (présent chez Marc et Matthieu). Son motif est théologique. « Je remets mon esprit » : l'esprit, c'est l'être vivant, ou la puissance de vie qui va au-delà de la mort. Quand Jésus remet son esprit à son père, il rapporte à leur lieu d'origine sa vie et sa mission. De plus, le choix du mot « père » à la place de « mon Dieu » personnalise la citation du psaume 31,6[88]. Le Jésus lucanien est absolument constant tout au long du récit de la Passion, priant le « Père » au commencement sur le mont des Oliviers et « le Père » à la fin sur le lieu de la crucifixion, ou colline du Crâne. Le tableau doit rester imprimé dans l'esprit des lecteurs ou des auditeurs qui vont devenir disciples de Jésus. La prière d'agonie de Jésus proclame avec confiance que le pouvoir des ténèbres n'a pas été capable de le séparer de son Père[89].

La résurrection avec Matthieu

La résurrection qui tient à la fois du miraculeux et du spectaculaire ne pouvait être reprise ailleurs que chez Matthieu. Connaissant l'attention qu'il porte à la présence de la communauté et du monde humain et terrestre dans ses écrits[90], nous ne sommes pas étonnés de retrouver ici l'effroi des gardes qui surveillent le tombeau, l'apparition de l'ange descendu du ciel[91], les soldats « comme morts » de peur, les onze disciples en Galilée, bref, toutes des scènes au caractère humain et poignant (Mt 27, 64, 28, 2–7 et 28, 12–15 ; AP ch.13). Ni Marc, ni Luc, ni Jean n'en font autant. Toutes

[88] Cf. R.E. Brown, cité dans la note 4, 1173–1176.

[89] « J'envoie sur vous ce que mon père a promis » dit-il en Lc 24,49. Cf. Lc 9,26 : quand Jésus reviendra à la fin des temps, ce sera le Fils de l'homme « dans la gloire du Père ».

[90] L'évocation de la femme de Pilate, des enfants de Bethléem, de la fuite en Egypte, des aveugles, de Véronique (non nommée chez Mt), de Barabbas et du Christ, du lavement des mains et de l'affirmation de Pilate de son innocence, du dépouillement de Jésus, jusqu'à la notion du « motif » de la condamnation à mettre sur la pancarte (Mt 27, 21–22/24–25/et 20, 29–34 ; AP 6–8).

[91] L'ange à l'aspect de l'éclair, son vêtement blanc comme la neige sont des détails descriptifs de type pictural.

ces descriptions seyent à merveille à une scène de théâtre : le tremblement de terre, le bruit et le mouvement, l'apparition d'en haut, la luminosité et la blancheur, tout est à voir et à entendre et l'aspect visuel de la scène est à son paroxysme. Tout l'irrationnel, l'incompréhensible, l'insaisissable est focalisé sur un tableau vivant et plus expressif à lui seul que les mots lus. Face à ce spectacle, seul Matthieu aura un mot pour rassurer : « je sais que vous cherchez Jésus ». L'auteur des AP tenait là un moyen extraordinaire pour marquer l'auditeur et surtout le spectateur et il a exploité cette source à bon escient. L'histoire de la garde du tombeau chez Matthieu est un important segment du récit de l'ensevelissement. La pointe en est essentielle, car elle rassemble trois objectifs de la discussion : a) elle est polémique, car elle réfute une histoire qui circulait chez les Juifs selon laquelle les disciples de Jésus auraient dérobé son corps, puis frauduleusement proclamé sa résurrection. La question de l'achat du mensonge (polémique de la tromperie) est une face de l'histoire, l'échec de la tentative en est une autre et porte son sens. b) elle est apologétique : l'histoire prouve que Jésus a accompli ce qu'il avait dit : « après trois jours, je ressusciterai ». c) elle est christologique, dans la mesure où elle révèle l'identité entre le ressuscité et le personnage de Jésus. Le message est que Dieu fait triompher le divin Fils sur ses ennemis, même quand ceux-ci représentent apparemment la toute-puissance de Rome et les autorités suprêmes des Juifs. Les événements stupéfiants qui surviennent, comme le séisme ou l'intervention de l'ange, sont une dramatisation de la puissance de Dieu. Si l'historicité de ce passage peut être mise en doute, admettons que la vérité communiquée par un drame peut parfois s'exprimer plus efficacement dans l'esprit des gens qu'une vérité communiquée par l'histoire. Et c'est probablement l'objectif primordial qu'avait en tête l'auteur des AP!

L'ensevelissement de Jésus par Joseph d'Arimathée sera le prétexte à un développement propre aux AP. En effet son intervention va provoquer la colère des Juifs qui vont l'enfermer. Une véritable enquête judiciaire menée par les Juifs eux-mêmes sera lancée dès qu'on découvrira les disparitions de Joseph et de Jésus. Luc fera un portrait plus détaillé de Joseph d'Arimathée que les autres évangélistes : il est présenté comme un conseiller juif bon et juste qui n'avait pas été d'accord avec le verdict et les actes du conseil des Juifs[92]. Il reste jusqu'à ce moment de l'histoire un disciple secret par peur des Juifs, jusqu'à ce qu'il entre, avec Nicodème[93], son ad-

[92] Lc 23,50–51 ; AP 11,3.

[93] Comme Joseph, Nicodème était naguère venu trouver Jésus de nuit ; comme le Joseph marcien, Nicodème était membre du sanhédrin, un maître en Israël ; comme le Joseph lucanien, Nicodème contestait le verdict de ses collègues du sanhédrin contre Jésus. Et enfin, comme le Joseph de Jean, il agit publiquement en faveur de Jésus, et fait donc ainsi preuve de plus de courage qu'il n'en avait montré jusqu'alors.

joint, dans une catégorie de nouveaux fidèles proches de celle des disciples. On peut s'attendre à voir désormais la portée de l'action publique de Joseph et de Nicodème. Elle les conduira à porter un fort témoignage à Jésus après la résurrection. Et c'est précisément ce qui va se passer dans les AP. Le récit du miracle de la libération de Joseph va porter un coup fatal aux Juifs : ceux-ci vivent la même surprise que les gardes au tombeau et ils décident d'écouter tous les témoins liés à l'histoire de Jésus : Lévi et son père ainsi que les trois Galiléens qui parleront de l'ascension du Christ.

La mission universelle et l'ascension du Christ

L'intervention, au ch.14, des trois Galiléens Phinès, Adas et Esaïe témoins de l'enseignement de Jésus avec ses disciples permet de donner un relief à la simple mention des onze disciples de Matthieu[94] et laisse surtout l'occasion à l'auteur d'introduire un extrait de ce qu'on trouve dans l'appendice de Marc[95] : l'invitation à proclamer l'évangile au monde entier et ce qui s'ensuit [96]. Ces témoignages mettent en relief la portée pédagogique et évangélisatrice du message. Jésus a enseigné à ses disciples ce qui relevait du dessein de Dieu. Suite au combat qu'il a mené contre ses opposants, Jésus s'est élevé dans les cieux. L'ascension sera évoquée (Mc 16,19 ; AP 14,1) par les 3 Galiléens qui viendront l'un après l'autre témoigner de ce qu'ils ont vu et comment Jésus s'élevait dans les airs. Puis quatre autres docteurs prennent la parole et citent des textes tirés de l'AT et de Luc[97] rappelant des ascensions célèbres de l'histoire : Hénoch, Moïse, Jésus. Anne et Caïphe approuvent ces interventions pour Hénoch et Moïse, mais ils ne manquent pas d'attirer l'attention sur la malédiction concernant l'homme « pendu au bois » (Dt 21,23 ; AP 16,3,2). En revanche, la foule, sans réserve, se convertit à Jésus comme le manifeste l'hymne au Seigneur qui achève le récit et réinterprète christologiquement des versets vétérotestamentaires. Comment ne pas voir là un message direct à la communauté : la crucifixion a marqué le dernier combat de Jésus, et sa résurrection, dont

---

[94] Mt 28,16 : « or les 11 disciples partirent pour la Galilée, pour la montagne où Jésus leur avait ordonné d'aller».

[95] La manifestation du Ressuscité à Marie de Magdala et aux disciples et son invitation à aller proclamer l'évangile à toute la création.

[96] Appendice de Mc 16,15–18 : Et il leur dit : « étant partis par le monde tout entier, proclamez l'évangile à toute la création ; celui qui croira et sera baptisé sera sauvé, celui qui ne croira pas sera condamné ; or les signes que voici accompagneront ceux qui ont cru ; par mon nom ils chasseront les démons, ils parleront en langues nouvelles, ils saisiront des serpents et, s'ils boivent quelque chose de mortel, il ne leur fera aucun mal ; ils imposeront les mains aux malades et ils s'en trouveront bien ».

[97] AP 16,3,1 : Dt 19,15 ; Gn 5,24 ; Dt 34, 5–6 ; Lc 2,34 ; Ex 23,20.

témoignent ouvertement les trois Galiléens, permet le rétablissement des humains, le retour d'un peuple nouveau, par la reconnaissance successive de tous les témoins interrogés. Le ministère de Jésus marqué par son enseignement et ses messages au peuple doit être reconnu comme un service rendu à la personne humaine tout entière.

Conclusion

L'auteur des AP nous présente une vision didactique, apologétique et sotériologique de la Passion du Christ. S'il la construit sur la base d'un drame liturgique, avec scènes de miracles, dialogues et décors, inscrite dans une unité de temps et de lieu – tous étant des caractéristiques appropriées au théâtre – c'est sans doute pour exercer auprès de ses spectateurs un impact visuel plus marquant que la simple lecture des faits. Par sa théâtralité il offrait à un public qui n'était pas forcément versé dans les lettres une possibilité d'entrer dans le message biblique avec plus de facilité, plus directement, d'une manière plus palpable et sans doute doté d'une plus grande force de conviction. Par son déroulement essentiellement le premier jour du triduum et enrichie par maintes manifestations à caractère liturgique, la pièce peut s'intégrer dans un contexte de veillée pascale. Le cadre du procès permettra par ailleurs d'apporter une certaine autorité judiciaire et politique à l'interrogatoire de Pilate et mettra en valeur les révélations de Jésus. Comme pourrait le laisser entendre l'intitulé du texte « Actes de Pilate[98] », Pilate a le beau rôle : il est soucieux de faire une enquête rigoureuse en approfondissant son interrogatoire et il accorde plus de crédit aux témoins favorables à Jésus qu'à ses adversaires. Seule sa frayeur explique qu'il ait cédé aux pressions des Juifs. Son attachement à la cause de Jésus est manifeste[99]. Nicodème, qui apparaît dans un titre ultérieur « Evangile de Nicodème», aura lui un rôle plutôt symbolique : son cheminement personnel (extérieur aux AP) est à l'image du peuple hésitant qui finit par devenir un fervent disciple du Christ[100]. L'ensemble du texte est une charge contre les autorités juives : leur mauvaise foi est dénoncée et elles sont obligées de s'avouer vaincues. Par contre les nombreuses formes de té-

[98] A comprendre comme « Actes commis sous le gouvernement de Pilate ».

[99] Il se manifestera par son jeûne et celui de sa femme, lorsqu'il apprend du centurion ce qui est arrivé au matin de Pâques (11,2).

[100] A la suite de cette étude, nous serions tentée d'appliquer le titre « Actes de Pilate » à la première partie du texte qui se terminerait avec le jeûne de Pilate et de sa femme (ch. 1–11) et le titre d' « Evangile de Nicodème », à la seconde partie marquée par l'aboutissement de l'enquête où « la bonne nouvelle », c'est-à-dire l'« Evangile », a été unanimement reçue (ch. 12–16).

moignages favorables à Jésus, provenant de milieux étrangers au christianisme, dénotent une volonté de l'auteur d'accentuer l'universalité de la reconnaissance.

L'auteur des AP choisit ses sources parmi les quatre évangiles en vue de mener à bien son objectif. Chez Jean, disciple de l'élévation et de la glorification du Fils, il puisera dans la richesse spirituelle du vocabulaire : il démontrera l'incapacité de s'entendre entre mondes différents tels que celui des Juifs ou de Pilate, tout en laissant transparaître une volonté apologétique du monde divin. Chez Matthieu, qui invite le Ressuscité à être présent au milieu de la communauté, il saisira le message social avec ses manifestations à caractère si humain : celles-ci lui permettront de disculper Pilate et plus loin de réfuter les fausses allégations juives, de prouver que tout s'accomplit suivant les paroles de Jésus et que le Fils triomphe devant les puissances juives ou romaines. Chez Luc qui offre son optimisme et son ouverture à la grâce divine aux plus démunis, il relèvera l'échange au Golgotha : la vision sotériologique y est parfaitement claire. Chez Marc qui rappelle à tous les disciples du Christ la mission qui leur incombe : « va dans le monde entier et prêche l'Evangile à toute la création », il reprend le message pour l'ancrer au cœur évangélisateur des AP. Toutes ces reprises se concentrent sur l'objectif ultime : une conversion progressive mais radicale des propres accusateurs du Christ et une reconnaissance générale de la véracité du message, de la mort, de la résurrection et de l'ascension de Jésus, fils de Marie et de Joseph.

„Tota paradisi clauis tuus sanguis est“

Die Blutzeugen und ihre Auferstehung in der frühchristlichen Märtyrerliteratur

PETER GEMEINHARDT

Um das Jahr 165 n. Chr. standen in Rom sieben Christen als Angeklagte vor dem Stadtpräfekten Quintus Junius Rusticus: der Philosoph und Lehrer Justin und seine sechs Schüler, darunter mit Charito auch eine Frau.[1] Sie waren „zur Zeit der verwerflichen Gesetze zu Gunsten der Idolatrie“ verhaftet worden[2], und entsprechend lautete die Anklage auf Verweigerung des Opfers für die traditionellen Götter Roms – eine Verweigerung, für die die Christen seit Jahrzehnten notorisch waren, so dass streng genommen das religiös exklusivierende Bekenntnis zu Christus Grund zur Verurteilung war.[3] Rusticus versicherte sich, dass sämtliche Angeklagten dieses Bekenntnis – Χριστιανός εἰμι – abgelegt hatten. Doch im Unterschied zu manchen anderen Richtern ließ er es nicht bei dieser Feststellung und beim Versuch, die Versammlungsräume der christlichen Gemeinde zu identifizieren, bewenden[4], sondern wollte mehr über den christlichen Glauben wissen, an dem ein offensichtlich gebildeter Mann wie Justin so starrsinnig festhielt. Vor allem an einem Thema hatte der Rusticus Interesse:

> „Der Präfekt sagte zu Justin: ‚Wenn du jetzt ausgepeitscht und geköpft wirst, glaubst du, dass du dann in den Himmel aufsteigen wirst?‘ Justin sagte: ‚So hoffe ich aufgrund meiner Standhaftigkeit, wenn ich dies hier erdulde. Ich weiß, dass auf die, welche ein rechtes Leben führen, die göttliche Gabe wartet bis zum Tag des Weltendes.‘ Der Präfekt Rusti-

[1] Mit H. MUSURILLO, The Acts of the Christian Martyrs, Oxford 1972, XIX ist der kürzeren griechischen Rezension (A) der Vorzug gegenüber der bekannteren Rezension B zu geben.– Zitate aus Märtyrerakten folgen grundsätzlich der Edition von Musurillo. Die Abkürzungen der Märtyrerakten und anderen patristischen Quellenschriften erfolgen nach: Lexikon der antiken christlichen Literatur, hg. von S. DÖPP/W. GEERLINGS, Freiburg u.a. [3]2002.

[2] M. Just. 1 = 42,4: Ἐν τῷ καιρῷ τῶν ἀνόμων προσταγμάτων τῆς εἰδωλολατρείας.

[3] M. Just. 5,6 = 46,12f.: οἱ μὴ βουληθέντες ἐπιθῦσαι τοῖς θεοῖς, φραγελλωθέντες ἀπαχθήτωσαν τῇ τῶν νόμων ἀκολουθίᾳ.

[4] Vgl. M. Just. 3,1–3 = 44,3–10.

cus sagte: ‚Also meinst du wirklich, dass du aufsteigen wirst?‘ Justin entgegnete: ‚Ich meine das nicht nur, sondern ich bin vollkommen davon überzeugt!‘“[5]

Offensichtlich reichte Rusticus diese Auskunft, denn er kehrte abrupt zum eigentlichen Ziel des Verhörs zurück: „Wenn du nicht gehorchst [sc. und opferst], wird du bestraft werden“ – worauf Justin bekräftigte: „Wir vertrauen darauf, dass wir, wenn uns die Strafe trifft, gerettet werden.“[6]

Das Martyrium Justins und seiner Schüler ist möglicherweise das erste[7], jedenfalls aber eines der eindrücklichsten Beispiele dafür, welche Rolle das Thema der Auferstehung von den Toten für die frühe christliche Märtyrertheologie spielte.[8] Für die Zeitgenossen war dies der *articulus stantis et cadentis ecclesiae* schlechthin: „Die Zuversicht der Christen ist die Auferstehung von den Toten. Wir sind, was wir sind, weil wir daran glauben“, so Tertullian.[9] Dabei war diese Zuversicht alles andere als unangefochten. Dass die Toten mit Leib und Seele, präziser gesagt: mit *Fleisch* und Seele dereinst auferstehen würden, um sich Gottes Gericht zu stellen, musste vor allem gegen „gnostische“, d.h. dualistisch denkende christliche Gruppen

---

[5] M. Just. 5,1–3 = 46,4–9: Ὁ ἔπαρχος Ἰουστίνῳ λέγει· Ἐὰν μαστιγωθεὶς ἀποκεφαλισθῇς, πέπεισαι ὅτι μέλλεις ἀναβαίνειν εἰς τὸν οὐρανόν; Ἰουστῖνος εἶπεν· Ἐλπίζω ἐκ τῆς ὑπομονῆς ἐὰν ὑπομείνω· οἶδα δὲ ὅτι καὶ τοῖς ὀρθῶς βιώσασιν παραμένει [τὸ θεῖον χάρισμα] μέχρι τῆς ἐκπυρώσεως. Ῥούστικος ἔπαρχος εἶπεν· Τοῦτο οὖν ὑπονοεῖς, ὅτι ἀναβήσῃ; Ἰουστῖνος εἶπεν· Οὐχ ὑπονοῶ, ἀλλ᾽ ἀκριβῶς πέπεισμαι. Zu dieser Passage vgl. G. KRETSCHMAR, Auferstehung des Fleisches. Zur Frühgeschichte einer theologischen Lehrformel, in: Leben angesichts des Todes. Beiträge zum theologischen Problem des Todes. FS H. THIELICKE, Tübingen 1968, 101–137, hier 130.

[6] M. Just. 5,4f. = 46,9–11: Ῥούστικος ἔπαρχος εἶπεν· Εἰ μὴ πείθεσθε, τιμωρηθήσεσθε. Ἰουστῖνος εἶπεν· Δι᾽ εὐχῆς ἔχομεν τιμωρηθέντες σωθῆναι.

[7] Möglicherweise stammt das Martyrium Polycarpi (dazu ausführlich unten) erst aus der Zeit um 177 und nicht, wie oft zu lesen, von 155/56; die Datierung hängt wesentlich davon ab, ob man darin eine Reaktion auf das Erstarken des Montanismus in Kleinasien sieht (so G. BUSCHMANN, Martyrium Polycarpi – Eine formkritische Studie. Ein Beitrag zur Frage nach der Entstehung der Gattung Märtyrerakte, BZNW 70, Berlin/New York 1994), der kaum vor 170 anzutreffen ist.

[8] Allerdings weist W.C. WEINRICH, Death and Martyrdom: An Important Aspect of Early Christian Eschatology, in: Concordia Theological Quarterly 66 (2002), 327–338, hier 327f. darauf hin, dass im Kontext einer Gerichtsverhandlung keineswegs immer die Hoffnung auf die Auferstehung zur Sprache gebracht wurde, sondern vielfach auch der Glaube an Gott den Schöpfer, so in M. Apoll. 2 = 90,10–12: Χριστιανός εἰμι· καὶ διὰ τοῦτο τὸν θεὸν τὸν ποιήσαντα τὸν οὐρανὸν καὶ τὴν γῆν καὶ τὴν θάλασσαν καὶ πάντα τὰ ἐν αὐτοῖς [Apg 4,24; vgl. Ex 20,11] σέβομαι καὶ φοβοῦμαι. – Im Folgenden geht es um eine theologische Thematik, die in kerygmatischen Texten verhandelt wird, als welche Märtyrerakten (ungeachtet ihrer literarischen Protokollform) grundsätzlich anzusehen sind. Es wird dagegen nicht nach dem historischen Sachgehalt des Geschilderten gefragt. Für meine Ausführungen ist allein relevant, was noch so skurrile Hinrichtungsszenen oder spektakuläre Visionsberichte bezüglich der Auferstehung theologisch aussagen.

[9] Tert. resurr. 1,1 = CChr.SL 2, 921,2f. Borleffs: „*Fiducia christianorum resurrectio mortuorum; illam credentes, sumus.*“

verteidigt werden.[10] Bei philosophisch informierten Kritikern des Christentums stieß die Auferstehung ebenso auf Unverständnis: Celsus nannte die Christen ein „körperverliebtes Geschlecht“ (φιλοσώματον γένος)[11], und der Präfekt in Ägypten, Culcianus, fragte bei Bischof Phileas von Thmuis, den er 306 zu verurteilen hatte, gleich zweimal nach, ob dieser nicht nur von der Seele, sondern wirklich vom Körper spreche: „Dieses Fleisch soll auferstehen?“[12] Schließlich musste sich der Glaube an die Auferstehung im Angesicht des Todes bewähren, wenn Christen um ihres Christuszeugnisses willen auf denkbar grausame Art und Weise hingerichtet und damit zu „Blutzeugen“ wurden, wie Justin und seine Schüler.

Es ist dieser letzte Aspekt, dem im Folgenden Aufmerksamkeit geschenkt werden soll: Welche Rolle spielt der Auferstehungsglaube in der literarischen Präsentation des Zeugentodes in Märtyrerakten und -passionen? Und wie wird über Geschick und Verbleib der Märtyrer in der zeitgenössischen Theologie reflektiert? Damit wird ein Stück Rezeptionsgeschichte der biblischen Auferstehungstraditionen greifbar, das deutlich zu machen vermag, wie ein nur schwer plausibel zu machender biblischer Topos für das Christentum gerade in der Zeit der „verwerflichen Gesetze“ unmittelbare Lebensrelevanz erlangen und behalten konnte.[13]

---

[10] Vgl. die Glaubensregel in Tert. praescr. 13,5 = FC 42, 256,13–17 Schleyer sowie schon das Insistieren des Ignatius von Antiochien darauf, dass Christus „nach der Auferstehung im Fleisch ist“ (Smyrn. 3,1 = Die Apostolischen Väter. Griechisch-deutsche Parallelausgabe, hg. von A. LINDEMANN/H. PAULSEN, Tübingen 1992, 226,20f.: μετὰ τὴν ἀνάστασιν ἐν σαρκὶ ὄντα); vgl. auch Just. dial. 80,5 = PTS 47, 209,31f. Marcovich.

[11] Orig. Cels. VII 36 = GCS Orig. II, 186,18 Koetschau; vgl. auch Celsus’ Argument gegen die Auferstehung in Cels. V 14 = a.a.O. 15,14f.: ἀλλ’ οὔτι γε τὰ αἰσχρὰ ὁ θεὸς δύναται οὐδὲ τὰ παρὰ φύσιν βούλεται. Zur paganen Kritik an der christlichen Auferstehungshoffnung vgl. K. SCHNEIDER, Studien zur Entfaltung der altkirchlichen Theologie der Auferstehung, Hereditas 14, Bonn 1999, 124–263; C.J. SETZER, Resurrection of the Body in Early Judaism and Early Christianity. Doctrine, Community, and Self-Definition, Boston/Leiden 2004, 99–108.

[12] A. Phileae nach Pap. Bodmer XX, Z. 54–58 = 332,4–8: Κουλκιανός εἶπεν· Ἡ σὰρξ αὕτη ἀν[ίσ]ταται; αὖθι[ς] κα[τ]απλησσόμενος εἶπεν· Ἡ σὰ[ρξ αὕτ]η ἀνίσταται; Φιλέας [εἶπεν· Ἡ σὰρ]ξ αὕτη ἀνίσταται … (es folgen Textverluste). Vgl. KRETSCHMAR, Auferstehung des Fleisches (s. Anm. 5), 101.

[13] Die folgenden Untersuchungen streben keine Vollständigkeit an, was die Auseinandersetzung mit der Sekundärliteratur betrifft; das gilt zumal für die oft intrikaten Einleitungsfragen zu den Märtyrerakten. Auch die antike Martyrologie als solche kann hier nur ausschnittsweise betrachtet werden (vgl. zum Phänomen und seiner Erforschung demnächst P. GEMEINHARDT, Märtyrer und Martyriumsdeutungen von der Antike bis zur Reformation, in: ZKG 120, 2009 [im Druck], hier auch ausführliche Literaturangaben). Das Verhältnis von Martyrium und Auferstehung im hier zu untersuchenden Quellenbestand thematisieren u.a. K. HOLL, Die Vorstellung vom Märtyrer und die Märtyrerakten in ihrer geschichtlichen Entwicklung, in: DERS., Gesammelte Aufsätze zur Kirchengeschichte II, Tübingen 1928 (= Darmstadt 1964), 68–102, bes. 72f.; U. KELLERMANN, Auferstanden in

1. Hoffnung über den Tod hinaus

Eines der berühmtesten Gebete der Kirchengeschichte entstammt dem Martyriumsbericht über Bischof Polykarp von Smyrna. Dieser war hochbetagt verhaftet worden, hatte gegenüber dem Prokonsul L. Statius Quadratus erfolgreich das Opfer für Götter und Kaiser verweigert und sah nun auf dem Scheiterhaufen dem Tod entgegen. Polykarp wandte sich im Gebet an Gott:

> „Ich lobe dich, dass du mich dieses Tages und dieser Stunde für würdig hieltest, in der Zahl der Märtyrer Anteil zu bekommen an dem Kelch deines Christus zur Auferstehung des ewigen Lebens von Seele und Leib in der Unvergänglichkeit des Heiligen Geistes…“.[14]

Der Text vereint auf knappem Raum wesentliche Charakteristika der frühchristlichen Deutung des Martyriums: das individuelle Datum, das liturgisch kommemoriert wurde; die Gemeinschaft der Märtyrer; der Bezug auf Jesu Passionserfahrung und die Hoffnung auf die ganzheitliche Auferstehung des Blutzeugen zu einem unvergänglichen Sein bei Christus. Im Martyrium des Polykarp hat sich der Begriff des μάρτυς terminologisch und

---

den Himmel. 2 Makkabäer 7 und die Auferstehung der Märtyrer, SBS 95, Stuttgart 1979, bes. 130–134; V. SAXER, Bible et Hagiographie. Textes et thèmes bibliques dans les Actes des martyrs authentiques des premiers siècles, Bern u.a. 1986, bes. 231–234; C. WALKER BYNUM, The Resurrection of the Body in Western Christianity: 200–1336. Lectures on the History of Religions N.S. 15, New York 1995, bes. 43–51. Zur Sicht der Auferstehung in der Alten Kirche vgl. allgemein R. STAATS, Auferstehung II/2: Alte Kirche, in: TRE 4 (1979), 513–529, bes. 517–519 sowie zuletzt SETZER, Resurrection of the Body (wie Anm. 11), 71–98; H. SONNEMANS, „Hellenisierung“ des biblischen Glaubens? Zur Lehrentwicklung in den ersten Jahrhunderten, in: Auferstehung der Toten. Ein Hoffnungsentwurf im Blick heutiger Wissenschaften, hg. von H. KESSLER, Darmstadt 2004, 72–93; B. STUBENRAUCH, Auferstehung des Fleisches? Zum Proprium christlichen Glaubens in Motiven patristischer Theologie, in: RQ 101 (2006), 147–156; U. VOLP, Gedanken zum Auferstehungsverständnis in der Alten Kirche, in: ZNT 19 (2007), 35–43. Zum Rekurs auf die Bibel in der antiken Hagiographie vgl. Th. BAUMEISTER, Der Rekurs auf die Bibel als Mittel zur Darstellung heiliger Geschichte in der altchristlichen Hagiographie, in: Normieren – Tradieren – Inszenieren. Das Christentum als Buchreligion, hg. von A. HOLZEM, Darmstadt 2004, 55–71 (mit besonderem Augenmerk auf das *Martyrium Polycarpi* und die *Passio Perpetuae et Felicitatis*) sowie M. VAN UYTFANGHE, La typologie de la sainteté en Occident vers la fin de l'Antiquité (avec une attention spéciale aux modèles bibliques), in: Scrivere di santi. Atti del II Convegno di studio dell'Associazione italiana per lo studio della santità, dei culti e dell'agiografia, Napoli, 22–25 ottobre 1997, hg. von G. LUONGO, Rom 1998, 17–48.

[14] M. Polyc. 14,2 = 12,25–28: εὐλογῶ σε, ὅτι ἠξίωσάς με τῆς ἡμέρας καὶ ὥρας ταύτης, τοῦ λαβεῖν μέρος ἐν ἀριθμῷ τῶν μαρτύρων ἐν τῷ ποτηρίῳ τοῦ Χριστοῦ σου εἰς ἀνάστασιν ζωῆς αἰωνίου ψυχῆς τε καὶ σώματος ἐν ἀφθαρσίᾳ πνεύματος ἁγίου. Übers. Th. BAUMEISTER, Genese und Entfaltung der altkirchlichen Theologie des Martyriums, TC 8, Bern u.a. 1991, 79.

theologisch zum *Blut-Zeugen* verengt – das Zeugnis wird zwar auch durch das worthafte Bekenntnis vor dem Prokonsul abgelegt, doch läuft die ganze Darstellung auf den Tod des Zeugen hinaus, der ihn als echten Nachahmer Christi (μιμητὴς Χριστοῦ) erweist und das Wortzeugnis so erst authentifiziert.[15] Umso enger wird der Zusammenhang zwischen Tod und Auferstehung geknüpft: Dass der Märtyrer durch den Tod zum Leben gelangt, ist kein kontingentes Widerfahrnis, sondern die Grundbedingung dafür, dass er den Tod willig, ja freudig auf sich nimmt. Bereits Ignatius von Antiochien († um 110) brachte dies auf die Formel: „Schön ist es, von der Welt fort zu Gott hin unterzugehen, damit ich in ihm aufgehe."[16] Tod und Auferstehung erscheinen als zwei Momente *einer* Bewegung, die von der Gemeinschaft mit Christus umfangen ist: „Wenn ich gelitten habe, werde ich ein Freigelassener Jesu Christi sein und in ihm als Freier auferstehen."[17] Am Ende des Todes steht das Leben, und der angehende Märtyrer fürchtet nichts mehr, als dass die römische Gemeinde in letzter Sekunde seine Hinrichtung und damit den Durchbruch zum wahren Leben vereitelt: „Hindert mich nicht zu leben, wollt nicht, dass ich sterbe!"[18]

Auch gegenüber den Behörden machten Märtyrer deutlich, was sie aus ihrer Perspektive erwartete: Als Pionius von seinem Richter vorgehalten wurde, er eile dem Tod entgegen, konterte jener: „Nicht zum Tod, zum Leben eile ich!"[19] Der Fortgang der Erzählung macht deutlich, dass die Schilderung des Martyriums nicht zuerst apologetischen, sondern kerygmatischen Zwecken dient: Als Pionius bereits auf dem Scheiterhaufen festge-

---

[15] Zum Begriff des μιμητής vgl. M. Polyc. 1,2; 17,3 = 2,12; 16,4f.; M. Lugd. 2,2 = 82,10f.; Ign. Ant. Rom. 6,3 = 214,7f. Lindemann/Paulsen: μιμητὴς τοῦ πάθους τοῦ θεοῦ μου.

[16] Ign. Ant. Rom. 2.2 = 210,4f. Lindemann/Paulsen: Καλὸν τὸ δῦναι ἀπὸ κόσμου πρὸς θεόν, ἵνα εἰς αὐτὸν ἀνατείλω. Vgl. Th. BAUMEISTER, Die Anfänge der Theologie des Martyriums, MBTh 45, Münster 1980, 282f. 299f. zum Thema der Auferstehung bei Ignatius und Polykarp und zum Verhältnis beider. Zur Debatte über die Datierung der Ignatianen, die sich derzeit wieder dem frühen 2. Jahrhundert zuneigt, vgl. F.R. PROSTMEIER, Ignatius von Antiochien, in: LACL (s. Anm. 1), 346–348.

[17] Ign. Ant. Rom. 4,3 = 212,4f. Lindemann/Paulsen: 'Αλλ' ἐὰν πάθω, ἀπελεύθερος γενήσομαι 'Ιησοῦ Χριστοῦ καὶ ἀναστήσομαι ἐν αὐτῷ ἐλεύθερος. Vgl. BYNUM, The Resurrection of the Body (s. Anm. 13), 27.

[18] Ign. Ant. Rom. 6,2 = 214,4f. Lindemann/Paulsen: μὴ ἐμποδίσητέ μοι ζῆναι, μὴ θελήσητέ με ἀποθανεῖν.

[19] M. Pion. 20,5 = 162,15f.: ἐλέχθη αὐτῷ· Τί σπεύδεις ἐπὶ τὸν θάνατον; ἀπεκρίνατο· Οὐκ ἐπὶ τὸν θάνατον ἀλλ' ἐπὶ τὴν ζωήν. Eus. h.e. IV 15,47 = GCS Eusebius II/1, 352,21–354,1 Schwartz datiert dieses Martyrium in die Zeit Polykarps, doch tatsächlich dürfte es sich um eine Begebenheit während der decischen Verfolgung (249–251) handeln. Zum Motiv des Eilens vgl. auch M. Lugd. 1,6 = 62,20: ἔσπευδον πρὸς Χριστόν und die Anspielung auf Pred 12,7 in P. Montan. 7,4 = 218,27f.: *„Ad deum suum spiritus properat."*

nagelt war und ein letztes Angebot, die Nägel zu entfernen, abgelehnt hatte, versank er für kurze Zeit in tiefes Nachdenken und meinte dann: „Deswegen eile ich, damit ich schneller auferweckt werde, auf dass die Auferstehung von den Toten erkennbar werde.“[20] Sein anonymer Hagiograph konstatierte, Pionius sei „nach seinem Sieg in dem großen Kampf durch die enge Pforte in das weite und große Licht“ eingegangen.[21] Die qualvolle Hinrichtung war also nicht ein Ort der Vernichtung, wie von den Richtern der Christen intendiert, sondern bereits der Ort, an dem zugleich die Erhaltung und die Heilung des Leibes durch Gott deutlich wurden. Pionius war bereits „vom Tod zum Leben durchgedrungen“ (Joh 5,24).

Eine solche Erwartung durchzieht die frühchristlichen Märtyrerakten. Flavian, der während der valerianischen Verfolgung zwei Tage länger als sein Gefährte Montanus auf die Hinrichtung warten musste, tröstete sich damit, „jener dritte Tag nach der zweitägigen Pause“ sei „nicht ein Tag des Leidens, sondern gleichsam der Auferstehung.“[22] Die Zeit im Gefängnis galt hier also gewissermaßen als vorweggenommene Hadesfahrt, die für den Märtyrer – wie für Christus – am dritten Tag schon wieder endete. Vor seinem Tod hatte Flavian noch einmal Gelegenheit, seinen Peinigern das Grunddatum der christlichen Hoffnung zu erläutern:

> „Wir leben, auch wenn wir sterben (vgl. 2 Kor 6,9); wir werden nicht vom Tod überwunden, sondern wir überwinden ihn. Und wenn jemand ‚zur Erkenntnis der Wahrheit gelangen‘ will (1 Tim 2,4), dann muss er ebenfalls Christ werden.“[23]

Diese Umkehrung der augenfälligen Konfiguration von Leben und Tod erklärt einerseits, dass schon bald der Todestag des Märtyrers als sein „Geburts-Tag“ (*dies natalis*) begangen wurde. „Das Geborenwerden steht mir bevor“, bekundete Ignatius.[24] Aus der Perspektive der Überlebenden formuliert das Polykarpmartyrium, künftig möge „die Feier des Geburtstages seines Zeugnisses“ begangen werden.[25] Dass hieraus tatsächlich eine liturgische Praxis erwuchs, bestätigen einerseits Inschriften[26], andererseits Cy-

---

[20] M. Pion. 21,4 = 164,2f.: Διὰ τοῦτο σπεύδω ἵνα θᾶττον ἐγερθῶ, δηλῶν τὴν ἐκ νεκρῶν ἀνάστασιν.

[21] M. Pion. 22,1 = 164,19–21: καὶ τὸν μέγαν ἀγῶνα νικήσας διῆλθε διὰ τῆς στενῆς θύρας εἰς τὸ πλατὺ καὶ μέγα φῶς.

[22] P. Montan. 17,3 = 230,22f.: *„dies ille post biduum tertius non quasi passionis sed quasi resurrectionis dies sustinebatur.“*

[23] P. Montan. 19,6 = 232,19–21: *„uiuere nos etiam cum occidimur; nec uinci morte sed uincere; et ipsos quoque, si uellent ‚peruenire ad notitiam ueritatis‘, etiam Christianos esse debere.“*

[24] Ign. Ant. Rom. 6,1 = 214,3f. Lindemann/Paulsen: ὁ δὲ τοκετός μοι ἐπίκειται.

[25] M. Polyc. 18,3 = 16,13: τὸν τοῦ μαρτυρίου αὐτοῦ ἡμέραν γενέθλιον.

[26] ILCV 2114a (Rom, ursprünglicher Fundort unbekannt): *„sanctis martyribus. Tiburtio, Baleriano et Maximo, quorum natales est XVIII kalendas Maias“*; ILCV 2116 = CIL III 9545 (Salona): *„natale S[epti]mi mart[yri]s die XIIII ka. Maia[s]“*; vgl. dazu U.

prians Mahnung, auch die Todestage der Konfessoren während der decischen Verfolgung aufzuzeichnen, „auf dass wir ihr Gedächtnis wie auch das der Märtyrer feiern können“.[27] Offenbar regte sich bei den römischen Behörden schon bald die Ahnung, dass im ortsbezogenen Gedächtnis des auferstandenen Märtyrers – der durch seinen Leichnam, später auch durch weitere Reliquien als dauerhaft präsent geglaubt wurde – eine wesentliche Kraftquelle für die Christen liegen mochte: Angeblich auf Betreiben von jüdischer Seite ließ der für Polykarps Hinrichtung verantwortliche Zenturio dessen Körper verbrennen; doch konnte die Gemeinde sich glücklicherweise dennoch seiner Gebeine versichern.[28] Das misslang bei den Christen, die um 177 in Lyon und Vienne die Hinrichtung zahlreicher Glaubensgenossen erleben mussten. Hier wurde die Asche der Verstorbenen von den Römern gezielt in die Rhône gestreut:

> „Dies taten sie in der Annahme, sie könnten Gott besiegen und die Auferstehung der Toten verhindern. Diese [sc. die Märtyrer] sollten, wie sie sagten, ‚keine Hoffnung auf Auferstehung haben; weil sie auf ihre Auferstehung vertrauen, führen sie eine fremde und neue Religion bei uns ein, verachten die Qualen und gehen bereitwillig und mit Freude in den Tod; jetzt wollen wir sehen, ob sie auferstehen werden und ob ihr Gott ihnen helfen und sie aus unseren Händen entreißen kann.‘“[29]

Hier wird die in dem o.g. Zitat von Tertullian und bei zahlreichen anderen Theologen betonte zentrale Bedeutung der Auferstehung für den christlichen Glauben bezeichnenderweise durch die „Heiden“ handgreiflich bestätigt: Auf der Grundlage der philosophischen Kritik eines Celsus hätte man die Christen doch eigentlich ihre Toten bestatten und sie ihrem nichtigen Glauben an die Auferstehung frönen lassen können. Doch scheint in der Umwelt des Christentums präzise wahrgenommen worden zu sein, dass hier mehr und anderes als die platonische Anthropologie auf dem Spiel stand: Der Mut, den Märtyrer und Märtyrerinnen bewiesen, speiste sich gerade aus der Hoffnung, dass sie nicht aus der Hand Gottes gerissen werden könnten, und dies nicht im Sinne einer dualistisch grundierten Verachtung des Körpers, die irdische Leiden schlicht als gegenstandslos hätte

---

VOLP, Tod und Ritual in den christlichen Gemeinden der Antike, SVigChr 65, Leiden/Boston 2002, 181 Anm. 370.

[27] Cypr. ep. 12,2 = CChr.SL 3B, 69,31–33 Diercks: *„ut conmemorationes eorum inter memorias martyrum celebrare possimus.“*

[28] Vgl. M. Polyc. 17,1–18,2 = 14,21–16,11.

[29] M. Lugd. 1,63 = 80,35–82,4: καὶ ταῦτ᾽ ἔπραττον ὡς δυνάμενοι νικῆσαι τὸν θεὸν καὶ ἀφελέσθαι αὐτῶν τὴν παλιγγενεσίαν ἵνα, ὡς ἔλεγον ἐκεῖνοι, μηδὲ ἐλπίδα σχῶσιν ἀναστάσεως, ἐφ᾽ ᾗ πεποιθότες ξένην τινὰ καὶ καινὴν ἡμῖν εἰσάγουσι θρησκείαν καὶ καταφρονοῦσι τῶν δεινῶν, ἕτοιμοι καὶ μετὰ χαρᾶς ἥκοντες ἐπὶ τὸν θάνατον. νῦν ἴδωμεν εἰ ἀναστήσονται καὶ εἰ δύναται βοηθῆσαι αὐτοῖς ὁ θεὸς αὐτῶν καὶ ἐξελέσθαι ἐκ τῶν χειρῶν ἡμῶν (Übers. P. GUYOT/R. KLEIN, Das frühe Christentum bis zum Ende der Verfolgungen. Eine Dokumentation I, Darmstadt 1993, 91).

erscheinen lassen, sondern durch die Erwartung, eben mit Leib und Seele aufzuerstehen.[30] Der geschundene Körper war Schauplatz des Kampfes mit dem Teufel, den die Märtyrer in der Deutung ihrer Hagiographen erfolgreich ausfochten, und der Sieg wurde durch nichts so eindrucksvoll illustriert wie durch die Zusage der leiblichen Auferstehung.[31] Das erklärt die detailreichen, oft makaber anmutenden und einem gewissen Voyeurismus nicht abholden Schilderungen der Verletzungen, die den Christen zugefügt wurden: je blutiger das Leiden, desto glorreicher die Bewahrung, deren Protagonisten und Adressaten gewiss sein durften.[32] Caroline Walker Bynum weist zu Recht darauf hin, dass hier die apologetischen und martyriologischen Dimensionen der Diskussion über die Auferstehung (s.o.) ineinander laufen:

> „Apologists such as Tertullian, Irenaeus, and Justin (himself ‚the martyr') spoke of resurrection as God's gift to all bodies but especially to those that experienced suffering and partition in prison or the arena. Their images of stasis, hardening, and reassemblage in heaven gave to mortal flesh the promise of victory over what martyrs, and those who admired them, feared most: excruciating pain in the moment of dying and dishonor to the cadaver after death."[33]

---

[30] Entsprechend wurde im Zuge der großen Christenverfolgung unter Kaiser Valerian (257–260) den Christen die Benutzung ihrer Friedhöfe untersagt – in der durchaus zutreffenden Erwartung, sie damit (und mit der Ausschaltung der Klerikerelite) entscheidend treffen zu können (vgl. den Bericht des Dionysius von Alexandrien über Valerians Maßnahmen bei Eus. h.e. VII 11,10 = GCS Eusebius II/2, 654,24–656,5 Schwartz, sowie die Aufhebung dieses Verbots durch Gallienus nach Eus. h.e. VII 13,2 = aaO. 666,14–23).

[31] Vgl. BYNUM, The Resurrection of the Body (s. Anm. 13), 49: „Thus resurrection is the ultimate victory, for it brings together the scattered bits of the church's heroes and heroines, providing for them the quiet sepulchre their executioners might prohibit and prevent."

[32] Vgl. dazu G. CLARK, Bodies and Blood: The Late Antique Debate on Martyrdom, Virginity and Resurrection, in: Changing Bodies, Changing Meaning. Studies on the Human Body in Antiquity, hg. von D. MONTSERRAT, London 1998, 99–115. Die Grenze des Zumutbaren war bezeichnenderweise bei der Sexualität erreicht: Christliche Frauen wurden auf alle erdenklichen Weisen gefoltert – doch verloren sie nie ihre Jungfräulichkeit bzw. wurden wunderbar vor sexueller Erniedrigung bewahrt. Spätestens mit dem Ende der Verfolgungen verschob sich der Akzent auf die Virginität, d.h. Trägerinnen der „Doppelkrone" des Märtyrertums und der Jungfräulichkeit wie Agnes bahnten den Weg für die Substitution der Blutzeugenschaft durch das lebenslängliche Martyrium der Asketen und Asketinnen. M.A. TILLEY, The Ascetic Body and the (Un)Making of the World of the Martyr, in: JAAR 59 (1991), 467–480, hier 472 verweist für den Gedanken, dass die für die Auferstehung nötige Reinheit nur durch Askese erreicht bzw. bewahrt werden könne (weshalb ein freiwilliges, spontanes Martyrium unangemessen erschienen sei), u.a. auf Acta Pauli et Theclae 3,12 (AAAp I, 244,3f. Lipsius): Ἄλλως ἀνάστασιν ὑμῖν οὐκ ἔστιν, ἐὰν μὴ ἁγνοὶ μείνητε καὶ τὴν σάρκα μὴ μολύνητε ἀλλὰ τηρήσητε ἁγνήν.

[33] BYNUM, The Resurrection of the Body (s. Anm. 13), 45.

Die Berichte über das Vorenthalten der Leichen lassen die schwere Anfechtung erkennen, die eine verweigerte Bestattung hervorrufen konnte: Mochte der Tote auch in jedem Fall bei Gott sein (und zwar sofort, dazu s.u.), bildeten doch seine „Überreste“ (Reliquien) den Haftpunkt für die Frömmigkeit der (für diesmal) Zurückgebliebenen – „zum Gedächtnis derer, die zuvor gekämpft haben, und zur Übung und Vorbereitung für die, denen dies bevorsteht“.[34] Dabei war für die frühen Martyriumsschilderungen die Auferstehung der Getöteten aus sich heraus evident und musste nicht eigens durch deren postmortale Wirksamkeit belegt werden – durch Heilungen oder Exorzismen, die später z.B. Ambrosius von Mailand als Kriterien nennt.[35] Doch war aller eschatologischen Reflexion zum Trotz auch schon früher das Grab der irdische Angelpunkt der Auferstehungshoffnung und in diesem Sinne durchaus eine Voraussetzung, um an die Aufnahme der Märtyrer zu Gott glauben zu können.[36]

2. Grenzgänge zwischen Tod und Leben

Die (drohende oder tatsächliche) Verweigerung einer Bestattung wurde vor allem dadurch aufgefangen, dass sich im Vollzug des Martyriums die Grenze zwischen Tod und Leben als durchlässig erwies – und zwar in beiderlei Richtung. Schon als noch Lebende waren die Märtyrer nicht mehr von dieser Welt: Sie hatten das himmlische Ziel vor Augen und Christus zur Seite. Die grausamen Folterungen zeigten daher, „daß die edlen Märtyrer Christi in jener Stunde gequält außerhalb des Fleisches weilten, mehr noch, daß der Herr ihnen zur Seite stand und mit ihnen redete.“[37] Analog dazu wurde in Lyon Sanctus, während man ihn verbrannte, von der Quelle des Lebenswassers gestärkt, die aus Christi Seite floss (Joh 7,38).[38] Dem in

[34] M. Polyc. 18,3 = 16,13–15: εἴς τε τὴν τῶν προηθληκότων μνήμην καὶ τῶν μελλόντων ἄσκησίν τε καὶ ἑτοιμασίαν. Zum Totengedenken an Polykarps Grab vgl. VOLP, Tod und Ritual (s. Anm. 26), 231.

[35] Vgl. dagegen Ambrosius' Ausführungen zur Translation der Reliquien von Gervasius und Protasius im Jahr 386 (ep. 77,9 = CSEL 82/3, 131,81–132,86 Zelzer): *„Non immerito autem plerique hanc martyrum resurrectionem appellant, videro tamen utrum ibi nobis certi martyres resurrexerint. Cognovistis immo vidistis ipsi multos a daemoniis purgatos, plurimos etiam ubi vestem sanctorum manibus contigerunt his quibus laborabant debilitatibus absolutos."* Dazu vgl. VOLP, Tod und Ritual (s. Anm. 26), 116–118.

[36] Vgl. BYNUM, The Resurrection of the Body (s. Anm. 13), 48 mit Verweis auf Min. Fel. Oct. 11,5; 34,10; 38,4 = M. Minucius Felix, Octavius, hg. und übers. von B. KYTZLER, München 1965, 76–78.188.204.

[37] M. Polyc. 2,2 = 2,24–26: ἐπιδεικνυμένους ἅπασιν ἡμῖν, ὅτι ἐκείνῃ τῇ ὥρᾳ βασανιζόμενοι τῆς σαρκὸς ἀπεδήμουν οἱ μάρτυρες τοῦ Χριστοῦ, μᾶλλον δὲ ὅτι παρεστὼς ὁ κύριος ὡμίλει αὐτοῖς.

[38] M. Lugd. 1,22 = 68,13–17; vgl. ebd. 1,28 = 70,15–17.

Karthago verurteilten Flavian erschien vor seinem eigenen Tod der bereits „gekrönte“ Successus, der „fleischliche Augen mit engelsgleichem Glanz blendete“.[39] Flavian hatte darüber hinaus eine Erscheinung seines bereits hingerichteten Bischofs Cyprian, der ihm mit tröstlichen Worten versicherte:

„Ein anderes Fleisch leidet, wenn die Seele im Himmel ist. Der Körper spürt dies überhaupt nicht, wenn sich der Geist vollkommen Gott hingibt.“[40]

Die Rettung der Seele konnte ihre Schatten dergestalt voraus werfen, dass z.B. die Märtyrer von Lyon und Vienne plötzlich „den Wohlgeruch Christi verströmten“[41] oder der Versuch, Polykarp zu verbrennen, dazu führte, dass sich der Duft von Weihrauch verbreitete, worin sich dessen Wunsch, als Opfer von Gott angenommen zu werden, sinnlich ausdrückte.[42] So sehr die frühen Märtyrerakten kerygmatische Literatur waren und sich an Christen wandten, so wenig war doch eine solche Antizipation des himmlischen Fortlebens „nur“ Glaubenssache. Gelegentlich waren solche Erfahrungen sogar Nichtchristen zugänglich, wie eine Episode während der Verhandlung gegen Marianus und Jacobus im numidischen Cirta zeigt:

„Einer der Brüder, der mit dabei stand, hatte die Augen der Heiden auf sich gezogen, weil ob der Gnade seines bevorstehenden Leidens Christus aus seinen Augen und aus seinem ganzen Gesicht hervor leuchtete. Da sie ihn mit ihren aufgewühlten und rasenden Sinnen fragten, ob er zur selben Religion und zum selben Namen [sc. Christi] gehöre wie jene, erwarb er sich durch sein augenblickliches Bekenntnis die Freude, den Märtyrern beigesellt zu werden.“[43]

Es ist ein gängiges Motiv in frühchristlichen Märtyrerakten, dass im Laufe einer Verhandlung auch weitere Christen als solche erkannt und umgehend verurteilt wurden. Der Akzent liegt freilich darauf, dass der ungenannte Bruder mit seinem (noch nicht einmal beschlossenen) Tod auch die verhei-

---

[39] P. Montan. 21,8 = 234,30f.: *„cuius effigies difficulter agnosceretur, eo quod carnales oculos angelico splendore percuteret.“*

[40] P. Montan. 21,4 = 234,13–15: *„Alia caro patitur cum animus in caelo est. nequaquam corpus hoc sentit, cum se Deo tota mens deuouit.“*

[41] M. Lugd. 1,35 = 72,19f.: τὴν εὐωδίαν ὀδωδότες ἅμα τὴν Χριστοῦ (vgl. 2 Kor 2,15).

[42] M. Polyc. 15,2 = 14,10f.: καὶ γὰρ εὐωδίας τοσαύτης ἀντελαβόμεθα ὡς λιβανωτοῦ πνέοντος ἢ ἄλλου τινὸς τῶν τιμίων ἀρωμάτων. Vgl. auch die Dufterfahrung in der Vision des Saturus (P. Perp. 13,8 = 122,10f.).

[43] P. Mar. Iac. 9,2f. = 206,20–25: *„et ecce unus e circumstantibus fratribus nostris omnium in se gentilium conuertit oculos, quod iam per gratiam proximae passionis Christus in eius ore et facie relucebat. cumque ex eo turbulentis et furentibus animis quaereretur an eiusdem et ipse esset religionis et nominis, rapuit tam dulcem promptissima confessione comitatum“*; Übers. K. GAMBER, Sie gaben Zeugnis. Authentische Berichte über Märtyrer der Frühkirche, Studia patristica et liturgica. Beiheft 6, Regensburg 1982, 87, ergänzt.

ßene Herrlichkeit so intensiv antizipierte, dass selbst die Ungläubigen dies bemerkten. Der Todgeweihte wurde also zum leibhaften Medium der Verkündigung, bevor er auch nur von weltlichen Mächten identifiziert und ergriffen worden war – womit auch deutlich wird, dass sich Martyrien letztlich nur auf Geheiß Gottes ereignen konnten und nicht etwa als investigative Erfolge der „Heiden" verbuchbar waren. Der namenlose Christ in Cirta bezeugte in besonderer Weise, was von Märtyrern insgesamt galt: Mit ihnen öffnete sich „ein Sichtfenster, durch welches der Glaube das ihm verheißene jenseitige Heil erkennen kann".[44]

Lebten die Märtyrer in der letzten Zeit vor ihrem Tod in der Wahrnehmung ihrer Begleiter schon unter einem offenen Himmel, so waren sie auch nach ihrem Tod nicht einfach weg, wie die Erscheinungen verblichener Glaubensgenossen vor Flavian zeigten. Freilich geschah dies nur selten vor „Heiden" und auch dann kaum einmal so spektakulär wie in den apokryphen Paulusakten, wo der getötete Apostel seinem Peiniger, Kaiser Nero, höchstpersönlich erschien, wie er es bereits zu Lebzeiten angekündigt hatte:

> „Kaiser, nicht nur für kurze Zeit lebe ich meinem König! Das aber wisse: Auch wenn du mich wirst enthaupten lassen, werde ich Folgendes tun: wieder auferweckt, werde ich dir erscheinen, damit du erkennst, dass ich nicht gestorben bin, sondern lebe meinem König Jesus Christus, der den ganzen Erdkreis richten wird."[45]

Gemeinsam mit Fructuosus, der dem Aemilianus erschien, der ihn 259 zum Scheiterhaufen verurteilt hatte[46], bildet Paulus eher eine Ausnahme: Adressaten von Erscheinungen oder Visionen waren in den meisten Fällen Christen. Fructuosus zeigte sich im Bedarfsfall allerdings auch kritisch seinen Anhängern gegenüber, die seine Asche eifersüchtig für sich behalten wollten – was anscheinend seine Chancen auf leibliche Auferstehung beeinträchtigte.[47] Zwei Christen, die im Haus des Aemilianus arbeiteten, sahen dagegen bereits zuvor „den Himmel geöffnet und den heiligen Bischof Fructuosus mit seinen Diakonen – die Pfähle, an die man sie gebunden hat-

---

[44] M. OHST, Beobachtungen zu den Anfängen des christlichen Heiligenkultes, in: Frömmigkeitsformen in Mittelalter und Renaissance, hg. von J. LAUDAGE, Studia humaniora 37, Düsseldorf 2004, 1–28, hier 16.

[45] Martyrium Pauli 4,1 = O. ZWIERLEIN, Petrus in Rom. Die literarischen Zeugnisse. Mit einer kritischen Edition der Martyrien des Petrus und Paulus auf neuer handschriftlicher Grundlage, UaLG 96, Berlin/New York 2009, 438,5–9: Καῖσαρ, οὐ πρὸς ὀλίγον καιρὸν ἐγὼ ζῶ τῷ βασιλεῖ μου· τοῦτο δὲ γίνωσκε· κἄν με τραχηλοκοπήσῃς, τοῦτω ποιήσω· αὖθις ἐγερθεὶς ἐμφανισθήσομαί σοι, εἰς τὸ γνῶναί σε ὅτι οὐκ ἀπέθανον, ἀλλὰ ζῶ τῷ ἐμῷ βασιλεῖ Ἰησοῦ Χριστοῦ, τῷ κρινοῦντι πᾶσαν τὴν οἰκουμένην. (Übers. aaO. 439).

[46] P. Fructuos. 7,1 = 184,3–6.

[47] Ebd. 6,1–3 = 182,11–184,2.

te, waren noch unversehrt! – gekrönt gen Himmel strebend.“[48] Jacobus, der in Cirta während der valerianischen Verfolgung zu Tode kam, berichtete, er habe in seiner Zelle eine Vision gehabt: Der bereits hingerichtete Agapius habe mit anderen Märtyrern ein himmlisches Festmahl gefeiert, und dem staunenden Jacobus sowie seinem Gefährten Marianus sei gesagt worden: „Warum eilt ihr [dabei zu sein]? Freut euch und jauchzt: Schon morgen werdet auch ihr mit uns speisen!“[49] Ganz ähnlich erwartete Fructuosus freudig die Hinrichtung, „um mit den Märtyrern und Propheten im Paradies, ‚das der Herr denen bereitet hat, die ihn lieben‘ (1 Kor 2,9), das Fest zu feiern“.[50] Zuvor hatte er sich durch Fasten auf das Martyrium – und damit auf die Auferstehung – vorbereitet.[51] Die *Passio Perpetuae et Felicitatis* berichtet von einer Vision des Saturus, der gemeinsam mit Perpetua schon einmal den Thronsaal Gottes betreten durfte und dort vier Mitmärtyrer antraf;[52] der Protagonistin selbst wurde in einer nächtlichen Vision ihr Leidensweg und dessen erfolgreiches Absolvieren angekündigt.[53] Dem Veteranen Julius, der unter Diokletian den Tod fand, wurden gar herzliche Grüße an einen bereits hingerichteten Valentio aufgetragen, was jener auch getreulich auszurichten versprach, nicht ohne den Absender Isichius zu mahnen: „Eile, mein Bruder, mir nachzufolgen!“[54] Das Gebet, das Julius vor seiner Hinrichtung sprach, nahm wiederum Bezug auf die archetypische Himmelsvision eines biblischen Protomärtyrers: „Herr Jesus Christus, um dessen Namen willen ich dies erleide, ich bitte dich: Erweise mir die Ehre, meinen Geist unter deine heiligen Märtyrer aufzunehmen!“[55] Um nichts anderes bat Stephanus, als er gesteinigt wurde (Apg 7,59), hierin selbst Jesu Wort am Kreuz (Lk 23,46) aufnehmend. Und der Mut, den die Märtyrer in der Wahrnehmung der Christen und auch der „Heiden“ an den

[48] Ebd. 5,1 = 182,5–7: „*ostendebant Fructuosum cum diaconibus suis, adhuc stipitibus quibus ligati fuerant permanentibus, ad caelum ascendentes coronatos.*“

[49] P. Mar. Iac. 11,6 = 208,26f.: „*Quid properatis? gaudete et exultate, cras enim nobiscum et ipsi caenabitis.*“ Vgl. auch die Gerichtsvision ebd. 6,6–15 = 202,1–23.

[50] P. Fructuos. 3,3 = 180,1–3: „*uti cum martyribus et prophetis in paradiso ‚quem praeparauit Deus amantibus se‘ solueret stationem.*“ Zum Bild des himmlischen Festmahls der Märtyrer vgl. auch Dionysius von Alexandrien bei Eus. h.e. VII 22,4 = GCS Eusebius II/2, 680,4–8 Schwartz.

[51] Vgl. P. Fructuos. 3,2 = 178,28–31; dazu BYNUM, The Resurrection of the Body (s. Anm. 13), 40f. sowie bereits TILLEY, The Ascetic Body (s. Anm. 32), 472.

[52] P. Perp. 11,9 = 120,10–13.

[53] Ebd. 4,3–10 = 110,12–112,5.

[54] A. Julii 4,2f. = 264,12–16: „*[Isichius dicebat:] Plurimum etiam saluta, posco, fratrem Valentionem famulum Dei, qui nos iam per bonam confessionem praecessit ad Dominum. Iulius uero osculatus Isichium dixit: Festina, frater, uenire. mandata autem tua illa audiet quem salutasti.*“

[55] Ebd. 4,4 = 264,17–19: „*Domine Iesu Christe, pro cuius nomine haec patior, te deprecor ut cum tuis sanctis martyribus spiritum meum suscipere digneris.*“

Tag legten, speiste sich aus der Gewissheit, dass die Erfüllung dieser Bitte wie bei Jesus, so auch bei seinen Nachfolgern nicht zweifelhaft sein würde.

3. Der direkte Weg ins Paradies

Im ältesten Stück christlicher lateinischer Literatur, dem Martyrium der Scillitaner (um 180), beantwortet einer der Todgeweihten, Nartzalus, den Urteilsspruch des Richters mit einem Lobpreis: „Heute sind wir Märtyrer im Himmel – Gott sei Dank!“[56] Die Hinrichtung mit dem Schwert erfolgte umgehend, was in einigen Handschriften wie folgt kommentiert wird: „Und so wurden sie alle zugleich durch das Martyrium gekrönt, und sie herrschen mit dem Vater und dem Sohn und dem Heiligen Geist in alle Ewigkeit.“[57] Das Martyrium befördert die *imitatores Christi* also unmittelbar zu diesem in den Himmel.[58] Sie erfreuen sich dort ewigen Lebens mit allen Heiligen[59], empfangen den „Kranz der Unsterblichkeit“[60], ja sogar göttliche Macht: Sie thronen mit Christus bzw. Gott und herrschen mit ihnen.[61] Im Hintergrund steht dabei die Vision des tausendjährigen Friedensreiches aus der Offenbarung des Johannes:

„Und ich sah die Seelen derer, die enthauptet waren um des Zeugnisses von Jesus und um des Wortes Gottes willen (διὰ τὴν μαρτυρίαν Ἰησοῦ καὶ διὰ τὸν λόγον τοῦ θεοῦ), und die nicht angebetet hatten das Tier und sein Bild und die sein Zeichen nicht angenommen hatten an ihre Stirn und auf ihre Hand; diese wurden lebendig und regierten mit Christus tausend Jahre... Dies ist die erste Auferstehung (ἡ ἀνάστασις ἡ πρώτη)“ (Offb 20,4f.).

---

[56] P. Scill. 15 = 88,26: *„Hodie martyres in caelis sumus: Deo gratias!“*

[57] Ebd. 17 = 88 App.: *„Et ita omnes simul martyrio coronati sunt, et regnant cum Patre et Filio et Spiritu sancto per omnia secula seculorum.“*

[58] M. Lugd. 2,7 = 84,10. Vgl. VOLP, Gedanken zum Auferstehungsverständnis (s. Anm. 13), 36: „Auf das Amphitheater folgt die Himmelfahrt.“

[59] M. Das. 4,4 = 274,27f.: καὶ μετὰ θάνατον ζωὴν αἰώνιον κληρονομήσω μετὰ πάντων τῶν ἁγίων.

[60] M. Lugd. 1,36.42 = 72,33; 74,27: τὸν (μέγαν) τῆς ἀφθαρσίας στέφανον; vgl. auch M. Polyc. 17,1 = 14,23f.; P. Perp. 19,2 = 126,23f.; P. Fructuos. 7,2 = 184,9; P. Maximil. 3,2 = 248,13f.; A. Agap. 2,4 = 282,17.

[61] Zum Stehen zur Rechten Christi vgl. etwa P. Fructuos. 7,2 = 184,10–12. In Herm. vis. III 1,9 = 344,23f. Lindemann/Paulsen wird der Erzähler belehrt, dass der Platz auf der rechten Seite Christi explizit den Märtyrern vorbehalten ist. Vgl. Dion. Alex. bei Eus. h.e. VI 42,5 = GCS Eusebius II/2, 610,26–28 Schwartz: οἱ θεῖοι μάρτυρες παρ' ἡμῖν, οἱ νῦν τοῦ Χριστοῦ πάρεδροι καὶ τῆς βασιλείας αὐτοῦ κοινωνοὶ καὶ μέτοχοι τῆς κρίσεως αὐτοῦ καὶ συνδικάζοντες αὐτῷ. Zum Regieren mit Gott vgl. auch P. Montan. 22,2 = 236,13–15. Nach Orig. mart. 28 = GCS Origenes I, 24,17–23 Koetschau ist das Martyrium der „Kelch des Heils“ (ποτήριον σωτηρίου); wer ihn trinkt, wird im Himmel mit Jesus herrschen (vgl. Mk 10,38–40).

Dem Kaiser die προσκύνησις zu verweigern war auch die Ursituation der späteren Martyrien, die Herrschaft mit Christus entsprechend die denkbar eindrücklichste Hoffnungsperspektive. Doch beschreibt der Seher Johannes die Auferstehung der Blutzeugen als einen futurischen Vorgang: Die Eröffnung des fünften Siegels offenbart „unten am Altar die Seelen derer, die versiegelt worden waren (τὰς ψυχὰς τῶν ἐσφραγμένων) um des Wortes Gottes und um ihres Zeugnisses willen" (Offb 6,9); doch auf ihr Schreien nach Rettung und Gerechtigkeit werden sie damit vertröstet, „dass sie ruhen müssten noch eine kleine Zeit, bis vollzählig dazukämen ihre Mitknechte und Brüder, die auch noch getötet werden sollten wie sie" (Offb 6,11). Das „weiße Gewand" (στολὴ λευκή), das den Wartenden übergeben wird, steht zweifellos mit der Taufe in Zusammenhang und lässt gemeinsam mit dem Ausdruck der „Versiegelung" erkennen, dass die Auferstehung der Getöteten als solche nicht fraglich ist, aber eben noch in der Zukunft liegt: Die Taufe durch das Zeugnis ist nur der erste Schritt auf diesem Weg.

Die frühchristlichen Martyriumsschilderungen und -deutungen setzen hier einen anderen Akzent. Stand für die Offenbarung ganz die Situation der Bedrängnis im Vordergrund (wie auch immer man diese historisch verortet[62]), so rang wenige Jahrzehnte später Hermas mit den ganz anderen Schwierigkeiten des christlichen Lebens nach der Taufe und vor dem Tod. Bekanntlich stieß er dabei zur Konzession der einmaligen Chance zur zweiten Buße für Christen, die nach der Taufe gesündigt hatten, vor. Rettung würden demnach auch die Christen erfahren, die für den Namen des Gottessohnes gelitten hätten – sonst wären sie aufgrund der Schwere ihrer Sünden verloren gewesen.[63] Durch das Vergießen ihres eigenen Blutes gereinigt zu werden, erwartete auch die karthagische Christin Felicitas, die sich durch die Geburt ihres Kindes befleckt hatte – sie ging „von einem Blutbad zum anderen, von der Hebamme zum Retiarier".[64] Die Verunreinigung musste also beseitigt werden, um das Ziel des Martyriums, die Gemeinschaft mit Christus, zu erreichen.

---

[62] Die traditionelle Datierung in die Zeit Domitians (81–96) wird zunehmend fraglich, da sich eine Verfolgung unter diesem Kaiser nicht zweifelsfrei nachweisen lässt. Zuletzt versuchte Th. WITULSKI, Die Johannesoffenbarung und Kaiser Hadrian. Studien zur Datierung der neutestamentlichen Apokalypse, FRLANT 221, Göttingen 2007, Offb in die Zeit Hadrians (117–138) zu verschieben – allerdings ebenfalls nicht restlos überzeugend.

[63] Herm. sim. IX 28,6 = 526,3–5 Lindemann/Paulsen: αἱ γὰρ ἁμαρτίαι ὑμῶν κατεβάρησαν, καὶ εἰ μὴ πεπόνθατε ἕνεκεν τοῦ ὀνόματος κυρίου, διὰ τὰς ἁμαρτίας ὑμῶν τεθνήκειτε [ἂν] τῷ θεῷ.

[64] P. Perp. 18,3 = 126,3–6: *„Item Felicitas, saluam se peperisse gaudens ut as bestias pugnaret, a sanguine ad sanguinem, ab obstetrice ad retiarium, lotura post partum baptismo secundo."* Eine „zweite Taufe" im Stadion durch sein eigenes Blut erlebte auch Saturus (a.a.O. 21,2 = 128,28f.).

Ins selbe Horn stieß Tertullian, der Wasser- und Bluttaufe in enger Zusammengehörigkeit sah. Wer mit Wasser getauft worden sei, müsse dies mit seinem eigenen Blut wiederholen: „Dies ist die Taufe, die das Reinigungsbad Wirklichkeit werden läßt, auch wenn man es nicht empfangen hat, und es zurückgibt, wenn man es zunichte gemacht hat."[65] Den Zusammenhang mit der Auferstehung explizierte schließlich Cyprian in seinem Mahnschreiben an Fortunatus:

Die Bluttaufe sei „eine Taufe, nach der niemand mehr sündigt, eine Taufe, die das Wachstum unseres Glaubens zur Vollendung bringt, eine Taufe, die uns bei unserem Abscheiden von der Welt sofort mit Gott vereinigt! Bei der Wassertaufe empfängt man Vergebung der Sünden, bei der Bluttaufe die Krone der Tugenden."[66]

Anhand des Bildes der Auferstehung wird eine Überzeugung artikuliert, die in wechselnden Gestalten für die frühchristliche Martyriumstheologie grundlegend ist: Auferstehung ist für die Märtyrer keine Verheißung von Künftigem, sondern Inbegriff der Gegenwart als Sein bei Gott und bei Christus. Die Märtyrer sind nicht nur *liberati*, sondern bereits *coronati*;[67] und damit ist nichts anderes gemeint als die Ansicht des Ignatius von Antiochien, das Ziel des Martyriums sei es, „Gottes teilhaftig werden" (θεοῦ ἐπιτυχεῖν).[68] Das prononcierte „Heute" der scillitanischen Märtyrer klingt

---

[65] Tert. bapt. 16,2 = FC 76, 202,13f. Schleyer: *„Hic est baptismus qui lavacrum et non acceptum repraesentat et perditum reddit!"*

[66] Cypr. Fort. praef. 4 = CChr.SL 3, 185,64–68 Weber: *„baptisma post quod nemo iam peccat, baptisma quod fidei nostrae incrementa consummat, baptisma quod nos de mundo recedentes statim deo copulat. In aquae baptismo accipitur peccatorum remissa, in sanguinis corona uirtutum"* (Übers. J. BAER, BKV 34, Kempten/München 1918, 349). Eine analoge Unterscheidung von normalen Christen und Märtyrern kennt auch die Syrische Didascalia, cap. XX = Didascalia Apostolorum. The Syriac Version, transl. by R.H. CONNELLY, Oxford 1929, 174,23–32: „If then He raises up all men – as he said by Isaiah: ‚All flesh shall see the salvation of God' [Jes 40,5; 52,10] –, much more will He quicken and raise up the faithful; and (yet more) again will He quicken and raise up the faithful of the faithful, who are the martyrs, and establish them in great glory and make them His counsellors. For to mere disciples, those who believe in Him, He has promised to give an everlasting glory, as of the luminaries which fail not, with more abundant light, that they may be shining for all time [cf. Dan 12,3]."

[67] Tert. Scorp. 6,1f. = CChr.SL 2, 1079,6–11 Reifferscheid/Wissowa: *„Euulsum enim de diaboli gula per fidem iam et per uirtutem inculcatorem eius uoluit efficere, ne solummodo euasisset, uerum etiam euicisset inimicum. Amauit, qui uocauerat in salutem, inuitare et ad gloriam, ut qui gaudeamus liberati, exultemus etiam coronati."* Vgl. W. BÄHNK, Von der Notwendigkeit des Leidens. Die Theologie des Martyriums bei Tertullian, FKDG 78, Göttingen 2001, 222; allgemein zur Überzeugung von der direkten Aufnahme in den Himmel vgl. bereits HOLL, Die Vorstellung vom Märtyrer (s. Anm. 13), 86.

[68] Vgl. Ign. Ant. Magn. 14; Trall. 12,2; 13,3; Rom. 1,2; 2,1; 4,1; 9,2; Smyrn. 11,1; Pol. 2,3; 7,1 = 198,13; 206,1.14f.; 208,16.19f.; 210,17; 216,14; 232,13; 236,13; 238,27 Lindemann/Paulsen; vgl. auch Rom. 5,3 = a.a.O. 212,16: Ἰησοῦ Χριστοῦ ἐπιτύχω. Nach N. BROX, Zeuge und Märtyrer. Untersuchungen zur frühchristlichen Zeugnis-Terminolo-

in zahllosen weiteren Texten an und nach: Schon der 1. Clemensbrief betonte, Petrus und Paulus hätten beide Zeugnis abgelegt (μαρτυρήσας) und seien daraufhin „an den gebührenden Ort der Herrlichkeit" gelangt.[69] Polykarps Gebet, dessen Beginn bereits zitiert wurde (s.o. bei Anm. 14), fuhr fort: „Unter ihnen [sc. den früheren Märtyrern] möchte ich *heute* vor dir angenommen werden als ein reiches und wohlgefälliges Opfer…".[70] Der standhafte Kriegsdienstverweigerer Maximilian begegnete der Drohung, er werde elendig zu Grunde gehen, mit dem Satz: „Ich werde nicht zu Grunde gehen, und wenn ich diese Welt verlasse, wird meine Seele mit Christus, meinem Herrn, leben."[71] Als Fructuosus ins Gefängnis gebracht wurde, schien sich dessen Tor buchstäblich zu sträuben, denjenigen in das schmutzige Innere einzulassen, für den schon eine „himmlische Wohnung" (*caeleste habitaculum*) bereit stand.[72] Die *Passio Perpetuae* artikulierte die unmittelbare Aufnahme in den Himmel im Medium einer Vision des Saturus:

„Gelitten hatten wir und das Fleisch abgestreift, da begannen wir von vier Engeln gen Osten getragen zu werden, deren Hände uns nicht berührten… Und als wir von der ersten Welt befreit waren, sahen wir ein unermessliches Licht, und ich sagte zu Perpetua: ‚Das ist es, was uns der Herr verheißen hat; seine Verheißung haben wir empfangen."[73]

---

gie, StANT 5, München 1961, 209–211 handelt es sich hier schon deshalb nicht um einen martyriologischen *terminus technicus*, weil die Teilhabe an Gott nach Ignatius das Ziel eines jeden Christen sei, das der Märtyrer allerdings mit Sicherheit erreicht. Vgl. dazu auch K. BOMMES, Weizen Gottes. Untersuchungen zur Theologie des Martyriums bei Ignatius von Antiochien, Theoph. 27, Köln 1976, 243f.; SCHNEIDER, Studien zur Entfaltung (s. Anm. 11), 61f.

[69] 1 Clem 5,4–7 (FC 15, 76,4–25 Schneider); vgl. Polyc. Phil. 9,2 = 252,5–7 Lindemann/Paulsen; M. Lugd. 2,3 = 82,22–24. Allerdings ist hier, wie BROX, Zeuge und Märtyrer (s. Anm. 68), 201 betont, nicht der Tod das Zeugnis, sondern die *zuvor* ertragene Mühe. Gegen H. VON CAMPENHAUSEN, Die Idee des Martyriums in der Alten Kirche, Göttingen (1936) ²1964, 54 wird die Zeugnisabgabe nicht „unmittelbar als Befreiung von dieser Welt verstanden."

[70] M. Polyc. 14,2 = 12,28f.: ἐν οἷς προσδεχθείην ἐνώπιόν σου σήμερον ἐν θυσίᾳ πίονι καὶ προσδεκτῇ.

[71] P. Maximil. 2,11 = 248,4f.: *„Ego non pereo; et si de saeculo exiero, uiuit anima mea cum Christo Domino meo."*

[72] P. Fructuos. 17,1 = 230,17.

[73] P. Perp. 11,2.4 = 118,27–29.30–120,2: *„Passi, inquit, eramus, et exiuimus de carne, et coepimus ferri a quattuor angelis in orientem, quorum manus nos non tangebant… et liberato primo mundo uidimus lucem inmensam, et dixi Perpetuae: Hoc est quod nobis Dominus promittebat: percepimus promissionem."* Vgl. dazu SAXER, Bible et Hagiographie (s. Anm. 13), 234f. Den Aufstieg der Märtyrer zum Himmel und ihre Aufnahme unter Engel und Himmelsmächte beschreiben auch die römischen Konfessoren bei Cypr. ep. 31,2 = CChr.SL 3B, 153,33–37 Diercks: *„Ex tuis ergo litteris uidimus gloriosos illos martyrum triumphos et oculis nostris quodammodo caelum illos petentes prosecuti sumus et inter angelos ac potestates dominationes que caelestes constitutos quasi contemplati sumus."*

Wie Perpetua selbst in ihrer Vision von der Himmelsleiter durch Christus persönlich in Empfang genommen wurde,[74] so musste nach Origenes Jesu Botschaft wie ein scheidendes Schwert wirken (vgl. Mt 10,34), „damit das Wort *für jetzt* den himmlischen Teil von uns in Empfang nehme und *später*, wenn wir es nicht mehr verdienen, in zwei Teile getrennt zu sein, uns vollständig zu Himmlischen mache.“[75] Mag das dahinter stehende Konzept des inneren, himmlischen Menschen auch sehr spekulativ[76] und mit der Vorstellung einer Auferstehung des Fleisches kaum vereinbar wirken, so ist doch festzuhalten, dass die sofortige Anteilhabe des Märtyrers an der Herrlichkeit Christi nicht nur für Origenes, sondern auch schon für Clemens von Alexandrien feststand:

„Guten Mutes kommt er [sc. der standhafte Märtyrer] nun zum Herrn, seinem Freund, für den er den Leib gerne hingegeben hat, dazu auch die Seele, wie es die Richter erwartet hatten, und er hört von unserem Erlöser die Begrüßung ‚lieber Bruder‘, um es mit dem Dichterwort zu sagen, wegen der Ähnlichkeit des Lebens.“[77]

Ebenso konnte nach Tertullian kein Zweifel daran bestehen, dass die Märtyrer unverweilt in den Himmel eilten und dort „die Krone der Unvergänglichkeit, die Belohnung mit der engelsgleichen Substanz, das Bürgerrecht im Himmel und die Herrlichkeit in alle Ewigkeit“ empfingen.[78] Und auch Cyprian betonte verschiedentlich, dass die verstorbenen Märtyrer den verdienten Preis für ihre Standhaftigkeit längst empfangen hätten, nämlich „die Vollendung der Tugend und die himmlische Krone“.[79] Das konnte auch nicht erstaunen, wurden die Blutzeugen doch nicht nur im Himmel erwartet, vielmehr kam Christus ihnen, wie gesehen, in ihrem Leiden entgegen:

„Ihr wisst ja, dass ihr unter den Augen des Herrn kämpft, der zugegen ist, und dass ihr durch das Bekenntnis seines Namens zu seiner Herrlichkeit gelangt. Und er beschränkt sich nicht etwa darauf, seinen Dienern nur zuzusehen, sondern er selbst ringt in uns, er

---

[74] P. Perp. 4,9 = 110,29f.: *„et leuauit caput et aspexit me et dixit mihi: Bene uenisti, τέκνον.“*

[75] Orig. mart. 37 = GCS Origenes II, 35,3–5 Koetschau: ἵν’ ἐπὶ τοῦ παρόντος τὸν ἐπουράνιον ἡμῶν παραλαβὼν ὕστερον ἀξίους γενομένους τοῦ μὴ διχοτομηθῆναι ἡμᾶς ἐξ ὅλων ποιήσῃ ἐπουρανίους (Übers. E. FRÜCHTEL, BGrL 5, Stuttgart 1973, 108).

[76] Vgl. FRÜCHTEL, BGrL 5 (s. Anm. 75), 129 (Komm. z. St.).

[77] Clem. Al. str. IV 14,2 = SC 463, 78,11–15 van den Hoek: Εὐθαρσήσας τοίνυν πρὸς φίλον τὸν κύριον, ὑπὲρ οὗ καὶ τὸ σῶμα ἑκὼν ἐπιδέδωκεν, πρὸς δὲ καὶ τὴν ψυχήν, ὡς οἱ δικασταὶ προσεδόκησαν, ἔρχεται, φίλε κασίγνητε ποιητικῶς τε ἀκούσας πρὸς τοῦ σωτῆρος ἡμῶν διὰ τὴν τοῦ βίου ὁμοιότητα (Übers. BAUMEISTER, Genese [s. Anm. 14] 129).

[78] Tert. mart. 3,3 = CChr.SL 1, 5,24–26 Dekkers: *„corona aeternitatis, brabium angelicae substantiae, politia in caelis, gloria in saecula saeculorum.“*

[79] Cypr. ep. 10,4 = CChr.SL 3B, 53,89f. Diercks: *„consummatio uirtutis et corona caelestis“*.

selbst kämpft an unserer Seite, er selbst ist es, der in unserem heißen Wettstreit zugleich krönt und gekrönt wird.“[80]

Christus, der die Märtyrer nach Leiden, Tod und Auferstehung im Himmel empfangen würde, war während des ganzen Prozesses dabei, ja gab sich selbst ein weiteres Mal hin – weshalb am guten Ausgang des Kampfes kein Zweifel bestehen konnte, wenn es sich um einen *guten* Kampf, d.h. um das geforderte Zeugnis für Christus handelte, das ohne Verzögerung zur Unsterblichkeit führte.[81] Wiederholt rief Cyprian verurteilten und vom Tod bedrohten Christen in Erinnerung, dass Christus nicht erst am Ende ihres Weges auf sie wartete, sondern schon jetzt in ihrer Bedrängnis, sei es im Kerker, im Bergwerk oder in Erwartung der Hinrichtung, an ihrer Seite war. Weil von Christus her für die Märtyrer und Konfessoren die Grenze zwischen Erde und Himmel durchlässig war, konnte umgekehrt die Aufnahme in die himmlische Gemeinschaft mit Christus, d.h. Auferstehung und ewiges Leben, vor Augen gestellt werden, ohne zynisch zu wirken:

„Täglich erwartet ihr mit Freuden den heilbringenden Tag eures Hingangs, und, jeden Augenblick im Begriff, aus der Welt zu scheiden, eilt ihr den euch Märtyrern verheißenen Geschenken und den himmlischen Behausungen zu, um nach dieser Finsternis der Welt das glänzendste Licht zu schauen und eine Herrlichkeit zu empfangen, die alle Leiden und Kämpfe überstrahlt.“[82]

4. Das eschatologische Proprium des Martyriums

Wenn nun im vorstehenden Abschnitt die Unmittelbarkeit der Aufnahme in den Himmel betont wurde, ließe sich fragen, ob das denn etwas Besonderes sei – und wie denn die anderen Christen nach ihrem Tod die Zeit bis zum Jüngsten Gericht verbringen würden. Diese Frage greift tief in das eschatologische Denken der Alten Kirche ein und soll hier nur insoweit verfolgt werden, als sich daraus eine Präzisierung des Verhältnisses von Märtyrertod und Auferstehung ergibt. Die Debatte über einen „Zwischenzustand“ in der späteren Patristik oder gar in der mittelalterlichen Scholastik muss und kann hier dagegen außer Betracht bleiben. In den patristischen Quellen wird ein solcher Unterschied zwischen dem Zeitpunkt der Aufer-

---

[80] Ebd. 10,4 = CChr.SL 3B, 53,94–98 Diercks: *„scientes uos sub oculis praesentis domini dimicare, confessione nominis eius ad ipsius gloriam peruenire, qui non sic est ut seruos suos tantum spectet, sed ipse luctatur in nobis, ipse congreditur, ipse in certamine agonis nostri et coronat pariter et coronatur.“*

[81] Vgl. Cypr. mortal. 3 = CChr.SL 3A, 18,38–41 Simonetti.

[82] Cypr. ep. 76,7 = CChr.SL 3C, 615,142–146 Diercks: *„Expectatis cotidie laeti profectionis uestrae salutarem diem et iam iam que de saeculo recessuri ad martyrum munera et domicilia diuina properatis, post has mundi tenebras uisuri candidissimam lucem et accepturi maiorem passionibus omnibus et conflictationibus claritatem.“*

stehung der Märtyrer und der anderen Christen nur von einem Autor explizit ventiliert – Tertullian, dem hier entsprechend die Aufmerksamkeit zu gelten hat.[83]

Der *locus classicus* findet sich in *De anima*, einem ca. 210 entstandenen „theologischen Lehrbuch der Psychologie“[84], das wiederum in zeitlicher Nachbarschaft zu den hier ebenfalls relevanten Traktaten *De resurrectione mortuorum* und *Scorpiace* steht. Die Schrift über die Seele wendet sich gegen gnostische und spiritualistische Seelenlehren und befasst sich in einem abschließenden Gedankengang eben mit dem Aufenthaltsort der Seelen der Verstorbenen bis zum Jüngsten Gericht.[85] Tertullian übte einerseits scharfe Kritik an Vorstellungen, wie sie in Platons *Phaidon* zum Ausdruck kamen, dass nämlich nur die Seelen der Philosophen zur Unsterblichkeit gelangen, während die übrigen Seelen in der Unterwelt landen, in „einer Art Schoß der Erde, in den aller Schmutz und alle Unreinheit der Welt zusammenfließt“.[86] Tertullian bestritt diese pejorativen Attribute der Unterwelt, die er als einen „verborgenen Abgrund mitten in ihren [sc. der Erde] Eingeweiden“[87] beschrieb. In diesen sei Christus hinabgestiegen und habe dort „den Erzvätern und Propheten Kunde von seiner Sendung gegeben“.[88] Von hier aus erschien es nun andererseits ganz unangemessen, wenn gewisse Christen „allzu stolz die Seelen der Gläubigen für die Unterwelt zu gut finden“ – würden sie doch fahrlässig die Aussicht ausschlagen, „daß sie in Abrahams Schoß die Auferstehung erwarten dürfen.“[89] Entgegen den o.g. Stellen aus den Märtyrerakten, wonach die Märtyrer im Himmel bereits von den Patriarchen und Propheten empfangen würden, sah Tertullian *alle*

---

[83] Zum Folgenden vgl. bereits VON CAMPENHAUSEN, Idee des Martyriums (s. Anm. 69), 125, ausführlich BÄHNK, Notwendigkeit des Leidens (s. Anm. 67), 220–232. Zum weiteren patristischen Kontext vgl. A. MERKT, Das Fegefeuer. Entstehung und Funktion einer Idee, Darmstadt 2005, bes. 33–40.

[84] E. SCHULZ-FLÜGEL, Tertullian, in: LACL (s. Anm. 1), 668–672, hier 669; vgl. ebd. zu den im Folgenden vorausgesetzten Datierungen.

[85] In welcher Weise die Frage nach einer schon erfolgten Auferstehung um 200 ein Thema war, zeigen z.B. auch die Acta Pauli et Theclae 3,14 = AAAp I 245,5f. Lipsius: ἀνιστάμεθα θεὸν ἐπεγνωκότες ἀληθῆ (2 Tim 2,18).

[86] Tert. anim. 54,4 = CChr.SL 2, 861,19f. Waszink: *„gremium terrae, quo omnes labes mundialium sordium [confluunt]“*; Übers. hier und im Folgenden nach: Tertullian, Über die Seele (De anima). Das Zeugnis der Seele (De testimonio animae). Vom Ursprung der Seele (De censu animae), hg. und übers. von J.H. Waszink (BAW), Zürich/München 1980, 171–173; angespielt wird – gezielt verzeichnend – auf Passagen aus Plat. Phaid. 109bc; 111e–112a.

[87] Tert. anim. 55,1 = 862,6 W.: *„inferioribus adhuc abyssis superstructo“.*

[88] Ebd. 55,2 = 862,11f. W.: *„et illic patriarchas et prophetas compotes sui faceret.“*

[89] Ebd. 55,2 = 862,13–16 W.: *„qui satis superbe non putent animas fidelium inferis dignas, serui super dominum et discipuli super magistrum, aspernati, si forte, in Abrahae sinu expectandae resurrectionis solacium capere.“*

Verstorbenen aller Zeiten, Nichtchristen wie Christen, in der Unterwelt auf die Auferstehung warten – was sogar für die Apostel hätte gelten müssen, wären diese an der Wende zum 3. Jahrhundert nicht längst als Märtyrer verehrt worden.[90] Tertullian schloss apodiktisch:

„Für keinen steht der Himmel offen, solange die Erde noch besteht, um nicht zu sagen, solange sie noch eingeschlossen ist; erst bei der Vollendung der Welt werden die Reiche der Himmel aufgeschlossen."[91]

Ganz ähnlich betont die im gleichen Zeitraum verfasste Schrift *De resurrectione mortuorum*, eine sofortige Aufnahme ins Paradies statt in die Unterwelt gründe allein in den *martyrii praerogativa*.[92] Die Argumentation richtete sich gegen eine Position, der zu Folge die Seelen der Christen gleich nach dem Tod in den Himmel kämen – anders als die der Heiden; andernfalls wäre Christi Tod ja umsonst gewesen. Offensichtlich wurden auch die Erzväter und Propheten bereits im Paradies vermutet.[93] Dem widersprach Tertullian hier wie auch in *De anima* vehement, und zwar mit dem Argument, „daß die dem Johannes im Geiste enthüllte Gegend des Paradieses, die unter dem Altar liegt, keine anderen Seelen aufweist als die der Märtyrer!"[94] Ebenso habe auch Perpetua, die *fortissima martyr*, „bei der Enthüllung des Paradieses am Tag ihres Leidens dort nur Märtyrer" gesehen.[95] Tertullian schloss, dass die „in Adam Verstorbenen" keinen Zutritt zum Paradies hätten, anders als die „in Christus Verstorbenen" – womit nichts anderes als der Zeugentod für Christus gemeint war. Denn gemäß dem Fortgang seiner Argumentation anerkannte Tertullian den Menschen als rechten Christen im Grunde nur,

[90] Dazu vgl. A. ANGENENDT, Heilige und Reliquien. Die Geschichte ihres Kultes vom frühen Christentum bis zur Gegenwart, München 1994, 38.

[91] Tert. anim. 55,3 = 862,23–25 W.: „*Nulli patet caelum terra adhuc salua, ne dixerim clausa. Cum transactione enim mundi reserabuntur regna caelorum.*"

[92] Tert. resurr. 43,3 = CChr.SL 2, 978,12–979,14 Borleffs: „*Nemo enim peregrinatus a corpore statim immoratur penes dominum, nisi ex martyrii praerogatiua, paradiso scilicet, non inferis, deuersurus.*" Vgl. BÄHNK, Notwendigkeit des Leidens (s. Anm. 67), 225.

[93] Vgl. Tert. anim. 55,4 = 862,27–29 W.; vgl. auch adv. Marc. IV 34,13 = CChr.SL 1, 638,10–17 Kroymann.

[94] Tert. anim. 55,4 = 862,29–31 W.: „*Et quomodo Iohanni in spiritu paradisi regio reuelata, quae subicitur altari, nullas alias animas apud se praeter martyrum ostendit?*"

[95] Tert. anim. 55,4 = 862,32f. W.: „*Quomodo Perpetua, fortissima martyr, sub die passionis in reuelatione paradisi solos illic martyras uidit?*" Vgl. P. Perp. 13,8 = 122,9f. Tertullian schreibt hier offenbar eine Vision des Saturus der Perpetua zu. Während Saturus aber „viele Brüder und unter diesen auch Märtyrer" (*multos fratres sed et martyras*) sah, spitzt Tertullian das Erlebnis auf die alleinige Präsenz der Märtyrer zu (BÄHNK, Notwendigkeit des Leidens [s. Anm. 67] 225 Anm. 575).

„wenn du für Gott stirbst, wie der Paraklet mahnt, nicht in Fieberträumen und auf Kissen weich gebettet, sondern im Martyrium, wenn du dein Kreuz auf dich nimmst und dem Herrn folgst, wie er selbst gebot.“[96]

Diese Passage gibt nun deutlich zu erkennen, dass Tertullian sich nicht nur von der Frontstellung gegen gnostisierende Christen leiten ließ, sondern auch von seiner mittlerweile hervortretenden montanistischen Prägung. Der Aufruf, nicht an Fieber, sondern durch das Martyrium zu sterben, wurde von ihm andernorts als Orakel einer montanistischen Prophetin zitiert.[97] Die Erwartung, dass nur das Martyrium zur sofortigen Aufnahme in den Himmel führte, die den anderen Heiden und Christen verwehrt bleiben musste, speiste sich aus dem Bewusstsein, dass ohnehin nur eine begrenzte Zahl an Christen zu dieser Standhaftigkeit in der Lage sein würde; umso eitler erschien die Hoffnung, ohne Vergießen eigenen Blutes ins Paradies zu gelangen. Der „Zwischenzustand“, der sich für alle Nichtmärtyrer aus dieser Perspektive ergab, war also nicht nur der Abwehr der gnostischen Lehren geschuldet, sondern auch der innerchristlichen Auseinandersetzung um die Notwendigkeit des Zeugentodes, der für Tertullian hier als konstitutiv für die unmittelbare Auferstehung galt:

„Der einzige Schlüssel zum Paradies ist dein Blut!“[98]

Es ist durchaus signifikant, dass Tertullian ein gutes Jahrzehnt zuvor im *Apologeticum*, das sich an eine pagane Leserschaft richtete, mit dem Martyrium nicht den Zugang zum Paradies, sondern die Verbreitung der Christen auf der Erde assoziiert hatte: „Zahlreicher werden wir, so oft wir von euch niedergemäht werden: Ein Same ist das Blut der Christen.“[99] Damit war gerade nicht eine exklusive Paradiesverheißung nur für Märtyrer gemeint, vielmehr wurde hier (und in zeitlicher Nähe ebenso in *De patientia*) *allen* Gläubigen das Paradies in Aussicht gestellt.[100] Umgekehrt lag ihm auch in früheren Schriften der Gedanke einer besonderen Dignität der Märtyrer nicht ferne: *„aqua vocati sanguine electi“* sind die wahren Christen

---

[96] Tert. anim. 55,5 = 863,36–40 W.: *„Agnosce itaque differentiam ethnici et fidelis in morte, si pro deo occumbas, ut paracletus monet, non in mollibus febribus et in lectulis, sed in martyriis, si crucem tuam tollas et sequaris dominum, ut ipse praecepit.“*

[97] Vgl. Tert. fug. 9,4 = CChr.SL 2, 1147,39–41 Thierry.

[98] Tert. anim. 55,5 = 863,40 W.: *„Tota paradisi clauis tuus sanguis est.“* Vgl. auch Tert. Scorp. 6,11 = CChr.SL 2, 1081,19–21 Reifferscheid/Wissowa: *„Sanguinem hominis deus concupiscit? et tamen ausim dicere, si et homo regnum dei, si et homo certam salutem, si et homo secundam regenerationem.“* Zur Differenz von *salus* und *certa salus* vgl. BÄHNK, Notwendigkeit des Leidens (s. Anm. 67), 224; zur Heilswirksamkeit des Blutes bezüglich der Auferstehung vgl. ANGENENDT, Heilige und Reliquien (s. Anm. 90), 64.

[99] Tert. Apol. 50,13 = 222 Becker: *„plures efficimur, quotiens metimur a vobis: semen est sanguis Christianorum.“*

[100] Tert. Apol. 47,13 = 210 Becker; pat. 9,5 = CChr.SL 2, 309,18–310,19 Borleffs; vgl. BÄHNK, Notwendigkeit des Leidens (s. Anm. 67), 228f. mit Anm. 590.

nach *De baptismo*.[101] Zu unterscheiden sind also nicht in erster Linie streng abgrenzbare Lebens- und Schaffensphasen Tertullians, sondern die sich wandelnden argumentativen Stoßrichtungen: Im *Apologeticum* galt der Blick nicht dem Eschaton, sondern der Lebenswelt, aus der die Christen durch Hinrichtungen nicht zu vertreiben sein würden, wie den paganen Statthaltern eingeschärft werden sollte; in *De anima* und *Scorpiace* wurde mit der Zusage des unmittelbaren Paradieseseintritts einerseits der Aufruf zum Martyrium verstärkt, andererseits die gnostische Hoffnung auf ein allzu billig erworbenes ewiges Leben gedämpft. Das Paradox liegt darin, dass den Märtyrern erspart bleibt, was Christus erdulden musste, nämlich der Aufenthalt im Hades – und damit wurden sie, wie Wiebke Bähnk zu Recht herausgestellt hat, „letztlich genau das, was Tertullian in bezug auf die anderen Gläubigen ironisch ablehnt: *‚servi super dominum et discipuli super magistrum‘*."[102]

Die Reflexion darüber, dass nach Offb 20,4 am Altar nur die Märtyrer weilten, diente also nicht einer freitragenden Spekulation über Zwischenzustände, sondern handfesten pastoralen und kontroverstheologischen Zwecken. Und das macht Tertullian zu einem zwar prononcierten, möglicherweise aber wenig repräsentativen Zeugen eines zeitlichen Unterschiedes zwischen der Auferstehung der Christen im Allgemeinen und der Märtyrer im Besonderen.[103] Dass es generell keine unmittelbare Aufnahme nach dem Tod in den Himmel gebe, betonten zwar auch Justin und Irenäus,[104] und dass sich die Märtyrer nach ihrem Leiden sofort der Gemeinschaft mit Christus erfreuen könnten, war *opinio communis* des späten 2. und 3. Jahrhunderts. Doch zueinander in Beziehung gesetzt wurde beides zuerst – und vorläufig nur – bei Tertullian. Schon Cyprian sah dagegen die Seelen *aller* Gläubigen im Himmel auf die zweite Auferstehung, d.h. auf

---

[101] Tert. bapt. 16,2 = FC 76, 202,10 Schleyer.

[102] BÄHNK, Notwendigkeit des Leidens (s. Anm. 67), 226f. mit Tert. anim. 55,2 = 862,14f. W.

[103] Dies wird nicht beachtet in der auf Tertullian Bezug nehmenden Passage über die Fortexistenz der Seele nach dem Tod bei ANGENENDT, Heilige und Reliquien (s. Anm. 90), 102f. B. DALEY, Eschatologie. In der Schrift und Patristik, HDG IV 7a, Freiburg u.a. 1986, 113 postuliert eine „frühere Tradition" für die Theorie eines Zwischenzustandes, die Tertullian „deutlicher als jeder andere Schriftsteller vor ihm" entwickelt habe; eine solche Tradition macht SCHNEIDER, Studien zur Entfaltung (s. Anm. 11), 62 bei Ign. Ant. Rom. 6,2 dingfest, wonach die Seele in himmlischen Gefilden auf die Auferstehung des Fleisches warten müsse – eine Unterscheidung, die sich bei Ignatius in dieser Trennschärfe kaum substantiieren lässt. Vgl. dagegen bereits VON CAMPENHAUSEN, Idee des Martyriums (s. Anm. 69), 125–127 Anm. 8.

[104] Vgl. Just. dial. 80,4 = PTS 47, 209,21–25 Marcovich; Iren. haer. IV 33,9; V 31,2 = SC 100, 820,151–154; SC 153, 394,45–47 Rousseau/Doutreleau.

die des Fleisches, warten.[105] Im Unterschied zum montanistischen Mahner Tertullian musste er neben den Märtyrern und Konfessoren die Masse der Gemeindeglieder im Blick behalten, von denen sich bekanntlich viele als *lapsi* entpuppten. Für den Seelsorger der Großstadtgemeinde in einer schweren Verfolgungszeit veränderte sich die eschatologische Perspektive – und damit auch die Wahrnehmung der biblischen Ansatzpunkte der Auferstehungshoffnung.

5. Die Auferstehung der Märtyrer: Eschatologisches Hoffnungszeichen für alle

Die Forschungsdiskussion der letzten Jahrzehnte hat gezeigt, dass zwischen der Forderung der (Leidens-) Nachfolge Christi im Neuen Testament und der Martyriumstheologie der frühen Kirche zwar deutliche Kontinuitätslinien bestehen, aber keineswegs Deckungsgleichheit herrscht. Das gilt im Allgemeinen für die Zuspitzung des Zeugenbegriffs auf das Blutzeugnis als einzigem Kennzeichen eines μάρτυς. Und es gilt im Besonderen für das Verständnis der Auferstehung, die im Grunde nur in einer neutestamentlichen Schrift mit dem Gedanken der Blutzeugenschaft zusammen gebracht wird: in der Offenbarung des Johannes. So ist in einem letzten Schritt nach der Aufnahme und Fortentwicklung der hier vorliegenden Ansätze zu fragen, wie sie für die frühchristliche Martyriumsdeutung maßgeblich wurden.

Wie gesehen, standen die martyriologischen *loci classici* Offb 6,9–11 und 20,4–6 bei Tertullian Pate für die Auffassung, allein die Märtyrer gelangten in der ersten Auferstehung unmittelbar zu Christus, während alle anderen, Christen wie Heiden, auf das Jüngste Gericht und die allgemeine Totenauferweckung warten müssten. Exegetisch wird man der Offenbarung des Johannes durch eine solche Beschränkung der „Siegersprüche" auf ein Proprium der Märtyrer kaum gerecht.[106] Vielmehr sind den Empfängern des „weißen Gewandes" von Offb 6,11 auch die Christen von Sar-

[105] Vgl. Cypr. mortal. 21 = CChr.SL 3A, 28,362–365 Simonetti; dazu G. GRESHAKE/J. KREMER, Resurrectio mortuorum. Zum theologischen Verständnis der leiblichen Auferstehung, Darmstadt ²1992, 209; O. KAMPERT, Das Sterben der Heiligen. Sterbeberichte unblutiger Märtyrer in der lateinischen Hagiographie des Vierten bis Sechsten Jahrhunderts, MThA 53, Altenberge 1998, 125.

[106] So aber pointiert bei Tert. Scorp. 12,9 = CChr.SL 2, 1093,22f. Reifferscheid/Wissowa: *„Quinam isti tam beati uictores, nisi proprie martyres?"* In diesem Sinne interpretiert auch VON CAMPENHAUSEN, Idee des Martyriums (s. Anm. 69), 45 mit Anm. 5, die Offenbarung; anders B. KOWALSKI, „... sie werden Priester Gottes und des Messias sein; und sie werden König sein mit ihm – tausend Jahre lang" (Offb 20,6): Martyrium und Auferstehung in der Offenbarung, in: SNTU.A 26 (2001), 139–163, hier 149f.156.

des zur Seite zu stellen, die ihre Reinheit bewahrt haben (Offb 3,4f.), sowie die „Überwinder" in Philadelphia und Laodicea (Offb 3,10f.20f.).[107] Für einen weiter gefassten Begriff von „Gerechten" in der Offenbarung spricht nicht nur der Textbefund, sondern auch der Konsens der Forschungen zum frühchristlichen Martyriumsverständnis, wonach die Einengung des Begriffs μάρτυς auf den *Blut*-Zeugen eine Entwicklung der nachneutestamentlichen Zeit ist: Sie vollzieht sich zwischen Ignatius von Antiochien und dem Hirten des Hermas, bei denen die Sache, nicht aber die Terminologie zu finden ist, und dem Polykarpmartyrium, das bereits eine ausgebildete Martyriumsbegrifflichkeit bezeugt. Der Blick auf die Offenbarung lehrt aber auch, dass die Vorstellung des Martyriums im Sinne der Blutzeugenschaft bereits innerhalb der nachmals kanonischen Schriften zu finden ist – denen Ignatius und Hermas zeitlich gesehen ja durchaus nahe stehen. Zwischen Vorstellung und Begriff ist daher – im Sinne einer präzisen Rekonstruktion der Kontinuität des theologischen Denkens der frühen Christen über spätere Kanonsgrenzen hinaus – zu unterscheiden.[108] Die Kontinuität in der Sache lässt aber den Schluss zu, dass das Verständnis des Martyriums – gegen die These von Campenhausens – keineswegs symptomatisch für ein „frühkatholisches" Selbstmissverständnis der Christenheit des 2. Jahrhunderts ist. Mindestens in einer der späteren kanonischen Schriften des Neuen Testaments bahnte sich diese Entwicklung schon an – kanonsgeschichtlich gesehen freilich am Rand, wurde doch die Offenbarung des Johannes zumal in der griechischen patristischen Theologie noch Jahrhunderte lang kritisch beäugt.

---

[107] Zur Forschungsdiskussion vgl. BÄHNK, Notwendigkeit des Leidens (s. Anm. 67), 223 Anm. 563; 224 Anm. 567, hier bes. zum „weißen Gewand", das nach Herm. sim. VIII 2,3 = 466,17f. Lindemann/Paulsen *alle* Gerechten erhalten, wobei nach vis. III 2,1 = a.a.O. 346,4–9 die Märtyrer zwar einen relativen Vorrang des Ruhmes genießen, ansonsten aber *allen* Christen τὰ αὐτὰ δῶρα καὶ αἱ αὐταὶ ἐπαγγελίαι gelten. Vgl. dazu auch BROX, Zeuge und Märtyrer (s. Anm. 68), 225f.

[108] Entsprechend stiften Äußerungen wie die folgende von KOWALSKI, „Priester Gottes und des Messias" (s. Anm. 106), 156 eher Verwirrung: „Auferstehung wird in Offb 20,4 denen verheißen, die nicht den Römischen Kaiser verehrt haben, und das müssen nicht zwangsläufig Märtyrer sein. Distanz zum Römischen Kaiserkult und eine klare Entscheidung für den christlichen Glauben sind die Voraussetzungen, um Auferstehung zu erreichen." Begründet wird dies mit Verweis auf Offb 18,24: „Dort sind allein die Propheten und Heiligen (προφητῶν καὶ ἁγίων) – zwei Termini für die Christen in der Offb – genannt, aber auch alle (πάντων τῶν ἐσφραγμένων ἐπὶ τῆς γῆς), die auf dieser Erde geschlachtet worden sind" (a.a.O. 150). Das heißt aber doch nichts anderes, als dass die Märtyrer nicht als terminologisch distinkte Gruppe präsent sind, während die Pointe in der Sache der Zeugnisgabe liegt – und genau das haben ja die Propheten getan, auf die in der frühchristlichen Martyrologie vielfach rekurriert wird (vgl. A.-M. SCHWEMER, Prophet, Zeuge und Märtyrer: zur Entstehung des Märtyrerbegriffs im frühesten Christentum, in: ZThK 96 [1999], 320–350).

Für die Frage nach Martyrium und Auferstehung heißt dies im Umkehrschluss, dass eher Unklarheit entsteht, wenn das Wortfeld „Martyrium" für die Interpretation neutestamentlicher Schriften verwendet und für diese wiederum eine Vertrautheit mit einer quasi kanonischen jüdischen Märtyrertheologie postuliert wird, so dass eine mehr oder weniger gerade Linie von den Makkabäern bis zu Polykarp gezogen wird.[109] Gewiss leidet Paulus um Christi willen und wünscht sich in Phil 1,23 sogar, die Welt zu verlassen und bei Christus zu sein (wobei σὺν Χριστῷ εἶναι nur hier als endzeitliche, ansonsten als irdische Gemeinschaft verstanden wird); aber es fehlt nicht nur die spätere Terminologie, vor allem ist der Wunsch zu sterben und aufzuerstehen (Phil 3,10f.) nicht die Erfüllung des Zeugnisauftrags, vielmehr wäre der Tod im Gefängnis die *Befreiung* von diesem Auftrag und dem daraus resultierenden Leiden.[110] Das unterscheidet Paulus von den späteren Märtyrern, deren Auftrag *ausschließlich* durch den Tod erfüllt wird (unbeschadet aller Verkündigungselemente vor dem Richter oder auf dem Richtplatz, die es gab, die aber, wie eingangs an Justin gezeigt, nicht den Kern der Martyriumsvorstellung berühren). Paulus' Rolle als Apostel ist dagegen nicht auf die des Blutzeugen zu reduzieren. Es sei daran erinnert, dass das Neue Testament selbst ohne Schilderungen des Todes der Apostel Paulus oder Petrus auskommt – ein Mangel, der ein Jahrhundert später durch die apokryphen Apostelakten „behoben" wurde, wodurch die Wort- nun auch zu expliziten Blutzeugen wurden.

---

[109] So bes. KELLERMANN, Auferstanden in den Himmel (s. Anm. 13). Das Problem seiner Deutung zeigt sich prägnant am Fazit zur Analyse der neutestamentlichen Belege: Es „bleibt festzustellen, *daß die Texte dem hellenistischen Judenchristentum und seinem Milieu entstammen.* Den Gedanken der Rehabilitierung als Begründung für die Notwendigkeit einer besonderen Märtyrerauferstehung sucht man im Neuen Testament vergeblich. Er deutet sich höchstens verhalten in Offb 6,9–11 und 20,4–6 an. Nach der grundlegenden Entdeckung in 2 Makk 7 scheint er inzwischen in der jüdischen und der sich aus ihr ableitenden urchristlichen Glaubensgeschichte selbstverständlich geworden zu sein" (a.a.O. 129). So richtig der Rekurs auf den hellenistisch-jüdischen Kontext ist, so sehr bleibt dagegen die Vertrautheit der neutestamentlichen Autoren mit den makkabäischen Märtyrern als normativen Vorbildern ein traditionsgeschichtliches Postulat. Ähnlich wie Kellermann votierte bereits T.E. POLLARD, Martyrdom and Resurrection in the New Testament, in: BJRL 55 (1972/73), 240–251, hier 245f., der zudem die jüdische Martyriumstheologie auch in der synoptischen Passionsgeschichte am Werke sieht: Nach Lk 23,43 sei Jesus zwischen zwei κακοῦργοι („criminals") gekreuzigt worden, nach Mt 27,38 par Mk 15,27 dagegen zwischen zwei λῃσταί („rebels", „freedom-fighters"). Jesu Wort an den reuigen Schächer signalisiere, dass er ihn als Mitkämpfer für Gottes Sache anerkenne: „The ‚thief', like Jesus, is suffering martyrdom, and will therefore receive the martyr's reward of instant resurrection with Jesus."

[110] Gegen die Deutung bei KELLERMANN, Auferstanden in den Himmel (s. Anm. 13), 113, der zu Folge sich im Philipperbrief der Prototyp der „christologischen Uminterpretation" finde, „die für die urchristliche und altkirchliche Märtyrererwartung grundlegend wird."

Die Bedeutung der biblischen Auferstehungsvorstellung für Verständnis und Deutung des Martyriums in der frühen Kirche partizipiert damit letztlich an derselben Entwicklung wie der Zeugenbegriff überhaupt: Es tritt eine begriffliche und sachliche Verengung ein, durch welche die ursprüngliche Bandbreite der Auferstehungshoffnung auf eine bestimmte Gruppe von Christen konzentriert wird – nicht um sie anderen Christen eschatologisch vorzuenthalten, wohl aber, um angesichts der auf Dauer gestellten Existenz der Kirche in der Welt die Unselbstverständlichkeit der himmlischen Gemeinschaft mit Christus einzuschärfen. Wenn die Pointe bei Tertullian in der scharfen Abhebung zweier Aufenthaltsbereiche der Märtyrer und aller anderen Menschen bis zum jüngsten Gericht liegt, so steht dagegen in räumlicher und zeitlicher Nähe das Insistieren Cyprians darauf, dass das Paradies *allen* Gläubigen (wenn auch nicht den „Heiden" und auch nicht den „Schismatikern") offen steht. Jenseits solcher pointierten Alternativen bemühen sich die Märtyrerakten grundsätzlich darum, das ursprünglich apokalyptisch grundierte Konzept der Auferstehung in ein lebensweltlich anschlussfähiges Theologumenon zu überführen. Sofern mit Tertullian, wie eingangs zitiert, gilt: „Wir sind, was wir sind, weil wir daran glauben!", wird mit der Rezeption und Transformation der biblischen Auferstehungshoffnung in den frühen Märtyrerakten *in nuce* der Inkulturationsprozess des Christentums in eine Welt greifbar, in der es geschichtlich existierte, von der es sich aber stets eschatologisch unterschieden wusste.

Geschichten von der Erscheinung des Auferstandenen in nichtkanonischen Schriften und die Entwicklung der Ostertradition[1]

JUDITH HARTENSTEIN

1. Einführung

In den Schlusskapiteln der kanonischen Evangelien finden sich einige Geschichten, in denen sich Jesus nach seiner Auferstehung seinen Jüngerinnen und Jüngern zeigt, sie von seiner Auferstehung überzeugt und sie beauftragt. Die Unterschiede und Widersprüche zwischen diesen Geschichten bieten erhebliche Schwierigkeiten für die historische Rekonstruktion der ursprünglichen Ereignisse und für die Erklärung der Traditionsentwicklung.[2] Die Situation wird noch komplizierter, wenn auch nichtkanonische Literatur einbezogen wird. Denn auch in einigen apokryphen Evangelien werden Erscheinungen des Auferstandenen erzählt, die noch vielfältiger sind.

In meinem Beitrag will ich nicht bei den ältesten Zeugnissen, die sich m.E. in den kanonischen Evangelien finden, ansetzen, sondern bei den späteren apokryphen Schriften. Auch und gerade weil die Erscheinungsgeschichten dort in Einzelheiten, Kontexten und Inhalt so unterschiedlich sind, lässt sich nach einer gemeinsamen Grundstruktur fragen. Sie weisen

---

[1] Erweiterte Fassung des Vortrags „Non-canonical appearance stories and the development of the resurrection tradition", gehalten beim SBL Annual Meeting 2007 in der Christian Apocrypha Section.

[2] Derzeit besteht m.E. die Tendenz, den historischen Wert der Ostergeschichten in den Evangelien insgesamt gering zu veranschlagen, primäre Bedeutung kommt dagegen dem Zeugnis des Paulus zu, der allerdings keine Geschichten über Erscheinungen bietet. Vgl. z.B. J. BECKER, Die Auferstehung Jesu Christi nach dem Neuen Testament. Ostererfahrung und Osterverständnis im Urchristentum, Tübingen 2007, 251; K. WENGST, Ostern – Ein wirkliches Gleichnis, eine wahre Geschichte. Zum neutestamentlichen Zeugnis von der Auferweckung Jesu, München 1991, 68; U. WILCKENS, Theologie des Neuen Testaments I, Teilband 2: Jesu Tod und Auferstehung und die Entstehung der Kirche aus Juden und Heiden, Neukirchen-Vluyn 2003, 144. Diese Gewichtung erscheint mir grundsätzlich richtig ebenso wie der Ansatz, die Osterkapitel im Kontext der Theologie der jeweiligen Evangelien zu verstehen. Die Frage nach der Entstehung des disparaten Befundes in den erhaltenen Evangelien ist damit aber noch nicht erledigt.

Merkmale auf, die es ermöglichen, sie trotz aller Differenzen als „Erscheinungsgeschichten" zu klassifizieren und diese Form dabei genauer zu definieren. Von diesem Ausgangspunkt aus sollen dann auch die Geschichten in den kanonischen Evangelien in den Blick kommen. Ich versuche dabei, aus den Beobachtungen von Übereinstimmungen und Besonderheiten Rückschlüsse für die Entwicklung der Form zu ziehen. Es geht mir also nicht um einen Vergleich von Einzelgeschichten, der z.B. eine literarische Abhängigkeit zeigen oder widerlegen könnte. Auch eine historische Auswertung der Geschichten ist nicht mein Anliegen, obwohl ich denke, dass meine These zur Entwicklung der Form auch Konsequenzen für sie hat. Mein Ansatz ist vielmehr formgeschichtlich im Sinne einer Analyse von literarisch vorliegenden Zeugnissen auf ihre Gattungsmerkmale hin.

2. Erscheinungen Jesu in apokryphen Evangelien und die Form von Erscheinungsgeschichten

2.1 Überblick

Nicht alle frühchristlichen Evangelien berichten von einer Erscheinung des Auferstandenen, weil dieser Stoff nicht überall Thema ist. So bietet Q zwar einen eschatologischen Ausblick, aber keine Passions- und Ostergeschichten. Das Thomasevangelium (EvThom) enthält noch weniger Erzählung und kommt ebenfalls ohne Erscheinungen des Auferstandenen aus.[3] Der Dialog des Erlösers (Dial NHC III,5) besteht zwar aus einem einigermaßen durchgehenden Dialog zwischen Jesus und seinen Jüngerinnen und Jüngern, aber ohne eine Erscheinungserzählung. Dadurch ist unklar, ob dieses Gespräch vor- oder nachösterlich zu verorten ist. In der ursprünglichen Fassung des MkEv endet die Passionsgeschichte mit der Erscheinung eines Engels vor einigen Jüngerinnen – auf diese Geschichte werde ich später noch eingehen – und enthält keine Erscheinungen des Auferstandenen selbst.

Bei manchen apokryphen Evangelien ist das Fehlen von Erscheinungsgeschichten vermutlich durch den schlechten Erhaltungszustand bedingt. So bricht der Text des Petrusevangeliums (EvPetr) am Anfang einer Geschichte ab, die wohl von einer Erscheinung Jesu am See Genezareth erzählte.[4] Erhalten ist aber ein Fragment des Hebräerevangeliums (EvHebr)

---

[3] Die Auferstehung Jesu spielt im EvThom grundsätzlich keine Rolle; vgl. zu dieser Frage J. HARTENSTEIN, Charakterisierung im Dialog. Maria Magdalena, Petrus, Thomas und die Mutter Jesu im Johannesevangelium im Kontext anderer frühchristlicher Darstellungen, NTOA/StUNT 64, Göttingen 2007, 256f.

[4] Bei weiteren, noch kürzeren Fragmenten von unbekannten Evangelien lassen sich praktisch keine Aussagen machen. Selbst beim Unbekannten Berliner Evangelium

mit einer kurzen Erzählung von einer Erscheinung Jesu vor Jakobus. Auch der sekundär an Mk 16,8 angeschlossene längere Markusschluss enthält eine ausgeführte Erscheinungsgeschichte vor den elf Jüngern und zwei kurze Erwähnungen von Erscheinungen.

Eine größere Zahl von Geschichten findet sich in Schriften, die mit einer Erscheinung Jesu nach seiner Auferstehung vor seinen Jüngerinnen und Jüngern beginnen und sie als Rahmenerzählung für einen Dialog nutzen, der den Hauptteil der Schrift ausmacht. Zu diesen Erscheinungsevangelien[5] – oft, aber nicht immer, aus dem Fund von Nag Hammadi – gehören die Weisheit Jesu Christi (SJC), das Apokryphon des Johannes (AJ), der Brief des Petrus an Philippus (EpPt), die erste Apokalypse des Jakobus (1ApcJac), der Brief des Jakobus (EpJac) und die Pistis Sophia (Pist Soph).[6] Die Epistula Apostolorum (EpAp) ist eine Schrift der gleichen Gattung, aber mit anderer inhaltlicher – nämlich antignostischer – Ausrichtung. Weitere Erscheinungen sind in apokryphen Apostelakten enthalten. So enthalten die Taten des Petrus und der zwölf Apostel (ActPt NHC VI,1) eine ausführliche Erscheinungserzählung während der Reisen der Apostel.[7]

2.2 Die Erscheinungsgeschichte der SJC

Ein typisches Beispiel ist die SJC, in der eine Erscheinung Jesu den Anfang der Schrift und den Rahmen für einen belehrenden Dialog bildet:

(UBE), von dem Abschnitte einer Art Abschiedsrede erhalten sind, die auch einen Vorverweis auf Osterereignisse enthalten, ist nicht sicher, ob Erscheinungsgeschichten zum Bestand des Evangeliums gehörten; vgl. J. HARTENSTEIN, Das Petrusevangelium als Evangelium, in: T.J. KRAUS/T. NICKLAS (Hg.), Das Evangelium nach Petrus. Text, Kontexte, Intertexte, TU 158, Berlin/New York 2007, 159–181, hier 170f.

[5] Ich finde diese Bezeichnung besonders passend, weil sie die gemeinten Schriften klar charakterisiert und eingrenzt, während die verbreitete Bezeichnung Dialogevangelien für sehr unterschiedliche Schriften stehen kann. Vgl. zur weiteren Begründung J. HARTENSTEIN, Dialogische Evangelien – Einleitung, erscheint in: C. MARKSCHIES / J. SCHRÄTER (Hg.), Antike christliche Apokryphen: Evangelien. Begründet von Edgar Hennecke. Siebte, völlig neu bearbeitete Auflage, Tübingen 2010.

[6] Das Mariaevangelium (EvMar) hat wahrscheinlich ebenfalls mit einer Erscheinung begonnen, aber die ersten Seiten der Schrift sind nicht erhalten.

[7] Die EpPt bietet neben der Erscheinungsgeschichte am Anfang, die den Dialog rahmt, der den Großteil der Schrift ausmacht, mindestens eine weitere Erscheinung Jesu während der weiteren Erlebnisse der Jünger. Die 2ApcJac besteht aus der Wiedergabe einer Rede des Jakobus vor seinem Martyrium, in der er seinerseits Worte aus einem Gespräch mit Jesus zitiert. Ob das Zusammentreffen der beiden für dieses Gespräch als eine nachösterliche Erscheinung zu verstehen ist (so W.-P. FUNK, Die zweite Apokalypse des Jakobus, in: NTApo I^6, 264–275, hier 265), scheint mir allerdings nicht sicher. Vor allem die beiläufige Beteiligung der Mutter des Jakobus spricht m.E. für eine Szene aus dem irdischen Leben Jesu.

SJC BG p.77,9–80,3: Nach seiner Auferstehung von den Toten, als seine zwölf Jünger und sieben Frauen, die ihm Jüngerinnen waren, nach Galiläa kamen, auf den Berg, der *(p.78)* ‚Weissagung und Freude' genannt wird, wobei sie nun ratlos waren über das Wesen des Alls und den Heilsplan und die heilige Vorsehung und die Vortrefflichkeit der Mächte (und) über alles, was der Erlöser mit ihnen macht im Geheimnis des heiligen Heilsplanes, da erschien ihnen der Erlöser, nicht in seiner früheren Gestalt, sondern in unsichtbarem Geist. Sein Aussehen aber war das Aussehen eines großen Lichtengels. *(p.79)* Seine Art aber werde ich nicht beschreiben können. Kein sterbliches Fleisch wird sie tragen können, sondern nur ein reines, vollkommenes Fleisch, wie er sich uns zeigte auf dem Berg, der ‚Ölberg' genannt wird, in Galiläa. Er sagte: „Friede sei mit euch! Meinen Frieden gebe ich euch." Und sie wunderten sich alle und fürchteten sich. Der Erlöser lachte. Er sagte zu ihnen: „Über was denkt ihr nach? Worüber seid ihr ratlos? Wonach sucht ihr?" Philippus sagte: *(p.80)* „Über das Wesen des Alls und den Heilsplan des Erlösers[8]."

Auf diesen Anfang folgen Belehrungen über den obersten Gott, seine Emanationen und den Aufbau der Himmel. Die Beziehung dieser Geschichte zur Erscheinung Jesu vor den Elf in Mt 28,16–20 fällt ebenso ins Auge wie die Besonderheiten. Gemeinsam ist das Grundgerüst der Erzählung: Auf dem Berg in Galiläa, zu dem die Jüngerinnen und Jünger von Jesus gesandt wurden, begegnet er ihnen mit himmlischer Vollmacht und gibt wesentliche Belehrungen. Über das MtEv hinaus bietet die SJC einen Namen für den Berg, die Beteiligung von Jüngerinnen und eine ausführliche Beschreibung des Erschienenen. Grundsätzlich anders ist der Inhalt der nach der Erscheinung folgenden Rede Jesu, dem auch schon die Ratlosigkeit und die Fragen der Jüngerinnen und Jünger am Anfang entsprechen. Es ist wahrscheinlich, dass die SJC das MtEv (und vermutlich auch weitere Evangelien) kennt und die Schlusserscheinung mit eigenen Akzenten ausgestaltet.[9]

Die Geschichte hat einen klaren Aufbau: Zunächst wird die Situation mit Ort, Zeit und beteiligten Personen beschrieben, wobei die ratlose Stimmung der Jünger und Jüngerinnen ausführlich dargestellt wird. Dann wird die Erscheinung selbst geschildert, in der der himmlische Charakter des Erscheinenden betont wird. Schließlich bilden der Gruß Jesu und die Reaktion darauf einen kurzen Dialog bevor zu den ausführlichen Offenbarungen übergeleitet wird, die den Hauptteil der Schrift ausmachen. Diese enden mit einigen konkreten Aufforderungen Jesu, dann verschwindet er wieder und die Jünger und Jüngerinnen beginnen zu predigen.

In der SJC und in vergleichbaren Schriften bereitet die Erscheinung Jesu seine Belehrungen vor, indem sie Zeit, Ort und Beteiligte einführt und

---

[8] „Der Erlöser" ist in SJC NHC III schon Subjekt des nächsten Satzes. – Übersetzung JH.

[9] Vgl. zur ausführlichen Darlegung und Auswertung der Parallelen und Differenzen J. HARTENSTEIN, Die zweite Lehre. Erscheinungen des Auferstandenen als Rahmenerzählungen frühchristlicher Dialoge, TU 146, Berlin 2000, 57–62.

vor allem den Offenbarer vorstellt. Die himmlischen Elemente in der Erscheinung zeigen die überirdische Herkunft dessen, der erscheint. Zugleich macht die Erzählung aber auch deutlich, dass es sich wirklich um den den Jüngern und Jüngerinnen bekannten Jesus handelt, obwohl er anders aussieht und sie eigentlich verlassen hat.[10] Durch die Erscheinungserzählung wird der himmlische Offenbarer auf die Erde platziert, mitten in das normale Leben hinein.[11]

2.3 Erscheinungsgeschichten in der Antike und ihre typische Form

Diese grundlegende Struktur ist nicht auf Erscheinungen des auferstandenen Jesus beschränkt. In der jüdischen und paganen Antike gibt es eine Fülle von vergleichbaren Geschichten. Klaus Berger sieht als zentrales Kennzeichen dieser Texte, die er Visionsberichte nennt, die „Schaltstelle", an der eine neue Ebene eingeführt wird. Jemand erscheint, wird gesehen oder steht auch nur einfach da – jedenfalls wird sprachlich der Einbruch einer himmlischen Wirklichkeit in die normal-irdische Erzählung signalisiert.[12] Zur Ausgangsebene gehören auch die Reaktionen der Empfangenden und am Ende das Verschwinden sowie weitere Ereignisse wie die Umsetzung eines erhaltenen Auftrags; die Einzelheiten sind nicht spezifisch, sondern begegnen auch unabhängig von Visionen. Die andere Ebene bildet die Botschaft, die in der Vision übermittelt wird. Ihr Inhalt selbst ist variabel und ebenfalls nicht spezifisch an Visionen gebunden. Immer ist die Botschaft aber mit überirdischer Autorität ausgestattet, die sie durch die Art der Übermittlung bekommt. Durch die Erscheinung werden die Empfangenden – oft bedeutende Einzelpersonen – besonders hervorgehoben.[13] Die Geschichten sind in sich geschlossene Einheiten, die in unterschiedlichen Kontexten verwendet werden können.

Solche Erscheinungsgeschichten[14] werden in der paganen Antike von verschiedenen Göttern oder verstorbenen Menschen erzählt. Häufig handelt es sich um Erscheinungen im Schlaf oder Traumgesichte. Inhaltlich

---

[10] Vgl. HARTENSTEIN, Lehre (s. Anm. 10), 281.

[11] Erscheinungsevangelien unterscheiden sich darin grundlegend von Himmelsreisen, in denen ein normaler Mensch in den Himmel gehoben wird, dort Dinge sieht und wesentliche Belehrungen erhält.

[12] Vgl. K. BERGER, Formgeschichte des Neues Testaments, Heidelberg 1984, 281; DERS., Visionsberichte. Formgeschichtliche Bemerkungen über pagane hellenistische Texte und ihre frühchristlichen Analogien, in: K. BERGER/F. VOUGA/M. WOLTER/D. ZELLER (Hg.), Studien und Texte zur Formgeschichte, TANZ 7, Tübingen 1992, 177–225, hier 201f.

[13] Vgl. BERGER, Visionsberichte (s. Anm. 13), 202f.

[14] Trotz meiner Anlehnung an die Beschreibung von Berger ziehe ich diese Bezeichnung der Texte vor, da das Element „Vision" m.E. im heutigen Sprachgebrauch impliziert, dass die Ereignisse nicht real stattfinden.

sind sowohl ganz konkrete Anweisungen oder Ankündigungen möglich, als auch bildliche Visionen, die erst noch – oft nach Abschluss der Erscheinung – gedeutet werden müssen.[15] Typisch ist jedenfalls, dass die Schaltstelle zum Wechsel der Ebene durch eindeutige Begrifflichkeit (Erscheinen, Gesicht ...) oder durch den unmittelbaren Zusammenhang deutlich wird. Eine Beschreibung der erscheinenden Person ist möglich, kann aber auch fehlen.

Im AT ist es manchmal Gott selbst oder öfter sein Engel, der erscheint, um herausgehobene Personen zu beauftragen (so z.B. Moses in Ex 3,1–4,17; Gideon in Ri 6,11–24) oder ihnen etwas anzukündigen (z.B. die Geburt Isaaks in Gen 18,1–15; die Geburt Simsons in Ri 13,2–5.9–20). Auch hier ist der Übergang zur himmlischen Wirklichkeit sprachlich klar erkennbar. Oft genügt einfach die Erwähnung der Erscheinung, an die sich dann eine Rede anschließt, die durch dieses Erscheinen qualifiziert ist.[16] Mitunter muss die Identität des Erscheinenden aber noch geklärt werden, bevor dann eine Botschaft als eigentlicher Inhalt der Erscheinung übermittelt wird.

2.4 Weitere Beispiele aus apokryphen Evangelien

Die SJC entspricht genau dieser Grundstruktur von antiken Erscheinungen. Die Schaltstelle ist durch das Verb „erscheinen" (ⲟⲩⲱⲛϩ) markiert und der himmlische Charakter des Erscheinenden wird in der Beschreibung deutlich. Auch die Reaktion der Jünger und Jüngerinnen gehört noch zu diesem einleitenden Teil. Die Belehrung als Inhalt der Vision umfasst dann nahezu die gesamte Schrift. Sie ist viel länger als in den meisten anderen Geschichten, aber das Verhältnis zwischen Erscheinung und Botschaft ist trotzdem genau dasselbe: Die Rahmenerzählung mit der Erscheinung eröffnet eine neue Ebene, auf der dann die Botschaft übermittelt werden kann. Wie in anderen Erscheinungsgeschichten gilt die Erscheinung bedeutenden Personen, nämlich der Gruppe aus zwölf Jüngern und sieben Jüngerinnen. Trotz Anknüpfung an schon bekannte Jesustradition ist die Erzählung selbstständig, sie bildet sogar eine eigene Schrift.

In anderen Erscheinungsevangelien sieht es ähnlich aus: In AJ und EpPt ist der himmlische Charakter der Erscheinung ähnlich wie in SJC oder noch stärker betont. In EpJac und 1ApcJac erscheint Jesus dagegen einfach ohne weitere himmlische Begleitumstände. Da sein Status nach der Auferstehung aber vorausgesetzt werden kann, ist auch dies ausreichend, um einen Kontakt zu einer himmlischen Person herzustellen:

---

[15] Vgl. die Auflistung der Beispiele bei BERGER, Visionsberichte (s. Anm. 13), 177–200, und ihre Auswertung.

[16] Vgl. R. RENDTORFF, Die Offenbarungsvorstellungen im Alten Israel, in: KuD Beiheft 1 (1961), 21–41, hier 24f.

EpJac NHC I p.2,7–39: [Als] aber alle zwölf Jünger zugleich beisammen saßen und als sie sich an das erinnerten, was der Erlöser einem jeden von ihnen gesagt hatte – sei es im Verborgenen, sei es öffentlich – und als sie es zu Büchern [ordneten], schrieb ich, was in [jener (Geheimlehre)] steht. Siehe, da erschien der Erlöser – [nachdem] er von [uns] gegangen war und [wir] auf ihn gewartet hatten – und zwar 550 Tage nachdem er von den Toten auferstanden war. Wir sagten zu ihm: „Bist du weggegangen und hast du dich von uns entfernt?“[17] Jesus aber sagte: „Nein, aber ich werde weggehen zu dem Ort, von dem ich gekommen bin. Wenn ihr mit mir kommen wollt, so kommt!“ Sie antworteten alle und sagten: „Wenn du uns befiehlst, kommen wir mit.“ Er sagte: „Wahrlich, ich sage euch: Niemand wird jemals in das Reich der Himmel eingehen, wenn ich es ihm befehle, sondern (ihr werdet eingehen,) weil ihr erfüllt seid. Überlasst mir Jakobus und Petrus, damit ich sie erfülle.“ Und nachdem er die beiden gerufen hatte, nahm er sie beiseite. Den Übrigen befahl er, sich (weiter) mit dem zu beschäftigen, womit sie (gerade) beschäftigt waren.[18]

Auf diese Szene folgen die Belehrungen an Jakobus und Petrus. Auch hier wird das Erscheinen (ⲟⲩⲱⲛϩ ⲁⲃⲁⲗ) sprachlich eindeutig festgehalten; statt himmlischer Begleitumstände gibt es zwar nur einen Verweis auf die Auferstehung, aber der stellt ebenfalls klar, dass es sich nicht einfach um eine Begegnung mit dem irdischen Jesus handelt. Der kurze Dialog mit den Jüngern dient weniger zur Identifizierung von Jesus als zur Klärung, wer nun die Offenbarungen erhalten soll; die eigentliche Botschaft folgt nach der Trennung der Beteiligten. Die Erscheinung dient also auch hier dazu, die Bedingungen herzustellen, unter denen die Botschaft als himmlische Offenbarung ergehen kann. Die Bedeutsamkeit der Personen wird noch dadurch unterstrichen, dass zwei besonders würdige Jünger ausgewählt werden.

Etwas anders und schwieriger zu greifen ist der Fall der EpAp, in der ebenfalls eine Erscheinung Jesu die Rahmenerzählung für seine ausführlichen Belehrungen bietet:

EpAp 9,1–12,4 (kopt I,11–V,5): 9,1 Dieser, von dem [wir] bezeugen, dass er der Herr ist, dieser, der [gekreuzigt] wurde durch Pontius Pilatus [und] Archelaos in der Mitte von zwei Räubern. 9,3 [Und] er [wurde] begraben an einem Ort, der heißt (II) [Schädel-(stätte)]. 9,4 Sie gingen zu jenem Ort, zählend [drei] Frauen, Maria, die zu Martha gehörende, <und Martha> und Maria [Magdalena]. 9,5 Sie nahmen Salbe, um sie [auf] seinen Leib zu gießen, indem sie weinten und trauerten über [das, was] geschehen war. 9,6 Als sie sich aber dem [Grab] näherten, blickten sie hinein; sie fanden den Leib nicht. 10,1 Als [sie] aber trauerten und weinten, erschien [ihnen] der Herr. Er sprach zu ihnen: „Um wen weint ihr? Fahrt nun nicht fort zu weinen! Ich bin es, nach dem ihr sucht. 10,2 Aber eine von euch soll zu euren Brüdern gehen und sagen: ‚Kommt, der Lehrer stand auf von den [Toten]!‘“ 10,3 Martha kam, sie sagte es uns. 10,4 Wir sprachen zu ihr: „Was willst [du]

---

[17] Der Satz kann auch als Vorwurf verstanden und übersetzt werden: „Du bist weggegangen und du hast dich von uns entfernt!“

[18] Übersetzung aus: J. HARTENSTEIN/U.-K. PLISCH, Der Brief des Jakobus (NHC I,2), in: H.-M. SCHENKE/H.-G. BETHGE/U.U. KAISER (Hg.), Nag Hammadi Deutsch. 1. Band: NHC I,1–V,1, GCS NF 8, Koptisch-Gnostische Schriften II, Berlin/New York, 11–26.

von (wörtl. mit) uns, o Frau? Dieser, der [gestorben] ist, [wurde] begraben, und ist es möglich, dass er lebt?" 10,5 Wir [glaubten] ihr nicht, dass der Erlöser auferstanden war von den Toten. 10,6 Da[(III)]rauf ging sie zum Herrn, sie sprach zu ihm: „Keiner von ihnen hat mir geglaubt, dass du lebst." 10,7 Er sprach: „Eine andere von euch soll zu ihnen gehen und es ihnen wieder sagen." 10,8 Maria kam, sie sagte es uns wieder, und wir glaubten ihr nicht. 10,9 Sie kehrte zurück zum Herrn. Auch sie sagte es ihm. 11,1 Darauf sprach der Herr zu Maria und ihren Schwestern: „Lasst uns zu ihnen gehen!" 11,2 Und er kam, er fand uns drinnen. Er rief uns heraus. 11,3 Wir aber dachten, dass es ein Gespenst sei. Wir glaubten nicht, dass es der Herr ist. 11,4 Darauf [sprach er] zu uns: „Kommt, fürchtet euch nicht. Ich [bin eurer Lehrer], dieser auch, den du, Petrus, dreimal [verleugnet] hast, und jetzt [verleugnest] du wieder?" 11,5 Wir aber kamen zu ihm, zweifelnd in [unserem] Herzen, dass (oder: ob) er es vielleicht nicht ist. 11,6 Darauf sprach er zu [uns]: „Weshalb zweifelt ihr noch und seid ihr ungläubig? Ich bin der, der zu euch gesprochen hat über mein Fleisch und mein Sterben und mein Auferstehen. 11,7 Damit ihr erkennt, dass ich es bin: Petrus, lege deine Finger in die Nägelmale meiner Hände. Und auch du, Thomas, lege deine Finger in die Lanzenstiche meiner Seite. Du aber, Andreas, betrachte meine Füße und sieh, ob sie nicht anhaften an der Erde. 11,8 Denn es ist geschrieben im Propheten: ‚Der Fuß von einem Dämonengespenst haftet nicht auf der Erde.'" 12,1 Wir aber [berü]hrten ihn, so dass wir wahrhaftig erkannten, dass [er auferstanden] war im Fleisch. 12,2 Und wir warfen uns nieder auf unser [Gesicht], bekennend unsere Sünden, dass wir [Ungläubige] gewesen waren. 12,3 Darauf sprach der Herr, unser Erlöser: „Ste[ht auf], und ich werde euch offenbaren die (Dinge), die oberhalb der Himmel sind, und die in den Himmeln und eure Ruhe, die im Himmelreich ist. 12,4 Denn mein [Vater] gab mir die Vollmacht, euch hinaufzunehmen und die, die an mich glauben."[19]

Nach dieser Erzählung von Jesu Erscheinung folgt ein ausführliches Gespräch mit den Jüngern; die EpAp entspricht in ihrer Form Erscheinungsevangelien wie der SJC. Streng genommen sind die Belehrungen jedoch nicht Teil der Erscheinungsgeschichte, sondern werden neu im Rückblick eingeleitet (EpAp 13,1: „Die (Dinge) aber, die er offenbart hat, diese sind es, die er sagt: ..."). Zudem ist auch die Erscheinung selbst ungewöhnlich, weil Jesus zunächst den am Grab trauernden Frauen erscheint (ⲟⲩⲱⲛϩ ⲁⲃⲁⲗ), und dann, nachdem er sie mehrmals vergeblich zu den Jüngern geschickt hat, selbst zu ihnen geht. Es findet also innerhalb der Erscheinung ein Ortswechsel und ein Wechsel der beteiligten Personen statt, der vor allem zur langwierigen aber gründlichen Überzeugung der Jünger von Jesu leiblicher Auferstehung dient. Jesus wird von den Jüngern (namentlich Petrus, Thomas und Andreas) betastet und geprüft, wobei deutliche Anklänge an die Thomasgeschichte in Joh 20 bzw. an Lk 24,36–51 bestehen.[20]

Obwohl Jesus nicht verschwindet und den Jüngern neu erscheint, kann die gesamte Erzählung auch als enge Verbindung von zwei Erscheinungsgeschichten verstanden werden: Zunächst erscheint er den Frauen, wobei

[19] Übersetzung der koptischen Handschrift der EpAp JH, vgl. HARTENSTEIN, Lehre (s. Anm. 10), 108–110.

[20] Vgl. HARTENSTEIN, Lehre (s. Anm. 10), 121–123.

zur Erscheinung auch die Selbstvorstellung gehört; die Botschaft ist dann der Auftrag, zu den Jüngern zu gehen und ihnen die Auferstehung Jesu zu verkünden (EpAp 10,1f). Die zweite „Erscheinungsgeschichte" besteht dann im Zusammentreffen Jesu mit den Jüngern, bei der der überirdische Charakter der Begegnung nur indirekt durch die Fehlwahrnehmung und mühsame Überzeugung der Jünger deutlich wird. Die Botschaft liegt in der Ankündigung von himmlischen Offenbarungen, die die weitere Schrift dann ausführt. Trotzdem ist das Zusammentreffen mit den Jüngern ungewöhnlich, nicht nur, weil es keine Erscheinung ist, sondern auch, weil die Leiblichkeit des Auferstandenen ein eigenes inhaltliches Anliegen ist – es geht nicht nur um die Identifikation des Erschienenen.

Eine andere Art von Erscheinungsgeschichte ist in ActPt (NHC VI,1) enthalten. Die Jünger sind unterwegs, um das Evangelium zu verkündigen, und treffen in einer Stadt einen Fremden, der ihnen den gefährlichen Weg zu einem weiteren Ort erklärt. Als sie diesen schließlich erreichen, begegnen sie ihm in der Gestalt eines Arztes wieder, ohne ihn zu erkennen:

ActPt NHC VI p.8,13–10,13: Siehe, da kam Lithargoël heraus, in einer anderen Gestalt als der, die wir kannten, (nämlich) in der Gestalt eines Arztes, der ein Arzneikästchen unter der Achsel trug und dem ein Schüler mit einem Koffer voller Arznei folgte. Doch wir erkannten ihn nicht. Da ergriff Petrus das Wort und sprach zu ihm: „Wir bitten dich um die Freundlichkeit, uns, weil wir hier fremd sind, zum Haus des Lithargoël zu führen, bevor es Abend wird." Er sprach: „Ich werde es euch aufrichtigen Herzens zeigen. Aber ich wundere mich darüber, dass ihr diesen guten Menschen kennt. Denn er zeigt sich keineswegs jedermann, weil er selbst der Sohn eines großen Königs ist. Rastet ein wenig; ich will inzwischen hingehen und diesen Mann (, zu dem ich gerade unterwegs bin,) gesund machen; dann komme ich zurück." Und er beeilte sich und kam schnell *(p.9)* zurück. Er sprach zu Petrus: „Petrus!" Petrus aber erschrak darüber, dass er seinen Namen ‚Petrus' kannte. Petrus antwortete dem Erlöser: „Woher kennst du mich, dass du mich beim Namen rufen konntest?" Da antwortete Lithargoël: „Ich will dich (etwas) fragen: Wer hat dir diesen Namen ‚Petrus' gegeben?" Er sprach zu ihm: „Jesus Christus war es, der Sohn des lebendigen Gottes; er hat mir diesen Namen gegeben." Er antwortete und sprach: „Ich bin es! Erkenne mich, Petrus!" Er entledigte sich des Gewandes, das er trug und durch das er sich uns unkenntlich gemacht hatte. Als er uns (auf diese Weise) wahrhaftig enthüllt hatte, dass er es sei, warfen wir uns zu Boden und erwiesen ihm Verehrung – wir waren elf Jünger. Er streckte die Hand aus und ließ uns aufstehen. Wir sprachen mit ihm demütig. Unsere Köpfe waren schamhaft zu Boden gesenkt, als wir sagten: „Was du willst, das wollen wir tun! Aber gib uns auch die nötige Kraft, um allezeit zu tun, was dir wohlgefällt." Er überreichte ihnen das Medizinkästchen und den Koffer, den der Schüler hatte, und gab ihnen folgende Anweisung *(p.10)* mit den Worten: „Kehrt zurück [zu der] Stadt, aus der ihr gekommen seid, die da heißt ‚Wohne (und) weile auf Geduld!', und lehrt alle, die zum Glauben an meinen Namen gekommen sind, dass (auch) ich geduldet habe in Mühsalen des Glaubens. Ich selbst werde euch euren Lohn geben. Den Armen jener Stadt sollt ihr geben, was sie zum Leben brauchen, bis ich ihnen jenes bessere (Gut) gebe, wovon ich <ihnen> gesagt habe: ‚Ich werde es euch zum Geschenk machen'." ...[21]

Es folgen zwei Rückfragen bzw. Einwände von Petrus und Johannes, die von Jesus beantwortet werden. In dieser Geschichte wird nicht ausdrücklich von einem Erscheinen Jesu gesprochen, denn er ist schon unerkannt anwesend. Aber indem er sich im Gespräch durch sein Wissen, das kein Fremder haben könnte, zu erkennen gibt, wird trotzdem ein Wechsel der Ebene in der Erzählung signalisiert. Die Reaktion der Jünger entspricht deshalb auch der in anderen Erscheinungen, bevor die Botschaft, eine Belehrung über ihre Mission, gegeben wird.[22] Die Geschichte hat Ähnlichkeit mit der Erscheinung Jesu vor Maria Magdalena in Joh 20, weil wie dort eine unerwartete Namensanrede zum Erkennen des Erschienenen führt. Auch mit der Emmausgeschichte ist das anfängliche Nichterkennen gemeinsam, anders als dort schließt sich an das Erkennen aber ein Auftrag Jesu an. Dieser erinnert an die Aussendungen in anderen Erscheinungen vor der Gruppe, hat aber in der Betonung der Armenfürsorge einen ganz eigenen Akzent.

Die EpPt bietet neben der ausführlichen Erscheinungsgeschichte zu Beginn der Schrift, die wie in SJC ein belehrendes Gespräch einschließt, Erlebnisse der Jünger in der Art einer Apostelgeschichte. Zu ihnen gehört ganz am Ende eine weitere Erscheinung:

EpPt NHC VIII p.140,13–27: Und sie versammelten sich miteinander und küssten sich, [indem sie] sagten: „Amen." Da erschien Jesus, der ihnen sagte: „Friede sei mit euch [allen] und allen denen, die an meinen Namen glauben. Wenn ihr aber geht, wird euch Freude und Gnade und Kraft zuteil werden. Seid aber unverzagt, siehe ich bin ewig mit euch." Dann trennten sich die Apostel in die vier Worte, um zu predigen. Und sie gingen in der Kraft Jesu in Frieden.[23]

---

[21] Übersetzung: H.-M. SCHENKE, Die Taten des Petrus und der zwölf Apostel (NHC VI,1), in: H.-M. SCHENKE/H.-G. BETHGE/U.U. KAISER (Hg.), Nag Hammadi Deutsch. 2. Band: NHC V,2–XIII,1, BG 1 und 4, GCS NF 12, Koptisch-Gnostische Schriften III, Berlin/New York 2003, 443–453.

[22] Nach BERGER, vgl. Visionsberichte (s. Anm. 13), 203, zeichnen sich Epiphanien dadurch aus, dass eine himmlische Gestalt nicht erscheint, sondern einfach anwesend ist und erst im Nachhinein identifiziert wird. Er sieht auch die Möglichkeit einer Verbindung und von fließenden Übergängen zwischen Epiphanien und Visionsberichten, für die m.E. die Geschichte aus ActPt ein Beispiel ist.

[23] Übersetzung JH, vgl. HARTENSTEIN, Lehre (s. Anm. 10), 181. In der Abschrift der EpPt aus Codex Tchacos (CT) fehlt der Anfang der Geschichte wegen einer Textlücke. Der wichtigste Unterschied liegt darin, dass diese Textfassung eine ausdrückliche Aufforderung zum Aufbruch enthält, bevor die Verheißungen ergehen (EpPt CT p.9,4f). Möglicherweise ist dies ursprünglicher als die Fassung in NHC VIII, in der der Aufbruch nur das Umfeld der Zusage bildet. Direkt vorher in der Schrift ist schon von der Verkündigung der Jünger die Rede, eine erneute Aufforderung zum Aufbruch steht in einer gewissen Spannung dazu und könnte deshalb abgemildert worden sein.

Diese Erscheinungsgeschichte ist sehr knapp, enthält aber alle typischen Elemente. Das Erscheinen Jesu wird ohne nähere Beschreibung festgestellt (ⲟⲩⲱⲛϩ ⲉⲃⲟⲗ), zur Kontaktaufnahme dient ein Gruß und die Botschaft besteht in einer Verheißung für den weiteren Weg der Jünger. Damit passt sie gut als Abschluss der Gesamtschrift.

Eine Erscheinung Jesu vor Jakobus aus dem EvHebr zitiert Hieronymus:

Hier.vir.ill. II: Als aber der Herr das Leintuch dem Knecht des Priesters gegeben hatte, ging er zu Jakobus und erschien ihm. Jakobus hatte nämlich geschworen, dass er nicht mehr essen werde von jener Stunde an, in der er den Kelch des Herrn getrunken hatte, bis er ihn auferstehen sehen würde von den Schlafenden. Und wiederum sagt der Herr etwas später: „Bringt Tisch und Brot!" Und sogleich wird hinzugefügt: Er nahm das Brot und dankte und brach es und gab es Jakobus, dem Gerechten, und sagte zu ihm: „Mein Bruder, iss dein Brot, denn der Menschensohn ist auferstanden von den Schlafenden."[24]

Es sieht so aus, als ob Hieronymus die Geschichte aus dem EvHebr nicht einfach vollständig zitiert, sondern kürzt und mit eigenen Bemerkungen mischt. Die Aufforderung Jesu, einen Tisch und Brot zu bringen, wird mit dem Hinweis eingeleitet, dass er dies etwas später sagt – vermutlich ist dies nicht Bestandteil der eigentlichen Erzählung, sondern eine Bemerkung, die auf eine Auslassung verweist. Hier könnte eine Beschreibung oder eine direkte Reaktion des Jakobus weggefallen sein. Auch der Rückblick auf den Schwur des Jakobus kann eine Erläuterung von Hieronymus sein, er ist aber auch als Bestandteil der Erzählung vorstellbar. Trotz dieser Unklarheit, wie die Geschichte genau aussah, wird deutlich, dass ihr ein Beweis für Jesu Auferweckung vorausgeht. Es ist dann ausdrücklich vom Erscheinen (*appareo*) Jesu vor Jakobus die Rede. Diese Erscheinung bereitet die Botschaft an ihn vor.

Der so genannte längere Markusschluss enthält ebenfalls eine ausgeführte Erzählung vom Erscheinen Jesu vor seinen elf Jüngern (Mk 16,14–20):

14 Später aber erschien er den Elf, als sie zu Tisch lagen, und tadelte ihren Unglauben und die Hartherzigkeit, dass sie denen, die ihn auferstanden gesehen hatten, nicht geglaubt hatten. 15 Und er sagte ihnen: „Geht in die ganze Welt und verkündigt jedem Geschöpf das Evangelium. 16 Wer glaubt und getauft ist, wird gerettet werden, wer aber nicht glaubt, wird verurteilt werden. 17 Diese Zeichen werden die Glaubenden begleiten: In meinem Namen werden sie Dämonen austreiben; sie werden in neuen Sprachen reden; 18 und mit den Händen werden sie Schlangen hochheben; und wenn sie etwas Tödliches trinken, wird es ihnen nicht schaden; auf Kranke werden sie die Hände legen und sie werden gesund werden." 19 Nachdem der Herr Jesus nun mit ihnen geredet hatte, wurde er aufgenommen in den Himmel und setzte sich zur Rechten Gottes. 20 Sie aber gingen

[24] Übersetzung: D. LÜHRMANN, Fragmente apokryph gewordener Evangelien in griechischer und lateinischer Sprache, MThSt 59, Marburg 2000, 52f.

los und verkündigten überall, wobei der Herr mitwirkte und die Rede durch die begleitenden Zeichen bekräftigte.[25]

In dieser Geschichte ist die Erscheinung mit einem typischen Begriff bezeichnet (φανερόω). Eine nähere Beschreibung oder eine Reaktion fehlen, dafür schließt ein Tadel am Unglauben der Jünger an die vorausgehende Erzählung an und bezieht auf diese Weise die dort vorliegende Reaktion der Gruppe ein. Das Schwergewicht der Geschichte liegt dann auf der Botschaft, in der die Jünger zur Mission aufgefordert werden (Mk 16,15–18).

Alle diese Geschichten enthalten zwei Teile: eine Erscheinung und eine Botschaft. In den Einzelheiten von beiden Teilen gibt es große Unterschiede, sie können auch länger oder kürzer sein, aber es sind jeweils beide Teile nötig, und zwar in einer besonderen Beziehung: Die Erscheinung bereitet die Botschaft vor, indem sie die neue Ebene der himmlischen Wirklichkeit eröffnet. Sie ist dadurch von zentraler Wichtigkeit, aber nur in Beziehung zur Botschaft, die Erscheinung hat ihren Zweck nicht in sich selbst.[26] Eine Erscheinungsgeschichte, die keine Botschaft enthält, ist nicht sinnvoll. Die Botschaft wiederum ist, auch wenn es natürlich eine Beziehung zum Erscheinenden und zu den Empfängern und Empfängerinnen gibt, unabhängig von der konkreten Situation. Ihr Inhalt ist nahezu beliebig, hat aber durch die Einbindung eine zusätzliche Bedeutung als himmlische Offenbarung.

Formal lässt sich festhalten, dass die apokryphen Erscheinungen Jesu den Ebenenwechsel durch die Erscheinung sprachlich klar signalisieren, meist durch eine ausdrückliche Benennung als Erscheinung, aber auch durch weitere Begleitumstände. Auch die Klärung der Identität des Erschienenen ist Bestandteil der Erscheinung. Die Empfänger und Empfängerinnen haben große Bedeutung: Es handelt sich um wichtige Personen wie Petrus, Jakobus oder die ganze Gruppe, denen auch eine entsprechend bedeutsame Mitteilung gemacht wird. Der Inhalt der Botschaft ist völlig unterschiedlich. Alle Geschichten sind in sich relativ geschlossene Größen, die in unterschiedlichen Kontexten stehen: Bei den Erscheinungsevangelien bildet die gesamte Schrift (oder ein großer Teil von ihr) eine einzige Erscheinungsgeschichte, in der die Botschaft enorm ausgeweitet ist. Erscheinungen können aber wie in ActPt (ähnlich auch in EpPt) Teil einer Apostelgeschichte sein oder sie können zu einer Passionsgeschichte gehören

---

[25] Übersetzung JH. Die beiden vorausgehenden Episoden im sekundären Markusschluss sind keine Erscheinungsgeschichten, denn die Erscheinung wird jeweils nur festgestellt (Mk 16,9.12). Diese Stücke sind am ehesten mit der Formeltradition 1Kor 15,5–8; Lk 24,34 verwandt, aber variantenreicher formuliert. Narrativ entfaltet wird jeweils nur die Übermittlung dieses Erlebnisses und die Reaktion darauf (Mk 16,10f.13).

[26] Nur in der EpAp bekommt die Überzeugung der Jünger von der Leiblichkeit des Auferstandenen eine eigene inhaltliche Relevanz.

bzw. an sie angefügt sein. Die Auferstehung Jesu ist dabei aber fast immer ausdrücklich vorausgesetzt.[27]

2.5 Typische Erscheinungsgeschichten im Neuen Testament

Auch im NT finden sich Erscheinungsgeschichten, die nach dem gleichen Prinzip aufgebaut sind. In der Geschichte von der Erscheinung Jesu vor Paulus in Apg 9,3–9 sieht Paulus zunächst ein Licht und hört eine Stimme, die ihn anspricht und sich selbst vorstellt – dann bekommt er den Auftrag, nach Damaskus zu gehen und auf weitere Anweisungen zu warten. Die Botschaft ist hier sehr knapp,[28] aber sie ist klar von der Erscheinung unterschieden, die zur Identifikation des Erschienenen führt und sie so vorbereitet. Ein spezifischer Begriff für „Erscheinen" ist nicht verwendet, was vielleicht daran liegt, dass nicht eine einzelne Person erscheint, sondern Licht und eine Stimme.[29] Durch die begleitenden Umstände ist der himmlische Charakter der Erscheinung jedenfalls gesichert. Die Geschichte ist als selbstständige Größe in die Apg integriert.

Das MkEv endet in 16,1–8 mit der Erscheinung eines Engels vor den Frauen, die das Grab besuchen. Die Beschreibung der Person, die im Grab sitzt, und die erschreckte Reaktion der Frauen verweisen auf den überirdischen Charakter des Jünglings, der durch seine typische Beruhigung bestätigt wird. Dann gibt er ihnen die Botschaft von Jesu Auferstehung und beauftragt sie damit, die Jünger und Jüngerinnen nach Galiläa zu schicken. Hier liegt alles Gewicht auf der Botschaft, deren Offenbarungscharakter durch die Erscheinung gesichert ist.

Eine weitere Erscheinungsgeschichte gibt es in Offb 1,9–20. Hier ist der Beginn des überirdischen Erlebnisses als ein Geistgeschehen (ἐγενόμην ἐν πνεύματι) eingeleitet, Johannes hört dann eine Stimme und sieht eine Gestalt, die ausführlich beschrieben wird. Nachdem der Erschienene sich vorgestellt hat, folgt als Botschaft das Diktat der Briefe an die Gemeinden (Offb 2,1–3,22).[30] Auch hier dient die Erscheinung zur Vorbereitung und Legitimation der Botschaft.

---

[27] Auch hier ist die EpAp die Ausnahme.

[28] In der späteren Wiederholung dieser Geschichte in Apg 26,12–18 gewinnt die Botschaft an Gewicht und umfasst Berufung und Auftrag.

[29] Eine solche Kombination begegnet auch in der ersten Erscheinungsgeschichte der EpPt, dort aber mit einem eindeutigen Begriff verbunden (EpPt NHC VIII p.134,9–14).

[30] Offb 4,1 bedeutet einen Neuansatz, weil Johannes nun in himmlische Bereiche aufsteigt und dort Visionen sieht; die Erscheinungsgeschichte geht hier in eine Art Himmelsreise über.

3. Erscheinungen Jesu in den Osterkapiteln der kanonischen Evangelien

Die kanonischen Ostergeschichten von der Erscheinung Jesu zeigen manche Übereinstimmungen mit den bisher behandelten, aber auch einige Besonderheiten. Insgesamt gibt es acht Geschichten: Im MtEv findet sich die Begegnung Jesu mit zwei Marien (Mt 28,9f) und mit den elf Jüngern auf dem Berg (Mt 28,16–20). Auch das LkEv erzählt zwei Geschichten von den beiden Jüngern auf dem Weg nach Emmaus (Lk 24,13–35) und von der in Jerusalem versammelten Gruppe (Lk 24,36–51). Im JohEv gibt es die Geschichte von Maria Magdalena am Grab (Joh 20,14–18), eine Geschichte von der im Haus versammelten Gruppe der Jünger und Jüngerinnen (Joh 20,19–23) und eine weitere eine Woche später mit Anwesenheit des Thomas (Joh 20,26–29), und schließlich eine Erscheinung vor der Siebenergruppe am See Genezareth (Joh 21,1–14).

Keine dieser Geschichten spricht ausdrücklich davon, dass Jesus erscheint, indem ein entsprechender Begriff benutzt wird. Die Jünger und Jüngerinnen begegnen Jesus, sehen ihn, er kommt zu ihnen oder steht in ihrer Mitte.[31] Dieses Fehlen von typischem Vokabular unterscheidet diese Geschichten von den nichtkanonischen Geschichten, aber auch von den kurzen Erwähnungen von Erscheinungen ohne ausgeführte Erzählung in 1Kor 15,5–8 und Lk 24,34.[32] Auch überirdische Begleitumstände der Erscheinungen wie Licht oder ein besonderes Aussehen des Erschienenen werden nicht erwähnt.[33] Auf den ersten Blick sehen die Geschichten nicht sehr nach Erscheinungen aus – einige von ihnen könnten ohne weiteres als normale Zusammentreffen mit Jesus verstanden werden, wenn sie an einem anderen Ort im Evangelium platziert wären.[34] Ihre Bedeutung als Er-

---

[31] Nur in Joh 21,1.14 wird die Geschichte als Erscheinung zusammengefasst und dabei φανερόω verwendet, aber das ist nicht Teil der Erzählung.

[32] Vgl. J. ALSUP, The Post-Resurrection Appearance Stories of the Gospel Tradition, Stuttgart 1975, 60f.

[33] Nur in Joh 20,19.26 könnte das Auftreten Jesu trotz geschlossener Türen einen solchen überirdischen Begleitumstand bilden, aber dies ist kein Zeichen, das das Kommen Jesu eindeutig als eine himmlische Erscheinung charakterisiert. In einigen Geschichten gibt es zunächst Probleme, Jesus zu erkennen. Dies ist eine spezifische Variante der Identifikation des Erschienenen, der sich nicht selbst vorstellt, sondern sich langsam erkennen lässt. In der Emmausgeschichte und in der Geschichte von Maria Magdalena liegt die Pointe des Nichterkennens jedoch gerade im Bezug zur Passionsgeschichte, die Jünger und Jüngerinnen erkennen Jesus nicht nur einfach nicht, sondern halten ihn für tot, obwohl er mit ihnen redet.

[34] Dies unterscheidet die Geschichten in den Osterkapiteln z.B. von der Verklärung (Mk 9,2–8), die oft als eine vorverlegte Erscheinung des Auferstandenen angesehen wird, bei der der Erscheinungscharakter aber viel ausgeprägter ist. Diese Geschichte ist besonders komplex, weil es drei beteiligte Gruppen und eigentlich zwei Erscheinungsvorgänge

scheinungsgeschichten erhalten die Erzählungen wesentlich durch den Kontext der Passionsgeschichte, sie sind keine selbstständigen Geschichten, die in verschiedene Zusammenhänge eingebunden werden könnten.

Von den beteiligten Personen her gelten einige der neutestamentlichen Erscheinungsgeschichten der Gesamtgruppe, andere weniger bedeutenden Person wie den Emmausjüngern oder Maria Magdalena und der anderen Maria. Zentral wichtige Einzelpersonen wie Petrus oder Jakobus fehlen, begegnen aber sowohl in der Auflistung in 1Kor 15 als auch in nichtkanonischen Geschichten.[35]

Trotz dieser Unterschiede ist der Ablauf der neutestamentlichen und apokryphen Erscheinungen des Auferstandenen durchaus ähnlich. In seiner formgeschichtlichen Untersuchung der neutestamentlichen Geschichten erkennt Charles H. Dodd fünf charakteristische Elemente: Zuerst wird die Situation beschrieben, dann folgt die Erscheinung Jesu, sein Gruß und das Erkennen durch die Jünger und Jüngerinnen und schließlich ergeht ein Auftrag.[36] Diese Struktur passt sehr gut zu apokryphen Erscheinungen – sogar besser als zu manchen der kanonischen Geschichten. Dodds Modell zeigt also zunächst die nahe Verwandtschaft aller Geschichten.

Rudolf Bultmann bietet dagegen eine formgeschichtliche Analyse, mit der sich die Unterschiede genauer erfassen lassen. Er sieht zwei Hauptmotive in den Erscheinungsgeschichten: den Nachweis der Auferstehung Jesu durch seine Erscheinung und den Missionsauftrag.[37] Die Geschichten können das eine oder das andere Motiv in den Vordergrund stellen, aber bei

---

gibt: Einerseits wird Jesus vor den Augen der Jünger verwandelt (9,2f) und es ergeht eine Botschaft aus der Wolke an sie (9,7). Die Verwandlung kann gut als die Schaltstelle zum Wechsel der Ebene angesehen werden, die hier keine Erscheinung ist, weil Jesus schon vorher da ist; sie dient gut zur Vorbereitung der dann ergehenden himmlischen Botschaft. Andererseits erscheinen aber auch Elia und Mose (9,4) und bringen eine Botschaft, die in der Erzählung aber nicht ausgeführt wird, sondern nur von Jesus gehört. Die Geschichte ist also kein besonders typisches Beispiel einer Erscheinungsgeschichte, lässt sich aber als eine Variante verstehen. In der Form ist sie m.E. eher mit den Erscheinungen Jesu in Apg 9 oder Offb 1 verwandt als mit den Ostergeschichten.

[35] Die Erwähnung einer Erscheinung vor Petrus in Lk 24,34 ist keine ausgeführte Geschichte, sondern entspricht formal 1Kor 15,5, ist also ein Stück Formeltradition in einem narrativen Kontext. Unklar ist allerdings, ob Maria Magdalena als bedeutende Person angesehen wird. M.E. ist sie in Mt 28,9f deutlich eine Nebenfigur, während ihr in Joh 20,14–18 größeres Gewicht zukommt. Vgl. J. HARTENSTEIN, Mary Magdalene the Apostle: A Re-interpretation of Literary Traditions?, in: lectio difficilior 1/2007 (http://www.lectio.unibe.ch), 4.

[36] Vgl. C.H. DODD, Die Erscheinungen des auferstandenen Christus. Ein Essay zur Formkritik der Evangelien, in: P. HOFFMANN (Hg.), Zur neutestamentlichen Überlieferung von der Auferstehung Jesu, WdF 522, Darmstadt 1988, 297–330, hier 299f. Ähnlich auch ALSUP, Appearance Stories (s. Anm. 33), 190.211f.

[37] Vgl. R. BULTMANN, Die Geschichte der synoptischen Tradition, FRLANT 29, Göttingen [10]1995, 312f.

den meisten sind beide vorhanden, wobei der Missionsauftrag in der Botschaft, die der Erschienene übermittelt, steckt, während die Auferstehung Jesu durch seine Erscheinung bis zum Erkennen durch die Jüngerinnen und Jünger deutlich wird. Diese Betrachtung zeigt, dass die Erscheinung Jesu in den neutestamentlichen Ostergeschichten nicht nur die Botschaft vorbereitet, sondern eine eigene inhaltliche Bedeutung hat. Die Tatsache, dass Jesus nach seiner Kreuzigung wieder mit seinen Jüngern und Jüngerinnen zusammentrifft, erweist seine Auferweckung. Es ist deshalb möglich, eine Geschichte auf die Erscheinung zu beschränken: Die Emmausgeschichte endet, als Jesus erkannt wird, er übermittelt keinen Auftrag.

Im Gegensatz dazu setzen die nichtkanonischen Erscheinungsgeschichten ebenso wie die Erscheinung Jesu vor Paulus in Apg 9 oder vor Johannes in Offb 1 die Auferstehung Jesu schon voraus.[38] Dies wird wie in SJC und EpJac ausdrücklich am Beginn der Geschichte festgestellt oder kann aus dem Kontext erschlossen werden. Im ersten Teil der Geschichte muss der Erschienene identifiziert werden, bevor er dann seine Botschaft gibt, aber die Jünger und Jüngerinnen bzw. die Leser und Leserinnen erfahren nicht erst durch die Begegnung von der Auferweckung.[39] Bei den Angelophanien im Grab ist die Auferstehung Jesu dagegen Teil der Botschaft, die der Engel übermittelt. Die beiden Hauptteile Erscheinung und Botschaft haben also bei den Geschichten in den kanonischen Evangelien je eigenes Gewicht, die Erscheinung ist nicht in erster Linie die Schaltstelle, an der die Ebene gewechselt und so die Botschaft vorbereitet wird.

Sowohl Bultmann als auch Dodd gehen von den kanonischen Erscheinungsgeschichten aus, nichtkanonische Geschichten kommen bei Dodd nur am Rande als spätere und deutlich andersartige Entwicklung in den Blick.[40] Auch in meiner Sicht sind die nichtkanonischen Erscheinungsgeschichten später abgefasst und die meisten von ihnen setzen klar die kanonischen Evangelien voraus. Trotzdem scheint ihre Form typischen Erscheinungsgeschichten stärker zu entsprechen, insbesondere im Verhältnis zwischen Erscheinung und Botschaft. Oder von der anderen Seite betrachtet: Im Vergleich mit ihnen wird deutlich, wie untypisch die „Erscheinungen" Jesu in den Schlusskapiteln der kanonischen Evangelien eigentlich sind. Diese Geschichten haben einige besondere Charakteristika: Sie brau-

[38] Eine Ausnahme ist die EpAp, in der zwar die Botschaft stark ausgebaut ist, aber auch die Überzeugung von der Auferweckung bzw. von der Leiblichkeit des Erschienenen eine große Rolle spielt.

[39] Aus der Sicht des Paulus ist die Auferstehung Jesu in Apg 9 allerdings schon eine Neuigkeit, denn Paulus selbst hat vorher bestimmt nicht an sie geglaubt. Aber die Apg erzählt nicht aus der Perspektive des Paulus, und für die Leserinnen und Leser ist die Auferstehung Jesu längst klar – ein Motiv „Nachweis der Auferstehung" lässt sich in der Geschichte jedenfalls nicht erkennen.

[40] Vgl. DODD, Erscheinungen (s. Anm. 37), 312f.

chen den Kontext der Passionsgeschichte, um überhaupt als Erscheinungen erkennbar zu sein; sie betonen den übernatürlichen Charakter der Erscheinung nicht durch Begleitumstände; sie benutzen nicht einmal einschlägige Begrifflichkeit. In ihrem Kontext ist ihr eines Ziel, die Auferstehung Jesu zu zeigen, und zwar indem seine Erscheinung oder, besser gesagt, die Begegnung mit ihm erzählt wird. Die Botschaft, die Jesus dann übermittelt, gibt der Erscheinung ein weiteres Thema, meist den Auftrag zur Mission.

4. Entwicklungen

Welche Folgerungen lassen sich nun aus dem Befund ziehen? M.E. ist eine Entwicklungstendenz erkennbar, wenn die Erscheinungsgeschichten in früheren Schriften (den kanonischen Evangelien) mit denen in späteren verglichen werden: Die Geschichten werden unabhängiger von der Passionsgeschichte und nähern sich der allgemein üblichen Gestalt von Erscheinungsgeschichten an. Dazu gehört, dass die Botschaft größeres Gewicht bekommt, ohne dass ein inhaltlicher Bezug zur Erscheinung besteht, die zu ihrer Vorbereitung dient. Gleichzeitig wird auch die Erscheinung selbst typischer ausgestaltet, insbesondere durch die Verwendung von einschlägigen Begriffen für das Erscheinen, aber mitunter auch durch weitere Beschreibungen und überirdische Elemente. Auch die Bedeutung der beteiligten Personen nimmt zu. Schließlich begegnen die Geschichten als in sich geschlossene Größen in ganz unterschiedlichen Zusammenhängen.

Eine ähnliche Entwicklung wie zwischen kanonischen und nichtkanonischen Geschichten lässt sich auch in den Erscheinungsgeschichten in den neutestamentlichen Evangelien erkennen, wenn die Differenzen zwischen ihnen ausgewertet werden. Die Geschichte, die formal am meisten Ähnlichkeit mit apokryphen und allgemeinantiken Erscheinungsgeschichten hat, ist die Erscheinung Jesu vor den elf Jüngern in Galiläa (Mt 28,16–20).[41] Ihre Verbindung zur Passionsgeschichte ist relativ locker: Zeitlich ist der Abstand zu den Passionsereignissen unbestimmt und auch inhaltlich ist die Auferweckung Jesu kein Thema mehr, sondern durch die vorausgehenden Geschichten schon geklärt.[42] Die Erscheinung selbst ist äußerst

[41] Vgl. BECKER, Auferstehung (s. Anm. 2), 35f, der Gleiches allerdings auch in Mt 28,9f sieht.

[42] Allerdings kann der Zweifel einiger Jünger in 28,17 als Zweifel an der Auferstehung Jesu gedeutet werden. Die Erzählung geht auf diesen Punkt aber nicht weiter ein, und insgesamt scheint es mir plausibler, den Zweifel als eine Verzagtheit, wie sie sonst im MtEv als Kleinglaube bezeichnet wird, zu verstehen, die sich auf den folgenden Auftrag bezieht. So ausführlich L. OBERLINNER, „... sie zweifelten aber“ (Mt 28,17b): Eine Anmerkung zur matthäischen Ekklesiologie, in: Salz der Erde – Licht der Welt, FS Anton Vögtle, Stuttgart 1991, 375–400, hier 388f passim.

knapp geschildert, während der Botschaft alles Gewicht zukommt. Auch wenn der Erschienene nicht beschrieben wird und kein eindeutiger Begriff für das Erscheinen verwendet wird, so ist die Geschichte doch gut als eine himmlische Erscheinung verstehbar, die dem Auftrag Nachdruck verleiht.[43] Auch die beteiligten Personen sind eine zentrale Gruppe. Gerade diese Geschichte ist nun aller Wahrscheinlichkeit nach eine redaktionelle Bildung des MtEv auf der Basis von Mk 16,7; es gibt keinen Grund zur Annahme, dass sie schon vorher mündlich überliefert wurde.[44]

Auch bei anderen Geschichten zeigen sich gerade in einer ausführlichen und wichtigen Botschaft Jesu redaktionelle Tendenzen des jeweiligen Evangeliums. So wird in Lk 24,44–49 schon eine Überleitung zur Apg gestaltet und in allen drei Geschichten in Joh 20 gehören die Botschaften von Aufstieg und Aussendung und die Seligpreisung der nichtsehenden Glaubenden in einen größeren johanneischen Zusammenhang. Es lässt sich nicht mehr erkennen, wie die Worte Jesu in einer früheren eventuell mündlichen Fassung der Geschichte ausgesehen haben könnten. An ihrem jetzigen Ort im Evangelium haben die Geschichten mit den letzten Worten Jesu eine wesentliche Funktion als Abschluss der Gesamtschrift. Wenn also bei der Abfassung der Evangelien die Geschichten überarbeitet wurden, so dass die Botschaft Jesu bei seiner Erscheinung an Bedeutung gewinnt und inhaltlich unabhängig von der Erscheinungssituation und dem Kontext Passionsgeschichte wird, entspricht dies genau der Tendenz zur Ausprägung gerade der typischen Züge von Erscheinungsgeschichten.[45]

Nach meinen bisherigen Überlegungen zu den Entwicklungen zwischen den schriftlich erhaltenen Geschichten lassen sich jetzt vielleicht auch einige Vermutungen über die mündliche Phase der Überlieferung ziehen. Auch wenn sich die Gestalt nicht im einzelnen rekonstruieren lässt, gehe ich davon aus, dass Mt 28,9f; Lk 24,13–35 und Lk 24,36–53 zumindest jeweils in einem Grundbestand auf ältere Tradition zurückgehen, was spätere Überarbeitung nicht ausschließt.[46] Schon hier zeigt sich, dass die Ge-

---

[43] Die himmlische Vollmacht Jesu wird zwar nicht in der Erzählung deutlich gemacht, aber in seinen eigenen Worten zu Beginn der Botschaft behauptet (Mt 28,18).

[44] Vgl. J. LANGE, Das Erscheinen des Auferstandenen im Evangelium nach Matthäus. Eine traditions- und redaktionsgeschichtliche Untersuchung zu Mt 28,16–20, Würzburg 1973, 438 passim; BECKER, Auferstehung (s. Anm. 2), 38f. Vorsichtiger ist U. LUZ, Das Evangelium nach Matthäus: 4. Teilband Mt 26–28, EKK I/4, Düsseldorf u.a. 2002, 431f., der die sprachliche Eigenständigkeit sieht, aber eine zugrunde liegende Tradition auch nicht ausschließt.

[45] Vgl. auch BULTMANN, Geschichte (s. Anm. 38), 313f., zur Begründung des Missionsauftrags als spätere Entwicklung.

[46] Dass ich Mt 28,16–20 für eine Bildung des Evangelisten auf Basis von Mk 16,7 halte, habe ich oben schon erläutert. Das JohEv setzt m.E. die synoptischen Evangelien voraus, in ihm zeigt sich also eine weitere Bearbeitungsstufe, es eignet sich nicht zur Re-

schichten mit den weniger zentralen Personen ein Übergewicht haben – entsprechend einer Entwicklung, in der die Bedeutung der Zeuginnen und Zeugen gestärkt wird. Und es ist auch auffällig, dass zur Emmausgeschichte überhaupt keine Botschaft des Erschienenen gehört, sie endet, als Jesus erkannt wird.[47] Die Begegnung der beiden Frauen mit Jesus Mt 28,9f enthält eine Botschaft, die im Wesentlichen die Botschaft des Engels wiederholt. Dies gilt oft als Indiz für eine redaktionelle Bildung dieser Geschichte,[48] könnte aber auch ein Hinweis sein, dass eine mündliche Fassung keine oder keine nennenswerte Botschaft umfasste.

Insgesamt ist es plausibel, die Entwicklungstendenz von den kanonischen zu den apokryphen Geschichten auch in die andere Richtung, auf die mündliche Überlieferung hin, zu verlängern. Und dann wäre eine solche Vorstufe von „Erscheinungen" des Auferstandenen vielleicht noch untypischer als die ältesten schriftlich erhaltenen Geschichten: Keine Erscheinungsterminologie, Personen ohne große Bedeutung, vielleicht keine Botschaft und eine enge Bindung an die Passionsgeschichte, ohne die die Geschichten nicht verständlich sind. Es sind gerade die Geschichten, die sich nicht mit der Aufzählung in 1Kor 15 überschneiden, die so in den Mittelpunkt des Interesses rücken. Meine Überlegungen bestätigen Untersuchungen, dass es sich um ganz unterschiedliche Traditionen handelt.[49] M.E. lohnt es deshalb, auch den historischen Wert gerade dieser Ostergeschichten neu zu prüfen.

5. Ergebnis

Mein Blick auf die Erscheinungsgeschichten in apokryphen Schriften hat gezeigt, dass sie bei allen Unterschieden in Einzelheiten eine gemeinsame Struktur aufweisen, die auch insgesamt für antike Erscheinungsgeschichten typisch ist: Sie enthalten mit Erscheinung und Botschaft zwei Teile, wobei die Erscheinung mit allen Begleitumständen und der Klärung der Identität

---

konstruktion von Vorstufen. Diese Frage ist hier aber nicht von entscheidender Bedeutung, da Joh 20,14–18 eine Parallele zu Mt 28,9f und Joh 20,19–23 zu Lk 24,36–53 bildet, während Joh 20,26–29 wohl eine johanneische Ausgestaltung eines Einzelzuges dieser Geschichte ist. Auch bei Unabhängigkeit des JohEv würde sich die Zahl der mündlich überlieferten Geschichten nicht erweitern.

[47] Das ausführliche Weggespräch hat eine andere Funktion, da es die Passion deutet und dazu voraussetzt, dass die beiden noch nicht von der Auferstehung wissen. Formal ist es jedenfalls weit von einer Botschaft entfernt, die durch eine Erscheinung mit Wechsel der Ebene vorbereitet wird.

[48] So ALSUP, Post-Resurrection (s. Anm. 33), 109f; BECKER, Auferstehung (s. Anm. 2), 36–38; H. GRASS, Ostergeschehen und Osterberichte, Göttingen [2]1962, 27f.

[49] Vgl. ALSUP, Post-Resurrection (s. Anm. 33), 56–61.

des Erschienenen der Vorbereitung dient, indem sie eine neue Ebene einer übernatürlichen Wirklichkeit eröffnet, in der dann die Botschaft ergeht. Typisch ist weiterhin, dass es sich um in sich geschlossene Geschichten handelt, die in verschiedene Kontexte eingebunden sein können und die Auferstehung Jesu jeweils schon voraussetzen. Die Erscheinung gilt bedeutenden Personen bzw. der Jüngergruppe und wird sprachlich durch spezifische Begrifflichkeit und oft weitere Umstände eindeutig signalisiert.

Im Vergleich mit den apokryphen Erscheinungsgeschichten wird der eigene Charakter der Geschichten von der Begegnung mit Jesus in den Osterkapiteln der kanonischen Evangelien offensichtlich. Die „Erscheinung" Jesu ist dort nicht nur Vorbereitung für eine himmlische Botschaft, sondern zeigt durch die enge Anbindung an die Passionsgeschichte zunächst seine Auferstehung. Spezifische Begriffe für Erscheinen fehlen und es sind auch eher unbedeutende Personen beteiligt. Innerhalb der literarischen Zeugnisse ist eine Entwicklung erkennbar, in der sich die Ostergeschichten allmählich dem typischen Charakter von Erscheinungsgeschichten annähern – und ich vermute, dass die ältere mündliche Überlieferung noch deutlich untypischer war.

Über dieses konkrete Ergebnis hinaus hoffe ich gezeigt zu haben, dass apokryphe Evangelien nutzbringend in eine formgeschichtliche Untersuchung einbezogen werden können, und zwar auch dann, wenn sie – wie in diesem Fall – gerade nicht eine besonders ursprüngliche Gestalt von Geschichten bewahrt haben.

Qur'ānic Perspectives on Jesus' Death and the Apocryphal *Acts of John*

CORNELIA B. HORN

The Qur'ān reflects knowledge of main events in the life of Jesus of Nazareth. Central among these are his conception and birth, instructions he offered to his disciples, as well as his death, resurrection, and/or ascension.[1] Many of the details of these *topoi* of Jesus' life can be identified with the four Gospels of the New Testament, while other material is reflected only in apocryphal Christian sources, much of it found in texts dating to before the emergence of the Qur'ān. By the early seventh century, Jewish and Christian communities already laid claim to a substantial history of composing and rewriting para-Biblical stories. This realm of pseudepigraphical and apocryphal literature has to be considered in order to properly evaluate the Qur'ān's contribution to writing religious text. Despite a century of work tracing the source-critical aspects of the Qur'ān's Christian material, this aspect of comparative analysis is neither treated exhaustively nor often in a satisfactory manner.

In recent years, scholars of the textual history of the Qur'ān are dedicating renewed efforts at reconstructing the details of the transmission of the Qur'ānic text from oral witness to written artifact. Manuscript evidence for the early history of Qur'ān manuscripts is now available in high-quality reproductions.[2] This line of research is gaining momentum with the estab-

---

[1] For studies of the Qur'ānic portrayal of Jesus of Nazareth, see among others the works by N. Robinson, *Christ in Islam and Christianity* (Albany 1991); E.G. Parrinder, *Jesus in the Qur'ān* (London 1965 and 1976); H. Räisänen, *Das koranische Jesusbild: Ein Beitrag zur Theologie des Korans* (Helsinki 1971); M. Hayek, *Le Christ de l'Islam* (Paris 1959); and J. Robson, "Muhammadan Teaching about Jesus", *The Moslem World* 29 (1939), 37–54. Significant parts of the present research were carried out while I was a Fellow of Byzantine Studies at Dumbarton Oaks, Harvard University's Research Institute for Byzantine, Pre-Columbian, and Garden and Landscape Studies. The collegial atmosphere and intellectual exchange among the fellows and directors of study of all three areas inspired and supported my investigations into the relationship between what may appear to some to be marginal forms of Christian expression and the rise of a world-religion-in-the-making, i.e., Islam, in late antique times. It is with gratitude that I dedicate this article to my 2007–2008 colleagues at Dumbarton Oaks.

[2] See for example F. Déroche and S. Noja Noseda (eds.), *Les manuscrits du style hiǧāzī. 1, le manuscrit arabe 328 (a) de la Bibliothèque nationale de France* (Sources de la

lishment of multi-year research enterprises such as the *Corpus Coranicum* Project at the Freie Universität in Berlin, Germany, part of whose envisioned results come close to the creation of an *apparatus criticus* for all Qur'ānic manuscripts investigated. At some point in the future work like that might make it possible to establish a critical text of the Qur'ān.[3] A second component of the *Corpus Coranicum*'s proposed work in tandem with the text-criticism of the Qur'ān consists of writing a commentary on Islam's holy book as a document of late antique religious history.[4] This effort is based on the realization that the text of the Qur'ān did not emerge in a vacuum, but rather addressed an audience that included Jews, Christians, Manichaeans, adherents of native Arabian religions, and others. In order to understand the message of any text, including a sacred one, it is crucial for the interpreter to take into account the traditions, oral and written, with which the work's audience was familiar. As much as there is no reason to doubt that those segments of the Qur'ān's audience that consisted of Jews and Christians were familiar with Biblical narratives derived from both the Hebrew Bible and the New Testament, that repertoire of Biblical stories was not restricted to precise reproductions of such narratives as found in the canonical texts. The presentation of biblical figures in the Qur'ān generally serves to illustrate the authenticity of Muhammad's message, the eventual victory of his struggle and by extension that of the *ummah* against their enemies, and other historiographical and biographical aspects of Muhammad and the early Muslim community. Earlier Jewish

transmission manuscrite du texte coranique 1, Projet amari 1; Lesa, Italy and Paris 1998). Some of the results of new work on fragments of early Qur'ān manuscripts also appear in print. See for example A. Fedeli, "The Evidence of Variant Readings in Qur'ānic Manuscripts", in *Die dunklen Anfänge. Neue Forschungen zur Entstehung und frühen Geschichte des Islam* (ed. K.-H. Ohlig and G.-R. Puin; Berlin 2006), 298–316; H.-C. Graf von Bothmer, K.-H. Ohlig, and G.-R. Puin, "Neue Wege der Koranforschung", *magazin forschung (Universität des Saarlandes, Saarbrücken)* 1 (1999), 33–46; and G.-R. Puin, "Observations on Early Qur'an Manuscripts in San'a", in *The Qur'an as Text* (ed. St. Wild; Islamic Philosophy, Theology, and Science 27; Leiden, New York and Cologne 1996), 107–111.

[3] For some discussion of the cache of manuscripts underlying a significant part of the *Corpus Coranicum* project, see A. Higgins, "The Lost Archive", *The Wall Street Journal* (Online US Edition) (January 12, 2008), http://online.wsj.com/public/article_print/SB120008793352784631.html [accessed April 17, 2008]; and the response by M. Marx, "The lost archive, the myth of philology, and the study of the Qur'an" (dated January 16, 2008).

[4] For the *Corpus Coranicum* Project and its goals, see http://www.bbaw.de/bbaw/Forschung/Forschungsprojekte/Coran/de/Startseite (accessed April 17, 2008): "Das Vorhaben 'Corpus Coranicum' beinhaltet zwei weitgehend unbearbeitete Felder der Koranforschung: (1) die Dokumentation des Korantextes in seiner handschriftlichen und mündlichen Überlieferungsgestalt und (2) einen umfassenden Kommentar, der den Text im Rahmen seines historischen Entstehungskontextes auslegt."

and Christian stories were in part simply adopted to identify Islam with the monotheism of Jewish and Christian prophetic revelation, as well as to create an early portrait of the first Muslims that would be paradigmatic for later generations. Hence, these stories were not uncritically adopted wholesale, but were selectively edited. In the case of Jesus, the many different and in some ways conflicting traditions about his life, death, and resurrection provided a wide choice from which to cull a portrait that fit the identity of the Qur'ānic community. When research into the Qur'ān's own creative rewriting of ancient narratives demonstrates the ingenuity and liberty with which older stories were reworked, a necessary step in measuring the level of such creative production of compositions consists in discerning to what extent the new Qur'ānic narrative is similar to or different from creative rewritings of Jewish and Christian texts that had already been produced in those respective communities prior to the rise of Islam. By the early seventh century, Jewish and Christian communities already laid claim to a substantial history of composing and rewriting para-Biblical stories. This realm of pseudepigraphical and apocryphal literature has to be considered in order to properly evaluate the Qur'ān's contribution to writing religious text.

On other occasions I have addressed questions arising from the observation of parallels between apocryphal infancy gospels, especially the *Protevangelium of James* and the *Infancy Gospel of Thomas*, and early Islamic literature, particularly the Qur'ān.[5] In conjunction with those articles, also the present work forms part of a larger research project that aims at filling a *lacuna* in history-of-religions scholarship concerning the early Islamic period. What is still lacking is a systematic treatment of the question of the relationship between Christian apocryphal traditions and the formation of the Qur'ān, with regard to both its text and early interpretations thereof.

As it is situated within the larger mosaic of the study of Sacred Scriptures and their interdependencies in the Ancient Middle East, this article focuses on the examination of aspects of possible connections between Christian apocryphal and Qur'ānic representations of Jesus' death. In its first segment, this contribution reexamines the Qur'ān's portrayal of scenes related to the end of Jesus' life. The second part treats the presenta-

[5] See C.B. Horn, "Einige Schnittstellen handschriftlicher Überlieferungen christlicher syrischer Apokryphen und ihre Erträge für das Verständnis ausgewählter Traditionen im Qur'ān", in *Akten des Symposiums der Deutschsprachigen Syrologen (Berlin 2006)* (ed. R. Voigt; forthcoming); EAD., "Mary between Bible and Qur'ān: Soundings into the Transmission and Reception History of the *Protoevangelium of James* on the Basis of Selected Literary Sources in Coptic and Copto-Arabic and of Art Historical Evidence Pertaining to Egypt", *Islam and Muslim-Christian Relations* 18.4 (2007), 509–538; and EAD., "Intersections: The Reception History of the *Protoevangelium of James* in Sources from the Christian East and in the Qur'ān", *Apocrypha* 17 (2006), 113–150.

tion of this theme in selected apocryphal literature, specifically the apocryphal *Acts of John*. This article argues that from the realm of available late antique parallels to the Qur'ān's account of the constellations of factors at the time of Christ's death, the narrative offered in the apocryphal *Acts of John* provides the closest parallel text.

Although it is a relevant issue, this article cannot achieve a detailed discussion of the definition of apocryphal literature and of the relationship between Gnostic and apocryphal texts.[6] For the immediate purposes of the present work a shorthand characterization has to suffice. I consider as apocryphal those texts and traditions that deal with figures or events known from the canonical Biblical text, here in particular the New Testament, and that contain details or larger passages, which supply information that is not found in the canonical material.[7]

The Qur'ān and Jesus' Death

The multiple traditions concerning Jesus at the background of the formation of the Qur'ān are clearly illustrated in the presentation of his death. The Qur'ān offers an ambiguous perspective on Jesus' passion. At times it seems to acknowledge that Jesus died, and at others it appears to cast doubt upon the reality of this event. Aspects of the Qur'ān's presentation of the theme reflect different periods in the chronology of individual sū-

---

[6] A fuller study of the question at stake here has to examine the relevance of scenes of Jesus' crucifixion found in the apocryphal *Acts of John* compared with scenes in the *Gospel of Peter*, the *Apocalypse of Peter* from Nag Hammadi, the *First Apocalypse of James* also from Nag Hammadi, the *Letter of Peter to Philip*, the *Second Treatise of the Great Seth*, and their impact on Islamic literature and exegesis.

[7] For the discussion of what ought to be considered as characteristics of apocryphal literature see for example S.J. Patterson, "Apocrypha: New Testament Apocrypha", in *The Anchor Bible Dictionary* (vol. 1; New York 1992), 294–297; S.C. Mimouni, "Le concept d'apocryphité dans le christianisme ancien et médiéval. Réflexions en guise d'introduction", in *Apocryphité. Histoire d'un concept transversal aux religions du Livre. En hommage à Pierre Geoltrain* (ed. S.C. Mimouni; BEHE.SR 113; Turnhout 2002), 1–21; T. Nicklas, "Semiotik – Intertextualität – Apokryphität: Eine Annäherung an den Begriff 'christlicher Apokryphen'", *Apocrypha* 17 (2006), 55–78; and P. Piovanelli, "Qu'est-ce qu'un 'écrit apocryphe chrétien', et comment ça marche? Quelques suggestions pour une herméneutique apocryphe", in *Pierre Geoltrain ou Comment 'Faire l'histoire' des religions? Le chantier des 'origines', les méthodes du doute et la conversation contemporaine entre les disciplines* (ed. S.C. Mimouni and I. Ullern-Weité; BEHE.SR 128. Histoire et prosopographie de la section des sciences religieuses 2; Turnhout 2006), 173–186.

ras.[8] In verses that witness to the earlier periods of the revelatory process, it is beyond question for the text that Jesus died and was resurrected. In *Sūrat Maryam* [19]:31–34, a section which is dated to the Meccan period, the newborn Jesus miraculously speaks in the cradle, saying among other wondrous things that Allah pronounced peace upon the day of his birth, the day of his death (*wayawma 'amūtu*), and the day of his resurrection (*yawma 'ub'athu ḥayyan*) (v. 34). Scholars have recognized this verse as evidence that the Qur'ān did or at least could conceive of the possibility of Jesus' death.[9] Other sections in sūras that are traditionally assigned to the Medinan period also contain passages that can be understood as referencing the possibility of Jesus' death. *Sūrat al-'Imrān* [3]:55 has God say "O Jesus! Behold! I am gathering you (*mutawaffīka*) and causing you to ascend to Me (*rāfi'uka 'ilayya*)"; *Sūrat al-Mā'idah* [5]:117 has Jesus declare "I was a witness of them while I dwelt among them, and when You took me (*falammā tawaffaytanī*) You were the watcher over them." In both instances the verbal forms derived from the root *w-f-y*, in line with Qur'ānic usage of these words in other instances, can be understood "as indicating the death of Jesus."[10]

Although elements of thought that consider the possibility of Jesus' death are detectable also during the Medinan period, it is in material from the stage of the community's history when the newly established group of Muhammad's followers had settled in Medina that strong statements of a

[8] Important work of establishing a relative chronology of sūras to one another as well as of discerning earlier and later portions within individual sūras was achieved with the publication of Th. Nöldeke, *Geschichte des Qorāns. Erster Teil: Über den Ursprung des Qorāns* (2nd ed. rev. by F. Schwally; Leipzig 1909; repr. Hildesheim 1961), 58–234. Also W. Rudolph, *Die Abhängigkeit des Qorans von Judentum und Christentum* (Stuttgart 1922), 82, observed relevant differences between sūras from the Meccan and the Medinan periods. See also W.M. Watt, *Bell's Introduction to the Qur'an* (Islamic Surveys 8; Edinburgh 1970), ch. 7.

[9] J. Henninger, *Spuren christlicher Glaubenswahrheiten im Koran* (Schriftenreihe der Neuen Zeitschrift für Missionswissenschaft / Les Cahiers de la Nouvelle Revue de science missionaire 10; Schöneck/Beckenried [Schweiz] 1951), 25. The contributions collected in this work first appeared as a series of articles in *Neue Zeitschrift für Missionswissenschaft / Nouvelle Revue de science missionaire* 1.2 (1945), 135–140; 1.4 (1945), 304–314; 2.2 (1946), 109–122; 3.2 (1947), 128–140; 3.4 (1947), 290–301; 4.2 (1948), 129–141; 4.4 (1948), 284–293; 5.2 (1949), 127–140; 5.4 (1949), 290–300; 6.3 (1950), 207–217; and 6.4 (1950), 284–297.

[10] See the discussion of the usage of these verbal forms in B.T. Lawson, "The Crucifixion of Jesus in the Qur'ān and Qur'ānic Commentary. A Historical Survey", *The Bulletin of the Henry Martyn Institute of Islamic Studies* 10.2 (1991), 34–62, here 38. For a consideration of the interpretation of verses related to the death of Jesus in the Qur'ān in more recent Islamic interpretation, see also B.T. Lawson, "The Crucifixion of Jesus in the Qur'ān and Qur'ānic Commentary. A Historical Survey. Part II", *The Bulletin of the Henry Martyn Institute of Islamic Studies* 10.3 (1991), 6–40.

rejection of claims to knowledge of details concerning Jesus' death appear.[11] In *Sūrat al-Nisā'* [4] from the Medinan period, the Qur'ān seems to question whether Jesus did undergo death, or whether he was not rather taken up into heaven by God, thus by-passing death altogether. The crucial text in *Sūrat al-Nisā'* also reveals a context of dispute between different parties and their respective perspectives concerning Jesus' death.

The most explicit and developed treatment of questions relating to Jesus' death and crucifixion in the Qur'ān occurs at *Sūrat al-Nisā'* [4]:157–158. This passage is embedded in the context of a list of criticisms raised against *ahlu lkitāb*, the People of the Book, an expression used here as a reference to the Jews, but possibly taking into account a larger group of people. At this instance, the Qur'ān rejects the claim that the *ahlu lkitāb* killed or crucified "Christ Jesus, the son of Maryam, the Apostle of God" (*Sūrat al-Nisā'* [4]:157).[12] The wording of verse 157 places particular emphasis on this negation: "they did not kill him (*mā qatalūhu*)," "they did not crucify him (*wamā ṣalabūhu*)," and at the end of the verse "they did not really kill him (*wa ma qatalūhu yaqiynan*)."[13] It may not be an exaggeration to see in the whole of this verse a formulation that explicitly rejected the Christian claim, based on the witness of the New Testament and other early Christian texts, that Jesus was crucified and died.

Sūrat al-Nisā' [4]:158 states that "God raised him [i.e., Jesus] up to himself (*bal rafa'ahu llāhu 'ilayhi*)." For the text Jesus was no longer perceived as being among the living on earth. Yet the act through which Jesus was transported from the world here below into the hereafter was not that of any human being, killing or even crucifying him. Rather, what removed Jesus from this earth was God's action, viewed as a positive undertaking.[14]

The reader of *Sūrat al-Nisā'* [4]:153–162 notes that one of the accusations of crimes of the Jews which the text formulates was that of claiming

---

[11] John of Damascus, *De haeresibus* 100/101 (ed. and tr. Migne, Patrologia Graeca 94.765–766; ed. and tr. D.J. Sahas, *John of Damascus on Islam. The 'Heresy of the Ismaelites'* [Leiden 1972], 132–135), may be the earliest Christian reaction to the Qur'ān's seeming denial of Jesus' crucifixion.

[12] For some discussion of the names and epithets which the Qur'ān used to designate Jesus, see M. Hayek, "L'origine des termes Isa, al-Masih (Jesus-Christ) dans le Coran", *L'Orient Chrétien* 7 (1962), 223–254 and 365–382; J.A. Bellamy, "Textual Criticism of the Koran", *JAOS* 121.1 (2001), 1–6, here 6; J.A. Bellamy, "A Further Note on 'Īsā", *JAOS* 122.3 (2002), 587–588; and Parrinder, *Jesus in the Qur'an* (n. 1), 22–54.

[13] See also H. Grégoire, "Mahomet et le Monophysisme", in *Mélanges Charles Diehl. Premier Volume: Histoire* (Études sur l'histoire et sur l'art de Byzance; Paris 1930), 107–119, here 114.

[14] For an insightful and sensitive reading of the Qur'ān and early Islamic interpretation on Jesus' death see the work by L. Stanislaus, "Jesus' Crucifixion, Death and Elevation in Islam: An Effort at Comprehension", *Journal of the Henry Martyn Institute* 17.2 (1998), 59–74.

responsibility for the death of Jesus. Yet it is precisely this death, which verse 157 expressly rejects. Compare this to the verses of *Sūrat al-'Imrān* [3]:54–57, in which the Jews as at least a subgroup of the People of the Book also are associated with the end of Jesus' life on earth. To be sure, *Sūrat al-Nisā'* [4]:157 stands in a line of negative criticism of the Jews for challenging their leaders to have God send down to them written revelations and laws for worshipping idols, for transgressing against the covenant and the laws of God, for rejecting God's signs, blaspheming, rejecting faith, and uttering false charges against Jesus' mother Mary. Given the voluminous *adversus Iudaeos* tradition within Christianity,[15] sources can readily be found that charge the Jews with having killed not only Jesus as a human person, but even God present in and through Jesus. As the earliest statement to that effect one may point to Melito of Sardis' formulation in *Peri Pascha*.[16] Vitriolic anti-Jewish polemic can be read in numerous other early Christian writers as well, including influential late antique authors from the Syriac-speaking realm like Ephraem, whose poetry and prose were available in the milieu into which Islam expanded early on.[17] The

---

[15] See for example the discussions in S. Krauss, "The Jews in the Works of the Church Fathers", *JQR* 5.1 (1892), 122–157, 6.1 (1893), 82–99, and 6.2 (1894), 225–261; R. Radford Ruether, "The *Adversus Judaeos* Tradition in the Church Fathers: The Exegesis of Christian Anti-Judaism", in *Essential Papers on Judaism and Christianity in Conflict: From Late Antiquity to the Reformation* (ed. J. Cohen; New York 1991), 174–189; M. Simon, "Christian Anti-Semitism", in *ibid.*, 131–173; and M.S. Taylor, *Anti-Judaism and the Early Christian Identity: A Critique of Scholarly Consensus* (New York 1995). For *adversus Judaeos* sentiments in the broader cultural context in the ancient world, see for example P. Schäfer, *Judeophobia: Attitudes toward the Jews in the Ancient World* (Cambridge, Mass. 1997).

[16] Melito of Sardis, *Peri Pascha* 96 (ed. O. Perler, *Méliton de Sardes. Sur la Pâque et Fragments*; Sources Chrétiennes 123 [Paris 1966], 116, l. 735); and E. Werner, "Melito of Sardes: The First Poet of Deicide", *HUCA* 37 (1966), 191–210. For discussions of the development of earlier sentiments, see for example J.D. Crossan, *Who Killed Jesus? Exposing the Roots of Anti-Semitism in the Gospel Story of the Death of Jesus* (New York 1995).

[17] On Ephraem's anti-Jewish polemic, see for example C.B. Horn, "The Holy Spirit and the Jews: Ephraem the Syrian on the Rending of the Temple Veil", in progress; C.C. Shepardson, *Anti-Judaism and Christian Orthodoxy: Ephrem's Hymns in Fourth-Century Syria* (Patristic Monographs Series; Washington, DC 2008); D. Cerbelaud, "L'anti-judaïsme dans les hymnes *de Pascha* d'Éphrem le Syrien", *ParOr* 20 (1995), 201–207; P.J. Botha, "The Poetic Face of Rhetoric: Ephrem's Polemics against the Jews and Heretics in *Contra Haereses* XXV", *Acta Patristica et Byzantina* 2 (1991), 16–36; K. McVey, "The Anti-Judaic Polemic of Ephrem Syrus' Hymns on the Nativity", in *Of Scribes and Scrolls: Studies on the Hebrew Bible, Intertestamental Judaism, and Christian Origins* (ed. H.W. Attridge, J.J. Collins, and Th.H. Tobin; New York 1990), 229–240; and A.P. Hayman, "The Image of the Jew in the Syriac Anti-Jewish Polemical Literature", in *"To See Ourselves as Others See Us": Christians, Jews, "Others" in Late Antiquity* (ed. J. Neusner, E.S. Frerichs, and C. McCracken-Flesher; Chico, Calif. 1985), 423–441. For

works of apocryphal Christian writers also were among such highly critical anti-Jewish voices.[18]

It has been noted that early Christian liturgical prayers that were observed on Good Friday and that primarily consisted of the recitation of long lists of accusations against the Jews for having sinned against God's commands and expectations in various ways, are rather close in structure to the arrangement of the content of *Sūrat al-Nisā'* [4]:153–162.[19] For the Qur'ān the problem was not that the Jews might have killed Jesus. Rather, the text accused them of falsely having claimed to have committed an act, which from the Qur'ān's perspective either did not really happen or did not take place in the manner in which they claimed it did.

---

discussions of the connection between ideas developed in the works of Ephraem the Syrian and other late antique Syriac writers and the Qur'ān see for example T. Andrae, *Der Ursprung des Islams und das Christentum* (KHÅ 1923–1925; Uppsala and Stockholm 1926). Yet given that at times (e.g., pp. 80 [174], 89 [183], or 103 [197]) Andrae relied on texts which modern scholarship no longer ascribes to Ephraem, a reexamination and reevaluation of the material and its transmission would be necessary to better determine the proposed relationship.

[18] For literature on Jews in Christian apocryphal works, see for example J.D. Shannon, *"'For Good Work Do They Wish to Kill Him?': Narrative Critique of the Acts of Pilate"* (M.A. thesis, University of Missouri; Columbia, Missouri 2006); T. Nicklas, "Die 'Juden' im Petrusevangelium (PCair 10759): ein Testfall", *NTS* 47.2 (2001), 206–221; J.R. Mueller, "Anti-Judaism in the New Testament Apocrypha. A Preliminary Survey", in *Anti-Semitism and Early Christianity. Issues of Polemic and Faith* (ed. C.A. Evans and D.A. Hagner; Minneapolis 1993), 253–268; B. Dehandschutter, "Anti-Judaism in the Apocrypha", *StPat* 19 (1989), 345–350; and M. Lowe, "*Ioudaioi* of the Apocrypha: A Fresh Approach to the Gospel of James, Pseudo-Thomas, Peter, and Nicodemus", *NT* 23 (1981), 56–90. A fuller study of this topic is in preparation.

[19] See H. Busse, "*Bāb Ḥiṭṭa*: Qur'ān 2:58 and the Entry into Jerusalem", *Jerusalem Studies in Arabic and Islam* 22 (1998), 1–17, here 15–16. Busse noted that the commandment "*udkhulū l-bāba sujjadan*, as mentioned in the Qur'ān" has "roots [that] l[ie] in the Biblical story of the building of the sanctuary in the desert told in Exodus chaps. 25–31, and in the psalms of the liturgy of the opening of the gate, particularly Psalm 24. In the Qur'ān, it is included in a list of commandments and divine favors to which the Israelites answered with disobedience and rebellion." Busse then pointed out the existence of "a literary genre which developed very early in Christian liturgy in the East, called *Improperia*, the enumeration of God's complaints about His disobedient and ungrateful people. The *Improperia* were recited on Good Friday. Their starting point is the exodus of the children of Israel from Egypt; their apex the crucifixion of Jesus." Even if one does not have to suggest "a direct relation of the Qur'ān to the *Improperia*, it is interesting to note" with Busse "that in Sūra 4:153–159, which includes the order to enter through the gate submissively, the enumeration of God's favors followed by the misdeeds of the Israelites is exactly the same." For further discussion of the *Improperia*, see also A. Baumstark, "Die Idiomela der byzantinischen Karfreitagshoren in syrischer Überlieferung", *OrChr* 25/26 (1928–1929), 232–247.

Several reconstructions of the intentions behind the passage in *Sūrat al-Nisā'* [4]:153–162 are possible. The Qur'ān may have responded with its perspective to accusations of the Jews as murderers of Christ, as frequently raised by Christians during the centuries. Alternatively, it took issue with possible confessions on the part of the Jews themselves of having killed Jesus, perhaps a less likely proposition. It also is conceivable that the Qur'ān incorporated a perspective that can be found as an accusation in Christian texts, like for example the *Gospel of Peter*, namely that the Jews, once having accomplished putting Jesus to death, then insisted on demonstrating that he had really died while at the same time trying to counteract, negate, and ideally eliminate any signs of his resurrection for fear of not being proven wrong and guilty of having killed an innocent victim or of not being convicted for lack of faith in the face of the miracle of the resurrection.[20] Independent of what one might discern as the intention of the text, *Sūrat al-Nisā'* [4]:153–162 censured in an indirect manner the Jews' rejection of Jesus as a prophet. Verse 159 formulated that everyone "must believe in him [i.e., likely Jesus] before his [i.e., the believer's] death." If the death envisioned here was not the believer's death, this comment would constitute "a transformation of the two-part soteriology of Paul and the Synoptic gospels."[21] Irrespective of when precisely that envisioned death of Jesus occurred, which all the while in this verse as well is at least seen as a possibility, on the Day of Judgment the Jews were to be charged not with killing Jesus, but with their lack of belief in him. This then was the overall concern of verses 157–158, not so much with whether or not Jesus died, but rather with the Jews' refusal of accepting him as the Messiah. Such a reading of the text is well in line with early Islamic interpretation of the passage at the hands of the *mufassirūna*.[22]

Sūrat al-Nisā' [4]:157 expanded upon its statement that the People of the Book, including the Jews, did not crucify Jesus and it offered a short phrase, "*walākin šubbiha lahum*," as an explanation for why the Jews might erroneously have believed they had done so. Throughout the range of discussions of what precisely the Qur'ān has to say on the question of Jesus' death, this particular, brief statement in verse 157 is recognized as the crux of the matter of the Qur'ān's perspective on Jesus' death.[23] How

---

[20] See for example *Gospel of Peter* VI.23, VII.25, VIII.28–30, IX.47–48, X.38, and XII.50.52 (ed. and tr. M.G. Mara, *Évangile de Pierre*; Sources Chrétiennes 201 [Paris 2006], 50–55 and 58–63). For a discussion of the characterization of the Jews in the *Gospel of Peter* see Nicklas, "'Juden' im Petrusevangelium" (n. 18).

[21] R.R. Phenix Jr., oral communication.

[22] See also Lawson, "The Crucifixion of Jesus in the Qur'ān", Part I (n. 10), 37.

[23] See for example Stanislaus, "Jesus' Crucifixion" (n. 14), 61–63; Lawson, "The Crucifixion of Jesus in the Qur'ān", Part I (n. 10), 39–41; Parrinder, *Jesus in the Qur'ān* (n. 1), 108. See also M. Borrmans, "Muslims and the Mystery of the Cross: Rejection or

precisely to understand this phrase has given rise to numerous explanations, translations, and interpretations.

The phrase *walākin shubbiha lahum* has been rendered in translations into Western languages with emphasis on different connotations of the range of meaning of the words in question. One can find renditions like "but he was counterfeited for them" (Bell), "but [the matter] was made dubious to them" (Maulvi Muhammad Ali), "it appeared to them such" or "it appeared so unto them" (Massignon, Yusuf 'Ali, Stansilaus), "it only seemed to them they did so" ('Abduh), "he was made a resemblance unto them" (Din), or "only a likeness of that was shown to them" (Arberry).[24] The earliest Christian readings of the passage understood that the Qur'ān here spoke of the Jews only having crucified Jesus' shadow (ἐσταύρωσαν τὴν σκιὰν αὐτοῦ).[25] A translation that would try to stay closest to the literal rendering of the phrase could offer "and/but he/it was made similar for/to them." Also, it is well known that the step from translating a phrase to interpreting its meaning is open to much variation and diversity. Some exegetes understand the phrase to indicate, in the context of *Sūrat al-Nisā'* [4]:157, that "they did not crucify him, but someone else [who looked] like him."[26] The underlying interpretation that someone else was substituted for Jesus before the crucifixion without the onlookers having noticed that exchange can safely be labeled as the one interpretation that most frequently is presented in the traditional exegesis of this verse.[27] The range of figures who are named as substitutes for Jesus extends across the representative sample of Simon of Cyrene, Judas, Pilate, the apostle Peter, one of Jesus' disciples, one of the thirteen disciples named Serjes, a Jew, another Jew named Naṭyânûs, the guard whom the Jews had placed over Jesus, a criminal, or one of Jesus' enemies.[28] Although not all of the various identifica-

---

Incomprehension?", *Encounter: Documents for Muslim-Christian Understanding*, vol. 2, n. 25 (1976), 1–13, here 1–4; J. Jomier, *Bible et Coran* (Paris 1959), 115–118; Hayek, *Le Christ de l'Islam* (n. 1), 217–218, see also 230–239; Robson, "Muhammadan Teaching about Jesus" (n. 1), 40; M. Din, "The Crucifixion in the Koran", *The Moslem World* 14 (1924), 23–29; E.E. Elder, "The Crucifixion in the Koran", *The Moslem World* 13 (1923), 242–258.

[24] Stanislaus, "Jesus' Crucifixion" (n. 14), 61–62; Din, "Crucifixion in the Koran" (n. 23), 29; and Lawson, "The Crucifixion of Jesus in the Qur'ān," Part I (n. 10), 34.

[25] John of Damascus, *De haeresibus* 100/101 (ed. and tr. Migne, *Patrologia Graeca* 94.765B; ed. and tr. Sahas, *John of Damascus on Islam*, 78 and 132–133).

[26] See for example Henninger, *Spuren christlicher Glaubenswahrheiten* (n. 9), 26.

[27] See especially the documentation offered in the discussions of Elder, "Crucifixion in the Koran" (n. 23), 245–251; and Lawson, "The Crucifixion of Jesus in the Qur'ān", Part I (n. 10), 45–52.

[28] See Elder, "Crucifixion in the Koran" (n. 23), 245; Parrinder, *Jesus in the Qur'ān* (n. 1), 111–112; Borrmans, "Muslims and the Mystery of the Cross" (n. 23), 3–4; Stanis-

tions of Jesus' substitute that are advanced in Islamic exegesis can be matched in Christian texts, there is a remarkable parallel between this Islamic tradition and earlier Gnostic speculations.[29]

Another line of interpretation of the phrase *walākin šubbiha lahum* examines whether some level of awareness of specific Christian doctrinal disputes concerning more contemporary aspects of Christological reflections as they surfaced in fifth- through seventh-century mainline Christendom might have formed the backdrop for the Qur'ān's choice of this clause. In the context of a study of the relationship between Muhammad and anti-Chalcedonian thought, Henri Grégoire offered as an alternative interpretation the suggestion to render the phrase *walākin šubbiha lahum* by "the matter was made unclear / uncertain to them."[30] Grégoire took the Arabic expression as a close equivalent of either of the Greek phrases "ἐφαντάσθη αὐτοῖς" or "ἔδοξεν αὐτοῖς", both to be translated as "it seemed / appeared to them." For him, this expression could reveal either an underlying docetic sentiment, or alternatively an extreme form of the so-called "Monophysite" perspective.[31] Grégoire's interpretation found its followers who understood the phrase to mean "it merely seemed to them so" and who more specifically adopted his explanation that the context for the Qur'ān's comment at this instance consisted of an awareness of or even a certain level of familiarity with ideas promoted by a group known as Aphthartodocetists.[32] These Christians were adherents of a distinctive teaching within the fold of the anti-Chalcedonian movement. At times they were known as Phantasiasts or Julianists, the later name being derived from one of their best-known representatives, Julian of Halicarnassus.[33] Whereas a comprehensive study of Aphthartodocetic thought and its history remains a

---

laus, "Jesus' Crucifixion" (n. 14), 63–64; and Lawson, "The Crucifixion of Jesus in the Qur'ān," Part I (n. 10), 45–48 and 50–52.

[29] A detailed analysis of this parallel is reserved for a separate study.

[30] Grégoire, "Mahomet et le Monophysisme" (n. 13), 114: "la chose fut rendue incertaine ou obscure pour eux."

[31] Ibid. 114 and 116. On matters of terminology for various participants in the Christological controversies of the fifth- and subsequent centuries, see S.P. Brock, "The 'Nestorian' Church: a lamentable misnomer", in *The Church of the East: Life and Thought* (ed. J.F. Coakley and K. Parry; BJRL 78.3; Manchester 1996), 23–35, reprinted in S. Brock, *Fire from Heaven. Studies in Syriac Theology and Liturgy* (Variorum Collected Studies 863; Aldershot, England, and Burlington, Vermont 2006), 1–14, here 4, favors the term "Henophysites."

[32] For some considerations of the teachings of Aphthartodocetists and those labelled as such within the context of doctrinal debates concerning Christology, see for example A. Grillmeier, with the assistance of Th. Hainthaler, *Jesus der Christus im Glauben der Kirche* (vol. 2/2: *Die Kirche von Konstantinopel im 6. Jahrhundert*) (Freiburg i. Br., Basel, and Vienna 1989), 83–116, 224–241, and 489–495.

[33] Henninger, *Spuren christlicher Glaubenswahrheiten* (n. 9), 28–29.

desideratum,[34] scholars who refer to it tend to characterize it as a form of docetism of the variant that Christ's human body did not share all aspects of the human body, but was aphthartos, "incorruptible".

More recent studies of the relationship between Christianity and Islam in the ancient Middle East favor Grégoire's model when considering a possible doctrinal Christian background for *Sūrat al-Nisā'* [4]:157. Employing both great diligence and ingenuity when studying the connections between Christianity in South Arabia, especially the regions of Najrān, and the areas of Mecca and Medina, Irfan Shahîd considered the influence of Aphthartodocetic thought as a subtext for the "Qur'ānic rejection of Christ's divinity" in the context of references to Jesus' death.[35] When evaluating such a proposition, it is important to distinguish between what Aphthartodocetists themselves thought and how some of their opponents represented their teachings. When looked at carefully, one has to acknowledge the lack of internal evidence from Aphthartodocetic sources regarding their denial of Jesus' death.

The identification of Aphthartodocetism as the immediate context for the Qur'ān's statement "*walākin šubbiha lahum*" in *Sūrat al-Nisā'* [4]:157 as well as the same verse's comment that "they did not really kill him" is rendered less likely if one examines carefully the precise nature of Aphthartodocetic claims about Jesus' death. Assumptions that Aphthartodocetists saw Christ's body as not really having been subject to death cannot be substantiated in the texts that are available as sources for the thought of the adherents of that movement. Such a claim rather is to be found in texts written about them by their opponents.[36] In his *Chronicle*, for example, Pseudo-Zachariah Rhetor includes a record of an exchange of letters between Severus of Antioch and Julian of Halicarnassus, which shows how Severus, seen through the lens of Zachariah, ascribed such a claim to them.[37] Pseudo-Zachariah's witness is of interest as a document for the

[34] The only monograph-length treatment on related matters is R. Draguet, *Julien d' Halicarnasse et sa controverse avec Sévère d'Antioche sur l'incorruptibilité du corps du Christ. Étude d'histoire littéraire et doctrinale suivie des Fragments dogmatiques de Julien (texte syriaque et traduction grecque)* (Louvain 1924).

[35] I. Shahîd, "Islam and *Oriens Christianus*: Makka 610–622 AD," in *The Encounter of Eastern Christianity with Early Islam* (ed. E. Grypeou, M. Swanson, and D. Thomas, The History of Christian-Muslim Relations 5; Leiden and Boston 2006), 9–31, here 19.

[36] For this observation see also J. Jarry, "La Sourate IV et les soi-disant origines Julianistes de l'Islam," *PIFAO. Annales Islamologiques* IX (Cairo 1970), 1–7, here 1: "les julianistes n'étaient phantasiastes que pour leur adversaires."

[37] Pseudo-Zachariah Rhetor, *Chronicle* 9.9–13 (ed. and tr. E.W. Brooks, *Historia ecclesiastica Zachariae Rhetori vulgo adscripta*, CSCO 84 and 88, Scriptores Syri 3/6 [Paris 1921; and Lovanii 1929], 101–113 [Syriac] & 70–78 [Latin]; tr. F.J. Hamilton and E.W. Brooks, *The Syriac Chronicle, Known as That of Zachariah of Mitylene* [London 1899], 232–244; a new translation and commentary by R.R. Phenix, G. Greatrex, and C.

spread of Severus' misrepresentation of Julian's ideas. Yet in their genuine writings Aphthartodocetists expressed quite clearly that they thought Christ really died.[38] He voluntarily accepted suffering and thus could be described as ἀπαθὴς ἐν τοῖς πάθεσιν and ἀθάνατος ἐν τῷ θανάτῳ. In fragments of Julian of Halicarnassus' works, for example, one can read that "in his flesh, which he [took] from us and which is like ours, the Lord truly suffered and died."[39] The Aphthartodocetists' teaching of Christ's bodily incorruption did not have to entail that he was not subject to death, and, if one judges the views of this group on the merits of their own writings, for all intents and purposes, they do not seem to have proclaimed so.

A further problem consists in the relative dearth of evidence for the spread of Aphthartodocetists into Southern Arabia at the time. While anti-Chalcedonian Christianity had spread widely in the areas around the Red Sea and to the South,[40] evidence for the presence of the followers of Julian of Halicarnass and the influence of his teachings in that region is restricted to the witness of the twelfth-century *Chronicle* of Michael the Syrian, which had identified a certain Sergius and Moses as sixth-century Julianist bishops of Najrān.[41] As a non-Julianist, anti-Chalcedonian supporter of Severus of Antioch, Michael the Syrian cannot be regarded as an impartial

---

Horn is in preparation for Translated Texts for Historians, University of Liverpool Press). See also Michael the Syrian, *Chronicle*, bk. 9, ch. 31 (ed. and tr. J.-B. Chabot, *Chronique de Michel le Syrien, Patriarche Jacobite d'Antioche [1166–1199]*, Tome [II] [Fascicule II] [Paris 1902], 321, col. 2 [Syriac] & 265 [French]).

[38] See Draguet, *Julien d'Halicarnasse* (n. 34), 138; and D.G.K. Taylor, "The Christology of the Syriac Psalm Commentary (AD 541/2) of Daniel of Ṣalaḥ and the Phantasiast Controversy," *StPatr* 35 (2001), 508–515, here 511.

[39] Julian of Halicarnassus, *Fragmenta Dogmatica* 132 (ed. Draguet, *Julien d'Halicarnasse*, 38* [Syriac] and 73* [Greek])

[40] See Shahîd, "Islam and *Oriens Christianus*" (n. 35), 19; for some discussion of specific groups at the origins of this expansion of anti-Chalcedonian groups into this area, see also C. Horn, "A Chapter in the Pre-History of the Christological Controversies in Arabic: Readings from the Works of John Rufus," in *Actes du 7ᵉ Congrès International des Études Arabes Chrétiennes (Sayyidat al-Bir, septembre 2004), Tome 1*, ed. S. Khalil Samir, S.J. (CEDRAC), *ParOr* 30 (2005), 133–156.

[41] See Michael the Syrian, *Chronicle*, bk. 9, ch. 31 (ed. and tr. Chabot, *Chronique de Michel le Syrien*, vol. 2, 320, col. 3 [Syriac] & 264, col. 1 [French]): "Le malheureux Eutropius vase inutile, ajouta à sa malice et ordonna dis évêques qu'il envoya de tous côtés, pour être les avocats de l'hérésie des Phantasiastes. L'un d'eux descendit à Ḥirta de Beit Na'aman, et dans le pays des Ḥimyarites. Il s'appelait Sergius. Il avait été un ascète et avait reçu la tonsure: il devint un vase inutile; il induisit en erreur et pervertit ces contrées. Ils ordonna des prêtres, et après avoir passé trois ans dans le pays des Ḥimyarites, il établit à sa place comme évêque un certain Moïse; lui-même mourut, dans le pays des Ḥimyarites." See also Shahîd, "Islam and *Oriens Christianus*" (n. 35), 19, fn. 37. For a discussion of the value of the witness of Michael the Syrian on the spread of Aphthartodocetists to Arabia, see also Jarry, "La Sourate IV" (n. 36), 4.

witness. Much as the label "Manichaean," also that of "Aphthartodocetist" was a convenient tag to affix to inconvenient opponents. It is known and well documented that in the sixth century Julianists were present in Egypt as well as in northern Syria and in the areas reaching into the Caucasus. As a general assumption it is certainly possible to think of them as also having been on site in Najrān in Southern Arabia. Yet earlier than Michael the Syrian's *Chronicle*, there is no further data available for their presumed presence there.

The preceding discussion has laid out in some detail why the hypothesis of Aphthartodocetic ideas as a potential doctrinal Christian subtext for *Sūrat al-Nisā'* [4]:157 is not strong enough to suffice as an explanation. This examination is based on the vantage points of the Aphthartodocetic writings concerning Christ's death and the availability of data about the spread of adherents of this movement on the Southern Arabian peninsula in the seventh and eighth centuries. The inquiry into possible conversation partners or texts promoted by them, whom and which the Qur'ān may have engaged with its comments on Jesus' death in the verse in question however does not have to be abandoned. Instead, it is possible to introduce other perspectives represented in Christian texts that offer a possible parallel to *Sūrat al Nisā'* [4]:157 159 and thus an opportunity to understand perhaps more precisely which positions the Qur'ān chose to side with, adopt with modifications, or respond to.

Parallel Accounts in Apocryphal Literature

In his study of parallels between Biblical narratives and the Qur'ān, Heinrich Speyer also evaluated apocryphal texts as potential contributors to the world of ideas with which Qur'ānic passages stand in parallel. His discussion of material from the apocryphal Acts of Apostles, however, only dealt with a small number of references.[42] Yet already Theodor Nöldeke and Friedrich Schwally were convinced that "the main source, from which Muhammad derived his knowledge, was to a lesser extent the Bible and to a greater extent extra-canonical, liturgical, and dogmatic writ-

[42] H. Speyer, *Die biblischen Erzählungen im Qur'an* (Hildesheim 1931, repr. 1971), 59, 62, and 331. Recent years have seen a significant increase of studies of figures known both to the Bible and the Qur'ān. See for example J.C. Reeves, "Some explorations of the intertwining of Bible and Qur'ān," in *Bible and Qur'ān: Essays in Scriptural Intertextuality* (ed. J.C. Reeves, SBL Symposium Series 24; Atlanta 2003), 43–60; or M.O. Opeloye, "The Account of Joseph (Yusuf [A.S.]) in the Qur'ān and the Bible," *Hamdard Islamicus* 18 (1995), 85–96

ings."[43] Developing a line of inquiry into apocryphal material that was suggested in 1923 by E.E. Elder and in 2006 by Stéphane Ruspoli,[44] the present article proposes that other passages from the apocryphal Acts of Apostles, specifically from the *Acts of John*, can fruitfully be compared to the Qur'ān's account of events pertaining to the end of Jesus' life.

The Apocryphal John and Muhammad: Sharing Revelations about Jesus on the Cross?

The *Acts of John* constitutes a text that has not been preserved as a whole. The text was condemned at the Second Council of Nicaea in 787 and given its subsequently restricted transmission, one section of this long apocryphal narrative, *Acts of John* 87–105, the portion that is of particular relevance for the present discussion, has come down to modern times as attested only in two sources.[45] Of these two witnesses, only Austrian National Library, MS Vienna hist. gr. 63, fols. 51v–55v, dated to 1319, is complete.[46] Nevertheless, that the passage in question here was not the result of composition only in the year 787 or subsequent to it emerges from the fact that at that time the *Acts of John* already had been circulating widely enough for the council fathers to have become aware of it and to have felt the need to examine it and express judgment upon it. To what precise point in time or even century prior to 787 one can date the existence or spread of knowledge of the relevant section of the *Acts of John*, a passage also known as the *Gospel of the Acts of John*, is another question. The answer to that question depends on details of the reception history of the *Acts of John* in the wider milieu of religious life in the Middle and Near East in antiquity as well as upon one's perception of the integrity and overall structure of the original composition of the *Acts of John*.[47] The

---

[43] Nöldeke and Schwally, *Geschichte des Qorāns* (n. 8), 8.

[44] Elder, "Crucifixion in the Koran" (n. 23), 255; and St. Ruspoli, "Quelques réflexions sur le 'docétisme' dans la Christologie ancienne et l'Islam," in *Pierre Geoltrain ou Comment 'Faire l'histoire' des religions? Le chantier des 'origines', les méthodes du doute et la conversation contemporaine entre les disciplines* (ed. S.C. Mimouni and I. Ullern-Weité, BEHE.SR 128. Histoire et prosopographie de la section des sciences religieuses 2; Turnhout 2006), 247–260.

[45] *Acts of John* 87–105 (ed. and tr. E. Junod and J.-D. Kaestli, *Acta Iohannis. Praefatio – Textus*, CC.Series Apocryphorum 1 [Turnhout 1983], 188–217).

[46] See Junod and Kaestli, *Acta Iohannis. Praefatio – Textus*, 26.

[47] For a study of the spread of the apocryphal *Acts of John* in the ancient world, see E. Junod and J.-D. Kaestli, *L'histoire des Actes Apocryphes des Apôtres du IIIe au IXe siècle: Le cas des Actes de Jean* (Cahiers de la RThPh 7; Genève, Lausanne, and Neuchâtel 1982).

whole range of aspects relevant for the study of this passage in conjunction with the Qur'ānic material cannot be examined in the present context. Yet if this article is able to lay out the close proximity between the passage in the *Acts of John* and *Sūrat al-Nisā'* [4]:157–159, it will have reached an immediate goal.

As far as one can tell from the extant evidence, for the ancient copyist of the *Acts of John*, the focus of the section at *Acts of John* 87–105 was on Christ's revelation of "the mystery of the Cross (τοῦ σταυροῦ τὸ μυστήριον)."[48] This 19-paragraph-long section has been regarded as the theologically most relevant, interesting, and revealing passage of the whole text. Yet much about this passage is debated, including its precise placement within the narrative as a whole. In their critical reconstruction of the text, Eric Junod and Jean-Daniel Kaestli have treated the passage as the description of an event taking place during John's stay at Ephesus, following the Andronicus and Drusiana cycle up to Andronicus's conversion.[49]

As the passage focuses the reader's attention on the "mystery of the Cross," themes related to suffering occur frequently and in variation. In the first part of the text, the section known as Hymn of the Dance, the reader is left with a sense of being drawn into a reenactment of the Last Supper.[50] *Acts of John* 94–96 features the well-known hymn sung in accompaniment of a ritual dance between Jesus and a crown of his twelve disciples. Prominent in the latter portion of the hymn is language that is related to the theme of suffering, on the one hand announcing suffering "the Lord" "has to endure," on the other hand creating an atmosphere of tension concerning the reality of suffering by suggesting repeatedly that knowledge of suffering also entails its absence. In two consecutive verses the hymn restates twice that the one who knows suffering possesses the state of "non-suffering."[51]

---

[48] *Acts of John* title preceding 87 (ed. and tr. Junod and Kaestli, *Acta Iohannis. Praefatio – Textus*, 188–189).

[49] *Ibid.* 87–105 (ed. and tr. Junod and Kaestli, *Acta Iohannis. Praefatio –Textus*, 188; see also the discussion on pp. 86–91).

[50] See also M. Pulver, "Jesu Reigen und Kreuzigung nach den Johannesakten", *Eranos-Jahrbuch* 9 (1942), 141–177; see also *Acta Iohannis. Textus alii – Commentarius, Indices* (ed. and tr. E. Junod and J.-D. Kaestli; CC.Series Apocryphorum 2; Turnhout 1983), 595–596.

[51] *Acts of John* 96 (ed. and tr. Junod and Kaestli, *Acta Iohannis. Praefatio – Textus*, 204–205, here 205, l. 14): εἰ τὸ πάσχειν ᾔδεις, τὸ μὴ παθεῖν ἂν εἶχες; and *ibid.* (pp. 206–207, here 207, l. 15): τὸ παθεῖν σύγγνωθι καὶ τὸ μὴ παθεῖν ἕξεις.

In *Acts of John* 97 the apostle John, who is not able to endure seeing Jesus suffer, is said to have fled to a cave on the Mount of Olives.[52] Subsequently that site offers a location and venue for a revelation of Jesus that is imparted exclusively to John. The revelation itself focuses on the explanation of the true nature of the scene of suffering on the cross that played in front of the people's eyes down below in Jerusalem.[53] Instead of insisting that what had happened on the wood of the cross down below was real, "the Lord" showed John a cross of light surrounded by a great crowd, which had no single form (μίαν μορφὴν μὴ ἔχοντα).[54] On the cross itself John saw "one form and a same likeness (μορφὴ μία καὶ ἰδέα ὁμοία),"[55] a phrase that suggests that whatever John saw was in the form and likeness of "the Lord." Yet John saw Jesus directly standing at the foot of the Cross. The formulation of "a form and a same likeness" as description of the figure on the cross of light that John became enabled to perceive is a detail that is crucial for the argument of the present discussion.

In the relevant passage, the *Acts of John* offers a sequence of comments that present a perception of the cruelties of the crucifixion as accessible to the eyes of the members of the crowds on the grounds in Jerusalem. The "Lord" made known to John that indeed for those below he was being crucified, "τῷ κάτω ὄχλῳ ἐν Ἱεροσολύμοις σταυροῦμαι."[56] Although the text does not give a more specific name to "the crowd below in Jerusalem" at this instance, an earlier comment in the context of introducing the Hymn of the Dance had spoken of "the Lord" going to be taken hold of by "the lawless Jews who were under the reign of the lawless serpent (ὑπὸ τῶν ἀνόμων καὶ ὑπὸ ἀνόμου ὄφεως νομοθετουμένων Ἰουδαίων)."[57] The reader is left to conclude that the Jews were not only the ones into whose hands "the Lord" was given over, but that they also were at least among those who brought him to the Cross. This passage does not involve a self-claim on the part of the Jews of having killed Jesus. Nevertheless it participates in a set of apocryphal as well as other early Christian, patristic texts that recast the

---

[52] *Ibid.* 97 (ed. and tr. Junod and Kaestli, *Acta Iohannis. Praefatio – Textus*, 206–209). See there especially p. 207, ll. 4–5: ἀλλ' ἔφυγον εἰς τὸ ὄρος; and p. 209, l. 7: ἐν μέσῳ τοῦ σπηλαίου.

[53] *Ibid.* 97 (ed. and tr. Junod and Kaestli, *Acta Iohannis. Praefatio – Textus*, 206–209).

[54] *Ibid.* 98 (ed. and tr. Junod and Kaestli, *Acta Iohannis. Praefatio – Textus*, 208–209; especially p. 209, l. 2).

[55] *Ibid.* 98 (ed. and tr. Junod and Kaestli, *Acta Iohannis. Praefatio – Textus*, 208–209; especially p. 209, l. 3).

[56] *Ibid.* 97 (ed. and tr. Junod and Kaestli, *Acta Iohannis. Praefatio – Textus*, 208–209; especially p. 209, ll. 8–9).

[57] *Ibid.* 94 (ed. and tr. Junod and Kaestli, *Acta Iohannis. Praefatio – Textus*, 198–199; especially p. 199, ll. 1–2).

storyline of Jesus' crucifixion in a way that implicates the Jews in Jesus' death, beyond what Matthew and Luke's passion accounts constructed when those texts accused the Jews and implied them as responsible for Jesus' death on the Cross.[58]

The text from the end of *Acts of John* 97 through the beginning of paragraph 98 treats the reality of the Lord's crucifixion as a problem, all the while suggesting that to some people who were present, or rather to most, it seemed that the crucifixion actually had taken place. Yet what had occurred was that "a form and unique likeness" of "the Lord" had remained on the cross, while the "real" Lord had already left, perhaps had never been on the cross. In addition to seeing the appearance of the cross of light with the "unique form and same likeness" on it, John also received a verbal explanation through the voice of the Lord, telling him among other things that he, i.e., the Lord, was not, or no longer, the one on the Cross (οὐδὲ ἐγώ εἰμι ὁ ἐπὶ τοῦ σταυροῦ).[59] Moreover, the "Lord" also explained to John that "he was named, what he was not, while not being what he was for the many (ὃ οὐκ εἰμὶ ἐνομίσθην, μὴ ὢν ὃ εἰμὶ τοῖς πολλοῖς)," and that "what they say about [him] [wa]s vile and unworthy of [him] (ἀλλ' ὅ τι με ἐροῦσιν ταπεινὸν καὶ οὐκ ἐμοῦ ἄξιον)."[60]

This detailed account, the presentation of which can be observed in this section of the *Acts of John* at which the author manages to establish connections of different elements with one another, is in close parallel to *Sūrat al-Nisā'* [4]:157. In that Qur'ānic passage the statement is presented that those who claimed to have killed Christ Jesus in fact "did not crucify him." Yet the Qur'ān does not formulate that no crucifixion had taken place. It merely says that they, i.e., the People of the Book, including the Jews, did not put Jesus to death through crucifixion. This leaves open the possibility that someone or something, not fully identical with Jesus, for instance "a unique form and same likeness" to Jesus, or perhaps only a part of Jesus, for instance his human nature, could have suffered on the Cross. The verbal form *šubbiha*, "was made similar," corresponds rather well with the nominal phrase ἰδέα ὁμοία, "same likeness," of the description found in *Acts of John* 98. In appearance, in both accounts Jesus seemed to be dying on the Cross. Yet knowledge that this was not really the case, but only was perceived as such was exclusive knowledge, was knowledge only accessi-

---

[58] For a recent discussion of how specific texts of apocryphal Acts, for example, the *Acts of Pilate*, engage in this process of implicating the Jews in responsibility for the crucifixion, see also Shannon, "For Good Work Do They Wish to Kill Him?" (n. 18).

[59] *Acts of John* 99 (ed. and tr. Junod and Kaestli, *Acta Iohannis. Praefatio – Textus*, 211, l. 4).

[60] *Ibid.* 99 (ed. and tr. Junod and Kaestli, *Acta Iohannis. Praefatio – Textus*, 211, ll. 5–6 and 6–7).

ble to a single, selected individual, John in the one case and Muhammad as the recipient of the Qur'ānic revelation in the other, a person destined to hear the words of explanation.[61] A sentence like "nothing therefore of the things they want to say about me have I suffered (οὐδὲν οὖν ὧν μέλλουσιν λέγειν περὶ ἐμοῦ ἔπαθον),"[62] which the Lord speaks to John in the context of explaining the true nature of the mystery of the cross can easily be seen as representing at the same time a summary statement of what is unpacked a little more fully in *Sūrat al-Nisā'* [4]:157, where the Qur'ān argues that what the People of the Book say about Jesus and his being killed or crucified is not true. As the concluding statement of *Sūrat al-Nisā'* [4]:157 again emphatically formulates that "they did not really kill him," so does this sentence in the *Acts of John* emphasize the same negation regarding Jesus.

Sūrat al-Nisā' [4]:157 seems to have had in view not only one monolithic group of members of the Jewish community, who formulated clear statements about their having killed Christ Jesus. The same verse also proposes that there were "those who differ in this (*wa' inna alladhīna 'khtalafū fīhi*)" and thus had a variant perspective of these events. Yet of these people the Qur'ān does not approve either. Instead it places them in contrast to the sure knowledge of its own claim and characterizes them as people who are "full of doubts, with no knowledge" in this matter. Instead, all they have to follow is conjecture (*'illa 'ttibā'a lẓanni*). It is noteworthy that the *Acts of John* likewise presents a rather developed statement regarding differing opinions circulating about the reality or non-reality of what had occurred to "the Lord" on the Cross. In close proximity to the emphatically formulated denial of sufferings of Jesus, *Acts of John* 101 has "the Lord" bring to John's awareness that he heard contradictory claims that the Lord "is suffering and has not suffered, is not suffering and has suffered, is being pierced and was not beaten, was being hung up and was not hung up, that blood flowed down from him and did not flow."[63] The indecisiveness and indeterminacy of people speaking in such a manner is evident. The Qur'ān's representation of the second group, namely of those people who were full of doubts, matches up rather well with the respective characterization offered at *Acts of John* 101. Like *Sūrat al-Nisā'* [4]:157

---

[61] *Ibid.* 98 (ed. and tr. Junod and Kaestli, *Acta Iohannis. Praefatio – Textus*, 209, l. 8). That neither John nor Muhammad have to be construed as historical persons for the logic of this narrative construction to work is understood in the present discussion.

[62] *Ibid.* 101 (ed. and tr. Junod and Kaestli, *Acta Iohannis. Praefatio – Textus*, 213, l. 1).

[63] *Ibid.* 101 (ed. and tr. Junod and Kaestli, *Acta Iohannis. Praefatio—Textus*, 212–213, especially p. 213, ll. 6–9): ἀκούεις με παθόντα καὶ οὐκ ἔπαθον, μὴ παθόντα καὶ ἔπαθον· νυγέντα καὶ οὐκ ἐπλήγην· κρεμασθέντα καὶ οὐκ ἐκρεμάσθην· αἷμα ἐξ ἐμοῦ ῥεῦσαν καὶ οὐκ ἔρευσεν.

with its emphatically concluding affirmation that "they did not really kill him," also *Acts of John* 101 follows up on its presentation of the seemingly contradictory opinions about the Lord's fate with the emphatic summary statement that "in a word, what those say about me, these things I have not suffered, but what they do not say, those things I have undergone."[64] The match of the first part of this statement with the Qur'ānic approach to the question is evident. The portion that suggests as alternative that Jesus did undergo suffering in another form, which in *Acts of John* 101 subsequently is presented as being centered on ideas concerning the Logos, the Qur'ān does not share. Yet given the Qur'ān's interest in identifying 'Īsā ibn Mariam, that is, Jesus the son of Mary, as the word from God (*Sūrat al-'Imrān* [3]:45; *Sūrat al-Nisā'* [4]:171), the Logos-centered explanations of *Acts of John* 101 at least could have functioned as an element that attracted Muhammad's attention also at this instance.

Sūrat al-Nisā' [4]:158 follows upon the rejection of the claim that the People of the Book, including the Jews, had killed Jesus. By way of contrast, it professes instead that "God [had] raised him up unto Himself." In similar manner also *Acts of John* 102 condenses the revelation to John and concludes with a final item, namely that the Lord "was raised up without anyone of the crowd seeing him [ascend] (ἀνελήφθη μηδενὸς αὐτὸν θεασαμένου τῶν ὄχλων)."[65] A potential background for such a comment that for all practical purposes abbreviates the more customary references to a passion, resurrection, and ascension narrative into a statement concerning the death and ascension only may perhaps be sought in developments evidenced in Quartodeciman circles and their liturgical practices.[66] Whether such a context exerted influence in both the milieu of the origins of the apocryphal *Acts of John* and that of the Qur'ān separately or whether one might think rather of a derivative line of influence cannot be decided here.

The preceding detailed discussion has established a significant density of parallels between the Qur'ānic account related to claims of Jesus' death in *Sūrat al-Nisā'* [4] and the section from the apocryphal *Acts of John* at chapters 87–105,[67] that is relevant to that text's depiction of the scene of

---

[64] *Ibid.* 101 (ed. and tr. Junod and Kaestli, *Acta Iohannis. Praefatio—Textus*, 212–213, especially p. 213, ll. 9–11): καὶ ἁπλῶς ἃ ἐκεῖνοι λέγουσιν περὶ ἐμοῦ ταῦτα μὴ ἐσχηκέναι, ἃ δὲ μὴ λέγουσιν ἐκεῖνα πεπονθέναι.

[65] *Ibid.* 102 (ed. and tr. Junod and Kaestli, *Acta Iohannis. Praefatio – Textus*, 214–215, especially p. 215, ll. 2–3).

[66] For comments on Quartodeciman practices and their reflections in Syriac Christianity, see for example G.A.M. Rouwhorst, "Das manichaeische Bemafest und das Passafest der syrischen Christen", *VigChr* 35 (1981), 397–411, here 398–399.

[67] For a detailed examination of parallels between the *Gospel of Peter* and the *Gospel of the Acts of John* see I. Czachesz, "The Gospel of Peter and the Apocryphal Acts of the Apostles. Using Cognitive Science to Reconstruct Gospel Traditions", in *Das Evangeli-*

Christ's crucifixion, death, and ascension. No similarly dense and clear line of parallels emerges from any comparison between the Qur'ānic material and any other Christian apocryphal text, or any other Christian or Gnostic text that could be identified thus far.

Parallels from Apocryphal Docetic and Gnostic Texts from Nag Hammadi

The perspective which apocryphal *Acts of John* 97–102 offers on the exclusively spiritual nature of Jesus' crucifixion and its allegorical character is not unique for ancient Christian literature. An investigation which pursues as its goal to determine not only which parallels in these early Christian texts are closest to the text of the Qur'ān, but which also desires to explore the wider context of exegetical thought on the Qur'ānic text on that matter, has to take careful account of more remotely related parallels as well.

Especially in texts preserved at Nag Hammadi one finds a related emphasis on argumentation that calls into doubt the reality of Christ's death on the Cross. Jean-Marc Prieur has examined the motif of a seemingly living Cross or a Cross of light in the texts that have come to light at Nag Hammadi, as well as in apocryphal sources more widely.[68] Prieur observed a widespread tendency among authors of Christian texts to avoid emphasizing the reality of the scandal of the Cross and Christ's death at the Cross and instead to substitute the spiritual and symbolic dimensions of both the Cross and the crucifixion.[69] From among the texts that Prieur had examined parallels to the narrative that is offered in the Qur'ān at *Sūrat al-Nisā'* [4]:157–158 are found in the apocryphal *Gospel of Peter*, the so-called gnostic *Apocalypse of Peter* from Nag Hammadi, the *First Apocalypse of James* from Nag Hammadi, the *Letter of Peter to Philip*, and the *Second Treatise of the Great Seth*. Yet in all these cases, the parallels occur only in selected motifs and do not add up to a continuous parallel also on the level of the structure of the text. Moreover, although several scholars have pointed out that various so-called Gnostic texts contain parallels to the Qur'ānic story of Jesus' death in *Sūrat al-Nisā'* [4], in fact these Gnostic texts rather offer parallels to how later Islamic exegesis interpreted

um nach Petrus. Text, Kontexte, Intertexte (ed. T.J. Kraus and T. Nicklas; TU 158; Berlin and New York 2007), 245–261, here 245–247.

[68] J.-M. Prieur, "La croix vivante dans la littérature chrétienne du IIe siècle", *RHPhR* 79.4 (1999), 435–444; and id., *La croix chez les Pères (du IIe au début du IVe siècle)* (Cahiers de Biblia Patristica 8; Strasbourg 2006), 11–19, 39–43, 67–87, and 109–134.

[69] Prieur, "La croix vivante" (n. 68), 435 and 444.

the text of the Qur'ān, and not to the Qur'ān itself.[70] The same holds true for alleged parallels to views of Gnostic teachers, for example, Basilides, to whose religious systems access is preserved only in references to and summaries of their works in patristic authors. As one of the results of the research of this study it emerges rather clearly that the apocryphal *Acts of John*, and within them the so-called *Gospel of the Acts of John*, is the single text that shows distinct and sustained parallels to *Sūra Nisā'* [4]:157–158 on the level of narrative themes, diction and phraseology, as well as in the structure or sequence of the arrangement of themes.

That a parallel might exist between the *Acts of John* and *Sūrat al-Nisā'* [4] was at least intimated previously in the works of Elder and Ruspoli. Yet neither one of these authors undertook to carefully compare and thus establish the evidence for such a parallel. A follow-up question that arises from these results is how one might explain the possibility of such a close relationship, even down to the level of specific formulation, between the Medinan sūra's presentation at verses 157 to 158 and the passage in *Acts of John*. One proposition could be that the reception history of the *Acts of John* in the diverse religious milieu of the late antique and early medieval Mediterranean world and to the East of it contains the answer. The precise contours of details of that answer, however, have to remain as a story for another day.

[70] See for example the data collected in Elder, "Crucifixion in the Koran" (n. 23); and Lawson, "The Crucifixion of Jesus in the Qur'ān" (n. 10).

„Wahrlich, es ist Gottes Sohn, der geboren wurde aus der Jungfrau ...“

Passions- und Ostermotive in der *Dormitio Mariae* des Ps-Johannes

THOMAS R. KARMANN

Einleitung: Maria – ein verheißenes Kind?

Ein Leser, der die neutestamentlichen Kindheitsgeschichten kennt, wird erstaunt sein, wenn er erstmals das *Protevangelium Jacobi* aufschlägt.[1] Er wird in diesem Text nämlich mehrere Berührungen zwischen dem Geschick Jesu und dem Marias feststellen. Zwei Beispiele seien kurz vorgestellt: Das apokryphe Kindheitsevangelium enthält, wie das Neue Testament in Bezug auf Jesus, zwei Ankündigungen der Geburt Mariens. Wie Maria im Lukasevangelium so wird im *Protevangelium* die Geburt Marias ihrer Mutter Anna von einem Engel verkündet.[2] Wie Josef im Matthäusevangelium, so erhält auch der Vater Marias im *Protevangelium* eine Verheißung.[3] Außerdem geschieht die Empfängnis Mariens wie die ihres Soh-

---

[1] Zum *Protevangelium Jacobi* vgl. u.a. É. DE STRYCKER, La forme la plus ancienne du Protévangile de Jacques. Recherches sur le papyrus Bodmer 5 avec une édition critique du texte grec et une traduction annotée, SHG 33, Brüssel 1961. H.R. SMID, Protevangelium Jacobi. A Commentary, ANT 1, Assen 1965. O. CULLMANN, Kindheitsevangelien, in: W. SCHNEEMELCHER (Hg.), Neutestamentliche Apokryphen in deutscher Übersetzung I: Evangelien, Tübingen [6]1990, 334–349 (330–372). G. SCHNEIDER (Hg.), Apokryphe Kindheitsevangelien, FC 18, Freiburg i.Br. u.a. 1995, 21–34. Das Kindheitsevangelium ist wahrscheinlich in der zweiten Hälfte des 2. Jahrhunderts entstanden und somit wohl der älteste Text, in welchem Maria im Mittelpunkt des Interesses steht.

[2] Vgl. *Protev.* 4,1 (FC 18, 102). Lk 1,26–38. Auf sprachliche Berührungen zwischen der Verheißung Marias an Anna bzw. Joachim und biblischen Geburtsorakeln kann hier nicht näher eingegangen werden. Allein durch die Gattung Geburtsankündigung wird der Leser aber dazu veranlasst, den Text in Beziehung zu vergleichbaren Kindesverheißungen der Bibel, also auch zu Lk 1,26–38 zu setzen.

[3] Vgl. *Protev.* 4,2 (FC 18, 102). Mt 1,18–25. Zur Kindheitsgeschichte Marias im *Protevangelium* vgl. allgemein u.a. SMID, Protevangelium Jacobi (s. Anm. 1), 25–69. O. EHLEN, Leitbilder und romanhafte Züge in apokryphen Evangelientexten. Untersuchungen zur Motivik und Erzählstruktur (*anhand des Protevangelium Jacobi und der Acta Pilati Graec. B*), AwK 9, Stuttgart 2004, 102–126.

nes auf wunderbare Weise. Anna ist zwar nicht wie ihre Tochter eine Jungfrau, aber stattdessen unfruchtbar. Und in gewisser Weise scheint auch die Empfängnis Marias ohne Zutun eines Mannes zu geschehen.[4] Ein Leser des *Protevangeliums*, der das Neue Testament kennt, wird das Schicksal Marias mit dem ihres Sohnes in Beziehung setzen: Die Mutter Jesu erscheint in diesem apokryphen Text wie ihr Sohn im Neuen Testament als ein verheißenes Kind.[5]

Vor diesem Hintergrund stellt sich die Frage, ob es solche Parallelen auch in Bezug auf das Lebensende Marias gibt. Haben Texte, die den Tod Mariens schildern, Berührungen mit den neutestamentlichen Berichten über den Tod und die Auferstehung Jesu? Dieser Frage soll hier exemplarisch anhand der *Dormitio Mariae* des Ps-Johannes nachgegangen werden. Zunächst soll dieser Text aber im Rahmen der sog. *Transitus-Mariae*-Literatur kurz vorgestellt werden. Traditionell werden die Texte, die den Tod Mariens thematisieren, in der deutschsprachigen Forschung nicht zu den neutestamentlichen Apokryphen gerechnet, sondern als hagiographische Schriften angesehen. Abschließend wird deshalb ganz knapp noch der Frage nachgegangen, ob diese Zuordnung nicht zu einseitig ist.

Hintergrund: Die *Transitus-Mariae*-Literatur und die *Dormitio Mariae* des Ps-Johannes

Das Ende Marias ist im frühen Christentum wohl lange Zeit kaum ein Thema gewesen, noch in der zweiten Hälfte des vierten Jahrhunderts äußert sich Epiphanius von Salamis folgendermaßen hierzu: „Ihr Lebensende kennt nämlich niemand … ."[6] Dies scheint sich im Verlauf des fünften

---

[4] Vgl. *Protev.* 1–4 (FC 18, 96–104). In 4,4 (104) könnte ein Hinweis darauf vorliegen, dass auch Maria selbst in gewisser Weise „jungfräulich" empfangen wurde. Dort sagt Anna nämlich zu ihrem Mann, dem sie nach 40tägiger Abwesenheit begegnet: … ἰδοὺ ἐν γαστρὶ ἔληφα. In 4,2 (102) hatte der Engel Joachim bereits dasselbe mitgeteilt. Unmittelbar zuvor hatte der Engel Anna in 4,1 (102) aber folgende Botschaft überbracht: Συλλήμψεις καὶ γεννήσεις, … . Evtl. klingt hier bereits eine Vorstellung an, die später als *immaculata conceptio* interpretiert wurde.

[5] Es werden im *Protevangelium* „Züge, die in der alten Tradition Jesus vorbehalten bleiben, auf Maria übertragen". CULLMANN, Kindheitsevangelien (s. Anm. 1), 338. Durch die Gattung Geburtsorakel und die wunderbare Empfängnis wird Maria als einziges Mädchen in die Reihe biblischer Verheißungsträger eingeordnet; anders als etwa bei Ismael oder Samson erhalten hier aber sowohl die Mutter als auch der Vater eine Geburtsankündigung. Eine Parallele dazu findet sich nur bei Jesus, jedoch auch nur dann, wenn man Lk 1,26–38 und Mt 1,18–25 miteinander kombiniert.

[6] EPIPH., *haer.* 78, 23, 9 (GCS 37, 474): τὸ τέλος γὰρ αὐτῆς οὐδεὶς ἔγνω … . Epiphanius ist nach derzeitigem Textbefund wohl der erste, der über den Tod Mariens reflektiert, und zwar in seinem Mitte der 370er Jahre entstandenen *Panarion*, in der Auseinan-

Jahrhunderts dann aber geändert zu haben. Es ist nämlich eine Fülle verschiedener spätantiker Texte über den Tod Marias erhalten geblieben, die teilweise bis ins späte fünfte Jahrhundert zurückdatiert werden können. Inwieweit diese Erzählungen auf älteren Traditionen beruhen, ist schwer zu sagen.[7] Insgesamt gibt es über sechzig verschiedene Texte zum Lebensende Mariens, sie sind in Griechisch, Latein, Syrisch, Koptisch, Arabisch, Äthiopisch, Armenisch, Georgisch und Gälisch überliefert.[8]

---

dersetzung mit den sog. Antidikomarianiten und den Kollyridianern. Vgl. auch EPIPH., *haer.* 78, 11 (GCS 37, 461f). Die Aussagen des zypriotischen Bischofs könnten zwar darauf hinweisen, dass das Ende Marias zu seiner Zeit z.T. bereits auf Interesse stieß, andererseits zeigt sich aber, dass er selbst hierzu noch kaum feste Traditionen kannte. Epiphanius hält es nämlich für möglich, dass Maria „einfach" gestorben ist und begraben wurde, dass sie das Martyrium erlitt oder dass sie am Leben blieb, legt sich aber selbst nicht fest. Vgl. hierzu u.a. auch G. SÖLL, Mariologie, HDG 3/4, Freiburg i.Br. u.a. 1978, 69f. S.J. SHOEMAKER, Epiphanius of Salamis, the Kollyridians, and the Early Dormition Narratives: The Cult of the Virgin in the Fourth Century, in JECS 16 (2008), 371–401.

[7] Zur *Transitus-Mariae*-Literatur vgl. allgemein u.a. M. JUGIE, La mort et l'assomption de la Sainte Vierge. Étude historico-doctrinale, StT 114, Vatikan 1944. M. VAN ESBROECK, Aux origines de la Dormition de la Vierge. Études historiques sur les traditions orientales, CS 472, Aldershot 1995. S.C. MIMOUNI, Dormition et assomption de Marie. Histoire des traditions anciennes, ThH 98, Paris 1995. S.J. SHOEMAKER, Ancient Traditions of the Virgin Mary's Dormition and Assumption, OECS, Oxford 2002. Dass manche Motive und Vorlagen der *Transitus*-Berichte bis ins 2. Jahrhundert zurückreichen, wie in der Forschung z.T. behauptet wird, ist m.E. sehr fraglich. Vgl. z.B. F. MANNS, Le récit de la dormition de Marie (Vatican grec 1982). Contribution à l'étude des origines de l'exégèse chrétienne, SBF.CM 33, Jerusalem 1989, 201–226. Ein breiteres Interesse am Ende Mariens ist erst ab dem 5. Jahrhundert feststellbar, dies hängt sicherlich auch mit den „mariologischen Implikationen" des christologischen Streits zusammen. In der deutschsprachigen Forschung hat die *Transitus*-Literatur bislang nur wenig Aufmerksamkeit erhalten, Ausnahmen bilden die beiden wichtigen Arbeiten von M. HAIBACH-REINISCH, Ein neuer „Transitus Mariae" des Pseudo-Melito. Textkritische Ausgabe und Darlegung der Bedeutung dieser ursprünglicheren Fassung für Apokryphenforschung und lateinische und deutsche Dichtung des Mittelalters, BABVM 5, Rom 1962 und H. FÖRSTER, Transitus Mariae. Beiträge zur koptischen Überlieferung. Mit einer Edition von P. Vindob. K 7589, Cambridge Add 1876 8 und Paris BN Copte 129[17] ff. 28 und 29, GCS NF 14, Berlin/New York 2006. In der zuletzt genannten Monographie findet sich auch ein aktueller Forschungsüberblick zur *Transitus*-Literatur. Vgl. ebd. 67–97.

[8] Übersichten der einzelnen *Transitus*-Texte finden sich bei MIMOUNI, Dormition et assomption (s. Anm. 7), XIX–XXII. M. VAN ESBROECK, Les textes littéraires sur l'assomption avant le Xe siècle, in: DERS., Aux origines de la dormition (s. Anm. 7), 265–285, v.a. 266ff und SHOEMAKER, Ancient Traditions (s. Anm. 7), 419–428. Die Anzahl und Nummerierung der aufgeführten Texte weicht z.T. voneinander ab. Für die griechische Überlieferung sind darüber hinaus auch die slawischen Übersetzungen zu berücksichtigen. Zur griechischen *Transitus-Mariae*-Literatur vgl. neben den zuvor angeführten Arbeiten auch A. WENGER, L'assomption de la T.S. Vierge dans la tradition byzantine du VIe au Xe siècle. Études et documents, AOC 5, Paris 1955. B.E. DALEY, On the dormition of Mary. Early Patristic Homilies, Crestwood 1998. S.C. MIMOUNI/S.J.

Eine Klassifikation dieser Textgruppe ist äußerst schwierig, im Gefolge von COTHENET und MIMOUNI legt sich aber wohl eine Ordnung der Texte nach typo- und topologischen Gesichtspunkten nahe: Die ältesten Texte scheinen von einer Entschlafung Mariens im engeren Sinn auszugehen. Maria stirbt, Christus nimmt ihre Seele auf und bringt sie in den Himmel. Der Körper Marias wird beigesetzt, er bleibt aber unverwest und wird nach drei Tagen ins Paradies, teilweise auch an einen unbekannten Ort gebracht. In einigen koptischen und äthiopischen Traditionen kommt es nach 206 Tagen zu einer Wiedervereinigung von Körper und Seele Mariens, was als eine Art Auferstehung interpretiert werden kann. In manchen Texten stirbt Maria allerdings nicht, sie wird entrückt und mit Leib und Seele in den Himmel aufgenommen. Zum Teil geschieht die Aufnahme allerdings erst, nachdem Körper und Seele Mariens drei Tage getrennt waren. Fraglich ist, ob man bei diesen verschiedenen Traditionen von einer Entwicklung auszugehen hat oder ob ein Nebeneinander der Modelle anzunehmen ist.[9] Daneben können die *Transitus*-Texte aber auch nach örtlichen Gesichtspunkten geordnet werden. Das Haus Mariens und somit ihr Sterbeort, aber auch ihr Grab wurden nämlich teilweise bei Bethlehem, an verschiedenen Orten in und nahe Jerusalems sowie in Ephesus lokalisiert.[10]

Aus der Vielzahl der Texte wurde für unsere Fragestellung die unter dem Namen des Apostels Johannes[11] überlieferte *Dormitio Mariae* ausgewählt. Dies hat mehrere Gründe: Zum einen handelt es sich bei diesem Text um eine relativ alte, vielleicht die älteste erhaltene griechische Erzäh-

---

VOICU, La tradition grecque de la dormition et de l'assomption de Marie. Textes introduits, traduits et annotés, Paris 2003.

[9] Vgl. É. COTHENET, Marie dans les apocryphes, in: H. DU MANOIR (Hg.), Maria. Études sur la Sainte Vierge, Bd. 6, Paris 1961, 71–156, v.a. 117–148. MIMOUNI, Dormition et assomption (s. Anm. 7), v.a. 37–73 u. 345–352. Eine knappe Zusammenfassung der Ergebnisse MIMOUNIS findet sich auch bei H.-J. KLAUCK, Apokryphe Evangelien. Eine Einführung, Stuttgart [2]2005, 248f. Abweichende Versuche, die *Transitus*-Literatur zu klassifizieren, finden sich u.a. bei M. CLAYTON, The *Transitus Mariae*: The Tradition and Its Origins, Apocrypha 10 (1999), 74–98, v.a. 74ff, und SHOEMAKER, Ancient Traditions (s. Anm. 7), v.a. 142–204.

[10] Eine umfassende Aufarbeitung aller Traditionen zum Sterbe- und Bestattungsort Mariens, wie auch zu den damit zusammenhängenden Reliquien findet sich bei MIMOUNI, Dormition et assomption (s. Anm. 7), 353–645.

[11] Die Schrift hat folgenden Titel: Τοῦ ἁγίου Ἰωάννου τοῦ θεολόγου λόγος εἰς τὴν κοίμησιν τῆς ἁγίας θεοτόκου. Z.T. wird Johannes darüber hinaus in manchen Handschriften auch als Apostel und Evangelist bezeichnet. PS-JOH., *dorm.* (TISCHENDORF 95). Die angebliche Verfasserschaft des Johannes zeigt sich aber auch im Text selbst, dort findet sich nämlich z.T. eine autoptische Erzählperspektive, die aber nicht völlig konsequent durchgehalten wird. Vgl. z.B. ebd. 6–11 (TISCHENDORF 97f). M. BONNET, Bemerkungen über die ältesten Schriften von der Himmelfahrt Mariae, in ZWTh 23 (1880), 222–230 (222–247). Zu Johannes vgl. u.a. auch R.A. CULPEPPER, John, the Son of Zebedee. The Life of a Legend, Columbia 1994, v.a. 232–235.

lung über das Lebensende Mariens. Die Schrift des Ps-Johannes ist nach MIMOUNI auf das späte fünfte oder frühe sechste Jahrhundert zu datieren, vielleicht ist sie aber sogar älter.[12] Von den gerade vorgestellten Modellen vertritt der Text ebenfalls das älteste: Maria erleidet den Tod, ihre Seele wird von ihrem Sohn in Empfang genommen, der sie ins „himmlische Schatzhaus" bringt. Der Leib Mariens wird vor der Verwesung bewahrt und nach einem dreitägigen Aufenthalt im Grab ins Paradies überführt, das vom Himmel klar abgegrenzt ist.[13] Bezüglich der Ortsfrage scheint der Text eine Art Kompromiss anzubieten. Maria stirbt zwar in Jerusalem und wird in Getsemani beigesetzt, sie hat aber sowohl in Betlehem als auch in Jerusalem ein Haus.[14] Zum anderen handelt es sich bei diesem Text um eine sehr breit überlieferte Schrift, es gibt weit über fünfzig Handschriften in griechischer Sprache und daneben Übersetzungen ins Lateinische, Arabische, Georgische und Slawische. Außerdem scheint diese Schrift im byzantinischen Osten eine Art Standardüberlieferung bezüglich des Lebensendes Mariens darzustellen, die auch in der Liturgie Verwendung fand.[15]

---

[12] Vgl. MIMOUNI, Dormition et assomption (s. Anm. 7), 123f. Die Datierung der *Dormitio* ist in der Forschung umstritten, sie schwankt zwischen dem 4. und dem späten 6. Jahrhundert. Als Anhaltspunkt für eine zeitliche Fixierung wird in der Literatur häufig auf die Entstehung eines Marienfestes am 15. August rekurriert, doch ist auch die Rekonstruktion der Frühgeschichte dieses Festes nicht unproblematisch. Vgl. PS-JOH., *dorm.* 42 u. 37 (TISCHENDORF 109 u. 106f). Zum Marienfest am 15. August vgl. z.B. K. GAMBER, Zur Geschichte des Koimesis-Festes, in: CH. SCHAFFER, Koimesis – Der Heimgang Mariens. Das Entschlafungsbild in seiner Abhängigkeit von Legende und Theologie, SPLi 15, Regensburg 1985, 151–164. H. AUF DER MAUR, Feste und Gedenktage der Heiligen, in: Ders./PH. HARNONCOURT, Feiern im Rhythmus der Zeit, Bd. 2/1, GdK 6/1, Regensburg 1994, 123–127 (65–357). MIMOUNI, Dormition et assomption (s. Anm. 7), 371–471. Teilweise wird in der Forschung aber auch ein anderer *Transitus*-Text unter dem Namen des Johannes, nämlich der sog. *Transitus graecus «R»* (WENGER 210–241) als das älteste griechische Apokryphon zum Lebensende Mariens angesehen. Vgl. u.a. WENGER, L'assomption (s. Anm. 8), 31–67.

[13] Vgl. v.a. PS-JOH., *dorm.* 44f u. 48f (TISCHENDORF 109–112). MIMOUNI, Dormition et assomption (s. Anm. 7), 125ff. Zur dogmengeschichtlichen Entwicklung bezüglich des Endschicksals Marias im Osten vgl. allgemein u.a. SÖLL, Mariologie (s. Anm. 6), 112–129 u. 144ff.

[14] Vgl. v.a. PS-JOH., *dorm.* 4, 32 u. 48 (TISCHENDORF 96, 105 u. 111). MIMOUNI, Dormition et assomption (s. Anm. 7), 127, v.a. Anm. 37. Nach MIMOUNI ist der Text in Jerusalem entstanden. Vgl. ebd. 124.

[15] „La Dormition grecque de Pseudo-Jean est un des écrits les plus représentatifs de la tradition grecque sur le sort final de Marie." MIMOUNI/VOICU, La tradition grecque (s. Anm. 8), 31. Zur Überlieferung des Textes vgl. MIMOUNI, Dormition et assomption (s. Anm. 7), 118f. Es scheint darüber hinaus auch eine Beziehung der *Dormitio Mariae* zu syrischen *Transitus*-Texten zu geben. Zur liturgischen Verwendung des Textes vgl. S.C. MIMOUNI, La lecture liturgique et les apocryphes du Nouveau Testament. Le cas de la Dormitio grecque du Pseudo-Jean, in OCP 59 (1993), 403–425. Dass der „Sitz im Leben"

Hauptteil: Passions- und Ostermotive in der ps-johanneischen *Dormitio Mariae*

Die *Dormitio* des Ps-Johannes wurde erstmals 1805 von BERGER auf der Grundlage von zwei Handschriften ediert, 1866 veröffentlichte KONSTANTIN VON TISCHENDORF den Text unter Heranziehung von mindestens fünf weiteren Manuskripten nochmals. Weil eine moderne kritische Edition fehlt, muss auch weiterhin auf die Ausgabe TISCHENDORFS zurückgegriffen werden.[16] Da die Schrift bislang in der deutschsprachigen Forschung nur wenig Aufmerksamkeit fand,[17] wird sie im Folgenden relativ ausführlich vorgestellt. Dabei liegt der Fokus auf den Verbindungen dieses Textes zu und Anklängen an die neutestamentlichen Passions- und Ostererzählungen, eine durchgängige Kommentierung ist im Rahmen der vorliegenden Untersuchung natürlich nicht möglich.[18]

Der Grabbesuch Mariens

Die Erzählung des Ps-Johannes beginnt mit dem Besuch und dem Gebet Marias am Grab Jesu in Jerusalem, bereits im ersten Satz sind durch das Stichwort μνῆμα somit die Passions- und Ostererzählungen des Neuen Tes-

---

der *Dormitio* die Liturgie ist, zeigt sich an zahlreichen Stellen im Text. Vgl. z.B. PS-JOH., *dorm.* 1, 4f, 17 u. 21 (TISCHENDORF 95ff u. 100ff).

[16] Vgl. CANT 101 = BHG 1055f. F.-X. BERGER, in: J.CH. V. ARETIN, Beyträge zur Geschichte und Literatur, vorzüglich aus den Schätzen der Königl. Hof- und Centralbibliothek zu München, Bd. 5, München 1805, 629–663. K. V. TISCHENDORF, Apocalypses apocryphae Mosis, Esdrae, Pauli, Iohannis, item Mariae dormitio, additis evangeliorum et actum apocryphorum supplementis, Leipzig 1866, 95–112. Es wird im Folgenden die Kapitelzählung TISCHENDORFS übernommen. Dieser hat allerdings zweimal die Zahl 15 vergeben, deshalb wird hier zwischen 15 u. 15a unterschieden.

[17] Dies könnte sich aber künftig ändern. Im Gegensatz zu den Sammlungen apokrypher Schriften von E. HENNECKE und W. SCHNEEMELCHER hat H.-J. KLAUCK nämlich der *Transitus-Mariae*-Literatur in seiner Einführung zu den Apokryphen ein eigenes Kapitel gewidmet und dort als Beispiel für diese Texte eine moderne Übersetzung der *Dormitio Mariae* des Ps-Johannes vorgelegt. Vgl. KLAUCK, Apokryphe Evangelien (s. Anm. 9), 247–260. Dies hat auch den Verf. zur Beschäftigung mit diesem Text inspiriert. Anders als von KLAUCK vermutet, ist seine Übersetzung der *Dormitio Mariae* aber nicht die erste ins Deutsche, eine solche findet sich bereits bei F.A. v. LEHNER, Die Marienverehrung in den ersten Jahrhunderten, Stuttgart 1881, 244–253.

[18] Die ausführlichste Auseinandersetzung mit diesem Text findet sich m.W. bei MIMOUNI/VOICU, La tradition grecque (s. Anm. 8), 31–60. Die folgende Grobgliederung des Textes orientiert sich an MIMOUNI und VOICU sowie an KLAUCK, ist aber v.a. durch die hier zu verfolgende Fragestellung beeinflusst. Vgl. KLAUCK, Apokryphe Evangelien (s. Anm. 9), 250–258. MIMOUNI hat daneben auch eine Untergliederung der Schrift in vier Hauptteile (*dorm.* 1–3; 4–31; 32–45; 46–50) vorgeschlagen. Da diese v.a. topographische und liturgische Kriterien zu berücksichtigen sucht, erscheint sie im vorliegenden Kontext jedoch als wenig hilfreich. Vgl. MIMOUNI, La lecture liturgique (s. Anm. 15), 414–424.

taments als Bezugstexte für den Leser bzw. Hörer gegenwärtig.[19] Unmittelbar darauf berichtet der Text von der Reaktion der Juden auf diesen Grabbesuch, diese wenden sich nämlich an die Hohenpriester und beschweren sich über den täglichen Aufenthalt Mariens am Grab Christi (τῷ θείῳ τάφῳ). Damit sind schon zu Beginn des Apokryphons zwei Personengruppen (οἱ Ἰουδαῖοι und οἱ ἀρχιερεῖς) angesprochen, die hier in Opposition zu Maria treten, die der Leser aber bereits aus dem Neuen Testament als Gegner Jesu kennt.[20] Die Hohenpriester treten in der *Dormitio Mariae* dann auch sogleich in einer Weise auf, die an das Ende des Matthäusevangeliums erinnert. Es wird nämlich berichtet, dass sie Wächter (οἱ φύλακες) beauftragt hatten, welche unterbinden sollten, dass das Grabmal Jesu zum Gebet aufgesucht werde. Die Hohenpriester befragen die Wachen auch, ob sie Maria im Grab gesehen hätten, was diese allerdings verneinen. Ps-Johannes erklärt dies mit dem wunderbaren Eingreifen Gottes.[21]

Die Erzählung setzt hierauf nochmals neu ein und berichtet wiederum vom Gang Mariens zum Grab, allerdings nun mit einer Zeitangabe. Der letzte Besuch der Mutter Jesu an dessen Grab wird auf einen Freitag (παρασκευῆς οὔσης), also auf den Tag seines Todes und seiner Bestattung datiert. Ein Leser der *Dormitio Mariae* fühlt sich also von Beginn an nicht nur örtlich, sondern auch zeitlich an die Passion Christi erinnert.[22] Im Grab

---

[19] Vgl. PS-JOH., *dorm.* 1 (TISCHENDORF 95). Das Grab Jesu wird hier natürlich bereits als Gebetsstätte betrachtet: κατὰ τὸ εἰωθός. Wenn es zutrifft, wie von MIMOUNI angenommen, dass die verschiedenen Abschnitte der *Dormitio Mariae* mit der Liturgie Jerusalems in Verbindung stehen, dann ist wohl zu vermuten, dass *dorm.* 1–3 in Bezug zur Grabeskirche steht. Vgl. hierzu MIMOUNI, La lecture liturgique (s. Anm. 15), 418–424. Der Text verwendet im 1. Kapitel das Wort μνῆμα, das sich auch in Lk 23,53; 24,1 findet. In Mk 15,46; 16,2f.5.8 und Mt 27,60; 28,8 wird stattdessen μνημεῖον verwendet.

[20] Vgl. PS-JOH., *dorm.* 2 (TISCHENDORF 96). In den Evangelien werden die Hohenpriester 64-mal genannt, häufig als die Verantwortlichen für den Tod Jesu. Vgl. z.B. Mt 20,18; 26,3f.59; 27,1f.20.41. Die Juden pauschal als Feinde Jesu finden sich v.a. im Johannesevangelium, z.B. in Joh 18,12.14.31.35f.40; 19,7.12.15. Das Lexem τάφος wird in Mt 27,61.64.66; 28,1 für das Grab Jesu gebraucht.

[21] Vgl. PS-JOH., *dorm.* 2 (TISCHENDORF 96). Nach Mt 27,62–66 hatten die Hohenpriester dafür gesorgt, dass das Grab Jesu bewacht wurde, um den befürchteten Diebstahl seiner Leiche durch die Jünger zu verhindern. In Mt 28,11–15 wird berichtet, dass die Hohenpriester nach der Auferstehung Christi die Wachen bestachen, um diese zu verheimlichen. In der *Dormitio Mariae* werden hingegen von den Hohenpriestern Wachen beauftragt, um den Besuch des Grabes zum Gebet zu verhindern. Für einen Leser bzw. Hörer, der die ntl. Perikopen kennt und Verbindungen zu vorliegendem Text herstellt, erscheinen die Hohenpriester von Anfang an in einem äußerst negativen Licht. Sie kennen das Geheimnis der Auferstehung Christi, versuchen es allerdings zu vertuschen und wollen nun auch noch der Mutter Jesu den Zugang zum Grab ihres Sohnes versperren. Das Nomen φύλαξ ist für das Matthäusevangelium nur als Variante belegt.

[22] Vgl. PS-JOH., *dorm.* 3 (TISCHENDORF 96). Das Lexem παρασκευή findet sich in Mk 15,42; Mt 27,62; Lk 23,54 und Joh 19,14.31.42.

erscheint Maria nun der Erzengel Gabriel und kündigt ihr den baldigen Tod an. Durch die beteiligten Personen und die Form der Botschaft erinnert die Szene zwar in erster Linie an die lukanische Kindheitsgeschichte, durch den Ort des Geschehens werden darüber hinaus *en passant* aber auch die Angelophanien der neutestamentlichen Ostererzählungen eingespielt.[23]

Das Kommen der Apostel zu Maria

Der folgende Teil der ps-johanneischen Schrift spielt in Betlehem, die Verbindungen zu den Passionsberichten des Neuen Testaments sind hier viel geringer. Zunächst wird die Rückkehr Marias in den Geburtsort Jesu und ihr Gebet um das Kommen des Johannes und der übrigen Apostel geschildert.[24] Diesem Gebet folgt dann sogleich eine kurze Notiz über die wunderbare Ankunft des Johannes in Betlehem. Die Erzählung setzt ein besonderes Verhältnis zwischen Maria und dem Apostel voraus, Joh 19,26f. wird sogar wörtlich zitiert.[25]

Der Bericht über die Begegnung zwischen Johannes und der Mutter Jesu enthält mehrere Gebete, erzählerisch nicht ungeschickt klingen dabei bereits zentrale Themen des Textes an. Johannes wendet sich etwa mit folgenden Worten an Christus: „..., deine Mutter möge aus diesem Leben scheiden und Schrecken erfasse die, die dich gekreuzigt und nicht an dich geglaubt haben.“[26] Das Ende Mariens wird hier also in Verbindung ge-

---

[23] Vgl. PS-JOH., *dorm.* 3 (TISCHENDORF 96). Die Szene erinnert an Lk 1,26–38. Vgl. MIMOUNI/VOICU, La tradition grecque (s. Anm. 8), 39, Anm. 14. KLAUCK, Apokryphe Evangelien (s. Anm. 9), 259. Ein Leser, der die ntl. Osterberichte kennt, wird allerdings auch Bezüge zu diesen Texten herstellen. Vgl. z.B. Mt 28,1–8. Die Botschaft Gabriels an Maria besteht darin, dass sie, wie von ihr erbeten, bald sterben und zu ihrem Sohn in den Himmel gelangen wird.

[24] Vgl. PS-JOH., *dorm.* 4f (TISCHENDORF 96f). Ps-Johannes geht hier davon aus, dass Maria ein Haus in Betlehem hat, später wird ein weiteres in Jerusalem erwähnt. Die innige Beziehung zwischen Maria und Johannes klingt bereits an, er wird gesondert von den anderen Aposteln als erster genannt.

[25] Vgl. ebd. 6f (TISCHENDORF 97). In *dorm.* 7 wird ausdrücklich darauf hingewiesen, dass Maria sich bei der Begegnung mit Johannes an das Wort Jesu erinnerte: ἰδοὺ ἡ μήτηρ σου, καὶ ἰδοὺ ὁ υἱός σου. Im Gegensatz zur Johannespassion ist hier jedoch die Reihenfolge umgedreht und der Wortlaut weicht leicht ab. Die Erzählung des Ps-Johannes setzt die Identifikation des Lieblingsjüngers mit Johannes natürlich bereits voraus. Als Aufenthaltsort des Apostels wird in *dorm.* 6 Ephesus genannt. Mit der Ankunft des Johannes verändert sich auch die Erzählperspektive, der Jünger berichtet nun als Augenzeuge in Ich-Form, dies wird allerdings nicht völlig durchgehalten.

[26] Ebd. 8 (TISCHENDORF 97f): ... καὶ ἐξέλτῃ ἡ μήτηρ σου ἐκ τοῦ βίου τούτου, καὶ πτοηθῶσιν οἱ σταυρώσαντές σε καὶ μὴ πιστεύσαντες εἰς σέ. Mit dem Verbum σταυρόω wird ein deutlicher Bezug zwischen dem Tod Jesu und dem Marias hergestellt. Das Verb πτοέω könnte evtl. darüber hinaus aber auch die Ostererzählungen einspielen. Vgl. Lk 24,37. Darauf könnte auch die Formulierung: καὶ νῦν ποίησον θαυμάσια ἐνώπιον τῆς γεννησάσης σε im Gebet des Johannes hindeuten, die an Joh 20,30 erinnert.

bracht zu einer noch nicht näher bestimmten Gruppe, die für die Kreuzigung Jesu verantwortlich war. Wenige Zeilen später berichtet Maria jedoch Folgendes: „Die Juden haben geschworen, dass sie meinen Leib, wenn mein Ende kommt, verbrennen werden."[27] Auch wenn hier noch keine direkte Gleichsetzung stattfindet, so deutet sich diese doch schon an. Der Leser wird darauf vorbereitet, dass die Juden wie gegen Jesu auch gegen Maria vorgehen werden.

Daneben wird in den Gebeten aber auch schon das wunderbare Lebensende Marias thematisiert, bei ihrem Tod werden sich die Apostel versammeln, Christus wird erscheinen und ihr Leib wird unversehrt bleiben.[28] Gleich im Anschluss wird dann auch die Ankunft der Apostel in Betlehem erzählt und ihr Zusammentreffen mit Maria geschildert.[29] Auf die Bitte Mariens hin berichten die Apostel hierauf, wie und wo sie von ihrem bevorstehenden Tod erfahren haben und auf welche Weise sie in den Geburtsort Jesu gelangt sind.[30]

Jüdisches Vorgehen gegen Maria – Teil I

Auch der folgende Teil der *Dormitio Mariae* spielt sich noch größtenteils in Betlehem ab, Jerusalem gerät allerdings nun wieder verstärkt in den Blick. In der Geburtsstadt Jesu geschehen nun zahlreiche Zeichen und Wunder, die Kunde davon dringt auch in die Hauptstadt. Das Haus Ma-

---

[27] PS-JOH., *dorm.* 10 (TISCHENDORF 98): οἱ Ἰουδαῖοι ἐξωμόσαντο ἵνα ἐν τῷ τελειωθῆναί με τὸ σῶμά μου κατακαύσωσιν. V.a. im Johannesevangelium begegnen die Juden dem Leser pauschal als Gegner Jesu, hier werden sie nun, wie auch schon in *dorm.* 2, auch als Feinde Marias dargestellt. Die Formulierung: ἐν τῷ τελειωθῆναί με erinnert an Joh 19,30, die Passion Jesu könnte also auch hier wieder im Hintergrund stehen. Ein jüdischer Schwur wird auch in Apg 23,12.14.21 erwähnt, und zwar gegen Paulus. Dort wird allerdings das Verb ἀναθεματίζω verwendet.

[28] Vgl. PS-JOH., *dorm.* 8–11 (TISCHENDORF 97f). Erzählerisch nicht ungeschickt erwähnt Maria in *dorm.* 9 eine Verheißung Christi, dass er bei ihrem Tod zu ihr kommen werde. Johannes kündigt Maria in *dorm.* 10 mit Worten aus Ps 16,10 (15,10 LXX) an, dass ihr Körper trotz des jüdischen Schwurs nicht vernichtet werden wird. In Apg 2,27 u. 13,35 wird dieser Psalmvers auf die Auferstehung Christi bezogen. In *dorm.* 11 meldet sich dann der Hl. Geist selbst zu Wort, der die unmittelbar bevorstehende Ankunft der übrigen Apostel ankündigt.

[29] Vgl. PS-JOH., *dorm.* 12–15 (TISCHENDORF 99f). Die Apostelliste wirkt etwas eigenartig, es werden neben Johannes Petrus, Paulus, Thomas, Jakobus, Andreas, Philippus, Lukas, Simon Kananäus, Thaddäus und Markus genannt. Matthäus wird erst in *dorm.* 23 (TISCHENDORF 102) erwähnt. Von fünfen wird berichtet, dass sie bereits tot waren, vom Hl. Geist aber auferweckt wurden, um beim Sterben Mariens dabei zu sein. Vgl. hierzu MIMOUNI/VOICU, La tradition grecque (s. Anm. 8), 43f, Anm. 42–48.

[30] Vgl. PS-JOH., *dorm.* 15a–25 (TISCHENDORF 100–103). „Die Charakterisierung der einzelnen Apostel durch Zuschreibung von Tätigkeitsfeldern und durch Selbstberichte setzt ausgeführte Apostellegenden voraus. Wir nähern uns hier der Gattung der apokryphen Apostelakten." KLAUCK, Apokryphe Evangelien (s. Anm. 9), 259.

riens in Betlehem wird zu einer Wallfahrtsstätte, an der es zu Heilungen verschiedenster Art kommt. Dies führt auch bei den Bewohnern Jerusalems zu Bekehrungen und großer Freude.[31]

Als Reaktion auf diese Vorgänge erwähnt Ps-Johannes auf Seiten der jüdischen Priesterschaft (οἱ ἱερεῖς τῶν Ἰουδαίων), aber auch beim Volk (ἅμα τῷ λαῷ αὐτῶν) blankes Entsetzen und starken Neid. Weiter wird berichtet, dass deshalb beschlossen wurde, gegen Maria und die Apostel vorzugehen. In der Wendung πάλιν ... συμβούλιον ποιησάμενοι findet sich nun sogar ein überdeutlicher Bezug zur Passionsgeschichte, mit denselben Worten fällt der Hohe Rat ja laut Mk 15,1 das Todesurteil über Jesus. Hier sind es aber nicht nur die Ratsherren, sondern die Priester zusammen mit dem Volk, das kurz zuvor angesichts der wunderbaren Ereignisse in Betlehem noch in Festtagsstimmung war.[32] Sogleich wird auch ein jüdischer Trupp (τὸ πλῆθος τῶν Ἰουδαίων) ausgesandt, der aber aufgrund einer Vision nicht nach Betlehem gelangt, sondern unverrichteter Dinge nach Jerusalem zurückkehren muss.[33]

Dadurch noch mehr erzürnt wenden sich die Hohenpriester nun an den römischen Statthalter (πρὸς τὸν ἡγεμόνα). Der Leser bzw. Hörer wird dadurch sofort an den Prozess Jesu vor Pilatus erinnert.[34] Die jüdische Seite

---

[31] Vgl. PS-JOH., *dorm.* 26–28 (TISCHENDORF 103f). Evtl. kann man aus diesem Abschnitt bei Ps-Johannes darauf schließen, dass zur Zeit der Abfassung des Textes in oder bei Betlehem ein marianisches Wallfahrtszentrum bestand. Vgl. auch MIMOUNI, La lecture liturgique (s. Anm. 15), 421. Die in *dorm.* 27 berichteten Heilungen greifen natürlich ntl. Motive auf. Vgl. z.B. Lk 7,21f. Bei der Aufzählung der Wunder wird in *dorm.* 26 auch eine φωνὴ ὡς υἱοῦ ἀνθρώπου erwähnt. Dieser Ausdruck nimmt Dan 7,13 auf, der Menschensohn spielt aber auch in der synoptischen Passionstradition eine wichtige Rolle. Vgl. z.B. Mk 14,62. In *dorm.* 28 wird berichtet, dass in Jerusalem aufgrund der wunderbaren Ereignisse ein Fest begangen wurde (ἑόρταζον). Damit ist ebenfalls ein gewisser Bezug zur Passion Jesu hergestellt. Vgl. z.B. Mk 14,2; 15,6.

[32] Vgl. PS-JOH., *dorm.* 29 (TISCHENDORF 104). Für einen Leser, der die ntl. Passionserzählungen kennt, ist der Bezug zum Vorgehen des Hohen Rates gegen Jesus überdeutlich. Vgl. Mk 15,1; Mt 27,1. Das jüdische Vorgehen gegen Maria wird hier mit dem Beschluss gegen Jesus parallelisiert, letztlich ist es aber noch gesteigert. Es sind ja nicht nur die Priester, sondern auch das Volk, die gegen Maria vorgehen wollen. Evtl. ist mit dem Lexem λαός sogar ein Bezug zu Mt 27,25 hergestellt.

[33] Vgl. PS-JOH., *dorm.* 29 (TISCHENDORF 104). Das Wort πλῆθος kommt auch in Lk 23,1 vor, dort wird der Hohe Rat, der Jesus zu Pilatus überstellt, so bezeichnet.

[34] Vgl. PS-JOH., *dorm.* 30 (TISCHENDORF 104). Der Titel ἡγεμών begegnet v.a. im Matthäusevangelium (27,2.11.14f.21.27). Der röm. Statthalter wird bei Ps-Johannes nicht mit Namen genannt. Würde man die Erwähnung von Kaiser Tiberius in *dorm.* 30 ernst nehmen, könnte man hier, wie beim Prozess Jesu, Pilatus als Statthalter annehmen, der ja erst kurz vor dem Tod des Tiberius als Präfekt abgelöst wurde. Es ist allerdings fraglich, ob man beim Autor der *Dormitio Mariae* oder bei spätantiken bzw. mittelalterlichen Lesern derartige historische Kenntnisse voraussetzen kann. Zu Pilatus vgl. u.a. A. DEMANDT, Hände in Unschuld. Pontius Pilatus in der Geschichte, Köln u.a. 1999.

fordert vom Statthalter, er solle Maria aus Judäa vertreiben. Ihr wird unterstellt, dass sie den Untergang der jüdischen Nation (τὸ ἔθνος τῶν Ἰουδαίων) verursache.[35] Ähnlich wie Pilatus im Johannesevangelium weigert sich der namenlose römische Präfekt zunächst, die Forderungen der Juden einfach auszuführen. Daraufhin drohen ihm diese mit Beschwerde bei Kaiser Tiberius. Auch hier findet sich eine Berührung mit der johanneischen Passionsgeschichte.[36] Der Statthalter entsendet nun einen Tribun (χιλίαρχος) nach Betlehem, evtl. eine Reminiszenz an Joh 18,12, wo bei der Gefangennahme Jesu ebenfalls ein Offizier dieses Rangs erwähnt wird.[37]

Die Erzählung schwenkt jetzt wieder in das Haus Mariens nach Betlehem. Der Hl. Geist ruft Maria und die Apostel auf, den Ort zu verlassen, und versetzt sie sogleich in das Haus der Mutter Jesu nach Jerusalem.[38] Währenddessen trifft der Tribun in Betlehem ein. Als er Maria und die Jünger nicht finden kann, verhört er die Bewohner des Ortes, nimmt sie fest und bringt sie zum Statthalter nach Jerusalem.[39]

Jüdisches Vorgehen gegen Maria – Teil II

Als nun das Haus Marias in Jerusalem aufgrund von Wundern ebenfalls zu einer Art Wallfahrtsstätte wird, erfahren nach einigen Tagen auch der Präfekt und die Priesterschaft, dass sich die Mutter Jesu und die Apostel in der Stadt aufhalten.[40] Nach Ps-Johannes ziehen die Juden (ὁ λαὸς τῶν Ἰου-

---

[35] Vgl. PS-JOH., *dorm.* 30 (TISCHENDORF 104). Durch die Situation, v.a. aber durch das Verb κράζω mit einem darauf folgendem Imperativ wird der Leser an die Passion Jesu erinnert. Vgl. Mk 15,13f; Mt 27,23.

[36] Vgl. PS-JOH., *dorm.* 30 (TISCHENDORF 104f). Die *Dormitio Mariae* weist hier zwar kaum wörtliche (Ausnahme: καῖσαρ), aber starke inhaltliche Parallelen zu Joh 19,12 auf. Wie im Johannesevangelium bezüglich der Schuld am Tod Jesu wird auch hier die römische Seite entlastet und das Vorgehen gegen Maria und die Apostel allein den Juden angelastet.

[37] Vgl. PS-JOH., *dorm.* 30 (TISCHENDORF 105). Ein Tribun begegnet auch mehrfach in der Apostelgeschichte bei der Verhaftung des Paulus in Jerusalem und bei seiner Überführung nach Cäsarea. Vgl. Apg 21ff.

[38] Vgl. PS-JOH., *dorm.* 31f (TISCHENDORF 105). Der Hl. Geist informiert Maria und die Apostel in *dorm.* 31 u.a. darüber, dass sich die Juden gegen sie empören. Das dabei verwendete Verb στασιάζω erinnert an die jüdische στάσις gegen Paulus. Vgl. Apg 23,10; 24,5. In *dorm.* 32 wird nun erstmals auch ein Haus Marias in Jerusalem erwähnt. Vgl. hierzu MIMOUNI, La lecture liturgique (s. Anm. 15), 421f. Ders./VOICU, La tradition grecque (s. Anm. 8), 51f, Anm. 95. Zu den verschiedenen Traditionen um das Haus Mariens vgl. MIMOUNI, Dormition et assomption (s. Anm. 7), 473–548.

[39] Vgl. PS-JOH., *dorm.* 33 (TISCHENDORF 105f). Mit dem Verb κρατέω klingt evtl. die Verhaftung Jesu an, allerdings sind es hier ja die Betlehemiten, gegen die der Tribun vorgeht. Vgl. z.B. Mk 14,1.44.46.

[40] Vgl. PS-JOH., *dorm.* 34 (TISCHENDORF 106). Bereits in *dorm.* 32 wurde berichtet, dass sich Maria und die Apostel fünf Tage in ihrem Haus in Jerusalem aufhielten. Auch hier wird nun erwähnt, dass der Aufenthalt Mariens in der Stadt erst nach fünf Tagen be-

δαίων μετὰ καὶ τῶν ἱερέων) daraufhin zum Haus Mariens, um dieses niederzubrennen.[41] Der Statthalter beobachtet das Geschehen aus der Ferne (ἀπὸ μακρόθεν).[42] Als die Menge jedoch mit ihrem Vorhaben beginnen will, schlagen durch ein Wunder Flammen aus dem Haus und verbrennen eine große Anzahl der Angreifer (πλῆθος πολὺ τῶν Ἰουδαίων).[43]

Als Reaktion darauf berichtet die *Dormitio Mariae*, dass sich in Jerusalem Furcht breitmachte und Christus als Gott gepriesen wurde.[44] Unter den Juden soll es nun zu einer Spaltung gekommen sein, viele sollen zum Glauben gefunden haben.[45] Einen deutlichen Bezug zur Passionsgeschichte Jesu weist jedoch der Ausruf des Statthalters auf: „Wahrlich, Gottes Sohn ist es (ἐπ' ἀληθείας θεοῦ υἱός ἐστιν), der geboren wurde aus der Jungfrau, die ihr vertreiben wolltet. Dies sind nämlich die Zeichen eines wahren Gottes (θεοῦ ἀληθινοῦ)."[46] Wie der Hauptmann unterm Kreuz in Mk 15,39 und

---

kannt wurde. Das dahinter stehende zeitliche Schema ist allerdings nicht recht klar. Vgl. MIMOUNI/VOICU, La tradition grecque (s. Anm. 8), 52, Anm. 96.

[41] Vgl. PS-JOH., *dorm.* 35 (TISCHENDORF 106). Hier wird berichtet, dass die Juden mit Feuer und Holz gegen das Haus Mariens vorgehen. Aufgrund des Stichworts ξύλα könnte der Leser auch in *dorm.* 34 einen Bezug zur Verhaftung Jesu herstellen. Vgl. z.B. Mk 14,43.48.

[42] Vgl. PS-JOH., *dorm.* 35 (TISCHENDORF 106). Der Präfekt wird hier in Opposition zu den Juden gestellt. Diese greifen Maria an, er sieht nur zu. Das Verhalten des Statthalters erinnert an die Frauen, die die Kreuzigung Jesu aus der Distanz heraus verfolgten. Vgl. z.B. Mk 15,40.

[43] Vgl. PS-JOH., *dorm.* 35 (TISCHENDORF 106). In der lukanischen Passionserzählung findet sich die Wortfolge πολὺ πλῆθος τοῦ λαοῦ, diese Lexeme begegnen dem Leser auch hier. Allerdings ist in Lk 23,27 die Volksmenge, die beim Kreuzweg Jesu zugegen war, angesprochen.

[44] Vgl. PS-JOH., *dorm.* 35 (TISCHENDORF 106). Auch mit dem Stichwort φόβος könnten hier die ntl. Erzählungen vom Tod und der Auferstehung Jesu eingespielt sein. Vgl. Mk, 16,8; Mt 27,54; 28,4.8. Daneben könnte der Leser aber auch aufgrund des in *dorm.* 35 vorkommenden Verbums δοξάζω eine Verbindung zum Tod Jesu herstellen, in Lk 23,47 wird nämlich berichtet, dass der Centurio unterm Kreuz als Reaktion auf das Sterben Christi Gott pries.

[45] Vgl. PS-JOH., *dorm.* 36 (TISCHENDORF 106). Von einem σχίσμα unter den Juden als Reaktion auf die Verkündigung Jesu berichten Joh 7,43; 9,16 u. 10,19. Das eine große Anzahl Juden aufgrund von Wundern zum Glauben kommt, hat ebenfalls Parallelen im Johannesevangelium. Vgl. z.B. Joh 2,23.

[46] PS-JOH., *dorm.* 36 (TISCHENDORF 106). Die Parallele zu den ntl. Passionsberichten ist überdeutlich, allerdings ist die Darstellung im Vergleich zu diesen sogar noch gesteigert. Nicht die Juden, sondern ein Römer erkennt die Gottheit Jesu als erster an. Das Verb ἀνακράζω, das hier das Bekenntnis einleitet, wird auch in Lk 23,18 benutzt. Dort leitet das Verbum aber den Ruf der Juden ein, die den Tod Jesu fordern. Vgl. auch Mk 15,13f; Mt 27,23. In *dorm.* 36 ist es jedoch nicht, wie in Mk 15,39 bzw. Mt 27,54 ein Centurio, sondern der Präfekt selbst, der das Geschehen beobachtet und seinem Glauben Ausdruck verleiht.

Mt 27,54, so ist es auch hier der Vertreter des Römischen Reiches, der die Gottessohnschaft Christi anerkennt.

Das Kommen Christi und das Sterben Marias

Im folgenden Abschnitt der ps-johanneischen Schrift, der im Hause Marias in Jerusalem spielt, finden sich kaum Anspielungen auf die Passions- und Ostererzählungen des Neuen Testaments. Eine Ausnahme bildet die Datierung. In der *Dormitio Mariae* wird das Kommen Christi, der dem Sterben seiner Mutter beiwohnen will, auf einen Sonntag (κυριακῆς) datiert. Diesen Wochentag nennt der Text ausdrücklich auch als Tag des Einzugs Jesu in Jerusalem sowie als Tag seiner Auferstehung, daneben werden aber auch andere heilsgeschichtliche Ereignisse auf einen Sonntag datiert, nämlich die Verkündigung an Maria, Jesu Geburt und seine Wiederkunft am Ende der Zeiten.[47]

Im Anschluss daran wird nun von der Herabkunft Christi berichtet.[48] Das Zusammentreffen zwischen Maria und ihrem Sohn erinnert den Leser durch die Form der Anrede (Μαριάμ) an die Begegnung Maria Magdalenas mit dem Auferstandenen am Ostermorgen. Daneben finden sich jedoch vor allem Berührungen mit der Verkündigungsszene.[49] Christus verheißt seiner Mutter, dass ihr Körper ins Paradies versetzt und ihre Seele in den Himmel gelangen wird.[50] Maria bittet daraufhin für alle, die ihren Namen anrufen, Christus erhört ihre Bitte.[51] Mit knappen Worten wird hierauf das Sterben Mariens erwähnt, der Herr nimmt ihre Seele in Empfang, die Apostel beginnen mit der Bestattung des Leibes.[52]

Jüdisches Vorgehen gegen Maria – Teil III

Ein drittes Mal berichtet Ps-Johannes von einem jüdischen Angriff gegen Maria, die Berührungen zu den Passionserzählungen sind dabei allerdings

---

[47] Vgl. PS-JOH., *dorm.* 37 (TISCHENDORF 106f). Durch die Datierung des Sterbens Marias auf einen Sonntag wird dies natürlich u.a. auch in Bezug zur Auferstehung Jesu gesetzt. Vgl. z.B. Mk 16,2.

[48] Vgl. PS-JOH., *dorm.* 38 (TISCHENDORF 107).

[49] Vgl. ebd. 39 (TISCHENDORF 107f). Die Anrede Μαριάμ findet sich in Lk 1,30 u. Joh 20,16. Die Szene hat viele Berührungen mit Lk 1,26–38.

[50] Vgl. PS-JOH., *dorm.* 39 (TISCHENDORF 108). Durch das Stichwort ἐν τῷ παραδείσῳ könnte ein Leser, der den lukanischen Passionsbericht kennt, hier evtl. eine Verbindung zur Verheißung Jesu an den „guten Schächer" herstellen. Vgl. Lk 23,43.

[51] Vgl. PS-JOH., *dorm.* 40–43 (TISCHENDORF 108f). „Marias größte Aufgabe aber ist nicht das Heilen, sondern die Fürbitte. Sie wächst in ihre Rolle als *mediatrix*, als Vermittlerin hinein … ." KLAUCK, Apokryphe Evangelien (s. Anm. 9), 260.

[52] Vgl. PS-JOH., *dorm.* 44f (TISCHENDORF 109f). In *dorm.* 45 wird berichtet, dass das Sterben Marias von Wohlgeruch und Licht begleitet war, außerdem soll eine himmlische Stimme zu hören gewesen sein, die sagte: μακαρία σὺ ἐν γυναιξίν. Vgl. Lk 1,42; 11,27.

deutlich geringer. Ein gewisser Jephonias (Ἑβραῖός τις ὀνόματι Ἰεφωνίας γενναῖος) soll beim Trauerzug versucht haben, Hand an den Leichnam Mariens zu legen. Ein Engel verhindert dies, indem er dem Angreifer mit einem Feuerschwert die Hände abtrennt und sie in der Luft schweben lässt.[53]

Als Reaktion auf dieses Wunder sollen die Juden (πᾶς ὁ λαὸς τῶν Ἰουδαίων) ausgerufen haben: „Wirklich, ein wahrer Gott ist es (ὄντως ἀληθινὸς θεός ἐστιν), der geboren wurde von dir, Gottesmutter, allzeit jungfräuliche Maria."[54] Dieses Bekenntnis erinnert den Leser bzw. den Hörer wiederum an den Ausruf des römischen Hauptmanns unterm Kreuz, allerdings sind es hier nun Juden, die Christus als Gott und seine Mutter als Gottesgebärerin bekennen. Selbst Jephonias fleht Maria um Erbarmen an, woraufhin ihn Petrus wieder heilt. Dieser Abschnitt der *Dormitio Mariae* endet mit der Notiz, dass der Angreifer zum Glauben kommt und Christus als Gott verherrlicht.[55]

Abschluss

Der letzte Abschnitt der ps-johanneischen Schrift berichtet über die Bestattung Mariens. Die Apostel bringen ihren Leichnam nach Getsemani, dort setzen sie Maria in einem neuen Grab bei (ἐν μνημείῳ καινῷ). Auch wenn die Mutter Jesu an einem anderen Ort als ihr Sohn begraben wird, nämlich dort, wo dessen Passion begann, so stellt der Hinweis auf das bislang unbenutzte Grab doch einen deutlichen Bezug zum Begräbnis Jesu her.[56] Aus dem Grab strömt Duft nach Salböl und es erklingen die Lobgesänge der Engel. Letztere enden nach drei Tagen, dies wird als Zeichen für die Übertragung des Leibes Marias ins Paradies gewertet. Diese Zeitangabe (ἕως τριῶν ἡμερῶν bzw. πληρουμένης τῆς τρίτης ἡμέρας) erscheint dem Leser

---

[53] Vgl. Ps-Joh., *dorm.* 46 (Tischendorf 110). Mimouni/Voicu, La tradition grecque (s. Anm. 8), 57, Anm. 128f. Das Verbum βαστάζω, das hier für das Tragen der Leichnams Verwendung findet, begegnet in diesem Sinne auch in Joh 20,15.

[54] Ps-Joh., *dorm.* 47 (Tischendorf 110). Das Verb ἀνακράζω wurde schon in *dorm.* 36 verwendet, dort wurde das Bekenntnis des Präfekten damit eingeleitet, hier das der Juden. Für einen Leser, der die Passionsberichte des NT kennt, wird der Kontrast nun überdeutlich. In Lk 23,18 leitet das Verb ἀνακράζω die Forderung der Juden nach der Hinrichtung Jesu ein, hier bekennt sich das ganze Volk zu ihm und seiner Mutter, und zwar mit ähnlichen Worten wie der römische Centurio auf Golgota. Vgl. Mk 15,39; Mt 27,54; Lk 23,47.

[55] Vgl. Ps-Joh., *dorm.* 47 (Tischendorf 110f). Das Verb δοξάζω erinnert an den Hauptmann in Lk 23,47.

[56] Vgl. Ps-Joh., *dorm.* 48 (Tischendorf 111). Von einem neuen Grab wird bei der Bestattung Jesu ausdrücklich in Mt 27,60 u. Joh 19,41 gesprochen. Vgl. auch Lk 23,53. Auch durch die Ortsangabe wird beim Leser ein Bezug zur Passion Jesu hervorgerufen. Vgl. Mk 14,32; Mt 26,26. Zum Grab Mariens in Getsemani vgl. u.a. Mimouni, La lecture liturgique (s. Anm. 15), 422ff. Ders., Dormition et assomption (s. Anm. 7), 549–579. Ders./Voicu, La tradition grecque (s. Anm. 8), 58, Anm. 131.

natürlich ebenfalls als eine Parallele zu Christus: Wie dieser am dritten Tag auferstand, so wird der Leib Mariens zu diesem Zeitpunkt ins Paradies versetzt.[57]

Im Anschluss schildert Ps-Johannes eine Vision der Apostel: Sie sehen, wie der Leib Marias im Paradies von den Heiligen, darunter Elisabet, Anna, Abraham, Isaak, Jakob und David, als eine Art Reliquie verehrt wird. Die *Dormitio Mariae* endet hierauf mit einem Gebet der Apostel.[58]

Resümee: Maria – gestorben, begraben, nach drei Tagen ins Paradies versetzt?

Dass sich in einer christlichen Schrift der ausgehenden Antike, die Maria zum Inhalt hat, Berührungen zu den neutestamentlichen Kindheitsgeschichten finden, überrascht kaum.[59] Diese Texte sind in Blick auf Maria ja die qualitativ und quantitativ ergiebigsten des Neuen Testaments. Dass die *Dormitio Mariae* des Ps-Johannes allerdings in einem solchen Umfang Parallelen zu bzw. Anspielungen auf die Passions- und Ostererzählungen aufweist, ist doch in gewisser Weise erstaunlich.[60]

Fassen wir die wichtigsten Beobachtungen noch einmal zusammen: Die ps-johanneische Erzählung über den Tod Mariens verweist örtlich mehrfach auf die Leidensgeschichte Jesu. Maria stirbt wie ihr Sohn in Jerusalem. Die *Dormitio* beginnt im Grab Jesu, also auf Golgota, dort wo die Passion endet. Die Text über die *Koimesis* Mariens endet in Getsemani, also dort, wo die direkte Leidensgeschichte ihres Sohnes beginnt, und zwar wie bei Jesus in einem neuen Grab.[61]

---

[57] Vgl. PS-JOH., *dorm.* 48 (TISCHENDORF 111). Mit der Zeitspanne von drei Tagen ist hier natürlich ein deutlicher Bezug zur Auferstehung Jesu hergestellt. Vgl. z.B. 1Kor 15,4; Mt 27,63f; Lk 24,7.

[58] Vgl. PS-JOH., *dorm.* 49f (TISCHENDORF 111f). Die Überlieferung des Schlussteils der *Dormitio Mariae* des Ps-Johannes ist sehr uneinheitlich. Vgl. MIMOUNI/VOICU, La tradition grecque (s. Anm. 8), 60, Anm. 139.

[59] Vgl. KLAUCK, Apokryphe Evangelien (s. Anm. 9), 259. Die Angelophanie in *dorm.* 3 (TISCHENDORF 96) erinnert z.B. stark an Lk 1,26–38. Daneben finden sich mehrfach Anspielungen auf das Magnifikat, z.B. auf Lk 1,48f in *dorm.* 25 (TISCHENDORF 102f). Zu Maria in den ntl. Kindheitsgeschichten vgl. z.B. J. BECKER, Maria. Mutter Jesu und erwählte Jungfrau, Biblische Gestalten 4, Leipzig 2001, 94–196.

[60] Darauf hat HANS-JOSEF KLAUCK in seiner Einführung zu den ntl. Apokryphen aufmerksam gemacht, dies hat den Verf. zu vorliegendem Beitrag angeregt. Vgl. KLAUCK, Apokryphe Evangelien (s. Anm. 9), 259.

[61] Vgl. u.a. PS-JOH., *dorm.* 1–3, 32 u. 48 (TISCHENDORF 95f, 105 u. 111). Selbst die letzte Ortsangabe des Textes: ἐν τῷ παραδείσῳ in *dorm.* 49 (TISCHENDORF 112) ist aufgrund von Lk 23,43 nicht ohne jeglichen Bezug zur Leidensgeschichte Jesu.

Und auch mit Blick auf die Zeitstruktur finden sich Berührungen mit den Passions- und Osterberichten des Neuen Testaments. Die *Dormitio Mariae* beginnt an dem Wochentag, an dem Jesus stirbt. Maria begegnet ihrem Sohn an dem Wochentag, an dem dieser auferweckt wird und seinen Jüngern begegnet. Marias Tod und die Aufnahme ihrer Seele in den Himmel wird auf einen Sonntag datiert, also auf den Tag der Auferstehung und Himmelfahrt Jesu. Und auch das Drei-Tage-Schema findet sich in der Schrift unter dem Namen des Apostels Johannes. Maria wird zwar nicht am dritten Tag auferweckt wie ihr Sohn, doch nach drei Tagen wird ihr Leib vom Grab ins Paradies versetzt. Darüber hinaus stirbt Maria zur Zeit desselben Kaisers wie ihr Sohn, vielleicht sogar unter demselben Statthalter.[62]

Auch bei den auftretenden Personen finden sich Parallelen zwischen der Schrift des Ps-Johannes und den neutestamentlichen Erzählungen über das Leiden Jesu. Wie im Matthäusevangelium die Hohenpriester das Grab Jesu bewachen lassen, so wollen sie in der *Dormitio Mariae* mithilfe von Wachen verhindern, dass Maria das Grab aufsucht. Wie im Neuen Testament der Hohe Rat beschließt, gegen Jesus vorzugehen, so sind es hier nun die Priester und das Volk. Wie in den Evangelien, vor allem bei Johannes die Juden als Gegner Jesu dargestellt werden, so sind sie in der Erzählung über das Lebensende Mariens die Feinde seiner Mutter, sie wollen Maria letztlich wie ihren Sohn zu Tode bringen, sie wollen sie vertreiben, ihr Haus niederbrennen und ihren Leichnam vernichten.[63]

---

[62] Vgl. u.a. PS-JOH., *dorm.* 3, 37f u. 48 (TISCHENDORF 96, 107 u. 111). Dass Maria während der Herrschaft des Kaisers Tiberius aus dem Leben scheidet, geht aus *dorm.* 30 (TISCHENDORF 104f) hervor. Der römische Statthalter bleibt in der *Dormitio Mariae* zwar namenlos, „wirkt aber fast wie Pilatus". KLAUCK, Apokryphe Evangelien (s. Anm. 9), 259. Vielleicht ist mit dem Statthalter sogar Pilatus gemeint, ein Leser mit präzisen historischen Kenntnissen könnte ihn aufgrund der Nennung von Tiberius jedenfalls mit diesem identifizieren.

[63] Vgl. u.a. PS-JOH., *dorm.* 2, 8, 10, 29f, 34f u. 46 (TISCHENDORF 96ff, 104ff u. 110). Zum Antijudaismus der *Transitus-Mariae*-Literatur vgl. S.J. SHOEMAKER, "Let us Go and Burn her Body": The Image of the Jews in the Early Dormition Traditions, in ChH 68 (1999), 775–823. SHOEMAKER leuchtet in diesem Beitrag die politischen und theologischen Hintergründe, die in spätantik-frühbyzantinischer Zeit zu Konflikten zwischen Juden und Christen führten, und die Rolle, die Maria und die *Transitus*-Texte in diesen Auseinandersetzungen spielten, aus. Vgl. allgemein zum christlichen Antijudaismus in der Spätantike z.B. M. SIMON, Verus Israel. Étude sur les relations entre chrétiens et juifs dans l'empire romain (135-425), BEFAR 167, Paris ²1964. J. NEUSNER/E.S. FRERICHS (Hg.), "To See Ourselves as Other See Us". Christians, Jews, 'Others' in Late Antiquity, Chico 1985, sowie H. SCHRECKENBERG, Die christlichen Adversus-Judaeos-Texte und ihr literarisches und historisches Umfeld (1.–11. Jh.), EHS XXIII/172, Frankfurt a.M. u.a. ⁴1999.

Wie in den neutestamentlichen Passionsberichten so begegnen aber auch in der *Dormitio* des Ps-Johannes die römischen Autoritäten. Ähnlich wie im Neuen Testament erscheinen diese im Gegensatz zur jüdischen Seite auch hier in einem viel positiveren Licht. Die Hohenpriester wenden sich nämlich wie beim Prozess Jesu an den Statthalter. Wie im Johannesevangelium zögert dieser zunächst, gegen Maria vorzugehen, wird aber wie Pilatus mit dem Hinweis auf den Kaiser von den Juden dazu gezwungen. Wie bei den Synoptikern ein römischer Offizier unterm Kreuz die Bedeutung Jesu anerkennt, so ist es hier der Präfekt selbst, der sich zur Gottheit Christi und zu seiner jungfräulichen Mutter bekennt.[64]

Vor diesem Hintergrund kann man zu der eingangs gestellten Frage feststellen: Ein Leser, der die neutestamentlichen Passions- und Osterberichte kennt, wird bei der Lektüre der *Dormitio Mariae* „auch bei der sterbenden Gottesmutter", wie bei ihrem Sohn, „Spuren einer ‚Passion'"[65] entdecken, obwohl sie in dieser Erzählung keines gewaltsamen Todes stirbt. Wie bei Christus wird der Leser darüber hinaus auch bei Maria Hinweise auf eine Art Osterereignis entdecken. Maria wird in diesem Text zwar nicht wie ihr Sohn auferweckt und sie wird auch nicht in den Himmel aufgenommen, aber Christus bringt ihre Seele ins „himmlische Schatzhaus" und ihr Leib gelangt nach drei Tagen ins Paradies.[66] Das Endschicksal Mariens wird in der Erzählung des Ps-Johannes also deutlich in Bezug zu Tod und Auferstehung Christi gesetzt.[67]

Andererseits wird ein Leser, der die *Dormitio* kennt, bei der Lektüre der neutestamentlichen Leidensgeschichten auch Verbindungen zu diesem Text herstellen. Die Tendenzen der Evangelien, die römische Seite hinsichtlich des Todes Jesu zu entlasten und die Juden zu belasten, werden bei einem solchen Leser sicherlich noch verstärkt werden.[68] Es „ist nur ein schwacher Trost", dass bei Ps-Johannes schließlich ganz Israel zum Glauben an die Gottheit Christi gelangt und seine Mutter als *Theotokos* aner-

---

[64] Vgl. PS-JOH., *dorm.* 30 u. 35f (TISCHENDORF 104ff).

[65] KLAUCK, Apokryphe Evangelien (s. Anm. 9), 259.

[66] Vgl. PS-JOH., *dorm.* 44 u. 48f (TISCHENDORF 109 u. 111f). MIMOUNI, Dormition et assomption (s. Anm. 7), 125ff.

[67] Dass auch andere Texte der *Transitus*-Literatur Bezüge zu den ntl. Passions- und Ostererzählungen aufweisen, zeigt sich etwa im lateinisch überlieferten, Josef von Arimathäa zugeschriebenen *Liber de transitu*. Dort finden sich z.B. in den Kapiteln 17–21 (TISCHENDORF 119ff) Berührungen mit den ntl. Perikopen über das leere Grab (z.B. Mt 28,1–8) und dem ungläubigen Thomas (Joh 20,24–29). Es wäre sicherlich lohnend, die *Transitus-Mariae*-Texte systematisch auf derartige Motive zu untersuchen.

[68] „Auch hier müssen wir also die Tendenz konstatieren, die Verantwortung für das Leiden zunächst des Herrn und dann seiner Anhänger auf die jüdische Seite zu verschieben." KLAUCK, Apokryphe Evangelien (s. Anm. 9), 259.

kennt.[69] Maria wird in dieser Erzählung somit zwar letztlich zu einer Art Brücke zwischen Christen und Juden, leider ist sie das historisch betrachtet aber nicht geworden. Auch vor diesem Hintergrund wäre es wohl wichtig, die *Transitus-Mariae*-Literatur noch intensiver zu bearbeiten, denn auch diese Texte scheinen Ausdruck christlichen Antijudaismus' zu sein, ja diesen noch verstärkt zu haben.[70]

Ausblick: Ist die *Dormitio Mariae* ein Apokryphon oder ein hagiographischer Text?

Dass die zahlreichen Texte zum Lebensende Mariens in der deutschsprachigen Forschung bislang eher geringe Aufmerksamkeit erhalten haben, hängt u.a. wohl auch damit zusammen, dass die *Transitus-Mariae*-Literatur aufgrund ihrer späten Entstehung meist nicht zu den neutestamentlichen Apokryphen gerechnet wurde und deshalb z.B. keine Aufnahme in die bedeutende Sammlung SCHNEEMELCHERS fand.[71] Die *Transitus*-Berichte

---

[69] Ebd. In *dorm.* 47 (TISCHENDORF 110f) rufen die Juden beim Leichenzug Mariens mit ähnlichen Worten, wie bei den Synoptikern der römische Hauptmann unterm Kreuz, aus: ... ὄντως ἀληθινὸς θεός ἐστιν ὁ τεχθεὶς παρὰ σοῦ, θεοτόκε ἀειπάρθενε Μαρία. Vgl. Mk 15,39; Mt 27,54; Lk 23,47. Selbst Jephonias, der den Leichnam Marias angreifen wollte, verherrlicht schließlich Christus. Bei einem Leser, der das NT kennt, soll dies vielleicht die Hoffnung wecken, dass letztlich auch das Judentum wie das *Imperium Romanum* zum Glauben an Christus finden wird.

[70] „Brücken, die Juden und Christen miteinander verbinden hätten können, schlug Maria (...) nicht. Die jüdische Frau, die den christlichen Messias zur Welt gebracht hatte, ließ ein Bewußtsein der Zusammengehörigkeit nicht aufkommen. Maria trennte, grenzte aus, rief Kontroversen und Konflikte hervor." K. SCHREINER, Maria. Jungfrau, Mutter, Herrscherin, München/Wien 1994, 413. Vgl. zum mit Maria in irgendeiner Weise verbundenen Antijudaismus u.a. ebd. 413–462. J. HEIL/R. KAMPLING (Hg.), Maria – Tochter Sion? Mariologie, Marienfrömmigkeit und Judenfeindschaft, Paderborn/München 2001.

[71] Vgl. z.B. W. SCHNEEMELCHER, Haupteinleitung, in: DERS. (Hg.), Neutestamentliche Apokryphen in deutscher Übersetzung. Bd. 1: Evangelien, Tübingen [6]1990, v.a. 40–52 (1–61). SCHNEEMELCHER differenziert zwischen ntl. Apokryphen und hagiographischer Literatur, dafür greift er v.a. auf chronologische Kriterien zurück. Für ihn ist es „ein erheblicher Unterschied, ob ein Werk dieser Art vor oder nach der Mitte des 4. Jh. entstanden ist" (44). „Das führt" nach KLAUCK „z.B. dazu, dass ein Text wie der des Pseudo-Johannes im Deutschen bislang völlig unzugänglich blieb." KLAUCK, Apokryphe Evangelien (s. Anm. 9), 260. In anderssprachige Apokryphen-Sammlungen wurden z.T. *Transitus-Mariae*-Texte aufgenommen. Vgl. z.B. M. ERBETTA (Hg.), Gli apocrifi del Nuovo Testamento. Versione e commento. Bd. 1/2: Vangeli. Infanzia e passion di Cristo, assunzione di Maria, Turin 1981, 407–632. J.K. ELLIOTT (Hg.), Apocryphal New Testament. A Collection of Apocryphal Christian Literature in an English Translation, Oxford 1993, 689–723.

wurden daneben aber selbst von MIMOUNI als Teil der hagiographischen Literatur und nicht als Apokryphen angesehen.[72]

Abschließend soll hier auf der Grundlage der Arbeiten von TOBIAS NICKLAS und vor dem Hintergrund der oben vorgestellten Beobachtungen deshalb kurz gefragt werden, ob es nicht auch sinnvoll ist, die *Dormitio* des Ps-Johannes als christliches Apokryphon zu interpretieren. NICKLAS greift für seine Annäherung an den Begriff Apokryphität auf Ergebnisse der Semiotik und Intertextualitätsdebatte zurück und bestimmt solche Texte als apokryph, die nicht Teil der christlichen Bibel geworden sind, diese aber als eine Art „privilegierten Hypotext" voraussetzen, das heißt dass der Bezug zur Bibel, vor allem zum Neuen Testament für das Verständnis eines solchen Textes bedeutungsvoll ist.[73]

Wendet man diese Kriterien auf die hier behandelte Schrift an, so zeigt sich schnell, dass es sinnvoll ist, die *Dormitio Mariae* als christliches Apokryphon zu interpretieren. Die Erzählung des Ps-Johannes ist weder Teil der heutigen christlichen Bibel, noch scheint sie jemals irgendwo als ein solcher betrachtet worden zu sein.[74] Andererseits ist dieser Text ohne das

---

[72] Vgl. S.C. MIMOUNI, Les Transitus Mariae sont-ils vraiment des apocryphes? in StPatr 25 (1993), 122–128. MIMOUNI beantwortet die im Titel seines Aufsatzes gestellte Frage folgendermaßen: „Autrement dit, malgré leur mention dans le Décret gélasien, il apparait préférable de considérer les Transitus Mariae comme des écrits hagiographiques originaires de la Grande Église, plutôt que comme des écrits apocryphes originaires de communautés chrétiennes intersticielles" (128). Als Hintergrund für die Überlegungen MIMOUNIS ist folgende Notiz im *Decretum Gelasianum* zu nennen: *Liber qui appellatur Transitus sanctae Mariae – apocryphus. Decr. Gelas.* V, 6, 1 (TU 38/4,12). Es ist in der Forschung umstritten, welcher der *Transitus*-Texte hier genau im Blick ist. An MIMOUNIS Einschätzung ist v.a. der Umstand problematisch, dass er apokryph in diesem Aufsatz fast mit heterodox gleichsetzt, zumindest aber apokryphe Schriften als prinzipiell außerhalb der Großkirche stehend betrachtet. Dies trifft allerdings nur teilweise zu, wie z.B. ein Blick auf das einleitend angesprochene *Protevangelium Jacobi* zeigt.

[73] Vgl. T. NICKLAS, Semiotik – Intertextualität – Apokryphität. Eine Annäherung an den Begriff „christliche Apokryphen", in Apocrypha 17 (2006), 55–78. DERS., Gedanken zum Verhältnis zwischen christlichen Apokryphen und hagiographischer Literatur: Das Beispiel der Veronica-Traditionen, in NedThT 62 (2008), 45–63. Eine eingehende Auseinandersetzung mit den Thesen NICKLAS' – er versteht seine Annäherung an den Begriff Apokryphität aufgrund der Offenheit des Apokryphenbegriffs dezidiert nicht als Definition – muss hier aus Raumgründen unterbleiben, positiv sei nur hervorgehoben, dass er v.a. die Textualität christlicher Apokryphen herausstellt.

[74] Selbst wenn man, wie von MIMOUNI gezeigt, eine gewisse Liturgizität der Schrift des Ps-Johannes annimmt und andererseits Liturgizität als ein Kriterium von Kanonizität betrachtet, so wurde die *Dormitio* doch nie als Bestandteil des NT angesehen. Vgl. hierzu MIMOUNI, La lecture liturgique (s. Anm. 15), 403–425. Trotz der großen Verbreitung der Schrift zeigt sich durch manche Randnotizen in den Manuskripten auch, dass sie wohl aus dogmatischen Gründen bei ihren Kopisten nicht nur auf Zustimmung stieß. Vgl. MIMOUNI, Dormition et assomption (s. Anm. 7), 125.

Neue Testament kaum verstehbar. Die auftretenden Personen, die Orts- und Zeitangaben verweisen durchgängig auf die neutestamentlichen Schriften, wie hier beispielhaft anhand der Passions- und Ostermotive gezeigt wurde.[75] An einigen Stellen bleibt der Text der *Dormitio* wohl sogar unverständlich, wenn der Leser nicht Informationen aus dem Neuen Testament einspielt. So ist für das Verständnis des Kapitels 29 z.B. die Kenntnis von Mk 15,1 bzw. Mt 27,1 bedeutsam, ja letztlich unentbehrlich. Bei Ps-Johannes wird nämlich berichtet, dass die jüdische Priesterschaft und das Volk „wiederum einen Beschluss fassten (πάλιν ... συμβούλιον ποιησάμενοι)", und zwar diesmal gegen Maria.[76] Für einen Leser, der den Beschluss des Hohen Rates gegen Jesus aus dem Neuen Testament nicht kennt, ist der eben referierte Text, zumindest aber das Adverb πάλιν kaum verstehbar.

Wenn man jedoch, wie gerade geschehen, die ps-johanneische Erzählung aufgrund ihrer vielfachen Bezüge zu neutestamentlichen Schriften zu den christlichen Apokryphen rechnet, ist damit nicht ausgeschlossen, dass die *Dormitio Mariae* nicht auch sinnvoll als hagiographische Schrift interpretiert werden kann. Beide Zugangsweisen müssen sich nicht ausschließen, sondern können komplementär verstanden werden.[77] Die Schrift des Ps-Johannes handelt vom Ende Mariens, Maria wird als Heilige, ja als die Heilige schlechthin dargestellt. Der Text schildert sie als Fürsprecherin und Vermittlerin, die Wunder bei ihrem Tod führen den römischen Präfekten und schließlich sogar ganz Israel zum Glauben an Christus, für den Le-

[75] Dies könnte auch mit Blick auf andere ntl. Texte, z.B. Lk 1–2, nachgewiesen werden. Für NICKLAS gibt es darüber hinaus auch eine Art indirekte Apokryphität von Texten, und zwar bei Hypertextualität zu anderen christlichen Apokryphen. Vgl. NICKLAS, Semiotik – Intertextualität – Apokryphität (s. Anm. 73), 73. Auch dies findet sich in der *Dormitio Mariae*. Die Berichte der Apostel darüber, wie sie zu Maria nach Jerusalem gelangt sind, weisen nämlich z.B. deutliche Bezüge zu apokryphen Apostelakten auf. Vgl. u.a. PS-JOH., *dorm.* 20 (TISCHENDORF 101f).

[76] Ebd. 29 (TISCHENDORF 104).

[77] „Der Begriff ‚apokryph' (...) lebt vom Gegenüber oder besser dem Zueinander apokrypher zu biblischen Texten, der Begriff ‚hagiographisch' vom Fokus eines Textes auf einen oder mehrere Protagonisten, die als ‚heilig' bezeichnet werden können. Die beiden Definitionen hängen also mit verschiedenen Perspektiven auf die jeweiligen Texte zusammen. Damit ist es also durchaus möglich, dass ein Text beide Kriterien erfüllt: Dies zeigt sich schon daran, dass ja eine Vielzahl von Charakteren, die in der christlichen Bibel begegnen, in der katholischen Kirche, aber auch den Kirchen des Ostens als Heilige verehrt werden; besonders deutlich wird dies in Texten, in denen das Leben Marias oder eines der Apostel im Mittelpunkt steht." NICKLAS, Gedanken zum Verhältnis (s. Anm. 73), 51f. Es ist darüber hinaus aber auch einzuräumen, dass hagiographische Texte meist ebenfalls die Bibel als „privilegierten Hypotext" voraussetzen, „Heilige" werden häufig in Anlehnung an biblische Gestalten gezeichnet. Um hagiographische Schriften auch als Apokryphen interpretieren zu können, müssen diese wohl irgendwie in einem „biblischen Umfeld" verortet werden können.

ser wird Maria somit zum Symbol der Hoffnung.[78] Vor diesem Hintergrund ist es sicherlich berechtigt, die *Dormitio* auch als hagiographische Schrift zu bezeichnen.[79]

[78] Die *Dormitio* beginnt folgendermaßen: Τῆς παναγίας ἐνδόξου θεοτόκου καὶ ἀειπαρθένου Μαρίας … . PS-JOH., *dorm.* 1 (TISCHENDORF 95). Im Umfeld des Hauses Mariens in Betlehem und Jerusalem kommt es nach Darstellung des Ps-Johannes zu zahlreichen Wundern und Heilungen, die wiederum zu Bekehrungen führen. Vgl. ebd. 26ff u. 34ff (TISCHENDORF 103f u. 106). Auch bei der Bestattung Marias kommt es zu wundersamen Geschehnissen, sodass schließlich das ganze Volk ihren Sohn als Gott bekennt. Vgl. ebd. 46f (TISCHENDORF 110f). Marias Rolle als Fürsprecherin wird in diesem Text ausführlich thematisiert, und zwar unmittelbar vor ihrem Tod. Vgl. ebd. 40–43 (TISCHENDORF 108f). Zum altkirchlichen Hintergrund vgl. allgemein u.a. L. GAMBERO, Mary and the Fathers of the Church. The Blessed Virgin Mary in Patristic Thought, San Francisco 1999. A. CAMERON, The Cult of the Virgin in Late Antiquity: Religious Development and Myth-Making, in: R.N. SWANSON (Hg.), The Church and Mary. Papers Read at the 2001 Summer Meeting and the 2002 Winter Meeting of the Ecclesiastical History Society, Rochester 2004, 1–21. CH. MAUNDER (Hg.), The Origins of the Cult of the Virgin Mary, London/New York 2008.

[79] „Soll man einen solchen Text (…) überhaupt noch zu den ‚neutestamentlichen Apokryphen' oder den ‚antiken christlichen Apokryphen' rechnen? Die Berührungen mit Hagiographie (Heiligenlegenden), Homilie (Predigt) und Liturgie sind jedenfalls sehr stark, aber damit sind Grenzbereiche markiert, mit denen es immer wieder zu Überschneidungen kommt." KLAUCK, Apokryphe Evangelien (s. Anm. 9), 260. Nach NICKLAS ist die Entscheidung, ob man einen solchen Text als apokryph oder hagiographisch interpretiert, von der „Perspektive des Rezipienten" abhängig und muss somit kein Gegensatz sein. NICKLAS, Gedanken zum Verhältnis (s. Anm. 73), 52.

Passion and Resurrection Traditions in Early Jewish-Christian Gospels

PETRI LUOMANEN

1. Introduction

We know relatively little about early Jewish-Christian gospels for sure. Since no manuscripts of these gospels have survived, the evidence has to be gathered from fragmentary quotations preserved in the writings of the Church Fathers. Some of the surviving fragments also include passion and resurrection traditions that differ from the canonical gospels in some important respects. All the references are quite short and as such they do not allow any secure reconstructions of larger passion narratives from which they might have been taken. Yet it is possible to delineate some general tendencies in these narratives and to sketch their ideological and social-historical background by comparing them with their canonical counterparts and reflecting on their contents in the light of other information we have about early Jewish Christians.

This article focuses on *early* Jewish-Christian gospels. Therefore, it mainly deals with evidence from the first to the beginning of the fifth century, the last patristic sources being Epiphanius' and Jerome's writings.[1]

---

[1] If not indicated otherwise, the texts and the translations of patristic passages in this article are based on A.F.J. Klijn/G.J. Reinink, *Patristic Evidence for Jewish-Christian Sects* (NT.S 36; Leiden 1973), and A.F.J. Klijn, *Jewish-Christian Gospel Tradition* (SuppVigChr 17; Leiden 1992). I concur with Klijn, *Jewish-Christian Gospel Tradition*, 20, who thinks that, after Jerome, Greek and Latin writers usually depend on earlier sources. In addition to patristic references, there are two later translations of Matthew's gospel which have sometimes been presented as important sources of early Jewish-Christian gospel traditions: Shem Tob's Hebrew Matthew and the Coptic text of Matthew in the Schøyen Collection. G. Howard, *Hebrew Gospel of Matthew* (Macon, Ga. 1995), published the text and translation of Shem Tob's Matthew arguing for an early date of the text. Howard's interpretation was opposed – convincingly, in my view – by W.L. Petersen, Review of G. Howard, "The Gospel of Matthew according to a Primitive Hebrew Text", *JBL* 108 (1989), 722–726; id., "The Vorlage of Shem-Tob's 'Hebrew Matthew'", *NTS* 44 (1998), 490–512. Petersen argues for a later date of the text of the Hebrew Matthew, showing its connections to Diatessaronic readings and Old Latin translations. Another possible source for Shem Tob's Diatessaronic readings is a Catalan version of Matthew. Thus, J.V. Niclós, "L'Évangile en hébreu de Shem Tob Ibn Shaprut: Une traduction

I will mainly deal with four passages: Section 3 of this article deals with a fragment that Epiphanius quotes in his Medicine Chest (*Panarion* XXX 22,3–5). This passage from the gospel that was used by the Ebionites concerns the preparations of Jesus' last Passover meal. Sections 4 and 5 deal with two fragments that are in Jerome's Commentary on Matthew (*Comm. Matt.* 27,16; 27,51). I will first briefly present the contents of the two references (section 4), then discuss their origin (section 5). Section 6 of this article discusses Jerome's *Illustrious Men* where he tells about Jesus' appearance to the James the Just (*Vir. ill.* II). However, before dealing with these passages in detail, I will discuss two problems that pertain to larger literary and socio-historical contexts of the surviving passages: reconstruction of the early Jewish-Christian gospels and the definition of Jewish Christianity.

2. Tracing Literary and Socio-Historical Contexts for Jewish-Christian Gospel Fragments

Modern scholars have tried to reconstruct the number and the contents of the Jewish-Christian gospels on the basis of the Church Fathers' quotations and references. The publication of the third edition of Edgar Hennecke's Neutestamentliche Apokryphen in 1959 (edited by Wilhelm Schneemelcher)[2] and its English translation in 1963 more or less created a consensus in the German and English-speaking scholarly world about the number and character of Jewish-Christian gospels. Several text-books and general articles on apocryphal gospels have repeated the view according to which there were originally three Jewish-Christian gospels: the *Gospel of the He-*

---

d' origine judéo-catalane replacée dans son Sitz im Leben", *RB* 106 (1999), 358–407; J. Joosten, "The 'Gospel of Barnabas' and the Diatessaron", *HThR* 95 (2002), 73–96, esp. 80 n. 31. H.-M. Schenke (ed.), *Coptic Papyri I: Das Matthäus-Evangelium im mittelägyptischen Dialekt des Koptischen (Codex Schøyen)* (Manuscripts in the Schøyen Collection II; Oslo 2001), published the Coptic text of Matthew. He argues for the primitive character of the version, suggesting that both the Coptic Matthew and the canonical Matthew must depend on an earlier Hebrew version of Matthew which is also behind the Jewish-Christian gospels. Schenke clearly overestimates the value of the Coptic version as a testimony of an early version of the Gospel of Matthew. Nevertheless, the study of the Coptic Matthew is still in its infancy and more detailed text-critical research is needed. For an overview and further bibliography of Shem Tob's Matthew and the Coptic Matthew in the Schøyen Collection, see C.A. Evans, "The Jewish Christian Gospel Tradition", in *Jewish Believers in Jesus: The Early Centuries* (ed. O. Skarsaune and R. Hvalvik; Peabody, Mass. 2007), 241–277, here 267–276.

[2] E. Hennecke/W. Schneemelcher (eds.), *Neutestamentliche Apokryphen in deutscher Übersetzung: Evangelien* (3rd ed.; Tübingen 1959).

brews, the *Gospel of the Ebionites* and the *Gospel of the Nazarenes*.[3] In the following, I will call this the Three Gospel Hypothesis (TGH). An alternative reconstruction, favoured mainly by some French scholars, has counted two gospels: the *Gospel of the Ebionites* and the *Gospel of the Hebrews/Nazarenes*.[4]

During the past decade, more and more critical voices have been raised against different aspects of the threefold distinction which was presented in the third edition of Hennecke's collection by Philip Vielhauer and Georg Strecker. Scholars who have become more aware of the weaknesses of the TGH, are now either refraining from making any firm conclusions about the number and contents of the gospels – organizing their presentation according to the available sources, the Church Fathers[5] – or making adjustments to the threefold[6] or to the twofold distinction.

---

[3] Ph. Vielhauer/G. Strecker, "Jewish-Christian Gospels", in *New Testament Apocrypha: Gospels and Related Writings* (ed. E. Hennecke, W. Schneemelcher and R.M. Wilson; 2nd edition; Cambridge 1991), 134–177. Klijn, *Jewish-Christian Gospel Tradition* (n. 1), also argues for three Jewish-Christian gospels. In the first edition of Hennecke's collection, A. Meyer still assumed there were only two Jewish-Christian Gospels. Foundations for the distinction of three gospels were laid in Hennecke's second edition by H. Waitz, and the theory was developed further in the third edition by Vielhauer and Strecker. See A. Meyer, "Hebräerevangelium", in *Neutestamentliche Apokryphen* (ed. E. Hennecke; Tübingen 1904), 11–21; A. Meyer, "Ebionitenevangelium", in *ibid.*, 24–27; H. Waitz, "Die judenchristlichen Evangelien in der altkirchlichen Literatur", in *ibid.*, 10–17; H. Waitz, "Das Matthäusevangelium der Nazaräer (Nazaräerevangelium)", in *Neutestamentliche Apokryphen* (ed. E. Hennecke; Tübingen 1924), 17–32; H. Waitz, "Ebionäerevangelium oder Evangelium der Zwölf", in *ibid.*, 39–48; H. Waitz, "Hebräerevangelium", in *ibid.*, 48–55.

[4] For instance, S.C. Mimouni, *Le judéo-christianisme ancien: Essais historiques* (Paris 1998), 209–211, 215–216. Some scholars have also argued for only one Jewish-Christian gospel. W.L. Petersen has drawn attention to Diatessaronic readings in many of the quotations suggesting that all the fragments could as well be rooted in one and the same gospel that is somehow related to Tatian's Diatessaron. See, for instance, W.L. Petersen, *Tatian's Diatessaron: Its Creation, Dissemination, Significance and History in Scholarship* (SuppVigChr 25; Leiden 1994), 29–31, 39–41. Only one Jewish-Christian gospel is also presupposed by R.A. Pritz, *Nazarene Jewish Christianity: From the End of the New Testament Period Until Its Disappearance in the Fourth Century* (Leiden 1988), 83–86; P.L. Schmidt, "'Und es war geschrieben auf Hebräisch, Griechisch und Lateinisch': Hieronymus, das Hebräer-Evangelium und seine mittelalterliche Rezeption", *Filologia Mediolatina* 5 (1998), 49–93.

[5] Evans, "The Jewish Christian" (n. 1), 245–246.

[6] J. Frey, who is writing on Jewish-Christian Gospels in the "new Hennecke" = Chr. Markschies/J. Schröter (ed.), *Antike Christliche Apokryphen I: Evangelien* (Tübingen 2010), is critical of the close connection that has been assumed between the Gospel of Matthew and the Gospel of the Nazarenes. He is also revising Vielhauer and Strecker's reconstruction by bracketing the so-called "Ioudaikon" fragments (readings titled as τὸ Ἰουδαικόν) from the Gospel of the Nazarenes. See also, J. Frey, "Die Scholien nach dem

In this article, I argue for a theory that assumes only two Jewish-Christian apocryphal gospels: the *Gospel of the Ebionites* and the *Gospel of the Hebrews*. However, the theory deviates from both the TGH and the previous hypothesis that assumed two gospels because, in my view, the evidence indicates that in addition to two actual gospels, there was also a collection of anti-Rabbinic testimonies that Jerome had received from the Nazarenes.[7] This collection was prepared by making minor adjustments to the wording of an Aramaic translation of the canonical Matthew.[8] Consequently, in this reconstruction, the contents and the character of the *Gospel of the Hebrews* becomes different from what has previously been assumed in the twofold or the threefold distinction because five anti-Rabbinic passages, transmitted by Jerome, are excluded from the apocryphal Jewish-Christian gospels and all the rest – excluding the ones that are presented by Epiphanius and commonly attributed to the *Gospel of the Ebionites* – are assumed to be from the *Gospel of the Hebrews*.

The term "Jewish Christianity" has been much debated during the past decades.[9] It has been accused of being an anachronistic, "scholarly invention" that misleadingly gathers under one umbrella various groups with different ethnic backgrounds and practices.[10] Otherwise, it has been found too slippery and futile precisely because scholars have used it in so many ways.[11] Nonetheless, I find the traditional terminology still informative and helpful, provided its anachronistic character is kept in mind. Furthermore, because the multifaceted character of both Christianity and Judaism during the first centuries C.E. has become widely acknowledged, it follows that

---

'jüdischen Evangelium' und das sogenannte Nazoräer-Evangelium", *ZNW* 94 (2003), 122–137. I want to express my gratitude to Prof. Frey for information he has kindly provided in e-mail correspondence and for a manuscript of one of his forthcoming articles which I was able to use when writing this article (n. 33).

[7] For problems in Vielhauer and Strecker's reconstruction and more detailed argumentation of this theory, see P. Luomanen, "The Nazarenes' Gospel and Their Commentary on Isaiah Reconsidered", in *Proceedings of the Jewish Pseudepigrapha & Christian Apocrypha Section at the SBL International Meeting in Groningen, The Netherlands, July 25–28, 2004* (ed. P. Piovanelli; forthcoming).

[8] In the Three Gospel Hypothesis, these passages are usually attributed to the *Gospel of the Nazarenes*.

[9] For recent overviews of the discussion, see M. Jackson-McCabe, "What's in a Name? The Problem of 'Jewish Christianity'", in *Jewish Christianity Reconsidered: Rethinking Ancient Groups and Texts* (ed. M. Jackson-McCabe; Minneapolis 2007), 7–38; J.C. Paget, "The Definition of the Term Jewish Christian and Jewish Christianity in the History of Research", in *Jewish Christianity Reconsidered: Rethinking Ancient Groups and Texts* (ed. O. Skarsaune and R. Hvalvik; Peabody, Mass. 2007), 22–52.

[10] Thus, for instance, J.E. Taylor, "The Phenomenon of Early Jewish-Christianity: Reality or Scholarly Invention?", *VigChr* 44 (1990), 313–334.

[11] Paget, "Definition" (n. 9), 50–52.

we cannot postulate only one type of Jewish Christianity but several Jewish Christianities, the characters of which have to be determined more closely case by case. One way to do this is to discuss *Jewish-Christian profiles* of the groups or text by focusing on *indicators of Jewish Christianity.*[12]

Andrew Gregory has questioned whether it is justified to speak of *Jewish-Christian gospels* as a category that is somehow set apart from other canonical and apocryphal gospels.[13] Given our meager knowledge about the complete gospels, Gregory's point is well taken: as long as we do not have entire gospels available, it is hazardous to characterize the gospels *per se* as Jewish-Christian. It might, indeed, be more preferable to speak of apocryphal – these gospels are truly apocryphal! – gospels used by early Jewish Christians which would leave open the precise nature of the gospels.

Although Gregory's arguments are healthy reminders of how little we actually know about these gospels, his criterion of what counts as Jewish-Christian texts – the ones that deal with Law observance[14] – appears quite rigorous and perhaps not sensitive enough to the variety of ways Judaism essentially affected the identities of Christ believers during the first centuries C.E. Although Law observance was the bone of contention in many cases, in some other circumstances, other *indicators of Judaism* may have stamped the identities and border marking of the Christ believers, also leaving their mark on the gospels that were used by them to such a degree that it is justified to speak of Jewish Christians transmitting and reinterpreting *their* own gospel traditions. In the following, the discussion about the Nazarenes anti-rabbinic collection – which seems to have culminated

---

[12] *Indicators of Jewish Christianity* consist of, for instance, Jewish practices (circumcision, Sabbath observance, purity laws), characteristically Jewish ideas (Yahweh as the only God, the temple as Yahweh's abode, the Covenant), pedigree or ethnicity of the group, Jesus' role in worship (his degree of divinity), baptism in the name of Jesus or triune God as the entrance rite to the community. This kind of analysis gets closer to the social reality of ancient groups when the study of these – and other pertinent indicators that may appear in the sources – is combined with the question about their role in the marking of social borders between the insiders and the outsiders. For the approach and its application, see also P. Luomanen, "Where Did Another Rich Man Come From? The Jewish-Christian Profile of the Story About a Rich Man in the 'Gospel of the Hebrews' (Origen, Comm. in Matth. 15.14)", *VigChr* 57 (2003), 243–275, 267–274; id., "Ebionites and Nazarenes", in *Jewish Christianity Reconsidered: Rethinking Ancient Groups and Texts* (ed. M. Jackson-McCabe; Minneapolis, Minn. 2007), 81–118, 84–85, 98–102, 106–107, 114–117.

[13] A. Gregory, "Hindrance or Help: Does the Modern Category of 'Jewish-Christian Gospel' Distort our Understanding of the Texts to which it Refers?", *JSNT* (2006), 387–413.

[14] Ibid., 390–392.

in Jesus' passion – suitably illustrates this point. Although these pro-Pauline Christians were probably not conservative in their interpretation of Jewish Law, there were still strong Jewish components in their religious profile. Whether these were strong enough to grant them – or their version of Matthew's gospel – a label of Jewish-Christian will be discussed in more detail below.

3. Jesus' Passion in the *Gospel of the Ebionites*

3.1 Epiphanius on the Ebionites' Trickery

Although the reconstruction of early Jewish-Christian gospels is a controversial issue, scholars are usually quite unanimous in attributing the fragments in Epiphanius' *Panarion* to the *Gospel of the Ebionites*. This gospel has obviously been written in Greek after the synoptic gospels were written since it harmonizes wordings of all three of them, Matthew and Luke in particular. *Panarion* has the following description of Jesus' conversation with his disciples before the Last Supper where Epiphanius criticizes the wording of the *Gospel of the Ebionites*.

> But the Lord himself says in turn, "With desire I have desired to eat this Passover with you." And he said "this Passover," not simply "Passover," so that no one would practice it in accordance with his own notion. The Passover, as I said, was roast meat and the rest. But of their own will these people have lost sight of the consequence of the truth, and have altered the wording—which is evident to everyone from the sayings associated with it—and made the disciples say, "Where wilt thou that we prepare for thee to eat the Passover?" And the Lord, if you please, says, "Have I desired meat with desire, to eat this Passover with you?" But how can their tampering go undetected, when the consequence cries out that the "mu" and the "eta" are additions? Instead of saying ἐπιθυμίᾳ ἐπεθύμησα they added the μή as an afterthought. Christ actually said "With desire I have desired to eat this Passover with you." But they mislead themselves by writing in meat and making a false entry, and saying "Have I desired meat with desire, to eat this Passover with you?" But it is plainly demonstrated that he both kept the Passover, and, as I said, ate meat. (*Pan.* XXX 22,3–5).[15]

The disciples' question – as it is quoted by Epiphanius and as it appears to have been in the *Gospel of the Ebionites* – is paralleled only in Mark and Matthew (Mark 14:12; Matt 26:17). The wording of the *Gospel of the Ebionites* is closer to Matthew, the only difference being a slightly different word order. On the other hand, Jesus' answer is paralleled only in Luke (cf. Luke 22:15–18) because there is no parallel for this section in Mark or Matthew. Thus, in this section, the *Gospel of the Ebionites* seems to have

[15] Trans. F. Williams, *The Panarion of Epiphanius of Salamis: Book I (Sects 1–46)* (NHS 35; Leiden 1987).

used at least Matthew and Luke. It also seems obvious that there was some sort of passion narrative in the *Gospel of the Ebionites* and that it was composed, somewhat creatively, using Matthew and Luke, at least.

3.2 Reconstructing the Passion Narrative in the Gospel of the Ebionites

Unfortunately, Epiphanius does not present any other quotations from the *Gospel of the Ebionites* that could be located in the passion narrative. However, it is possible to draw some conclusions about the passion narrative on the basis of this passage and other passages Epiphanius quotes from the *Gospel of the Ebionites*, especially if we also make use of other information about the Ebionites practices and theology.[16] In the following, I intend to show that – given there was some coherence in the passion narrative and the ideology of the Ebionites – the wording of their gospel must have been, at some points, quite close to what we now can see in manuscript D in Luke.

Epiphanius' quotations from the *Gospel of the Ebionites* give the impression that Jesus has expressed his unwillingness to eat meat with his disciples as an answer to the disciples' question where Jesus wants them to prepare the Passover meal. This suggests that the *Gospel of the Ebionites* did not include Jesus' instructions to the disciples on how to find a location for the Passover meal. This is natural enough: if Jesus was not willing to eat the Paschal Lamb with the disciples, there was no need for him to give special instructions how to arrange such a meal.

On the other hand, we know from Irenaeus' and Epiphanius' descriptions that the Ebionites celebrated the Eucharist, but using only unleavened bread and water (Irenaeus, *Haer.* V 1,3; Epiphanius, *Pan.* XXX 16,1). Thus, there probably was a description of the institution of the Eucharist in their gospel, although the meal setting must have been an ordinary meal, not a Passover meal. Its wording must also have been different from what we have now in the synoptic gospels because – if the Ebionites celebrated the Eucharist only with water – blood/wine cannot have been mentioned in the actual institution. As a matter of fact, Jesus' words about the sacrificial

[16] It is clear that this kind of argumentation remains hypothetical since the logic is to try to figure out what there must have been or what there cannot have been in the Ebionites' passion narrative. This kind of argumentation, however, may not be too precarious since we have some examples of cases where the contents of the *Gospel of the Ebionites* cohere with information about the Ebionites from elsewhere. For instance, Epiphanius seems to know about the Ebionites' practice of not eating meat from his own experience – he probably met Ebionites in Cyprus where he was acting as bishop (*Pan.* XXX 15,3–4). Furthermore, he presents two examples from the *Gospel of the Ebionites* where the Ebionites have changed the synoptic wording in order to support their own practice. For a discussion of what Epiphanius knew from his own experience and what he derived from his sources, see Luomanen, "Ebionites and Nazarenes" (n. 12), 85–102.

significance of his own blood would have appeared quite problematic for the Ebionites whose Jesus condemned the sacrificial cult all together (*Pan.* XXX 16,5). Instead, there would have been room for words to the effect that the disciples were to abstain from drinking wine.

All the synoptic gospels have, in the passage on the Last Supper, Jesus' words that he will not be drinking wine until in the kingdom of God (Mark 14:25; Matt 26:29; Luke 22:18). However, in Luke this vow is the most outspoken since it is presented before the institution of the Eucharist and it is coupled with the words about not eating Passover – in the canonical Luke, Jesus yearns to eat Passover with his disciples but only for this last time before his passion. Next time will be in the kingdom of God.

Thus, there are two notable features that draw attention to Luke's version of the Last Supper if one tries to trace the closest possible point of comparison for the wording of the *Gospel of the Ebionites*: the wording of Jesus' answer in the *Gospel of the Ebionites* is paralleled only in Luke, and Jesus' vows not to eat Passover and not to drink wine are most vehement in Luke.

If one takes Luke's description of the Last Supper (Luke 22:15–20) as the starting point – assuming that the opening verse was formulated the way Epiphanius describes – would the story have been acceptable to the Ebionites? Jesus words about not eating Passover and not drinking wine before the Kingdom of God arrives (Luke 22:15–18) would cohere very well with the Ebionites' diet and their Eucharistic practice, which did not include meat or wine. It is even quite possible to interpret Luke 22:17–18 as an institution of a Eucharistic cup that contained water only. Verse 19 would also still be acceptable and even necessary as an institution of the Eucharistic bread although the words about the body "given for you" might have some suspicious sacrificial overtones. Problems begin with the second cup in verse 20 where Jesus' blood is assigned a sacrificial role.

As it happens, manuscript D, Old Latin and Old Syriac translations have a shorter version of the Last Supper in Luke, which conveniently ends precisely at the point where the story begins to be problematic from the Ebionite point of view, the last words being "this is my body." In the case of the Last Supper, the connection between the *Gospel of the Ebionites*, D, Old Latin and Old Syriac translations remains hypothetical but there are two other instances where the wording of the *Gospel of the Ebionites* demonstrably agrees with the same group of manuscripts supporting the view that the match between the presumed contents of the *Gospel of the Ebionites* and these manuscripts of Luke is not coincidental. First, in the description of Jesus' baptism (*Pan.* XXX 13,7–8), the *Gospel of the Ebionites* agrees with this same group of manuscripts against others by including Ps 2:7 at the end of the words sounding from the Heaven: "Today I have begotten you." Second, in Luke 3:21, manuscript D agrees with the *Gospel of the Ebionites* (and Mark) when it describes how the Spirit went *into* (εἰς) Jesus. This corresponds to one of the most characteristic features of the Ebionites' Christology – also typical of the Pseudo-Clementines – according to which the eternal Christ/Spirit entered the man called Jesus at his baptism.

Although there was significant development in the Ebionite movement from the mid-second century, when Irenaeus first refers to the Ebionites, to the end of the fourth century (Epiphanius), all the theological ideas that have come up during the preceding discussion have good chances of having been part of the Ebionites' symbolic universe from very early on.[17] Yet, there is no basis for using these Ebionite connections to support the view that D's reading should be taken as the original one in Luke's Last Supper[18] or that the *Gospel of the Ebionites* was one of Luke's sources.[19] Nevertheless, the Ebionite connections cast light on the theological motives behind the shortened Lukan text. Notably, the defenders of the longer

---

[17] The Ebionites' practice of using water in the Eucharist is attested by both Irenaeus and Epiphanius (cf. above). The idea of Christ/Spirit entering Jesus is more explicit in Epiphanius' description but also seems to be presupposed by Irenaeus when he compares the Ebionites' Christology with the Christology of Cerinthus (*Haer.* I 26,2; I agree with scholars who read here, on the basis Hippolytus' parallel "similiter" pro "non similiter." The Ebionites Christology was similar to the Christology of Cerinthus who separated Christ and Jesus). The critical attitude towards the sacrificial cult agrees with using water in the Eucharist, but it may also be rooted in the theology of the Hellenists in the early Jerusalem church – if the Ebionites' history can be traced back to them. For this hypothesis, and a more detailed discussion on the development of the Ebionite movement, see Luomanen, "Ebionites and Nazarenes" (n. 12), 85–102; id., "Sacrifices Abolished: The Last Supper in Luke (Codex Bezae) and in the *Gospel of the Ebionites*", in *Lux Humana, Lux Aeterna: Essays on Biblical and Related Themes in Honour of Lars Aejmelaeus* (ed. A. Mustakallio in collaboration with H. Leppä and H. Räisänen; Publications of Finnish Exegetical Society 89; Helsinki and Göttingen 2005), 186–208, 201–206.

[18] Westcott and Hort argued that when the Old Latin and the Old Syriac versions agreed with the Codex Bezae, they represented an older, non-interpolated text. This is precisely the case in Luke 22:19b–20. However, after the publication of the second edition of the Greek New Testament, where the so-called "Western non-interpolations" were abandoned, the Greek New Testament and Nestle-Aland editions have agreed on the longer Lukan text as the original reading. The manuscript evidence for the longer reading is overwhelming (provided one does not accept Westcott and Hort's principle), and literary critical considerations also support the view that the longer text stems from Luke's pen. Luke's distinctive diction is so clear in the passage that it is not possible to reconstruct any written source that Luke might have used. However, the possibility remains that Luke freely used an older Jewish-Christian tradition in the first half of the passage which he combined with more Pauline formulations in the second half. For more detailed discussion see Luomanen, "Sacrifices Abolished" (n. 17).

[19] In contrast to J.R. Edwards, "The *Gospel of the Ebionites* and the Gospel of Luke", *NTS* 48 (2002), 568–586.

reading have found it difficult to provide a satisfactory explanation for the genesis of the shorter reading. Once the Ebionite character of the shorter text is acknowledged, the shortening becomes more understandable.[20] The scribe who changed Luke's text here and in some other instances (see above) was, at least partly, influenced by Ebionite ideas. As such, the shorter reading also approximates the wording of the institution of the Eucharist as it must have stood in the *Gospel of the Ebionites*.

Since the *Gospel of the Ebionites* presumes that the Spirit entered Jesus when he was baptized by John, question arises whether the Spirit might have flown away at the time of his death. If the *Gospel of the Ebionites* was consistent with the Christology of the Ebionites as it is described by Epiphanius (cf. *Pan*. XXX 3,1–6; XXX 14,4; XXX 16,1), then there probably was also a description of the departure of the Spirit/Christ. The *Gospel of Peter* indicates that such beliefs were also expressed in the gospel narratives. In the *Gospel of Peter* 19, the Lord cries: "My power, power, you have forsaken me." Whether the Gospel of the Ebionites referred to Power, Christ or Spirit remains uncertain but on the basis of the key features of the Ebionite Christology, it is seems very likely that there was some sort of separation of the man Jesus and his heavenly occupant at the end of the gospel.

4. Passion Fragments in Jerome's Commentary on Matthew

Jerome's Commentary on Matthew (398 C.E.) contains an alternative interpretation of the name Barabbas in Matt 27:16:

> The name of this man is interpreted in the Gospel which is written according to the Hebrews as son of their master…

In this passage, Jerome appears to claim that in the gospel according to the Hebrews, the name Barabbas which means son of the/his father in Hebrew, was followed by an interpretation that the name means "son of their master." Scholars have found this reference problematic for two reasons. First, an interpretation of a Semitic name would seem unnecessary in a Semitic gospel. Second, Barabbas means "son of the/his father." Even the Greek accusative form Βαραββᾶν which is attested in the actual Greek text of the

[20] The inability of the defenders of the longer reading to provide a satisfactory reason for the shortening of the text is still considered to be the best argument for the shorter reading. J.A. Fitzmyer, *The Gospel according to Luke (X–XXIV): Introduction, Translation and Notes* (AncB 28A; New York 1985), 1388; J. Nolland, *Luke 18:35–24:53* (WBC 35C; Dallas, Tex. 1993), 1041.

passage[21] and would come closer to Jerome's interpretation – means, in Aramaic and Syriac, literally "son of *our* master/Rabbi," not "son of *their* master/Rabbi."[22]

However, as Lagrange has pointed out in this context the "interpretation" does not refer to a translation but to spelling/reading the name in such a way that it comes to mean the "son of *our* master" instead of the "son of (our) father." [23] In my view, if placed back in Matthew's narrative, the form "son of *our* master/Rabbi" is perfect in the mouth of the crowds. Jerome's "interpretation," for its part, expresses the same thing from his own, Christian point of view: the crowds wanted to free the "son of *their* master/Rabbi."

When Jerome is explaining the death of Jesus in the Gospel of Matthew he refers to the following difference he found in the gospel used by the Nazarenes:

> The veil of the temple has been rent and all the mysteries of the law which were formerly covered have been made public and have come over to the people of the gentiles. In the Gospel which we have already often mentioned we read that a lintel of an enormous size was broken and split. Josephus also tells that the angelic powers, once the overseers of the temple, at the same moment proclaimed: Let us go away from these places. (Comm. Matt. 27,51).

Jerome also refers to the same incident in one of his letters (*Epist.* CXX 8, a letter to Hedibia), with slightly different words: "a lintel of wonderful size of the temple collapsed."[24] Minor differences in the key words of the passage indicate that Jerome was not providing literal translations from the original but quoted the passage freely from his memory. Jerome had already discussed the "lifted" lintel of the temple in Isa 6:4 in his letter to Damasus some twenty years earlier (*Epist.* XVIII; sublatum est superliminare). According to Jerome, a Greek scholar interprets the "lifting" of the lintel as a sign of the coming destruction of the Jerusalem temple although many others think that, in Isaiah, the reference is to the moment when the veil of the temple will be rent. [25]

---

[21] In some Greek manuscripts the name is even written with double ρ. See Klijn, *Jewish-Christian Gospel Tradition* (n. 1), 93.

[22] Problems connected with Jerome's reference are extensively treated by Vielhauer/Strecker, "Jewish-Christian Gospels" (n. 3), 156–157.

[23] R.P. Lagrange, "L' Evangile selon les Hébreux", *RB* 31 (1922), II: 161–181 and III: 321–149, 329, followed by Klijn, *Jewish-Christian Gospel Tradition* (n. 1), 92.

[24] The Latin runs in *Epist.* CXX 8: superliminare templi mirae magnitudinis conruisse, and in *Comm. Matt.* 27,51: superliminare temple infinitae magnitudinis fractum esse. For the Latin text and translations, see Klijn, *Jewish-Christian Gospel Tradition* (n. 1), 93–94.

[25] Klijn, *Jewish-Christian Gospel Tradition* (n. 1), 96. Lifting of the lintel corresponds to the Greek text of Isa 6:4. This confirms that the idea about the lifted lintel of

Because the lifting or moving of the lintel of the temple is especially connected to the temple's future destruction by Greek commentators, it is probable that the reference to the breaking of the lintel was already in the Greek version of Matthew from which the Nazarenes' Aramaic translation was prepared.[26] While the renting of the veil is open to several interpretations,[27] the broken lintel is more clearly a sign of the future destruction of the temple.

The Nazarenes themselves were pro-Pauline and had nothing against the mission to the Gentiles.[28] Nevertheless, they were extremely critical of early Rabbis. In their exposition of Isaiah, they indicated that the Saviour had become to them "destruction and shame." (Jerome, *Comm. Isa.* 8:11–15). Thus, the interpretation which takes the broken lintel as a sign of the future destruction of the temple suits their thinking very well, although they probably were not responsible for the original phrasing in Matthew.

5. What did Jerome get from the Nazarenes?

Jerome's quotations present the most difficult problem for the reconstruction of early Jewish-Christian gospels. On the one hand, Jerome boasts that the Nazarenes who lived in Syrian Beroea let him copy Matthew's gospel in the original Hebrew that they were using. On the other hand, he presents so few quotations from this gospel that it is questionable whether he really possessed an entire copy of Matthew in Hebrew (or Aramaic/Syriac). Furthermore, some of the quotations he claims to have received from the Nazarenes are demonstrably taken from other Church Fathers.[29]

---

the temple as a sign of the future destruction was derived from commentators writing in Greek. The fact that Jerome does not refer to actual collapsing or breaking when he is writing to Damasus suggests that at that time he did not yet know about the wording in the gospel used by the Nazarenes.

[26] Notably, the interpretation of the name Barrabbas in the Nazarenes' version of Matthew (see above) also seems to presume the Greek accusative form (βαραββᾶν) which has inspired the twisted Aramaic reinterpretation of the name as "Son of our Master." Thus, there are traces in both fragments of an earlier Greek version from which the Nazarenes' gospel was translated.

[27] For different possibilities, see U. Luz, *Das Evangelium nach Matthäus (Mt 26–28)* (EKK II/4; Neukirchen and Düsseldorf 2002), 357–364.

[28] This becomes clear from the Nazarenes' exposition of Isaiah that Jerome quotes in his own Commentary on Isaiah (*Comm. Isa.* 9,1).

[29] Two obvious examples are a passage that is also found in Origen's writings but which Jerome claims to have translated from a "gospel edited according to the Hebrews" (cf. Jerome, *Comm. Mich.* 7,5–7; *Comm. Isa.* 40,9–11; *Comm. Ezech* 16,13; Origen, *Comm. Jo.* 2,12; *Hom. Jer.* 15,4), and a passage that is clearly derived from Ignatius of Antioch (Jerome, *Vir. ill.* XVI). For discussion, see, for instance, Vielhauer/Strecker, Je-

The theory which assumes three Jewish-Christian gospels solves the problem of Jerome's quotations by attributing Jerome's fragments to two gospels: the Gospel of the Hebrews and the Gospel of the Nazarenes. In Vielhauer and Strecker's reconstruction, a passage is attributed to the Gospel of the Nazarenes if it has indications of a Semitic basis or close affinity with the synoptic tradition, in particular with Matthew.[30] On the other hand, the non-synoptic character of a fragment signals the Gospel of the Hebrews as the likely original source of the quotation and Origen's writings as the source from which Jerome probably gathered his information.

The Three Gospel Hypothesis attributes the above-introduced fragments in Jerome's Commentary on Matthew to the Gospel of the Nazarenes.[31] However, I find the criteria of the TGH outdated and questionable. The TGH derives its idea about a synoptic type and a non-synoptic type of Jewish-Christian gospel from Waitz, who presented the distinction in the second edition of Hennecke's collection in 1924. At that time, the assumption was not as dubious as it is today, when we know from the Gospel of Thomas that synoptic type sayings can very well exist together with sayings with a more Gnostic orientation.[32] With the Gospel of Thomas available, one should not start with an assumption that makes a clear distinction between synoptic types of gospels and "Gnostic" types of gospels. Vielhauer and Strecker also make unsubstantiated assumptions about the close relationship that must have existed between the Gospel of the Nazarenes and the Gospel of Matthew.[33]

---

wish-Christian Gospels (n. 3), 143–145; Klijn, *Jewish-Christian Gospel Tradition* (n. 1), 52–55, 121–123.

[30] Vielhauer/Strecker, "Jewish-Christian Gospels" (n. 3), 148.

[31] Ibid., 162; Klijn, *Jewish-Christian Gospel Tradition* (n. 1), 91–97.

[32] Without going into the details of the recent discussion about the definition of Gnosticism, I think it is safe to say that the *Gospel of Thomas* betrays some Gnostic orientation although its character as a Gnostic writing can be questioned if compared with, for instance, Sethian Gnosticism. The alleged "Gnostic" features in the fragments attributed to the *Gospel of the Hebrews* are also quite far from classic Gnostic doctrines. It is this that makes the comparison of the "Gospel of the Hebrews" with the *Gospel of Thomas* informative. A helpful summary of the recent discussion on the character of Gnosticism is provided in A. Marjanen (ed.), *Was There a Gnostic Religion?* (Publications of the Finnish Exegetical Society 87, 2005).

[33] The Latest versions of the TGH have managed to escape some of the weaknesses. J. Frey, for instance, thinks that the Ioudaikon fragments cannot be connected to the *Gospel of the Nazarenes*. He also emphasizes that a close affinity with the Gospel of Matthew cannot be taken for granted. Frey, "Die Scholien nach dem 'jüdischen Evangelium'" (n. 6), 126–129; J. Frey, "Zur Vielgestaltigkeit judenchristlicher Evangelienüberlieferungen", in *Jesusüberlieferung in apokryphen Evangelien* (ed. J. Frey and J. Schröter; WUNT; Tübingen, 2010).

Although it seems clear that Jerome did not get an entire gospel from the Nazarenes, I find it justified to assume that he got some sort of collection of sayings from them. In order to avoid unfounded theological and literary presumptions about the character of the materials Jerome possibly received from the Nazarenes, I have sought more neutral and formal criteria for the basis of distinction.[34]

The criteria I have applied are as follows. First, Jerome only started to refer to the Nazarenes in 391–392. Earlier fragments can be excluded from the possible Nazarene collection. Second, fragments that are demonstrably derived from other Church Fathers can be excluded (see above, n. 29). Third, fragments where the translator is expressed in the first person plural ("we translated") or where Greek is mentioned as the language into which the translation was (also) made, can be excluded from the collection.

If one applies the above three criteria to Jerome's fragments, one is left with the following eight quotations:

1. *Comm. Matt.* 2,5 (398 C.E.)
2. *Comm. Matt.* 6,11 (398 C.E.)
3. *Comm. Matt.* 23,35 (398 C.E.)
4. *Comm. Matt.* 27,16 (398 C.E.)
5. *Comm. Matt.* 27,51 (398 C.E.)
6. *Comm. Isa.* 11,1–3 (408/10 C.E.)
7. *Comm. Ezech.* 18,5–9 (410/5 C.E.)
8. *Pelag.* III 2 (415 C.E.)

Notably, five of the remaining eight fragments are in Jerome's commentary on Matthew which already raises the question of whether the core of the collection Jerome received from the Nazarenes could be found in these fragments, especially because Jerome claims to have received from the Nazarenes a version of Matthew's gospel.[35]

---

[34] For a more detailed critical discussion of the TGH and the description of the reconstruction process, see Luomanen, The Nazarenes' Gospel (see n. 7), forthcoming.

[35] Furthermore, there are features in two of the three "non-Matthean" fragments (fragments 6–8 above) which make them less secure candidates for fragments derived from the Nazarenes. First, *Comm. Isa.* 11,1–3 is usually connected with another fragment that was excluded from the possible collection on the basis of the formal criteria. In *Comm. Isa.* 11,1–3, the Holy Spirit appears as Jesus' mother. This feature connects it to *Comm. Mich.* 7,6 which was excluded from the collection on the basis that Jerome is likely to have derived it from Origen. The TGH attributes both these fragments to the *Gospel of the Hebrews*. Second, *Pelag.* III 2 gives an exceptionally large number of names for the gospel from which the passage(s) were derived. The introduction to this fragment runs: "In the Gospel according to the Hebrews which was written in the Chaldaic and Syriac language but with Hebrew letters, and is used up to the present day by the Nazoreans, I mean that according to the Apostles, or, as many maintain, according to Matthew." The exceptionally high number of attributions (five if the language and script are counted as

At first sight, the Matthean fragments appear only as a collection of alternative readings of Matthew's text. However, if placed back in their original contexts, an interesting pattern appears. All the readings seem to be derived from Matthean passages that are highly critical of the Jewish people and their leaders. The collection even seems to have covered the time from Jesus' birth to his death:

1. Initial rejection of the newborn "king of the Jews" by Herod and "all Jerusalem" (Matt 2:5 in context).
2. Words of judgment upon the nation because of its treatment of the prophets (Matt 23:35 in context).
3. The nation's avowed responsibility for the death of Jesus, who died instead of a "son of their Rabbi" (Matt 27:16 in context).
4. Signs following Jesus' death prove him to have been "the son of God" (Matt 27:51 in context).
5. Even the Matthean version of the Lord's Prayer (Matt 6:11 in context) coheres very well with this collection because the Lord's Prayer is presented in Matthew as an alternative to Jewish prayer practices and similar criticisms of Jewish prayers and praying habits also characterize the Nazarenes' relation to the Rabbis (cf. Jerome, *Comm. Isa.* 8,19–22; *Epist.* CXII 13)

The hypothesis about the Nazarenes' anti-Rabbinic collection gets further support from comparison with the Nazarenes' Isaiah exposition that Jerome quotes extensively in his Commentary on Isaiah.[36]

If the above reconstruction is on the right track, it shows how the Nazarenes picked up key passages from Matthew's narrative that exemplified Jesus as the Son of God who was sent to his own people. From the very beginning, the people mistreated him like they had earlier done with their prophets. The story, which has obvious Deuteronomistic overtones, culmi-

---

one) in the introduction is probably due to the fact that Jerome presents two fragments in the same context and has placed all the relevant titles at the beginning of the first one.

[36] The reconstructed Matthean collection shares the following features with the passages Jerome quotes from the Nazarenes' Isaiah exegesis: (1) The Nazarenes' Isaiah commentary (Jerome, *Comm. Isa.* 9,1) refers to an Old Testament citation found only in Matthew (Matt 4:15–16). This proves that the Nazarenes used Matthew's gospel in their exegesis. (2) The most negative attitude towards the Rabbis. (3) A similar scribal method that attributes anti-Rabbinic meaning to Semitic names. In the Commentary on Isaiah, the names of Shammai and Hillel are interpreted as meaning scatterer and unholy. In the Matthean collection, Barrabban is interpreted as meaning the "son of their Rabbi." (4) Both collections are concerned with criticizing the prayer practices of the Rabbis. (5) In both collections, Jesus' position as the Son of God is the key topic (Jerome, *Comm. Isa.* 31,6–9; Jerome, *Comm. Isa.* 29,17–21; cf. the centurion's confession s after Jesus' death: "Truly this man was the Son of God."). (6) Both collections entertain hope for the Israelites' conversion and submission to their ruler (Matt 23:38; *Comm. Isa.* 31,6–9).

nates in Jesus' trial when the people choose "the son of their Rabbi" instead of Jesus the Son of God. However, Jesus is proven to be God's Son through the centurion's confession and signs accompanying his death which predict the future punishment: the destruction of the Temple.

If the Nazarenes' collection was based on the canonical Matthew, is it justified to call its fragments Jewish-Christian? As far as the question concerns only the *text* of the Nazarene's collection (cf. Gregory's critical questions, presented in the beginning of this article), the question is closely tied with the question about Matthew's Jewish-Christian character. I agree with Gregory that the Gospel of Matthew was edited in a community where strict Law observance was no longer required.[37] However, an understanding of the original audience or the community where the text was edited does not yet solve the question about the Jewish-Christian character of the text as it stands. The mere fact that the degree of Matthew's Judaism remains controversial among scholars shows that the text itself is also open to interpretations that locate it within Judaism. Thus, if applied to the case of the Nazarenes, from a theoretical point of view it is quite possible that, for the Nazarenes, the Gospel of Matthew was more Jewish than it was for it original editor.

Although a discussion of the Jewish Christianity of a *text as it stands* is informative to some extent,[38] I find it more interesting to try to describe and understand the social reality where the texts were interpreted and applied, if such information is available. As far as the Nazarenes' real-life Law observance is concerned, their interpretation of Matthew was not Jewish-Christian in Gregory's definition: the Nazarenes were so clearly pro-Pauline that their interpretation of Jewish Law must have been quite liberal.[39]

---

[37] Applying Stark and Bainbridge's definition of cult and sect movements, I have characterized Matthew's community as a Christian cult movement. See P. Luomanen, "The 'Sociology of Sectarianism' in Matthew: Modelling the Genesis of Early Jewish and Christian Communities", in *Fair Play: Diversity and Conflicts in Early Christianity: Essays in Honour of Heikki Räisänen* (ed. I. Dunderberg, C. Tuckett and K. Syreeni; NT.S 103; Leiden 2002), 107–130. Cf. Gregory, "Hindrance or Help" (n. 13), 405.

[38] In the light of the indicators of Jewish Christianity such a discussion would concern the questions how and to what extent a text propagates, supports, allows or prohibits Jewish and/or Christian ideas and practices. This would give a rough picture of what sort of Jewish-Christian thinking and practice is more likely or possible on the basis of a given text, but this does not yet determine how the text is used and interpreted in actual life.

[39] The Nazarenes' Isaiah exegesis in Jerome, *Comm. Isa.* 9,1: "When Christ came and his preaching shone out, the land of Zebulon and the land of Naphtali first of all were freed from the errors of the Scribes and the Pharisees and he shook off their shoulders the very heavy yoke of the Jewish traditions. Later, however, the preaching became more

However, a more nuanced picture of the Nazarenes' Jewish-Christian profile can be achieved with the help of the indicators of Jewish Christianity. The Nazarenes' ethnic identity, in terms of their language and knowledge of Jewish culture, the Rabbinic movement in particular, seems to have been even more pronounced than in the case of the editor of Matthew's gospel. The vigour with which the Nazarenes attacked the Rabbis gives very much the impression of a struggle over a common Jewish heritage. The Nazarenes were so closely tied with their Jewish compatriots that the teaching of the Rabbis could not simply be ignored. Instead, much effort was put on finding evidence in the Scriptures – we know of Isaiah and Matthew expositions – which would put their opponents in a bad light and justify the Nazarenes' own position. On the other hand, as regards the terms and consequences of being either inside or outside the Nazarene group, it seems that the Nazarenes possessed a clear Christian identity: Jews can be saved only by becoming Christians.[40] Thus, although the Nazarenes overall religious profile was clearly more to the Christian side, it was accompanied by such pronounced Jewish elements that to describe it simply as Christian without any further qualification would certainly give an oversimplified picture of their position and the strong bonds with which they were tied to their Jewish heritage.

6. Jesus' appearance to James the Just

In *Illustrious Men*, Jerome describes how Jesus appeared to his brother, James the Just:

...also the Gospel which is according to the Hebrews and which I have recently translated into Greek and Latin of which also Origen often makes use, says after the account of the resurrection of the Lord: But the Lord after he had given linen cloth to the servant of the priest, went to James and appeared to him (for James had sworn that he would not eat bread from the hour in which he drank the cup of the Lord until he had seen him rising again from those who sleep), and again, a little later, it says: Bring the table and bread, said the Lord. And immediately it is added: He brought bread and blessed and

---

dominant, that means the preaching was multiplied, through the Gospel of the apostle Paul who was the last of all the apostles..."

[40] Jerome, *Comm. Isa.* 31,6–9: "O sons of Israel who deny the Son of God with the most vicious opinion, turn to him and his apostles. If you will do this, you will reject all idols which to you were a cause of sin in the past and the devil will fall before you, not because of your powers but because of the compassion of God. And his young men, who a certain time earlier fought for him, will be tributaries of the Church and any of its power and stone will pass ...". I argue for this view in Luomanen, "The Nazarenes' Gospel" (n. 7), forthcoming.

broke it and gave it to James the Just and said to him: My brother, eat thy bread for the Son of Man is risen from those who sleep. (Jerome, *Vir. ill.* II).

Since Jerome refers to Greek as the target language of the translation and also refers to Origen, it is obvious the fragment represents a case where Jerome is relying on a Greek source, most probably Origen. This means that the passage probably dates from the second or early third century. The TGH attributes it to the Gospel of the Hebrews. The hypothesis that has been developed in this article also takes the Gospel of the Hebrews as a possible origin of the fragment, although it understands the character of the Gospel of the Hebrews somewhat differently, in closer relation to the synoptic gospels.[41]

The canonical gospels do not mention Jesus' appearance to James. On the contrary, in Mark, James appears in a critical light since he is listed together with Jesus' relatives (Mark 6:3) who go after Jesus because they think he is out of his mind (Mark 3:20–21.31). Paul lists James among the many witnesses of Jesus' resurrection (1 Cor 15:7) but by no means as the first one, as appears to be the case in Jerome's passage. Obviously, one of the central concerns of this fragment is to write James into the gospel narrative, attributing to him the role of being among the first witness of the resurrection which would better cohere with the high esteem in which he was held among early Christians.

As such, the passage suggests that the gospel from which it was taken included a passion narrative akin to the narratives in the synoptic gospels. It must have included at least the Last Supper, (most likely) a description of Jesus' death, and a story about his burial. The fragment suggests a setting where there are several witnesses to the resurrection,[42] among them a servant of the (high?) priest, to whom Jesus gives the linen cloth that has been used for burial, presumably as evidence of resurrection.[43]

In addition to giving James a role among the first witnesses, the fragment also exhibits other concerns. Why is the appearance connected to James' oath of not eating bread before he has seen the Son of Man risen? James the Just was known for his virtue and ascetic lifestyle (Eusebius, *Hist. eccl.* II 23 = SC 31, 85–90) but this hardly explains the passage be-

[41] As a matter of fact, points of contact between the *Gospel of the Hebrews* and the synoptic gospels would explain better the semicanonical position of the Gospel of the Hebrews in many of the references of the Church Fathers. See for instance, Eusebius, *Hist. eccl.* III 25.

[42] Cf. Matt 27:62–66; the *Gospel of Peter* 28–34 and the *Ioudaikon* in Cod. N.T. 1424.

[43] Thus, H.-J. Klauck, *Apocryphal Gospels: An Introduction* (London 2003), 42–43, following Waitz, "Hebräerevangelium" (n. 3), 49.

cause the point is not James' ascetic lifestyle in general but a specific vow which actually involves only a short-term abstinence.

Klauck sees here an apologetic argument: if James, a just man, deviates from his vow of not eating bread, the resurrection "has indeed taken place and the risen Lord has encouraged his brother to resume eating."[44] While I find it hard to see in the fragment the kind of apologetics for resurrection Klauck suggests – the apologetics seems to be channelled more directly through the group of witnesses to the resurrection – Klauck may be on the right track when he notes that the fragment makes a point of the fact that James resumes eating. Since the fragment also includes obvious traces of a Eucharistic setting – the table and the bread is prepared according to Jesus' instruction and Jesus breaks the bread – it would seem that the fragment intends to combine James with a practice of fasting that ends with the Eucharist, celebrated on the day of the resurrection.

One possible context where there would have been a need for such a legitimization of a practice of fasting is the so-called "Easter controversy" that arose towards the end of the second century between Asian and other dioceses (Eusebius, *Hist. eccl.* V 23–25 = SC 41, 66–72). When Victor became the bishop of Rome, he tried to excommunicate all the Asian churches who followed the Jewish practice and always celebrated Easter on the fourteenth of Nisan which could be any day of the week. According to Eusebius (*Hist. eccl.* V 23), several conferences and synods were held because of the controversy. The one that was arranged in Palestine was presided over by the bishops Theophilus of Caesarea and Narcissus of Jerusalem who defended the majority view according to which the Easter fast should always end on the day of the Saviour's resurrection, not on the fourteenth of Nisan. Eusebius also quotes Irenaeus who urged Victor to be tolerant and pointed out that the dispute was not only about the date of the Paschal festival but also about the correct practice of fasting (*Hist. eccl.* V 24). Notably, Eusebius states (V 25) that the Palestinian bishops, Narcissus and Theophilus, wrote a long defence of their practice which they claimed to have received from the apostolic succession. Since Narcissus was the bishop of Jerusalem, in his case, the apostolic succession would naturally go back to James the brother of Lord who was regarded as the first bishop of Jerusalem. Moreover, Eusebius quotes a passage from Narcissus and Theophilus where they point out that dioceses in Palestine and Alexandria exchange letters in order to secure that Easter is celebrated at the same time in both places.

Eusebius' information is significant for the interpretation of the present passage in two respects. First, it presents a natural context for a story about James the Just who did not end his "Paschal fast" on the fourteenth of Ni-

---

[44] Klauck, *Apocryphal Gospels* (n. 43), 43.

san when the Paschal lambs were slaughtered but waited, as he had vowed, until the day of the resurrection. Second, it shows how the story about Jerusalem's first bishop could have easily ended up in Alexandria and with Origen. If the passage was composed in the heat of the Easter dispute, then it probably does not represent the oldest stratum of the Gospel of the Hebrews since the first references to this gospel are by Papias and Hegesippus.[45] However, theoretically – even if it was later added to the Gospel of the Hebrews – it may well have been in the version that was quoted by the Alexandrian writers, Clement and Origen, in the beginning of the third century.[46]

7. Conclusion

The fact there are no manuscripts of early Jewish-Christian gospels currently available tells more about the preferences and power policy of the developing orthodoxy than about the relative importance of these gospels among Christ followers during the first centuries C.E. As a matter of fact, there are more quotations from these gospels and references to their contents in the writings of the Fathers than from any other apocryphal gospel. The character of the references also shows that the Fathers did not simply disagree with some of the contents of these gospels but even valued them,[47] and hoped to find in them information from some early Hebrew followers of Jesus.

The fragments connected to Jesus' passion and resurrection in the Jewish-Christian gospels discussed in this article come from three different gospels, two of which can be characterized as apocryphal: the Gospel of the Ebionites and the Gospel of the Hebrews. The third one, the Nazarenes' Aramaic gospel, seems to have been simply a slightly altered version of the canonical Matthew.

Epiphanius quotes the Gospel of the Ebionites in order to show how the Ebionites have twisted the wording of the true gospel in favour of their abstinence from meat. The reference is short but if combined with other information about the Ebionites' practices, the fragment opens a window

---

[45] Quoted in Eusebius, *Hist. eccl.* III 39,17 and IV 2,28. Papias' reference is controversial since some scholars think that the information about the source (the *Gospel of Hebrews*) comes from Eusebius. See, Vielhauer/Strecker, Jewish-Christian Gospels (n. 3), 138. In my view, this assumption is unsubstantiated; it only aims to support the TGH's hypothesis that the *Gospel of the Hebrews* originated in Egypt.

[46] For the date of the first Alexandrian references, see Klijn, *Jewish-Christian Gospel Tradition* (n. 1), 47–52.

[47] Thus, Frey, "Vielgestaltigkeit" (n. 33), forthcoming.

on the Ebionites' interpretation of passion narratives which may also have affected the manuscripts of the canonical gospels (Luke's D, Old Latin and Old Syriac versions). In this tradition, Jesus' death is not given any sacrificial meaning. It exemplifies the interpretative tradition of the Ebionites who were critical of the sacrificial cult in general. Although, in this regard, the Ebionites can be regarded as more Samaritan than Judaean, there are so many Jewish as well as Christian elements in their religious profile that they well deserve the label of Jewish Christian.

The Nazarenes' anti-Rabbinic collection – if correctly reconstructed in this article – shows how key elements in Matthew's passion narrative were reinterpreted and "updated" by Jewish Christians who had a similar, close love-hate-relationship with their Jewish compatriots as the original editor(s) of the gospel.[48] Consequently, if a full a translation this gospel were available, scholars would probably find it equally difficult to place it on the axis between Judaism and Christianity as they do the present canonical version of the Gospel of Matthew.

The fragment from the *Gospel of the Hebrews* gives James the Just a role in the passion narrative which corresponds to the high esteem in which he was held, especially among early Jewish Christians. Although James the Just was originally the spokesman of conservative Jewish Christians, his person was later embraced equally by proto-orthodox Christians, Jewish Christians of the Pseudo-Clementines as well as Gnostic circles.[49] Therefore, it is also difficult to give only one possible *Sitz im Leben* for the fragment that Jerome quotes in his *Illustrious Men*. Although the fragment possibly was in the *Gospel of the Hebrews*, it may also have served the needs of mainstream bishops in their dispute over the correct Easter practice. On the whole, the hypothesis about the *Gospel of the Hebrews* that has been developed in this article, because it locates both synoptic and strong Wisdom traditions in the *Gospel of the Hebrews*, might make it more understandable why traditions about James were embraced in so many early Christian circles.

---

[48] Although Matthean scholars disagree on whether Matthew should be placed intra muros or extra muros in relation to Judaism, it is largely acknowledged that Matthew struggles to make sense of his Jewish heritage in the light of the new commitment to Jesus. For an overview of the recent discussion, see W. Carter, "Matthew's Gospel: Jewish Christianity, Christian Judaism, or Neither?", in *Jewish Christianity Reconsidered; Rethinking Ancient Groups and Texts* (ed. M. Jackson-McCabe; Minneapolis 2007), 155–179.

[49] For an overview of the development of James traditions, see J. Painter, "Who Was James? Footprints as a Means of Identification", in *Jewish Christianity Reconsidered; Rethinking Ancient Groups and Texts* (ed. B. Chilton and J. Neusner; Louisville and London 2001), 10–65.

Because of the scantiness of the evidence, discussion about Jewish-Christian gospel traditions is bound to remain hypothetical. Although it is impossible to draw absolutely certain conclusions I hope I have succeeded in pointing out some interesting variations of the passion and resurrection traditions in early Jewish-Christian gospels, some of their characteristic features not known elsewhere, but also some examples of their close relationship with canonical passion and resurrection traditions. Obviously, there was not just one Jewish-Christian interpretation of Jesus' passion and resurrection, just like there was not just one Jewish Christianity but many, of which we would know even more if we had the entirety of Jewish-Christian gospels available.

Does the *Gospel of Judas* Rehabilitate Judas Iscariot?

ANTTI MARJANEN

1. Introduction[1]

The picture the canonical gospels paint of Judas Iscariot is gloomy and gets worse as the process of interpretation advances. In the Gospel of Mark, Judas is the one who hands Jesus over to his opponents although it is not entirely clear what his precise motivation is (14:10).[2] In Matthew, Luke and John there is no doubt. Judas acts out of love for money in Matthew and Luke (Matt 26:15; Luke 22:6) and as an agent of the Devil in Luke and John (Luke 22:3; John 6:70–71; 13:2, 27). Matthew informs his readers that after his treachery Judas Iscariot repented of his greed and committed suicide by hanging himself (27:5). Luke does not speak of Judas' remorse but describes his death as an act of divine punishment (Acts 1:18).

In some non-canonical texts from the second century and in later Christian tradition Judas' fate is depicted in ever more dramatic terms. Papias, a second-century apologist, reports that Judas swelled up so immensely that he could no longer pass through where a carriage could and that his stomach finally burst.[3] In the Middle Ages Judas Iscariot vies for the questionable prize of being the most notorious sinner of all times. In his famous description of Hell, Dante places Judas Iscariot in its ninth and lowest circle dedicated to traitors, in zone 4 which is even named Judecca after Judas Iscariot. Lucifer, whose treachery against God keeps him imprisoned here, uses each of his three faces and three mouths to chew on a sinner. Judas is in the middle mouth with his head inside, while the skin of his

---

[1] I am grateful to Ismo Dunderberg, Lance Jenott and Elaine Pagels for their helpful comments on the first draft of the article.

[2] Mark 14:10–11 does not state that Judas Iscariot hands over Jesus *if* he gets money, but Judas is rather given some money *since* he does it. Thus, Judas' motivation is not explicitly connected to greed in Mark.

[3] Papias' desription is transmitted by Apollinaris of Laodicea; see W. Schneemelcher, *Neutestamentliche Apokryphen* (vol. 2: Apostolisches, Apokalypsen und Verwandtes; 5th ed.; Tübingen 1989), 25.

back is continuously ripped by Lucifer's claws.[4] The negative character the portrait of Judas Iscariot tends to gain is not only reflected in Christian traditions but in Manichaean texts as well. According to *Kephalaia* 18.37–19.6, Judas Iscariot was at first called a good man and an apostle who was counted among the twelve. Then Satan entered him and Judas delivered Jesus into the hands of the Jews and was called "traitor" and "murderer." The Great Crucifixion Hymn of the Manichaeans combines the motif of satanic vexation with that of Judas' greed. It states that Satan "mounted the wretched Iscariot, a most dear believer among the disciples" and that Judas "abjured Truth for a bribe that the Jews gave him and gave up his own Lord and Teacher."[5]

The first reports of the newly published *Gospel of Judas* led us to understand that this text offered a new picture of Judas. It was claimed that it provided a rehabilitation of Judas and made him a paragon of the disciple of Jesus.[6] At the SBL Annual Meeting in Washington in 2006, where a well-attended panel discussion on the *Gospel of Judas* was held, the situation had somewhat changed.[7] Scholars had been given time to study the text more carefully. Some of them had also convened their own seminars on the text. In Washington, it became clear that some members of the panel as well as some among the audience no longer maintained that the *Gospel of Judas* contained a positive view of Judas Iscariot.[8] In fact, many thought that, together with the other disciples, Judas was seen in rather negative terms.[9] Still, some members of the panel, some from the

---

[4] Dante, *Divine Comedy* I 34. Brutus and Cassius, who were traitors to Julius Caesar, are devoured in the two mouths on either side of Judas.

[5] The reference was introduced by T. Sala in his paper "A Neglected Version of Judas" presented at the 2006 SBL Annual Meeting, November 18–21, Washington, D.C.

[6] This view was advocated by the first editors and English translators of the text in *The Gospel of Judas from Codex Tchacos* (ed. R. Kasser, M. Meyer, and G. Wurst; Washington, D.C. 2006).

[7] Besides the chair-person Nicola Denzey, the panel consisted of Craig A. Evans, Karen L. King, Marvin Meyer, Elaine Pagels, and John D. Turner.

[8] In some later seminars and conferences on the *Gospel of Judas* the polarization of views regarding the character of Judas Iscariot in the text has continued. For a listing and description of these seminars, see the preface of A.D. DeConick, *The Thirteenth Apostle: What the Gospel of Judas Really Says* (London 2007), xvii–xxi. The papers presented at the Sorbonne conference on October 27–28, 2007, have been published in *The Gospel of Judas in Context: Proceedings of the First International Conference on the Gospel of Judas* (ed. M. Scopello; NHMS 62; Leiden/Boston 2008).

[9] The most important representatives of the negative, "revisionist" – as it is nowadays called – view of Judas, who have published on the issue, are: L. Painchaud, "À propos de la (re)découverte de l'Évangile de Judas" *LThPh* 62 (2006), 553–568 (cf. also L. Painchaud, "Polemical Aspects of the *Gospel of Judas*", in Scopello [ed.], *The Gospel of Judas in Context* [n. 8], 171–186, esp. 177–184); B. Pearson, "Judas Iscariot and the *Gospel of Judas*" (Occasional Papers 51, The Institute for Antiquity and Christianity;

audience, as well as some scholars writing articles and books on the topic maintained the previous view, insisting that a favorable picture of Judas Iscariot could be found in the *Gospel of Judas*.[10] The whole discussion strayed rather far from any scholarly consensus. Thus, we find ourselves not only with every chance for a long-standing scholarly debate but also with a challenging case for scholarly research. The purpose of this paper is to ask whether or not the *Gospel of Judas*, among other things, attempts to rehabilitate Judas Iscariot who in the New Testament gospels and later Christian texts bears the label of the greatest villain of early Christianity.

Before I address this question directly, one fact has to be emphasized. Already before, but especially since the publication of the document, various media sources have raised considerable expectations as to the significance of the *Gospel of Judas* for our understanding of the earliest history of Christianity.[11] I want to stress that I regard the *Gospel of Judas* as a late

---

Claremont, Calif. 2007); DeConick, *The Thirteenth Apostle* (n. 8) (cf. also ead., "The Mystery of Betrayal: What Does the *Gospel of Judas* Really Say?", in Scopello [ed.], *The Gospel of Judas in Context* [n. 8], 239–264); J. Brankaer and H.-G. Bethge (eds.), *Codex Tchacos: Texte und Analysen* (TU 161; Berlin and New York 2007), 255–378; E. Thomassen, "Judasevangeliet og gnosticismen", in *Mellem venner og fjender: En folkebog om Judasevangeliet, tidig kristendom og gnosis* (ed. A.K. Petersen, J. Hyldahl and id.; Copenhagen 2008), 143–166, esp. 163–166 (cf. also E. Thomassen, "Is Judas Really the Hero of the *Gospel of Judas*?", in: Scopello [ed.], *The Gospel of Judas in Context* [n. 8], 157–170); A.K. Petersen, "Genskrevet Skrift: Judas som fortalt og som historisk figure", in Petersen, Hyldahl and Thomassen (ed.), *Mellem venner og fjender* (cf. the previous reference), 39–80, esp. 71–78; N.A. Pedersen, "Historien om Judasevangeliet", in *ibid.*, 81–117; J. Turner, "The Place of the *Gospel of Judas* in Sethian Tradition", in: Scopello (ed.), *The Gospel of Judas in Context* (n. 8), 187–237, esp. 214–216, 223–229.

[10] In addition to Kasser, Meyer, and Wurst (ed.), *The Gospel of Judas* (n. 6), the most important representatives of the positive view of Judas are: B.D. Ehrman, *The Lost Gospel of Judas Iscariot: A New Look at Betrayer and Betrayed* (Oxford 2006); P. Nagel, "Das Evangelium des Judas", *ZNW* 98 (2007), 213–276; E. Pagels and K.L. King, *Reading Judas: The Gospel of Judas and the Shaping of Christianity* (New York 2007).

[11] An internet version of a preliminary edition of the Coptic text of the *Gospel of Judas* by R. Kasser and G. Wurst was released by the National Geographic Society at Easter in 2006. At the same time the National Geographic Society published an English translation of the text based on the preliminary edition (Kasser, Meyer, and Wurst [ed.], *The Gospel of Judas* [n. 6]). The *editio princeps* of the text (R. Kasser, G. Wurst, M. Meyer, and F. Gaudard [ed.], *The Gospel of Judas together with the Letter of Peter to Philip, James, and a Book of Allogenes from Codex Tchacos* [Washington, D.C. 2007]) was published a year later. Already before these publications, some low-quality photographs of the text had circulated among scholars, and some pages of the Codex Tchacos had also been posted in the internet. These "pre-publications" generated much discussion both among scholars and a more general audience, which led to many interviews and popular articles on the *Gospel of Judas*, which were often somewhat sensational. The fact that some photographs of Codex Tchacos posted in the internet were not in fact, against

second-century writing, which does not change or provide anything for our reconstruction of the historical Jesus or Judas Iscariot. In fact, I find it likely that the text is the very one to which Irenaeus refers in his *Adversus haereses* (I 31.1), whether he had actually read it or knew it only by hear-say. Still, the *Gospel of Judas* is an important document of early Christianity. It represents a unique interpretation of second-century Christian faith which is reflected, for example, in a special understanding of cosmology, the mission of Jesus, and the role of martyrdom.

The characterization of Judas Iscariot in the *Gospel of Judas* will be treated under five headings: Judas Iscariot and the Twelve; Judas Iscariot as a Favorite Disciple of Jesus; Judas Iscariot and the Handing Over of Jesus; Judas Iscariot and the Holy Generation; The Function of Jesus in the Textual Strategy of the *Gospel of Judas*.

2. Judas Iscariot and the Twelve

Like the canonical gospels, the *Gospel of Judas* begins its portrayal of Jesus' public activity with the calling of the twelve disciples (*Gos. Judas* 33.13 15[12]; cf. e.g. Mark 1:16–20). Compared to the description of the twelve in the canonical gospels, the *Gospel of Judas* yields two outstanding features, however. First, in the canonical gospels the twelve may sometimes misunderstand the purposes of their master or act foolishly, but occasionally, they are also described as loyal and faithful followers of Jesus. In the *Gospel of Judas*, by contrast, the twelve are constantly criticized, even ridiculed by Jesus because of their false understandings or actions. Ultimately, they end up representing a position completely different from that of Jesus and the author of the text. Immediately after their calling they demonstrate a naïve and misguided trust in the effects of religious ritual (either a prayer of thanksgiving over a meal or the Eucharist) and totally misunderstand who God and Jesus are (33.26–34.18).

Later, when the twelve report their vision of Jewish priests making sacrifices, Jesus accuses them of being these very priests who present offerings to their (false) god (39.18–40.1). Furthermore, Jesus claims that, unlike the Jews who slaughter animals, the twelve disciples sacrifice their own children and when they do they do it in the name of Jesus. Sacrificing in the name of Jesus cannot refer to a concrete sacrificial act in a second

general understanding, from the *Gospel of Judas* but from the *Book of Allogenes* of the same manuscript further complicated and confused the situation.

[12] The references to the *Gospel of Judas* are given according to *editio princeps* of the Coptic text in Codex Tchacos. The first number indicates the page of the codex, and the number after the comma refers to the line of the page.

century context. The expression must have been used in a metaphorical sense. Note that Ignatius who refers to his future martyrdom can describe himself as "a sacrifice to God" (*Rom.* 4.2; cf. *Rom.* 2.2) and that the second-century martyrs of Lyons are also depicted as ones who "were sacrificed" (Eus. *Hist. eccl.* V 1.51).[13] In light of these passages, it is possible that when the author of the *Gospel of Judas* accuses the twelve of sacrificing their children, he is presenting a severe critique of certain (apostolic) Christian leaders. They not only supported other Christians facing martyrdom but they incited them to submit themselves to it.[14] Some said that martyrdom glorified Christ (e.g., Tertullian, *De fuga in persecutione* 9, where Tertullian approvingly quotes a Montanist oracle). Others portrayed martyrdom as the best means by which to gain access to God (cf. Ignatius, *Rom.* 4.1; *The Acts of Justin and Companions* C 4[15]). The author of the *Gospel of Judas* condemns this emphasis on the significance of martyrdom, more or less claiming that the twelve and their followers, the apostolic Christians, present a false view of God and in fact serve Saklas and Yaldabaoth, the rulers of chaos and the underworld (*Gos. Judas* 38.18–40.26; 51.5–23; 56.11–13). Therefore, such Christians will actually be condemned on the last day (40.25–26). That incitement to martyrdom is viewed as evil is underlined by the fact that the *Gospel of Judas* links it to many other actions that it treats as serious sins, including homosexuality and murder.[16]

---

[13] Brankaer and Bethge (*Codex Tchacos* [n. 9], 332–341, esp. 338) and Pedersen ("Historien om Judasevangeliet" [n. 9], 101–104) have suggested that the sacrificial scene of the disciples' vision is to be understood as a reference to Christian cultic actions, especially to the celebration of the Eucharist, which is seen as a non-acceptable continuation of the Jewish Temple sacrifice, practiced by the apostolic Christians who follow the example and the teaching of the twelve. Certainly, there are early Christian texts which use sacrificial terminology to describe the Eucharist (cf. *Did.* 14.2; Irenaeus, *haer.* IV 17.5). This interpretation is unlikely, however, since the idea of Eucharist as a sacrifice does not fit the scene in the *Gospel of Judas* where it is the cattle, i.e., the people being led astray, who are equated with an offering. For the same reason, the interpretation of Thomassen ("Judasevangeliet og gnosticismen" [n. 9], 165), according to which the polemical view of sacrifice broached in the *Gospel of Judas* is directed against the idea of the sacrificial death of Jesus, is not probable.

[14] This view is advocated by P. Townsend, E. Iricinschi, and L. Jenott, "The Betrayer's Gospel", *The New York Review* (June 8, 2006), 32–37, esp. 36; A. Marjanen and I. Dunderberg, *Juudaksen evankeliumi* (Helsinki 2006), 87–89; Pagels and King, *Reading Judas* (cf. above footnote 10), 43–57.

[15] For the text, see H. Musurillo, *The Acts of Christian Martyrs* (Oxford 1972), 59.

[16] The non-ascetic character of the *Gospel of Judas* is demonstrated by the fact that even fasting is included among the misdeeds of the priests the disciples see in their vision (40.12–13).

The second outstanding feature in the description of the twelve in the *Gospel of Judas* is that Judas Iscariot, although seemingly belonging to the group, is not really part of them. This is not already clear at the beginning of the document when the calling of the twelve is reported. It becomes obvious only after Jesus asks whether any of the twelve disciples is strong enough to bring out the perfect human and stand before him. Despite their assurances, none of them is able to do it, except for Judas, but at this point even he cannot look into the eyes of Jesus without turning his face aside (*Gos. Judas* 35.2–14). Nevertheless, Jesus recognizes Judas' strength, asking him to separate himself from the others so that he has to be replaced by somebody else (35.23–36.4). Unlike the Book of Acts, where Judas' replacement serves to reestablish the apostolic collegium for the benefit of the nascent Christian church, in the *Gospel of Judas* the replacement of Judas is a requirement of the false god whom the apostles serve.

After his separation from the rest of the disciples, Judas starts receiving special instruction from Jesus, and he also demonstrates more understanding of Jesus' teaching than the others do. When the twelve present their vision of the sacrificing priests Judas no longer seems to share that vision with the others. In fact, Judas later presents his own vision, which is introduced with a statement that implies that Judas is not or at least is no longer a part of the twelve (44.15–18). This impression is also confirmed when Jesus calls him the "thirteenth *daimōn*"[17] (44.21) and it is further

[17] The Greek word *daimōn* has been variously interpreted by scholars. Those who see it in light of a traditional Greek understanding render it "a lesser god" (K. King in Pagels and ead., *Reading Judas* [n. 10], 140–141) or "spirit" (M. Meyer in id. [ed.], *The Nag Hammadi Scriptures* [New York 2007], 764). Others, who conceive *daimōn* in terms of a Christian or Sethian understanding, suggest it should be translated as a "demon" and that Jesus' word indicates that Judas was an evil figure who only knew Jesus because he was a "demon" (Painchaud, "À propos de la (re)découverte de l'Évangile de Judas" [n. 9], 558–559; DeConick, *The Thirteenth Apostle* [n. 9], 48–51.110–124; Pedersen, "Historien om Judasevangeliet" [n. 9], 107; so also Birger Pearson in his paper at the 2007 SBL Annual Meeting in San Diego). Although all of these explanations are basically possible (early Christian and especially Sethian writers used the term *daimōn* with a negative connotation whereas other contemporary writers, such as Plutarch, Celsus and Plotinus, hold onto the classical philosophical position that daimons are divine or quasi-divine good intermediaries between highest divinities and humans; for this view, see D.B. Martin, *Inventing Superstition: From the Hippocratics to the Christians* [Cambridge, Mass. 2004], 93–108, 177–180, 189–192) none of them captures the gist of the text. The reference to Judas as the "thirteenth demon" should not be seen as a characterization of his spiritual or evil character. Rather, in its present context it underlines Jesus' attempt to curb the eagerness and impatience of Judas who wants to present his own alternative vision. At this point in the story Judas has not yet received the most decisive instruction from Jesus, the one by which he will realize his true identity. Even if Jesus' reference to Judas as a "thirteenth demon" were taken as a rebuke, one should not exaggerate its significance, although the term in Christian and especially Sethian texts does have a

corroborated by the content of the vision. In the vision, Judas sees himself being persecuted and stoned by the twelve (44.24–45.1). The special position of Judas Iscariot over against the other disciples is further underscored by the fact that, while Jesus may characterize him as "the thirteenth, and ... cursed by the other generations", nevertheless, he will rule over them (46.20–24). As in the canonical gospels, so also in the *Gospel of Judas*, Judas Iscariot is clearly distinguished from the other disciples of Jesus. In the canonical gospels it happens because of his involvement with the betrayal of Jesus. In the *Gospel of Judas* the distinction is due to the total lack of understanding by others and to Judas' ability to perceive the right character of the mission and message of Jesus.

3. Judas Iscariot as a Favorite Disciple of Jesus

My colleague Ismo Dunderberg and I have sought to advance the thesis that Judas' relationship to Jesus should be seen in terms of a specially favored disciple.[18] In early Christian literature, both within the canon ("Beloved Disciple" in the Gospel of John; Peter, James, John and sometimes Andrew in the Gospel of Mark) and outside it (e.g., Thomas in the *Gospel of Thomas*; Mary Magdalene in the *Gospel of Mary* and in the *Gospel of Philip*; James and Peter in the *Apocryphon of James* and James alone in the *First* and *Second Apocalypse of James*; Mary Magdalene, John, James, Matthew, and Philip in *Pistis Sophia I–III* and all the disciples in *Pistis Sophia IV*; Bartholomew in the *Questions of Bartholomew*) the phenomenon of a specially favored disciple appears frequently. This disciple is usually called "beloved", one who often understands more clearly the cause of

---

negative connotation. The word *daimōn* appears only once in the *Gospel of Judas*. Apart from this one instance, nobody, not even any assistant of Saklas, is called a demon in the extant part of the text. In that sense the use of the word does not link Judas with the evil characters of the mythological account in the *Gospel of Judas*. In fact, the use of the word *daimōn* as a characterization of a human being, for example a biblical figure, is an unusual feature in all Sethian texts. The closest parallel to the use of the word *daimōn* in connection with a human being is Jesus' strong rebuke directed to Peter in Mark 8:33 after Peter has tried to prevent Jesus from accomplishing his task. Jesus is said to call Peter Satan. Even this kind of reprimand does not signify the final judgment of this particular disciple. Similarly, in the *Gospel of Judas* Jesus' scolding can be taken as a temporary criticism of Judas' impatience and misunderstanding. The fact that Jesus is ready to continue a dialogue with Judas and listen to him confirms this.

[18] Marjanen and Dunderberg, *Juudaksen evankeliumi* (n. 14), 73–78. For our other studies on the the specially favored (or beloved) disciple motif, see I. Dunderberg, *The Beloved Disciple in Conflict? Revisiting the Gospels of John and Thomas* (Oxford 2006), 116–198; A. Marjanen, "Mary Magdalene, a Beloved Disciple", in *Mariam, the Magdalen, and the Mother* (ed. D. Good; Bloomington, Ind. 2005), 49–61.

Jesus than other disciples. Not infrequently, this disciple also interprets Jesus' words to the others, and functions as the source and the guarantor of the text deriving from the teaching or special revelation of Jesus. In some instances this special disciple may also come into a conflict with other disciples.

Although nowhere in the extant part of the *Gospel of Judas* is Judas characterized as "beloved", his portrait encompasses many features familiar from other texts containing the motif of a specially favored disciple. The beginning of the *Gospel of Judas* depicts Judas as the authenticator of the traditions found in the text. The *incipit* of the gospel confirms that the content is derived from secret conversations between Jesus and Judas (33.1–6). The (implied) reader of the text must assume that the message of this gospel, including the crucial cosmological teaching "that [no] human will see" (47.4–5), which I think has soteriological character, has come down to the reader through Judas Iscariot. Even if Judas has his own moments of weakness and misunderstanding (35.10–14; 44.18–21; 45.10–14), it is clear that he is the most perceptive of all the disciples, so that Jesus singles him out for special instruction (35.23–25; 47.1–5 etc.). Like Peter in the Gospel of Mark (8:29) or Thomas in the *Gospel of Thomas* (13), Judas is the only disciple in the *Gospel of Judas* who understands Jesus' real character and origin. From the beginning of the gospel Judas realizes that Jesus is not from this "generation", but from the immortal aeon of Barbelo, the divine female character familiar from so-called Sethian texts (35.17–19). It is no wonder that by the end of the gospel Judas receives a position of trust and may "sacrifice the man who bears" Jesus (56.19–21). The only typical characteristic of a "favorite disciple" Judas Iscariot lacks is that he does not really interpret the teachings of Jesus to other disciples. This is most likely due to the fact that the relationship between Judas and the rest of the disciples is so exacerbated that there is no possibility of communication between them after the initial separation.

4. Judas Iscariot and the Handing Over of Jesus

The text which has generated most discussion as far as the content of the *Gospel of Judas* is concerned is probably the passage in which Jesus states that Judas Iscariot "will sacrifice the man who bears" Jesus (56.19–21). The statement predicts the ending of the gospel in which it is said that, while approached by some scribes, Judas Iscariot received money and agreed to hand Jesus over to them (58.19–26). Before Jesus' words there is a lacuna in the text but the context makes it fairly clear that Jesus is talking about those who offer sacrifices to Saklas, thus doing something "that is evil" (56.17). After that Jesus continues to address Judas: "But you will exceed all of them. For you will sacrifice the man who bears me" (56.17–21). The text provokes many questions, but as to the view of Judas Iscariot in the *Gospel of Judas* two are especially important. First, in light of the negative connotation of sacrifice found elsewhere in the *Gospel of Judas*, should it also be taken here as a negative act? The second question is related to the first. If Judas Iscariot is said to exceed all those sacrificing to Saklas, does that mean that he is superior to them with regard to something that is positive or something that is negative?

Those scholars, most prominently Louis Painchaud, who insist that in the final analysis, the portrait of Judas Iscariot in the *Gospel of Judas* is negative, do not see any difference between sacrificing in 56.19–21 and in the dream of the twelve (38.1–26; 39.25–28). They think that in both cases it is to be seen as a negative act, which is in harmony with the purposes of Saklas (cf. 56.12–13), the inferior god. Therefore, by sacrificing Jesus, Judas Iscariot proves even worse than his apostolic colleagues who sacrifice their own children.[19] As in the *Concept of Our Great Power* (NHC VI, 4 41,15–24), so in the *Gospel of Judas*, according to Painchaud, when Judas betrays Jesus, he is thus considered to be an instrument of the archons in their war against the real God.[20]

Although Painchaud's arguments have to be taken seriously they do not carry enough weight to change the earlier features connected with the figure of Judas from positive to negative. If Jesus indicates here that Judas is the most evil disciple for forcing Jesus into martyrdom, the end of his address to Judas spoken later becomes totally inconceivable. In rather positive and encouraging terms, Jesus exhorts Judas as follows: "Look, you have been told everything. Lift up your eyes and look at the cloud and the light within it and the stars surrounding it. And the star that leads the way is your star" (57.15–20). To be sure, the stars[21] are somewhat ambiguous entities in the *Gospel of Judas*. Some stars/angels act definitely as evil guides or beings (e.g., 46.1–2; 51.8–52.14; 54.18–24; 55.14–20) but others may be taken as more positive entities or at least as being capable of

[19] Painchaud, "À propos de la (re)découverte" (n. 9), 557–558; similarly DeConick, *The Thirteenth Apostle* (n. 9), 57–59; Petersen, "Genskrevet Skrift" (n. 9), 76–77; Pedersen, "Historien om Judasevangeliet" (n. 9), 108; R. Falkenberg, "Kongerigets hemmeligheder – et forsøg på en fortolkning af Judasevangeliet", in *Mellem venner og fjender* (ed. A.K. Petersen, J. Hyldahl and E. Thomassen [n. 9]), 138.

[20] Painchaud put forward this view in the general discussion following the panel discussion at the SBL Annual Meeting in Washington, D.C., November 2006 (cf. now also Painchaud, "Polemical Aspects of the *Gospel of Judas*", in: Scopello [ed.], *The Gospel of Judas in Context* [n. 8], 178).

[21] Stars and angels, both ambiguous depending on their derivation, are very closely related in the *Gospel of Judas*.

functioning as positive entities, depending on whose stars/angels they are and what the situation is (42.7–8; 47.18–26). With the ending of Jesus' last speech the stars surrounding the luminous cloud (57.16–18), which is the dwelling place of Adamas and the incorruptible generation of Seth (48.21–49.6), seem to be positive entities. The same positive connotation would apply to the star of Judas "that leads the way" (57.19–20).[22]

If that interpretation is correct, the act of sacrificing which Judas is supposed to undertake, although it leads to martyrdom of Jesus, has a different meaning and function than the sacrifices carried out by the other disciples.[23] The earliest interpretation presented by various scholars was to see the sacrifice of Judas as an act through which Jesus was enabled to free himself from the mortal body (the "man who bears" Jesus) which fettered him to the earth.[24] It has nonetheless been pointed out by Elaine Pagels and Karen King that Jesus of the *Gospel of Judas* did not seem to have any difficulty in leaving his body and visiting the heavenly realm of the holy generation during his earthly ministry (36.15–17).[25] Therefore, they maintain that to see Judas' act as liberating Jesus from the bondage of his mortal body contradicts the ease with which the *Gospel of Judas* can speak elsewhere about Jesus' ability to leave his body. This type of apparent contradiction is not totally unusual in early Christian texts. A prime example would be Paul, who, in one instance, can speak of his "out-of-body"

---

[22] To be sure, the star of Judas had also misled him on an earlier occasion. This only suggests that astrological determinism is not a consistently negative feature in the *Gospel of Judas*; similarly S. Kim, "The *Gospel of Judas* and the Stars", in: Scopello (ed.), *The Gospel of Judas in Context* (n. 8), 293–309.

[23] In his paper "Judas, Other Disciples, and Ancient Anger Management" at the Codex Judas Congress in Houston, March 2008, Ismo Dunderberg argued that the anger Judas needs to muster in order to accomplish the task of sacrificing Jesus (cf. *Gos. Judas* 56.22) shows that he is not yet the "perfect human being" whom the ancient Greek philosophical tradition assumes to be capable of existing without anger. According to Dunderberg, Judas is not completely ignorant with regard to the challenges of moral development but he has not yet reached and will not reach its most advanced stage. Dunderberg's thesis is interesting but presupposes too readily that the description of Judas' anger in the *Gospel of Judas* is primarily rooted in Greek philosophical tradition. Another interpretive background, namely that of the Hebrew Bible, points to a more positive understanding of Judas' anger. The Hebrew Bible provides us with plenty of examples according to which the wrath of God and humans for the sake of a righteous cause is not only acceptable but desirable (in a private communication, Lance Jenott has especially called my attention to the righteous anger of Moses and Phinehas; Ex 32:7–20; Num 25:6–13). In addition, *On the Origin of the World*, a Nag Hammadi text displaying Sethian features, refers to Sabaoth, who having received some light from the light of Pistis Sophia turns to hate his father Yaldabaoth (103,32–104,13).

[24] So e.g., Ehrman, *The Lost Gospel of Judas Iscariot* (n. 10), 172.

[25] Pagels and King, *Reading Judas* (n. 10), 170–171 n. 4.

experience (2 Cor 12:1–4) while, in another text from the same letter, he longs for liberation from his "earthly house" (2 Cor 5:1–4).

Karen King may still be right that *Judas*' act implies more than simply delivering Jesus from his earthly bondage. She has suggested that the sacrifice of Jesus accomplished by Judas is to be seen "as a demonstration that the true spiritual nature of humanity is not flesh, nor can it be constrained by death."[26] The idea of Jesus' death as a successful attack against the powers of Hades and as a deliverance of the dead from the underworld is also found in another early Christian writing, namely the *Testimony of Truth* (NHC IX,3). Like the *Gospel of Judas*, this text allows a positive interpretation of the martyrdom of Jesus. It becomes instrumental in defeating the power of death although it criticizes Christians who submit to martyrdom hoping thereby to effect their salvation (31,22–34,1).[27] In light of the similarities between the *Gospel of Judas* and the *Testimony of Truth*, it is not impossible to combine a vehement criticism of martyrdom as a futile sacrifice with a positive understanding of Jesus' death as a martyr.

5. Judas Iscariot and the Holy Generation

One of the most difficult questions concerning Judas Iscariot in the *Gospel of Judas* is his relationship to the great and holy generation, mentioned for the first time in 36.16–17 or possibly in 36.8–9 and subsequently many times with slightly varying titles, including the "incorruptible [generation] of Seth" (49.5–6). Who then belong to the holy generation? The key passage which seems to identify the members of the holy generation and to distinguish them from the persons of mortal birth is 43.14–23. Jesus of the text states as follows: "The souls of every human generation will die. When these people (belonging to the holy generation), however, have completed the time of the kingdom and the spirit leaves them, their bodies will die, but their souls will be made alive, and they will be taken up."

According to this text, the members of the holy generation differ from the persons of mortal birth in one essential respect. They own a soul which is capable of making them alive after the life-giving spirit leaves them in their death, and therefore they are able to ascend to the heavenly realm of the holy generation. The persons of mortal birth, on the other hand, do not have a soul which can survive bodily death, and for that reason the depar-

[26] Ibid., 163.

[27] For the understanding of Jesus' death in the *Testimony of Truth*, see also M. Franzmann, *Jesus in the Nag Hammadi Writings* (Edinburgh 1996), 143–144.

ture of the spirit means a definitive death for them.[28] In the later cosmology, in which two angels, Michael and Gabriel, are said to have been assigned the task of giving lives to humans, the same division in human beings is seen. Michael gives spirit to everybody but no soul or at least no soul which guarantees the continuity of human life beyond physical death. Gabriel, for his part, is ordered to take care of the holy generation ("the great kingless generation"), and he provides them with both spirit and soul capable of making them alive and being taken up after the death of the body (53.18–25).

It is not only the specific – obviously pre-existent (57.9–14) – character of the soul, however, which makes the members of the holy generation distinct. They also have to know Jesus in the right way and be strong enough to bring out the perfect human in order to stand before Jesus (34.13–35.6). It is also possible that belonging to the holy generation includes some ethical consequences although they are not explicitly spelled out in the extant part of the text. According to the author of the *Gospel of Judas*, those of mortal birth have not only misunderstood the significance of martyrdom, they have also practiced various sexual sins, other acts of impurity, and general lawlessness. This suggests the members of the holy generation would be expected to obey higher moral standards. The rules of conduct cannot be too strict, however, since fasting is not seen as a requirement but as a reprehensible deed (39.18–40.20).

But does Judas belong to the holy generation? There is no text in the *Gospel of Judas*, which deals with the question of Judas' soul. Therefore, the anthropological discussion presented above does not settle the question of Judas' position. There are passages, however, especially at the beginning of the *Gospel of Judas*, which suggest that, despite all the features of the text which seem to portray Judas as a specially favored disciple, he would not belong to the holy generation. When Judas relates to Jesus his vision of the heavenly house and expresses his wish to enter it, Jesus seems to deny Judas' access altogether, since "no person of mortal birth is worthy to enter the house … for that place is reserved for the holy" (45.14–19).[29] The fact that Judas is introduced as "the thirteenth (daimon)"

---

[28] A similar interpretation is advocated by Karen King in Pagels and ead., *Reading Judas* (n. 10), 138–139, 159–160.

[29] Some scholars have also pointed out that in *Gos. Judas* 35.25–27 Jesus is said to impart "the mysteries of the kingdom" to Judas. At the same time Jesus states that Judas will not enter that kingdom. This is taken to indicate that Judas does not belong to the holy generation although Jesus reveals its secrets to him (so, e.g., Painchaud in his paper "A Tale of Two Kingdoms: The Mysteries of the *basileia* in the *Gospel of Judas*" presented at the SBL Annual Meeting in Washington, D.C., November 2006; Petersen, "Genskrevet Skrift" [n. 9], 74; Falkenberg, "Kongerigets hemmeligheder" [n. 19], 126–127). It is to be noted, however, that the kingdom in the *Gospel of Judas* is a somewhat

(44.21; 46.20) or as ruling over "the thirteenth aeon" (55.10–11) is also seen as an indication that although he is placed relatively high in the religious hierarchy, he never reaches the realm of the holy generation. In the *Apocalypse of Adam* the thirteenth kingdom is the highest one which has some understanding of the Savior but it still belongs to the lower world and is situated just below the generation without a king (82.10–19).[30] But is the thirteenth aeon of the *Gospel of Judas* to be evaluated in the same way as the thirteenth kingdom in the *Apocalypse of Adam*?[31] Does Judas appear "to be stuck in the lower cosmos, if at its highest level, the thirteenth aeon," as stated by Birger Pearson?[32]

In order to show that the metaphorical implication of numbers may easily vary in different writings one can point to the Nag Hammadi tractate *Marsanes* (NHC X,1) in which the thirteenth level does not belong to the lower world but represents the highest. In *Marsanes*, the thirteenth seal "speaks concerning [the] Silent One who was not [known], and the primacy of [the one who] was not distinguished" (4.21–23). In *Pistis Sophia* the thirteenth aeon is a positive place, clearly above the twelve chaotic aeons, in which Sophia dwells and into which she is again elevated after being temporarily removed from that place into lower aeons (178.11–17). At the same time it is also, at least initially, the dwelling place of Authades and Adamas, evil rulers of chaos and persecutors of Sophia, who are

---

obscure term. In the only instance in which the meaning of the term is unequivocal (43.18) it does not refer to the realm of the holy generation but to the visible world. Partly because of the fragmentary textual context, the other occurences of the term (45.26; 46.13; 53.14) are open to several interpretations but there is nothing in these passages which prevents one from understanding the kingdom in them in the same way as in 43.18, in other words, as a reference to the visible world in which persons of mortal birth dwell. In light of this, the kingdom in 35.25–26 to which Judas "will not (ultimately) go into" need not be the realm of the "great kingless (!) generation" (53,24) but the visible world in which the generation of persons of mortal birth, including the apostles and the representatives of apostolic Christianity, will remain. The fact that this causes Judas "to grieve much" (35.27) can be explained by the fact that his separation from his fellow-disciples makes them persecute and curse him (44.26–45.1; 46.21–22). These texts serve as a *vaticinium ex eventu* of what is happening to Judas in the apostolic tradition.

[30] This was pointed out by Painchaud in the Nordic Nag Hammadi and Gnosticism Network Seminar on the *Gospel of Judas* in Bergen, in August 2006.

[31] As indicated by Pearson ("Judas Iscariot and the *Gospel of Judas*" [n. 9], 11), the idea of thirteen aeons belonging to the sphere of Yaldabaoth, the evil creator, also appears in other Sethian writings, such as *Zostrianos* (NHC VIII 4,25–28) and the *Gospel of the Egyptians* (NHC III 63,17–18).

[32] Pearson, "Judas Iscariot and the *Gospel of Judas*" (n. 9), 11; similarly DeConick, *The Thirteenth Apostle* (n. 9), 110–113; Brankaer and Bethge, *Codex Tchacos* (n. 9), 347–348; Thomassen, "Judasevangeliet og gnosticismen" (n. 9), 166.

nevertheless forced to leave that place and go into chaos (168.11–19).[33] To be sure, a somewhat ambiguous parallel use of the number "thirteenth" in *Marsanes* and *Pistis Sophia* is no better argument for interpreting the relationship of Judas to the holy generation in the *Gospel of Judas* than that in the *Apocalypse of Adam* or other Sethian texts. Yet the point here is to show that none of these texts can be used without reservation for interpreting the meaning of the thirteenth in the *Gospel of Judas*.[34]

There is, however, a systematic textual development in the *Gospel of Judas* with regard to the position of Judas which might suggest that he is meant to be seen as a member of the holy generation in the text. At the beginning of the gospel, when Judas and the other disciples are asked to "bring out the perfect human and stand before" Jesus, even Judas, although he certainly comes closest to fulfilling Jesus' order, cannot look him in the eyes but has to turn away his face (35.10–14). Therefore, it is no wonder that after Judas presents his vision to Jesus and asks him whether he could enter the house of the holy generation that he has seen, Jesus denies his request rather harshly (45.14–19). Somewhat later when Jesus and Judas continue their conversation, Judas wonders what advantage he has received when Jesus has set him apart from his previous generation (46.16–18). At that point it is at least clear that Judas is no longer part of the apostolic group. The obvious confusion in 46.24–25 prevents us from seeing what is going to happen in the last days (46.24–47.1).[35] At least it is very likely, despite the fragmentary character of the text, that in the next part of the

[33] A. Marjanen, "The Figure of Authades in the Nag Hammadi and Related Documents", in: *Coptica – Gnostica – Manichaica: Mélanges offerts à Wolf-Peter Funk* (ed. by L. Painchaud and P.-H. Poirier; BCNH, Section "Études" 7; Quebec 2006), 575–577; similarly M. Meyer, "The Thirteenth Daimon: Judas and Sophia in the Gospel of Judas" [http://www.chapman.edu/meyer]; Pedersen, "Historien om Judasevangeliet" (n. 9), 107.

[34] Similarly Kim, "The *Gospel of Judas* and the Stars" (n. 22), 307.

[35] Scholars are debating whether the grammatical form *nekbōk* should be taken as a second person singular of the third future (for the form, see W.C. Till, *Koptische Dialektgrammatik mit Lesestücken und Wörterbuch* [München 1961], 55) or of the conjunctive (for the form, see B. Layton, *A Coptic Grammar with Chrestomathy and Glossary: Sahidic Dialect* [Wiesbaden 2000], 276). In the former case, which is grammatically more likely, the text clearly denies that the subject of the sentence will enter the holy generation, whereas the latter confirms it. Because of the confusion in the text (see Kasser, Wurst, Meyer, and Gaudard [ed.], *The Gospel of Judas* [n. 11]) it is not clear, however, whether the subject is really Judas. It is not even unequivocal that the two lines 46.25–47.1 after the textual confusion belongs to a speech of Jesus, since there is a new introduction of the speech ("Jesus said") in 47.1–2 (as pointed out by Tage Petersen in a private discussion). It may even be part of the speech of Judas in which he quotes what the other disciples have said to him. This may be too speculative, but in any case it is difficult to use this passage as a clear indication that Jesus denies Judas access to the holy generation.

dialogue Jesus moves on to teach him something which no human (obviously of mortal birth) is allowed to see (47.2–5). After the long cosmological account the description contains a new twist again. Jesus says to Judas: "Look, you have been told everything. Lift up your eyes and look at the cloud and the light within it and the stars surrounding it" (57.15–18). What is Judas supposed to see? A cloud? Yes. But above all, he is supposed to look at something no human (of mortal birth) will ever see. Whether or not it is Judas (and not Jesus) who enters the luminous cloud in 57.22–23,[36] it is certainly reasonable to conclude that the narrative development of the gospel has led Judas from the band of the disciples to the holy generation.[37] Whatever else the *Gospel of Judas* is, with regard to the status of Judas Iscariot, it can be taken as a story of development.

---

[36] It has been suggested that the use of conjunction *auō* ("and") before the verbal expression *affōk ehoun* ("he entered") could indicate the change of the subject from Judas to Jesus (so G. Schenke and S. Arai who are mentioned in Kasser, Wurst, Meyer, and Gaudard [ed.], *The Gospel of Judas* [n. 11], 233). This is possible but by no means necessary. The extension of a main clause with a past tense conjugation (*a-*) by another main clause can follow either an asyndetic pattern or a linkage with a conjunction (cf. Layton, *A Coptic Grammar* [n. 35], 260). One example of a clause linkage with the conjunction *auō* in the *Gospel of Judas* is in 48.17–21. As to its grammar and train of thought, the most natural way to read *Gos. Judas* 57.21–23 is to infer that it is Judas, not Jesus or anybody else, who enters the cloud.

[37] A similar interpretation of Judas Iscariot, who is making constant progress during his encounters with Jesus, is presented by Elaine Pagels in her paper "Baptism in *Gospel of Judas*: A Preliminary Inquiry" at the Codex Judas Congress in Houston (March 2008); Pagels maintains that Judas "serves as the paradigm of one, who having been born 'of mortal birth', doomed and hopeless, ... receives catechetical instruction that follows a traditional pattern of *warning* and *instruction* that culminates in *exhortation* intended to encourage the hearer to receive baptismal 'rebirth' into the 'great and holy race'." An interesting alternative interpretation of a positive Judas has been put forth by Falkenberg ("Kongerigets hemmeligheder" [cf. above footnote 18], 132–140; cf. also Ismo Dunderberg in his paper "Judas, Other Disciples, and Ancient Anger Management" at the Codex Judas Congress in Houston, March 2008). He is not completely sure whether Judas ever becomes part of the holy generation but he maintains that Judas is a similar figure as Sabaoth in *On the Origin of the World* (NHC II,5). It is possible that they both end up being intermediaries who are clearly above the evil Creator and his allies, including the twelve in the case of the *Gospel of Judas*, and they both also receive a special revelation. In spite of all that, they may not attain the highest realm of divinity. In his last essay on the *Gospel of Judas*, Marvin Meyer ("The Thirteenth Daimon" [n. 33]) has also presented a mediating view of Judas. Based on the similarities between Judas and Sophia in *Pistis Sophia*, who both reach to the thirteenth aeon and are called daimons, Meyer finds a typological relationship between them. They are necessarily not part of the holy generation but they are both redeemed and clearly placed above the chaos and its twelve aeons.

6. The Function of Judas in the Literary Strategy of the *Gospel of Judas*

Finally, I return to the title of the article and ask whether the *Gospel of Judas* rehabilitates Judas Iscariot and tries to change the picture the canonical gospels impart of him. I would say yes. Instead of depicting him as the greatest villain of earliest Christianity, he becomes the most favored disciple who seems to understand his master best and who mediates and authenticates the written description of his mission and message. The rehabilitation of Judas also takes place by means of correcting certain aspects of the canonical portrait of him and giving them a completely different interpretation. For example, the separation of Judas from other disciples is not due to his betrayal but to his greater perception of Jesus' teaching. Moreover, Judas does not commit suicide nor die in an accident but is being persecuted by other disciples.[38] The replacement of Judas does not serve the perfection of the apostolic collegium for the service of the Church but it is required by the inferior god. Judas is probably also regarded as a member of the holy generation and thus he could also serve as a role model for Christians. To be sure, this is not the most important function of Judas in the literary strategy of the author of the Gospel of Judas. Rather, he is pictured as Jesus' special disciple because, through him, the text can criticize the other disciples and the form of Christianity they represent.[39] In the highly polemical atmosphere of its day, especially with regard to the understanding of martyrdom, the use of Judas Iscariot as the most favored disciple of Jesus and as the authenticator of his message is an ingenious, if rather farfetched, attempt to undermine the credibility of apostolic Christianity. The author wants to underline that even Judas Iscariot, whom most Christians regarded as the traitor of Christianity, understood the core of Christianity better than those apostolic leaders who were most eagerly followed.

---

[38] This was pointed out by Ismo Dunderberg in a private communication.

[39] This was emphasized by Painchaud in the general discussion following the panel discussion at the SBL Annual Meeting in Washington, D.C., November 2006; similarly Petersen, "Genskrevet Skrift" (n. 9), 77–78; Thomassen, "Judasevangeliet og gnosticismen" (n. 9), 163–166. And although my overall interpretation of Judas's position in the *Gospel of Judas* differs from his, at this one point I very much agree with Painchaud.

Jesus' Suffering and Ethics: Patristic Exegesis Reconsidered

MARTIN MEISER

In patristic literature Jesus' death is not only understood as the basis of our salvation but also seen as an example for our moral life. With regard to some biblical passages this statement seems to be self-explanatory, yet it has certain implications to be discussed.

1. The New Testament's terms denoting this circumstance are conjunctions like ὡς, κάθως and γάρ. Jesus is rarely named as a paradigm;[1] more often the relevant texts speak about *mimesis*. However, in ancient Christian exegesis on Passion texts we find not only the idea, but very often also the terminology of example and imitation.

2. The death of prominent persons was a subject of its own interest in ancient times. Timon's Σίλλοι, to be found in Diogenes Laertios' *Lives and doctrines of famous philosophers*, are sometimes ridiculed, but there are traditions of a noble death[2] that have been a challenge for Christian proclamation. In the Greek world, the fates of Codros[3], Menoiceus[4], Leaina[5], Anaxarchos[6], Zeno of Elea[7], and especially the death of Socrates have

---

[1] For μίμησις cf. 1 Cor 11:1, for τύπος cf. 1 Cor 10:6.11; for ὑπόγραμμος cf. 1 Pt 2:21, for ὑπόδειγμα cf. Joh 13:15; Jas 5:10. The term παράδειγμα does not occur in the New Testament but it is a biblical term, cf. Ex 25:40 LXX.

[2] For an exhaustive collection of these traditions see A. Lumpe, "Exemplum", *RAC* VI (1966), 1229–1257; the Christian reception is listed pp. 1247–1252.

[3] Cf. Cicero, *Tusc.* 1,116; Velleius Paterculus, *Historiae Romanae* 1,2,1; cf. further Lactance, *div. inst.* III,12,22 = CSEL 19, 210; Jerome, *in Eph.* 1,7 = PL 26, 450 D – 451 A.

[4] Cf. Cicero, *Tusc.* I,116; Papinius Statius, *Thebaïs* X,762–77; cf. further Lactance, *div. inst.* III,12,22 = CSEL 19, 210.

[5] Cf. Pausanias, Description of Greece I,23 ; Plinius, *n.h.* VII,87; Tertullian, *apol.* 50,8 = CCL 1, 170.

[6] Cicero, *Tusc.* II,52; Valerius Maximus, Memorable Doings and Sayings III,3 ext. 4; Diogenes Laertios, *Vitae* IX,58–9; cf. further Origen, *Cels.* VII,53 = SC 150, 138.

[7] Cf. Plutarchus, *de Stoicis repugnandis* 37, 1051 D; Diogenes Laertius, Lives 9,26–28; cf. also Tertullian, *de anima* 58,5 = CCL 2, 868; Clement of Alexandria, *str.* IV,56,1 = GCS 15, 274.

to be mentioned, in Roman tradition the examples of Dido[8], Mucius Scaevola[9], Lucretia[10], Curtius[11], Decius[12], Hasdrubal's wife[13], Regulus[14], Cato the Younger[15], and Otho[16]. So we have to develop a theory of the history of Christian reception and non-reception of these traditions.[17]

3. In the second century, ancient critics of Christianity did not only repeat the gossip-like reproaches of thyestic meals and sexual misbehaviour[18] but also began to read Christian scriptures and to prove the absurdity of Christian faith. Therefore, we have to ask whether an influence of pagan criticism on Patristic exegesis can be ascertained or not.

4. The appreciation of non-Christian examples by Christian authors is part of the general and well disputed theme "Christians and pagan wisdom". Some authors hardly quoted pagan examples and were content with mere biblical examples. Other authors defended their use of pagan exam-

---

[8] Cf. also Tertullian, *ad martyres* 4,5 = CCL 1, 6; id., *ad nationes* 1,18,3 = CCL 1, 137.

[9] Cf. Livy, II,12,1–13,5 and especially Livy II,12,9: *et facere et pati fortia Romanum est*; Seneca, *ep.* 98,12; Valerius Maximus, Memorable Doings and Sayings III,3,1; Dio Cassius, Roman History LIII,8,3; cf. also Tertullian, *de anima* 58,5 = CCL 2, 868; Augustine, *de civitate Dei* V,18 = CSEL 40/1, 247–8.

[10] Cf. Cicero, *fin.* II,66; Quintilian, *inst.* V,11,10; cf. further Tertullian, *ad martyres* 4,4 = CCL 1,6.

[11] Cf. Livy, VII,6,3–5; Quintilian, *inst.* XII,2,30; Dio Cassius, Roman history LIII,8,3; cf. even Tertullian, *de testimonio animae* 4,9 = CCL 1, 180; Augustine, *de civitate Dei* 5,18 = CSEL 40/1, 248. There is a monument at the *Forum Romanum*.

[12] Cf. Livy, X,28,13–18; Quintilian, *inst.* XII,2,30; Dio Cassius, Roman History LIII,8,3. Cf. further Lactance, *div. inst.* III,12,22 = CSEL 19, 210.

[13] Polybius, Roman History 38,20,7; Strabo, *Geographica* XVII,3,14; cf. further Tertullian, *ad nationes* I,18,3 = CCL 1, 137; id., *apol.* 50,5 = CCL 1,170.

[14] Cf. Seneca, *ep.* 98,12; Seneca, *de providentia* 3,7–10; Quintilian, *inst.* XII,2,30; cf. further Tertullian, *de testimonio animae* 4,9 = CCL 1, 180; Augustine, *de civitate Dei* I,15 = CSEL 40/1, 27–30.

[15] Cf. Seneca, *de providentia* 2,10; id., *de constantia sapientis* 2,3; Plutarch, *Vita Catonis minoris* 69,2–3: Cato's death is a death for freedom. Velleius Paterculus, Historia Romana 2,49, gave only little comment.

[16] Cf. Dio Cassius, Roman History, LXIII,13,3.

[17] Cf. K. Döring, Exemplum Socratis, in *Studien zur Sokratesnachwirkung in der kynisch-stoischen Popularphilosophie der frühen Kaiserzeit und im frühen Christentum* (Hermes.E 42; Wiesbaden 1979). This is a useful, but, concerning Christianity, not an exhaustive book. For example, references to Origen's *Contra Celsum* are missing.

[18] These rebukes are only quoted by Christian authors, cf. Tertullian, *apol.* 7–9 = CCL 1, 98–105; Minucius Felix, *Octavius* 9,2–6 = CSEL 2, 13f.; Athenagoras, *suppl.* 31–36 = PTS 31, 99–112; analogies from pagan authors like Tacitus or Celsus are missing. According to Minucius Felix, *Octavius* 9,6 = CSEL 2, 13f., Fronto mentioned these issues in the assembly of the Roman senate.

ples by pointing out to how the Bible itself[19] and the Church fathers refer to pagan examples or used allegorical exegesis of the 'sack of Egypt' in Exod 12:35–36.[20]

The Example of Jesus

According to the New Testament the death of Jesus is not only the basis of our salvation but it has also ethical implications; self-denigration (Mark 10:45; Phil 2:6–8) and self-negation, i.e. the struggle against desires (Matt 16:24; Gal 5:24), willingness to subordination (1 Pt 2:21–23) and to suffering[21] are the main issues raised in patristic exegesis.[22]

The terminology of example and imitation mentioned above was part of a coherent and common ancient concept to clarify a doctrine or to admonish people without specific philosophical education to behave differently. Ancient Christians shared this concept and introduced this terminology in the exegesis of New Testament references which contain the idea but not the terms. This terminology is not only applied to comment on passages like Matt 16:24 parr.[23]; 20:28[24]; 26:42[25]; 26:50[26]; 27:40–43[27]; Luke

---

[19] Origen, *hom. in Luc.* 31,3 = FC 4/2, 314–316; Jerome, *ep.* 70,2,1 = CSEL 54, 701–2. Decisive are 1 Cor 15:33; Tit 1:12; Acts 17:28. Cf. further the references to Moses and Daniel in Basil of Caesarea, *ad adolescentes* 2 = PG 31, 568 C.

[20] Origen, *ep. ad Gregory the Thaumaturgos* 2 = SC 148, 188; Gregory of Nyssa, *vit. Mos.* II = GNO 7,1, 67–69; Augustine, *doctr. Christ.* II,144 = CSEL 80, 75.

[21] Hebr 13:12f; 1 Pet 4:12; Ignatius, *Rom.* 6,3.

[22] The phenomenon that a distinct event can be interpreted in multiple ways is analogous in pagan and Christian tradition: The death of Cato is commented on as death for *dignitas* (Valerius Maximus, Memorable Doings and Sayings III,2,14) and freedom (Seneca, *de constantia sapientis* 2,3), as an example of the fortitude in suffering (Seneca, *ep. moral.* 98,12), and as an example of the Stoic doctrine that death is no evil (Cicero, *Tusc.* 1,74).

[23] Hilary of Poitiers, *in Mt* = SC 258, 58; Beda Venerabilis, *Mc.* = CCL 120, 538; Leo I., *tract.* 70,4 = CCL 138 A, 429: *Dicente Domino: Qui non accipit crucem suam et sequitur me, non est me dignus, et dicente Apostolo: Si conpatimur, et conregnabimus, quis uere Christum passum, mortuum et resuscitatum colit, nisi qui cum ipso et patitur et moritur et resurgit?*

[24] Origen, *comm. in Mt* 16,8 = GCS 40, 497 admonishing the leaders of the church; Hilary of Poitiers, *Mt* 20,12 = SC 258, 116; Jerome, *in Matth.* 3,20,25 = SC 259, 96, quoted by Beda Venerabilis, *Mc* = CCL 120, 566: *Denique sui proponit exemplum.*

[25] Cyril of Alexandria, *in Mt* = PG 72, 456 A: The fact of the repetition of Jesus' plea proves that we are allowed to implore God repeatedly as well.

[26] Jesus accepts Judas' kiss – he teaches to love the enemies; cf. Hilary of Poitiers, *in Mt* 32,1 = SC 258, 240; Beda Venerabilis, *Mc.* = CCL 120, 618; id., *Lc.* = CCL 120, 387, pointing out to Ps 119:7.

[27] John Chrysostom, *hom. in Mt* 87,2 = PG 58, 771f.

23:34[28]; Gal 1:4[29]; 3:13[30]; Phil 2:5[31], but even to comment on ὕπαγε ὀπίσω μου in Matt 16:23[32], or Jesus' cry at the Cross (Ps 21:2 LXX = Matt 27:46).[33] According to Leo the Great Jesus' suffering as a whole is both sacrament of justification and example of demanded devotion[34], and the cross as punishment for low people is supposed to serve all people an opportunity for imitation.[35]

The criterion of ancient Christian exegesis was the usefulness for the Christian believers, and this concept of usefulness was biblically grounded in 2 Tim 3:16, but closely related to philosophical ideas of the Hellenistic world.[36]

The Death of Socrates in Ancient Literature

As far as the death of Socrates is concerned, it is not necessary to dispute whether Socrates himself understood his own death in a paradigmatic way or not. The fact is that his death has been understood as a moral example since the time of his pupils Xenophon and Plato. According to Xenophon, Socrates knew very well that his willingness to die would bear witness to the fact that he "wronged no man at any time, nor corrupted any man, but strove ever to make my companions better".[37] The Platonic Socrates addresses his accusers: "Do not … demand of me that I act before you in a

---

[28] Beda Venerabilis, *Lc.* = CCL 120, 403.

[29] Origen, *Cels.* II,11 = SC 132, 314.

[30] NHC 1,2, p. 13,20–25; Tertullian, *patient.* 8,3 = CC.L 1,308.

[31] Origen, *comm. in Mt* 16,8 = GCS 40, 497; Marius Victorinus, *in Phil* 2,5 = CSEL 83/2, 187; Pelagius, *in Phil* 2,5; Theodoret of Cyrus, *in Phil* = PG 82, 569 B.

[32] Hilary of Poitiers, *in Mt* = SC 258, 58. The reason for this positive interpretation of these words is the following context Matt 16:24, but also the positively nuanced ὀπίσω μου in Matt 4:19.

[33] Beda Venerabilis, *Mt* = PL 92, 125 A; Hrabanus Maurus, *in Mt* = PL 107, 1142 CD: *Et ostendit quam patientes et sperantes debeant esse inter flagella, qui peccatores sunt, quomo ipse ad immortalitatem non nisi per mortem transivit.*

[34] Leo I., *tract.* 67,5 = CCL 138 A, 411: *Ab omnipotenti enim medico duplex miseris remedium praeparatum est, cuius aliud est in sacrament, aliud in exemplo, ut per unum conferantur divina per aliud exigantur humana. Quia sicut Deus iustificationis est auctor, ita homo deuotionis est debitor.*

[35] Lactantius, *epit.* 46,3 = SC 335, 182: *Suscepit ergo id genus mortis quod solet humilibus inrogari, ut omnibus facultas daretur imitandi.* But Lactantius does not specify the issues of the imitation demanded from us.

[36] Cf. M. Sheridan, "The Concept of the 'Useful' as an Exegetical Tool in Patristic Exegesis", *StPatr* 39 (2006), 253–257, here 253.

[37] Xenophon, *Mem.* 4,8,10.

way which I consider neither honourable nor right nor pious."[38] Further: "if you kill me …, you will not injure me so much as yourselves. For neither Anytos nor Meletos could injure me; that would be impossible for I believe it is not God's will that a better man can be injured by a worse".[39] And he comments on Crito's announcement of the nearness of his death with these words: "good luck be with us! If this is the will of the gods, so be it."[40]

The death of some important people is told according to the outline of Socrates' death. It is disputed whether even they themselves understood their imminent death in this way.[41] The death of Socrates was a subject of reflections for example in times of danger for philosophers, especially in the first century C.E.: Philosophers had to endure banishment and death during the times of Nero, Vespasian and Domitian.[42]

Seneca quoted the example of Socrates as an example of an overwhelming multitude of troubles,[43] with regard not only to the death but to the whole life of the Athenian philosopher.[44] Thinking of Socrates' example as a positive one implies that he felt the impulse to become an example himself.[45]

According to Epictetus the Athenian philosopher this is the most important example of philosophic living in general. Two statements formulated in allusion to Socratic maxims are given in Epictetus' Enchiridion as advice, which we should, upon every occasion, have in mind: "they (scil. Anytos and Meletos) can kill me yet they cannot injure me" and "if this is the will of the gods, so be it".[46] Yet for Epictetus these sayings are not only general rules but also examples of the main doctrines of his own philosophy: The *dictum* on Anytos and Meletos demonstrated in Epictetus' view that for Socrates the essence of the good did not consist in the very life.[47] Epictetus concludes: "I have learned to see that everything that happens, when outside the realm of my moral purpose (ἀπροαίρετον), is nothing to me."[48] Socrates' word spoken to Crito teaches us to learn the meaning of

---

[38] Plato, Apology 35c; cf. Plato, *Crito* 54bc.

[39] Plato, Apology 30cd.

[40] Plato, *Crito* 43d.

[41] Cicero, *Tusc.* 1,74 and Plutarchus, *Cato minor* 69,3, concerning Cato the Younger.

[42] Cf. Tacitus, *ann.* 15,62, concerning Seneca; ibid. 16,32–34, concerning Thrasea Paetus.

[43] Seneca, *ep. moral.* 98,12.

[44] Seneca, *ep. moral.* 104,28.

[45] Seneca, *ep. moral.* 98,13.

[46] Epictetus, *Enchiridion* 53,3f.

[47] Epictetus, *Diss.* I,29,18.

[48] οὐδέν ἐστιν πρὸς ἐμέ. (1,19,24).

death, exile, prison, hemlock, and not to lament.[49] Not death itself is evil but our fear of death.[50] To be educated consists precisely in learning to desire everything exactly as it happens to be.[51]

Ancient Critics on the Story of Jesus' Passion

Jesus' cross caused mockery and despise from the very beginning of Christianity, and the oldest testimony of critique against Christianity did not speak of it very favourably.[52] The first specified critique is formulated within the "Word of truth" by the philosopher Celsus who did not simply repeat the well-known accusations against the Christians but had read the Gospels and therefore was more informed than his predecessors in anti-Christian criticism.

For Celsus Jesus' claim to be God was not only disapproved because of the fact of his suffering.[53] On the one hand, it was a well-known general problem in Greek philosophy to combine the notion of the good and unchangeable god with the idea of suffering; on the other hand, Celsus reads some details of the Gospels' Passion story as evidence against the Christian truth. If Jesus had really been God he would not have had to suffer corporal pains and would not have lamented in Gethsemane;[54] and if he really had been God he would have disappeared from the cross.[55] Even human beings like Heracles, Asclepios, Orpheus or the philosophers Anaxarchos and Epictetus mastering their imminent death in an honourable way were superior to Jesus: For him, it would have been better not to remain silent but to persuade his accusers by speaking freely and thus proving his innocence.[56] The stories told by the Gospels are not reports on real events but inventions by the disciples in order to cover up their master's misfor-

[49] Epictetus, *Diss.* I,4,24.

[50] Epictetus, *Diss.* II,1,14.

[51] Epictetus, *Diss.* I,12,15: τὸ παιδεύεσθαι τουτ' ἐστιν ἕκαστα οὕτω θέλειν ὡς γίνεται.

[52] Tacitus, *ann.* XV,44.

[53] Celsus, according to Origen, *Cels.* II,9.31 = SC 132, 300–302. 362. Julian the Apostate is said to have repeated this argument: *Ostendemus ... illlum nouum eius* (scil. *Diodori*) *Deum Galilaeum, quem aeternum fabulose praedicat, indigna morte et sepultura denudatum confictae a Diodoro deitatis* (Julian the Apostate, cited in Facundus of Hermiane, Pro defensione trium capitulorum 4,2,62 = CCL 90 A).

[54] Celsus, according to Origen, *Cels.* II,24 = SC 132, 348.

[55] Celsus, according to Origen, *Cels.* II,68 = SC 132, 444.

[56] Celsus, according to Origen, *Cels.* VII,53 = SC 150, 138.

tune.[57] Celsus certainly knew about Christians interpreting Jesus' punishment as teaching contempt for death,[58] but he did not consider this fact to be proof of a moral value of Christianity.

Porphyry repeats some of Celsus' critical remarks and lists explicitly the contradictions between Jesus' behaviour and some of his statements,[59] but he also focuses indirectly on the comparison of Jesus with Socrates when asking: "Why did Christ not say anything worthy of one who was worthy and divine, when brought to the high priest or to the governor? He could have educated his judge and onlookers and made them better men. Yet, he tolerated being beaten with a reed, spit at, and crowned with thorns – unlike Apollonius, who, after speaking frankly to the emperor Domitian, disappeared from the court. … even if Christ had to suffer according to God's orders, and was compelled to endure penalties, at least he should have tolerated his suffering with frankness, and spoken words of power and wisdom to his judge Pilate."[60] We remember: To make other people better men was the mission vindicated by Socrates.[61]

I would like to conclude this section with the following remarks: To combine the notion of the good and unchangeable God with the idea of suffering was a problem for ancient Greek philosophy in many ways, and, for early Christians, it was an issue not only on account of their own system and therefore often being disputed between Arians and Non-Arians[62], but also a problem pointed out to by ancient critics of Christianity.

Christian Reception of Non-Christian Noble Death

Examples of pagan self-offering are well-known to some Christian authors; the first occurrence to be mentioned here is 1 Clem 55:1.[63] To educated

---

[57] Celsus, according to Origen, *Cels.* II,15f = SC 132, 324–326; similarly Porphyry, Frgm. 15 Harnack (p. 50f) = Frgm. 169, R. Berchman, *Porphyry Against the Christians. Ancient Mediterranean and Medieval Texts and Contexts* (Studies in Platonism, Neoplatonism, and the Platonic Tradition 1; Leiden 2005), 194.

[58] Celsus, according to Origen, *Cels.* II,73 = SC 132, 458.

[59] Porphyry names the contradiction between Jesus' behaviour in Gethsemane and his saying "Do not fear because of those who can kill the body" (Porphyry, Frgm. 62 Harnack [p. 84] = Frgm. 174 Berchman [p. 197]).

[60] Porphyry, Frgm. 63 Harnack (p. 84f) = Frgm. 174 Berchman (p. 197).

[61] Xenophon, *Mem.* 4,8,10.

[62] Cf. Athanasius, *c. Ar.* III,26 = PG 26, 377 A – 380 B; Hilary of Poitiers, *in Mt* 31,2 = SC 238, 226.

[63] For the first half of 1 Clem 55,1 cf. the traditions retold in Cicero, *Tusc.* I,116; for the second half of 1 Clem 55,1 cf. the saying of Scipio Africanus quoted in Seneca, *ep.* 86,2: *causa tibi libertatis fui, ero et argumentum; exeo, si plus quam tibi expedit crevi.*

Christians, the details of Socrates' trial were well-known: in the ancient schools of rhetoric Socrates' trial was a regularly used paradigm,[64] and possibly Lucian even testifies Socrates' popularity with Christians even in the lower classes of Greco-Roman society.[65] The Christian reception of Socrates,[66] insofar it was a positive one, is a topic in Christian apology and hardly ever a topic of ethical admonition. Some Christians like Justin the martyr establish a community of fate between the Christian martyrs and Socrates: Both sides intended to enlighten their contemporaries on how to think of heavenly things appropriately;[67] both sides had to suffer punishment in the form of injury following a charge of atheism;[68] both sides are rehabilitated by the punishment of their accusers.[69] Justin frankly alludes to Socrates with the words "you can kill us but you cannot hurt us".[70] Clement of Alexandria quotes Plato's description of the just man tormented by his enemies[71] and draws a parallel to Wis 2:12f.[72] and 1 Cor 4:9,11[73].

Tertullian, Minucius Felix and Arnobius use the traditions of noble death in the Greco-Roman world with regard to *apologetic* interests. Tertullian attacks the Greco-Roman contempt for the Christian willingness to martyrdom: *uestris ista* (pagan examples of a noble death) *ad gloriam, nostris ad duritiam deputatis*[74]. In a milder tone Minucius Felix compares the Christian martyrs with Greco-Roman suffering heroes, and he concludes: If these heroes are honoured in Greco-Roman culture, Christians'

---

[64] E. Benz, "Christus und Sokrates in der Alten Kirche (Ein Beitrag zum altkirchlichen Verständnis des Märtyrers und des Martyriums)", *ZNW* 43 (1950/51), 195–224, here 219.

[65] Ibid., 220.

[66] Cf. ibid., passim; E. Fascher, Sokrates und Christus, *ZNW* 45 (1954), 1–41 = id., *Sokrates und Christus* (Leipzig 1959), 36–94.425–432.

[67] Justin, *1 apol.* 5,2–4 = PTS 38, 38f.; *M.Apoll.* 38 (Musurillo 100); cf. Tertullian, apology 14,7 = CCL 1,113.

[68] Justin, *2 apol.* 10,5 = PTS 38, 151; *M.Apoll.* 40f. (Musurillo 100); *M.Pion.* 17 (Musurillo 158); Athenagoras, *Suppl.* 31,1 = PTS 31, 99f. Justin, *2 apol.* 7(8),1 = PTS 38, 149, also underline the analogy between the fate of Jesus and the fate of Heraclitus and Musonius Rufus.

[69] Tertullian, apology 14,8 = CCL 1,113. Mara bar Sarapion (see J.B. Aufhauser, *Antike Jesuszeugnisse* [2nd ed.; Bonn 1925], 5–11) compares Socrates, Pythagoras, and the "wise king" of the Jews, Jesus.

[70] Justin, *1 apol.* 2,4 = PTS 38,33.

[71] Plato, *rep.* II, 361 E: "… the just man will have to endure the lash, the rack, chains, the branding-iron in his eyes, and finally, after every extremity of suffering, he will be crucified, and so will learn his lesson that not to be but to seem just is what we ought to desire."

[72] Clement of Alexandria, *str.* V,108,2f. = GCS 15, 398.

[73] Clement of Alexandria, *str.* IV,52,1f. = GCS 15, 272.

[74] Tertullian, *ad nationes* I,18,5 = CCL 1,137.

willingness to martyrdom is a proof of the truth of Christianity.[75] According to Arnobius, the noble death of Greco-Roman heroes justifies Christians worshipping Christ crucified.[76]

Not apology but exhortation determines the conclusion *a minori ad maius*: If even non-Christians are able to become heroes for the sake of earthly glory, how much should Christians be willing to suffer martyrdom.[77] Socrates sometimes serves as a paradigm of μακροθυμία and ὑπομονή.[78] Ps-Caesarius of Nazianzus calls Socrates, Antisthenes and Epictetus the examples of μακροθυμία; in comparison to these examples τῆς ἔξω παιδείας the Christians should not lag behind.[79]

However, other Christians reclaimed superiority with regard to Christian martyrs[80] or misused the Socratic confession "I go to die, and you to live; but which of us goes to the better lot, is known to none but God"[81] in order to refute the dogmatic philosophy of his successors[82] or had a negative notion of Greco-Roman martyrs in general.[83]

Within Christian *exegetical* writings, I have not found any references to Socrates. Even the nowadays discussed parallels between Acts 5:29 and Plato's apology[84] are rarely noted.[85] In the Acts of Apollonius, Socrates' death is commented by quoting Is 3:10, but this combination does not occur in the known commentaries on Isaiah[86] – we have to consider the brevity of the distinctive explanations even in the voluminous works. But also in Christian writings on martyrdom the suffering of Socrates is not mentioned at all. One reason could be the occurrence of martyrdoms in biblical

[75] Minucius Felix, *Oct.* 37,3–5 = CSEL 2, 52.

[76] Arnobius, *ad nationes* I,40 = CSEL 4, 26f.

[77] Cf. Tertullian, *apol.* 50,5–9 = CCL 1, 170; id., *mart.* 4,4–7 = CCL 1,6f.

[78] *Acta Phileae* 4,1–2.

[79] Ps-Caesarius of Nazianzus, *dial.* 4, *interr.* 192 = PG 38, 1172.

[80] Cf. Lactantius, *div. inst.* V,13,12–14 = SC 204, 196; cf. also Augustine, *de civitate Dei* I,24 = CSEL 40/1, 42–3.

[81] Plato, Apology 42 a.

[82] Ps-Justin, *Cohortatio ad Graecos* 36,2 = PTS 32, 73, alluding to Plato, apology 42a.

[83] Cf. Tertullian, *de anima* 1,1–6 = CCL 2, 781f; Gregory of Nazianzus, *or.* 4,70 = SC 309, 178–182; John Chrysostom, *hom. in Mt* 33,4 = PG 57, 392f.

[84] Plato, Apology 29d.

[85] Acts 5:29 is quoted as a word stimulating the willingness to suffer martyrdom, cf. Origen, *comm. in Rom* 9,27 = FC 2/5, 94; Dionysius of Alexandria, in Eusebius of Caesarea, *h.e.* 7,11,4–5 = GCS 9/2, 654; Athanasius of Alexandria, *c. Ar.* III,57 = PG 26, PG 441C – 444 A. Yet nowhere any parallel is drawn between Christian martyrdom and the fate of Socrates. In some commentaries to Acts 5,29 this parallel is missing also, cf. Beda Venerabilis, *retr.* = CCL 121, 128.

[86] I have controlled Euseb of Caesarea, *Is.* 29 = GCS 57, 23; Jerome, *in Is.* 16 = CC.SL 73 A, 683; Theodoret of Cyrus, *Is.* = SC 315, 214–216; Cyril of Alexandria, *Is.* 1,2 = PG 70, 108 C – 109 A; Procopius of Gaza, *Is.* = PG 87/2, 1904 D – 1905 B.

writings: The martyrdom of Eleazar (2 Macc 6) and the martyrdom of the seven sons and her mother mentioned in 2 Macc 7 are sometimes quoted,[87] and homilies on biblical martyrs like Abel or the Maccabees[88] or on Christian martyrs made it unnecessary to memorize the pagan Socrates.

Christian Apologetic Literature and Anti-Christian Polemic

According to Celsus, Jesus could have dodged his way of suffering if he had truly been God. Origen answers: neither did Socrates; he preferred to die according to his philosophy instead of living against his own teaching. Leonidas, at the Thermopyles, showed a similar attitude, Jesus and the Christians as well, though they knew that they had to die if they confessed the Christian faith.[89] But Origen's refutation is more far-reaching: The full purpose of Jesus' crucifixion is not intelligible by the very wording but by a symbolic meaning: We should follow our Lord in self-denigration and take up his cross and so would be crucified for the world and renounce any sin.[90] Explicitly, Origen explains Jesus' silence during the mockery in the praetorium (Matt 27:27–31) to be proof of steadfastness and self-control superior to any speech of the Greek philosophers.[91]

Jesus' announcements of his imminent suffering are in Christian literature clearly understood as sayings of Jesus himself; Celsus' theory of the invention of these sayings by the disciples is, at least, mentioned in Augustine's *De consensu evangelistarum*.[92]

Anti-Christian Polemics and Christian Exegesis

Some exegetes formulate general remarks concerning the passion of Jesus with possible allusions to the problems raised by anti-Christian critics. John Chrysostom and Augustine, at least, shortly refute the wrong opinion that Jesus' passion could be unworthy for him.[93] Explicit references to anti-Christian polemics occur only rarely in Christian exegetical writings.

---

[87] Origen, *mart.* 22–27 = GCS 1, 19–24; Cyprian, *ep.* 58,6,1 = CCL 3C, 327f.

[88] Eusebius Gallicanus, *hom.* 32 = CCL 101, 363–371.

[89] Origen, *Cels.* II,17 = SC 132, 330–332.

[90] Origen, *Cels.* II,69 = SC 132, 446–448.

[91] Origen, *Cels.* VII,55 = SC 150, 142.

[92] Augustine, *cons. ev.* 1,16/24 = CSEL 43, 22.

[93] John Chrysostom, *hom. in Mt* 54,4 = PG 58, 537; Augustine, *Io. ev. tr.* 60,2 = CCL 36, 478.

Some examples of ancient exegesis of the Passion stories, however, show that there is at least some indirect influence.

Jesus' announcements of his imminent suffering are generally understood as sayings of Jesus himself; Joh 10:18 excluded for ancient Christian authors the possibility that Jesus should not have known of his suffering.[94] In the commentaries on Matt 24:9 there is no hint at actual experiences. The mockery of the crucified Jesus is nowhere commented by the argument that Jesus' silence and his remaining on the cross would imply a teaching for believers to be patient under such sufferings.

Yet, there are some issues where the coincidence of anti-Christian critique and problems of Christian theology leads to exegetical efforts worthy to be noted here: Jesus' prayer at the Mount of Olives, his silence during the trial and the mockery, and his quotation of Ps 21:2 LXX on the cross.

The story of Jesus' struggle at the Mount of Olives contains two critical points for the Greco-Roman point of view as well as for Christian faith: Jesus' sorrow (Matt 26:37) and Jesus' plea (Matt 26:39,42).

Different positions are held up by Christians with regard to human affections. In a situation generally demanding apologetic efforts, Origen has to write with regard to two ideals of his pagan counterparts concerning Platonic theology and Stoic ethics: 1. God cannot suffer; 2. the wise man is free from affections. According to Origen's exegesis of Matt 26:37 mastered by these ideals, Jesus is only insofar affected by affections as he can demonstrate the truth of his saying "the spirit is willing but the flesh is weak" (Matt 26:41b).[95] Directly confronted with Celsus' polemics Origen justifies the pains of Jesus in another way: How should Jesus Christ be a paradigm for his followers in their dangerous situation, if he did not really have to undergo the pains?[96] Without explicit reference to an apologetic situation Hilary of Poitiers and Jerome offer a moral justification for Jesus: His sorrow does not result from his dread of death but from his compassion for the apostles who will fail (Matt 26:31) and – so only Jerome – to the Jewish nation that will be punished if Jesus is killed.[97] Augustine's exegesis is not apologetics but polemics: The Stoic struggle against affections is wrong, and his critique of this Stoic issue also concerns Christian ethics: The Christian should have affections: the affection of fear regarding men

[94] Referring to this problem Joh 10,18 is cited by Leo I., *tract.* e 68,2 = CCL 138 A, 415; Petrus Chrysologus, *serm.* 72 bis 1 = CCL 24 A.

[95] Origen, *comm. in Mt ser.* 90 = GCS 38, 205; similarly Tertullian, *or.* 4,5 = CCL 1, 260 interprets Jesus' plea Matt 26:39,42.

[96] Origen, *Cels.* II,25 = SC 132, 354.

[97] Hilary of Poitiers, *in Mt* 31,4 = SC 258, 230; Jerome, *in Mt* 26,37 = SC 259, 252.

who may be lost to Christ, the affection of joy if men are gained for Christ.[98]

Jesus' plea is interpreted as a plea not refusing the suffering in any way – with regard to the biblical announcements and to Jesus' consecration of his body and blood (Matt 26:28) it was impossible for ancient Christian authors that Jesus should have wished to evade the imminent passion. Hilary interpreted Jesus' prayer as a plea in favour of his followers to overcome the weakness of their flesh and their fear of death; Jesus' prayer is a help for us in the situation of martyrdom.[99] According to Origen and Jerome Jesus' prayer was a plea in favour of the Jewish nation: if the Jews killed him they would have no possibility of exculpation; Jesus wished to hinder God's punishment of them.[100] Other interpretations underline the spiritual implications: this prayer implies the admonition to follow God even against our own nature;[101] Jesus takes up our weakness in order to teach us to put the divine will before the human will;[102] Jesus' plea in Gethsemane can encourage us to repeated prayer[103] and shows what could be prayed for by somebody in fear: Because "we do not know how to pray as we ought to" (Rom 8:26), God mercifully denies the harmful things asked for.[104] Yet we find also other interpretations: Jesus has overcome the weakness of the flesh; therefore the apostles were willing to suffer martyrdom[105] in order to demonstrate the distinction between the one emotion excusing the weakness and the other emotion that he had chosen from the will of the Father for the reconciliation of the world.[106]

The silence of Jesus according to Matt 27:12 is interpreted as a consequence of his willingness to suffer: Jesus did not want to respond in order to prevent the possibility that he could be freed so that the usefulness of

---

[98] Augustine, *Io. ev. tr.* 60,3 = CCL 36, 479, mentioning fear, sadness, desire, joy. Augustine did not mention here (!) that according to the doctrine of some Stoics there are also allowed affections.

[99] Hilary of Poitiers, *in Mt* 31,10 = SC 258, 236 – 238.

[100] Origen, *Cels.* II,25 = SC 132, 354; Jerome, *in Mt* = SC 259, 254; Beda Venerabilis, *Lc.* = CCL 120, 385f.

[101] John Chrysostom, *hom. in Mt* 83,1 = PG 58, 746.

[102] Augustine, *Io ev. tr.* 52,3 = CCL 36, 447; Leo I., *tract.* 54,4 = CCL 138 A, 320; Maximus Confessor, *opusc.* 7 = PG 91, 80 D (concerning this issue within the frame of Christological debate cf. P.M. Blowers, "The Passion of Jesus Christ in Maximus the Confessor: A Reconsideration", *StPatr 37* [2001], 361–377, 368f.).

[103] Cyril of Alexandria, *in Mt* = PG 72, 456 AB.

[104] Leo I., *tract.* 56,2 = CCL 138 A, 330. Similarly Cyril of Alexandria, *in Lc* = PG 72, 921 B.

[105] Athanasius of Alexandria, *c. Ar.* 3,57 = PG 26, PG 441C – 444 A.

[106] Leo I., *tract.* 67,7 = CCL 138 A, 413.

the cross would be missing.[107] However, there is also a possible allusion to the anti-Christian critiques: According to John Chrysostom, any answer of Jesus would have been useless; there was no possibility of making the accusers better men.[108] The polemical comments on the mockery Matt 27:40–43 at least implicitly contribute to this reproach: Even if Jesus had descended from the Cross, the mockers had not become faithful to him.[109]

The cry at the cross is a cry of mercy *propter nos*[110] and *pro nobis*[111]. Jesus transfers our desolation in order to finish the curse upon us;[112] within himself Jesus depicts our existence[113]; Jesus uses words to be used by the human sinners.[114]

The continuation of Ps 21:2a LXX raises christological problems. Jerome comments on the distinctive Greek versions of this phrase. Symmachus and Aquila and the fifth and sixth edition render *gemitus mei*, i.e. the sigh of Jesus concerning Israel and its refutation to accept the salvation brought by him; the LXX-rendering *verba delictorum meorum* is not spoken in regard to himself but to the nation whose sins he had took up by his own body (cf. 1 Pt 2:24).[115] According to Augustine the phrase *longe a salute mea, uerba delictorum meorum* cannot be spoken by Christ with regard to himself because of the absence of sin (*qui peccatum non fecit, nec inuentus est dolus in ore eius*, 1 Pt 2:22) but is a plea for us: *Quomodo ergo dicit delictorum mea, nisi quia pro delictis nostris ipse precatur, et delicta nostra sua delicta fecit, ut iustitiam suam nostram iustitiam faceret.*[116]

---

[107] Jerome, *in Mt* = SC 259, 278, quoted also by Beda Venerabilis, *Mc.* = CCL 120, 626: *Iesus autem nihil respondere uoluit, ne crimen diluens dimitteretur a praeside et cruces utilitas differretur.*

[108] John Chrysostom, *hom. in Mt* 86,1 = PG 58, 764.

[109] Leo I., *tract.* 68,2 = CCL 138 A, 417.

[110] Maximus of Turin II., *hom.* 45 = PL 57, 330 A: *Haec autem dicit, ut manifestaret propter nos se esse derelictum, quorum peccata portabat, ac videntes disceremus et nos pro ipso sancto et iusto mori, cum pro peccatoribus et ille moreretur.*

[111] Leo, *serm.* 67,7 = CCL 138 A, 412f: *Vox ista ... doctrina est, non querela. Nam cum in Christo Dei et hominis una persona sit, nec ab eo potuerit relinqui a quo non poterat separari, pro nobis trepidis et infirmis interrogat cur caro pati metuens exaudita non fuerit.*

[112] (Ps?-)Athanasius of Alexandria, *exp. Ps.* = PG 27, 132 B: τὰ ἡμῶν εἰς ἑαυτὸν μετατιθεὶς ἵνα παύσῃ τὴν ἀράν.

[113] Gregor of Nazianzus, *or.* 30,5 = FC 22, 232: ἐν ἑαυτῷ ... τυποῖ τὸ ἡμέτερον.

[114] Cyril of Alexandria (Reuss, *Matthäuskommentare*, Frgm. 312); Beda Venerabilis, *Matt.* = PL 92, 125 A; Hrabanus Maurus, *in Mt* = PL 107, 1142 CD: *Ostenditque quantum flere debeant qui peccant, quando sic flevit qui nunquam peccavit.*

[115] Jerome, *in psalm* 21,2 = FC 79, 120–122.

[116] Augustine, *en. Ps.* 21, *serm.* 2,3 = CCL 38, 123.

Conclusion

The exegetical writings in the strict sense do not contain many clear allusions to pagan anti-Christian critics. Authors like Jerome feel free to allude to pagan critics[117] or not.[118] Regarding Leo I., the Venerable Bede and Raban Maur this can be explained by the fact of Christian dominion. John Chrysostom, however, perhaps a student of Libanius, knew the anti-Christian tendencies in the forth century very well; Jerome read Porphyry's attack while Augustine and Cyril of Alexandria were great apologists in any way. Why is a treatment of anti-Christian critics widely missing in their exegetical writings?

One point has to do with genre. The *Sitz im Leben* of the homily, addressing believers, seemed for most of these authors[119] not to be the proper occasion to include examples of pagan critique. Some fourth-century authors were even conscious of a revitalising well-educated paganism, combining philosophical thoughts with traditional theology. They felt being counterparts of that movement but were not sure whether believers were able to differentiate.

Finally, the Christian cosmos itself contained possibilities to formulate moral implications of the death of men. Willingness to martyrdom and implications of individual ethics were common biblical issues satisfying ordinary claims – so: why should the memory of Socrates be kept alive?

[117] Cf. Jerome, *in Gal* = CCL 77 A, 168.

[118] Cf. Jerome, *in Mt* = SC 259, 296.

[119] There are exceptions: Maximus of Turin, *hom.* 37,1f = CCL 23, 145 compares the myth of Odysseus' saving himself in the scene *Od.* 12, 39–54 with Christ who really saves the whole world.

Checks and Balances
Is Christ's Passion an Exemplum Only?
Patristic Interpretation of 1 Peter 2:21[1]

ANDREAS MERKT

Patristic literature abounds with quotations from the New Testament. Verses from 1 Peter, however, are only seldom quoted. There are a lot of ancient commentaries on the books of the New Testament. But what we hardly ever find are commentaries on the Catholic Epistles and especially on 1 Peter.

Within the few existing commentaries on 1 Peter almost every verse is covered. But one verse is regularly skipped by the commentators from Clement onwards: 1 Peter 2:21. Didymus for example comments on verse 18 and then continues with verse 23 leaving out verse 21 (and the verses around). It seems certain that this verse which calls Christ's Passion an *exemplum* floats outside the mainstream of ancient Christian literature. However, it can serve to highlight some of the difficulties and strengths of the *Novum Testamentum Patristicum* (NTP) project.[2]

The first difficulty I encountered in preparing the commentary on 1 Peter within the NTP series was the lack of ancient commentaries. I soon came to envy Martin Meiser, who had prepared Galatians, for the numerous commentaries on this letter which he could use as the backbone of his work whereas I had to search for 1 Peter receptions as if for a needle in a haystack. The problem I was confronted with was how to write a commentary without a commentary, to write a modern patristic commentary without having an ancient Christian commentary at my disposal. In order to avoid a sheer accumulation of material the findings had to be systematized by a mixture of chronological and thematic orders. At the same time, the NTP commentary should not alienate the patristic interpretation from its

---

[1] This article renders the paper I gave at a workshop during the XVth International Conference on Patristic Studies at the University of Oxford (August 6–11, 2007).

[2] The *Novum Testamentum Patristicum* is an international and interdenominational project which aims at an extensive documentation of the patristic reception and exegesis of the New Testament. The first volume (Galatians) appeared in 2007: Martin Meiser, Galater (NTP 9; Göttingen: Vandenhoeck & Ruprecht). Further information: www-ntp.uni-r.de.

original context and atmosphere. As for 1 Peter 2:21, we can clearly distinguish a reception which we might term "moral, parenetical, didactic" from a genuinely theological use of the verse.

The verse reads: "For you Christ suffered, leaving you an example, so that you may follow his footsteps."

1. Moral, Parenetical, Didactic Reception

First of all, the verse informs us about the way Christ taught: "Words would have been little," Augustine comments in one of his sermons, "had the example not been added."[3] Then we learn from this verse what the acceptance of his doctrine means. Being more than a merely cognitive act, it comprises imitating and following. This is said against those who believe that to be a Christian it suffices to be baptized and go to church. Following in the *forma sacramenti* is not enough, tells us Augustine. You have to follow Christ *in opere exempli* as well.[4]

The central aspect of Christ offering an example is also a matter of consent in patristic literature: it is his humility which has to be imitated first of all.[5] From 1 Peter 2:21 with its stress of Christ's suffering the ancient authors infer that there is one outstanding way of following Christ: martyrdom. Again it is especially Augustine who often quotes this verse when he preaches about martyrs. This traditional line of reception, however, gets into a crisis when it is adopted by Pelagians. Between 411 and 413 the early Pelagian author of *De divitiis* quotes this verse and then asks: In which respect do we have to imitate Christ? He replies: "In poverty, if I am right, not in wealth, not in *superbia*, but in humility ...."[6] This verse is quite popular among other Pelagians as well. And indeed, it fits their theology. No wonder, it is not only used parenetically but also theologically. Julian of Eclanum is, as far as I see, the first to exploit the verse theologically.

---

[3] *Sermo* 284,6 (PL 38,1292).

[4] *Sermo* 37,16 (Patrologia 13,134 Drobner).

[5] Cf. (Ps-) Makarios, *Logos* 55,4,3; 56,1,3; 64,4 (vgl. BGL 52,445f.448.486 Fitschen).

[6] Cf. *De divitiis* 9,5 (272,97–99 Kessler) und 10,1 (274,1f). Cf. A. Kessler, *Reichtumskritik und Pelagianismus. Die pelagianische Diatribe* de divitiis*: Situierung, Lesetext, Übersetzung, Kommentar* (Paradosis 43; Fribourg 1999). For the use of 1 Peter 2:21 in other Pelagian writings cf. Ps-Pelagius, *De castitate* 6,91 (137,5 Caspari; PLS 1,1464–1502); (Ps-?)Pelagius, *Epistula ad quandam matronam Christianam* 1 (RB 34 [1922] 266–274: 266,8 Morin) (cf. Y.-M. Duval, in: M. Soetard (ed.), *Valeurs dans le stoicisme*, Lille 1993, 215–243); Ps-Paulinus, *ep.* 2,12 (CSEL 29,445,8).

2. The Christological and Soteriological Interpretation

2.1 Julian's Use of 1 Peter 2:21

Against Augustine Julian quotes the verse together with the following sentence, the citation from Isaiah: *he did not commit sin, nor was deceit found on his lips.* As others before him he finds this statement confirmed by the Lord's saying: *The prince of this world comes, and he finds nothing in me* (John 14:30).

What is new with Julian is that he turns 1 Peter 2:22 which speaks of Christ's sinlessness into an argument against natural sin in general: He underlines that Peter "did not say: He assumed no sin, but: *He committed no sin.*[7] (...) If he had any thought of natural evil, he would have more carefully and precisely mentioned this point and would have written: Christ left us an example; he neither committed sin, nor did he inherit the sin which we contract by being born ... But if the apostle had this in mind, he would never have made mention of his example. After all, whom would he have presented to human beings for their imitation, if the nature of a strange flesh set him apart and if the difference of his substance undermined the severity of his teaching?"[8]

We see how Julian employs the call to follow in Christ's footsteps as an argument against natural sin (*in natura crimen, peccatum per naturale virus, naturale malum, peccatum naturale*): Christ can only be a real example for us if he shared our starting conditions. That means either: If there is a *peccatum naturale* in us then there is natural sin in him as well. This is, according to Julian, unthinkable. But this is how far, in his eyes, Augustine's impiety has gone. Or if Christ was born with a sinless nature then we must have been born without sin, too. Hence there cannot be natural sin. "And so it is established", Julian concludes, "that there is no innate sin, since Christ had none, who without loss to the honour of his deity became incarnate in order that he might be imitable by us."[9]

2.2 Augustine's Answer

Augustine's answer is twofold. On the one hand, he dismisses Julian's argumentum e silentio: "When he [Peter] was, of course, proposing to human beings an example in Christ for their imitation, what need was there for the

[7] Julian in: Augustinus, *Contra Iulianum opus imperfectum* 4,85 (CSEL 85/2,86,1–9 Zelzer). Translation: R. Teske, Answer to the Pelagians III: Unfinished Work in Answer to Julian (The Works of St. Augustine. A Translation for the 21st Century I/25; New York 1999), 451.

[8] Ibid. 4,86 (87,4–12).

[9] Ibid. 4,87 (89,34–36); transl. Teske 452.

apostle Peter to say anything about original sin?"[10] On the other hand, he tries to reduce Julian's argument ad absurdum. Of course, imitation cannot be related to anything beyond our will. Our nature however is beyond our will. We cannot bring about a state of being born without sin as Christ was. And we cannot bring about a state of being born "as he was born of the Holy Spirit and the Virgin Mary". But the question remains: If we are born in sin how can we imitate Christ at all? "(…) in order to imitate Christ," Augustine says, "our will is reformed, but in order to be free from original evil, our nature is reborn."[11] Hence, natural sin does not necessarily preclude, as Julian insinuates, that we follow Christ's example.

While in his *Opus imperfectum* Augustine directly replies to a Pelagian we find traces of the Pelagian controversy in other writings as well.

2.3 The influence of the Pelagian controversy on Augustine's use of 1 Peter 2:21

Thirty years ago Wilhelm Geerlings demonstrated in his study on "Christus exemplum" how Augustine's use of the term exemplum, in general, changes under the influence of Pelagianism. This insight, we may now add, also applies to Augustine's interpretation of 1 Peter 2:21. Traces of this debate can be found, as Geerlings has shown, even in some parts of the *Tractatus in Iohannis evangelium.*[12] This agrees with my findings about Augustine's use of 1 Peter 2:21 in this work.

In tractate 84 Augustine interprets John 15:13 ("Greater love than this no one has, that he lay down his life for his friends"). He cites 1 John 3:16 ("… as Christ has laid down his life for us, so we also ought to lay down our lives for the brethren")[13] and Proverbs 23:1–2 (LXX) ("If you shall sit to dine at the table of a powerful man, consider and understand the things that are set before you, and so put forth your hand, knowing that it is necessary for you to prepare such like"). The quotation from 1 Peter[14] follows and he comments: "This [following in Christ's footsteps] is what the holy martyrs did with intense love". After that he clarifies the difference between Christ's death and the death of martyrs and other human beings: Christ's death redeems. All the others have to be redeemed in order to be able to follow in his footsteps: "… we can do nothing without him … we, apart from him, cannot have life." To reinforce this point the text has been

---

[10] Ibid. 4,86 (87,14–17); transl. Teske 451.

[11] Ibid. (87,17–88,21).

[12] Cf. W. Geerlings, *Christus exemplum. Studien zur Christologie und Christusverkündigung Augustins* (Mainz 1978).

[13] *In Io. Tr.* 84,1,1 (CCL 36,536 Willems). Transl. Fathers of the Church 90 (1994) 133 Rettig.

[14] Ibid. 84,1,2 (CCL 36,537 Willems). Transl. 134.

interpolated, perhaps by Augustine himself. Nine manuscripts insert the sentence: "Someone could imitate him in his dying, no one could in his redeeming."[15]

In tractate 88 on John 15:20 and 21 the use of the verse appears even more clearly anti-Pelagian. At the very beginning Augustine quotes the verse and then states: "And if we do this [i.e. following in his steps], assuredly we do it with the assistance of him who said, 'Without me you can do nothing.' (John 15:5)"[16]

By the way, my work on Augustine's reception of 1 Peter 2:21 had a side-effect. It helped to date sermon 284 preached on the festal day of the martyrs Marianus and James. The chronologists discuss two dates: 397 and 418. A comparison with sermo 37 may help. In sermo 37 Augustine says: We have to follow his steps *non tantum in forma sacramenti, sed etiam in opere exempli.*[17] He thus emphasizes the *opus exempli* without mentioning that imitating this work presupposes grace. Of course, when he gave this homily in 397 he felt no need to stress this aspect. Things are quite different when he quotes the same verse in sermo 284 again. Here, too, he underlines that Christ taught not only by words but by giving an example. But now Augustine adds that Christ's teaching, namely his hanging on the cross, was at the same time the work of a physician, a *medicus*: "He hung from the cross, and healed." He healed by begging his father to forgive those who "know not what they do". "... he made his blood medicine (*medicamentum*)".

Then Augustine goes on to present Peter as the prototype of those following in Christ's footsteps. At first, Peter was presumptuous. He felt self-confident and thought himself able to follow Christ. But he betrayed him. "Peter had in fact presumed on his strength, had trusted in his own strength, not on the grace of God, but in his capacity to choose (*de libero arbitrio*)." Then the Lord looked at him and sent his Spirit. Peter became a witness.

From this example of Peter Augustine draws the general conclusion: "In so far as we can, my brothers, let us imitate in the Lord the example of the passion. But we will be able to imitate the example if we ask him for help, not going beyond what the Lord gives like Peter when he presumed but following and asking [praying] like Peter when he grew."[18] The difference between this sermon and sermo 37 is so manifest that it appears very improbable they were given in the same year. Sermo 284 seems to have anti-Pelagian overtones which best fit a dating in the year 418.

---

[15] Ibid. 84,1,3–2,1 with App.

[16] Ibid. 88,1,1; transl. 161.

[17] *Sermo* 37,16 (Patrologia 13,134 Drobner).

[18] *Sermo* 284,6 (PL 38,1292–1293).

2.4 After Augustine

Decades ago Basil Studer demonstrated that with Augustine and, even more, after him *exemplum et sacramentum* becomes an anti-Pelagian slogan.[19] Christ or his passion and dying is not only example but also saving mystery. Leo the Great explicitly links this slogan with the passage from 1 Peter. In sermo 63, held on Wednesday of Holy Week 452, he says: "Our Saviour, the son of God, gave both a mystery (*sacramentum*) and an example to all who believe in him, so that they might attain the one by being reborn, and arrive at the other by imitation. Blessed Peter the apostle teaches this, saying ...." Then the verses 21 to 24 are quoted. Although Leo does not comment on this passage we may assume that he finds the sacramental aspect of Christ's passion in verse 24: "He himself bore our sins in his own body on the cross, so that, dead to sin, we might live for holiness."[20]

These findings may be quite predictable: Pelagianism influenced the reception of 1 Peter 2:21 with its key term *exemplum* (Greek: ὑπογραμμός). However, a look into the future NTP commentary on 1 Peter will provide more detailed information. Because of its comprehensiveness the NTP is suited to widen our patristic horizon in general and regarding 1 Peter 2:21 in particular wc lcarn that thc dcbatc about thc tcrm *example* cannot bc reduced to the Pelagian controversy as modern scholarship seems to suggest. The christological and soteriological interpretation of Christ's portrayal as example or paradigm in 1 Peter is considerably older than the Pelagian controversy.

2.5 Back to Origen

The history of a christological reading of 1 Peter 2:21 begins, as far as I can see, with Origen's work against Celsus. Celsus had quoted a Jew who denied that Jesus actually had suffered pain. Origen replies by alluding to 1 Peter: If Jesus had not suffered how could he have been presented as a paradigm of patience and tolerance to those of his followers who were undenyably suffering?[21]

About the same time Origen wrote against Celsus, i.e. in his last years, he also delivered his homilies on Joshua.[22] Homily 8 deals with Joshua 8

---

[19] Cf. B. Studer, "'Sacramentum et exemplum' chez saint Augustin", *Recherches augustiniennes* 10 (1975), 87–141.

[20] Leo the Great, *Sermo* 63,4 (CCL 138A,384–385 Chavasse). Transl. Fathers of the Church 93 (1995) 274f. Freeland/Conway.

[21] Origenes, *Contra Celsum* 2,25 (SC 132,34–38 Borret).

[22] Of course, one has to consider the question of reliability of the form the text has come down to us, namely in Rufinus' Latin translation. Rufin himself gives a clue in his peroration to the *Commentary on the Epistle to the Romans*. He admits that he consi-

and especially with the "twofold wood". The "king of Ai" is said "to be hanged on the twofold wood" (Jos 8:29). "In this place", Origen comments, "a mystery is hidden very deeply. But with your prayers we shall attempt to uncover these things, not from our opinions but from the testimonies of divine Scripture."[23]

The twofold wood prefigures the "double reason for the cross of the Lord". One reason is stated by Peter in his letter: Christ was crucified to leave behind an example for us. The other reason is mentioned in Colossians 2:14–15: "What was contrary to us, he bore away from the midst, fixing it to his own cross; stripping principalities and authorities, he exposed them openly to public ridicule, triumphing over them on the wood of the cross." Thus the cross is a "token of victory over the Devil". Paul mentions both aspects of the cross in Galatians 6:14: "Let me not glory except in the cross of my Lord Jesus Christ, through whom the world has been crucified to me and I to the world." "You see", Origen comments, "that even here the Apostle brought forth a twofold understanding of the cross. For he says, that for him, two opposing things have been crucified: himself as a saint and the world as a sinner."[24]

Thus, long before Augustine and other anti-Pelagian authors, Origen demonstrates that in 1 Peter 2:21 we find only one aspect of the passion of Christ: the visible example he gave for imitation. This aspect has to be supplemented, by resorting to other verses, with the invisible aspect: The victory over the devil and over sin.

3. Conclusion

We may summarize the patristic interpretation of 1 Peter 2:21 as follows: What we read in this verse about the reason and aim of Christ's suffering is only one aspect which, if it is isolated, may lead to a Pelagian misunderstanding. This verse, however, has to be read in connection with verse 24,

derably changed the form of Origen's homilies on Leviticus from a hortatory to an expository style and that he even interpolated the homilies on Genesis and Exodus where he felt them wanting. Quite differently he translated the homilies on Joshua and a few others "just as we found them, literally and without great effort." (Simpliciter ut invenimus, et non multo cum labore transtulimus): Origenes, *Der Römerbriefkommentar des Origenes. Kritische Ausgabe der Übersetzung Rufins, Bücher 7–10*; ed. C.P. Hammond Bammel, aus dem Nachlass herausgegeben von H.J. Frede und H. Stanjek, AGLB 34 (1998), 861. Trans. Th.P. Scheck, Fathers of the Church 104, 311. This statement was confirmed by Annie Jaubert's philological studies in preparing the *Sources Chrétiennes* edition of the text: SC 71 (1960, corrected reprint 2000) 68–82.

[23] Origenes, *hom. in Jos*. 8,3 (SC 71,222 Jaubert).

[24] Ibid. (SC 71,224 Jaubert).

as Leo suggests. Furthermore it may be counterbalanced, as we learn from Origen, by the verses from Colossians and Galatians. Although it remains true that Christ, as 1 Peter says, suffered in order to give an example his suffering and death more deeply aimed at the destruction of the devil and his army. Its purpose is the death of sin. By baptism, which makes us dead to sin, we are enabled to follow Christ's example of holiness.

So much for the question of theological content. Beyond that, I would like to stress three points:

1. It is possible to write a patristic commentary on 1 Peter without a commentary. It is possible and feasible to reconstruct something like an unwritten commentary on 1 Peter. By collecting the incidental remarks on 1 Peter we may conjecture about what authors like Origen or Augustine would have said, had they written a commentary on 1 Peter.

2. The NTP commentary contributes to our understanding of the way ancient Christian authors used to read the Bible. They applied a kind of mental "windows system": Whenever they clicked on a biblical verse or term a window opened offering helpful links to other biblical passages. Some links only serve to corroborate an obvious understanding of a passage. That is the function, for example, of 1 John 3:16 to 1 Peter 2:21 and vice versa. Other links are used to offer checks and balances: This is what Galatians 6:14 and Colossians 2:14–15 do for 1 Peter 2:21. This method constrains the impact of single suggestive verses respectively of interpretations based on single verses or passages. This mechanism of the mutual elucidation of various verses reduces opportunities for exegetical tyranny or monopoly. This hermeneutics aims at maintaining a balance of interpretation within the canon. The obvious meaning of one verse is constrained by other verses.

3. The NTP will help to assess the significance not only of the scriptural context but also of the context of interpretation: the literary genre, liturgy, the context of a specific theological controversy and so on. For example, in 1 Peter 2:21 we can see how the liturgical context of the martyrs' feasts gave prominence to this verse and linked it to other verses popular in homilies on the martyrs. We also learn that sometimes context is overestimated: It is true that the Pelagian use of the verse provoked some clarifications which contributed to the anti-Pelagian slogan *exemplum et sacramentum*. However, as we learnt by going back to Origen, the idea of a twofold significance of the Passion is much older than the historical anti-Pelagianism and thus, in a certain sense, independent of this context. The biblical text itself seems to imply and supply a range of explanations which are made explicit on special occasions. The Pelagian controversy is only one of the many fascinating sounding boards which give a variety of different sounds and resonances to the voices of the New Testament.

Eine vergessene Textform von Apg 1,2

PATRICIO DE NAVASCUÉS

1. Einleitung

Die Textüberlieferung am Anfang der Apostelgeschichte gehört zu den am meisten diskutierten und kommentierten Problemen des lukanischen Doppelwerks. Der Grund hierfür ist klar: Der so genannte *westliche* oder D-Text (TW) und der *alexandrinische Text* (TA) weichen erheblich voneinander ab.[1]

Heute liest sich der Text, den die kritischen Editionen für Apg 1,1–2 üblicherweise bieten, folgendermaßen:[2]

Τὸν μὲν πρῶτον λόγον ἐποιησάμην περὶ πάντων, ὦ Θεόφιλε, ὧν ἤρξατο ὁ Ἰησοῦς ποιεῖν τε καὶ διδάσκειν, ἄχρι ἧς ἡμέρας ἐντειλάμενος τοῖς ἀποστόλοις διὰ πνεύματος ἁγίου οὓς ἐξελέξατο ἀνελήμφθη.

Laut textkritischem Apparat des *Greek New Testament. Fourth Revised Edition* (GNT) wird diese Lesart durch P^{74vid} ℵ A B C^{vid} E Ψ 33 36 81 181 307 453 610 614 945 1175 1409 1678 1739 1891 2344 *Byz Lect* $it^{c, dem, e, p, ph, ro, w}$ vg syr^{h} arm eth geo slav Basil Chrysostom Severian Nestorius gestützt. Im dortigen Apparat findet sich auch der Verweis auf die so genannte „westliche" Variante: // ἡμέρας ἀνελήμφθη ... καὶ ἐκέλευσεν κηρύσσειν τὸ Εὐαγγέλιον D $it^{(ar), d, (gig), (t)}$ (vg^{mss}) syr^{hmg} ($cop^{sa, meg}$) Augustinus Varimadum.

Schon am Anfang der Apg, das heißt, bereits im Proömium (Apg 1,1–11), muss sich der Herausgeber zwischen einer westlichen und der alexandrinischen Variante des Texteds entscheiden: Immerhin beschäftigt sich Apg 1,1–11 mit Fragen, die für das ganze Buch der Apostelgeschichte bedeutsam sind.

Zudem beschreibt Apg 1,1–11 – und gerade auch Apg 1,2 – ein wichtiges Ereignis, die „Himmelfahrt" Jesu. Wie bekannt, liegen nur wenige ex-

---

[1] Zur Frage der Textüberlieferung der Apostelgeschichte weiterführend vgl. u.a. T. NICKLAS/M. TILLY (Hg.), The Book of Acts as Church History. Text, Textual Traditions and Ancient Interpretations, BZNW 120, Berlin/New York 2003 [dort auch weiterführende Lit.].

[2] Vgl. R. SWANSON (Hg.), New Testament Greek Manuscripts. Acts, Sheffield 1998, 1.

plizit neutestamentliche Verweise auf die Himmelfahrt vor. Tatsächlich müssen wir uns mit Mk 16,19: ὁ μὲν οὖν κύριος Ἰησοῦς μετὰ τὸ λαλῆσαι αὐτοῖς ἀνελήμφθη εἰς τὸν οὐρανὸν καὶ ἐκάθισεν ἐκ δεξιῶν τοῦ θεοῦ, Lk 24,51: καὶ ἐγένετο ἐν τῷ εὐλογεῖν αὐτὸν αὐτοὺς διέστη ἀπ' αὐτῶν καὶ ἀνεφέρετο εἰς τὸν οὐρανόν und Apg 1,1–11 begnügen. In der neueren Forschungsgeschichte wurde vor dem Hintergrund, dass Mk 16,19 nicht zum ursprünglichen Mk-Text gehört und einige Textzeugen des lukanischen TW die Wendung ἀνεφέρετο εἰς τὸν οὐρανόν (in Lk 24,51) und das entscheidende Verb ἀνελήφθη (in Apg 1,2) auslassen, immer wieder angenommen, dass alles, was die Himmelfahrt Christi betrifft, erst in einer späteren Phase in den neutestamentlichen Text Eingang gefunden bzw. als Reaktion einer frühen christlichen Gemeinde eingearbeitet worden sei, die das Ziel verfolgt habe, die Figur Christi im Stil paganer und jüdischer Gestalten zu mythifizieren.

Auf den letztgenannten Vorschlag hat bereits im Jahr 1938 die Monographie von Victorien Larrañaga, *L'Ascension de Notre-Seigneur dans le Nouveau Testament*, Rom 1938, mit stichhaltigen Belegen reagiert. Larrañaga widerlegte die genannte Hypothese und zeigte, dass die Erzählung von der Himmelfahrt bereits im Originaltext des Proömiums der Apostelgeschichte belegt ist. Obwohl die Diskussion auch nach Larrañagas Arbeit weiterging, verteidigen heute nur noch wenige Autoren die Hypothese einer durch die Hinzufügung von ἀνελήφθη erfolgten Interpolation. Damit aber ist noch nicht die Frage beantwortet, wie sich die Entstehung der genannten Varianten des TA und TW erklären lässt.

Es ist deshalb wichtig zu beschreiben, wie die Auseinandersetzung um den Originaltext des lukanischen Doppelwerks (des TA oder des TW)[3] ebenso wie die um den Urtext der Erzählung von der Himmelfahrt[4] das Interesse moderner Textkritiker und Exegeten zwar bestimmt hat – man dabei aber trotzdem eine Textvariante übersehen hat. Dieser vergessenen Textvariante möchte sich der nun folgende Beitrag zuwenden:

Der textkritische Apparat des GNT entspricht in Wirklichkeit nämlich nicht genau dem tatsächlichen Befund bei den zitierten Textzeugen, stim-

---

[3] Eine gute Darstellung findet sich bei B.M. METZGER, A Textual Commentary on the Greek New Testament, London 1971, 259–272 (wenn auch Metzger auf diesen Seiten die Variante, die Gegenstand unserer Untersuchungen hier ist, nicht erwähnt). M.-E. BOISMARD, The Texts of Acts: A Problem of Literary Criticism?, in E.J. EPP/G.D. FEE (Hg.), New Testament Textual Criticism (FS B.M. Metzger), Oxford 1981, 147–157. Im Zusammenhang mit dem TW vgl. jüngst M.-É. BOISMARD, Le texte occidental des Actes des Apôtres. Édition nouvelle entièrement refondue, ÉtB. N.S. 40, Paris 2000 (auch in dieser Monographie wird unsere Variante nicht beachtet, da sie im TW nicht begegnet).

[4] Vgl. E.J. EPP, The Ascension in the Textual Tradition of Luke-Acts, in: New Testament Textual Criticism (s. Anm. 3), 131–145.

men doch weder syr^{h} noch Nestorius mit ℵ A B C E Ψ und dem Rest der Zeugen des TA überein.[5]

2. Das Syntagma διὰ πνεύματος ἁγίου

Ob man nun eher der TA- oder der TW-Variante zuneigt, um den Text in einer Übersetzung oder im Hinblick auf einen Kommentar genau zu verstehen, in jedem Falle ist es notwendig, ein Element genauer zu betrachten, dessen Zuordnung offen bleibt, das Syntagma διὰ πνεύματος ἁγίου. Der TA von Apg 1,2 lautet folgendermaßen: ἄχρι ἧς ἡμέρας ἐντειλάμενος τοῖς ἀποστόλοις διὰ πνεύματος ἁγίου οὓς ἐξελέξατο ἀνελήμφθη. Dies wirft natürlich die Frage auf, ob sich die Worte διὰ πνεύματος ἁγίου auf das Partizip ἐντειλάμενος oder auf die Verbform ἐξελέξατο beziehen.

Bereits A. Loisy[6] hat diese Schwierigkeit erkannt und bei seiner Übersetzung sehr vorsichtig betont: „jusq'au jour où, ayant donné, par l'Esprit-Saint, ses ordres aux apôtres qu'il s'était choisis, il fut enlevé". Im Kommentar lässt er beide Möglichkeiten offen: die, die ἐντειλάμενος mit διὰ πνεύματος ἁγίου und die, die διὰ πνεύματος ἁγίου mit ἐξελέξατο verbindet. Im Hinblick auf die erste erinnert er daran, wie das Evangelium nach Lukas bei mehr als einer Gelegenheit Jesus als jemanden darstellt, der in seinem Handeln vom Heiligen Geist geleitet wird (vgl. Lk 4,1.14.18). Auch jetzt, wo er seinen Jüngern gegenüber anordne, dass sie bis zur Aussendung des Heiligen Geistes in Jerusalem bleiben sollten, handle er „durch den Heiligen Geist" bewegt, *indem er Anweisungen durch den Geist gebe.* Loisy verweist hier auch auf Johannes Chrysostomus, *Hom. in Acta apostolorum* I (PG 60, 18). Auch dieser habe nach der Bedeutung des διὰ πνεύματος ἁγίου gefragt und sei zu dem Schluss gekommen, dass der Text mit besagter Wendung in rätselhafter Weise auf den Befehl Jesu, alle Völker zu lehren und zu taufen (vgl. Mt 28,19), sowie auf Jesu Art und Weise zu sprechen anspiele: Jesus verwende Worte, die Geist seien (vgl. Joh 6,63). Er befähige die Apostel, seine Worte zu verstehen und seine Weisungen zu erfüllen.

Allerdings sei es, wie Loisy meint, auch denkbar, dass es die Apostel seien, die, wie die Apg es immer wieder darstellt, „durch den Heiligen Geist" handelten (vgl. Apg 4,8; 7,55; 13,2), weil sie vom Herrn, „durch den Geist" inspiriert, ausgewählt worden seien (vgl. Lk 6,13).

Eine ganz andere Meinung vertrat E. Meyer, der Apg 1,2 für *unübersetzbar* hielt und deshalb für die These einer Interpolation plädierte. Die

---

5 Offensichtlich ist C hier lakunös. Vgl. SWANSON (Hg.), New Testament Greek Manuscripts. Acts (s. Anm. 2), 1.

6 A. LOISY, Les Actes des Apôtres, Paris 1920, 4–7.

Wendung διὰ πνεύματος ἁγίου hänge quasi in der Luft, ohne passend mit ἐντειλάμενος, mit ἐξελέξατο oder mit ἀνελήμφθη verbunden werden zu können. Seine Meinung begründete Meyer für die ersten beiden Varianten mit philologischen und theologischen Gründen, im dritten Fall dagegen beschränkte er sich auf die bloße Behauptung der Unmöglichkeit.[7]

E. Jacquier[8] wiederum entschied sich dafür, διὰ πνεύματος ἁγίου mit der Erwählung der Zwölf zu verbinden: „si mal venu que soit le texte, il n'y a donc pas lieu de le retoucher comme s'il avait été tardivement interpolé". Jacquier übersah dabei nicht den problematischen Charakter des lukanischen Texts, verteidigte aber gegen frühe Thesen einer Interpolation dessen Ursprünglichkeit.[9]

A.C. Clark[10] verstand den TW (bei ihm mit dem Symbol *Z* bezeichnet) als die Originalfassung der Apostelgeschichte, auf der in komprimierter Version der TA aufbaue. Apg 1,2 sei ursprünglich folgendermaßen formuliert gewesen: ἐν ᾗ ἡμέρα, τοὺς ἀποστόλους ἐξελέξατο διὰ πνεύματος ἁγίου **καὶ ἐκέλευσεν κηρύσσειν τὸ εὐαγγέλιον**.[11] Clark glaubte, dass der im lukanischen Urtext von Apg 1,2 erwähnte Tag der Tag der Erwählung der Zwölf sei und nicht der der Himmelfahrt Christi. Dieser Bezug sei erst später in einigen Handschriften von *Z* sozusagen als Ergebnis einer Har-

---

[7] E. MEYER, Der Eingang des zweiten Buchs. Die Interpolation der Himmelfahrt, in: Ursprung und Anfänge des Christentums I, Stuttgart 1921, 34–45, hier 37: „Die Brüchigkeit des Textes tritt denn auch gleich in v. 2 deutlich hervor. In der Mehrzahl der Handschriften lautet der Text ἄχρι ἧς ἡμέρας ἐντειλάμενος τοῖς ἀποστόλοις διὰ πνεύματος ἁγίου, οὓς ἐξελέξατο, ἀνελήμφθη. Das ist ganz unübersetzbar; διὰ πνεύματος ἁγίου schwebt völlig in der Luft; in den Relativsatz kann es seiner Stellung nach nicht gehören, und es wäre sehr wunderlich, wenn hervorgehoben werden sollte, dass Jesus bei der Auswahl der Apostel der Mitwirkung des heiligen Geistes bedurfte -ev. 6, 12 bereitet sich Jesus für ihre Auswahl die ganze Nacht hindurch durch Gebet vor, eine von Lukas selbst gestaltete Erweiterung des kurzen Berichts bei Marcus 3, 13. Noch weniger kann es mit ἀνελήμφθη verbunden werden. So bleibt nur übrig, es zu ἐντειλάμενος zu ziehen: ‚nachdem er ihnen durch den heiligen Geist Auftrag gegeben hatte'. Aber einen vernünftigen Sinn gibt das auch nicht. Zu ἐντειλάμενος fehlt das Objekt, und er hat ihnen den Auftrag nicht durch den heiligen Geist gegeben, sondern direkt, wohl aber ‚die Verheissung seines Vaters', d.i. eben den heiligen Geist, dafür versprochen. Eben das hat offenbar zu dessen Erwähnung den Anlaß gegeben; was gesagt werden sollte, ist, dass er ihnen für die Ausführung seines Auftrags die Mitwirkung des heiligen Geistes in Aussicht gestellt hat."

[8] E.-J. JACQUIER, Les Actes des Apôtres, Paris 1926, 136.

[9] So ist es der Fall bei K. LAKE/H.J. CADBURY, The Acts of the Apostles. Additional Notes, in: F.J. FOAKES JACKSON/K. LAKE (Hg.), The Beginnings of Christianity, Teil I, Bd. V, London 1933, 1–5.

[10] A.C. CLARK, The Acts of the Apostles. A Critical Edition with Introduction and Notes on Selected Passages, Oxford 1933.

[11] Fettgedruckt bietet Clark Hinzufügungen des *Codex Bezae* zum Text *Z* (d.h. dem genannten Text TW).

monisierung der Codices א A B C mittels Einfügung des Verbs ἀνελήμφθη[12] eingefügt worden (wie im *Codex Bezae* oder in der syrischen *Harklensis*).

M. Dibelius wiederum vertrat die These, dass die entsprechenden Passagen in Apg 1,2 wie in 4,25 mit dem Ziel eingefügt worden seien, das Handeln des Heiligen Geistes hervorzuheben. Jedoch bleibe in Apg 1,2 der Bezug der interpolierten Passage offen, denn das Syntagma διὰ πνεύματος ἁγίου passe weder zum Partizip ἐντειλάμενος noch zum Verb ἐξελέξατο.[13]

Im Gegensatz dazu glaubte E. Haenchen in seinem erstmals 1956 veröffentlichten Kommentar zur Apostelgeschichte, dass sich διὰ πνεύματος ἁγίου unverkennbar auf die Wahl der Apostel beziehe. Mit dieser Wendung habe Lukas die Stellung der Zwölf (nunmehr der Elf) als die bei ihrer Wahl durch den Geist legitimierte Kirche hervorheben wollen. Die eigentümliche Anordnung des Satzes durch Lukas, der διὰ πνεύματος ἁγίου dem οὓς ἐξελέξατο voranzustellte,[14] sei dem lukanischen Stil verdankt.

Wenig später verteidigte auch H. Conzelmann die Priorität des TA. Dennoch räumte auch er ein, dass διὰ πνεύματος ἁγίου weder zu ἐντειλάμενος noch zu ἐξελέξατο passe. Letztlich entschied er sich für einen Bezug auf ἐντειλάμενος. Die Aussage aus Apg 1,2 werde in Lk 24,44–49 näher spezifiziert. Später dann werde im TW das Verb ἀνελήμφθη in Apg 1,2, genauso wie ἀνεφέρετο εἰς τὸν οὐρανόν in Lk 24,51 mit dem Zweck ent-

---

[12] Vgl. CLARK, The Acts of the Apostles (s. Anm. 10), 336: „*D* and *c.Th* agree exactly, except that *c.Th.* places οὓς ἐξελέξατο before διὰ πνεύματος ἁγίου. They have been harmonized with Γ by the adoption of ἄχρι ἧς ἡμέρας and the addition of ἀνελήμφθη in a different collocation (after ἡμέρας instead of at the end of the sentence), with the consequential alteration ἐντειλάμενος τοῖς ἀποστόλοις οὓς ἐξελέξατο for the original τοὺς ἀποστόλους ἐξελέξατο of Aug[ab]. With these alien elements they combine the rest of the *Z* reading καὶ ἐκέλευσεν κηρύσσειν τὸ εὐαγγέλιον, omitted by Γ."

[13] M. DIBELIUS, The Text of Acts. An Urgent Critical Task, JR 21 (1941), 421–431; Deutsche Version: Der Text der Apostelgeschichte, in: ID., Aufsätze zur Apostelgeschichte, Göttingen 1968, 76–83. Auf Seite 81 sagt er: „Es ist nun die Beobachtung nicht unwichtig, dass auch in 1, 2 die Erwähnung des Heiligen Geistes an der schwierigsten Stelle des einleitenden Satzes vorkommt. Dort müsste man sie beziehen entweder auf das Gebot Jesu – und das ist nahezu unmöglich – oder auf die Auswahl der Jünger, und das erscheint fast noch unmöglicher. Jesus bedarf nicht des Heiligen Geistes, weder für seine Aufträge noch für seine Jüngerwahl. Hier und in 4,25 hätte dann also eine Anschauung, die man wohl als eine Theologie des Heiligen Geistes bezeichnen könnte, den Text beeinflusst."

[14] E. HAENCHEN, Die Apostelgeschichte, KeK, Göttingen [5]1968, 107–108: „ἄχρι ἧς ἡμέρας ἀνελήμφθη gibt den Endpunkt des Lk-Ev an, ἐντειλάμενος meint Jesu Worte Lk 24, 44–49. διὰ πνεύματος ἁγίου bezieht sich auf das Folgende, die Wahl der Apostel. Lukas verdeutlicht damit dem Leser die Autorität der Apostel: Jesus hat sie durch den hl. Geist erwählt und sie vor seinem Scheiden beauftragt."

fernt, die Schwierigkeiten des neutestamentlichen Gedankengangs zu beseitigen.[15]

Auch J. Munck diskutierte die Ambivalenz der Passage. In beiden Textvarianten spiele der Heilige Geist eine aktive Rolle, noch bevor das Pfingstfest erzählt werde. Leider ist nicht erkennbar, für welche Möglichkeit Munck sich letztlich entscheidet.[16]

J. Dupont dagegen erklärte sich als Anhänger der Verbindung von διὰ πνεύματος ἁγίου mit οὓς ἐξελέξατο und gab auch Gründe an, warum Lukas die logische Anordnung der Wendung umgekehrt habe.[17]

Duponts Meinung, die Erwähnung des Heiligen Geistes aus Apg 1,2 sei mit der Wahl der Zwölf in Lk 6,13 zu verbinden, haben sich verschiedene Autoren mit sehr ähnlichen Argumenten angeschlossen – genannt seien z.B. G. Schneider,[18] J. Roloff[19] oder R. Pesch[20]. Sie alle rekurrieren auf eine alte Erklärung T. Zahns: Da Jesus auf Grund der in Lk 3,22; 4,1.14 ge-

---

[15] H. Conzelmann, Die Apostelgeschichte, HNT 71, Tübingen 1963, 20: „διὰ πνεύματος ἁγίου passt weder zu ἐντειλάμενος noch zu ἐξελέξατο; Dibelius Aufs. 81 f. will den Passus streichen; lässt man ihn stehen, zieht man ihn besser zu ἐντειλάμενος (gegen Hae). Die Zeugen des ‚westlichen' Textes haben den Schaden auf verschiedene Weise zu heilen versucht; ihre Textformen sind durchweg sekundär und hängen mit dem W-Text von Lc 24, 50 ff. zusammen (sie streichen ἀνελήηφθη und in Lc 24, 51 ἀνεφέρετο εἰς οὐρανόν)."

[16] J. Munck, The Acts of the Apostles, AncB, New York 1967, 3. Ähnlich O. Bauernfeind, Kommentar und Studien zur Apostelgeschichte, WUNT 22, Tübingen 1980, 19–20.

[17] J. Dupont, Études sur les Actes des Apôtres, LeDiv 45, Paris 1967, 239: „Le prologue des Actes, quoi qu'on en ait dit, fait encore de l'excellent grec quand il écrit: ἄχρι ἧς ἡμέρας ἐντειλάμενος τοῖς ἀποστόλοις διὰ πνεύματος ἁγίου οὓς ἐξελέξατο ἀνελήμφθη (i, 2). Le complément circonstanciel διὰ πνεύματος ἁγίου est placé en evidence, et en même temps le pronom relatif est rapproché du verbe qu'il determine. Il y a là un tour de phrase très heureux et susceptible de plaire à une oreille grecque. Mais en même temps, le sens peut prêter à confusion: pour s'en rendre compte, il suffit de connaître un peu l'histoire ancienne du texte et l'histoire récente de son interprétation. Mais l'équivoque tient avant tout au fait qu'on a perdu le sens de la langue grecque et de sa flexibilité. La construction οὓς διὰ πνεύματος ἁγίου ἐξελέξατο eût été tout à faire claire, mais combien lourde! Luc est trop grec pour supporter tant de lourdeur, surtout dans une préface, et trop intelligent pour prévoir l'inintelligence de ses interprètes." Der selbe Autor bekräftigt etwas später mit gleicher Intensität seine Position: id., Nouvelles études sur les Actes des Apôtres, LeDiv 118, Paris 1984, 114, Anm. 5: „Possible à s'en tenir à un point de vue purement grammatical, la construction ‚après avoir donné dans l'Esprit Saint ses instructions aux apôtres qu'il avait choisis' doit être considérée comme fautive en raison 1° du rythme de la phrase (lire tout haut!), 2° du style du Luc (qui place en anaphore l'expression qu'il veut accentuer), 3° du contexte (qui rappelle l'ordre donné), et 4° du rapport avec Lc 6, 12–13 (relation entre prière et Esprit Saint dans la théologie de Luc)."

[18] G. Schneider, Die Apostelgeschichte, HThKNT V, 1, Freiburg 1980, 192–193.

[19] J. Roloff, Die Apostelgeschichte, NTD V, Göttingen 1981, 19.

[20] R. Pesch, Die Apostelgeschichte, EKK V/1, Zürich 1986, 61.

nannten Proklamation Träger des Heiligen Geistes ist, kann er von diesem Zeitpunkt an diesen an die Zwölf weitergeben.

F.F. Bruce dagegen bevorzugt die Lösung, die ἐντειλάμενος auf διὰ πνεύματος ἁγίου bezieht, und entdeckt darin ein die gesamte Apostelgeschichte, die man seiner Meinung nach *Geschichte des Heiligen Geistes* nennen könne, durchziehendes Leitmotiv. Von daher sollte der Auftrag zur Verkündigung des Evangeliums, den Jesus den Aposteln anvertraut habe, als Auftrag mit göttlicher Kraft verstanden werden.[21]

Einige Autoren bieten eine gute Zusammenfassung der Problematik, ohne sich für eine Variante zu entscheiden, die dann doch auf der Stufe einer Hypothese bleiben muss. Das ist auch bei J. Zmijewski der Fall, der jedoch geradezu *in extremis* eine bemerkenswerte Hypothese anbietet, auf die ich in Kürze zurückkommen werde.[22]

C.K. Barrett bezieht wie Bruce nicht nur aus linguistischen, sondern auch aus inhaltlichen Gründen das Syntagma διὰ πνεύματος ἁγίου auf den durch ἐντειλάμενος ausgedrückten Auftrag. Tatsächlich findet sich bei der Wahl in Lk 6,13 kein Hinweis auf den Heiligen Geist, dafür aber in den Anweisungen, die Jesus in Lk 24,49 und Apg 1,8 ausspricht.[23] Dagegen

---

[21] F.F. BRUCE, The Book of the Acts, NICNT, Grand Rapids 1989, 30–31: „It was ‚through the Holy Spirit' that Jesus gave his parting charge to the apostles. Almost invariably Luke restricts the designation ‚apostles' to the twelve men whom Jesus chose at an early stage in his ministry (Luke 6:13–16), except that Judas Iscariot was replaced by Matthias (as we are told later in this chapter). His charge to them made them the chief heralds of the good news which he had brought. The extension of the good news in the power of the Spirit is the theme of Acts. At his baptism Jesus had been ‚anointed' with the Holy Spirit and power (10:38), and more recently, in Paul's words, he had been ‚designated Son of God in power, according to the Spirit of holiness, by his resurrection from the dead' (Rom 1:4). In the Johannine account of the commission laid on his disciples by the risen Christ, he indicated the power by which they were to carry out their commision when he ‚breathed into them' and said, ‚Receive the Holy Spirit' (John 20:22). Luke makes it plain that it is by the power of that same Spirit that all the apostolic acts which he goes on to narrate were performed, so much so that some have suggested, as a theologically more appropriate title for his second volume, *The Acts of the Holy Spirit*."

[22] J. ZMIJEWSKI, Die Apostelgeschichte, RNT, Regensburg 1994, 46–47: „Doch dürfte es ... näherliegen, die Wendung ‚durch den Hl. Geist' ... in Bezug zu bringen ... vielleicht sogar darüber hinaus auch noch mit dem Himmelfahrtsgeschehen (das durch die Passivformulierung ‚er wurde aufgenommen' umschriebene Handeln Gottes würde dann als ein ‚in der Kraft des Hl. Geistes' erfolgendes charakterisiert)."

[23] C. K. BARRETT, A Critical and Exegetical Commentary on the Acts of the Apostles I, Edinburgh 1994, 69: „διὰ πνεύματος ἁγίου is awkwardly placed; the fact that the Western text is in this respect easier should probably be taken as an argument against its originality. It is probably better to take the phrase with ἐντειλάμενος than with ἐξελέξατο, both on linguistic grounds (the relative clause is most naturally taken to being with οὓς) and because, though there is no reference to the Holy Spirit in Luke's account of the

beharrt J. Taylor als Anhänger der TW-Variante auf der Verbindung zwischen Heiligem Geist und der Wahl nach Lk 6, wenngleich seiner Meinung nach auch auf Apg 13,2 angespielt wird.[24]

Schließlich äußerte sich auch J. Kilgallen kritisch gegenüber den vorgestellten Lösungsvorschlägen und fügte einen weiteren hinzu. Er denkt neu über die Bedeutung der Präposition διά nach – diese könne auch kausal übersetzt werden. Indem er die genannte Passage auf die Wahl der Apostel beziehe, wolle der lukanische Text zu verstehen geben, dass die Aussendung des Heiligen Geists über die Zwölf der Grund ihrer vorhergehenden Wahl war. Sie seien also bereits mit Blick darauf ausgewählt worden, dass eines Tages der Heilige Geist auf sie herabkommen möge.[25]

Es lässt sich also in der Tat beobachten, wie wenig die Interpretationen von Apg 1,2 zu einem *common sense* führten. Klar ersichtlich bleibt, dass diejenigen, die dem TW den Vorzug geben (Clark, Taylor), das Syntagma διὰ πνεύματος ἁγίου mit der Wahl der Zwölf verbinden wollen. Aber auch einige unter den Anhängern der TA-Variante (Jacquier, Haenchen, Dupont, Schneider, Roloff, Pesch) beziehen die Worte διὰ πνεύματος ἁγίου auf die Wahl der Apostel in Lk 6,13. Wieder andere entscheiden sich für eine Verbindung mit dem Auftrag aus Lk 24,44–49 (Conzelmann, Bruce, Barrett) oder stellen beide Varianten vor, ohne sich für klar eine zu entscheiden (Loisy, Munck, Bauernfeind, Zmijewski), manche lehnen schließlich beide mehr oder weniger entschieden ab (Meyer, Dibelius, Kilgallen). Dibelius' Vorschlag wiederum bestand darin, den Hinweis auf den Geist als eine durch dogmatische Gründe veranlasste spätere Hinzufügung anzusehen; Kilgallen schließlich setzt bei einem kausalen Verständnis der Präposition διά an.

Es ist klar, dass wir einen problematischen Text vor uns haben. Verschiedene Aspekte der Kritik von Meyer und Dibelius bleiben gültig und sind von Kilgallen neu formuliert wurden: Jesus entsende eben nicht den

---

choice of the Twelve, both the Lucan charges refer to the Spirit (Lk 24,49 ... the promise of my Father ... power from on high; and Acts 1.8).“

[24] J. TAYLOR, Les Actes des Apôtres, ÉtB. N.S. 41, Paris 2000, 9: „Par ailleurs, le TO rattache l'expression ‚par l'Esprit Saint' au choix des apôtres par Jésus tandis que, dans le TA, elle flotte maladroitement entre la prescription faite aux apôtres et leur choix par Jésus. Elle peut fort bien faire allusion à la prière qui précéda le choix des apôtres selon Lc 6, 12 même si l'Esprit Saint n'est pas expressément mentionné dans ce contexte. Il faut enfin se reporter à Ac 13,2, un verset ajouté par Act II au récit primitif: c'est l'Esprit Saint qui choisit Paul et Bernabé pour les envoyer en mission, et il le fait tandis que les disciples priaient et jeunaient. De même ici: c'est sous l'inspiration de l'Esprit Saint que Jésus a choisi ses apôtres.“

[25] J.J. KILGALLEN, „The Apostles Whom He Chose because of the Holy Spirit“. A Suggestion Regarding Acts 1,2, Bib. 81 (2000), 414–417.

Geist zu dem Zeitpunkt, zu dem er die Mission auf die Zwölf übertrage,[26] vielmehr fordert sie auf, bis zum Empfang seiner Kraft in Jerusalem zu bleiben (Apg 1,8), d.h. bis zum Empfang der Gabe des Hl. Geistes (an Pfingsten). Zugleich findet sich auch im Zusammenhang der Erzählung von der Wahl der Zwölf in Lk 6,13 keine Erwähnung des Geistes.[27] Und es ist auch (*gegen* Bruce) nicht zulässig, zur Lösung des Problems auf Passagen des Neuen Testaments außerhalb Lukasevangeliums zurückzugreifen, da Lukas ja eine interne Referenz auf sein eigenes Werk im Proömium der Apostelgeschichte macht.

Die Lösung von Meyer und Dibelius umgeht die Schwierigkeit durch die These einer späteren Interpolation, und auch die jüngste Hypothese Kilgallens muss angezweifelt werden: Schließlich hat διά im gesamten Neuen Testament nur ganz selten kausale Bedeutung und ist diese im lukanischen Doppelwerk sonst nirgends belegt.[28] Ist deswegen an andere Möglichkeiten, das Problem zu lösen, zu denken?

Unter allen erwähnten Hypothesen fällt die oben nur kurz angesprochene von J. Zmijewski heraus (vgl. oben). Besagter Autor diskutiert alle Möglichkeiten, das Syntagma διὰ πνεύματος ἁγίου zu verstehen. Seiner Meinung nach könne man es auf das Partizip ἐντειλάμενος (1), das Verb ἐξελέξατο (2) auf beide (3) sowie auf ἀνελήμφθη (4) beziehen. Mit den ersten drei Vorschlägen geht Zmijewski noch nicht über die Gedanken vieler anderer Autoren hinaus. Bemerkenswert jedoch ist seine vierte Möglichkeit. In der Tat findet sich unter den Varianten zu Apg 1,2, die Zmijewski anführt, keine, die das διὰ πνεύματος ἁγίου in Beziehung zu ἀνελήμφθη setzt. Dies aber ist genau der Sachverhalt, den ich hier in Erinnerung rufen will: die Existenz einer griechischen Variante, die das Syntagma διὰ πνεύματος ἁγίου unmittelbar vor das Verb ἀνελήμφθη setzt, was den Vorschlag

[26] Ebd., 414f: „For instance, one can, in regard to the first of the opinions above, assert that Jesus gave orders while under the influence of the Spirit, but one would be hard put to find any sure indication from the Gospel (especially Luke 24) that Jesus gave any orders at any time ‚under the influence of the Holy Spirit‘. [...] But that these texts (Luke 4,14.18) are the justification for saying that Jesus gave orders (we are dealing with the latter verses of Luke 24) while under the influence of the Holy Spirit is an argument that rates the qualification ‚possible‘, but not much more. [...] One simply does not understand that, in the resurrection chapter, Jesus was under the influence of the Spirit when he ordered his apostles to ‚stay in the city till you are clothed in power from on high‘ (Luke 24,49).“

[27] Ebd., 415: „In the story of Jesus’ choosing the Twelve (Luke 6,12–16), there is no reference to the influence of the Holy Spirit upon Jesus. True, he is described at prayer all night. This detail, copuled with the remarks noted above at Luke 4,14 and 4,18, might justify a later statement, that ‚under the influence of the Holy Spirit, Jesus chose the apostles‘. But again the conclusion drawn is ‚possible‘, but little more.“

[28] Ebd., 416: „It is an admittedly rare usage, and not found in Luke-Acts. Yet, rare as it is, it does exist, and so can be, grammatically speaking, a possible reading here.“

Zmijewskis nun noch interessanter macht. Mit dieser Variante eröffnet sich eine feste Basis, auf der der Bezug zwischen dem Syntagma διὰ πνεύματος ἁγίου und der Himmelfahrt Jesu diskutiert werden kann – ein Aspekt, der auch helfen kann, lukanische Theologie besser zu verstehen.

3. Die Version Harklensis und das patristische Zeugnis

Die als Harklensis bekannte syrische Version ist bisher kaum untersucht.[29] Trotzdem können wir Folgendes festhalten: Im Jahr 508/9 fertigte ein gewisser Polycarp im Auftrag des Philoxenos von Mabbug mit dem Ziel, die bisherige, als Peshitta bekannte syrische Version des Neuen Testaments zu verbessern, eine syrische Übersetzung des Neuen Testaments nach dem Kanon der syrischen Kirche an. Ungefähr hundert Jahre später, im Jahr 615/6, fügte Thomas von Harkel, Bischof von Mabbug, Randbemerkungen hinzu und revidierte den philoxenischen Text anhand ihm vorliegender griechischer Manuskripte aus dem Kloster Enaton (nahe Alexandria). Dank der Arbeit von Joseph White, der zwischen 1778 und 1803 in drei Bänden die besagte *versio Philoxeniana* publizierte, können wir heute auf diese Version zurückgreifen.

J. White allerdings zeigte im Zusammenhang mit dem von ihm gewählten Titel einen Optimismus, den wir heute nicht mehr teilen können: Das von ihm veröffentlichte Werk lässt sich eigentlich nicht als *Philoxeniana* betrachten, verfügte White doch über eine Version, die schon von Thomas von Harkel und anderen syrischen Autoren revidiert worden war. Wir wissen, wie weit sich der *philoxenianische* Text zuweilen von der *harklensischen* Revision unterschied. Neuere Studien haben außerdem gezeigt, dass der geistige Hintergrund, vor dem Polycarp im 6. Jh. seine Revision anfertigte, nicht derselbe war, der Thomas von Harkel ein Jahrhundert später prägte.

Tatsächlich war Polycarp, Chorbischof des Philoxenos, beauftragt, seine Version als Antwort auf ein konkretes Problem des Philoxenos hin anzufertigen: die syrische Kirche sollte mit neuen Bibelkommentaren (im Stil von Diodor und Theodor) ausgestattet werden, um die antichalkedonische monophysitische Lehre zu unterstützen. Für diese Kommentare benötigte

---

[29] Vgl. S. BROCK, Resolution of Philoxenian/Harclean Problem, in EPP/FEE (Hg.), New Testament Textual Criticism (s. Anm. 3), 325–343; A. JUCKEL, Introduction to the Ḥarklean Text, in G.A. KIRAZ (Hg.), Comparative Edition of the Syriac Gospels. Matthew, I, Leiden 1996, xxxi–lxxxii; F. RILLIET, Filosseno di Mabbug, in: A. DI BERARDINO (Hg.), Nuovo Dizionario Patristico e di Antichità Cristiane. F–O, Genova ²2007, 1968–1970; K. DEN BIESEN, Tommaso di Harqel, in: A. DI BERARDINO (Hg.), Nuovo Dizionario Patristico e di Antichità Cristiane. P–Z, Genova ²2008, 5404.

Philoxenos zunächst die Übersetzungsarbeit des Polycarp. Philoxenos kannte die Atmosphäre in Syrien (Edessa, Antiochien) sehr gut. Er vertrat und verteidigte dort die cyrillische gegen die nestorianische Lehre, hielt sich einige Zeit in Konstantinopel auf, war von 485 bis 518 Bischof von Mabbug (Hierapolis) und wurde schließlich nach Thrakien verbannt, wo er im Jahre 523 starb.

Ein Jahrhundert später fertigte Thomas von Harkel, ebenfalls Bischof von Mabbug, eine Revision an, in der er auch neutestamentliche Bücher berücksichtigte, die traditionell nicht zum syrischen Kanon gehörten (2 Petr, 2–3 Joh, Jud). Er begann diese Arbeit, als er von Kaiser Mauricius ins Exil nach Ägypten verbannt worden war. Dort widmete er sich im Jahr 615/6 im Kloster Enaton dieser Arbeit. Sie zielte einerseits darauf, den griechischen Text im Stil seiner Zeitgenossen Paulus von Tella, Paulus von Edessa und anderer anhand einer wörtlichen Übersetzung genauestens zu untersuchen und andererseits die unterschiedlichen Überlieferungen des griechischen und des syrischen Texts zu kennzeichnen. Auf diese Weise fügte er dem revidierten philoxenischen Text Randglossen mit Varianten hinzu. Bisweilen maß er Varianten, die von Philoxenos nicht beachtet worden waren, größere Bedeutung zu und ließ diese in den Text einfließen, während er die philoxenische Version in die Randglosse setzte.[30]

Aufgrund dieser Erkenntnisse lässt sich erschließen, dass das, was uns *via* Philoxenos – Thomas von Harkel erreicht, welche ja beide bestens in der griechischen und syrischen Kultur unterwiesen waren, eine syrische Version ist, die gut durch griechische Manuskripte gestützt ist. Angesichts der Fülle der heute verfügbaren griechischen Manuskripte des Neuen Testaments lässt sich allerdings nur äußerst schwer herausfinden, welcher

---

[30] JUCKEL, Introduction (s. Anm. 29), xxxv: „The main purpose of the Harklean margin is to display variant readings of the Greek New Testament text (translated into Syriac) so as to supply the reader with an enlarged knowledge of the Greek textual tradition. The readings are probably taken from the one (or two) Greek manuscripts upon which Thomas was relying alongside his special *Vorlage*. Another purpose of the margin is to annotate and to elucidate the Syriac translation by means of Greek marginalia which give the exact Greek background of the translation... While Philoxenus' intention was to create a correct *translation* of the New Testament, it is Thomas' intention to do more: to give, not only a correct translation, but also a comprehensive *display of New Testament textual traditions* (of both Greek and Syriac). It is a new dimension that Thomas adds to the work of his predecessor." Vgl. auch BROCK (s. Anm. 29), 343, Anm. 68. Im zweiten Kolophon des Werkes drückt der Autor es nach dem Bericht über die *Apostelgeschichte* und die *Katholischen Briefe* so aus: „Explicit liber sanctus Actuum Apostolicorum et Epistularum Catholicarum septem. Descriptus est autem ex exemplari accurato eorum qui versi sunt diebus memoriae piae Sancti Philoxeni Confessoris, Episcopi Mabugensis. Collatus est autem diligentia multa a me Thoma paupere ad exemplar Graecum valde accuratum et probatum in Antonia Alexandriae, urbis magnae, in monasterio sancto Antonianarum, sicut reliqui omnes libri, socii eius."

Text dem entsprechen könnte, was diese beiden syrischen Autoren in den Händen hielten.

In jedem Falle aber ist die Version Harklensis von großem Interesse für Apg 1,2. Ihr Text liest sich folgendermaßen:[31]

'ᵉdamā lᵉyawmā haw dᵉkad pᵉkad hᵉwā ēnūn lašlīḥē hānūn dagbā bᵉyad rūḥā qadīšā ēstalaq [„bis zu dem Tag, an dem er, nachdem er den Aposteln, die mittels des Hl. Geists erwählt worden waren, die Anweisungen gegeben hatte, aufgenommen wurde" bzw. „bis zu dem Tag, an dem er, nachdem er den Aposteln, die erwählt worden waren, die Anweisungen gegeben hatte, mittels des Hl. Geists aufgenommen wurde"].

Und in der Randbemerkung heißt es:

(*'ᵉdamā lᵉyawmā haw dᵉkad*) *ēstalaq kad pᵉkad lašlīḥē hānūn dagbā bᵉyad rūḥā qadīšā wapkad lᵉmakrāzū lēwangelīān* [„(bis zu dem Tag, an dem) er aufgenommen wurde, als er den Aposteln, die mittels des Hl. Geists erwählt worden waren, Anweisungen gegeben hatte und als er Anweisungen zur Verkündigung des Evangeliums gegeben hatte"].

Die meisten Experten haben sich aufgrund ihres Interesses am TW ganz auf die Randbemerkung konzentriert. Dabei hat offensichtlich niemand die Variante, die die syrische Übersetzung des Thomas von Harkel anbietet, bemerkt. In ihr geht das syrische Äquivalent des Syntagmas διὰ πνεύματος ἁγίου tatsächlich unmittelbar dem Verbum ἀνελήμφθη voraus. Das griechische Manuskript des Klosters Enaton, das Thomas von Harkel zu Anfang des 7. Jhs. zur Verfügung stand, bot also offenbar folgende Lesart: ἄχρι ἧς ἡμέρας ἐντειλάμενος τοῖς ἀποστόλοις οὓς ἐξελέξατο διὰ πνεύματος ἁγίου ἀνελήμφθη.

Nach dieser Variante könnte man διὰ πνεύματος ἁγίου mit ἐξελέξατο, aber auch mit ἀνελήμφθη kombinieren (indem man die Himmelfahrt Jesu auf das Handeln des Heiligen Geistes zurückführt). Eine noch für Zmijewski wenig wahrscheinliche Möglichkeit erhält so durch die griechische Textüberlieferung, die Thomas von Harkel bekannt war, neuen Rückhalt. Unmittelbar ergibt sich die Frage: Entspricht nach unserem Kenntnisstand auch irgendein griechischer Textzeuge dem, worauf sich Thomas von Harkel stützen konnte? Meines Wissens liegt uns keine Handschrift mit dieser Lesart vor;[32] dennoch besitzen wir Zeugen für diese lukanische Variante:

---

[31] Actuum Apostolorum et Epistolarum tam catholicarum quam paulinarum versio Syriaca Philoxeniana ex codice ms. Ridleiano in bibl. coll. nov. oxon. reposito nunc primum edita cum interpretatione et annotationibus Josephi White, s.t.p., Oxford 1799, 1.

[32] Handschrift 1505 (Athos, 8. Jh.) liest so: ἄχρι ἧς ἡμέρας ἐντειλάμενος τοῖς ἀποστόλοις διὰ πνεύματος ἁγίου ἀνελήμφθη. Ich glaube, dass es sich hier eher um einen Ausfall von οὓς ἐξελέξατο handelt, und nicht so sehr um eine Annäherung von διὰ πνεύματος ἁγίου an ἀνελήμφθη. Vgl. SWANSON, New Testament Greek Manuscripts. Acts (s. Anm. 2), 1; K. ALAND, Kurzgefasste Liste der griechischen Handschriften des Neuen Testaments, ANTTF 1, Berlin ²1994, 134

die altkirchlichen Autoren Nestorius, Eusebius von Dorylaeum und Cyrill von Alexandrien.

In einer Homilie, in der er gegen den Titel *Theotokos* für Maria polemisiert, spielt Nestorius[33] (vom Jahr 428 an Bischof von Konstantinopel), auf die angesprochene Stelle an. Es handelt sich um die Predigt *Saepe mecum fluctus*:[34]

πλείονα τὴν εἰς αὐτὸν κατασκευάζοντες ὕβριν καὶ τὸ πνεῦμα τῆς θείας ἀποτέμνουσι φύσεως, τὸ τὴν ἀνθρωπότητα αὐτοῦ διαπλάσαν (τὸ γὰρ ἐν τῇ Μαρίᾳ, φησί, γεννηθὲν ἐκ πνεύματός ἐστιν ἁγίου, (Mt 1,20), τὸ κατὰ δικαιοσύνην τὸ πλασθὲν ἀναπλάσαν (ἐφανερώθη, γάρ φησιν, ἐν σαρκί, ἐδικαιώθη ἐν πνεύματι, (1 Tim 3,16), τὸ δαίμοσιν αὐτὸν φοβερὸν ἐργασάμενον (ἐγώ, γάρ φησιν αὐτὸς ὁ κύριος, ἐν πνεύματι θεοῦ ἐκβάλλω τὰ δαιμόνια, (Mt 12,28), τὸ τὴν αὐτοῦ σάρκα πεποιημένον ναόν (τεθέαμαι, γάρ φησιν ὁ βαπτιστής, τὸ πνεῦμα καταβαῖνον ὡσεὶ περιστερὰν καὶ μένον ἐπ' αὐτόν, (Joh 1,32), τὸ τὴν ἀνάληψιν αὐτῷ τὴν εἰς οὐρανοὺς χαρισάμενον (ἐντειλάμενος, γάρ φησι, τοῖς ἀποστόλοις, οὓς ἐξελέξατο, διὰ πνεύματος ἁγίου ἀνελήφθη (Apg 1,2) – τοῦτο δή, τὸ τηλικαύτην τῷ Χριστῷ χαρισάμενον δόξαν, Χριστοῦ κατασκευάζουσι δοῦλον...

Wie es scheint, war der Hauptkritikpunkt des Nestorius der unangemessene Streit (ὕβρις) der Arianer und der Makedonianer über die Stellung des Heiligen Geistes. In seinem Bestreben, den Weg dieser Kritik zu verlassen und die göttliche Natur des Geistes zu verteidigen, zieht er verschiedene Schriftstellen der Bibel heran, die die göttliche Stellung des Geistes beweisen sollten. Dieser Geist habe in der Tat – nach Art des Schöpfers – im jungfräulichen Schoß Mariens die Natur Christi geformt (vgl. Mt 1,20), er habe sie auf eine neue Art (vgl. 1 Tim 3,16), furchterregend für die Dämonen (vgl. Mt 12,28), gebildet, Christi Fleisch in einen Tempel verwandelt (vgl. Joh 1,32) und ihm das Geschenk der Himmelfahrt verliehen (vgl. Apg 1,2).

Zweifellos liest also Nestorius, wenn er Apg 1,2 zitiert, nicht nur das Syntagma διὰ πνεύματος ἁγίου zwischen ἐξελέξατο und ἀνελήμφθη, sondern interpretiert es, indem er es auf das Verb ἀνελήμφθη und nicht auf ἐξελέξατο bezieht. Für Nestorius bewirkt der Heilige Geist die Himmelfahrt der menschlichen Natur Christi.

Nur wenig später, wohl um das Jahr 430, veröffentlicht Eusebius von Dorylaeum[35] (damals ein Laie aus Konstantinopel) sein Werk *Contestatio*, in dem er Argumente des Paul von Samosata und des Nestorius aneinanderreiht. Er will damit zeigen, dass der Bischof von Konstantinopel nur eine neue Variante der Häresie aus Samosata predige. So gebraucht der zu-

[33] Vgl. M. SIMONETTI, Nestorio-nestorianesimo, in: Nuovo Dizionario Patristico e di Antichità Cristiane. F–O (s. Anm. 29), 3482–3485.

[34] F. LOOFS, Nestoriana, Halle 1905, 293–294.

[35] Vgl. M. SIMONETTI, Eusebio di Dorileo, in: A. DI BERARDINO (Hg.), Nuovo Dizionario Patristico e di Antichità Cristiane. A–E, Genova ^{2}2006, 1854.

künftige Bischof erneut die Stelle der nestorianischen Predigt *Saepe mecum fluctus*, strukturiert sie aber seinem Zweck gemäß:[36]

Παῦλος (εἶπε)· Κρείττονα δὲ κατὰ πάντα, ἐπειδὴ ἐκ πνεύματος ἁγίου καὶ ἐξ ἐπαγγελιῶν καὶ ἐκ τῶν γεγραμμένων ἡ ἐπ᾽ αὐτῷ χάρις.

Νεστόριος (συμφώνως εἶπεν). τεθεάμαι γὰρ, φησὶ, τὸ πνεῦμα καταβαῖνον ὡσεὶ περιστερὰν καὶ μένον ἐπ᾽ αὐτόν, τὸ τὴν ἀνάληψιν αὐτῷ χαρισάμενον, - ἐντειλάμενος φησὶ, τοῖς ἀποστόλοις οὓς ἐξελέξατο, διὰ πνεύματος ἁγίου ἀνελήφθη, - τοῦτο δὴ τὸ τηλικαύτην Χριστῷ χαρισάμενον δόξαν.

So wie Paul von Samosata glaubte, dass Christus (der nicht identisch mit dem Logos sei) den Rest der Menschen aufgrund der Gnade, die auf ihn gemäß Verheißung und Schrift durch den Heiligen Geist herabgekommen sei, übertreffe, so bekräftige auch Nestorius das Verständnis der Herrlichkeit Christi als Frucht des Werks des Heiligen Geistes, der ihn in der Himmelfahrt mit herausragender Herrlichkeit ausgezeichnet habe, wie es dem Zitat in Apg 1,2 entspricht.

Im selben Jahr 430 schreibt Cyrill von Alexandrien[37] seine fünf Bücher *Adversus Nestorium*. Er zitiert erneut die ganze Passage von *Saepe mecum fluctus* und fügt einen Kommentar hinzu. Cyrill richtet seine Kritik gegen Nestorius, indem er betont, dass die menschliche Natur Christi in der Person mit dem Wort vereint sei und dass deswegen jedes Wort in Gemeinschaft mit dem Vater und seinem Geist keine eigene Legitimation durch die Unterstützung des Geistes benötige. Cyrill kritisiert Nestorius, indem er jedes Zitat, das Nestorius zum Beweis der Göttlichkeit des Heiligen Geistes heranzieht, durchgeht. Er tut dies nicht, weil er sich gegen die Göttlichkeit des Geistes wenden will, sondern weil sich für ihn solche Interpretationen der Schrift kompromittierend gegen die hypostatische Union des Wortes wenden. Wenn sich auch die Kritik des Nestorius hinsichtlich des Heiligen Geistes eigentlich gegen die Makedonianer richtet, so versteht Cyrill sie in Bezug auf Christus als entscheidenden Trennungsgrund.

Als er zum Zitat von Apg 1,2 kommt, schreibt Cyrill, vgl. *Adversus Nestorium* IV, 3:[38]

Οὐκ ἀμώμητον δὲ πρὸς τούτῳ φαίην ἂν, τὸ, ὡς ἐπ᾽ ἀνθρώπου κοινοῦ τὴν ἀνάληψιν αὐτῷ τὴν εἰς οὐρανὸν δεδωρῆσθαι λέγειν παρὰ τοῦ Πνεύματος· ἐπιλέκτους μὲν γὰρ ἐποιεῖτο τοὺς μαθητὰς διὰ τοῦ ἁγίου Πνεύματος, ἀνελήφθη γε μὴν ὡς θεός.

Cyrill hält es für tadelnswert zu glauben, dass Jesus, so als wäre er ein gewöhnlicher Mensch gewesen, für seine Himmelfahrt mit dem Geschenk

[36] EUSEBIUS DORYLAEUS, Contestatio, in: E. SCHWARTZ (Hg.), Acta Conciliorum oecumenicorum. Concilium universale Ephesenum I, 1, 1, Berlin 1927, 101–102.

[37] Vgl. M. SIMONETTI, Cirillo di Alessandria, in: Nuovo Dizionario Patristico e di Antichità Cristiane. A–E (s. Anm. 35) 1044–1049.

[38] PG 76, 185 A.

des Geistes bedacht worden sei. Laut Cyrill war dem nicht so. Die Erwähnung des Geistes im Text der Apg müsse in Relation zur Erwählung der Apostel verstanden werden. *Mittels des Hl. Geistes* habe Jesus sie zu Erwählten gemacht, während er wie Gott aufgenommen wurde.

Was den Gegenstand unserer Untersuchung angeht, wurzelt der Hauptaspekt der Kritik des Eusebius von Dorylaeum und Cyrills darin, dass beide den lukanischen Text, wie er von Nestorius zitiert wird, unverändert belassen. Die Stellung des Syntagmas διὰ πνεύματος ἁγίου im Vers diskutieren sie nicht. Man könnte also daraus schließen, dass sich in Konstantinopel wie in Alexandrien die griechischen Manuskripte von Apg 1,2 so lasen: ἐντειλάμενος τοῖς ἀποστόλοις οὓς ἐξελέξατο διὰ πνεύματος ἁγίου ἀνελήφθη. Eusebius von Dorylaeum übernimmt es jedenfalls so. Die Interpretation von Nestorius bezieht sich auf folgende Interpunktion: οὓς ἐξελέξατο, διὰ πνεύματος ἁγίου ἀνελήφθη. Cyrill erwidert auf jene Variante mit der folgenden Interpunktion: οὓς ἐξελέξατο διὰ πνεύματος ἁγίου, ἀνελήφθη.

Im selben Jahr 430 verfasst Johannes Cassianus auf Veranlassung des Erzdiakons Leo (des zukünftigen Leo des Großen) seine sieben Bücher *De incarnatione Domini contra Nestorium.* In VII,17,1–2 kommt er auf die lateinische Übersetzung von *Saepe mecum fluctus* zu sprechen, ein polemischer Unterton ist nicht zu verkennen:[39]

„Ais ergo in alia disputatione, immo in alia blasphemia tua: et spiritum de divina natura separavit, qui humanitatem eius creavit. Ait enim quia, *quod ex Maria natum est, de spiritu sancto est* (Mt 1,20). Qui et iustitia replevit quod creatum est. Ait enim: *apparuit in carne, iustificatus est in spiritu* (1 Tim 3,16). Item qui eum fecit et daemoniis metuendum. *Ego* enim, ait, *in spiritu dei eicio daemones* (Mt 12,28). Qui et carnem eius fecit templum: *vidi* enim *spiritum descendentem quasi columbam et manentem super eum* (Joh 1,32). Item qui ei donavit elevationem in caelum. Ait enim: *dans mandatum apostolis, quos elegit, per spiritum sanctum elevatus est* (Apg 1,2). Hunc denique qui tantam gloriam Christo donavit ...... omnis ergo in his blasphemia tua haec est, ut nihil Christus per se habuerit, sed nec ipse, ut tu ais, solitarius homo aliquid a verbo, id est a filio dei ceperit, sed totum in eo donum spiritus fuerit."

Später hält er sich ganz an die Kritik, die von Cyrill von Alexandrien vorgebracht wurde, vgl. VII, 22, 1:[40]

„Addis autem etiam hoc praedictis impietatibus tuis quod elevationem domino in caelum spiritus condonarit, ostendens scilicet sacrilego sensu tuo, quod tam inbecillum ac tam egenum dominum Iesum Christum fuisse credis, quod, nisi eum spiritus elevasset in caelum, adhuc hodie forsitan futurum aestimares in terra."

---

[39] CASSIANUS MASSILIENSIS, De incarnatione Domini contra Nestorium libri vii, ed. M. PETSCHENIG, CSEL 17, Wien 1888, 372–373.

[40] Ebd., 379–380.

Was uns nun aber grundsätzlich im Zusammenhang mit der Textkritik von Apg 1,2 interessiert, sind die folgenden Zeilen Cassians, vgl. VII, 22, 1–3:[41]

„Ad probationem autem dicti etiam testimonium sacrum adhibens ait, inquis, enim: *dans mandata apostolis, quos elegit, per spiritum sanctum elevatus est* (Apg 1,2). Quid te appellem, quid te aestimem, qui corrumpendo divinas litteras id agis, ne testimonia sacra habeant vim testimoniorum? Novum audaciae genus, quae id efficere argumentis nequitiae suae nititur, ut falsitatem veritas confirmare videatur. Non enim ita in apostolicis actibus dictum est, ut tu ais. Quid enim scriptura dicit? *Quae coepit Iesus facere et docere usque in diem qua praecipiens apostolis, per spiritum sanctum quos elegit, assumptus est* (Apg 1,1–2). Quod utique hyperbaton est et ita intellegendum: ‚quae coepit Iesus facere et docere usque in diem qua assumptus est, praecipiens apostolis, quos elegit per spiritum sanctum', ut responderi tibi forsitan amplius quam testimonio ipso in hac parte non habeat, quia sufficere utique ad plenum veritati debet integritas testimonii, si falsitati poterat satis esse corruptio."

Cassian stellt im Unterschied zu Eusebius und Cyrill den biblischen Text nach der Version des Nestorius (konkret Apg 1,2) in Frage und behauptet, dass dieser die Hl. Schriften verderbe, so dass „es scheine, dass die Wahrheit' (der Hl. Schriften) ‚den Fehler' (der Lehre) ‚bekräftige'". Zudem überliefert er im Folgenden den Text übereinstimmend mit der gängigen Version des TA. Dabei bezieht er unweigerlich die Worte διὰ πνεύματος ἁγίου auf die Erwählung der Apostel.

Möglicherweise fand Cassian in Gallien keine griechische oder lateinische Version (oder wollte sie nicht finden), die den Text von Apg 1,2 nach der Version des Nestorius wiedergab, und schloss daraus auf eine Textmanipulation, die der Letztgenannte zu verantworten habe. Im Gegensatz dazu legt auch die Selbstverständlichkeit, mit der Eusebius von Dorylaeum und Cyrill von Alexandrien die auch in der Version Harklensis belegte Variante des Nestorius anerkennen, nahe, dass das, was Cassian als korrumpierten Text angesehen hat, einfach in Gallien bzw. unter den Texten, die Cassian erreichbar waren, nicht belegt war.

Wie soll man schließlich diese vergessene Lesart von Apg 1,2 beurteilen? Aus grammatikalischer Sicht muss man zugestehen, dass sich die Variante viel besser in den Textduktus einfügt als jede andere der Lesarten, bei denen die Zuordnung von διὰ πνεύματος ἁγίου offen bleibt. Aus Sicht der kirchlichen Lehre führt die Lesart nicht wirklich zu den Problemen, die Cyrill zu entdecken glaubte, wie gleich zu zeigen sein wird. Liegt hier also der lukanische Originaltext vor, der später der Revision unterlag, die im TA überliefert wird, und die sich (womöglich) dank der Kontroverse um Nestorius und der Lösung Cassians durchsetzte? Vor einer allzu schnellen Antwort warnt uns die *Hom. in Acta apostolorum* I (PG 60, 18) des Johan-

[41] Ebd., 380.

nes Chrysostomus, wo der Bischof von Konstantinopel zu Beginn des 5. Jh. und vor Nestorius, Cyrill und Cassian, den Text bereits wie die Mehrheit der Textzeugen des TA (א A B E Ψ) liest, d.h. anders als die Version Harklensis, Nestorius, Eusebius von Dorylaeum und Cyrill.

Für den Moment kann man nur schließen, dass vom 5. bis 7. Jh. in Konstantinopel und Alexandrien (Thomas von Harkel arbeitete in einem Kloster nahe der ägyptischen Metropole) die genannten griechischen Varianten (die übliche des TA und der Harklensis) nebeneinander existierten und dass beide gut bezeugt waren.

Im folgenden Abschnitt gilt es nun noch etwas mehr über die theologischen Aspekte, die sich mit den Varianten verbinden, herauszufinden.

4. Einige theologische Aspekte

Wenn sich Nestorius von der allgemein gültigen Lehre entfernte, dann geschah das natürlich nicht auf Grund des Abschnitts aus *Saepe mecum fluctus*, den Cyrill so hart kritisierte. Eher könnte man Cyrill des Monophysitismus beschuldigen, der in den Passagen gegen Nestorius versteckt ist. Schließt etwa die Verteidigung der hypostatischen Union zwischen Wort und Fleisch die Aufhebung sämtlicher spezifischer Werke ein, die der Geist in der Menschheit des inkarnierten Wortes von Nazareth bis zur Himmelfahrt bewirkte? Diese Unklarheit ist es, die sich in der Kritik bemerkbar macht, die der Alexandriner diesbezüglich an Nestorius richtet.

Um dies zu bestätigen, wollen wir uns ansehen, wie die lukanische Stelle in der Zeit vor Nestorius interpretiert wurde. Leider findet sich Apg 1,2 nicht unter den am häufigsten zitierten Bibelstellen der frühen christlichen Literatur. Es gibt praktisch keine Spur von besagter Stelle in der vornizänischen Exegese. Später finden wir sie bei Basilius von Caesarea in den *Regulae morales* 70,1; bei Didymus (oder Ps.-Didymus) in *De trinitate* (PG 39, 933) und an anderen weniger bedeutenden Stellen. Die genannten Autoren gehen alle von der Lesart des TA aus.

Allerdings können wir bei einigen vornizänischen Autoren, sobald sie auf die Himmelfahrt Christi Bezug nehmen, einen Nachhall der Version Harklensis bemerken. Wenden wir uns zunächst Irenäus von Lyon zu. In *Adversus Haereses* III, 12, 5 schreibt er:[42]

„Hae voces Ecclesiae ex qua habuit omnis Ecclesia initium; hae voces civitatis magnae novi Testamenti civium; hae voces apostolorum, hae voces discipulorum Domini, eorum qui post adsumptionem Domini per Spiritum (μετὰ τὴν ἀνάληψιν τοῦ κυρίου διὰ τοῦ πνεύματος) et perfecti exstiterunt et invocaverunt Deum..."

[42] IRENAEUS, Adversus Haereses III, 2, edd. A. ROUSSEAU/L. DOUTRELEAU, SC 211, Paris 2002 (1974), 196.

Das griechische Original hat uns durch die Katenenüberlieferung erreicht und bestätigt die Zuverlässigkeit der lateinischen Übersetzung. Irenäus bezieht sich auf die Stimmen jener Jünger zu Pfingsten, die *nach der Himmelfahrt vom Herrn mittels des Hl. Geistes* vollkommen gemacht wurden.

Die Eigenschaft des Heiligen Geistes ist es, das Fleisch in den Himmel zu erheben. In der Tat sind der Heilige Geist und das Wort die beiden Hände, derer sich der Vater bedient, um den Mensch zu formen und in den Himmel zu führen. Obwohl es eine qualitative Differenz zwischen der Entrückung des Elija oder des Henoch (ins Paradies) und Jesus (in den Himmel) gibt, ist der Mechanismus derselbe; und so lesen wir bei Irenäus in einem Abschnitt, in dem er sich auf den Patriarchen und den Propheten bezieht (*Adversus Haereses* V, 5, 1):[43]

„Quid autem de illis dicamus, quandoquidem Enoch placens *Deo*, in quo *placuit* corpore *translatus est*, translationem justorum praemonstrans, et Helias sicut erat in plasmatis substantia *assumptus est*, assumptionem patrum prophetans? Et nihil impediit eos corpus in translationem et assumptionem eorum; per illas enim manus per quas in initio plasmati sunt, per ipsas assumptionem et translationem acceperunt. Assuetae enim erant in Adam manus Dei coaptare et tenere et bajulare suum plasma et ferre et *ponere* ubi ipsae vellent."

Das Fleisch von Adam, Henoch und Elias war genauso menschlich wie das Christi, so dass es die Unterstützung des Geistes vor dem Ereignis der zukünftigen Himmelfahrt benötigte. Dass im Falle Christi die Person das Wort ist, hebe die dem menschlichen Fleisch innewohnende Bedürftigkeit zu dessen fortschreitender Verwandlung und Vergöttlichung nicht auf (*contra* Cyrill).

Auch liest man in der *Didascalia* VI, 23, 8:[44]

„Ipsi ergo, qui potens est aperire aures cordium vestrorum, ut suscipiatis quae ministrata sunt eloquia Domini per evangelium et per doctrinam Iesu Christi Nazareni, qui crucifixus est sub Pontio Pilato et dormivit, ut evangelizaret Abraham et Isaac et Iacob et sanctis suis universis tam finem saeculi quam resurrectionem, quae erit mortuorum, et exsurrexit a mortuis, ut ostendat et det notis suis pignus resurrectionis, et in caelis susceptus per virtutem Dei et spiritus eius, et sedentis ad dexteram sedis omnipotentis Dei super Cherubin, qui *veniet cum virtute et gloria iudicare vivos et mortuos*..."

Und im entsprechenden Abschnitt der *Constitutiones* VI, 30, 9:[45]

τῷ δόντι ἡμῖν ἀρραβῶνα τῆς ἀναστάσεως ἑαυτὸν καὶ εἰς οὐρανοὺς ἀναληφθέντι διὰ τῆς δυνάμεως τοῦ θεοῦ καὶ πατρὸς αὐτοῦ...

---

[43] A. ORBE, Teología de san Ireneo I. Comentario al Libro V del „Adversus haereses", BAC Maior 25, Madrid 1985, 228–250 (lateinischer Text, Übersetzung und weitreichender Kommentar).

[44] Didascalia et Constitutiones Apostolorum, hg. von F.X. FUNK, I, Paderborn 1905, 382.

[45] Didascalia et Constitutiones Apostolorum (s. Anm. 44), 383.

Man findet hier – und ebensowenig bei Irenäus – keine Schwierigkeiten, die Himmelfahrt des Herrn als Werk des Geist oder als Machterweis Gottes zu beschreiben.[46]

Übereinstimmend mit der Problematik stoßen wir in den unterschiedlichen Himmelfahrtserzählungen von Elija, Henoch und anderen nicht nur auf die häufige Verwendung des Verbs ἀναλαμβάνω (wie im Fall von Apg 1,2), sondern auch (wenn auch auf unterschiedliche Weise) auf die Nennung einer Kraft, die diese Himmelfahrt bewirkt (Feuerwagen, Wirbelsturm, Geist), vgl. 2 Kön 2,11; Ez 8,3; 1 Makk 2,58; Sir 48,9; 49,14; 1 Hen 52,1; 70,2; 71,5; *Vita Adae* 25.

5. Zusammenfassung

Zusammenfassend bleibt zu sagen: Die syrische Version Harklensis, die auf der Basis griechischer Manuskripte im ägyptischen Kloster Enaton verfasst wurde, bestätigt genauso wie die Zeugnisse des Nestorius, Eusebius von Dorylaeum und Cyrill die Existenz einer griechischen Variante von Apg 1,2, in der das Syntagma διὰ πνεύματος ἁγίου unmittelbar vor dem Verb ἀνελήμφθη steht. Besagte Variante, die Cassian in Gallien zeitgleich zu Nestorius und Cyrill anscheinend nicht kannte, liest sich grammatikalisch viel flüssiger als die bekannten Lesarten (des TA oder des TW). Außerdem harmoniert sie theologisch gut mit der frühen Christologie, die nicht zögerte zu unterstreichen, dass die menschliche Natur Christi weiterhin der Unterstützung des Geistes bedurfte, um verherrlicht zu werden.

Die Polemik, die um Apg 1,2 zwischen Nestorius und Cyrill entstand, hat womöglich dazu beigetragen, dass diese Variante an den Rand ge-

[46] Etwas Ähnliches bemerkt man in der Erzählung des *Epistola apostolorum* 51, wo die *Wolke* (vgl. Apg 1,11) den *Geist* oder die *Verherrlichung* repräsentiert, vgl. C. SCHMIDT/I. WAJNBERG (Hg.) Gespräche Jesu mit seinen Jüngern nach der Auferstehung, TU 43, Leipzig 1919, 154: „Nachdem er dies gesagt und das Gespräch mit uns beendet hatte, sagte er uns wiederum: ‚Sehet, am dritten Tage und in der dritten Stunde wird derjenige kommen, der mich gesandt hat, damit ich mit ihm weggehe'. Und als (wie) er dies sprach, geschah Donner und Blitz und Erdbeben, und es rissen sich die Himmel auf, und es erschien eine lichte Wolke, die ihn emportrug. Und (es ertönten) die Stimmen vieler Engel, indem sie jubelten und lobpriesen und sagten: ‚Sammele uns, o Priester, zum Lichte der Herrlichkeit!' Und als sie dem Firmament sich genähert, vernahmen wir seine Stimme: ‚Gehet hin in Frieden'." Über die *Wolke* sagt SCHMIDT, 302: „Diese Lichtwolke hat aber eine besondere Bedeutung, denn der Herr hat verkündet, dass der Vater, der ihn gesandt, kommen und mit ihm weggehen würde. Sie ist also gleichsam die δόξα des Vaters, mit der der Sohn in das Lichtreich einzieht. Deshalb ist auch der Herr jetzt bei seinem Aufstieg nicht mehr wie beim Abstieg eine unbekannte Größe, vielmehr begleiten ihn Jubel und Lobpreis der Engel wie bei der Schilderung der Himmelfahrt in der Ascensio Jes. c. 11,22ff."

drängt wurde und man andere Lesarten (die ohne Zweifel schon zur Zeit des Chrysostomus existierten) bevorzugte, in denen das Syntagma διὰ πνεύματος ἁγίου fern vom finalen Verb ἀνελήμφθη platziert und deswegen mit dem Verb ἐξελέξατο oder mit dem Partizip ἐντειλάμενος verbunden werden musste. Zur endgültigen Klärung dieses Problems wäre es sicherlich wichtig, die Interpretationen dieser Stelle durch Apollinaris und seine Anhänger zu kennen, wie auch die der Makedonianer und der Pneumatomachen. Gerade im Konflikt mit Letzteren diskutierte Nestorius ja die genannte Stelle.

Sicherlich erlauben die heute verfügbaren Daten keinen Beweis, dass die Variante Harklensis von Apg 1,2 die originale Lesart des lukanischen Texts ist; ebenso wenig jedoch lässt sich das Gegenteil behaupten. Für diese Lesart würde sprechen, dass sie mit Leichtigkeit die grammatikalischen und theologischen Vieldeutigkeiten löst, mit denen mehr als ein Exeget des 20. Jahrhunderts Probleme hatte (Loisy, Meyer, Dibelius, Conzelmann, Munck, Zmijewski, Kilgallen). Deshalb verlangt diese Variante mehr Aufmerksamkeit, als ihr in Zeiten moderner Textkritik zugebilligt wurde. In jedem Falle sollte man sie mehr als bisher als einen Teil der an sich schon verwirrenden und komplizierten Überlieferungsgeschichte des Texts der Apostelgeschichte verstehen.

Leid, Kreuz und Kreuzesnachfolge bei Ignatius von Antiochien

TOBIAS NICKLAS

Zu den frühesten Zeugnissen christlicher Literatur außerhalb des Neuen Testaments gehören die Briefe des Ignatius von Antiochien.[1] Wahrscheinlich verfasst, als der Bischof bereits als Gefangener nach Rom unterwegs ist, wo ihn sein Martyrium erwartet, versuchen sie den Gemeinden von Ephesus, Magnesia, Tralles, Rom, Philadelphia und Smyrna sowie dem Bischof Polycarp von Smyrna in schwieriger Situation Ermahnung zum Durchhalten in Einheit wie zum Festhalten an Grunddaten des Glaubens zu sein – Letzteres in ganz konkreter, z.T. sehr polemischer Auseinanderset-

---

[1] Die Authentizität auch der Texte der mittleren Sammlung ist in den vergangenen Jahren immer wieder, v.a. von R.M. HÜBNER, Thesen zur Echtheit und Datierung der sieben Briefe des Ignatius von Antiochien, ZAC 1 (1997), 44–72; DERS./M. VINZENT, Der paradox Eine. Antignostischer Monarchianismus im zweiten Jahrhundert, VigChr.S 50, Leiden et al. 1999, und im Gefolge Hübners T. LECHNER, Ignatius adversus Valentinianos? Chronologische und theologiegeschichtliche Studien zu den Briefen des Ignatius, VigChr.S 47, Leiden et al. 1999, angezweifelt worden – man ordnete die Texte mit z.T. beachtlichen Beobachtungen als Pseudepigraphen erst in eine deutlich spätere Phase des 2. Jahrhunderts ein. Zur Kritik an HÜBNER und LECHNER vgl. z.B. A. LINDEMANN, Eine Antwort auf die ‚Thesen zur Echtheit und Datierung der sieben Briefe des Ignatius von Antiochien', ZAC 1 (1997), 185–194; G. SCHÖLLGEN, Die Ignatianen als pseudepigraphisches Briefcorpus. Anmerkungen zu den Thesen von Reinhard M. Hübner, ZAC 2 (1998), 16–25; M. EDWARDS, Ignatius and the Second Century: An Answer to R. Hübner, ZAC 2 (1998), 214–226; H.J. VOGT, Bemerkungen zur Echtheit der Ignatiusbriefe, ZAC 3 (1999), 50–63, A. BRENT, Ignatius of Antioch: A Martyr Bishop and the Origin of Episcopacy, London/New York 2007, 95–143, sowie P. FOSTER, The Epistles of Ignatius of Antioch, in: DERS. (Hg.), The Writings of the Apostolic Fathers, London/New York 2007, 80–107, hier 88–89, der allerdings selbst aus anderen Gründen zu einer späteren Datierung um 125–150 n.Chr. kommt. Vgl. auch die Zusammenfassungen der insgesamt äußerst differenzierten, im Grunde seit Jahrzehnten währenden Diskussion bei W. UEBELE, „Viele Verführer sind in die Welt ausgegangen": Die Gegner in den Briefen des Ignatius von Antiochien und in den Johannesbriefen, BWANT 151, Stuttgart/Berlin/Köln 2001, 20–27, sowie M. ISACSON, To Each Their Own Letter: Structure, Themes and Rhetorical Strategies in the Letters of Ignatius of Antioch, ConB.NT 42, Stockholm 2004, 12–14. – Ich selbst neige eher zur konservativeren Zuschreibung der Texte an Ignatius selbst und damit der Frühdatierung in das zweite Jahrzehnt des 2. Jahrhunderts (zwischen etwa 110 und 117 n.Chr.).

zung mit Gegnern.[2] Zudem verstehen sich die Briefe mehr oder minder als Vermächtnis des Bischofs, Abschiedsschreiben, ja im weitesten Sinne „Testament“.[3] In diesen Texten kommt der in sein eigenes Leiden gehende Ignatius immer wieder auf die Passion Christi zu sprechen, in deren Licht er auch sein eigenes Schicksal interpretiert.[4] Dabei zeigt er sich bekanntlich immer wieder vor allem von Gedanken des Paulus, vor allem aus dessen 1. Korintherbrief, den Ignatius zu kennen scheint,[5] beeinflusst. Die in

---

[2] Einen forschungsgeschichtlichen Überblick zu Versuchen der Rekonstruktion der Gegnerpositionen, die hier nicht im Mittelpunkt der Untersuchung stehen kann, bieten etwa C. MUNIER, Où en est la question d'Ignace d'Antioche? Bilan d'un siècle des recherches 1870–1988, ANRW 2.27.1 (1993), 359–484, hier 398–413, oder knapp M. MYLLYKOSKI, Wild Beasts and Rabid Dogs. The Riddle of the Heretics in the Letters of Ignatius, in: J. ÅDNA (Hg.), The Formation of the Early Church, WUNT 183, Tübingen 2005, 341–377, hier 345–350. Zum häufig bearbeiteten Thema vgl. auch C.K. BARRETT, Jews and Judaizers in the Epistles of Ignatius, in: R. HAMERTON-KELLY/R. SCROGGS (Hg.), Jews, Greeks and Christians. Religious Cultures in Late Antiquity. Essays in Honor of William David Davies, Leiden 1976, 220–244; A. DAVIDS, Irrtum und Häresie, Kairos 15 (1973), 165–187, hier 173–178; P.J. DONAHUE, Jewish Christianity in the Letters of Ignatius of Antioch, VigChr 32 (1978), 71–93; M.D. GOULDER, Ignatius' 'Docetists,' VigChr 53 (1999), 16–30; J.W. MARSHALL, The Objects of Ignatius' Wrath and Jewish Angelic Mediators, Journal of Ecclesiastical History 56 (2005), 1–23; J.L. SUMNEY, Those Who ‚Ignorantly Deny Him‘: The Opponents of Ignatius of Antioch, JECS 1 (1993), 345–365; W. UEBELE, Viele Verführer (s. Anm. 1), 20–92.

[3] Damit ist nicht gesagt, dass hier die literarische Form „Testament“ vorliege; zum Ausdruck gebracht sei vielmehr, dass die Tatsache, dass es sich um so etwas wie „letzte Worte“ des Bischofs an die jeweiligen Gemeinden handelt, ihnen auch ein besonderes Gewicht verleiht.

[4] Vielleicht müsste man hinzufügen, dass Ignatius sein Leiden im Licht des Leidens Christi wie auch des Leidens des Paulus interpretiert, wie D.M. REIS, Following in Paul's Footsteps: Mimēsis and Power in Ignatius of Antioch, in: A. GREGORY/C.M. TUCKETT (Hg.), Trajectories through the New Testament and the Apostolic Fathers, Oxford et al. 2005, 287–305, hier 293–300 zeigt, der von „Ignatius imitating Paul imitating Christ“ schreibt (293). Ähnliche Gedanken auch bei W. REBELL, Das Leidensverständnis bei Paulus und Ignatius von Antiochien, NTS 32 (1986), 457–465; sowie R.F. STOOPS, Jr., If I Suffer ... Epistolary Authority in Ignatius of Antioch, HThR 80 (1987),161–178, hier 168 und 177.

[5] Die Frage nach dem literarischen Verhältnis zwischen Texten der „Apostolischen Väter“ und neutestamentlich gewordener Schriften ist seit langer Zeit umstritten, da die Autoren des frühen und mittleren 2. Jahrhunderts neutestamentliche Schriften noch nicht mit formal als Zitate einleiteten oder gar an irgend einer Stelle auf ihre Vorlagen verwiesen. Eine Antwort ist – auch aufgrund der Verschiedenheit der in der neuzeitlichen Sammlung „Apostolische Väter“ zusammengestellten Texte – nicht pauschal zu geben. Auch die Briefe des Ignatius von Antiochien stellen den Exegeten, der sich für literarische Abhängigkeiten interessiert, vor Probleme. Ein Grund dafür, dass gerade in seinen Texten nur an wenigen Stellen sicher auf literarische Abhängigkeit zu „neutestamentlich gewordenen“ Texten geschlossen werden kann, mag sicherlich darin liegen, dass es sich hier eben nicht um theologische Traktate, die am Schreibtisch des Bischofs entstanden,

den Briefen des Ignatius entwickelte Kreuzestheologie ist also sicherlich stark durch die konkrete Situation, in die hinein sie entwickelt ist, beeinflusst, also Martyrium einerseits und Auseinandersetzung mit Gegnern andererseits, von denen zumindest einige ganz offensichtlich die Menschlichkeit Christi – und damit sein menschliches Leiden – abgestritten haben dürften.[6]

Wie aber sind die Aussagen des antiochenischen Bischofs zu Leiden und Kreuz Christi in seine theologische Gesamtkonzeption einzuordnen? Handelt es sich um mehr oder weniger verstreute, ad hoc entwickelte, der historischen Situation allein verdankte „Zufallsprodukte" oder lässt sich aus ihnen bzw. von ihnen her ein theologisches Gesamtsystem erkennen?

Eine Antwort auf diese Frage sei zunächst anhand einer Durchsicht entlang der verschiedenen, üblicherweise als echt anerkannten Ignatius-Briefe versucht. Die sich daraus ergebenden Gedankenstränge sollen dann erst in einem zweiten Schritt – soweit die Texte, die sicherlich nur Fragmente der Theologie des Ignatius wiedergeben, es zulassen – zusammengefasst werden.

---

handelt, sondern um Briefe auf dem Weg zum Martyrium in Rom. Trotzdem lassen sich zumindest einige Beobachtungen als konsensfähig herausschälen: In der m.W. jüngsten Studie zum Thema kommt Paul FOSTER zu dem Schluss, dass Ignatius sicher den 1. Korintherbrief, von dem er längere Passagen offensichtlich aus dem Gedächtnis zitieren konnte, kannte, und dass dies mit großer Wahrscheinlichkeit auch für die Briefe an die Epheser, sowie 1 und 2 Timotheus galt: In allen anderen Fällen empfiehlt FOSTER zumindest große Zurückhaltung – unter den Evangelien des Neuen Testaments lasse sich immerhin am ehesten eine Kenntnis des Matthäusevangeliums wahrscheinlich machen. Vgl. P. FOSTER, The Epistles of Ignatius of Antioch and the Writings that later formed the New Testament, in: A. GREGORY/C.M. TUCKETT (Hg.), The Reception of the New Testament in the Apostolic Fathers (The New Testament and the Apostolic Fathers), Oxford et al. 2005, 160–186, hier 185. – Zur Paulusrezeption des Ignatius vgl. zudem weiter A. LINDEMANN, Paulus im ältesten Christentum. Das Bild des Apostels und die Rezeption der paulinischen Theologie in der frühchristlichen Literatur bis Marcion, BHT 58, Tübingen 1979, 199–221, und DERS., Paul's Influence on ‚Clement' and Ignatius, in: A.F. GREGORY/C.M. TUCKETT (Hg.), Trajectories through the New Testament and the Apostolic Fathers, Oxford et al. 2005, 9–24, hier 16–24.

[6] Auf etwas mehr als einer Seite seines umfangreichen Kommentars zu den Briefen des Ignatius geht auch W.R. SCHOEDEL, Die Briefe des Ignatius von Antiochien: Ein Kommentar, München 1990, 68–69, auf das Thema „Leiden und Auferstehung" bei Ignatius ein; einen Abschnitt widmet dem Thema zudem die ältere Studie von K. BOMMES, Weizen Gottes: Untersuchungen zur Theologie des Martyriums bei Ignatius von Antiochien, Theophaneia 27, Köln/Bonn 1976, 51–56. W. REBELL, Das Leidensverständnis (s. Anm. 4), wiederum konzentriert sich v.a. auf das Verständnis der eigenen Leidensexistenz des Bischofs.

1. Der Brief an die Epheser

Welch bedeutende Rolle das Thema von Leid und Kreuz in Ignatius' Brief an die Epheser (*Eph.*) spielen wird, zeigt sich bereits in seinem Präskript. Ignatius bezeichnet die Gemeinde als „gesegnet", „geeint zu bleibender, unveränderlicher Herrlichkeit"[7], aber auch „auserwählt in wahrem Leiden" (ἐκλελεγμένην ἐν πάθει ἀληθινῷ). Damit sind im Grunde schon wichtige Grundlinien seines Gemeindeverständnisses angedeutet. Was aber ist mit dem „wahren Leiden" gemeint, das hier offensichtlich eine Art Ausgangspunkt der Auserwählung bildet? Es kann sich im Grunde bereits hier nur um das Leiden Christi handeln: Dafür spricht trotz des fehlenden Artikels vor πάθος die Tatsache, dass hier nicht davon die Rede ist, die Gemeinde sei *zum* Leiden auserwählt, sowie das Attribut ἀληθινός, dessen Adverbform Ignatius immer wieder (vgl. z.B. *Sm.* 1,2; *Trall.* 9,1) verwenden wird, um die Wahrheit des Leidens Christi gegenüber Gegnern zu verteidigen, die offensichtlich behaupten, Christus habe nur zum Schein gelitten.

Diese Deutung bestätigt sich bereits wenig später: Wenn in *Eph.* 1,1 die Gemeindemitglieder als „Nachahmer Gottes"[8] (μιμηταὶ θεοῦ), die „im Blut Gottes" (vgl. sonst „Blut Christi": *Trall.* 8,1; *Röm.* 7,3; *Phil.* Inscr.; 4; *Sm.* 1,1; 6,1; 12,2) wiederbelebt seien (ἀναζωπυρήσαντες ἐν αἵματι θεοῦ) bezeichnet werden, so verweist Ignatius damit nicht auf die Gefahr eigener Blutzeugenschaft der Gemeinde, sondern auf ihr Verhalten ihm, dem Gefangenen und zukünftigen Märtyrer, gegenüber. Gleichzeitig aber ist bereits ein Zueinander angesprochen, das für Ignatius' Verständnis von Christi Passion im Folgenden immer wieder von Bedeutung sein wird: Das Leiden und Sterben Christi hat für Ignatius soteriologische Bedeutung; zudem aber wird, wenn er von Wiederbelebung durch das „Blut Gottes" spricht, sicherlich auch ein sakramentaler Bezug – zum Empfang der Eu-

---

[7] W.R. SCHOEDEL, Die Briefe des Ignatius (s. Anm. 6), 69, schreibt: Mit dieser Bezeichnung „sieht Ignatius die christliche Kirche zu Ephesus als eine Manifestation der einen transzendenten Kirche an."

[8] Gemeint ist damit Christus, der bei Ignatius immer wieder als θεός bezeichnet werden kann. Zur Christologie des Ignatius vgl. weiterführend z.B. C.T. BROWN, The Gospel and Ignatius of Antioch, Studies in Biblical Literature 12, New York et al. 2000, 133–163, T.G. WEINANDY, The Apostolic Christology of Ignatius of Antioch: The Road to Chalcedon, in: A. GREGORY/C.M. TUCKETT (Hg.), Trajectories through the New Testament and the Apostolic Fathers, Oxford et al. 2005, 71–84 (sieht Ignatius als Bindeglied zwischen neutestamentlicher und späterer „orthodoxer" Christologie) sowie knapper P. FOSTER, The Epistle of Ignatius (s. Anm. 1), 98–100. Auffallend an dieser Bezeichnung ist natürlich, dass Ignatius zwar die Gemeinde bereits als „Nachahmer Christi", sich selbst aber erst als eine Art „werdender Jünger" (1,2) bezeichnet. Im rhetorischen Konzept des Briefes ist dies natürlich z.T. der *captatio benevolentiae* zu verdanken, wie auch M. ISACSON, To Each Their Own Letter (s. Anm. 1), 35–36, schreibt. Die Diskrepanz bleibt aber auffallend.

charistie – hergestellt, gleichzeitig aber auch eine ekklesiologische Linie gelegt: Gemeinde zu sein, bedeutet, dem Vorbild Christi[9] nachzueifern, so wie dies Ignatius nun tut, der, wie er in *Eph.* 1,2 schreibt, in Rom mit wilden Tieren kämpfen wird,[10] „um dadurch ein Jünger zu sein". Was er hier in Bezug auf sich selbst sagt, wird er später allgemeiner zum Ausdruck bringen: Wahre Jüngerschaft, d.h. Christsein im Vollsinn des Wortes, erfüllt sich für Ignatius erst im Sterben in Nachahmung Christi (vgl. auch 3,1; *Röm.* 4,2; 5,3). Dass dies in den Ignatiusbriefen nicht nur am Rande eine Rolle spielt, hat natürlich mit der besonderen Situation des Schreibers zu tun, der immer wieder auf dieses Thema zurückkommt und es dabei variiert: Gerade als Blutzeuge sieht Ignatius sich bzw. seinen Geist als „Sühnopfer" (περίψημα; 8,1) bzw. „Lösegeld" (ἀντίψυχον; 18,1; 21,1; *Sm.* 10,2; *Pol.* 2,3; 6,1) für die angesprochene Gemeinde, die Durchgangspunkt für diejenigen ist, die auf ihrem Weg zur Hinrichtung zu Gott kommen (12,2). Nicht nur das Leiden Christi, sondern sein eigener Tod als Märtyrer in Nachahmung Christi rückt somit in die Nähe eines Opfers.[11] Ob damit hier bereits ein Bezug zum eucharistischen Opfer zu sehen ist, ist allerdings fraglich.

Ein sakramentaler Bezug entsteht eher in *Eph.* 18,2, wenn auch auf noch einmal etwas anderer Ebene: Ignatius spricht hier z.T. nach Paaren geordnet entscheidende Eckdaten seines Glaubens an, die hier in Zusammenhang mit der οἰκονομία θεοῦ, d.h. der „Heilsökonomie" bzw. dem „Heilsplan Gottes" (vgl. hierzu auch *Eph.* 20,1), gesetzt sind: Dabei spricht er auch

---

[9] Dieses Vorbild wird wiederum durch den Bischof an die Gemeindemitglieder vermittelt, wie sich auch in der Forderung *Eph.* 1,3 zeigt, dass die Gemeinde dem Vorbild des Bischofs Onesimus nacheifern soll. Zum Verhältnis Gemeinde – Bischof vgl. auch die Aussagen in *Eph.* 4–6.

[10] H. PAULSEN, Die Briefe des Ignatius von Antiochia und der Brief des Polykarp von Smyrna. Zweite, neubearbeitete Auflage der Auslegung von Walter Bauer, HNT 18, Tübingen 1985, 26, schreibt hierzu: „Daß die Verurteilten nach Rom transportiert wurden, ist nicht außerordentlich (vgl. die Bestimmungen des Corpus iuris Dog. 48,19,31). Ignatius wurde dabei als ein rechtskräftig Verurteilter (also wohl kaum aufgrund einer Appellation!) nach Rom gebracht." Vgl. hier auch eine Liste mit anderen antik-christlichen Hinweisen auf den Tierkampf.

[11] Vgl. auch die Differenzierungen in der von Ignatius verwendeten Opfersprache: C. BUTTERWECK, ‚Martyriumssucht' in der Alten Kirche? Studien zur Darstellung und Deutung frühchristlicher Martyrien, BHT 87, Tübingen 1995, 29–30, etwa verweist in diesem Zusammenhang auf die Unterschiede zwischen der *peripsema* bzw. *antipsychon*-Terminologie und der nur im Römerbrief begegnenden Rede von der θυσία θεοῦ. Sie schreibt (30): „Ignatius will sein Martyrium als Zeugnis für die Wahrheit des Menschseins, des Leidens und Sterbens Christi den Bischöfen und Gemeinden zur Verfügung stellen, damit sie – von der Verfolgung verschont und nicht in dieser Weise zum Bekenntnis genötigt – im Kampf gegen die Gnostiker darauf verweisen können." Vgl. auch die Gedanken bei A. BRENT, Ignatius (s. Anm. 1), 45–49.

davon, dass Jesus, hier als „unser Gott" und „Christus" bezeichnet, geboren wurde und getauft, damit er *durch Leid* das Wasser reinige (ἐγεννήθη καὶ ἐβαπτίσθη, ἵνα τῷ πάθει τὸ ὕδωρ καθαρίσῃ). Die Rede von der Reinigung des Wassers ist sicherlich traditionell und dürfte tauftheologische Hintergründe haben;[12] Ignatius aber bindet die tauftheologische Aussage durch den Zusatz τῷ πάθει an seine Theologie des Leidens Christi an (vgl. hierzu schon Mk 10,38f.; Lk 12,50). Die reinigende Kraft der Taufe ist somit durch das heilbringende Leiden Christi erst ermöglicht. Die später entstehende Vorstellung, das Martyrium sei als eine Art von „zweiter Taufe" bzw. Bluttaufe zu verstehen,[13] ist in diesem Denken, das einerseits wahre Jüngerschaft an Leidensnachfolge[14] bindet, andererseits die Kraft der Taufe im Leiden Christi begründet sieht, so bereits *in nuce* vorbereitet.

Weitere Verbindungslinien finden sich auch in anderen Passagen des Textes: So wird das Thema des Leidens Christi auch in *Eph.* 7,2 angesprochen, einem Text, der den Eindruck macht, er sei aus den Bestandteilen eines traditionellen Glaubensbekenntnisses, vielleicht eines Christushymnus,[15] zusammengestellt, in dem Geburt, Tod und Auferstehung Christi miteinander in Verbindung gebracht werden.[16] Christus wird hier als einzi-

[12] Vgl. auch H. PAULSEN, Die Briefe des Ignatius (s. Anm. 10), 42, oder W. UEBELE, Viele Verführer (s. Anm. 1), 49. Eine Vielzahl erhellender altkirchlicher Parallelen bietet W.R. SCHOEDEL, Die Briefe des Ignatius (s. Anm. 6), 156–157.

[13] Vgl. hierzu auch T. NICKLAS, Gebete in frühchristlichen Märtyrerakten, in: H. KLEIN/V. MIHOC/K.-W. NIEBUHR (Hg.), Gebet im Neuen Testament. Sambata Konferenz, WUNT, Tübingen 2009 [im Druck].

[14] In diesem Zusammenhang zu erwähnen ist allerdings, dass Leidensnachfolge für Ignatius nicht nur (oder in erster Linie) das Martyrium bedeutet, sondern die „Vielzahl leidvoller Momente" wie C. BUTTERWECK, Martyriumssucht (s. Anm. 11), 31, betont. Vgl. weiterführend zum Thema „Nachfolge" auch D.M. REIS, Following (s. Anm. 4).

[15] Der Text wurde seit R. DEICHGRÄBER, Gotteshymnus und Christushymnus in der frühen Christenheit, StUNT 5, Göttingen 1967, 155, immer wieder als „hymnisch" bezeichnet oder mit einem „Hymnus" verglichen. W.R. SCHOEDEL, Die Briefe des Ignatius (s. Anm. 6), 118, jedoch sieht Melitos Paschahomilie als „Schlüssel zur Form dieser Stelle. Denn nichts ist charakteristischer für eine Homilie als Folgen paralleler, für rhetorische Wirkung zusammengehäufter Ausdrücke."

[16] Bereits dieser Text dürfte der Auseinandersetzung mit „doketischen" Gegnern dienen, W. UEBELE, Viele Verführer (s. Anm. 1), 57, geht noch weiter und spricht von „Vertreter[n] eines radikalen, „monophysitischen" Doketismus," während etwa M. MYLLYKOSKI, Wild Beasts (s. Anm. 2), 373, selbst zögert, von „Doketen" zu sprechen, und Parallelen zur Lehre des Cerinth erkennt. Kritisch auch M. GOULDER, Docetists (s. Anm. 2), der aufgrund der angeblich prophetischen, possessionistischen Christologie der Gegner Nähen zu ebionitischen Judenchristen ausmachen will. Wie dem auch sei: Ich verwende den Begriff „Doketismus" hier und später in dem von N. BROX, „Doketismus" – eine Problemanzeige, ZKG 95 (1984), 301–314, hier 309, zunächst vorgetragenen sehr weiten Sinne. Dieser bezeichnet zunächst als entscheidenden Aspekt für die Bezeichnung einer Christologie als „doketisch" die Auffassung, „daß Christus nur scheinbar ... Mensch war,

ger „Arzt" (ἰατρός) bezeichnet, dann folgen antithetisch aufgereihte Attribute: Dabei bildet wohl das erste Paar „fleischlich und geistlich" den Schlüssel für das Zueinander der folgenden „gezeugt und ungezeugt", „aus Maria[17] und aus Gott", stellen doch für Ignatius „Fleisch und Geist zwei Sphären oder Dimensionen dar, von denen sich die erste auf die menschliche, die zweite auf die göttliche Wirklichkeit bezieht."[18] Für unsere Fragestellung interessant sind zunächst die Antithesen ἐν σαρκὶ γενόμενος θεός und ἐν θανάτῳ ζωὴ ἀληθινή. Dem „in Fleisch" steht dabei das „im Tode" gegenüber: gerade weil Christus *im Fleisch* „göttlich" bzw. „als (ein) Gott" *geboren* ist, kommt ihm auch *im Tode* wahres (ewiges) Leben zu. Als „im Fleisch" bzw. „aus Maria" Geborener aber ist Christus zunächst *dem Leiden ausgesetzt* (παθητός), dann aber als Gott und im Tode *leidenslos* bzw. *leidensunfähig* (ἀπαθής). Als solcher aber ist Christus „Herr" und „Arzt". Während die soteriologische Linie über die Verbindung zum Begriff des „Arztes" hier nur angedeutet ist, schreibt Ignatius seine Deutung des Christusleidens hier ganz klar in die Christologie ein; diese aber verbindet hier auch strukturell sehr deutlich die Pole der Anthropologie und der Gottesvorstellung, die hier als Gegensätze ausgedrückt sind, welche in Christus gleichwohl vereint sind.

Zu den für unsere Fragestellung sicherlich wichtigsten Passagen des Briefs an die Epheser gehört Abschnitt 9, wo Ignatius in Auseinandersetzung mit seinen Gegnern erneut soteriologische und ekklesiologische Dimensionen miteinander verknüpft: Die Glieder der Gemeinde werden als „Steine für den Tempel/des Tempels des Vaters" (λίθοι ναοῦ πατρός; 9,1) bezeichnet. Damit scheinen zwei in frühchristlichen Texten immer wieder zu findende Traditionslinien miteinander verknüpft zu sein: einerseits die Vorstellung, dass die Mitglieder der Gemeinde als „Steine" bzw. „lebendige Steine" (z.B. Eph 2,20–22; 1 Petr 2,4–6) miteinander ein Gebäude bilden, andererseits die Idee eines himmlischen Tempels (Hebr 11,10; 12,22; Offb 21–22; *Hermas Vis.* 3; *Sim.* 9)[19], den sich Ignatius offensichtlich noch

---

ganz gleich wie das Zustandekommen oder Ins-Werk-setzen dieses Scheins aussah". Da es mir hier nicht darauf ankommt, die Auffassungen der verschiedenen von Ignatius bekämpften Gruppierungen genauer zu beschreiben, werde ich nicht näher auf die sich daraus ergebenden Differenzierungsmöglichkeiten („Zwei-Naturen und Zwei-Personen-Vorstellung", „strenger ‚Monophysitismus'" oder „Bild der Tarnkappe") eingehen, die BROX im selben Beitrag (309) beschreibt.

[17] Zur Bedeutung Marias bzw. der Jungfräulichkeit Marias für die Theologie des Ignatius vgl. weiterführend P. FOSTER, Epistles of Ignatius (s. Anm. 1), 100–101.

[18] W.R. SCHOEDEL, Die Briefe des Ignatius (s. Anm. 6), 117.

[19] Das hier entwickelte Bild hindert Ignatius nicht daran, wenig später von den einzelnen Glaubenden als „Tempeln Gottes" zu sprechen, in denen Gott lebe (*Eph.* 15,3). Das Bild des Tempels begegnet auch in anderen Texten des Ignatius: vgl. z.B. *Magn.* 7,2, wo es zusammen mit anderen Bildern für die Einheit der Gemeinde steht.

als im Aufbau begriffen vorstellt. Die anschließende Bilderfolge jedenfalls lebt von dieser Vorstellung: Die Steine sind „vorbereitet/zubereitet" für das Bauwerk/den Bau Gott des Vaters. Um aber dorthin zu gelangen, haben sie eine μηχανῆ, d.h. eine Maschine, eine Art „Kran", nötig, durch den sie „nach oben gehoben" (ἀναφέρω) werden.[20] Bei dieser „Hebemaschine" handelt es sich um das Kreuz. Interessanterweise ist das Bild damit aber noch nicht vollendet: Um nach oben zu gelangen, ist zudem ein Seil nötig – der heilige Geist –, aber auch der eigene Einsatz, der durch die im Folgenden noch häufig begegnende, für Ignatius enorm wichtige Dyas „Glaube" und „Liebe" beschrieben wird.[21] Erneut steht das Kreuz Christi hier also im Zentrum einer Denkkonstellation: Muss den bisherigen Verbindungslinien zusätzlich eine eschatologische Komponente zugefügt werden? Wenn das Ziel des Lebens eines Glaubenden, das von Ignatius auch als „ewiges Leben" (z.B. *Eph.* 7,2; 18,1 usw.) bezeichnet werden kann, hier als „himmlischer Tempel" vorgestellt ist, der nur über die μηχανῆ des Kreuzes erreicht werden kann, dann ist hier zumindest eine individual-, wenn nicht auch eine im Ansatz universaleschatologische Komponente zu erkennen.

Dass die Heilstat Christi am Kreuz für Ignatius tatsächlich als Teil ein kosmischen Geschehens betrachtet werden kann, zeigt sich später, wenn er Jungfräulichkeit Mariens, Geburt Christi und seinen Tod als μυστήρια κραυγῆς (19,1), d.h. als „Mysterien eines Schreies"[22], vollbracht im

[20] Die Vorstellung, dass das Kreuz zum Hinaufheben der Christen dient, findet sich auch in leichter Variation in den späteren Texten Hippolyt, *Antichr.* 59 (Bild eines Schiffs und der Leiter zur Rahe hinauf), oder Methodius, *Porph.* 1,7–10 (Verwendung der Idee vom Hebekran). Hierzu auch H. PAULSEN, Die Briefe des Ignatius (s. Anm. 10), 35, und W.R. SCHOEDEL, Die Briefe des Ignatius (s. Anm. 6), 126. Man könnte in diesem Zusammenhang auch auf gnostische Parallelen wie etwa die in den *Johannesakten* 97–102 überlieferte Szene vom Lichtkreuz verweisen, durch dessen Stamm die Lichtfunken nach oben kommen. Entscheidender Unterschied in diesem Kontext aber ist die in den *Johannesakten* enthaltene Polemik gegen das Leiden Christi am Holzkreuz.

[21] „Glaube" und „Liebe" begegnen bei Ignatius häufig nebeneinander (*Eph.* 9,1; 14,1–2; *Magn* 1,2; 13,1; *Trall* 8,1, *Röm inscr.*, *Phil.* 11,2) – er übernimmt diese Zusammenstellung wahrscheinlich aus der frühchristlichen Tradition. Zur Liebe als Komplement des Glaubens bei Ignatius von Antiochien vgl. auch P. MEINHOLD, Die Ethik des Ignatius, in: Studien zu Ignatius von Antiochien, Veröffentlichungen des Instituts für Europäische Geschichte Mainz 97, Wiesbaden 1979, 67–77, hier 70.

[22] Das Wort μυστήριον begegnet einerseits im Umfeld von Mysterienkulten, der Sprachgebrauch des Ignatius aber dürfte von Paulus beeinflusst sein (Röm 11,25; womöglich 1 Kor 2,1), dessen Begriffsverwendung ihren Hintergrund in frühjüdischen Vorstellungen findet. Dort begegnet der Begriff meist in Verbindung mit besonders qualifizierten göttlichen Geheimnissen, die gerne in Bezug zu Eschatologie und Kosmologie stehen. Wichtig daran ist die Vorstellung, dass diese Geheimnisse dem irdischen Menschen in seiner vergänglichen Welt nur mit Hilfe spezieller Offenbarungen eröffnet werden können. Ignatius geht hier noch weiter: Nicht einmal der Fürst dieser Weltzeit habe

„Schweigen Gottes“ (ἐν ἡσυχίᾳ θεοῦ)[23], bezeichnet, welche dem „Archonten dieses Äons“ verborgen geblieben seien. Erst das Aufleuchten eines Sterns von unsagbarem Licht habe diese Geheimnisse den Äonen offenbar gemacht, von da an sei alle Magie aufgelöst und jede Fessel des Bösen verschwunden (19,2–3):[24] Interessant daran ist, dass Ignatius offensichtlich Jungfräulichkeit Mariens, Geburt Christi und seinen Tod als drei auf gleicher Ebene liegende heilsgeschichtliche Ereignisse auffasst, die als „Offenbarung Gottes auf menschliche Weise“ verstanden werden können, welche die alte Herrschaft zerstört und „in die Neuheit ewigen Lebens“ (εἰς καινότητα ἀϊδίου ζωῆς) sowie zur „Auflösung des Todes“ (θανάτου κατάλυσις) geführt haben (19,3).

Der Brief an die Epheser bietet aber noch weitere für das vorliegende Thema interessante Passagen:

– *Eph.* 16,1–2 setzt Ignatius das Thema Kreuz nun, wie später in anderen Zusammenhängen noch öfter zu beobachten sein wird, in polemischem Kontext ein. Er bezeichnet seine Gegner, auf deren Lehre er zumindest hier nicht näher eingeht, als „Häuserverwüster“ (οἰκοφθόροι) und spielt damit sicherlich auf das kurz vorher erwähnte „Wohnen“ Christi (κατοικέω), der hier wieder als „Gott“ bezeichnet ist, in den Gläubigen an, die damit seine „Tempel“ sind. Diese Zerstörer werden die Basileia Gottes nicht erben (vgl. 1 Kor 6,9–10; 15,50; Eph 5,5).[25] Ihnen und ihren Anhängern prophezeit Ignatius vielmehr, dass sie „in das unauslöschliche Feuer“ (εἰς τὸ πῦρ τὸ ἄσβεστον) gehen werden, weil sie „schmutzig“ bzw. „befleckt“ sind (ῥυπαρός). Der Grund dafür ist, dass sie „den Glauben Gottes (bzw. den Glauben an Gott), für den Jesus Christus gekreuzigt worden ist, durch schlechte Lehre verwüstet (φθείρω)“ (16,2) haben. Ist damit zum Ausdruck gebracht, dass erst die Kreuzigung Christi den Glauben ermöglicht hat? Dies legen

---

die Geheimnisse erkennen können. Zur Verwendung des Begriffs bei Ignatius vgl. A. BRENT, Ignatius (s. Anm. 1), 71–94. – Zu Versuchen, die geheimnisvolle Rede von den „Mysterien eines Schreis“ zu deuten, vgl. weiterführend auch T. LECHNER, Ignatius (s. Anm. 1), 255–261.

[23] Das „Schweigen“ wird gerne als „Charakteristik der göttlichen Sphäre“ (H. PAULSEN, Die Briefe des Ignatius [s. Anm. 10], 43) aufgefasst. Damit entsteht ein Bezug zu *Eph.* 6,1, wo vom Schweigen des Bischofs die Rede ist, womit womöglich die Gottesnähe des Bischofs zum Ausdruck gebracht ist. Zu anderen Deutungen vom Schweigen des Bischofs vgl. aber auch H.A. MAIER, The Politics of the Silent Bishop: Silence and Persuasion in Ignatius of Antioch, JThS 55 (2004), 503–519.

[24] Der so genannte „Sternhymnus“ von *Eph.* 18,1–20,1 wurde wiederholt zum Gegenstand der Forschung. Zur Forschungsgeschichte vgl. z.B. T. LECHNER, Ignatius (s. Anm. 1), 246–252.

[25] Ich würde allerdings zögern, die Rede von den „Häuserverwüstern“ so sehr von 1 Kor 6,9f. her zu interpretieren, wie dies immer wieder geschah. Es muss hier keineswegs an „Ehebruch“ oder „unzüchtiges Verhalten“ gedacht werden. So aber z.B. W.R. SCHOEDEL, Die Briefe des Ignatius (s. Anm. 6), 148–149.

Parallelstellen wie *Magn.* 9,1 und *Trall.* 2,1 durchaus nahe (vgl. auch Justin, *dial.* 91; 131).[26] Die Auseinandersetzung mit den Gegnern wird in *Eph.* 17,1 fortgesetzt. Da der Text nun von der ἀφθαρσία der Kirche, hier vielleicht am ehesten als „Unverwüstlichkeit" zu verstehen, spricht, wodurch eine Kette zur Erwähnung der „Häuserverwüster" und ihrer Tätigkeit des „Verwüstens" entsteht, ist es durchaus denkbar, dass auch die geheimnisvolle Aussage aus 17,1, der Herr habe „Salbe auf sein Haupt genommen" (μύρον ἔλαβεν ἐπὶ τῆς κεφαλῆς αὐτοῦ), um der Kirche Unverwüstlichkeit „zuzuduften,"[27] sich zumindest im weitesten Sinne auf die Passion Christi bezieht.[28] Die ekklesiologische Dimension von Ignatius' Denken über das Leiden Christi wäre hier dann besonders weit ausgezeichnet: Das Leid Christi hätte dann nicht nur Einfluss auf die Christusnachfolge der einzelnen Christen, sein Bezug auf Tod und Auferstehung bzw. ewiges Leben von Gott her eröffne gleichzeitig die Unvergänglichkeit der Kirche, die weder durch Häretiker noch durch Verfolgungen gefährdet werden kann.

– Bereits kurz angesprochen wurde *Eph.* 18,1, wo Ignatius seinen Geist zunächst als „Sühnopfer des Kreuzes" (περίψημα ... σταυροῦ) bezeichnet, dann aber vom „σκάνδαλον des Kreuzes" spricht:

ἐστιν σκάνδαλον τοῖς ἀπίστουσιν, ἡμῖν δὲ σωτηρία καὶ ζωὴ αἰώνιος. ποῦ σόφος; ποῦ συζητήτης; ποῦ καύχησις τῶν λεγομένων συνετῶν;

„Es ist ein Anstoß den Ungläubigen, uns aber Heil und ewiges Leben. Wo ist ein Weiser, wo ein Disputator, wo das Rühmen derer, die man Verständige nennt?"

So sehr hier die Parallele zu 1Kor 1,19–20 (vgl. auch Röm 3,27) ins Auge fällt,[29] so sehr zeigt sich auch der Unterschied in der Argumentationsrichtung: Während Paulus das vor dem Hintergrund von Jes 29,14 LXX entwickelte Argument theologisch, d.h. in seine Rede von der Kraft Gottes, die sich in scheinbarer Schwachheit zeigt, und der Weisheit Gottes, die auf die Welt töricht wirkt, einbettet, tritt diese *theo*logische Verbindungslinie für Ignatius zurück. Ihm geht es um eine soteriologische und damit verbunden wohl (individual)eschatologische Komponente: Das Kreuz Christi, das den

[26] Zu dieser Parallele vgl. auch H. PAULSEN, Die Briefe des Ignatius (s. Anm. 10), 53.

[27] Diese schöne Übersetzung des Verbums πνέω findet sich auch bei A. LINDEMANN/H. PAULSEN, Die Apostolischen Väter, Tübingen 1992, 189. Sie erklärt sich aufgrund der Geruchsmetaphorik des Abschnitts, in dem auch vom „Gestank" der gegnerischen Lehre die Rede ist. Zu traditionsgeschichtlichem Vergleichsmaterial vgl. W.R. SCHOEDEL, Die Briefe des Ignatius (s. Anm. 6), 150–151.

[28] M. ISACSON, To Each Their Own Letter (s. Anm. 1), 66, vermutet einen Bezug zur Todes-Salbung Jesu in Betanien. W.R. SCHOEDEL, Die Briefe des Ignatius (s. Anm. 6), 151, hält Mt 26,7 für besonders nahe, verweist aber auch auf Joh 12,3 und 20,22.

[29] M. ISACSON, To Each Their Own Letter (s. Anm. 1), 68 n. 96, erkennt im Kontext weitere, wenn auch vagere Anspielungen auf 1 Kor 1, so dass sich der gesamte Abschnitt ab *Eph.* 17 auf 1 Kor 1 beziehe.

Unglaubenden „Skandal" ist, wird den Glaubenden zu Heil und ewigem Leben. Die veränderte Stoßrichtung ist verständlich, denn als Christus Nachfolgender, der nun seinen Tod in *imitatio Christi* zu erwarten hat, ist für Ignatius natürlich vor allem die auch ihm Heil bringende paradoxe Konsequenz des Kreuzestodes – „ewiges Leben" – bedeutsam.[30]

Mit der Durchsicht des Epheserbriefs sind bereits wichtige Grundlinien einer Kreuzes- und Leidenstheologie des Ignatius angezeigt, andere Briefe aber bestätigen nicht nur das Bisherige, sondern bieten durchaus noch weitere Aspekte. Dies allerdings geschieht mit unterschiedlicher Schwerpunktsetzung und Gewichtigkeit:

2. Der Brief an die Magnesier

Im Vergleich zum Brief an die Epheser treten im Brief an die Gemeinde von Magnesia (*Magn.*) die Aussagen über Passion und Kreuz Christi etwas zurück, Ignatius geht es hier vor allem um die Einheit der Gemeinde zunächst mit Gott und Christus, dann aber auch mit dem Bischof.[31] Auch hier warnt Ignatius vor Irrlehrern, hier vor der Gefahr des „Judaisierens" von Christen (*Magn.* 8–9),[32] demgegenüber er scharf die Trennlinie zwischen „Judentum" (Ἰουδαϊσμός) und „Christentum" (Χριστιανισμός) hervorhebt (*Magn.* 10,3). Was ist mit der Aussage gemeint, dass, wer weiter dem Judentum entsprechend lebt, bekenne, „die Gnade nicht empfangen zu haben" (χάριν μὴ εἰληφέναι; 8,1)? Das Thema „Gnade" spielt bei Ignatius ja nur am Rande eine Rolle, zumindest einmal (*Sm.* 6,1) aber zeigt sich, dass auch sie vom Kreuz Christi her verstanden werden kann. Eine sichere Antwort auf die Frage scheint mir hier aber nicht möglich.

Ignatius betont weiter, dass er Vorsorge dafür treffen wolle, dass die Gemeinde nicht „an die Angelhaken des Irrtums" (εἰς τὰ ἄγκιστρα τῆς κε-

---

[30] Dies passt auch sehr gut zu den in *Eph.* 19,2–3 geäußerten Gedanken über das Heil.

[31] So auch M. ISACSON, To Each Their Own Letter (s. Anm. 1), 100. Zur Herleitung und Bedeutung der kirchlichen Einheit bei Ignatius vgl. z.B. H. PAULSEN, Studien zur Theologie des Ignatius von Antiochien, Forschungen zur Kirchen- und Dogmengeschichte 29, Göttingen 1978, 132–144.

[32] W. UEBELE, Viele Verführer (s. Anm. 1), 59, spricht im Zusammenhang mit den Irrlehrern in Magnesia von einer „Verschmelzung von Gnosis (bzw. Doketismus) und ‚Judaismus'" (59); M. MYLLYKOSKI, Wild Beasts (s. Anm. 2), 373, erkennt Parallelen zu dem jüdisch-christlichen Modell der *Anabathmoi Jakobou* (ps-Clem. Rec. 1,27–71), „that attributes to the prophets and priests a salvation-historical function that would threaten to relativize the Ignatian gospel."

νοδοξίας)[33] gerät, sondern weiterhin fest an Geburt, Leiden und Auferstehung Christi glaubt (*Magn.* 11). Diese Trias erinnert an die in *Eph.* 19,1 erwähnten drei Geheimnisse (vgl. auch *Trall.* 9; *Phil.* 9,2; *Sm.* 1).[34] Interessanterweise fehlt hier nun aber die Jungfräulichkeit Mariens und wird demgegenüber die ἀνάστασις erwähnt. Letztere – und überraschenderweise nicht das Leiden – wird zudem konkret in die Zeit der Amtsverwaltung des Pontius Pilatus verankert (*Magn.* 11; vgl. auch *Trall.* 9,1; *Sm.* 1,2): Leid und Auferstehung Christi, „wahrhaftig und gewiss vollbracht durch Jesus Christus" (πραχθέντα ἀληθῶς καὶ βεβαίως ὑπὸ Ἰησοῦ Χριστοῦ), bilden somit ein historisch greifbares Fundament des Glaubens, an dem die Gemeinde festhalten soll, um gerettet zu werden.

Der Hintergrund der Tatsache, dass Ignatius hier so sehr die Auferstehung Christi betont, zeigt sich im vorausgehenden Kontext: Gegen die judaisierenden Gegner betont er, dass es nun nicht mehr angebracht sei, den Sabbat zu halten (σαββατίζειν), sondern dass nun dem Herrentag entsprechend gelebt werden müsse (*Magn.* 9,1), da an diesem Tage mit der Auferstehung Christi auch das Leben der Christen – „durch ihn und seinen Tod" (δι' αὐτοῦ καὶ τοῦ θανάτου αὐτοῦ) – aufgegangen sei.[35] Dieses von einigen bestrittene „Mysterium"[36] bilde die Grundlage des Glaubens, seinetwillen hielten die Christen stand, um Jünger Christi zu werden. Deutlicher als in *Eph.* 16,2 ist hier ausgesprochen, dass für Ignatius der Tod Christi offensichtlich Glauben ermöglicht und damit zum Ausgangspunkt auch des Lebens der Glaubenden wird.

Das Ignatius ja immer wieder umtreibende, hier nur angedeutete Thema des Standhaltens auch der Christen auf das Vorbild Christi hin wird an anderer Stelle, in einer Allegorie auf Münzen und ihre Prägung, ausführlicher angesprochen. *Magn.* 5,1 spricht vom Ziel aller menschlichen Taten bzw. den beiden Zukunftsmöglichkeiten – ein jeder gehe nämlich an „seinen Ort". Dieser Gedanke wird durch eine Art von Gleichnis weitergeführt:[37]

---

[33] Vgl. zur Übersetzung auch H. PAULSEN, Die Briefe des Ignatius (s. Anm. 10), 55: „κενοδοξία ist hier nicht wie Phld 1,1 ... die Sucht nach eitlem Ruhm, sondern, wie Weish 14,14, der törichte Wahn, der Irrtum."

[34] Zur Verbindung der Heilsdaten Geburt, Leiden und Auferstehung vgl. auch *Kerygma Petri* frg. 4 bei Clemens Alex. *Strom.* 6,15,128.

[35] Die Tatsache, dass Ignatius hier solchen Wert auf den Sonntag legt, lässt mich an der These von W. UEBELE, Viele Verführer (s. Anm. 1), 66, zweifeln, dass der Vorwurf des „Judaismus" nichts mit der Befolgung jüdischer Bräuche, sondern alleine mit der Art der Gegner, die Schrift auszulegen, zu tun habe. – Zum Sonntag als dem Tag, in dem bereits in der frühen Kirche Gottesdienst gefeiert wurde, vgl. z.B. 1 Kor 16,1–3; Apg 20,7–12; Offb 1,10; *Barn.* 15,9; Justin, *dial.* 138.

[36] Zum Begriff des μυστήριον vgl. oben Anm. 22.

[37] Übersetzung angelehnt an A. LINDEMANN/H. PAULSEN, Die Apostolischen Väter (s. Anm. 27), 193–195. – Die Verwendung eines aus dem Münzwesens stammenden Bildes mag traditionsgeschichtlich zunächst einmal vage an Jesu Antwort auf die Frage nach der

Magn. 5,2:

ὥσπερ γάρ ἐστιν νομίσματα δύο, ὃ μὲν θεοῦ, ὃ δὲ κόσμου, καὶ ἕκαστον αὐτῶν ἴδιον χαρακτῆρα ἐπικείμενον ἔχει, οἱ ἄπιστοι τοῦ κόσμου τούτου, οἱ δὲ πιστοὶ ἐν ἀγάπῃ χαρακτῆρα θεοῦ πατρὸς διὰ Ἰησοῦ Χριστοῦ, δι' οὗ ἐὰν μὴ αὐθαιρέτως ἔχομεν τὸ ἀποθανεῖν εἰς τὸ αὐτοῦ πάθος, τὸ ζῆν αὐτοῦ οὐκ ἔστιν ἐν ἡμῖν.

„So wie es nämlich zwei Münzen gibt, die Gottes und die der Welt, und eine jede von ihnen ihre Prägung trägt, die Ungläubigen die dieser Welt, die Gläubigen aber in Liebe die Prägung Gottes des Vaters durch Jesus Christus, durch den, wenn wir nicht freiwillig das Sterben auf sein Leiden hin haben, sein Leben nicht in uns ist."

Das Gleichnis zeugt von einem klaren Dualismus zwischen der Zugehörigkeit zur Welt, der die Ungläubigen zuzuordnen sind, und der Zugehörigkeit zu Gott der Glaubenden. Wichtig dabei ist der abschließende Konditionalsatz: Das entscheidende Kriterium, wer als Glaubender bzw. wer als Ungläubiger einzuordnen ist, besteht darin, dass der Glaubende „freiwillig das Sterben auf sein Leiden hin hat". Zugehörigkeit zu Gott entscheidet sich also in der eigenen Position dem Leiden Christi gegenüber, ja im Grunde in der eigenen Bereitschaft dem Leiden Christi auch durch den Tod nachzufolgen.[38]

Wie sehr Ekklesiologie für Ignatius mit zumindest der Bereitschaft zur Leidensnachfolge Christi zu tun hat, aus der heraus dann erst ewiges Leben möglich wird, zeigt sich nun auch in der Polemik gegen Judentum und Judaisierer. Ganz offensichtlich sieht Ignatius bereits die Propheten Israels als vom Judentum getrennt an: Für ihn gehören sie zur Kirche, denn auch sie hätten nicht dem Judentum entsprechend, sondern gemäß Christi Jesu

---

kaiserlichen Steuer (Mk 12,13–17 par.) erinnern, wo die Prägung einer Münze ebenfalls über ihre Zugehörigkeit entscheidet; weniger überzeugend erscheint mir dagegen die von H. PAULSEN, Die Briefe des Ignatius (s. Anm. 10), 50, und W.R. SCHOEDEL, Die Briefe des Ignatius (s. Anm. 6), 193, angeführte Parallele des Agraphons „Werdet kundige Geldwechsler" – der Bezug besteht im Grunde nur aus der Verwendung gemeinsamer Bildwelten. J.-P. LOTZ, Ignatius and Concord: The Background and Use of the Language of Concord in the Letters of Ignatius of Antioch, Patristic Studies 8, New York et al. 2007, 60–63, dagegen deutet das Gleichnis vor dem Hintergrund der Prägung von Münzen mit dem Bild der Göttin Ὁμόνοια, um die immer gefährdete, z.T. nach Konflikten neu gewonnene Eintracht zwischen rivalisierenden Städten Kleinasiens zum Ausdruck zu bringen. Mit der Verwendung des Bildes habe Ignatius in seinem eigenen Ringen um die Einheit der Gemeinden an die Probleme der fortwährenden Rivalitäten zwischen den Städten Asiens erinnern wollen, eine Nuance, die im Kontext sicherlich eine Rolle gespielt haben mag, m.E. der Deutung des Textes aber nichts entscheidend Neues hinzuzufügen vermag.

[38] Vgl. ähnlich W.R. SCHOEDEL, Die Briefe des Ignatius (s. Anm. 6), 193: „Folglich wird ein Christ durch die Bereitschaft zu leiden, wie der Herr litt ..., geprägt; demütige Unterwerfung unter den Bischof wird offensichtlich als Folgeerscheinung dieser Bereitschaft angesehen."

(κατὰ Χριστὸν Ἰησοῦν) gelebt (*Magn.* 8,2).[39] Dadurch aber gilt für sie die gleiche Logik wie für die Glaubenden seiner Zeit: Bereits sie seien im Grunde in einer Form der Christusnachfolge *vor* Christus verfolgt (*Magn.* 8,2; vgl. Mt 5,12; 23,29–32; Mk 12,1–9; Lk 11,47–51; Irenäus, *haer.* 4,33,9), dann aber schließlich auch von den Toten auferweckt worden (*Magn.* 9,2).

3. Der Brief an die Traller

Eine ganz zentrale Rolle spielt das Thema Kreuz und wahrhaftiges Leiden Christi wieder im Brief an die Traller (*Trall.*), wo es erneut (s.a. *Eph.*) bereits im Präskript auftaucht. Mit der Aussage, die Traller hätten Frieden im bzw. durch das Leiden Christi, bereitet Ignatius hier bereits die späteren Ermahnungen vor, auf keinen Fall den Gegnern, hier zumindest in einem weiten Sinne wohl „Doketen,“[40] zu folgen.

Trall. 2–3 entwirft die Vorstellung einer bereits klar hierarchisch aufgebauten, gleichzeitig auf Christus und sein Leiden hin zentrierten Kirche:[41] Von der Gemeinde wird Unterordnung unter den Bischof wie unter Christus verlangt (*Trall.* 2,1), was an das in *Magn.* 3,2 entwickelte Bild vom sichtbaren und dem unsichtbaren Bischof, d.h. Christus, erinnert. Ist es gerade die Leidensnachfolge des Bischofs, die ihn Christus so nahe werden lässt? Dies ist zumindest hier nicht ausgesagt (vgl. aber *Trall.* 4,2). Eher möchte man meinen, dass dem Bischof die Aufgabe zukommt, die Gemeinde dahingehend zu leiten, dass sie nicht in die Irre geführt wird, sondern am Glauben an Christus, „der um unseretwillen gestorben ist“ (δι' ἡμᾶς ἀποθανόντα; 2,1), festhält und dadurch, d.h. „glaubend an seinen Tod dem Sterben entflieht“ (ἵνα πιστεύσαντες εἰς τὸν θάνατον αὐτοῦ τὸ ἀποθανεῖν ἐκφύγετε). Damit ist nicht nur der Gedanke des Präskripts wieder aufgegriffen, dass die Gemeinde von Tralles „Frieden hat im Fleisch und

[39] Das sich daraus ergebende Verhältnis des Ignatius zu den Schriften und Traditionen Israels scheint mir vor diesem Hintergrund als nicht unproblematisch: Einerseits lehnt er ganz offensichtlich das „Judentum“ ab, andererseits versucht er zumindest Teile der Traditionen Israels für das Christentum zu retten. Dies geschieht hier, indem er die Propheten Israel entgegenstellt.

[40] Zum Begriff „Doketismus“ s. Anm. 16. W. UEBELE, Viele Verführer (s. Anm. 1), 74, hält auch in diesem Falle eine „ ‚monophysitische‘ Spielart der Gnosis“ für wahrscheinlich; vgl. aber z.B. die Einwände von M. MYLLYKOSKI, Wild Beasts (s. Anm. 2), 373.

[41] Grundlegend zu kirchlichen Ämtern und Theologie der Kirche bei Ignatius siehe auch C. MUNIER, Question d'Ignace d'Antioche (s. Anm. 2), 413–424. 440–448 [Forschungsgeschichte], sowie zur Ekklesiologie H. PAULSEN, Studien zur Theologie (s. Anm. 31), 145–157.

Geist durch das Leiden Jesu Christi, unserer Hoffnung auf die Auferstehung in ihn," diese Logik fügt sich m.E. auch gut in den Rest des Schreibens: Ignatius sieht die Gemeinde ja offenbar in besonderer Weise von Irrlehrern bedroht, die behaupten, dass Christus nur zum Schein gelitten habe (*Trall.* 10). Deren Wirken sieht er als so bedrohlich, dass er es als „hinterhältige Anschläge des Teufels" (*Trall.* 8,1; vgl. auch *Phil.* 6,2) bezeichnen kann: Auch in ihrem Widerstand gegen Irrlehrer stehen die Christen also in einer Auseinandersetzung von kosmischer Bedeutung. Gerade in diesem Kontext stößt Ignatius zu einer wahrlich kühnen Identifikation durch: „Glaube" ist σάρξ τοῦ κυρίου, Liebe αἷμα Ἰησοῦ Χριστοῦ (*Trall.* 8,1). Schärfer könnte der unüberwindliche und keinen Kompromiss duldende Gegensatz zu den Gegnern nicht zum Ausdruck gebracht werden als durch diese Identifikation zweier bei Ignatius immer wieder begegnender Grunddimensionen des Christseins mit Aussagen, die unmittelbar mit dem menschlichen Leiden Christi zusammenhängen.[42]

Das Thema beschäftigt ihn weiter: Etwas später (*Trall.* 9,1) scheint Ignatius ein Traditionsstück zu zitieren oder zumindest zu verarbeiten. Dabei stellt er heraus, dass Christus aus dem Geschlecht Davids sowie aus Maria stamme, vor allem aber, dass er „*wahrhaftig* geboren wurde, aß und trank, *wahrhaftig* verfolgt wurde unter Pontius Pilatus, *wahrhaftig* gekreuzigt wurde und starb, während die Himmlischen und die Irdischen und die Unterirdischen zusahen, er auch *wahrhaftig* auferweckt wurde von den Toten, als ihn sein Vater auferweckte, er auch dem Gleichnis entsprechend uns, die ihm Glaubenden so auferwecken wird – sein Vater in Christus Jesus, ohne den wir das *wahre* Leben nicht haben" (*Trall.* 9,1-2).[43] Vier Mal also wird mit dem Adverb ἀληθῶς betont, dass die genannten Geschehnisse des menschlichen Lebens Christi, die gleichzeitig die Glaubensgrundlage der Traller bilden, „wahrhaftig" geschehen seien. Gegen die Gegner hebt Ignatius hervor, dass Glauben an Christus und damit an die Heilsereignisse seines *menschlichen* Lebens, das in die Auferweckung durch den Vater führte, die einzige Möglichkeit bedeutet, ebenso auferweckt werden zu können. Ohne den wahrhaft lebenden Christus kann für Ignatius auch der Glaubende nicht wahres Leben erlangen. Kreuz und Leiden sind in diesem Abschnitt zwar nur einer von mehreren Gedanken einer Reihe, die auf die Möglichkeit des Glaubenden, ewiges Leben zu erlangen, hinführt. Zwar kann keines der Glieder dieser Kette herausgebrochen werden, allerdings werden Kreuzestod und Auferweckung breiter als die anderen Aussagen ausgeführt und erfahren damit eine besondere Betonung. Zudem zeigt sich

---

[42] Ob zudem ein Bezug zur Eucharistie hergestellt werden soll, ist fraglich, wie auch W.R. SCHOEDEL, Die Briefe des Ignatius (s. Anm. 6), 247, herausarbeitet.

[43] Übersetzung angelehnt an A. LINDEMANN/H. PAULSEN, Die Apostolischen Väter (s. Anm. 27), 205.

der Schwerpunkt auf den Aussagen zum Leiden Christi sicherlich auch daran, dass direkt im Anschluss an *Trall.* 9 gerade dieses Element aus der Reihe hervorgehoben wird. Während die als gottlos und ungläubig bezeichneten Gegner[44] behaupten, Christus habe nur zum Schein gelitten (*Trall.* 10), führt Ignatius womöglich in Anknüpfung an 1Kor 15,32 das Beispiel seines eigenen Schicksals an.[45] Er argumentiert so von den Konsequenzen des Denkens der Gegner her. Sein Leiden als Gefangener und kommender Blutzeuge wäre dann tatsächlich ein grundloses Sterben, da dieser Tod weder echte Christusnachfolge sein, noch den Bischof als einen wahren Jünger Christi erweisen könnte. Damit ist natürlich nicht das Argument der Gegner in seinem Fundament getroffen[46] – es zeigt sich aber auch aus negativer Sicht, wie sehr Kreuz und Leiden Christi nicht nur für die Christologie und Soteriologie, sondern auch für das Kirchenverständnis und natürlich konkret vor allem auch für das Selbstverständnis des Ignatius als baldiger Märtyrer von tragender Bedeutung sind.

Die Bedeutung des Kreuzes für das Kirchenbild des Ignatius wird direkt im Anschluss (*Trall.* 11) noch einmal mit einem eindrucksvollen Bild vertieft: Die Gegner erscheinen als „schlechte Seitentriebe," deren Früchte todbringend (θανατηφόρον) sind (11,1).[47] Damit ist im Grunde der bereits in *Trall.* 9 zum Ausdruck gebrachte Gedanke umformuliert: Glauben im Sinne des Ignatius führt zu ewigem Leben, den Gegnern nachzufolgen, aber in den Tod. Dem Bild der schlechten Seitentriebe wird sogleich ein Gegenbild entgegengestellt: Die wahren Jünger sind κλάδοι τοῦ σταυροῦ, „Zweige des Kreuzes" also, das hier im verwendeten Bild hier offensichtlich die Rolle des Baums einnimmt, ihre Frucht dagegen ist „unvergänglich" (ἄφθαρτος): Dies erinnert natürlich an das johanneische Bild vom Weinstock und seinen Reben (Joh 15), das Bild des Weinstocks ist dabei aber durch das Kreuz ersetzt,[48] möglicherweise aber liegt hier auch bereits die Idee vor, dass das Kreuz mit dem Baum des Lebens im Paradies zu

---

44 Mit diesen Bezeichnungen stellt Ignatius die Gegner natürlich bereits als außerhalb der Kirchengemeinschaft stehend dar – Kompromisse mit einem derartigen Denken sind für ihn, wie oben angedeutet, nicht möglich.

45 Die Frage nach einer möglichen literarischen Abhängigkeit des Textes von 1 Kor 15,32 wird kontrovers behandelt.

46 Dass Ignatius aber offensichtlich die sich aus dem doketischen Denken der Gegner ergebende Konsequenz richtig erkannt hat, zeigt sich auch bei einem Blick auf Irenäus, *haer.* 3,18,5.

47 Auf dieser Linie liegen auch die Bezeichnungen der Gegner als „Teufelsgewächs" (*Eph.* 10,3) und schlechte Gewächse (*Phil.* 3,1) bzw. die Darstellung der gegnerischen Lehre als „fremdartiges Gewächs" (*Trall.* 6,1). Hierzu weiterführend auch W. UEBELE, Viele Verführer (s. Anm. 1), 28–29. – Zum Wort θανατηφόρον allgemein vgl. weiterführend die Beispiele bei W.R. SCHOEDEL, Die Briefe des Ignatius (s. Anm. 6), 258.

48 So auch M. WALTER, Gemeinde als Leib Christi. Untersuchungen zum Corpus Paulinum und zu den ‚Apostolischen Vätern', NTOA 49, Freiburg, CH/Göttingen 2001, 268.

identifizieren sei, wie sich dies bereits in Offb 2,7 und 22,1–2 andeutet (vgl. auch *Barn.* 11,6–8; Justin, *dial.* 86,1–8).[49] Wie auch immer: Im Verhältnis zum Kreuz entscheidet sich für Ignatius Jüngerschaft; nur wer seinen Glauben an der Wahrhaftigkeit des heilsbringenden Kreuzestodes Christi ausrichtet und von ihm her bestimmt, kann unvergängliche Frucht bringen. Doch das Bild geht weiter – und greift nun ganz offensichtlich paulinische bzw. deuteropaulinische Vorstellungen (1Kor 12,12–27; Eph 1,22–23; 4,12.15–16.25; Kol 1,18a.24; 2,19; 3.15) von der Kirche als dem Leib Christi auf (vgl. sonst nur *Sm.* 1,2):[50]

Δι᾽ οὗ ἐν τῷ πάθει αὐτοῦ προσκαλεῖται ὑμᾶς ὄντας μέλη αὐτοῦ. οὐ δύναται οὖν κεφαλὴ χωρὶς γεννηθῆναι ἄνευ μελῶν, τοῦ θεοῦ ἕνωσιν ἐπαγγελλομένου, ὅ ἐστιν αὐτός.

Durch es (i.e. das Kreuz) beruft er euch in seinem Leiden, die ihr seine Glieder seid. Nicht kann das Haupt ohne Glieder von Neuem geboren werden, während Gott Einheit verspricht, was er selbst ist.

Christus wird in diesem Bild ähnlich dem Kolosser- oder Epheserbrief als Haupt des Leibes der Kirche gesehen, gleichzeitig ist er ihr einheitsstiftendes Prinzip, dessen „neue Geburt" auch für ihre Glieder neue Geburt verheißt: Im Vergleich zu den genannten deuteropaulinischen Texten aber verschiebt sich das Bild noch einmal deutlich: Wo Kol und Eph den entscheidenden Wert auf die kosmische Bedeutung Christi und der mit ihm verbundenen Kirche legen, setzt Ignatius zwei Bilder nebeneinander, wodurch ein Zueinander entsteht, das bei zu genauem Hinsehen widersprüchlich erscheint. Die Glaubenden werden verstanden als „Zweige des Kreuzes" einerseits, dann aber werden sie als seine Glieder zu Christus gerufen, der wiederum als ihr Haupt zu gelten hat. Ich denke nicht, dass der Text nun möchte, dass diese beiden Bilder zu eng ineinander verflochten werden – viel mehr kommt es auf das beiden gemeinsame Element des Bezugs zum Kreuz an: Gerade in der Auseinandersetzung mit den Leugnern des Leidens Christi setzt Ignatius den Akzent darauf, dass es der *gekreuzigte* Christus sei, der die an ihn Glaubenden zu sich ruft und der als Haupt der Kirche zu verstehen ist, deren Gläubige sich (auch) als Zweige des Kreuzesstammes begreifen dürfen.

---

[49] Vgl. hierzu auch A. BRENT, Ignatius and Polycarp: The Transformation of New Testament Traditions in the Context of Mystery Cults, in: A. GREGORY/C.M. TUCKETT (Hg.), Trajectories through the New Testament and the Apostolic Fathers, Oxford et al. 2005, 325–349, hier 326–327.

[50] Weiterführend hierzu v.a. M. WALTER, Gemeinde als Leib Christi (s. Anm. 48).

4. Der Brief an die Römer

Im Brief an die Römer (*Röm.*) verschieben sich die Akzente erneut: Im Zentrum steht der bereits im Brief an die Gemeinde von Ephesus betonte Gedanke, dass erst das Martyrium Ignatius zum wahren Jünger Christi werden lasse. Die Betonung dieses Gedankens wie auch die hier immer wieder zum Ausdruck gebrachte Martyriumssehnsucht des Ignatius hängt womöglich mit der Angst des Bischofs zusammen, dass die Gemeinde von Rom sein Martyrium in letzter Minute noch verhindern könnte (vgl. *Röm.* 1,2; 2,1; 4,1; 7,2).[51] An späterer Stelle kann er diese Gefahr gar als Versuch der Verführung durch den „Archonten dieses Äons" (*Röm.* 7,1) bezeichnen.

So stellt er in immer neuen Variationen die Bedeutung seines Märtyrertodes für seine wahre Jüngerschaft (*Röm.* 3,2; 4,2–3; 5,1.3), ja für sein wahres Menschsein (6,2) heraus. Er kann den Tod als Märtyrer mit einer Neugeburt vergleichen (6,2), will sich von der Materie, die ihn an die Welt und die widergöttlichen Mächte bindet, lösen[52] und „reines Licht" (6,2) erlangen bzw. fühlt bereits „lebendiges Wasser" (7,2; vgl. Joh 4,7–15; 6,35; 7,37–38; Offb 7,17; 21,6; 22,2.17) in sich wirken.

Immer wieder scheint er seinen zu erwartenden Tod selbst in die Nähe eines Sakraments zu rücken, indem er sich als „Weizen Gottes" (σῖτος θεοῦ), „Brot des Christus" (ἄρτος τοῦ Χριστοῦ) oder „Opfer für Gott" (θεοῦ θυσία) bezeichnet (*Röm.* 4,1–2; vgl. auch 2,2).[53] Dies ist ihm ganz offensichtlich deswegen möglich, weil er auch die Eucharistie ganz klar aus einem Zusammenhang mit dem Sterben Christi heraus versteht. So schreibt er in *Röm.* 7,3:

---

[51] Weiterführende Spekulationen zu den konkreten juristischen wie auch sonstigen Möglichkeiten möglicherweise einflussreicher Mitglieder der christlichen Gemeinde Roms sind aber kaum angebracht. Belege zu Versuchen christlicher Gemeinden, gefangene Glaubensbrüder frei zu bekommen, bietet H. PAULSEN, Die Briefe des Ignatius (s. Anm. 10), 70: Lucian, *de morte Peregrini* 112; Eusebius von Caesarea, *h.e.* 6,40; Apostolische Konstitutionen 4,9; 5,1,2; *syrDid* 18; Cyprian, *ep.* 62,4.

[52] P. MEINHOLD, Episkope – Pneumatiker – Märtyrer. Zur Deutung der Selbstaussagen des Ignatius von Antiochien, in: Studien zu Ignatius von Antiochien, Veröffentlichungen des Instituts für Europäische Geschichte Mainz 97, Wiesbaden 1979, 1–19, hier 14–15, spricht daher von einem dualistischen Weltbild des Ignatius, das ihn mit gnostischem Denken verbinde, ohne ihn deswegen zum Gnostiker zu machen.

[53] Kritisch allerdings W.R. SCHOEDEL, Die Briefe des Ignatius (s. Anm. 6), 282, der davon ausgeht, Ignatius habe das Bild „wohl eher aus dem Bereich des Brotbackens, um die Verwandlung auszudrücken, der er als Ergebnis des Martyriums entgegenblickte," entnommen. Dies ist durchaus denkbar, trotzdem lässt sich bei der Lektüre die Assoziation dieser Bilder mit der Eucharistie nicht völlig ausblenden.

Ἄρτον θεοῦ θέλω, ὅ ἐστιν σὰρξ Ἰησοῦ Χριστοῦ, τοῦ ἐκ σπέρματος Δαυιδ, καὶ πόμα θέλω τὸ αἷμα αὐτοῦ, ὅ ἐστιν ἀγάπη ἄφθαρτος.

„Brot Gottes will ich, das ist Fleisch Jesu Christi, der aus dem Samen Davids ist, und zum Trank will ich sein Blut, das ist unvergängliche Liebe."

Mit der Rede vom „Brot Gottes" (vgl. schon *Eph.* 5,2) wie auch dem „Fleisch und Blut Jesu Christi" ist hier natürlich an Abendmahlsterminologie angeknüpft. Das Zueinander von „Brot" und „Unvergänglichkeit" erinnert an Aspekte der Brotrede Jesu im Johannesevangelium (vgl. z.B. Joh 6,27.33.35), ohne auf literarische Abhängigkeiten schließen zu lassen. Fleisch und Blut Christi in der Eucharistie zu empfangen bedeutet für Ignatius Zugang zur „unvergänglichen Liebe"[54] Gottes, welche wiederum erst ewiges Leben ermöglicht.

Das letztlich eschatologische Ziel der eigenen Christusnachfolge über „Feuer, Kreuz, Kämpfe mit wilden Tieren etc." (*Röm.* 5,3) formuliert er so: μόνον ἵνα Ἰησοῦ Χριστοῦ ἐπιτύχω.[55] Das Verbum ἐπιτυγχάνω lässt hier verschiedene Deutungen zu – ich würde so weit gehen, den Satz mit „alleine, damit ich Jesu Christi teilhaftig werde"[56] zu übersetzen. Er will εἰς Ἰησοῦν Χριστόν sterben, also wörtlich „in Jesus Christus hinein", Christus, den er im unmittelbaren Kontext als „für uns Gestorbenen" (ὑπὲρ ἡμῶν ἀποθανόντα) und „um unseretwillen Auferstandenen" (δι' ἡμᾶς ἀναστάντα) bezeichnet. So bittet Ignatius darum, die Gemeinde möge ihm gewähren, „Nachahmer des Leidens meines Gottes zu sein" (μιμητὴν εἶναι τοῦ πάθους τοῦ θεοῦ μου; 6,3; vgl. *Eph.* 1,1)[57], was für jeden verständlich sei, der Christus tatsächlich in sich habe. So kann Ignatius hier gar so weit gehen, davon zu schreiben, dass er sich in Liebe nach dem Sterben sehne

---

[54] Mit der ἀγάπη dürfte auch hier wieder der bei Ignatius regelmäßig begegnende Zentralbegriff der „Liebe" angesprochen und nicht ein Terminus Technicus im Sinne eines „Liebesmahls" verwendet sein, wie auch H. PAULSEN, Die Briefe des Ignatius (s. Anm. 10), 77, betont.

[55] Zu dieser Formulierung bzw. dem θεοῦ ἐπιτυγχάνειν als Kernaussage ignatianischer Eschatologie vgl. H. LOHMANN, Drohung und Verheißung: Exegetische Untersuchungen zur Eschatologie bei den Apostolischen Vätern, BZNW 55, Berlin/New York 1989, 174.

[56] A. LINDEMANN/H. PAULSEN, Apostolische Väter (s. Anm. 27), 213, übersetzen etwas vorsichtiger mit: „nur dass ich zu Christus gelange." Vgl. auch die parallelen Formulierungen *Röm.* 1,2; 2,1 und 4,1, wo Ignatius das Ziel als θεοῦ ἐπιτυχεῖν bezeichnet, also „Gottes teilhaftig werden".

[57] W.R. SCHOEDEL, Die Briefe des Ignatius (s. Anm. 6), 292, schreibt hierzu: „Dieser Satz beleuchtet wirkungsvoll, wie sehr Ignatius das christliche Leben im allgemeinen, vor allem aber das Leben des Märtyrers, unter der Herrschaft der Gestalt des gekreuzigten Herrn sieht." – Vgl. hierzu auch die späteren Aussagen in Märtyrertexten wie *M. Polyc.* 17,3 oder Eusebius von Caesarea, *h.e.* 5,2,2 (Brief der Gemeinden von Lyon und Vienne).

(*Röm.* 7,2). Auch diese Liebe (hier: ἔρως) sei „gekreuzigt", verstehe sich also vom Kreuz her, ein Gedanke, der an Gal 6,14 erinnert.[58]

5. Der Brief an die Philadelphier

Der Brief an die Gemeinde von Philadelphia (*Phil.*) bestätigt weitgehend die bisher herausgearbeiteten Grundlinien: Bereits im Präskript betont Ignatius ganz besonders das ihn offensichtlich gerade hier bewegende Problem der Einheit der Kirche (vgl. aber auch etwa *Phil.* 2,1–2; 3,1–3; 7,2; 8,1; 9,1),[59] spricht daneben aber auch von ihrem überzeugten Festhalten an Leiden und Auferstehung Christi.

Auch in der Gemeinde von Philadelphia scheint es Auseinandersetzungen mit Gegnern zu geben, Ignatius geht auf deren Lehre aber nicht näher ein. Die Nähe mancher Aussagen zur Argumentation im Brief an die Magnesier aber lässt vermuten, dass Ignatius es hier mit einer ähnlichen Gruppe zu tun haben dürfte.[60] Aufschlussreich erscheint mir *Phil.* 3,3, wo es heißt, dass derjenige, der „in fremdartiger Gesinnung" bzw. „Meinung" (γνώμη) wandle,[61] sich nicht „mit dem Leiden", d.h. dem Leiden Christi, in Übereinstimmung befinde. Parallel dazu heißt es, dass, wer einem „Spalter" folge, das Reich Gottes nicht erben könne. Das Leiden Christi wird hier also erneut nicht nur zu einer Basis des Glaubens, sondern das Festhalten daran auch als einzige Möglichkeit, das Heil zu erlangen, angesehen.

Auch das bereits aus *Magn.* 9,3 bekannte Motiv, dass bereits die Propheten das Evangelium vorverkündet hätten, begegnet wieder (*Phil.* 5,2; vgl. auch pln. Eph 2,20), zunächst einmal allgemeiner als im oben genannten Schreiben, dann aber noch einmal konkreter auf Leiden und Auferstehung Christi hin bezogen. Ganz offensichtlich hat die Auseinandersetzung mit den Gegnern auch mit unterschiedlicher Auslegung der Schriften Isra-

---

[58] Zur Konkretisierung von Gal 6,14 als Bereitschaft zum Martyrium vgl. auch die Beispiele bei M. MEISER, Galater (NTP 9), Göttingen 2007, 312 n. 30.

[59] Vgl. auch J. SPEIGL, Ignatius in Philadelphia: Ereignisse und Anliegen in den Ignatiusbriefen, VigChr 41 (1987), 360–376, hier 361, der auf die häufige Verwendung des Begriffs „Spaltung" in *Phil.* verweist.

[60] Nachdenkenswert erscheint mir der bei M. MYLLYKOSKI, Wild Beasts (s. Anm. 2), 354–364. 373, vorgebrachte und bereits (s. Anm. 6) erwähnte Alternativvorschlag zu den häufig wiederholten Ideen, es gehe hier um die Auseinandersetzung mit „Doketen". Eine eindeutige Rekonstruktion der Gegnerposition aber lassen die Texte m.E. nicht mehr zu.

[61] Der „fremdartigen Gesinnung" steht im Denken des Ignatius immer wieder die „Gesinnung Gottes" bzw. „Christi" (z.B. *Eph.* 3,2), die des Bischofs (*Polyc.* 4,1; 5,2), die „auf Gott hin" (*Röm.* 7,1; *Phil.* 1,2) sowie die „in Gott" (*Polyc.* 1,1) gegenüber. Hierzu vgl. auch H. PAULSEN, Die Briefe des Ignatius (s. Anm. 10), 82.

els – hier als die (in einem Archiv bewahrten) „Urkunden“ bzw. „Akten“ (ἀρχεῖα; *Phil.* 8,2)[62] bezeichnet – zu tun. Ganz offensichtlich sehen beide Gruppen die „Urkunden“ als Grundlage ihrer Argumentation über die Wahrheit des Evangeliums an.[63] Der Gegnergruppe, die bestimmte Aussagen des Evangeliums nicht in den Urkunden findet,[64] setzt Ignatius nicht nur sein „Es steht geschrieben“ gegenüber. Wegen des damit weiterhin bestehenden Zweifels der Gegner gewichtet er die „Urkunden“ neu (*Phil.* 8,2):

ἐμοὶ δέ ἀρχεῖά ἐστιν Ἰησοῦς Χριστός, τὰ ἄθικτα ἀρχεῖα ὁ σταυρὸς αὐτοῦ καὶ ὁ θάνατος καὶ ἡ ἀνάστασις αὐτοῦ καὶ ἡ πίστις ἡ δι᾽ αὐτοῦ ...

„Meine Urkunden aber ist Jesus Christus, die heiligen Urkunden sein Kreuz, sein Tod, seine Auferstehung und der Glaube durch ihn ...“

Damit sind die Schriften Israels, des „Alten Testaments“, im wahrsten Sinne des Wortes enorm relativiert, d.h. in einen neuen Bezug gesetzt. Ihrer Rolle als Schriften *Israels* sind sie im Grunde verlustig gegangen – wie sehr sie als Schriften *der Kirche* gesehen werden, die sich von Israel abgrenzt, zeigt sich, wenn Ignatius wenig später eine Reihe von Gestalten erwähnt – Abraham, Isaak, Jakob, die Propheten –, die in Einheit mit der Kirche bereits durch Christus, die Tür, zum Vater (vgl. parallel Joh 10,7,9; 14,6), eingegangen seien (*Phil.* 9,1). So nimmt er einen hermeneutischen Perspektivenwechsel vor, wie er im frühen Christentum immer wieder zu beobachten ist:[65] Das Alte Testament – hier die Schriften der Propheten – sind „gemäß der Christuslehre“ (κατὰ χριστομαθίαν; *Phil.* 8,2), von Christi Ankunft[66], seinem Leiden und seiner Auferstehung her, zu deuten, „denn

[62] Zur textkritischen Problematik vgl. H. PAULSEN, Die Briefe des Ignatius (s. Anm. 10), 86.

[63] J. SPEIGL, Ignatius in Philadelphia (s. Anm. 59), 364, argumentiert sogar noch etwas vorsichtiger, spricht davon, dass die „Urkunden“ als Bekenntnisgrundlage einer Seite zu gelten hätten, und das AT zu ihnen dazugehört haben dürfte.

[64] Für diese Interpretation des Abschnitts setzt sich z.B. C.E. HILL, Ignatius, ‚the Gospel‘, and the Gospels, in: A. GREGORY/C.M. TUCKETT (Hg.), Trajectories through the New Testament and the Apostolic Fathers, Oxford et al. 2005, 267–285, hier 272, ein. Ob damit seiner (vorsichtig vorgebrachten) Folgerung, mit „Evangelium“ sei womöglich schon ein geschriebenes Dokument gemeint (273), zu folgen ist, möchte ich doch aber eher bezweifeln.

[65] C.K. BARRETT, Jews and Judaizers (s. Anm. 2), 229, weist in diesem Zusammenhang etwa auf die Nähe zu Justin, *dial.* 90,1. Vgl. aber auch die Beispiele bei T. NICKLAS, Christliche Apokryphen als Spiegel der Vielfalt frühchristlichen Lebens: Schlaglichter, Beispiele und methodische Probleme, ASE 23 (2006), 27–44.

[66] Gemeint ist hier sicherlich die Geburt Christi, nicht die endzeitliche Parusie, wie auch H. PAULSEN, Die Briefe des Ignatius (s. Anm. 10), 87, herausstellt.

die geliebten Propheten haben auf ihn hin verkündigt“[67] (*Phil.* 9,2). Wer dies in den Schriften Israels nicht zu erkennen vermag, interpretiert nach dieser Denkweise bereits ihre Grundintention falsch.[68]

6. Der Brief an die Gemeinde von Smyrna

Vielleicht noch stärker als die bisherigen Schreiben ist der Brief an die Gemeinde von Smyrna (*Sm.*) durch die Auseinandersetzung mit wohl zumindest in einem weiten Sinne „doketischen“ Gegnern geprägt.[69] So begegnet das Thema „Passion Christi“ bereits in den ersten Abschnitten, aber auch in der Salutatio (*Sm.* 12,2) und bildet so geradezu eine Art thematischen Rahmens um den Text, in dem tatsächlich eine Vielzahl für unser Thema bedeutsamer Aussagen des antiochenischen Bischofs zu finden sind. Zwar zeigen sich viele der begegnenden Argumentationsmuster mehr oder minder als Wiederholungen bzw. Variationen zu Bekanntem aus den anderen Texten, in der Fülle der Aussagen lassen sich aber auch einige neue Linien erkennen.

Wie sehr das Thema Ignatius beschäftigt, zeigt sich schon in dem an *Trall.* 9 und 11 erinnernden Eingangsabschnitt, in dem er zunächst den Glauben der Smyrnäer lobt und diesen als – offensichtlich in allen Herausforderungen, ihn zu verändern und damit zu verfälschen – „unbeweglich“ (ἀκίνητος) bezeichnet. Die Smyrnäer seien „wie Angenagelte am Kreuz des Herrn Jesus Christus im Fleisch wie auch im Geist und Befestigte in der Liebe im Blut Christi“ (*Sm.* 1,1). Erneut begegnen in diesem Lob also die für Ignatius so wichtigen beiden Grunddimensionen „Glaube“ und „Liebe“: Wie sehr im Denken des Ignatius für *beide Größen* das Kreuzesleiden Christi als entscheidend angesehen wird, zeigt sich darin, dass er die verlangte Unbeweglichkeit von Glauben und Liebe mit dem „Angenageltsein“ am Kreuz Christi vergleicht. H. Paulsen schreibt hierzu: „[E]s schwebt das Bild vor, daß der Glaube wegen der Annagelung an das Kreuz

---

[67] Übersetzung übereinstimmend mit der bei A. LINDEMANN/H. PAULSEN, Apostolische Väter (s. Anm. 27), 225.

[68] Den damit zu verbindenden Vorwurf, Ignatius verweigere den Gegnern damit die Diskussion, erkennt J. SPEIGL, Ignatius in Philadelphia (s. Anm. 59), 364, durchaus an, verweist aber darauf, dass dies „nicht aufgrund von Gesprächsunfähigkeit, sondern wegen der Kürze der nur zur Verfügung stehenden Zeit und wegen der Martyriumssituation, die immer stark auf ein Bekenntnis zudrängte,“ nachzuvollziehen sei.

[69] W. UEBELE, Viele Verführer (s. Anm. 1), 91, spricht deswegen in diesem Zusammenhang erneut von einer „radikale[n] Form“ des Doketismus. Vgl. aber auch die kritische Haltung von M. MYLLYKOSKI, Wild Beasts (s. Anm. 2), 373.

sich nicht von dem wahren πάθος Christi zu entfernen vermag."[70] Gleiches gilt im ignatianischen Denken für die Liebe. Damit lässt sich dieses Bild vielleicht als eine Variation der in *Trall.* 11 zum Ausdruck gebrachten Vorstellung begreifen, welche die Glieder der Kirche als „Zweige des Kreuzes" begreift, die vom Kreuz her auch ihre Frucht entwickeln können. Dass Ignatius entgegen seiner bildhaften Betonung der Festigkeit ihres Glaubens und ihrer Liebe offensichtlich doch in Sorge um die Situation in Smyrna ist, zeigt sich allerdings, wenn er gleich im Anschluss daran – ähnlich *Trall.* 9,1–2 oder *Eph.* 18,2 in einer Art Bekenntnis mit sicherlich traditionellem Hintergrund – die Wahrhaftigkeit entscheidender Heilsdaten betont (*Sm.* 1,1–2). Erneut sind die Heilsdaten in Paaren angegeben, wobei die erste Aussage jeweils durch Verwendung des Adverbs ἀληθῶς bekräftigt wird und beim letzten Paar, auf welches alle Aussagen wie in einer Klimax hinführen, die Glieder nicht nur am breitesten ausgezeichnet, sondern durch einen ἵνα-Satz miteinander verbunden sind: [71]

- *wahrhaftig* aus dem Geschlecht Davids dem Fleisch nach / Sohn Gottes nach Willen und Kraft Gottes
- *wahrhaftig* geboren aus einer Jungfrau / getauft von Johannes ...
- *wahrhaftig* ... angenagelt für uns im Fleisch / damit er ... ein Wahrzeichen aufrichte ... durch die Auferstehung ...

Um die „Wahrhaftigkeit" der Kreuzigung zu betonen, bedient sich Ignatius dabei über die Bekräftigung mit ἀληθῶς hinaus des Mittels, dass er erneut davon spricht, dass Christus „angenagelt" (καθηλωμένον) wurde, dass dies „im Fleisch" (ἐν σαρκί) und – in der obigen Strukturdarstellung noch nicht gezeigt – „unter Pontius Pilatus und Herodes, dem Tetrarchen", also eingebettet in einen nachprüfbaren historischen Kontext, geschah (*Sm.* 1,2). Drastischer könnte ein Glaubensbekenntnis das menschliche Leiden und Sterben Christi wohl kaum zum Ausdruck bringen. Die besondere Heilsrelevanz gerade des Kreuzesgeschehens wird nun aber auch durch zwei Brüche in der Struktur des Bekenntnisses zum Ausdruck gebracht:

– Von der Aussage zur Kreuzigung Jesu ist der Relativsatz ἀφ' οὗ καρποῦ ἡμεῖς ἀπὸ τοῦ θεομακαρίστου αὐτοῦ πάθους („eine Frucht, von der wir sind, von seinem gottseligen Leiden") abhängig: Damit wird doppelt, durch den Anschluss an die Aussage über die Kreuzigung Christi und die Parallelisierung mit ἀπὸ τοῦ ... die Bedeutung des Leidens Christi für die

[70] H. PAULSEN, Die Briefe des Ignatius (s. Anm. 10), 91. Womöglich ist hier das paulinische Thema des mit Christus Gekreuzigt-Seins (Gal 2,19) weitergeführt. Vgl. z.B. W.R. SCHOEDEL, Die Briefe des Ignatius (s. Anm. 6), 345.

[71] Übersetzungen hier angelehnt an A. LINDEMANN/H. PAULSEN, Apostolische Väter (s. Anm. 27), 227. Eine ausführliche Analyse der Einzelelemente des Bekenntnistextes bietet W.R. SCHOEDEL, Die Briefe des Ignatius (s. Anm. 6), 345–350.

Christen angesprochen: Erneut (s.o. *Eph.* 16,1–2; *Magn.* 9,1; *Trall.* 2,1), vielleicht aber eindringlicher als bisher begegnet die Aussage, dass es letztlich das Leiden Christi ist, das erst den Glauben ermöglicht – und damit die Glaubenden als seine „Frucht" hat. Dass damit das aus *Trall.* 11 bekannte Bild vom Kreuzesstamm, seinen Zweigen und Früchten noch einmal deutlich variiert ist, ist für die Argumentation kein Problem.

– Wie oben angedeutet aber führt die das Bekenntnis abschließende Aussage zur Auferstehung nun nicht einfach die bisherige Reihung fort, sondern ist durch einen Finalsatz an die Aussage über den Kreuzestod Christi angeschlossen. Ziel des Leidens Christi ist es, „in alle Ewigkeiten ein Wahrzeichen aufzurichten" (ἵνα ἄρῃ σύσσημον εἰς τοὺς αἰῶνας).[72] Dies geschieht „durch" bzw. „vermittelst der Auferstehung" (διὰ τῆς ἀναστάσεως) – Auferstehung also wird somit als ewiges Ziel des Leidens Christi mit diesem auf direkte Weise verknüpft. Diese Auferstehung wiederum bezieht sich nicht nur auf Christus allein, sondern geschieht im Blick auf bzw. für „seine Heiligen und Gläubigen, seien sie Juden, seien sie unter den Heiden" (εἰς τοὺς ἁγίους καὶ πιστοὺς αὐτοῦ, εἴτε ἐν Ἰουδαίοις εἴτε ἐν ἔθνεσιν; vgl. pln Eph 2,16). Obwohl diese also letztlich aus beiden ursprünglich getrennten Gruppen – Juden und Heiden – zusammenkommen, werden sie aufgrund der Auferstehung Christi doch geeint „in dem *einen* Leib seiner Kirche" (ἐν ἑνὶ σώματι τῆς ἐκκλεσίας αὐτοῦ; vgl. parallel Justin, *dial.* 26,1–4). Das Kreuz Christi ist hier somit nicht nur in direkter Verbindung mit der Auferstehung gesehen, es wird so zum Ausgangspunkt des Heils und zum Prinzip der Einheit der Kirche aus Juden und Heiden. Ist die Bezeichnung der Kirche als „Leib" hier bewusst angefügt? Dann geht die Verbindung womöglich noch weiter: Der *eine* Leib der Kirche Christi steht dann in Entsprechung mit dem *einen* Leib des wahrhaft Gekreuzigten.

Dass ihm in der gesamten Reihe das Aussagenpaar zu Kreuz und Auferstehung am wichtigsten ist, zeigt sich auch im direkt folgenden Abschnitt *Sm.* 2, wo Ignatius seine Argumentation nun auf die konkrete Situation, die Auseinandersetzung mit den offensichtlich doketischen Gegnern, zur Anwendung bringt. Die Argumentation erinnert an *Trall.* 10, allerdings wird ein stärkerer Wert auf die Auferstehung gelegt[73], die – als fleischliche Auf-

[72] Das Bild vom σύσσημον stammt aus dem militärischen Bereich und weist in die Richtung von Gedanken einer *militia Christi*, wie sie dann in *Polyc.* vermehrt begegnet. Der Hintergrund ist, wie W.R. SCHOEDEL, Die Briefe des Ignatius (s. Anm. 6), 349, jedoch bemerkt, bei Texten wie Jes 5,26; 49,22; 62,10 zu suchen.

[73] Hier ist – anders als z.B. *Trall.* 9,2 und *Sm.*7,1 – sogar von der Selbsterweckung Christi die Rede (vgl. z.B. die traditionsgeschichtlichen Parallelen Joh 2,19; 10,17–18).

erstehung – auch in *Sm.* 3 ausführlich zur Sprache kommen wird, vielleicht noch deutlicher als in *Trall.* 10 werden die Gegner zudem dämonisiert.[74]

Die Auseinandersetzung mit den Gegnern durchzieht nun weiter *Sm.* 3, wo die Körperlichkeit auch der Auferstehung Christi thematisiert ist. Ab Abschnitt 4 kommt Ignatius wieder zu seiner eigenen Person zurück. Sehr ähnlich *Trall.* 10 argumentiert er mit seinem eigenen Schicksal, die kleine Verschiebung gegenüber *Trall.* besteht darin, dass Ignatius hier von sich selbst als „nur zum Schein gefesselt" spricht, hätte Christus nur zum Schein gelitten. Was auf den ersten Blick noch nicht unbedingt logisch wirkt,[75] klärt sich im weiteren Verlauf der Argumentation. Gerade, wenn er „nahe dem Schwert" (ἐγγὺς μαχαίρας) sei, sei er auch „nahe Gott" (ἐγγὺς θεοῦ), wenn er „mitten unter den Tieren" (μεταξὺ θηρίων) sei, auch „mitten in Gott" (μεταξὺ θεοῦ).[76] Ist mit „Gott" hier erneut Christus gemeint? Ich denke, ja, denn Ignatius schließt die Aussage an, dass er dies alles „im Namen Jesu Christi" erleide.[77] Vor allem aber rundet sich das Argument mit einem Gedanken, der sich auch in späteren christlichen Märtyrerakten immer wieder angedeutet findet: Das Leiden des Märtyrers ist nur deswegen erträglich, weil Christus, der selbst „vollkommener Mensch" (τελείος ἄνθρωπος) geworden ist, mitleidet (συμπαθεῖν) und so dem Leidenden Kraft verleiht. Das Durchhalten der Blutzeugen im Leiden ist so nicht nur im Sinne einer Nachahmung Christi verstanden, sondern umgekehrt als Erweis des Beistands dessen, der selbst durch Leid zur Auferstehung gelangte – nun aber seinen Anhängern im Leid beisteht. Diese Argumentationslinie ist es, die Ignatius das Leiden der Märtyrer in eine Reihe mit den Worten der Propheten, das Gesetz Mose und das Evangelium stellen lässt (*Sm.* 5,1): Für ihn zeugt all dies von Christus, seinem Leiden und seiner Auferstehung (vgl. auch *Sm.* 7,2).

Eine weitere Variation bisheriger Gedanken begegnet in *Sm.* 6,1: In einer an Gal 1,8 erinnernden Argumentation wird die Bedeutung des Glaubens – hier an das Blut Christi – nicht nur für den Menschen, sondern auch für die „Himmlischen" (τὰ ἐπουράνια), die „Herrlichkeit der Engel" (ἡ δόξα τῶν ἀγγέλων) sowie die „sichtbaren und unsichtbaren Archonten" (οἱ ἄρχοντες ὁρατοί τε καὶ ἀόρατοι) hervorgehoben: Nicht nur für den Menschen geht es im Glauben an das Leiden Christi um die Chance auf ewiges

---

[74] Hier wird wohl eine Aussage der Gegner, Christus sei „körperlos" (ἀσώματος) gewesen, aufgenommen und gegen sie selbst gewandt: Nicht Christus sondern die Gegner seien körperlos und dadurch „dämonisch".

[75] M. ISACSON, To Each Their Own Letter (s. Anm. 1), 164, etwa schreibt in diesem Zusammenhang: „The argument is totally dependent on his own credibility."

[76] H. PAULSEN, Die Briefe des Ignatius (s. Anm. 10), 94, verweist auf die traditionsgeschichtliche Parallelität zu EvThom 82.

[77] Zum Leiden „im Namen Jesu Christi" in antiken Märtyrerakten vgl. die entsprechenden Gedanken in T. NICKLAS, Gebete (s. Anm. 13) [im Druck].

Heil – auch über die genannten Mächte kommt, so sie nicht glauben, das Gericht.[78] Selbst himmlische Hierarchien zählten so letztlich nichts, komme es doch alleine auf „Glaube und Liebe" an, „denen gegenüber nichts den Vorzug genießt" (ὧν οὐδὲν προκέκριται; 6,1). In diesem Kontext ist nun auch von der Gnade Jesu Christi, die sich ganz offensichtlich im Heil des Kreuzesereignisses erweist, die Rede – der Gedanke ist aber kaum aus dem Kontext entwickelt, es zeigt sich hier nur, dass er im Denken des Ignatius offensichtlich nicht ganz fehlt, andererseits aber zumindest in den von ihm überlieferten Texten nur am Rande eine Rolle spielt (vgl. aber auch *Magn.* 8,1).

Über den Hinweis auf die Liebe in 6,1 entwickelt Ignatius zudem eine letzte, vielleicht im Gegensatz zu den anderen am wenigstens konsequent verfolgte Linie: Wenn die christliche Liebe in solch engem Bezug zum Kreuzesereignis steht, wie das bereits mehrfach formuliert wurde (s.o. etwa *Sm.* 1,1), dann haben die „irreführenden Meinungen" der Gegner im Hinblick auf die Gnade Jesu Christi[79] auch ethische Konsequenzen (*Sm.* 6,2): Da den Gegnern nichts an der Liebe liegt, liegt ihnen auch nicht an den praktischen Taten der Liebe: Sie kümmern sich nicht um Witwen und Waisen, Bedrängte, Gefesselte noch Freigelassene, noch Hungernde und Dürstende.[80] Ob diese Vorwürfe an die Gegner zutreffen, sei dahingestellt; wichtig ist damit, dass sich, positiv gewendet, selbst die ethische Praxis der liebenden Solidarität, die christliche Gemeinden ja gerade auch für Außenseiter der Gesellschaft, sozial Bedrohte und Benachteiligte attraktiv machte, für Ignatius aus dem Kreuzesleiden Christi ergibt.

Etwas später wirft Ignatius den Gegnern vor, sich auch der Eucharistie zu enthalten (*Sm.* 7,1).[81] Dass er diese hier als Fleisch des Retters Jesu Christi bezeichnet, das vom Vater auferweckt wurde, ist auch in anderen Texten bereits zur Sprache gekommen (s.o. etwa *Röm.* 7,3). Hinzu kommt wohl aus der Tradition (vgl. z.B. 1Kor 15,3-5) das sonst nicht erwähnte Leiden *für unsere Sünden*: Das Thema der grundsätzlichen Sündigkeit und Erlösungsbedürftigkeit des Menschen, das etwa Paulus so sehr umtreibt, hat Ignatius zumindest in den von ihm erhaltenen Briefen offensichtlich kaum beschäftigt; hier begegnet es zumindest einmal geradezu *en passant.*

---

[78] H. PAULSEN, Die Briefe des Ignatius (s. Anm. 10), 95, verweist auf Jud 6; Joh 12,31; 16,11; Offb 19,20 und 20,10 als frühchristliche Parallelen zu dem Gedanken, dass auch Engel und Geister gerichtet werden.

[79] Zur Gnade in diesem Zusammenhang vgl. auch W.R. SCHOEDEL, Die Briefe des Ignatius (s. Anm. 6), 373.

[80] Eine Vielzahl traditionsgeschichtlicher Parallelen zu den Gliedern dieser Reihe bietet H. PAULSEN, Die Briefe des Ignatius (s. Anm. 10), 95.

[81] Das Ignatius auch hier wohl übertreibt bzw. seine Vorwürfe nicht ganz gerechtfertigt sind, zeigt W.R. SCHOEDEL, Die Briefe des Ignatius (s. Anm. 6), 375.

7. Der Brief an Polycarp

Zuletzt sei wenigstens kurz noch auf den Brief an Polycarp (*Polyc.*) eingegangen, der zumindest auf den ersten Blick kaum Neues zum Thema zu erbringen scheint, da sich der Text, der ja an einen Bischof gerichtet ist, besonders für praktische Aufgaben der Gemeindeleitung interessiert. An mehreren Stellen spricht Ignatius wieder von der heilbringenden Kraft seines eigenen Martyriums (*Polyc.* 2,3; 6,1), was sich – wie in den anderen Texten entwickelt – nur aus seinem Verständnis der Passion Christi selbst erklärt. Hier entwickelt Ignatius auch Gedanken in die Richtung einer *Militia Christi*, etwa wenn er von Kämpfern („Athleten") spricht, die sich zwar „schlagen lassen" müssen (δέρεσθαι), um dann doch zu siegen (*Polyc.* 3,1; vgl. auch 1,3; 2,3; 6,1–2). Wie bereits im *Eph.* 7,2 wird Christus als Leidensunfähiger, der um unseretwillen leidensfähig wurde und (im Leid) standhielt (*Polyc.* 3,2), gezeichnet.

Vielleicht aber lässt sich auch von *Polyc.* her noch eine weitere Dimension des Themas erkennen: Auch wenn die Verbindungslinien hier nicht explizit gemacht sind, zeigen sich doch einige Indizien, die darauf verweisen, dass auch das hier entwickelte Ideal bischöflichen Wirkens vom Bild des im Fleisch leidenden Christus bestimmt ist. So betont Ignatius die Aufgabe des Bischofs, sich um die Einheit bzw. Einigung der Gemeinden zu sorgen (*Polyc.* 1,2), auch für den Bischof ist die christliche Liebe ein entscheidender Leitfaden (*Polyc.* 1,2) seines Handelns und Ertragens, was sich in gerade den Handlungen zeigt wie der in *Polyc.* 4,1 beispielhaft erwähnten Versorgung der Witwen, die laut *Sm.* 6,2 von den doketischen Gegnern wegen ihrer Verachtung des Kreuzes unterlassen wird. Aufgabe des Bischofs ist es „standzuhalten" bzw. „zu ertragen" (ὑπομένειν; *Polyc.* 3,1), wodurch er Christus gleicher wird, der ebenfalls „standgehalten" hat (*Polyc.* 3,2 s.o. 3,1). Erst dieses Bild des Bischofs macht das hierarchische Amtsverständnis des Ignatius auch theologisch nachvollziehbarer: Hauptaufgabe des Bischofs ist es in diesem Verständnis, in seinem der Einheit dienenden Handeln der Gemeinde dauerhaft Christus, den Gekreuzigten und Auferstandenen vor Augen zu führen.

Fazit

Die systematische Zusammenfassung theologischer Aussagen, die sich über ein Corpus von Briefen verteilen, die *ad hoc*, also aus konkreter Veranlassung heraus, ja gar auf eine konkrete Notsituation hin verfasst sind, ist methodisch natürlich nie ganz unproblematisch: Das Corpus der erhaltenen Briefe des Märtyrerbischofs Ignatius von Antiochien darf nicht mit einem theologischen Kompendium verwechselt werden, das mehr oder weniger eine „Summe" der Theologie des Autors darstellen möchte. So manche Schwerpunktsetzung mag sich aus der Perspektive des Autors verstehen, der in Erwartung seines baldigen Todes den angeschriebenen Gemeinden so etwas wie eine Art „brieflichen Testaments" hinterlassen möchte, um ihnen in bedrohter Situation eine Art Wegweiser zu geben. Trotz allem aber ergibt sich aus der Zusammenschau der Gedanken des antiochenischen Bischofs doch ein sehr beeindruckendes Gesamtbild. Es mag in Teilen Aspekten der historischen Situation verdankt sein, in die hinein die Texte verfasst sind – der Erwartung eines eigenen leidvollen Todes als Blutzeuge und des Auftretens (wohl zumindest im weitesten Sinne) „doketischer" Gegner – das Theologumenon vom wahrhaftigen Kreuzesleiden des Jesu Christi, der für Ignatius als Mensch und als Gott (wenn auch wahrscheinlich in subordinatianistischer Weise) verstanden wird, bildet für das theologische Denken des Bischofs einen, wenn nicht den entscheidenden Kernpunkt, aus dem eine Vielzahl anderer theologischer Dimensionen, besonders Christologie, Soteriologie, Ekklesiologie, Sakramentenverständnis und zumindest bestimmte Dimensionen der Ethik, weniger deutlich auch Eschatologie und Kosmologie, heraus entwickelt sind, während die Dimensionen der Gnadenlehre (vgl. aber *Magn.* präskr.; *Sm.* 6,1) oder auch der Vorstellung von der im Kreuz zu überwindenden Sünde des Menschen (vor allem im Vergleich zu Paulus) sehr deutlich zurücktreten (vgl. nur *Sm.* 7,1).

1. Christologie

In der konkreten Auseinandersetzung mit Gegnern, von denen zumindest einige (recht deutlich in Ephesus, Tralles, Smyrna) ganz offensichtlich das Bekenntnis zur wahren Menschlichkeit Christi ablehnen, betont Ignatius z.T. in offensichtlich von ihm überarbeiteten traditionellen Credo-Formeln bzw. überkommenem Material entscheidende Heilsdaten (z.B. *Eph.* 7,2; *Magn.* 11; *Trall.* 9,1–2; *Sm.* 1,1–2). Dabei werden gerne Aspekte, die die wahre Menschlichkeit Christi betonen, antithetisch solchen, in denen seine Göttlichkeit zum Ausdruck gebracht wird, gegenübergestellt (vgl. z.B. *Eph* 7,2). Betont aber wird die Menschlichkeit und hier gerne vor allem die Tatsächlichkeit des menschlichen, d.h. fleischlichen Leidens Christi, das zudem zu einem konkreten historischen Zeitpunkt – unter Pontius Pilatus (und Herodes) – zu datieren ist (z.B. *Sm.* 1,2). Dabei aber wird keineswegs die Göttlichkeit Christi vernachlässigt, sondern auf das Zueinander von beidem Wert gelegt: Die Verbindung von Menschlichkeit – und damit Leidensfähigkeit bzw. wahrem Leiden – und Göttlichkeit, d.h. Leidensunfähigkeit (*Eph.* 7,2) ermögliche so auch das Heil des Menschen. Damit aber ist bereits die Brücke zur Soteriologie geschlagen:

2. Soteriologie

Immer wieder zeigt sich, wie sehr Ignatius das Leiden Christi als ein entscheidendes Datum seiner Soteriologie entwickelt, indem er zunächst die Möglichkeit der Auferstehung Christi ins ewige Leben eng an sein Kreuzesleiden anbindet, im getreuen Festhalten am Zueinander der beiden Glaubensinhalte aber zugleich die Möglichkeit des Heils für den Glaubenden selbst erkennt. Wie Paulus versteht Ignatius das Kreuz Christi als ein *Skandalon*, anders als dieser entwickelt er diese Idee aber nicht theologisch, sondern in erster Linie soteriologisch weiter: Das Kreuz wird dem Glaubenden aus Juden und Heiden (*Sm.* 1,2) zu Heil und ewigem Leben – und selbst für himmlische Wesen und Engel (*Sm.* 6,1) entscheidet sich Heil im Glauben an das Kreuz. Dies kann auf unterschiedliche Weise formuliert sein: Erst im Blut Gottes, d.h. Christi, sei die Gemeinde „wiederbelebt" (*Eph.* 1,1); erst im Tode Christi sei wahres, ewiges Leben ermöglicht worden (*Eph.* 7,2), was daran liegt, dass Gott im Fleisch geboren sei. Entsprechend dem Gleichnis der Auferweckung des wahrhaft gekreuzigten Christus werde der Vater auch die Glaubenden auferwecken (*Trall.* 9,1–2), und im Leiden Christi werde durch die Auferstehung für alle Zeiten ein Wahrzeichen aufgerichtet (*Sm.* 1,2).

Dies aber ist nicht die einzige Möglichkeit, mit der Ignatius soteriologische Gedanken an seine Vorstellung vom Kreuz anbindet. Wenn die Christen Steine für den (wohl als himmlisch verstandenen) Tempel des Vaters (*Eph.* 9,1) sind, dann müssen sie für dieses ewige Bauwerk nicht nur vorbereitet, sondern auch zu ihm emporgehoben werden: Dies geschieht durch den „Kran" des Kreuzes, das Seil des Geistes wie auch den eigenen Einsatz in Glaube und Liebe.

3. Ekklesiologie

Dies ermöglicht Ignatius, entscheidende Aspekte seines Verständnisses der *Kirche* in engem Zusammenhang mit seiner Idee des Kreuzesleidens Christi zu entwickeln. Das „Leiden", mit dem Ignatius ganz offensichtlich das Kreuz Christi versteht, unter das aber wohl auch andere Ereignisse der Passion Christi subsumiert werden können (vgl. z.B. die Todessalbung *Eph.* 17,1), wird immer wieder als Ausgangspunkt bzw. als Ermöglichung, an anderen Stellen als eine Art Fundament des Christseins überhaupt verstanden (vgl. z.B. *Eph.* 16,1-2; *Magn.* 9,1; *Trall.* 2,1): Die Gemeinden sind auserwählt im Leiden Christi (*Eph. präskr.*), sie werden verstanden als Frucht des Leidens Christi (*Sm.* 1,2) bzw. sollen festhalten an den entscheidenden Heilsdaten, zu denen immer auch das manchmal sogar besonders hervorgehobene Leiden Christi gezählt wird (*Eph.* 19,1; *Magn.* 11; *Trall.* 9; *Phil.* 9,2; *Sm.* 1). Das Leiden Christi ermögliche Frieden (*Trall.*

Präskr.; 2,1), vor allem aber die für Ignatius so wichtige Einheit der Kirche:

So können die Christen als Zweige des Kreuzes angesehen werden (*Trall.* 11), womit wohl das alttestamentliche Bild des Lebensbaums im Paradies (Gen 2,7) weitergeführt ist: Frucht kann die Gemeinde so nur über ihre Verbindung zum Kreuzesstamm bringen – ihre Gegner dagegen sind schlechte Seitentriebe mit todbringender Frucht (*Trall.* 11,1). Ähnlich eindrucksvoll ist auch das in *Sm.* 1,1 verwendete Bild vom „unbeweglichen" Glauben der Smyrnäer, deren Glaube wie Liebe geradezu „angenagelt" nicht vom Kreuz Christi entfernt werden kann.

Ignatius aber hat ganz offensichtlich nicht nur die irdische Kirche im Blick – immer wieder betont er mit verschiedenen, durchaus der Tradition verpflichteten Bildern auch deren himmlische Dimension. Christen sind für ihn Steine des wohl als im Himmel befindlich verstandenen Tempels des Vaters (*Eph.* 9,1), die über den Kran des Kreuzes nach oben gehoben werden; oder Glieder des Leibes Christi, die von Christus durch das Kreuz in seinem Leiden berufen sind (*Trall.* 11,2), des einen Leibes des Gekreuzigten, in dem Juden und Heiden zur Einheit werden (*Sm.* 1,2).

Bekanntlich legt Ignatius in seiner konkreten Darstellung der Kirche bereits überraschend viel Wert auf eine recht weit entwickelte Ämterhierarchie, v.a. einen monarchianischen Episkopat. Obwohl die Verbindungslinien nicht immer ganz eindeutig sind, halte ich es für wahrscheinlich, dass auch das Ideal bischöflichen Wirkens nicht nur am Vorbild Christi, sondern dem Vorbild des leidend-gekreuzigten Christus ausgerichtet ist. Die Gemeinde hat sich unter den Bischof wie unter Christus unterzuordnen, der ja als unsichtbarer Bischof (*Magn.* 3,2) bezeichnet werden kann. Die Nähe des Bischofs zu Christus aber scheint besondere Implikationen im Hinblick auf dessen eigene Leidensnachfolge (*Trall.* 4,2) wie auch seine Vorbildrolle in der kosmischen Auseinandersetzung der Kirche (*Polyc.* 1,3; 2,3; 3,1–2; 6,1–2), im Ringen um ihre Einheit (*Polyc.* 1,2) wie auch in ihrer konkreten ethischen Gesinnung zu haben (*Polyc.* 1,2; 4,1).

4. Sakramentenverständnis

Bereits die Verbindung von Leiden Christi und Blut Christi ermöglicht Ignatius auch die Anbindung seines Eucharistieverständnisses an seine Kreuzestheologie. So spricht er vom „Brot Gottes", das als „Fleisch Jesu Christi" zu verstehen ist, oder dem Trank seines Blutes, der unvergänglichen Liebe (*Röm.* 7,3). Womöglich hängt auch der in *Sm.* 7,1 vorgebrachte Vorwurf an die Gegner damit zusammen: Wer die Wahrhaftigkeit des menschlichen Lebens und Leidens Christi ablehnt, hat so auch nicht Teil an der Eucharistie, dem Fleisch des Retters Jesus Christus.

Doch nicht nur die Eucharistie wird bei Ignatius vom Leiden Christi her verstanden; *Eph.* 18,2 deutet zumindest an, dass dies auch für die Taufe gilt, das Christus durch sein Leid das Wasser gereinigt habe. Wie sehr dieses Denken etwa mit der Vorstellung, dass Kirche erst durch das Leiden Christi ermöglicht sei, zusammenhängt, lässt sich aber aufgrund der knappen Bemerkung leider nicht mehr erhellen.

Ist auch der Tod des Märtyrers in Nachfolge Christi als „Sakrament" verstanden? Texte, in denen Ignatius als „Weizen Gottes", „Brot Christi" oder „Opfer für Gott" (*Röm.* 4,1–2) bezeichnet, ermöglichen zumindest derartige Assoziationen – sie zwingen aber noch nicht zu dieser Folgerung.

5. Nachfolge Christi

Als im Leiden Christi Auserwählte sollen sich die Christen als Nachahmer Gottes, d.h. Christi verstehen (*Eph.* 1,1; 3,1; *Röm.* 3,2; 4,2; 5,3); dabei kann Ignatius zumindest, wenn er über sich selbst spricht, an mancher Stelle so weit gehen, zu behaupten, dass er erst in seiner persönlichen Kreuzesnachfolge als Märtyrer zum Jünger Jesu (*Eph.* 1,2), ja neu geboren werde (*Röm.* 6,2). Dies mag sicherlich in dieser Extremform der konkreten Situation verdankt sein, in der die Briefe abgefasst sind; vor allem aber wenn er den Glauben als „Fleisch des Herrn" und die Liebe als „Blut Jesu Christi" (*Trall.* 8,1) bezeichnet, wird deutlich, wie sehr Christsein für Ignatius vom Leiden Christi her zu bestimmen hat. Nicht nur sei das wahrhaftige Leiden Christi der einzige Grund für die Leidensnachfolge auch der Christen bis hinein in den Tod (*Trall.* 10), auch umgekehrt könne das Leiden der Zeugen geradezu als Beweis für das wahrhaftige Leiden Christi verstanden werden (*Sm.* 4): Nur weil Christus, der vollkommene Mensch, tatsächlich mit dem Märtyrer mitleidet und ihm so Kraft gibt, kann dieser sein Leid tatsächlich auch ertragen.

Neben dieser Konzentration auf das eigene Schicksal scheint für Ignatius aber auch die Kreuzesnachfolge jedes einzelnen Christen auch jenseits des Martyriums konkrete ethische Konsequenzen zu haben: So ist die „Liebe", die das Leben der Glaubenden bestimmen soll, bei Ignatius theologisch so eng an das Kreuzesleiden Christi angebunden (vgl. v.a. *Trall.* 8,1), dass sich somit auch die konkreten Taten der Liebe, die das Gemeindeleben ausmachen, vom Kreuzesleiden her verstehen, bzw. umgekehrt Ignatius den Gegnern, die die Wahrhaftigkeit des Leidens Christi ablehnen, vorwerfen, es auch an Taten der Liebe mangeln zu lassen (*Sm.* 6,2). Christen sind so wie Münzen in Liebe geprägt von Gott, dies aber heißt, dass sie im Gegenüber zur Welt „das Sterben auf sein Leiden hin haben" (*Magn.* 5,2).

6. Eschatologie

Weniger deutlich sind auch eschatologische Aussagen an die Kreuzestheologie des Ignatius angebunden, sie fehlen jedoch nicht völlig. Der Weg geht dabei z.B. über die Soteriologie: Festhalten im Glauben an das Kreuz ermöglicht dem Glaubenden nicht nur ewiges Leben; so sehr das Bild des Kreuzes als Kran (*Eph.* 9), der den Gliedern der Kirche ermöglicht, ihren endzeitlichen Ort als Steine des himmlischen Tempels zu erreichen, zunächst soteriologische wie ekklesiologische Dimensionen besitzt, so sehr sollte doch auch die eschatologische Komponente, wenn auch im Text kaum zum Ausdruck gebracht, nicht vollkommen vernachlässigt werden. Deutlicher ausgedrückt wird das eschatologische Ziel, das Ignatius für sich selbst erhofft, an anderer Stelle: Als Nachahmer des Leidens Christi (*Röm.* 6,3) habe er Sehnsucht nach dem Tode, damit er „Christus erlange" bzw. gar „seiner teilhaftig werde" (*Röm.* 5,3).

Umgekehrt kann Ignatius aber auch betonen, dass die Ablehnung des Bekenntnisses zum Leiden Christi und die damit einhergehende „Verwüstung" des Glaubens, „für den Christus gekreuzigt wurde," den Menschen ins „unauslöschliche Feuer" (*Eph.* 16) führt.

7. Kreuz und Kosmos

All die entscheidenden Daten des Lebens, Sterbens und Auferstehens Christi wie auch des Ringens der Glieder der Kirche um das Heil werden bei Ignatius als Teil einer kosmischen Auseinandersetzung gesehen: So gehört der Tod Christi zu den geheimnisvollen Mysterien des Schreies (*Eph.* 19,1), die in ihrer Heilsbedeutsamkeit dem Archonten dieses Äons bzw. dem Fürsten dieser Welt verborgen blieben und somit die Überwindung der Macht des Todes ins ewige Leben hinein ermöglichten (*Eph.* 19,3). Am Bekenntnis zum Leid Christi entscheide sich für Menschen, aber auch für alle himmlischen Wesen, selbst die Engel (*Sm.* 6,1) Zugehörigkeit zu Gott bzw. Christus oder Zugehörigkeit zur Welt der Ungläubigen, wodurch das Wirken der Irrlehrer, die das Bekenntnis zum Leiden Christi ablehnen, für Ignatius letztlich als Wirken des Teufels (*Trall.* 8,1; *Phil.* 6,2; vgl. auch *Sm.* 2) verstanden werden kann, demgegenüber der Bischof und seine Gemeinde wie Christus „standzuhalten" haben (*Polyc.* 3,1–2).

The Passion Narrative in the *Sibylline Oracles*

JEAN-MICHEL ROESSLI*

Introduction

The question of the relationship between apocryphal and canonical Scriptures is fascinating, but it has to be asked in different ways depending on the apocryphal text under study. In this paper I look at the way the passion narratives are retold in the *Sibylline Oracles*. The question is to be asked specifically for the Sibyls who are "vaticinating" in Books 1, 6, and 8 of the collection. A special place must be given to the first Book,[1] because in it the Sibyl predicts not only the advent of Christ, his passion, and his res-

* I wish to thank warmly Dr. Alicia Batten and Dr. Paul Laverdure for their valuable help in editing this text.

[1] This book consists of 400 hexameters, an important part of which – verses 1 to 323 – is probably the work of a Jewish author of the turning point of our era, "rewritten" by a Christian who intended to complete it by adding a long section on Jesus and his earthly ministry. Most scholars see Books 1 and 2, separated in the manuscripts by a colophon, as a single writing. Some date its composition in the second or third century of the Christian era. Some others consider that there is no reason to distinguish a primitive Jewish stratum and a Christian rewriting, and conclude that the double Book 1–2 is an entirely Christian work of the second, third or fifth century (see the conclusion below). For recent studies of this double book, see J.L. Lightfoot, *The Sibylline Oracles. With Introduction, Translation, and Commentary on the First and Second Books* (Oxford 2008); O. Waßmuth, *Sibyllinische Orakel 1/2: Ein apokalyptisches Dokument des kleinasiatischen Judentums und seine christliche Adaption. Studien und Kommentar* (to be published in the series "Ancient Judaism and Early Christianity" at Brill, Leiden, in 2010); and T. Beech, *A Socio-Rhetorical Analysis of the Development and Function of the Noah-Flood Narrative in* Sibylline Oracles 1–2 (Ph.D. Thesis submitted to the Faculty of Theology, Saint Paul University, Ottawa, February 2008). A first review of J.L. Lightfoot's book was published by A. Kachuk in *Bryn Mawr Classical Review*, June 21, 2008; very recently a shorter review has been published by G.L. Watley in *The Classical Review* 59/1 (2009), 101–103 (who is about to finish his own dissertation on the *Sibylline Oracles* 1–2). See also M. Monaca, *Oracoli Sibillini* (Testi patristici 199; Rome 2008). Translations of the *Sibylline Oracles* are taken from J.J. Collins, "The Sibylline Oracles," in *The Old Testament Pseudepigrapha* (ed. by J.H. Charlesworth; vol. 1: *Apocalyptic Literature and Testaments*; Garden City, N.Y. 1983), 317–472 (unless otherwise stated). The Greek text, sometimes emended, is taken from J. Geffcken, *Die Oracula Sibyllina* (GCS 8; Leipzig 1902; repr. Berlin 1967).

urrection but, still more surprisingly, she also predicts the gospel and the end of the prophets (vv. 382 and 386). This means that the Sibyl, who is a pagan prophetess, considers herself to be on the same level as the prophets, prophesying the history of salvation with them, and also completes them, explaining that their promises are realised in Jesus. And she even pretends to a kind of superiority, since she predicts the teachings of the gospels (v. 382) and the end of prophecy (v. 386). In order to realize this divinatory fiction – since it is obviously a fiction – the Sibyl intends to use both the prophets and the Gospels, often combining the two, either by implicit allusions, or by literal quotations, or even by precise lexical borrowings. In order to build her passion narrative, the Sibyl selects elements from both canonical and apocryphal traditions, sometimes identified and sometimes not, which she illustrates with texts from the prophets.

The Passion Narrative in Books 1, 6 and 8 of the Sibylline Oracles (*Sibyllina Oracula*)

Thus this paper analyzes textual fragments related to the passion in Books 1, 6, and 8 of the *Sibylline Oracles* and compares them with the corresponding passages in the New Testament. Subsequently, the paper evaluates the Sibyl's rewriting, points of contact between her work and the canonical Scriptures, possible dependencies, and discrepancies.

Sib Or 1:365–366 and Sib Or 8:287–290

In the *Sibylline Oracles*, the passion narrative proper starts with Christ's scourging, when he receives blows and spit. We find the scourging in *Sib Or* 1:365–366 and *Sib Or* 8:287–289, while the canonical narrative can be read in Matt 26:67 and 27:30; Mark 14:65 and 15:19, and Luke 22:63–65.

Sib Or 1:365–366	*Sib Or 8:287–290*
	εἰς ἀνόμων χεῖρας καὶ ἀπίστων ὕστερον ἥξει, Later he will come into the hands of lawless and faithless men,
καὶ τότε δὴ κολάφους καὶ πτύσματα φαρμακόεντα Then indeed Israel, with abominable lips,	δώσουσιν δὲ θεῷ ῥαπίσματα χερσὶν ἀνάγνοις and they will give blows to God with unholy hands
Ἰσραὴλ δώσει μυσαροῖς ἐνὶ χείλεσι τούτῳ And poisonous spittings, will give this man blows.	καὶ στόμασιν μιαροῖς ἐμπτύσματα φαρμακόεντα, and poisonous spittings with polluted mouths.
	δώσει δ' εἰς μάστιγας ἀναπλώσας τότε νῶτον·

Then he will stretch out his back and give it
to the whips.

Luke's narrative, where there is no mention of the spit, is too different from the text in the *Sibylline Oracles* to have served as a source for the Sibyl. We can thus set it aside. The words ῥαπίσματα and ἐμπτύσματα of *Sib Or* 8:288–289, however, reveal a close kinship with Matthew's narrative, where we find the corresponding verbs ἐμπτύω and ῥαπίζω in Matt 26:67, and the verb ἐμπτύω alone in Matt 27:30. The same terms ῥαπίσματα and ἐμπτύσματα also show a link with Mark's narrative, where in 14:65 we find the verbs ἐμπτύω and the substantive ῥαπίσματα in the dative plural. Nevertheless, since Mark is closer to Luke than to Matthew and we have set aside the third evangelist, we can conclude for now that the closest parallel is with Matthew. Several other passages in the *Sibylline Oracles* confirm that Matthew was the Gospel *par excellence*, as is generally the case for most Christian apocalyptic literature of the second and third centuries.

In the case of *Sib Or* 1:365, the kinship with Matt seems to be particularly clear, since Matt 26:67 uses κολαφίζω and ἐμπτύω, while the Sibylline verse combines the substantives κολάφους and πτύσματα; an abbreviated form of ἐμπτύσματα in *Sib Or* 8:288.

In the canonical Gospels the spit upon Jesus is mentioned twice and in two different contexts. In Matt 26:67 // Mark 14:65 it is done in front of the Sanhedrin, while in Matt 27:30 // Mark 15:19 it is done by the Roman soldiers.[2] The context is not defined clearly in the *Sibylline Oracles*. But in *Sib Or* 1:365–366, the responsibility for the scourging is explicitly stated: it is Israel. "*Then indeed Israel, with abominable lips, / and poisonous spittings, will give this man blows.*" This anti-Judaism is not new in Book 1 of the *Sibylline Oracles*, since it appears earlier, in lines 360–361: "*And then Israel, intoxicated, will not perceive / nor yet will she hear, afflicted with weak ears.*" Yet, in Book 8 the Sibyl leaves the identity of the guilty party vague, because she introduces the scourging by saying that the Logos "*will come into the hands of lawless and faithless men*" – Jesus is called this two lines earlier (v. 285: "*and the Logos, who creates forms, to whom everything is subject*"). Who these *lawless and faithless men* are cannot be easily determined. Nevertheless, we may wonder if the words ἀνόμοι and ἀπίστοι refer to the Romans rather than to the Jews, because the latter had received the Law ("νόμος"), which is not the case for the Romans.[3] But we

---

[2] In the fourth Gospel, Jesus is also struck twice, the first time by one of the guards of the High Priest (John 18:22: ῥάπισμα), the second time by the Roman soldiers (John 19:3: ῥαπίσματα).

[3] T. Nicklas, "Apokryphe Passionstraditionen im Vergleich: Petrusevangelium und Sibyllinische Orakel (Buch VIII)", in *Das Evangelium nach Petrus. Text, Kontexte, Inter-*

can also wonder if the use of these two adjectival nouns does not distinguish two categories of unbelievers: on the one hand, the Romans, deprived of the Law (ἀνόμοι), and, on the other hand, the Jews, who are faithless (ἀπίστοι). If so, the two adjectival nouns would echo the Gospel narrative, where Jews and Romans alternately participate in the trial of Jesus. It is true that earlier in Book 8 (v. 220: "*Both faithful and faithless men will see God*"), specifically in the acrostic poem narrating Christ's parousia and the Last Judgment, these two words are used interchangeably in order to contrast "*just*" with "*unjust*" or "*faithful*" with "*faithless*."[4] But some lines earlier in Book 1 (vv. 362–363), where the anti-Jewish polemic is obvious, the Sibyl announces that "*when the raging wrath of the Most High comes upon the Hebrews / it will also take faith away from them.*" In the eyes of this Sibyl, there are Jews who are faithless (ἀπίστοι).

In Book 8 (v. 290), the scene continues with a line which does not have any parallel in Book 1: "*Then he will stretch out his back and give it to the whips.*"[5] The source here is not found in the canonical Gospels but in the third song of the suffering Servant of Isa 50:6 (NRSV): "*I gave my back to those who struck me, and my cheeks to those who pulled out the beard; I did not hide my face from insult and spitting.*"[6] Three key words of this biblical verse are to be found in the scourging narrative in Book 8 of the *Sibylline Oracles*: μάστιγας, ῥαπίσματα, and ἐμπτυσμάτων, with one difference: in the third song of the suffering Servant the scourging precedes the blows and the spit. The process of rewriting in this section of Book 8 is similar to what we read in the *Epistle of Barnabas* 5:14 which quotes Isa

---

texte (ed. by T.J. Kraus & T. Nicklas; TU 158; Berlin and New York 2007), 263–279, here 270.

[4] *Ibid.*

[5] Lactantius (*Divine Institutes*, 4:18:15), Augustine (*City of God*, 18:23:2), and the author of the *Tübingen Theosophy* (Beatrice, *Anonymi Monophysitae Theosophia. An Attempt at Reconstruction* [VigChr.S 56; Leiden, Boston and Cologne 2001], 55,225 = Erbse, *Fragmente griechischer Theosophien* [Hamburger Arbeiten zur Altertumswissenschaft 4; Hamburg 1941], 10,274) have a slightly different text: "*But he will give for their blows simply a holy back.*" The last is the epitome of a collection of pagan testimonia compiled at the end of the 5th or at the beginning of the 6th century of our era and which relies mostly on Lactantius: see the bibliography in Beatrice and Lightfoot (n. 1), passim.

[6] Isa 50:6 LXX: Τὸν νῶτόν μου δέδωκα εἰς μάστιγας, τὰς δὲ σιαγόνας μου εἰς ῥαπίσματα, τὸ δὲ πρόσωπόν μου οὐκ ἀπέστρεψα ἀπὸ αἰσχύνης ἐμπτυσμάτων. – ἔμπτυσμα is a *hapax legomenon* in Isaiah. This biblical verse is also the background of Matt 26:67; cf. U. Luz, *Matthew 21–28. A Commentary* (Hermeneia; Minneapolis 2005), 448, n. 11. Jesus' prediction of the Son of Man's sufferings in the Synoptics (Mark 10:34 and parallels) is surely inspired by this verse of Isaiah; see D.J. Moo, *The Old Testament in the Gospel Passion Narratives* (Sheffield 1983), 88–89 and 139–144.

50:6–7 without 6b–7a: "*Again he says, 'See! I have set my back to whips and my cheeks to blows; and I have set my face as a hard rock.*'"[7]

It must be pointed out that, although they sometimes differ from each other, the two passages from the *Sibylline Oracles* both qualify the spit upon Jesus' face as φαρμακόεντα, i.e. "*poisonous*" or "*venomous.*" This is not the case in the biblical text. Now, if the canonical Gospels merely say that Jesus received spit on his face, literally "*in his eyes,*" the *Sibylline Oracles* are more interested in stating that the spit comes from "*abominable*" or "*unclean lips*" (1:366) and "*polluted mouths*" (8:289). Although the adjectives are not the same, the idea of "*unclean lips*" in *Sib Or* 1:366 surely comes from Isa 6:5, where the prophet accuses himself and the people to whom he belongs, that is to say, Israel, of having "*unclean lips*" (ἀκάθαρτα χείλη ἔχων ἐν μέσῳ λαοῦ ἀκάθαρτα χείλη ἔχοντος). This parallel seems to be more than likely, because the verses quoted (*Sib Or* 1:360–361, 369–371) are a free rewriting of the same chapter in the Book of Isa 6:9–10, where Israel is accused of stubbornness and stupidity: "*And he said, "Go and say to this people: 'Keep listening, but do not comprehend; keep looking, but do not understand.' Make the mind of this people dull, and stop their ears, and shut their eyes, so that they may not look with their eyes, and listen with their ears, and comprehend with their minds, and turn and be healed.*" (NRSV)[8] *Sib Or* 8:289 is much less explicit in its accusation on this point.

Some scholars state that these verses of the *Sibylline Oracles* (8:287–290) are reminiscent of the *Gospel of Peter* 9[9], but this is unproven. A detailed comparison shows that the differences are more important than the

---

[7] *Barn.* 5:14: Καὶ πάλιν λέγει· Ἰδού, τέθεικά μου τὸν νῶτον εἰς μάστιγας, καὶ τὰς σιαγόνας εἰς ῥαπίσματα, τὸ δὲ πρόσωπόν μου ἔθηκα ὡς στερεὰν πέτραν. Translation by B.D. Ehrman in: *The Apostolic Fathers* (vol. 1; Loeb Classical Library; Cambridge, Mass. 2003); reprint in: id., *Lost Scriptures. Books that Did Not Make It into the New Testament* (Oxford 2003), 224.

[8] Isa 6:9–10 LXX: καὶ εἶπε Πορεύθητι καὶ εἶπον τῷ λαῷ τούτῳ Ἀκοῇ ἀκούσετε καὶ οὐ μὴ συνῆτε καὶ βλέποντες βλέψετε καὶ οὐ μὴ ἴδητε· ἐπαχύνθη γὰρ ἡ καρδία τοῦ λαοῦ τούτου, καὶ τοῖς ὠσὶν αὐτῶν βαρέως ἤκουσαν καὶ τοὺς ὀφθαλμοὺς αὐτῶν ἐκάμμυσαν, μήποτε ἴδωσι τοῖς ὀφθαλμοῖς καὶ τοῖς ὠσὶν ἀκούσωσι καὶ τῇ καρδίᾳ συνῶσι καὶ ἐπιστρέψωσι καὶ ἰάσομαι αὐτούς.

[9] *Gospel of Peter* 9: "*Others standing there were spitting in his face; some slapped his cheeks; others were beating him with a reed; and some began to flog him, saying, 'This is how we should honor the Son of God!'*" Καὶ ἕτεροι ἑστῶτες ἐνέπτυον αὐτοῦ ταῖς ὄψεσι καὶ ἄλλοι τὰς σιαγόνας αὐτοῦ ἐράπισαν, ἕτεροι καλάμῳ ἔνυσσον αὐτὸν καὶ τινες αὐτὸν ἐμάστιζον λέγοντες· ταύτῃ τῇ τιμῇ τιμήσωμεν τὸν υἱὸν τοῦ θεοῦ. Translated by Ehrman, *Lost Scriptures* (n. 7), 32; on the critical text cf. T.J. Kraus / T. Nicklas, *Das Petrusevangelium und die Petrusapokalypse. Die griechischen Fragmente mit deutscher und englischer Übersetzung* (GCS NF 11; Neutestamentliche Apokryphen 1; Berlin and New York 2004).

similarities, and the latter are better explained by the imagery of the suffering Servant in Isa 50:6 than by a literary dependence between both texts.[10]

It is interesting to note that the verses 287-290 of *Sib Or* 8 are quoted after Isa 50:5–6 and Ps 34:15–16 in the *Divine Institutes* of Lactantius (4:18:15), written at the beginning of the fourth century of our era, as proofs of pagan prophecies of Christ's Passion.[11] Augustine also cites them, but in Latin, in his *City of God* 18:23:2, after he presents and discusses the Sibyl's famous acrostic. The Bishop of Hippo attempts to gather into a coherent unity those verses of the *Sibylline Oracles* spread throughout Lactantius' work, "*to support the progression of his argument,*" as Augustine says. It must be pointed out that all of the 17 verses gathered by Augustine refer to the Passion of Jesus:

Afterwards, says she [= the Sibyl], he shall fall into the unjust hands of unbelievers; they shall strike God with unclean hands and shall spit upon him the poisonous spittle of their impure mouths; but he shall simply give over his holy back to their whips.[12] And silently he shall take their blows so that none may know what word, or whence, He comes to speak to hell as he is crowned with thorns.[13] For meat they have given him gall, and for drink, vinegar; this is the kind of hospitality they shall show him at table.[14] Thou fool – not to have recognized thy God, displaying himself before the minds of men; instead, you crowned him with thorns and brewed him the cup of bitter-tasting gall.[15] But the veil of the temple shall be rent; and at midday there shall be a night of pitch-blackness lasting for three hours.[16] And, having died, he shall sleep the sleep of death for three days; then he shall come back from hell to the daylight; the first of the arisen, establishing the beginning of resurrection for those whom he has recalled.[17] (*The City of God*, 18:23:2)[18]

---

[10] This is also the point of view of Nicklas, "Apokryphe Passionstraditionen" (n. 3), 270–271. See also L. Vaganay, *L'évangile de Pierre* (ÉtB; Paris 1930), 164–165. Vaganay's conclusions have been accepted by Mara, *Évangile de Pierre* (SC 201; Paris 1973; ²2006). 23; Ead., *Il Vangelo di Pietro* (Scritti delle origini cristiane 30; Bologna 2003), 19; M. Erbetta, *Gli apocrifi del Nuovo Testamento. Vangeli I.1: Scritti affini ai vangeli canonici – composizione gnostiche – materiale illustrativo* (Torino 1975), 141; J. Denker, *Die theologiegeschichtliche Stellung des Petrusevangeliums. Ein Beitrag zur Geschichte des Doketismus* (EHS XXIII.36; Bern and Frankfurt, Main 1975), 19–20.

[11] They can also be found in the *Tübingen Theosophy* (Beatrice [n. 5], 55,222–225 = Erbse [n. 5], 10,271–274).

[12] *Sib Or* 8:287–290; Lactantius, *Div. Inst.*, 4:18:15.

[13] *Sib Or* 8:292–294; Lactantius, *Div. Inst.*, 4:18:17.

[14] *Sib Or* 8:303–304; Lactantius, *Div. Inst.*, 4:18:19.

[15] *Sib Or* 6:22–24; Lactantius, *Div. Inst.*, 4:18:20.

[16] *Sib Or* 8:305–306; Lactantius, *Div. Inst.*, 4:19:5.

[17] *Sib Or* 8:312–314; Lactantius, *Div. Inst.*, 4:19:10.

[18] Augustinus, *The City of God*, 18:23:2: "in manus iniquas", inquit, "infidelium postea ueniet; dabunt autem deo alapas manibus incestis et inpurato ore exspuent uenenatos sputus; dabit uero ad uerbera simpliciter sanctum dorsum." "et colaphos accipiens tacebit, ne quis agnoscat, quod uerbum uel unde uenit, ut inferis loquatur et corona spinea coronetur." "ad cibum autem fel et ad sitim acetum dederunt; inhospitalitatis hanc mon-

These verses come mainly from Book 8 of the *Sibylline Oracles* (except three verses coming from Book 6). Book 1 apparently was unknown to Lactantius (and consequently to Augustine, who relied on the latter for his knowledge of these lines).

Sib Or 8:292–293

The first Book of the *Sibyllline Oracles* jumps directly from the scourging and the spit to the food and drink given to Jesus on the Cross (1:367).

But in Book 8, verses 292–293, there is an interesting development in Jesus' attitude at the scourging: "*Beaten, he will be silent, lest anyone recognize who he is, whose son, and whence he came, so that he may speak to the dead.*" The blows are noted by the same verb, κολαφίζω, that we find in Matt 26:65 and Mark 14:65. This is nothing new, except that the order of events here is closer to the canonical Gospels than in Book 1. As for Jesus' silence, the four Gospels mention it (Matt 26:63; 27:13; Mark 14:61; 15:4; Luke 23:9; John 19:9) twice in both Matthew and Mark, first in front of the Sanhedrin, and second before Pilate. In Luke and John, only Jesus' refusal to answer to Pilate is mentioned. The Gospels never use the verb for silence, σιγάω, which the *Sibylline Oracles* might be using for metric reasons. The *Sibylline Oracles* do not mention any specific interrogation, while the canonical Gospels relate several. But the expression τίς τίνος ὤν in the *Oracles* could well echo a question about Jesus' messianic mandate and divine filiation, as is read in Matt 26:63, Mark 14:61, and Luke 22:67. Furthermore, Lactantius and those who rely on him present a variant: "... *so that no one may know / that he is the Word, and whence he comes,*"[19] which tends to confirm this interpretation.

---

strabunt mensam." "ipsa enim insipiens tuum deum non intellexisti, ludentem mortalium mentibus, sed et spinis coronasti et horridum fel miscuisti." "templi uero uelum scindetur; et medio die nox erit tenebrosa nimis in tribus horis." "et morte morietur tribus diebus somno suscepto; et tunc ab inferis regressus ad lucem ueniet primus resurrectionis principio reuocatis ostenso." Translated by G.G. Walsh, and D.J. Honan, *Writings of Saint Augustine* (vol. 8, in: *The Fathers of the Church. A New Translation*; vol. 24; New York 1954), 117. On this topic, see J.-M. Roessli, "Augustin, les sibylles, et les *Oracles sibyllins,*" in: *Augustinus afer. Saint Augustin: africanité et universalité. Actes du colloque international, Alger-Annaba, 1–7 avril 2001* (ed. by P.-Y. Fux, J.-M. Roessli and O. Wermelinger; Paradosis 45/1; Fribourg 2003), 263–286, here 275–276. I corrected the mistranslated "*so that none may know the source or the meaning of the word he addresses to hell*" with "*so that none may know what word, or whence, He comes to speak to hell.*"

[19] Lactantius (*Div. Inst.*, 4:18:17), Augustine (*City of God*, 18:23:2), and the author of the *Tübingen Theosophy* (Beatrice [n. 5], 55,230 = Erbse [n. 5], 10,281): τίς λόγος ἤ; quod uerbum uel unde uenit.

Sib Or 1	*Sib Or 8:292–293*
	καὶ κολαφιζόμενος σιγήσει, μή τις ἐπιγνῷ, Beaten, he will be silent, lest anyone recognize τίς τίνος ὢν πόθεν ἦλθεν, ἵνα φθιμένοισι λαλήσει, who he is, whose son, and whence he came, so that he may speak to the dead;

The subsequent question, πόθεν ἦλθεν, used indirectly in the *Oracles*, might also well echo Pilate's question about Jesus' kingship in Jn 19:9: πόθεν εἶ σύ; "*Where are you from?*"

There is some doubt about the subordinate clause: ἵνα φθιμένοισι λαλήσει. Should it be interpreted in connection with these three indirect questions: "... *who he is, whose son, and whence he came*"? If this is the case, the Sibyl certainly wants to emphasize that the Word can speak to the dead because of his filiation and his divine identity: "*lest anyone recognize who he is, whose son, and whence he came to speak to the dead.*" There is another possible reading. Nothing prevents this subordinate clause, introduced by ἵνα, from being connected to the main verb of the sentence. Thus, if the Word chooses to keep silent and refuses to reveal his identity, it is in order to speak to the dead: "*he will be silent, lest anyone recognize who he is, whose son, and whence he came, so that he may speak to the dead.*" I do not think it is grammatically and syntactically possible or even necessary to choose between these two readings, which corresponds very well to the multiple meanings inherent to the *Sibylline Oracles*. Whatever the case, this subordinate clause anticipates the ultimate goal of the Word's Passion, which is not only to redeem the dead, but also to speak to them (v. 293).

A more direct source for the Word's silence at this instance may not be found in the Synoptic Gospels but in the Book of Isaiah. Isaiah writes about the suffering Servant in 53:7: "*He was oppressed, and he was afflicted, yet he did not open his mouth; like a lamb that is led to the slaughter, and like a sheep that before its shearers is silent, so he did not open his mouth.*" (NRSV)[20] Lactantius notes it and connects it to the Sibylline verses.[21]

---

[20] Isa 53:7 LXX: καὶ αὐτὸς διὰ τὸ κεκακῶσθαι οὐκ ἀνοίγει τὸ στόμα· ὡς πρόβατον ἐπὶ σφαγὴν ἤχθη καὶ ὡς ἀμνὸς ἐναντίον τοῦ κείροντος αὐτὸν ἄφωνος οὕτως οὐκ ἀνοίγει τὸ στόμα αὐτοῦ.

[21] Lactantius, *Div. Inst.*, 4:18:16–17: "*Likewise of His Silence, which He kept tenaciously even unto death, Isaiah spoke again thus: "He was led as a sheep to the slaughter, and he was as a lamb before his shearers, without a word, and thus he did not open his mouth."* (Isa 53:7) *And the above-mentioned Sibyl: "And receiving the blows he will be silent, so that no one may know what the word is or whence he comes, in order that he*

The *Gospel of Peter* also presents Jesus' silence, but it is the Lord's silence on the Cross, and with a totally different meaning from the one in the *Sibylline Oracles*. The apocryphal gospel (v. 10) adds: "*But he was silent, as if he felt no pain.*"[22] Leaving aside the question of whether any docetism is present in this assertion,[23] it is certain that Jesus, the Lord (κύριος), is silent to hide his sufferings and not to keep a secret.

In Book 8 of the *Sibylline Oracles*, the Word's silence has a totally different function; its role precisely is to conceal, at least for a while, the meaning of his suffering in salvation history. Jesus, portrayed earlier as the creative Word of all things and the Saviour of the dead (vv. 285–286), is actually going to become the one who speaks to the dead (v. 293). The contrast between Jesus' silence in front of the living during his Passion and his willingness to speak to the dead after his own death, is very striking. Everything unfolds as if the Word wanted somehow to save his word for those who had lost it. This contrast furthermore reveals a very interesting rhetorical structure. At the beginning of creation the Word is (v. 285). At the end of times, that is to say, at the Last Judgement, he speaks with the dead. In the meantime, during his trial, the Word is silent, because he must not be recognized as such by the living, as the variant transmitted by Lactantius and his successors stresses: "*so that no one may know / that he is the Word, and whence he comes.*" Nowhere to my knowledge, even in the canonical Gospels, has the Passion such a strategic position between creation and eschatology.[24]

Sib Or 8:294–298 and Sib Or 1:373–374a

Book 8 (vv. 294–296) of the *Sibylline Oracles* continues to narrate Jesus' crowning with thorns and the piercing of his sides. In so doing, the Sibyl combines two separate episodes of the New Testament: the mockery of Jesus with a crown of thorns and a reed before his crucifixion (Matt 27:29 and Mark 15:17), and the piercing of his side with a spear when he is on the Cross (John 19:34). The language used by the Sibyl leaves no doubt. The expression στέφανον ἀκάνθινον is directly borrowed from Matt and Mark, while πλευρὰς νύξουσιν ("*they pierced his sides*") is an almost exact copy of the Johannine phrase: τὴν πλευρὰν ἐνύξεν ("*[one of the soldiers]*

---

might address the lowly and wear a crown of thorns." [*Sib Or* 8:292–294a] (Translated by M.F. McDonald, in: *The Fathers of the Church. A New Translation* [vol. 49; New York 1964]), 293.

[22] Ehrman, *Lost Scriptures* (n. 7), 32. See Mara, *Évangile de Pierre* (n. 9), 106–111.

[23] See, e.g., G.W. McCant, "The Gospel of Peter: Docetism Reconsidered," *NTS* 30 (1984), 258–273; P.M. Head, "On the Christology of the Gospel of Peter," *VigChr* 46 (1992), 209–224.

[24] As Nicklas, "Apokryphe Passionstraditionen" (n. 3), 272 rightly emphasized it.

pierced his side with a spear"), except that *Sib Or* 8:296 uses the plural while John and *Sib Or* 1:373 maintain the singular. As for the spear (λόγχη) in John, it is replaced by the reed (κάλαμος) of Mark and Matt. By the choice of the verb *νύσσω*, "*to pierce,*" the Sibyl may well have intended to imply the realization of Zechariah's prophecy (12:10b): "*When they look on the one whom they have pierced, they shall mourn for him, as one mourns for an only child, and weep bitterly over him, as one weeps over a first-born*" (NRSV).[25]

Sib Or 1:372–374a	*Sib Or 8:[302] 294–296*
ἀλλ᾽ ὅταν ἐκπετάσῃ χεῖρας καὶ πάντα μετρήσῃ	[ἐκπετάσει χεῖρας καὶ κόσμον ἅπαντα μετρήσει,
But when he will stretch out his hands and measure all,	He will stretch out his hands and measure the entire world.]
καὶ στέφανον φορέσῃ τὸν ἀκάνθινον ἠδέ τε πλευράν	καὶ στέφανον φορέσει τὸν ἀκάνθινον ἐκ γὰρ ἀκανθῶν
and bear the crown of thorns – and they will stab	and he will wear the crown of thorns. For, made of thorns,
	τὸ στέφος ἐκλεκτῶν αἰώνιών ἐστιν ἄγαλμα,
	the crown is the eternal array of chosen men.
	πλευρὰς νύξουσιν καλάμῳ διὰ τὸν νόμον αὐτῶν
νύξωσιν καλάμοισι νόμου χάριν ... his side with reeds according to the law...	They will stab his sides with a reed on account of their law.
	ἐκ καλάμων γὰρ σειομένων ὑπὸ πνεύματος ἄλλου
	For by reeds shaken by another wind
	προσκλίματα ψυχῆς ἐστράφη ὀργῆς καὶ ἀμοιβῆς
	the inclinations of the soul are turned from the wrath and change.

In order to illuminate this theological "midrash," which borrows much from both the canonical Gospels and the Prophets, Book 8 proposes two interesting new exegeses: one about the crown of thorns, the other about the reed.

In the first, the Sibyl explains (vv. 295–296), rather surprisingly, that, thanks to its thorns, the crown becomes "*the eternal array of the elected*

---

[25] Zech 12,10b LXX: ἄνθ᾽ ὧν κατωρχήσαντο καὶ κόψονται ἐπ᾽ αὐτὸν κοπετὸν ὡς ἐπ᾽ ἀγαπητὸν καὶ ὀδυνηθήσονται ὀδύνην ὡς ἐπὶ πρωτοτόκῳ. As Nicklas, "Apokryphe Passionstraditionen" (n. 3), 273, n. 48 noticed, this prophet's quotation was widespread in the early Christian literature: *Barn.* 7:8–9; *Proto-Gospel of James*, 24:3; Justin, *Dial.* 32:2; *Apol.* 52:11; Irenaeus, *haer.* 4:33:11, etc.

ones."[26] In so doing, she distances herself from the canonical Gospels (and from the *Gospel of Peter* 8, which is very close to the canonical Gospels on this matter), for whom the crown is the emblem of a humiliated King stripped of his kingdom (*Spottkönig* in German). She transforms the crown into an eternal "*array*" (ἄγαλμα), a symbol *par excellence* of election. With this exegesis, which Lactantius might allude to in his *Divine Institutes* 4:26:21,[27] the Sibyl emphasizes once again the close link between the Passion and eschatological redemption.

In the second exegesis, that of the reed, the text of vv. 297–298 is unfortunately unclear. I translate it so: "*For by reeds shaken by another wind / the inclinations of the soul are turned from wrath and change.*"[28] We can

---

[26] My translation. Collins translates it in the following manner: "*For, made of thorns, the crown of chosen men is an eternal delight.*" Compare with J.-M. Roessli, "Les *Oracles sibyllins*: Livre 6, 7 et 8 (vv. 217–428)," in: *Écrits apocryphes chrétiens*, (ed. by P. Geoltrain and J.-D. Kaestli, Index established by J.-M. Roessli and S. Voicu; Bibliothèque de la Pléiade 516, t. 2; Paris 2005), 1045–1083 (reprint 2006), here 1076: "*Car c'est en raison de ses épines que la couronne des élus est une parure éternelle.*" The *Tübingen Theosophy* has the same text as the classes of manuscripts Φ and Ψ: "τὸ στέφος ἐκλεκτῶν ἁγίων αἰώνιον ἥξει," "*For out of thorns shall ever come the crown of holy ones elect,*" translated by M.S. Terry, *The Sibylline Oracles Translated from the Greek Into English Blank Verse* (New York and Cincinnati 1890), 189; see also id., *The Sibylline Oracles. Translated from The Greek into English Blank Verse, New Edition Revised After the Text of Rzach* (New York and Cincinnati 1899 [reprint New York 1973]), 60: "*For of thorns is the crown an ornament / Elect, eternal.*"

[27] Lactantius, *Div. Inst.*, 4:26:21: "Nam corona spinea capiti eius imposita id declarabat fore ut diuinam sibi plebem de nocentibus congregaret. Corona enim dicitur circumstans in orbem populus." "*For the placing of a crown of thorns upon His head, declared that it would come to pass that He would gather to Himself a holy people from those who were guilty. For people standing around in a circle are called a corona.*" (Translated by W. Fletcher, *The Ante-Nicene Fathers*, edited by A. Roberts, J. Donaldson, and A. Cleveland Coxe [vol. VII; Buffalo, N.Y. 1886], 128). See also Clement of Alexandria, *Paedagogue*, 2:8:74:1–3. This exegesis (*Sib Or* 8:295–296) anticipates the interpretation of *Sib Or* 8:302, which Lactantius clearly alludes to later in the same chapter of *Divine Institutes,* 4:26:36); cf. below the discussion on *Sib Or* 8:302.

[28] I slightly corrected the first hemistich of Collins' translation: "*For by winds [sic!] shaken by another wind...*" Instead of the verb "to turn from" (ἐστράφη) of Ψ, one could also chose the variant "to nourish" (ἐτράφη) of Φ. In that case, these verses would be translated as follows: "*For from reeds shaken by another wind the inclinations of the soul were nourished of wrath and change.*" Most scholars do not translate these lines, as they are considered to be corrupted. See nevertheless Terry, *Sibylline Oracles* (1890, n. 26), 189: "*For from the reeds by another spirit moved / Was he brought up for judgments of the soul, / And wrath and recompense,*" id., *Sibylline Oracles* (1899, n. 26), 60: "*For of reeds shaken by another spirit / Were nourished inclinations of the soul, / Of anger and revenge*") or E. Massaux, *Influence de l'évangile selon saint Matthieu sur la littérature chrétienne avant Irénée* (Universitas Catholica Lovaniensis II.42; Louvain/Gembloux 1950), 235: "*Car par un autre des roseaux qui vacillaient au vent, l'âme a été amenée au jugement de la colère et de la rétribution,*" Roessli, "Les *Oracles sibyllins*" (n. 26),

certainly recognize an allusion to John the Baptist. First Jesus asks (Matt 11:7 and Luke 7:24): "*What did you go out into the wilderness to look at? A reed shaken by the wind?*" Secondly, there is a reminder of the Baptist's preaching (Matt and Luke 3:7): "*You brood of vipers! Who warned you to flee from the wrath to come?*" The link with the Passion is hard to establish, but it is possible that the reed with which Jesus was beaten reminds the readers of the imminence of Judgment, which John the Baptist announced.[29] In this case, the Sibyl of Book 8 intends to connect the Word's passion with the Last Judgment, as Nicklas inclines to think on the basis of the passion narrative's position after the parousia's acrostic in Book 8:217–250.[30]

The juxtaposition of the verb νύσσω and the substantive κάλαμος can also be found in the *Gospel of Peter* 9, quoted above. Peter also makes the reed stroke an act of derision preceding the Crucifixion, just as in *Sib Or* 8:296, without saying that the reed pierces Jesus' side. The same can be found in the Gnostic and docetic section of *Acts of John* 97 ("... *'John, for the people below in Jerusalem I am being crucified and pierced with lances and reeds and given vinegar and gall to drink. But to you I am speaking, and listen to what I speak.' Jesus then goes on to reveal to John the true meaning of the crucifixion, concluding, 'So then, I have suffered none of those things which they will say of me,'*")[31] which dates back to the second century Syria, and is found the *Oracle of Baalbek*, lines 74–75 ("*And they will pierce his side with a reed (stake) and will not harm*

1076–77: "*Car c'est des roseaux secoués par un autre vent / que les inclinations de l'âme se sont détournées de la colère et du châtiment,*" and Monaca, *Oracoli Sibillini* (n. 1), 176: "*Dalle canne agitate dal vento, poi, un altro si alimentò / guardando al giudizio della passione dell'anima e alla redenzione.*"

[29] John the Baptist is alluded to in *Sib Or* 1:336–343, but nowhere else in Book 8, so that Waßmuth, *Sibyllinische Orakel* (n. 1) considers that *Sib Or* 8, with its highly developed christology, was no longer interested in the figure of the Baptist. On Matt 11:7, see Hilary of Poitiers, *In Matt.*, 11:4 and Ambrose of Milan, *In Lucam*, 5:104–106; in the latter, the reed becomes the very flesh of Christ. I thank Agnès Bastit for these references.

[30] Nicklas, "Apokryphe Passionstraditionen" (n. 3), but see also below note 34.

[31] Translated by R.E. Van Voorst, "Extracanonical Passion Narratives," in: *The Death of Jesus in Early Christianity* (ed. by J.T. Carroll and J.B. Green; Peabody, Mass. 1995), 151, n. 6 (Curiously, this author does not mention the *Sibylline Oracles* at all.) On this text, see *Acta Iohannis. Textus alii, commentarius, indices*, (ed. by E. Junod and J.-D. Kaestli; CC.SA 2; Turnhout 1983), 581–677; id., "Les Actes de Jean," in *Écrits apocryphes chrétiens* (ed. by F. Bovon and P. Geoltrain; Bibliothèque de la Pléiade; t. 1; Paris 1997), 973–1037, here 979–981. Let us note that the *Acts of John* combine the plural of John 19:34 (λόγχη, "spear" or "lance") and the plural of Matt 11:7 and 27:29 (κάλαμος, "reeds"). On Matt 27:29, see Hilary of Poitiers, *In Matt.*, 33:3 and Ambrose of Milan, *In Lucam*, 10:105–106; in the latter, the reed represents Christ's humanity. I thank Agnès Bastit for these references.

him,")[32] except that in these texts the stroke is given during the Crucifixion itself, as in the first Book of the *Sibylline Oracles*.[33] No direct borrowing can be established between the *Gospel of Peter*, the *Acts of John*, and the *Sibylline Oracles*, but it is likely that the *Oracle of Baalbek* follows the *Sibylline Oracles* on this point.

Book 1 of the *Sibylline Oracles* also presents the crown of thorns and the piercing of the Lord's side with reeds, but it happens during the Crucifixion, and only one side of the Lord is pierced, as in the Gospel of John. Unlike in Book 8, no exegesis is given. In Book 1 the scene is presented as follows: after a violent accusation against Israel and its people (vv. 369b–371), the Sibyl narrates Jesus' crucifixion itself. She does it in an extraordinary manner. Isolated from its context, the language the Sibyl uses could have a totally different meaning. It could express Jesus' or God's lordship over the universe. In the *Oracles* it is also a barely veiled allusion to Jesus' crucifixion (vv. 372–373): "*But when he will stretch out his hands and measure all, / and bear the crown of thorns – and they will stab.*"

The same idea can also be found in Book 8 (v. 302): "*He will stretch out his hands and measure the entire world.*" It comes later, after the crown of thorns, and it forms an independent sentence. It could have, even more than in Book 1, a totally different meaning if isolated from its context.[34]

---

[32] P.J. Alexander, *The Oracle of Baalbek. The Tiburtine Sibyl in Greek Dress* (Dumbarton Oaks Studies; Washington 1967), 13: καὶ κάλαμῳ νύξουσιν αὐτοῦ τὴν πλευρὰν καὶ οὐδὲν ἀδικήσουσιν αὐτόν. The *Oracle of Baalbek* is not the original version of the better known Latin *Tiburtine Sibyl*, but an amplified version, dating back to the beginning of the sixth century, of the original Greek version of the latter which is to be dated to the fourth century. There are also versions of the *Tiburtine Sibyl* in Arabic and Ethiopic; on this, see J. Schleifer, "Die Erzählung der Sibylle: ein Apokryph. Nach den karschunischen, arabischen und äthiopischen Handschriften zu London, Oxford, Paris und Rom," *Denkschriften der Kaiserlichen Akademie der Wissenschaften. Philosophisch-historische Klasse* 53 (1910), 1–80; R.Y. Ebied and M.J.L. Young, "A Newly-Discovered Version of the Arabic Sibylline Prophecy," *OrChr* 60 (1976), 83–94; id., "An Unrecorded Arabic Version of a Sibylline Prophecy," *OrChrP* 43 (1977), 279–307; as well as translations into old French; on this, see J. Haffen, *Contribution à l'étude de la Sibylle médiévale. Étude et édition du MS. B.N., F. FR. 25407 fol. 160v–172v : Le livre de Sibille* (Annales littéraires de l'Université de Besançon 296; Paris 1984); J. Baroin and J. Haffen, *La Prophétie de la Sibylle Tiburtine. Édition des MSS B.N. FR. 375 et Rennes B.M. FR. 593* (Annales littéraires de l'Université de Besançon 355; Paris 1987). In all of these versions only one side of Jesus is pierced, while the *Acts of John* remain silent on this point.

[33] Both texts are mentioned by Lightfoot, *The Sibylline Oracles* (n. 1), 437.

[34] Ch. Alexandre (*Oracula Sibyllina* [Paris 1841], 281, note to 302; *Oracula Sibyllina* [Paris 1869], 237, note to 302ff.) proposed to move this verse after 298. It must be noted that in most of the manuscripts of the *Sibylline Oracles* the order of the verses in Book 8 is very chaotic. That is the reason why I personally would not give so much weight and

In both cases, of course, the context alludes to, as well as interprets, the Crucifixion. By this very positive reading of the Crucifixion, the Sibyl reinforces the link she wants to draw between the Passion and Salvation, as Lactantius also understands it, when he inserts a Latin version of this line in the fourth Book of his *Divine Institutes*: "*Therefore in His suffering* He stretched forth His hands and measured out the world, *that even then He might show that a great multitude, collected together out of all languages and tribes, from the rising of the sun even to his setting, was about to come under His wings, and to receive on their foreheads that great and lofty sign.*"[35] Many other patristic and apocryphal texts confirm this interpretation of the Crucifixion, in which the Crucified takes the whole world under his protection.[36]

---

credit as Nicklas, "Apokryphe Passionstraditionen" (n. 3) does to the literary context – narrower or broader – of the passion narrative in the *Sibylline Oracles*. Nobody has followed Alexandre on this point. In my opinion, verse 302 is in its right position after the announcement of the abrogation of the Law by Jesus in the preceding verses (vv. 299–301); see below.

[35] Lactantius, *Div. Inst.*, 4:26:36: "Extendit ergo in passione manus suas orbemque dimensus est, ut iam tunc ostenderet ab ortu solis usque ad occasum magnum populum ex omnibus linguis et tribubus congregatum sub alas suas esse uenturum signumque illud maximum atque sublime frontibus suis suscepturum." Translated by Fletcher, *Ante-Nicene Fathers* (n. 27), 129. Cf. Rev 7:1–4; 14:1. Cf. *Sib Or* 8:302.

[36] Irenaeus of Lyon, *haer.*, 5 Frg. gr. 16:10 ff.: "*Through the extension of the hands of a divine person, gathering together the two peoples to one God...*" [= 5:17:4 (inspired by Eph 3:18): "*This word, then, what was hidden from us, did the dispensation of the tree make manifest, as I have already remarked. For as we lost it by means of a tree, by means of a tree again was it made manifest to all, showing the height, the length, the breadth, the depth in itself; and, as a certain man among our predecessors observed, through the extension of the hands of a divine person, gathering together the two peoples to one God. For these were two hands, because there were two peoples scattered to the ends of the earth; but there was one head in the middle, as there is but one God, who is above all, and through all, and in us all.*" (Translated by A. Roberts and W. Rambaut, *Ante-Nicene Fathers* [ed. by A. Roberts, J. Donaldson, and A. Cleveland Coxe; vol. 1; Buffalo, N.Y. 1885]); Hippolytus, *The Antichrist*, 61: "*... Jesus Christ, who, in stretching forth His holy hands on the holy tree, unfolded two wings, the right and the left, and called to Him all who believed upon Him, and covered them as a hen her chickens.*" (Translated by Ph. Schaff, *Ante-Nicene Fathers* [ed. by A. Roberts, J. Donaldson, and A. Cleveland Coxe; vol. 5; Buffalo, N.Y. 1885]); Lactantius, *Div. Inst.*, 4:26:21, quoted above in n. 27 in relation to *Sib Or* 8:295–296. See also the *Ode of Solomon* 27:2–3 (M. Lattke, *Oden Salomos. Text, Übersetzung, Kommentar. Teil 2. Oden 15–28* [NTOA 41/2; Fribourg and Göttingen 2001], 253–256); *Ode of Solomon* 42:1–2 (id., *Oden Salomos. Text, Übersetzung, Kommentar. Teil 3. Oden 29–42* [NTOA 41/3; Fribourg and Göttingen 2005], 249–252; English translation: *The Odes of Solomon: A Commentary*, Minneapolis 2009); *Sib Or* 5:257 and 8:251 (about Moses).

Sib Or 8:299–301 and Sib Or 1:332

But before this evocation of the crucifixion (v. 302), the Sibyl of Book 8 prophesies the dissolution of the Law by Jesus (vv. 299–301): "*But when all these things of which I have spoken are fulfilled, / then for him every law will be dissolved which from the beginning / was given in decrees to men, on account of a disobedient people.*" These lines seem to be deeply influenced by the Paul of *Galatians* and, in a certain way, of *Romans*. The same idea, even more explicit and polemical, is found in the already mentioned *Oracle of Baalbek*, lines 41–42, where Jesus is said to dissolve the Law of the Hebrews in order to establish and impose his own law: "*He will dissolve the Law of the Hebrews and establish his own law, and his law will reign.*"[37] In Book 8 the reference to the Law of the Hebrews is alluded to indirectly by the mention of "*a disobedient people*" (διὰ λαὸν ἀπειθῆ)[38]. Paul J. Alexander, the editor of the *Oracle of Baalbek*, correlated the Sibyl's prophecy that Jesus will destroy the Jewish Law with Marcion's "*doctrine of the fundamental opposition of Law and Gospel.*"[39] We know that "in his *Antitheses* Marcion deleted Jesus' saying (Matt 5:17) that he had not come to destroy the Law or the Prophets and inserted into his version of the Gospel of Luke a Jewish charge before Pilate that Jesus '*was destroying the Law and the Prophets.*'[40] Later Marcionists then incorporated into their gospel the words of Jesus himself which said the very opposite of Matt 5:17: '*Do you believe that I have come to fulfil the Law or the Prophets? I have come to destroy, but not to fulfil.*'"[41]

---

[37] Alexander, *Oracle of Baalbek* (n. 32), 12: λύσει τὸν νόμον τῶν Ἑβραίων καὶ ἴδιον νόμον στήσει, καὶ βασιλεύσει ὁ νόμος αὐτοῦ.

[38] I do not follow Nicklas, "Apokryphe Passionstraditionen" (n. 3), 273, n. 47, for whom what is meant by "*every law*" (or also, and maybe better, by "*the whole law*," πᾶς νόμος) is unclear and may not be related to the Jewish Law, because of this allusion to "*a disobedient people*". This expression is also found in *Sib Or* 1:204; 3:668; and 6:11 (after correction), where it obviously refers to the Jewish people. But above all, I do not think it could relate to any other law than to the Law of the Hebrews, as is confirmed by the *Oracle of Baalbek*. This is also J.H. Charlesworth's view ("Jewish and Christian Self-Definition in the Christian Additions to the Apocryphal Writings," in: E.P. Sanders [ed.], *Jewish and Christian Self-Definition* [vol. 2; London 1980], 27–55 and 310–315, here 53). See, however, Nicklas, "Apokryphe Passionstraditionen" (n. 3), 275, where he identifies the law of *Sib Or* 8:307 with the Jewish Torah. Curiously, Nicklas does not seem to link *Sib Or* 8:299–301 to *Sib Or* 8:307–309; see below.

[39] Alexander, *Oracle of Baalbek* (n. 32), 72.

[40] *Ibid.*, n. 27.

[41] *Ibid.*, 72. Alexander quotes Isidore of Pelusa, *Ep.* I.371, and refers, of course, to A. von Harnack, *Marcion: Das Evangelium vom fremden Gott* (TU 15; Berlin ²1924), 80 and 261; 173 and 235; 369ff. See also Nicklas, "Apokryphe Passionstraditionen" (n. 3), 278.

Sib Or 1:332	*Sib Or 8:299–301*
	ἀλλ᾽ ὅτε ταῦτά γε πάντα τελειωθῇ ἅπερ εἶπον,
	But when all these things of which I have spoken are fulfilled,
αὐτὸς πληρώσει δε θεοῦ νόμον, οὐ καταλύσει	εἰς αὐτὸν τότε πᾶς λύεται νομος, ὅστις ἀπ᾽ ἀρχῆς
He will fulfil the Law of God – he will not destroy it –	then for him every law will be dissolved which from the beginning
	δόγμασιν ἀνθρώποις ἐδόθη διὰ λαὸν ἀπειθῆ.
	was given in decrees to men, on account of a disobedient people.

The exegesis of Book 8 strongly contrasts with the assertion of Book 1 of the *Sibylline Oracles* (v. 332): "*He will fulfil the Law of God – he will not destroy it –*", which echoes Matt 5:17 ("*Do not believe that I have come to destroy the Law and the prophets; I have not come to destroy but to fulfil,*")[42] except that the Sibyl speaks more precisely of the "*Law of God,*"[43] omits the prophets, and predicts this right at the beginning of her "Gospel epitome" in Book 1. The *Tiburtine Sibyl*, as well as the medieval translations of this text in old French, will say almost the same thing: "*He will fulfil the Law of the Hebrews and make additions to it,*"[44] with the substitu-

[42] See Lightfoot, *The Sibylline Oracles* (n. 1), 427, who refers to D.A. Hagner, *Matthew 1–13* (WBC 33A; Columbia 1993), 105–106, for the meaning of the verb πληρῶσαι. The same explanation can be read in a note to Matt 5:17 in the ecumenical French translation of the New Testament (TOB), Paris ³1989. For Jesus and the Law, Lightfoot also refers to R.S. McConnell, *Law and Prophecy in Matthew's Gospel: The Authority and Use of the Old Testament in the Gospel of St. Matthew* (Dissertation; Basel 1969), 6–100.

[43] As in *Sib Or* 3:256, 276, 284, 580, 600, 686, 719, 757, 768; 7:128 and 11:37; on this, see R. Buitenwerf, *Book III of the* Sibylline Oracles *and its Social Setting, With an Introduction, Translation, and Commentary* (SVTP 17; Leiden and Boston 2003), 339–342.

[44] E. Sackur, *Sibyllinische Texte und Untersuchungen. Pseudo-Methodius, Adso und die tiburtinische Sibylle* (Halle 1898; reprint Turin 1963), 179, line 28. For a French translation of this text, see R. Basset, *Les apocryphes éthiopiens. X. La sagesse de Sibylle* (Paris 1900). In the manuscripts edited by J. Haffen, *Contribution* (n. 32), 116, one reads: "La Lei aemplira / E la soie ajoindra" (vv. 249–250), and by Barouin and Haffen, *La Prophétie* (n. 32), 89: "e aemplira le loy des Hebrius et ajoustera ses propres choses a une chose" (27c, ll. 91–92). According to the abstracts of two other old French versions of the *Tiburtine Sibyl* (M. Le Merrer, "Des sibylles à la sapience dans la tradition médiévale," *Mélanges de l'École française de Rome. Moyen Âge* 98 [1986], 13–33, here 24: "*Il déposera la loi judaïque et suscitera une nouvelle loi*," and Ph. Verdier, "La naissance à Rome de la vision de l'Ara Coeli. Un aspect de l'utopie de la paix perpétuelle à travers un thème iconographique," *Mélanges de l'École française de Rome. Moyen Âge* 94 [1982], 85–119, here 94: "*Il remplacera l'ancienne loi par la loi nouvelle,*") it is not

tion of the "*Law of God*" with the "*Law of the Hebrews,*" and the idea that Jesus will add something to it.

Sib Or 1:367–368a and Sib Or 8:303–304

How do the two Sibylline Books (*Sib Or* 1:367–368a and *Sib Or* 8:303–304) present the episode of the Passion regarding the drink given to Jesus, in comparison with the canonical Gospels?

Or Sib 1, 367[–371]	*Or Sib 8, 303–304*
εἰς δὲ τὸ βρῶμα χολὴν καὶ εἰς ποτὸν ὄξος ἄκρατον	εἰς δὲ τὸ βρῶμα χολὴν καὶ πιεῖν ὄξος ἔδωκαν·
For food they will give him gall and for drink	They gave him gall for food and vinegar to drink.
δυσσεβέως δώσουσι κακῷ βεβολημένοι οἴστρῳ	τῆς ἀφιλοξενίης ταύτην δείξουσι τράπεζαν.
unmixed vinegar, impiously, smitten in breast	They will show forth this table of inhospitality.
στήθεα καὶ κραδίην, ἀτὰρ ὄμμασιν οὐκ ἐσορῶντες	
and heart with an evil craze, not seeing with their eyes	
τυφλότεροι σπαλάκων, φοβερώτεροι ἑρπυστήρων	
more blind than blind rats, more terrible than poisonous	
θηρῶν ἰοβόλων, βαρέι πεπεδημένοι ὕπνῳ	
Creeping beasts, shackled with heavy sleep.	

Each of the canonical Gospels narrates how Jesus "*was given drink*" at the Crucifixion (Matt 27:34,48; Mark 15:36; Luke 23:26, and John 19:29) and all of them mention the vinegar, but only Matt 27:34 speaks of "*gall,*" without saying that this is given "*as a meal*" and without associating it with vinegar. According to Matthew it is mingled with wine. The most relevant parallel for the Sibylline verses is found in Ps 68:22 LXX, "*They gave me also gall for my meat; and in my thirst they gave me vinegar to drink,*"[45] as Lactantius also writes in his *Divine Institutes* (4:18:18).[46] Al-

---

impossible that some medieval translations of the *Tiburtine Sibyl* have kept the memory of the doubts or controversies concerning Jesus' attitude towards the Law.

[45] Ps 68:22 LXX: καὶ ἔδωκαν εἰς τὸ βρῶμά μου χολὴν καὶ εἰς τὴν δίψαν μου ἐπότισέν με ὄξος.

[46] Lactantius, *Div. Inst.*, 4:18:18–19: "*But respecting the food and the drink which they offered to Him before they fastened Him to the cross, David thus speaks in the sixty-eighth Psalm:* 'And they gave me gall for my meat; and in my thirst they gave me vinegar to drink.' *The Sibyl foretold that this also would happen:* 'They gave me gall for my food, and for my thirst vinegar; this inhospitable table they will show.' [*Sib Or* 8:303–

most every word used by the Sibyl is found in the biblical text: εἰς τὸ βρῶμα, χολήν, ὄξος; only the verb πίνω of *Sib Or* 8:303 is somewhat different, but its meaning is not far from ποτίζω ("*to give to drink*"), of which we have the substantive in *Sib Or* 1:367. In the case of *Sib Or* 8:303, the kinship goes even further, since we find the same form, ἔδωκαν, which is an aorist in a context where a future tense would be expected, as in the following and preceding verses. It can legitimately be asked if the Sibyl of Book 8 had merely copied from the *Septuagint* without adapting it to the temporal framework of the oracular discourse, which requires a future tense. It is still more probable that this is the case since the following verse (v. 304) alludes to a table, τράπεζα, of inhospitality, the source of which is certainly found in the next verse of the same Psalm 68:23 LXX.[47] The Sibyl ironically and sarcastically summarizes, with this laconic clause: "*they will show forth this table of inhospitality,*" what Jesus' meal will be during the Passion. Taken as a whole, the sequence of verses 288–304 shows that Book 8 of the *Sibylline Oracles* tries to connect the sufferings of the Incarnate Word both with the suffering Servant in Isaiah and the Just in Psalm 68 LXX. Book 1 completes its oracle with a further development of Isa 6:9–10 quoted above in relation to *Sib Or* 1:360–361. These lines (vv. 369–371) are intended to heighten the accusation against Israel: "*Impiously, smitten in breast / and heart with an evil craze, not seeing with their eyes / more blind than blind rats, more terrible than poisonous / creeping beasts, shackled with heavy sleep.*[48]

Clearly, verse 22 of Psalm 68 LXX also inspired the evangelists, even if John alone alludes to it without quoting it explicitly (John 19:28–29, "*in order to fulfil the Scripture.*") It is almost certain that Matthew was inspired by it, since he replaces the myrrh mingled with wine with the gall, when Jesus arrives on Golgotha.[49] Thus, Matthew changes the wine mixed with myrrh into a disgusting and humiliating drink and, in so doing, he

304]" (Translated by Fletcher, *Ante-Nicene Fathers* [n. 27], 120–121). Nicklas, "Apokryphe Passionstraditionen" (n. 3), 274, n. 51, notes that the link between Jesus' meal on the Cross and Ps 68:22 LXX was already drawn by Origen, *Commentary on Matthew*, ser. 137 to Mt 27:47–49.

[47] Also mentioned by Nicklas, "Apokryphe Passionstraditionen" (n. 3), 273, and Lightfoot, *The Sibylline Oracles* (n. 1), 436, who rightly points out that the Sibyl does not mention Jesus' clothes, as does Matt 27:35, a detail inspired by Ps 21:19 (20:18 LXX).

[48] Cf. Lightfoot, *The Sibylline Oracles* (n. 1), 436 for a discussion. On the proverbial blindness of blind rats, see W. Schrage, τυφλός, τυφλόω, *ThWNT* 8 (1969), 270–294, here 275–77.

[49] The Antiochian recension of Matthew also replaces the wine by vinegar, which is a further proof of the influence of Ps 68:22 LXX. See also Nicklas, "Apokryphe Passionstraditionen" (n. 3), 274, n. 52.

changes an act of compassion into an act of nasty mockery. The *Gospel of Peter*, the *Epistle of Barnabas*, and Melito of Sardis' *On Pascha*[50] come still closer to the spirit of Psalm 68:22 LXX than Matthew, but the Sibyl is the most strongly inspired by this verse, since she never speaks of wine, or vinegar, mingled with gall, but of gall alone which, furthermore, is not called a drink but is presented as food, as in Psalm 68:22 LXX. From Matthew to the *Sibylline Oracles*, we can see an increase in nastiness, and in order to realize it, the latter draw directly from the text of the LXX.[51]

Finally, in Book 6 of the *Sibylline Oracles*, the shortest of the collection, the entire Passion of Jesus – the "*Son of the Immortal*" in this Book – is epitomized by these two items: the crown of thorns and the drink mixed with gall. The Passion is expressed here with a remarkable economy (21–25): "*For you alone, land of Sodom, is destined calamity. / For you were malicious, and did not recognize your own God / When he came with mortal eyes. But you crowned him / with acanthus, and terrible gall you mixed / for insult and drink. That will cause you calamity.*"[52] Lines 22–24 are quoted in the same passage of the *Divine Institutes* mentioned above (4:18:19),[53] in relation to Psalm 68:22 LXX. The same anti-Judaism, which is found in Book 1 of the *Sibylline Oracles*, appears in this violent judgement, where all Israel is identified with Sodom.

---

[50] *Gospel of Peter*, 16: "*And someone of them said: 'Give him to drink gall with vinegary wine.' And having made a mixture, they gave to drink*;" *Barn.* 7:3: "*When fixed to the cross, He had given Him to drink vinegar and gall*;" *Barn.* 7:5: "*Because to me, who am to offer my flesh for the sins of my new people, you are to give gall with vinegar to drink*;" Melito of Sardis, *On Pascha*, 79:573:574: "*You prepared for Him sharp nails and false witnesses and ropes and scourges and vinegar and gall*;" 582–583: "*While you had wine to drink and bread to eat, He had vinegar and gall.*" See Mara, *Évangile de Pierre* (n. 9), 129–132, although she does not mention the *Sibylline Oracles*; Nicklas, "Apokryphe Passionstraditionen" (n. 3), 274, n. 52.

[51] See Moo, *The Old Testament* (n. 6), 249–252 and 278–280 and Massaux, *Influence* (n. 28), 89.

[52] My own translation. For a detailed study of this short hymn, see M.D. Usher, "The Sixth Sibylline Oracle as a Literary Hymn," *Greek, Roman and Byzantine Studies* 36 (1995), 25–49, and J.-M. Roessli, "Le VI[e] livre des *Oracles sibyllins,*" in: *Les Sibylles. Actes des VIII[e] Entretiens de La Garenne Lemot, Nantes 18–20 octobre 2001*, (ed. By J. Pigeaud; Nantes 2005), 203–230. An exhaustive bibliography of the previous scholarship on this book will be found there.

[53] Lactantius, *Div. Inst.*, 4:18:19: "*And another Sibyl rebukes the land of Judaea in these verses:* 'For you, entertaining hurtful thoughts, did not recognize your God sporting with mortal thoughts; but crowned Him with a crown of thorns, and mingled dreadful gall.' [*Sib Or* 6:22–24]" (Translated by Fletcher, *Ante-Nicene Fathers* [n. 27], 120–121.) Lactantius has another variant in the first hemistich of verse 23, which explains the difference in translation; on this, see Roessli, "Le VI[e] livre des *Oracles sibyllins*" (n. 52), 226–227.

Sib Or 1:375–378 and Sib Or 8:305–309

The *Sibylline Oracles* go immediately from the pseudo-meal offered to Jesus to the tearing of the Temple veil and to the darkness in the middle of the day. The first Book reverses the order of the events, as do the canonical Gospels; the eighth Book prefers to have the tearing of the veil before the darkness.

Sib Or 1:375–378	*Sib Or 8:305–309*
νύξ ἔσται σκοτόεσσα πελώριος ἤματι μέσσῳ There will be monstrous dark night in midday	ναοῦ δὲ σχισθῇ τὸ πέτασμα καὶ ἤματι μέσσῳ The veil of the Temple will be rent, and in midday
καὶ τότε δὴ ναὸς Σολομώνιος ἀνθρώποισιν And then indeed the temple of Solomon will effect	νύξ ἔσται σκοτόεσσα πελώριος ἐν τρισὶν ὥραις. there will be dark monstrous night for three hours.
σῆμα μέγ' ἐκελέσει, ὁπόταν' Αιδωνέος οἶκον a great sign for men, when he goes to the house of Hades	
βέσεται ἀγγέλλων ἐπαναστασίην τεθνεῶσιν. Announcing the resurrection to the dead.	
	οὐκέτι γὰρ κρυφίῳ τε νόμῳ ναῷ τε λατρεύειν For it has been again revealed that there would no longer be obedience to a temple
	φαντασίαις κόσμου κεκαλυμμένῳ αὖτις ἐδείχθη nor to a secret law hidden behind the illusions of the world,
	αὐθέντου καταβάντος ἐπὶ χθονὸς ἀενάοιο. when the eternal sovereign came down to earth.

The two events are narrated in the Synoptics (Matt 27:51; Mark 15:38; Luke 23:45; and Matt 27:45; Mark 15:33; Luke 23:34), but the treatment in the *Sibylline Oracles* is quite different.

Apart from the reverse order of the two events, Book 8 is very close in its formulation to the Synoptics, since the substantive ναός and the verb σχίζω are found in it. Only the word πέτασμα replaces, for obvious metric reasons, the composite word καταπέτασμα of the Synoptics. Furthermore, Book 8 seems to link the tearing of the veil and the coming of the Word on earth to the lifting of all restrictions on reaching God (v. 307–309): "*For it has been again revealed that there would no longer be obedience to a temple / nor to a secret law hidden behind the illusions of the world, / once the eternal sovereign has come down to earth.*"[54] These verses are certainly to be read in relation to lines 299–301, as if they were written to follow them ("*For it has been* again *revealed...*"). They also refer to one of the possible interpretations of Matt 27:51 ("*At that moment the curtain of the temple was torn in two, from top to bottom,*" [NRSV]) the veil of the sanctuary pointing possibly both to the veil separating the parvis of the Temple itself – the renting of which opens up access to the presence of God to the pagans – as well as to the veil separating the Holy place from the Holy of Holies – the tearing of which means the end of the priesthood of the Ancient Covenant.[55] This is not the same in the first book, where the Sibyl takes some liberties in describing the Temple (ναός) as "Solomonian" – as she does again later (v. 393).[56] She predicts not the tearing of the veil – which is totally absent in this version of the narrative – but that a great sign (σῆμα) would echo from the Temple. This imagery belongs to the sibylline repertoire of signs (σήματα) and prodigies (*Sib Or* 4:56; 12:74; 14:221, and, above all, *Sib Or* 8:244).[57]

However, as stated above, the darkness which had covered the earth is known to the Synoptics (Matt 27:45, Mark 15:33, and Luke 23:44) and happens after the tearing of the veil, contrary to what happens in Book 8. In the Synoptics there is darkness from the sixth to the ninth hour, i.e. for three hours, but it is not said that it was night during the day. The *Gospel of Peter* again shows kinship with the *Sibylline Oracles*, because it, too, speaks of darkness at midday (v. 15): "*it was noon and darkness came over*

[54] My translation. Collins' translation is: "*For no longer with secret law and temple must one serve / the phantoms of the world. That which had been hidden was again made manifest / when the eternal sovereign came down to earth.*" Compare also with Terry, *Sibylline Oracles* (1899, n. 26), 60: "*For it was no more pointed out again / How to serve secret temple and the law / Which had been covered with the world's displays, / When the Eternal came himself on earth,*" and with Roessli, "Les oracles sibyllins" (n. 26), 1077: "*Car il fut à nouveau révélé qu'on ne servirait plus un temple / et une loi secrète qui se cache dans les images du monde, / une fois le souverain éternel descendu sur terre.*" A similar idea is found later in 8:326–328: "*... appearing gentle to all so that he* [the king Jesus] *may lift our yoke / of slavery, hard to bear, which lies on our neck / and undo the godless ordinances and constraining bonds.*" See Lightfoot, *The Sibylline Oracles* (n. 1), 438, who refers to Hagner, *Matthew 14–28* (n. 42), 849. See also Nicklas, "Apokryphe Passionstraditionen" (n. 3), 275, who rightly identifies the law of *Sib Or* 8:307 with the Jewish Torah, and wonders sceptically (n. 54) if the "secret law" of this verse has something to do with the secret revelation added to the Torah, of which the apocalyptic tradition speaks.

[55] See note to Matt 27:51 (TOB [n. 42]).

[56] The adjective Σολομώνιος is found only here and in *Sib Or* 3:167, 214 in the Judaeo-Hellenistic literature.

[57] See Lightfoot, *The Sibylline Oracles* (n. 1), 437.

all of Judea."[58] The *Gospel of Peter* differs when this happens abruptly before the drinking scene and because the drink consists in a mixture of gall and vinegar (v. 16), something we do not find in the *Sibylline Oracles*.

So, it seems that once again the *Gospel of Peter* and the *Sibylline Oracles* drew on common sources, without necessarily depending on each other, since we find as many points of convergence as points of divergence between them.[59]

Patristic tradition[60] saw in the miraculous darkness at Calvary the accomplishment of the prophecies by Amos 8:9 "*'On that day,' says the Lord GOD, 'I will make the sun go down at noon, and darken the earth in broad daylight'*" and Jer 15:9: "… *her sun went down while it was yet day.*"[61] Lactantius offers a good example, since he refers to these biblical prophecies before quoting our Sibylline verses:

> Therefore, being lifted up and nailed to the cross, He cried to the Lord with a loud voice, and of His own accord gave up His spirit. And at the same hour there was an earthquake; and the veil of the temple, which separated the two tabernacles, was rent into two parts; and the sun suddenly withdrew its light, and there was darkness from the sixth even to the ninth hour. Of which event the prophet Amos testifies: 'And it shall come to pass in that day, says the Lord, that the sun shall go down at noon, and the daylight shall be darkened; and I will turn your feasts into mourning, and your songs into lamentation.' Also Jeremiah: 'She who brings forth is affrighted, and vexed in spirit; her sun is gone down while it was yet mid-day; she hath been ashamed and confounded; and the residue of them will I give to the sword in the sight of their enemies.' And the Sibyl: 'And the veil of the temple shall be rent, and at midday there shall be dark vast night for three hours.'[62]

---

[58] *Gospel of Peter*, v. 15a: ἦν δὲ μεσημβρία καὶ σκότος κατέσχε πᾶσαν τὴν Ἰουδαίαν. Translated by Ehrman, *Lost Scriptures* (n. 7), 32. See Nicklas, "Apokryphe Passionstraditionen" (n. 3), 274.

[59] On this, see, of course, Nicklas, "Apokryphe Passionstraditionen" (n. 3), who did not take Books 1 and 6 into account in his comparison.

[60] Irenaeus, *haer.*, 4:33:12; Tertullian, *Against the Jews*, 10; *Against Marcion*, 4:42; Cyprian, *Testimonia*, 2:23; Eusebius, *Evangelical Demonstration*, 10:6:1; Aphraate, *Homelies*, 1:11; Cyril of Jerusalem, *Cat.*, 13:25.

[61] Amos 8:9 LXX: δύσεται ὁ ἥλιος μεσημβρίας. Jer 15:9: ἐπέδυ ὁ ἥλιος αὐτῇ ἔτι μεσούσης τῆς ἡμέρας. See E. Massaux, *Influence* (n. 28), 89–90.

[62] Lactantius, *Div. Inst.*, 4:19:2–5: "Suspensus igitur et adfixus exclamauit ad Deum uoce magna et ultro spiritum posuit. Et eadem hora terrae motus factus est et uelum templi quod separabat duo tabernacula scissum est in duas partes et sol repente subductus est et ab hora sexta usque in nonam tenebrae fuerunt. Qua de re Amos propheta testatur: 'Et erit in illo die, dicit Dominus, occidet sol meridie et obtenebricabitur dies lucis: et conuertam dies festos uestros in luctum et cantica uestra in lamentationem.' Item Hieremias: 'Exterrita est quae parit et taediuit anima, et subiuit sol ei, cum adhuc medius dies esset, contusa est et maledicta: reliquos eorum in gladium dabo in conspectu inimicorum eorum.' Et Sibylla: [Or sib 8,305–306]" (Translated by W. Fletcher, *Ante-Nicene Fathers* [n. 27], 122.)

Neither the Sibyl in Book 1 nor the Sibyl in Book 8 mentions the simultaneous earthquake of Matt 27:51 ("*The earth shook, and the rocks were split*") and parallels.[63]

Sib Or 1:377b–380 and Sib Or 8:310–314

In Book 1 the sound or sign (σῆμα) which resounds in the Temple coincides with the descent of Christ into Hell.[64] In Book 8 the descent happens when the veil of the temple is rent and the night comes in midday. This event seems present in the NT (cf. 1 Cor 15:20: "*the first fruits* (ἀπαρχή) *of those who have died,*" and perhaps 1 Pet 3:19: "*in which also he* [Christ] *went and made a proclamation to the spirits in prison*"), where it is connected to prophetic expectations. When Lactantius cites *Sib Or* 8:312–314 in his *Divine Institutes* (4:19:10), he does it in relation to Psalm 3:6 [3:5] and 16 (15):10, and above all Hos 6:2 ("*After two days he will revive us; on the third day he will raise us up, that we may live before him*") and 13:13-14 ("*The pangs of childbirth come for him, but he is an unwise son; for now he does not present himself at the mouth of the womb. Shall I ransom them from the power of Sheol? Shall I redeem them from Death? O Death, where are your plagues? O Sheol, where is your destruction? Compassion is hidden from my eyes.*" [NRSV]) But the Christian tradition, especially at the beginning, has a hard time agreeing about what Christ actually said when he was in Hell.[65] The *Sibylline Oracles* reflect this diversity of views. In Book 1, Christ is presented as proclaiming the resurrection of the dead without any exception (v. 378). In Book 8, however, he offers hope for all the saints (v. 310-311; cf. v. 227), and announces the end of time and the last day (v. 311). Verse 312 goes further in promising that Christ will put an end to death: "*And he will complete the fate of death when he has slept the third day.*" It is also in this way that Lactantius understood it: "*And the Sibyl, too, said that he would impose a terminus on death after a sleep of three days:* 'And the sleep of death having been undergone, he shall be dead for three days. And then coming back from the dead he shall come to light, the first of resurrection, showing the beginning to those called.' (*Sib Or* 8:312-314)"[66]

---

[63] Lightfoot, *The Sibylline Oracles* (n. 1), 437.

[64] 'Αιδωνέος is probably a poetic form of 'Αιδης (8:310) rather than the genitive of Adonis ('Αιδωνεύς), as Collins believed and which I correct.

[65] On this topic, see R. Gounelle, *La descente du Christ aux enfers. Institutionalisation d'une croyance* (CEA; Série Antiquité 162; Paris 2000); id. (ed.), *La descente du Christ aux enfers* (Supplément Cahiers Évangile 128; Paris 2004), although he says nothing about the *Sibylline Oracles*.

[66] Lactantius, *Div. Inst.*, 4:19:10: "Et ideo Sibylla impositurum esse morti terminum dixit post tridui somnum: [*Sib Or* 8:312–314]" (Translated by M.F. McDonald, in *The*

Sib Or 1:377b–380

... ὁπόταν 'Αιδωνέος οἶκον
... when he goes to the house of Hades

βήσεται ἀγγέλλων ἐπαναστασίην τεθνεῶσιν
Announcing the resurrection to the dead.
αὐτὰρ ἐπὴν ἔλθῃ τρισὶν ἤμασιν ἐς φάος αὖτις
When he comes again in three days to the light
καὶ δείξῃ θνητοῖσι τύπον καὶ πάντα διδάξῃ
and shows his wounds and teaches all...

Sib Or 8:310–314

ἥξει δ' εἰς'Αΐδην ἀγγέλλων ἐλπίδα πᾶσιν
He will come to the Hades announcing hope for all
τοῖς ἁγίοις, τέλος αἰώνων καὶ ἔσχατον ἦμαρ
the holy ones, the end of ages and last day,
καὶ θανάτου μοῖραν τελέσει τρίτον ἦμαρ ὑπνώσας
and he will complete the fate of death when he has slept the third day.
καὶ τότ' ἀπὸ φθιμένων ἀναλύσας εἰς φάος ἥξει
And then, returning from the dead, he will come to light,
πρῶτος ἀναστάσεως κλητοῖς ἀρχὴν ὑποδείξας
first of the resurrection, showing a beginning to the elect...

Conclusion

When one examines the relationships between the Scriptures and the Books of the *Sibylline Oracles* considered in this paper, it can be concluded that the latter reveal clear affinity with the Gospel of Matthew, as is frequently the case for several Christian literary works written before the third century. They also show the faint influence of other canonical writings, of certain apocrypha and, of course, of the Prophets. However, we find no explicit quotations from Mark and Luke in Books 6 and 8,[67] while Mark shows up in Book 1 by a short allusion to the story of John the Baptist's murder (1:342–343) and an apparent verbal similarity (1:373).[68] In Book 1 there are still more episodes closely copied from Matthew than in Books 6 and 8, and some passages specifically reflect the vocabulary of John (1:373–374, and 1:340–341 and 360–361 for episodes other than the passion narrative), which does not seem to be the case in Books 6 and 8.

Fathers of the Church. A New Translation, vol. 49; New York 1964, 297–298). The passion narrative ends here. Books 1 and 8 continue with the apparition of the Resurrected and his ascension to heaven (*Sib Or* 1:380–381 and 8:318–320), preceded in 8:315–317 by an exegesis of the baptism.

[67] See Massaux, *Influence* (n. 28), 80–98, for the last point 97. See also W.-D. Köhler, *Die Rezeption des Matthäusevangeliums in der Zeit vor Irenäus* (WUNT II.24; Tübingen 1987).

[68] Lightfoot, *The Sibylline Oracles* (n. 1), 426 finds a single – perhaps accidental – echo of Luke (*Sib Or* 1:371).

The main difference consists of opposing views on Jesus' attitude towards the Law. The Sibyl of Book 1 asserts that he "*will fulfil*" it (v. 332), while the Sibyl of Book 8 insists that he will abolish it and all what is connected to it (vv. 300–301; 307–309, 326b–328, quoted by Lactantius in *Div. Inst.* 7:18:8.)[69] Furthermore, Book 8 is much more interested in mystical and typological interpretations and its language is much more metaphorical, sometimes even a bit florid (see, e. g., *Sib Or* 8:294–298).

The juxtaposition and combination of various Gospel sources cause us to think that the authors of these works could have used a Gospel harmony, since there is evidence for such harmonies for this period (second and third centuries).[70] Nevertheless, the *Oracles* are sometimes too eclectic for a harmony, although some episodes might reflect such an approach, for example, the fusion of two episodes: the mockery of Jesus with a crown of thorns and a reed before the crucifixion and the piercing of his side during the crucifixion in 1:373-374 and 8:294-296.

In fact, the Sibyl seems particularly interested in the Gospel narratives which have a prophetic background or which explicitly quote prophetic texts. Thus, the Sibyl shows an inclination for Matthew and other New Testament writings which incorporate prophetic testimonies applicable to Christ. So, for example, the obstinate refusal of Israel to recognize Jesus as the Messiah in *Sib Or* 1:360–364; 368–371, is read alongside Isa 6, quoted in the Gospels and the Acts. The bad treatment reserved to the Messiah in *Sib Or* 1:365–366 and *Sib Or* 8:288–290 is also inspired by Isa 50 and 53, which are themselves paraphrased in the Synoptics. The same thing happens with the gall and the vinegar which come from Psalm 68 LXX, alluded to by John and clearly reinterpreted by Matthew. The Sibyls oscillate constantly between the Gospels, the Prophets as quoted in the Gospels, and the original prophetic sources, sometimes through a New Testament citation (*Sib Or* 1:365–366: πτύσματα; *Sib Or* 8:289: ἐμπτύσματα; *Sib Or* 1:367 and 8:303: χολή and ὄξος), sometimes not (*Sib Or* 1:365–366: "*unclean lips;*" *Sib Or* 8:299: "*polluted mouths*;" *Sib Or* 1:375: "*a monstrous dark night in midday*;" *Sib Or* 8:306: "*dark monstrous night for three hours*,") while adopting a way of reading the Prophets which derives directly from the canonical Gospels. The Sibyls of these Books belong therefore to currents of early Christian exegesis of Scriptures in which they embody a pa-

[69] Lactantius, *Div. Inst.*, 7:18:8: "*He will take away the intolerable yoke of slavery which is placed on our neck, and he will do away with impious laws and violent chains.*" (Translated by W. Fletcher, *The Ante-Nicene Fathers* [n. 27], 116.)

[70] Tatian's *Diatessaron* is the first known Harmony of the four Gospels, but Tatian's teacher, Justin, seems to have already known such a synoptic harmony. See also Nicklas, "Apokryphe Passionstraditionen" (n. 3), 274, n. 52, and Lightfoot, *The Sibylline Oracles* (n. 1), 426–427.

gan prophetess supposed to prophecy the Gospels alongside with the Hebrew Prophets, towards whom the Sibyl of Book 1 even pretends to distance herself, since she announces their end (v. 386).

Regarding the Passion narrative, two different perceptions can be seen in these books of the *Sibylline* collection. Books 1 and 6 are extremely hostile to the Jews (1:360–371; 387; 6:21–25): they are responsible for the Messiah's death. This aspect is also found in the *Gospel of Peter*,[71] but it does not imply that there is a literary dependence between these texts. Nothing of this has any parallel in Book 8, where the Jews are never named and Jesus' enemies hardly identifiable, except by their impiety (v. 287). If Book 1 is openly polemical against Israel, at the same time it is favourable to the mission to the Gentiles (ἔθνη; vv. 345–347 and 383–384), which could mean that his author "*sees himself primarily in terms of the Gentiles and not as a sect of, or development, from Israel.*"[72] Unlike him, the author of Book 8 seems to be simultaneously concerned by the conversion of both the Jews and the pagans (v. 316b–317: "*so that, born from above, they may no longer serve the lawless customs of the world,*"[73] v. 324: "*Rejoice, holy daughter of Sion, who have suffered much,*"[74] v. 332: "*Set aside the former [gods or customs] and wash from his blood.*")

In Book 1 (v. 364) Jesus is called Son of God (παῖς θεοῦ), while in Book 8 (v. 288) he is named God (θεός). These two titles, of which we have other examples (*Sib Or* 1:324, 331 and *Sib Or* 8:242, 249–250), reflect different christologies. Although too vague to be connected with a specific Gospel, the christology of Book 1 is rather close to the canonical tradition, while Book 8 reflects a form of "*modalist monarchianism*", in which Father and Son are perfectly identified. We have other striking examples of this in Book 6 (vv. 22–24) of the *Sibylline Oracles*, which I believe is one of the earliest Christian compositions of the collection (A.D. 150–250): "*For you were malicious, and did not recognize your own* God / *When he came with mortal eyes. But you crowned him / with acanthus, and*

[71] On this, see T. Nicklas, "Die Juden im Petrusevangelium (PCair 10759). Ein Testfall," *NTS* 47 (2001), 206–221, as well as J.D. Crossan's and J. Verheyden's contributions in: Kraus/Nicklas (eds.), *Das Evangelium nach Petrus* (n. 3), 117–134 and 281–300.

[72] Charlesworth, "Jewish and Christian Self-Definition" (n. 38), 50.

[73] These "*lawless customs of the world*" might refer to the pagan as well as to the Jewish practices.

[74] See Isa 62:11 and, above all, Zec 9:9: "*Rejoice greatly, O daughter Zion! Shout aloud, O daughter Jerusalem! Lo, your king comes to you; triumphant and victorious is he, humble and riding on a donkey, on a colt, the foal of a donkey*" [NRSV]), this one quoted by Matt 21:5 and John 12:15.

terrible gall you mixed...,"[75] as well as in Book 7 (v. 53: "*because they did not recognize* God,") vv. 66–67: "*Wretched one, you did not recognize your* God, *whom once Jordan washed three times, and the Spirit flew like a dove.*")[76]

The Christian authors who quote the Sibyls of our books do so in order to show the concord (συμφονία) between the message of the Old Testament and that of the (supposed) pagan prophecies.[77] Thus Lactantius, in the fourth book of his *Divine Institutes*, draws heavily on the christological section of Book 8 (vv. 272–314), citing first an Old Testament prophecy, then a passage of Book 8 which is supposed to corroborate it. As we have seen, Lactantius often quotes the very biblical passage on which the Sibyl relies, and presents her text as if it was an independent prediction (cf. *Sib Or* 8:287–790 in *Div. Inst.* 4:18:13–15; *Sib Or* 8:303–304 and *Sib Or* 6:22-24 in *Div. Inst.* 4:18:18–20). In so doing, Lactantius is the Sibyl's ideal reader, since he interprets her exactly as she hopes to be interpreted, simultaneously "*raising and dismissing the possibility of forgery*."[78] Lactantius, in using 8:272–314, shows no other interest than in the narrative parts of the section, in other words, in the predictions of events related to the life of Jesus. He passes over the theological reflections which constitute a main feature of Book 8 (cf. vv. 279–286; 295–298; 299–301; 307–311) and which differentiates it so strongly from Book 1. Lactantius' use of the *Sibylline Oracles* will be followed by the author of the *Tübingen Theosophy*,

---

[75] My translation. *Sib Or* 6:22–23: αὐτὴ γὰρ δύσφρων τὸν σὸν θεὸν οὐκ ἐνόησας / ἐλθόντα θνητοῖσιν ἐν ὄμμασιν· ἀλλ᾽ ἀπ᾽ ἀκάνθης ... – Strikingly, neither the name of Jesus or his designation as "Christ" appears in this book. It is also the case in the preserved fragments of the *Gospel of Peter*; see Nicklas, "Apokryphe Passionstraditionen" (n. 3), 267, n. 20.

[76] My translation. *Sib Or* 7:53: ὅτι δὴ θεὸν οὐκ ἐνόησαν. *Sib Or* 7:66–67: τλήμων, οὐκ ἔγνως τὸν σὸν θεόν, ὃν ποτ᾽ ἔλουσεν / Ἰόρδανος ἐν τριτάτοισι καὶ ἔπτατο πνεῦμα πελεί᾽ ὥς. For a French translation and a commentary on Books 6, 7 and 8 of the *Sibylline Oracles*, see Roessli, "Les oracles sibyllins" (n. 26), as well as my dissertation on this topic to be published in the *Series apocryphorum* of the *Corpus Christianorum*.

[77] See J.-M. Roessli, "Catalogues de sibylles, recueil(s) de *Libri Sibyllini* et corpus des *Oracula Sibyllina*. Remarques sur la formation et la constitution de quelques collections oraculaires dans les mondes gréco-romain, juif et chrétien," in E. Norelli (ed.), *Recueils normatifs et canons dans l'antiquité. Perspectives nouvelles sur la formation des canons juif et chrétien dans leur contexte culturel. Actes du colloque organisé dans le cadre du programme plurifacultaire "La Bible à la croisée des savoirs" de l'Université de Genève, 11–12 avril 2002* (PIRSB 3; Lausanne 2004), 47–68, here 64.

[78] Lightfoot, *The Sibylline Oracles* (n. 1), 425. See Lactantius, *Div. Inst.*, 4:15:26: "His testimoniis quidam reuicti eo confugere ut aiant non esse illa carmina Sibyllina, sed a nostris ficta atque composita." "*Some, refuted by these testimonies, are accustomed to have recourse to the assertion that these poems were not by the Sibyls, but made up and composed by our own writers.*" (Translated by Fletcher, *Ante-Nicene Fathers* [n. 27], 116.)

who sees the Sibyl as "*a seer in accord with the holy prophets*."[79] Let us note that the parallelism between the supposed pagan prophecies of the Sibyls and that of the Hebrew prophets is at the origin of the iconographical correlation that Christian art will draw from the eleventh century onwards and which will bring the artists to juxtapose Sibyls and Hebrew Prophets in a single scene.[80]

From the fact that Lactantius and early Christian literature before the *Tübingen Theosophy* (5th-6th century)[81] cite both Books 8 and 6 and not Book 1, some scholars have concluded that Book 8 is prior to Book 1. In a further step it has been assumed that Book 1 derived from Book 8, until Kurfess argued that both Books had drawn independently from the New Testament and that similarities between them were accidental.[82] With Waßmuth and Lightfoot, I consider that the numerous similarities between the two books militate against a total independence of the two books. More recently, Olaf Waßmuth, following Kurfess, argued for the priority of Book 1 over Book 8, among other reasons because its theology is more complex and sophisticated. This divergence of views explains the difficulty in dating Book 1 and 8, particularly Book 1, some arguing for a Christian rewriting of a Jewish oracle in the middle of the second century (Friedlieb, Collins, Waßmuth)[83], some in the third (Geffcken)[84], and finally

---

[79] *Tübingen Theosophy*, § 10 (Erbse [n. 5], 80,294): ὡς δὲ σύμφωνός τις ἡ πρόμαντις τῶν προφετῶν."

[80] See E. Mâle, *L'art religieux du XIIIe siècle en France* (Paris 1919 [1898]), 339–343; id., *L'art religieux de la fin du Moyen Âge en France* (Paris 1949 [1908]), 254–279; L. Réau, *Iconographie de l'art chrétien* (II, 1; Paris 1956), 420–430; G. Seib, "Sibyllen," in: E. Kirschbaum (ed.), *Lexikon der christlichen Ikonographie* 4 (1972), 150–153; Redaktion, "Propheten," in: id. (ed.), *o. l.* 3 (1972), 461–462; F. Gay, "Sibille," in *Enciclopedia dell'arte medievale* X (1999), 586–589.

[81] If we except a possible allusion to *Sib Or* 1:283ff. in the *Constantine's Discourse to the Assembly of the Saints* (18,2), dated between 313 and 325 (see J.-M. Roessli, "Vies et métamorphoses de la Sibylle," review article about M. Bouquet and F. Morzadec (eds.), *La Sibylle. Parole et représentation* [Collection « Interférences »], Rennes 2004, and about J. Pigeaud (ed.), *Les Sibylles. Actes des VIIIe Entretiens de La Garenne Lemot, 18 au 20 octobre 2001*, Nantes 2005, in *Revue de l'histoire des religions* 224/2 [2007] 253–271, here 259–260), the first textual evidence for Books 1 and 2 comes from the *Tübingen Theosophy*.

[82] A. Kurfess, "Oracula Sibyllina I/II", *ZNW* 40 (1941), 151–165, here 159–160.

[83] J.H. Friedlieb, Χρησμοὶ σιβυλλιακοί. *Oracula Sibyllina ad fidem codd. mscr. quotquot extant recensuit, praetextis prolegomenis illustravit, versione Germanica instruxit, annotationes criticas et indices rerum et verborum locupletissimos adiecit*, Leipzig 1852 / *Die sibyllinischen Weissagungen, vollstaendig gesammelt nach neuer Handschriftenvergleichung, mit kritischem Commentare und metrischer deutscher Uebersetzung* (Leipzig 1852), XIV–XXII and LIX; Collins, "The Sibylline Oracles" (n. 1); Waßmuth, *Sibyllinische Orakel 1/2* (n. 1).

some seeing in Books 1 and 2 a Christian composition of the second (Lightfoot [n. 1], 149), the third (Alexandre)[85] or the fifth century (Bleek, Goodman).[86] Whatever the priority, what is important to understand is that the author who wrote after felt free to use his sources (Bible and *Sibylline Oracles*) in his own way.

[84] J. Geffcken, *Komposition und Entstehungszeit der Oracula Sibyllina* (TU 8.1; Leipzig 1902), 47–53.

[85] Ch. Alexandre, *Oracula Sibyllina* (vol. 2, *Excursus ad Sibyllinos libros*, V, cap. x. *De primo libro et secundo*; Paris 1856), 389–401.

[86] F. Bleek, "Ueber die Entstehung und Zusammensetzung der uns in 8 Büchern erhaltenen Sammlung Sibyllinischer Orakel; eine kritische Untersuchung mit besonderer Rücksicht auf Thorlacius," *ThZ* 1 (1819), 120–246, here 167–197; M. Goodman, "The Sibylline Oracles," in *The History of the Jewish People in the Age of Jesus Christ (175 B.C.–A.D. 135)* (ed. G. Schürer; revised and edited by G. Vermes, F. Millar and M. Goodman; vol. III.1; Edinburgh 1986), 618–654, here 645.

Origen's Interpretation of 1 Corinthians 15

RIEMER ROUKEMA

What did Origen really think about the resurrection of the dead? In his extant works he often deals with this theme, and his views have been investigated in numerous papers and books. The publications of Henri Crouzel deserve to be mentioned here,[1] but many other scholars also went into this subject.[2] This contribution is devoted to Origen's interpretation of 1 Corinthians 15 (more precisely: 1 Cor 15:12–55), Paul's famous chapter on the resurrection.[3]

---

[1] See especially H. Crouzel, "Les critiques adressées par Méthode et ses contemporains à la doctrine origénienne du corps ressuscité", *Gr.* 53 (1972), 679–716; id., "Les prophéties de la résurrection selon Origène", in *Forma Futuri: Studi in onore del cardinale Michele Pellegrino* (Torino 1975), 980–992; id., "La 'première' et la 'seconde' résurrection des hommes d'après Origène", *Did(L)* 3 (1973), 3–19; id., "Le thème platonicien du 'véhicule de l'âme' chez Origène", *Did(L)* 7 (1977), 225–238; id., "Mort et immortalité selon Origène", *BLE* 79 (1978), 19–38, 81–96, 181–196; id., "La doctrine origénienne du corps ressuscité", *BLE* 81 (1980), 175–200, 241–266; id., "Différences entre les ressuscités selon Origène", in *Jenseitsvorstellungen in Antike und Christentum: Gedenkschrift für Alfred Stuiber* (JAC.E 9; Münster 1982), 107–116; id., "Quand le Fils transmet le Royaume à Dieu son Père", *StMiss* 33 (1984), 359–384; see also footnote 30.

[2] See, e.g., F. Altermath, *Du corps psychique au corps spirituel. Interprétation de 1 Cor. 15,35–49 par les auteurs chrétiens des quatre premiers siècles* (BGBE 18; Tübingen 1977); D.G. Bostock, "Quality and Corporeity in Origen", in *Origeniana Secunda* (ed. H. Crouzel and A. Quacquarelli; Roma 1980), 323–337; A. Vítores, *Identidad entre el cuerpo muerto y resucitado en Orígenes segun el "De Resurrectione" de Metodio de Olimpo* (Jerusalem 1981); G. Dorival, "Origène et la résurrection de la chair", in *Origeniana Quarta* (ed. L. Lies; IThS 19; Innsbruck and Vienna 1987), 291–321; L.R. Hennessey, "A Philosophical Issue in Origen's Eschatology: The Three Senses of Incorporeality", in *Origeniana Quinta* (ed. R.J. Daly; BEThL 105; Leuven 1992), 373–380; H.S. Schibli, "Origen, Didymus, and the Vehicle of the Soul", ibid., 381–391; J.F. Dechow, "Origen and Corporeality: The Case of Methodius' *On the Resurrection*", ibid., 509–518; M.J. Edwards, "Origen no Gnostic; or, on the Corporeality of Man", *JThS* 43 (1992), 23–37; H.S. Benjamins, "Methodius von Olympus, *Über die Auferstehung*. Gegen Origenes und gegen Porphyrius?", in *Origeniana Septima* (ed. W.A. Bienert and U. Kühneweg; BEThL 137; Leuven 1999), 91–98; A.-C. Jacobsen, *Kødets opstandelse? Menneske og målet hos Irenæus og Origenes* (Copenhagen 2002), 166–188, 236–269, 279–297. See also footnote 17.

[3] A French version of this paper was published as R. Roukema, "La résurrection des morts dans l'interprétation origénienne de *1 Corinthiens* 15", in *La résurrection chez les*

1 Corinthians 15:12–23

According to 1 Cor 15:12 some Corinthian Christians said that there is no resurrection of the dead. In his reaction, Paul sees an inextricable link between the resurrection of Christ and the resurrection of those who believe in him. In his catenae fragments Origen explains that Christ's resurrection took place in his carnal body (σάρξ). To the "heterodox" who "want to allegorize the resurrection of the human beings" he says that in that case "they also have to allegorize the resurrection of the Saviour".[4] However, he admits that "each heresy" acknowledges that Christ has risen from the dead. Origen refers to Col 1:18, where Christ is called "the first-born from the dead", which implies that the resurrection of human beings should resemble the resurrection of Christ, which took place in the body. He refutes the view of those who confess the resurrection of Christ but deny the general resurrection of the dead, whether they say so openly or secretly. Thus Origen reproduces Paul's argument that the resurrection of Christ, being the first fruits of those who have died (1 Cor 15:20), and the resurrection of the dead belong together.[5] Of course, this interpretation is aimed at the Gnostics. For example, in the *Gospel of Philip* the resurrection is a spiritual experience situated in the earthly life of Christ and of those who come to know the true *gnosis*.[6]

In his *Dialogue with Heraclides* Origen also refers to Christ as the first fruit of the resurrection (1 Cor 15:20.23). Against the docetic view that Christ had a spiritual body Origen maintains that Christ's body had become a corpse, which is impossible for a spiritual body.[7] He says that Christ's human body is the foundation of the salvation of mankind; for

Pères (ed. J.-M. Prieur; CBiPa 7; Strasbourg 2003), 161–177; see also id., *De uitleg van Paulus' eerste brief aan de Corinthiërs in de tweede en derde eeuw* (Kampen 1996), 221–260.

[4] Fragm in Ep ad Cor 81 = C. Jenkins, "Origen on I Corinthians IV", *JThS* 10 (1909), 29–51 (44–45); see the corrections by C.H. Turner, "Notes on the Text of Origen's Commentary on I Corinthians", *JThS* 10 (1909), 270–276 (274); cf. Origenes, De Resurrectione, in Pamphilus, Apol pro Origene 130, l. 22–24 = SC 464, 212; PG 17, 595B.

[5] Fragm in Ep ad Cor 83; 84, l. 2–32 = JThS 10 (1909) 45–46; cf. his Comm in Titum, in Pamphilus, Apol pro Origene 33 l. 74–78 = SC 464, 88; PG 17, 556A.

[6] Evangelium Philippi 19; 21; 55; 59; 79; 83 (translation and numbering B. Layton, *The Gnostic Scriptures: A New Translation with Annotations and Introduction* [Garden City, New York 1987], 329–353); cf. Tertullian, De resurrectione mortuorum 19, 2–6 = CCSL 2, 944–945. It is noteworthy that the spiritualization of the resurrection also occurs in the deutero-Pauline epistles (Col 2:12; 3:1; Eph 2:6), and that it is contested in 2 Tim 2:18.

[7] Dial cum Heracl 5, l. 8–23 = SC 67, 66.

"those who say that the body of the Saviour was spiritual reject the salvation of the human body".[8] So far Origen seems an orthodox Church Father.

In his *Commentary on the Gospel of Matthew*, however, Origen quotes the Corinthian assertion that "there is no resurrection of the dead" (1 Cor 15:12) in another context, namely with respect to the Sadducees who also denied this belief (Mat 22:23). He explains that the Sadducees did not only reject the resurrection of the flesh, but also the immortality of the soul and even its survival after death.[9] In a digression Origen supposes that the Corinthians who denied the resurrection of the dead also rejected, as the Sadducees did, the survival of the soul after death; for about them Paul wrote (in Origen's reading): "If for this life we have hoped only in Christ, we are of all people most to be pitied" (1 Cor 15:19).[10] This argument implies that Origen asks whether those who believe in the survival of the soul after death can hope in Christ, not only for their earthly lives, but also for the hereafter, although they do not believe in the resurrection of the dead. His response to this suggestion is that "someone who rejects the resurrection of the dead as the Church believes it, even though he has been misled, has not fully hoped only in Christ". But after this implicit confirmation of the Church's faith Origen refers to the specific tenet of the resurrection of the *flesh*. He hypothesizes: "If the resurrection in which the crowd believes is not true, has not someone who rejects it for this life hoped only in Christ, (believing that) the soul will survive, although it will not recover its former body, but will put on something ethereal and better?" Origen's answer reads that "we are not of all people most to be pitied if we say that the soul lives and survives, but if we do not cover her with this body and if we do not say that she will recover it".[11] In these allusive words Origen expresses his view that someone who believes that in the resurrection the soul will put on an ethereal body, did hope in Christ. This implies that according to

---

[8] Ibid. 7, l. 7–9 = SC 67, 70.

[9] Comm in Mat XVII, 29 = GCS 40, 665, l. 22–666 l. 19.

[10] Ibid. = GCS 40, 666, l. 24–31. According to this quotation Origen reads εἰς ἐν τῇ ζωῇ ταύτῃ ἠλπικότες ἐσμὲν ἐν Χριστῷ μόνον, which corresponds with the later Majority Text. The "Alexandrian" reading that has been preferred in the 27th edition of the *Novum Testamentum Graece* (ed. B. and K. Aland et al.) is: εἰ ἐν τῇ ζωῇ ταύτῃ ἐν Χριστῷ ἠλπικότες ἐσμὲν μόνον. Most modern commentators relate μόνον with "in this life", and this may also have been Origen's understanding. It is also possible to apply μόνον to the whole sentence. Cf. D.D. Hannah, *The Text of I Corinthians in the Writings of Origen* (NTGF.TA 4; Atlanta 1997), 149–150; C.K. Barrett, *The First Epistle to the Corinthians* (BNTC; London [2]1971), 349–350; G.D. Fee, *The First Epistle to the Corinthians* (NICNT; Grand Rapids, Mi. 1987), 744–745; A.C. Thiselton, *The First Epistle to the Corinthians* (NIGTC; Grand Rapids, Mi. 2000), 1221–1222.

[11] Comm in Mat XVII, 29 = GCS 40, 666, l. 32–667, l. 19. For the interpretation of l. 8–14 as a question, see the translation and note by H.J. Vogt, *Origenes. Der Kommentar zum Evangelium nach Matthäus II* (BGrL 30; Stuttgart 1990), 282, 318.

Origen Paul did not criticize this understanding of the resurrection. We will see that this conception of a resurrection in an ethereal body represents precisely Origen's own conviction. Thus he implicitly defended himself against his adversaries who accused him that he did not truly believe in the resurrection of the flesh.

In the following section of his digression Origen argues once more that in 1 Cor 15 Paul wrote especially against those who totally denied the resurrection, as the Sadducees did, and not against those who advocated a qualified view of it. From the same chapter he quotes: "If the dead are not raised at all, why are people baptized on their behalf? And why are we putting ourselves in danger every hour? If with merely human hopes I fought with wild animals at Ephesus, what would I have gained by it? If the dead are not raised, 'Let us eat and drink, for tomorrow we die'" (1 Cor 15:29b.30.32). Repeating the hypothesis that the popular conception of the resurrection of the flesh is not correct, Origen asks some rhetorical questions: "Why would this entail that it is in vain that we put ourselves in danger when we struggle for the salvation of our souls? (...) Why would this entail: 'Let us eat and drink, for tomorrow we die'?"[12] Here Origen clearly does not argue against the heretics, but against those who did not accept his view of the resurrection of the dead, which itself his adversaries considered heretical. In order to testify that – formally, at least – he did share the popular belief of the Church he concludes his digression by quoting Is 40:5, "all flesh shall see God's salvation", Job 19:25–26 LXX, "eternal is He who shall deliver me on the earth, and who will raise my skin that endures all these things", and Paul, Rom 8:11, "he will give life to your mortal bodies through his Spirit that dwells in you".[13] We may conclude that in his own way Origen did believe that the flesh will rise, but we will see that he supposed that it will be transformed and will lose the material features of the earthly body.

In his interpretation of 1 Cor 15:20: "But in fact Christ has been raised from the dead, the first fruits of those who have died", which has been preserved in the catenae, he wonders if Christ is the first fruits of all or of many. He finds the solution of this dilemma in 1 Cor 15:22, where Paul says: "for as all die in Adam, so all will be made alive in Christ", which means that not only the righteous will be made alive.[14] At the same time

[12] Comm in Mat XVII, 29 = GCS 40, 667, l. 20–668, l. 8.

[13] Ibid. = GCS 40, 668 l. 9–19. For the reference to Is 40,5, cf. Tertullian, De res mort 59,3 = CCSL 2, 1007; it appears that Isaiah 40,5 was quoted by "heretics" in the discussion on the resurrection.

[14] Fragm in Ep in Cor 84, l. 72–86 = JThS 10 (1909) 47–48; it seems correct that Jenkins, "Origen" (n. 4) added in l. 86: ἀλλὰ πάντες ζωοποιηθήσονται. See also Comm in Joh XX, 224 = SC 290, 268; Comm in Ep ad Rom V, 2, l. 155–158 = AGLB 33, 398–399; PG 14, 1025B.

Origen takes account of the anxious reaction of a Christian who concludes from this that he endures so much trouble (for the Christian faith) in vain if Christ is the first fruits of *all* who have died and *all* will be made alive in him. Origen replies that Paul adds: "but each in his own order" (1 Cor 15:23). In his understanding this means that each person will experience the resurrection depending on his life style and merits.[15] In his *Commentary on Isaiah* he explains "each in his own order" by distinguishing between the first resurrection of the righteous and the second resurrection of the sinners who will be punished (cf. Apoc 20:6).[16] We will see later that according to Origen even the sinners who will be risen in order to be punished will still have a chance to be purified and to submit themselves to Christ.

1 Corinthians 15:24–28

In the following section Paul writes that after the coming of Christ and the resurrection of the dead Christ will subject those who will subject themselves to him to the Father, including his enemies, and that subsequently he will subject himself to the Father, so that God will be all in all (1 Cor 15:24–28). Origen has often quoted these verses, and several detailed publications have been devoted to his interpretation.[17] For this reason we will give only a short survey of his understanding of this passage.

Whereas Irenaeus and Tertullian thought that it is God who will subject all his enemies under the feet of Christ (1 Cor 15:25),[18] Origen thinks that Christ is the subject of θῇ in this verse. He says that the end will resemble the beginning and that it will take place "when each person will be punished according to his sins". In the present time Christ reigns until he will

[15] Fragm in Ep ad Cor 84 l. 86–89 = JThS 10 (1909) 48; Hom in Num 1,3,2–3 = SC 415, 40–44; Hom in Jer 8,6 = SC 232, 368–370; Comm in Joh XXXII, 27–29 = SC 385, 198–200; cf. Crouzel, "Différences" (n. 1).

[16] In Pamphilus, Apol pro Origene 137, l. 1–26 = SC 464, 220–222; PG 17, 597BC; Crouzel, "La 'première' et la 'seconde' résurrection" (n. 1), 8, shows that this interpretation of Apoc 20:6 is exceptional in Origen's works.

[17] E. Schendel, *Herrschaft und Unterwerfung Christi. 1. Korinther 15,24–28 in Exegese und Theologie der Väter bis zum Ausgang des 4. Jahrhunderts* (BGBE 12; Tübingen 1971), 81–110; J. Rius-Camps, "La hipótesis origeniana sobre el fin último (*peri telous*). Intento de valoración", in *Arché e Telos. L'antropologia di Origene e di Gregorio di Nissa. Analisi storico-religiosa* (ed. U. Bianchi and H. Crouzel; Milano 1981), 58–117; Crouzel, "Quand le Fils…" (n. 1).

[18] Irenaeus, Adv Haer V, 36, 2 = SC 153, 460; Tertullianus, Adv Marc V,9,6 = CCSL 1, 689–690.

put all his enemies under his feet.[19] As long as the hostile powers seduce human beings to sin Christ, the Lamb of God, takes away their sin, until all sin will be taken away from the whole world (cf. Jn 1:29).[20] In the end all enemies will be subjected to Christ, including the "last enemy", death (1 Cor 15:26). According to Origen this last enemy is not the common death, which arrives when the soul is separated from the body, but the devil, who causes the death of the soul by separating it from God by means of sin.[21] On the one hand Origen says with Paul that the hostile powers, including the last enemy, will be destroyed (1 Cor 15:24.26).[22] On the other hand he supposes that it will not be the substance of the last enemy that will perish, since his substance has been made by God, but only "his intention and hostile will, who do not come from God but from himself"; for "nothing is incurable for its Creator".[23] Although Origen can say in a sermon that when someone, like the last enemy, will be subjected by force, he will not find favour anymore, we may assume that he expressed his real opinion in his treatise *On First Principles*, where he says that all powers will be subjected "by Wisdom, i.e., by the Logos, and not by force and necessity".[24] According to Origen both the hostile powers and all human beings are destined to this voluntary submission to Christ. He thinks that the slowness and the negligence of human beings delay the final reconciliation of the world with God.[25] Yet finally, when all creatures will have subjected themselves to Christ, he will subject himself to the Father. In this way all things will in Christ subject themselves to the Father, so that God will be all in all.[26] This is the *apokatastasis*, in which the only activity that will remain for the creatures is to contemplate God.[27] In his *Commentary on Romans* Origen says that then "there will be no more human beings, since all have

---

[19] De Princ I, 6, 1–2, l. 20–45 = SC 252, 194–196.

[20] Comm in Joh I, 233–235 = SC 120, 175–177; VI, 295–296 = SC 157, 352–354.

[21] Comm in Ep ad Rom VI, 6, l. 24–39 = AGLB 33, 480–481; PG 14, 1068AB; Comm in Joh XX, 363–365 = SC 290, 332–334.

[22] Comm in Joh XXXII, 29–32; 39 = SC 385, 200; 204; Comm in Ep ad Rom V, 1, l. 562–567 = AGLB 33, 387; PG 14, 1019BC; Comm in Ep ad Rom V, 7, l. 74–78 = AGLB 33, 420; PG 14, 1036D.

[23] De Princ III, 6, 5, l. 134–144 = SC 268, 244.

[24] Hom in Jos 16, 3 = SC 71, 364; De Princ I, 2, 10, l. 376–380 = SC 252, 136; De Princ III, 5, 8, l. 214–221 = SC 268, 232.

[25] Comm in Ep ad Rom IX, 41, l. 87–103 = AGLB 34, 776; PG 14, 1243BC.

[26] De Princ I, 7, 5, l. 192–198 = SC 252, 220; De Princ III, 5, 6–7, l. 171–213 = SC 268, 230–232; De Orat 25, 2–3 = GCS 3, 358, l. 17–21; 359, l. 1–15; Hom in Lev 7, 2, l. 68–92 = SC 286, 312–314; Hom in Ps 36, 2, 1, l. 23–89 = SC 411, 94–98; Comm in Cant prologus 4, 20 = SC 375, 160; Comm Ser in Mat 55 = GCS 38, 126, l. 8–29; Comm in Ep ad Rom VI, 5, l. 72–77 = AGLB 33, 475; PG 14, 1065D.

[27] Comm in Joh I, 91–92 = SC 120, 106–108; De Princ II, 3, 5, l. 196–210 = SC 252, 262; De Princ III, 5, 7, l. 209–213 (in Latin: *restitutio*) = SC 268, 232.

become gods".[28] In his treatise *On First Principles* he gives his readers the choice between three hypotheses about the human condition at that time: 1. either they will not have any bodies at all; 2. or the substance of the human body will become ethereal; 3. or the earth, the planets and the fixed stars will dissolve to nothing, whereas the saints will stay in another sphere of heaven.[29] As for this last possibility Origen does not specify the condition of the human body in that sphere. In this text Origen does not disclose which of the three hypotheses he prefers. As we said already, we will see that he supposes that in the end the human bodies will have a ethereal substance.

Origen's conception of the *apokatastasis* has been strongly rejected, both during his life and in the subsequent centuries. To mention only one example: in a *Letter to his Friends in Alexandria* Origen defends himself against the accusation that he would have said that the devil would be saved. The Valentinian Candidus ascribed this opinion to him, and Demetrius, the bishop of Alexandria, seems to have given credence to this incrimination. But Origen calls it slander and says that it falls to the Lord to reproach the devil or not.[30] In reality Origen supposed, however, that the devil is free to convert or not, since like all creatures he has a free will.[31]

We can deduce from Origen's interpretation of this passage that he understands Paul's apocalyptic scenario as a long process, or perhaps we should say: as an endless process, depending on the slowness or the progress of each creature that is gifted with reason.

---

[28] Comm in Ep ad Rom V,1 = J. Scherer, *Le Commentaire d'Origène sur Rom. III.5–V.7 d'après les extraits du papyrus N° 88748 du Musée du Caire et les fragments de la Philocalie et du Vaticanus gr. 762: essai de reconstitution du texte et de la pensée des tomes V et VI du "Commentaire sur l'Épître aux Romains"* (Cairo 1957), 128, l. 12–16; cf. Rufinus's translation of Origenes, Comm in Ep ad Rom III,1, l. 155–156: *sancti quique erunt sicut angeli Dei* = AGLB 16, 199; PG 14, 926A.

[29] De Princ II, 3, 7 in Hieronymus, Epistulae 124, 5 = J. Labourt, *Jérôme. Lettres. Texte établi et traduit VII* (Paris 1961), 101, l. 12–26; SC 253, 154 and in Rufinus's translation (SC 252, 270–272); cf. De Princ I, 6, 4; II, 3, 3; = SC 252, 204–206; 256–258; De Princ III, 6, 1–3 = SC 268, 234–242.

[30] In Hieronymus, Apol adv Rufinum II, 18–19 = SC 303, 148–156 and Rufinus, De adult libr Origenis 7 = SC 464, 296–304; see H. Crouzel, "A Letter from Origen 'To Friends in Alexandria'", in *The Heritage of the Early Church: Essays in Honor of G.V. Florovsky* (ed. D. Neiman and M. Schatkin; OrChrA 195; Rome 1973), 135–150.

[31] See R. Roukema, "'Die Liebe kommt nie zu Fall' (1 Korinther 13,8a) als Argument des Origenes gegen einen neuen Abfall der Seelen von Gott", in *Origeniana Septima. Origenes in den Auseinandersetzungen des 4. Jahrhunderts* (ed. W. Bienert and U. Kühneweg; BEThL 137; Leuven 1999), 15–23.

1 Corinthians 15:29–34

In our discussion of 1 Cor 15:12–23 we already saw a reference to 1 Cor 15:29b.30.32. Here we add a remark that Origen made on 1 Cor 15:33–34, where Paul says: "Do not be deceived: 'Bad company ruins good morals'. Come to a sober and right mind and sin no more; for some people have no knowledge of God. I say this to your shame." In his *Commentary on Romans* Origen explains that by these words Paul warns the negligent Christians who want to profit from the apparent universalism of the preceding discourse, where the apostle said that "all will be made alive in Christ" and "then comes the end, when he hands over the kingdom to God the Father" (1 Cor 15:22.24).[32] In our previous section on this passage we saw that Origen addressed the concern of the anxious Christian who worried why he had to endure sufferings for his faith if *all* will be made alive in Christ, but here he warns lax Christians who think that the future resurrection in Christ is already guaranteed, even when there are no traces of sanctification in their lives.

1 Corinthians 15:35–49

Next, Paul tries to explain what sort of bodies there will be in the resurrection. He gives the image of the seed and the wheat or some other grain (1 Cor 15:37), to which Origen adds the example of the human seed that will develop into a human being and the example of the result of pruning a fig tree as arguments for the resurrection of the dead.[33] He explains by means of the Stoic concept of the σπερματικὸς λόγος that God has sown his *logos*, which makes that the different seeds will become, for example, an ear or a tree. He supposes that, likewise, the human being has also got a σπερματικὸς λόγος which brings about that in the resurrection a new body will germinate. However, this body will not consist of flesh, but it will be spiritual, according to 1 Cor 15:44. Origen interprets the term "spiritual" as "ethereal" (*aethereum*), and thinks that this suits the kingdom of heaven.[34]

---

[32] Comm in Ep ad Rom V, 1, l. 90–110 = AGLB 33, 363–364; PG 14, 1006D–1007A.

[33] Fragm in Ep ad Cor 84, l. 33–45; 87 = *JThS* 10 (1909), 46–47; see the corrections of the punctuation proposed by C.H. Turner, *JThS* 10 (1909), 276 (n. 4).

[34] Stromata, in Hieronymus, Contra Joh Hieros 26, l. 7–20 = CCSL 79A, 43–44 (for the attribution of this text to Origen's Stromata, see P. Nautin, *Origène, sa vie et son œuvre* [CAnt 1; Paris 1977], 296–300); Comm in Ps 1, in Methodius, De resurrectione I, 24, 5 = GCS 27, 249–250; cf. De Princ I, 6, 4, l. 182–185; II,10,3, l. 102–114 = SC 252, 206; 380–382; Fragm in Ep ad Cor 84, l. 45–57 = JThS 10 (1909), 47; Contra Celsum V, 18–19 = SC 147, 56–62; Contra Celsum VII, 32 = SC 150, 84–88.

It is important for Origen that there will be a corporeal resurrection and that it will not only concern the soul. He thinks it would be absurd if the body which, together with the soul, has suffered for Christ and has resisted its own natural vices and passions, would not be compensated for this, and that only the soul would be crowned.[35] In order to clarify his view of the resurrection he not only draws on the Stoic σπερματικὸς λόγος, but also on the concept of εἶδος in its Platonic and Aristotelian sense of "form" as opposed to matter, and on the concept of οὐσία, "essence". He holds that the material body cannot rise again, since in its earthly existence it is liable to change from day to day; so which body should then be raised? However, the human identity cannot only be found in the soul, but also in the εἶδος and the οὐσία of the body, which in the resurrection will be given back to the soul. According to Origen the resurrection body will be spiritual, which means that it will have the same εἶδος and the same οὐσία as the earthly body, without being material.[36]

Origen gives an allegorical interpretation of the flesh of animals, birds, and fishes, which Paul enumerates in 1 Cor 15:39. He disputes the idea that a sinner is destined to receive an animal body, as some adherents of metempsychosis supposed,[37] and he explains that the sinners will receive bodies according to their sins, which means that their condition may be comparable to the dumb animals. Likewise he also says that those who will rise in glory will not receive the body of the sun, the moon, or a star, which Paul mentions in 1 Cor 15:41; he explains that by these terms the apostle points to the future glory and brightness of the righteous and of their blessed dwellings.[38]

In Paul's terms Origen explains that although the righteous have been sown in a physical (ψυχικός) body in perishability, dishonour, and weakness, they will be raised in a spiritual body in imperishability, glory, and power (1 Cor 15:42–44).[39] Tentatively he relates this "psychic body" to the

---

[35] De Resurrectione, in Pamphilus, Apol pro Origene 128 = SC 464, 208–210; PG 17, 594AB.

[36] Comm in Ps 1, in Methodius, De Resurrectione I, 22, 2 – 23, 2 = GCS 27, 244–247; cf. De Princ I praefatio 5 = SC 252, 82–84; De Resurrectione, in Pamphilus, Apol pro Origene 130 = SC 464, 210–214; PG 17, 594C–595C. See Crouzel, "Critiques" (n. 1), 688–692; Vítores, *Identidad* (n. 2), 88–89, 99–115, and Dorival, "Origène et la résurrection" (n. 2), 292–295.

[37] See, e.g., Plato, Phaedo 81E; Phaedrus 249B; Timaeus 42C; Plotinus, Enneades III, 4, 2; IV, 3, 12; VI, 7, 6–7; Augustinus, De Civ Dei X, 30 = BAug 34, 538.

[38] De Resurrectione, in Pamphilus, Apol pro Origene 134, l. 17–34 = SC 464, 216–218; PG 17, 596C–597A; cf. De Princ II, 10, 2–3 = SC 252, 376–382; Hom in Jos 10, 1 = SC 71, 270; Comm in Mat X, 3 = SC 162, 150; Contra Celsum IV, 30 = SC 136, 254–256.

[39] Comm in Isaiam XXVIII, in Pamphilus, Apol pro Origene 137, l. 1–10; 139 = SC 464, 220; 224; PG 17, 597B; 598BC.

fall of the souls (ψυχαί) from their original and heavenly condition of νοῦς. According to this speculation God has created earthly bodies for the fallen souls, so that the earthly body can be called "psychic". In the resurrection however the body will not be psychic anymore, since it will have returned to its original state.[40] Origen expects that it can last innumerable ages until the body will reach the very fine, pure, and splendid condition that is characteristic of spiritual bodies.[41] Yet it appears that Origen hesitates to say that the final condition of the spiritual bodies will be incorporeal, since incorporeality is proper only to God.[42] We will come back to the question of the final incorporeality of the creatures.

Origen uses Paul's distinction between the first and the last Adam and between the first man from the earth and the second man from heaven (1 Cor 15:45–49) mainly with regard to human life in this world. He understands that Paul speaks about Adam and Christ[43] and applies this passage to the conversion of the human being to Christ, which entails that one is led by the Spirit and already bears "the image of the heavenly" (1 Cor 15:49).[44] Sometimes however Origen quotes this passage in order to explain what it means that in the resurrection the human being will have a spiritual body.[45]

1 Corinthians 15:50–55

Next, Paul says that "flesh and blood cannot inherit the kingdom of God, nor does the perishable inherit the imperishable" (1 Cor 15:50). For Origen this means that in the resurrection we will rid ourselves of the earthly quality of our bodies, so that they will be spiritual, whereas their εἶδος will be preserved.[46] In other terms, the earthly body will be changed into its heav-

---

[40] De Princ II, 8, 2–4, l. 78–190 = SC 252, 340–349; see Altermath, *Corps psychique* (n. 2), 110–116.

[41] De Princ III, 6, 4–6, especially l. 167–176 = SC 268, 242–250.

[42] De Princ I, 6, 4, l. 175–182; II, 2, 2, l. 24–32 = SC 252, 206; 246–248; De Princ III, 6, 7–9; IV, 3, 15, l. 491–496 = SC 268, 250–254; 396–398.

[43] Comm in Joh I, 108; I, 225 = SC 120, 116; 170; Hom in Jos 8, 6 = SC 71, 234.

[44] Fragm in Gen 1, 26 = PG 12, 96AB; Hom in Gen 9, 2 = SC 7[bis], 242; Hom in Jer 8, 2, l. 35–51 = SC 232, 360–362; Comm in Rom V, 1, l. 209–232 = AGLB 33, 369–370; PG 14, 1010A–C. Cf. Altermath, *Corps psychique* (n. 2), 116–119.

[45] Contra Celsum V, 19, l. 8–23 = SC 147, 60 (on p. 61 the translation "nous porterons" is to be corrected to "portons"); De Princ III, 6, 5, l. 153–163 = SC 268, 246. Origen reads the aorist subjunctive φορέσωμεν, "let us bear"; see Hannah, *Text* (n. 10), 166–167, who erroneously refers to Contra Celsum V, 20.

[46] Comm in Ps 1, in Methodius, De Resurrectione I, 23, 2–3 = GCS 27, 246–247; cf. De Princ II, 10, 3 = SC 252, 380–382; Contra Celsum V, 19 = SC 147, 60; Stromata, in Hieronymus, Contra Joh Hieros 25, l. 10–26 = CCSL 79A, 41–42.

enly οὐσία.[47] In Origen's understanding the following clause, "We will not all die, but we will all be changed" (1 Cor 15:51),[48] concerns those Christians who are called "we who are alive" in 1 Thess 4:15. They are those whose bodies are dead because of sin, and whose spirits are alive because of righteousness (Rom 8:10). They lead a spiritual life and for this reason they will immediately be transformed to incorruptibility. Consequently Origen identifies "the dead" who "will be raised imperishable" (1 Cor 15:52) with "the dead in Christ" mentioned in 1 Thess 4:16. He explains that they are the Christians who have sinned and who are called "dead" in spite of their penance and the expiation of their sins. Elsewhere he says that they are those who continue to sin in spite of their faith in Christ. Because they are most in need of the resurrection and God wants them also to be saved, he will transform them like "those who are alive".[49]

Although in the texts mentioned in the preceding footnote Origen quotes Paul's terms "the moment", "the twinkling of an eye", and "the last trumpet" (1 Cor 15:52), he does not go into their precise meaning. This is not strange; for him it would be unthinkable that in a last moment a real trumpet will sound to announce the general resurrection. However, the notion of a distinct moment occurs in his following passage: "When the judgement day will have come and at the voice of the archangel (cf. 1 Thess 4:16) and the sound of the last trumpet the earth will shake (cf. Hebr 12:26), then the seeds will move immediately and in a moment they will germinate the dead, yet not their flesh, and neither will they restore them in their former shapes".[50] We will come back to Origen's difficulty to reconcile this notion of a precise moment and his remarks on the spiritual development of each individual.

Paul continues: "For this perishable body must put on imperishability, and this mortal body must put on immortality" (1 Cor 15:53). Origen explains that the perishable and mortal matter of the body shall put on a perfect soul that adorns it and covers it mortal nature, so that the body will be spiritual and covered by imperishability and immortality. Origen is aware that his readers may be surprised by this notion of a perfect soul that the body will put on as a cloak and compares this soul with Christ whom the saints have to put on (Rom 13:14). When, after a long period, the body will

[47] De Oratione 26, 6 = GCS 3, 363, l. 17–22.

[48] Origen reads: οὐ πάντες κοιμηθησόμεθα πάντες δὲ ἀλλαγησόμεθα; see Contra Celsum V, 17, l. 7–8 = SC 147, 56 and Hannah, *Text* (n. 10), 168–169, who erroneously refers to Contra Celsum V, 18.

[49] Comm in Thess III, in Hieronymus, Epistulae 119, 9–10 = ed. J. Labourt, *Jérôme. Lettres. Texte établi et traduit VI* (Paris 1958), 111–115; Comm in Joh XX, 231–233 = SC 290, 270–272; cf. Contra Celsum II, 65 = SC 132, 440; Contra Celsum V,17 = SC 147, 56.

[50] Stromata, in Hieronymus, Contra Joh Hieros 26, l. 20–24 = CCSL 79A, 44.

have put on this perfect soul, it will consequently have put on imperishability and immortality.[51] For this notion of the perfect soul Origen was inspired by Plato's *Timaeus*.[52]

This interpretation of 1 Cor 15:53 occurs in his treatise *On First Principles*. Origen is more specific about this verse in his *Commentary on the Gospel of John*, where he says that something corporeal cannot be transformed unto something incorporeal. He underlines there that the perishable and mortal nature will *put on* imperishability and immortality, and that this does not imply that it will be transformed unto imperishability and immortality.[53] Elsewhere Origen quotes this verse as a testimony to the sanctification of the earthly life, as an anticipation of the eschatological resurrection.[54] Paul continues that after the body has put on imperishability and immortality "death has been swallowed up in victory" (1 Cor 15:54). Origen says that the same thing is expressed previously when Paul wrote about the final destruction of death as the last enemy in 1 Cor 15:26.[55] In 1 Cor 15:55 he reads: "Death, where is your sting? Hades, where is your victory?"[56] He explains that the dead, who have left their earthly bodies and dwell in finer and purer bodies, can henceforth neither be overcome by death nor wounded by its sting. Their material nature will gradually disappear, death will finally be swallowed, and God will be all in all.[57]

In Rufinus's version of *On First Principles* Origen asks whether in the end the rational creatures will be completely incorporeal. In this version he answers with an objection. He supposes that in case the rational creatures, thanks to their free will, would fall again from their blissful condition, God would have to create bodies for them once again.[58] We are to understand that this is not desirable. However, although Origen considers the possibility of a new fall in several texts,[59] it is less sure whether this was his decisive reason to reject the final incorporeality. Should we give credit to the testimonies of Jerome and the emperor Justinian who said that Origen sup-

[51] De Princ II, 3, 2 = SC 252, 250–256.

[52] This is suggested by Bostock, "Quality" (n. 2), 336–337, who refers to Timaeus 34B; 36E.

[53] Comm in Joh XIII, 429–430 = SC 222, 268.

[54] De Oratione 25, 3 = GCS 3, 359, l. 11–15; cf. Contra Celsum VII, 32, l. 25–42 = SC 150, 86–88.

[55] Contra Celsum VI, 36, l. 1–8 = SC 147, 264–266.

[56] De Oratione 25, 3 = GCS 3, 359, l. 10; cf. Hannah, *Text* (n. 10), 172–173.

[57] De Princ II, 3, 3, l. 100–120 = SC 252, 256; De Princ III, 6, 3, l. 66–87 = SC 268, 240.

[58] De Princ II, 3, 3, l. 120–142 = SC 252, 256–258; cf. De Princ III, 6, 3, l. 87–95 = SC 268, 240–242.

[59] Cf. Roukema, "Die Liebe kommt nie zu Fall" (n. 31).

posed that the final state of the rational creatures would be incorporeal?[60] It is true that even in Rufinus's version Origen gives his readers the choice to decide whether the creatures' final state would be corporeal or incorporeal.[61] As we said before, Origen supposed that the end will always resemble the beginning, which means that the end will be the restoration of the initial state of creation.[62] So the question is whether Origen thought that in the beginning the rational creatures were created incorporeal or that they were not. According to a testimony preserved by Procopius of Gaza (5th–6th century) Origen appears to have supposed that in the beginning the rational creatures had received luminous bodies.[63] This implies that prior to their fall the creatures had fine bodies that correspond with the ethereal bodies that are destined for the resurrection, as we saw above. We can conclude that Origen reserves absolute incorporeality only to God.[64] This conclusion corresponds with the remark in his *Commentary on the Gospel of John*, where he maintains that something corporeal cannot be transformed into something incorporeal.[65]

Origen also refers to the sting of death (1 Cor 15:55). He says it was made blunt by Christ who preached salvation to the spirits who were imprisoned in Hades (cf. 1 Pet 3:19; 4:6), so that they could go to heaven.[66] He quotes the same verse as an exhortation to the believers to lead a spiritual life, so that the last enemy, death, will be destroyed in them and Christ says in them: "death, where is your sting? Hades, where is your victory?"[67] Once more we see that in Origen's understanding the resurrection and the disappearance of death are not only eschatological events, but have to start in earthly life already. We still have to clarify how Origen can on the one hand speak about a distinct moment of the resurrection, whereas on the other he explains repeatedly that it will be long before the risen body reaches its final condition of spiritual body that has put on imperishability and immortality.[68] In fact, according to Origen the ascent and the spiritual

---

[60] Hieronymus, Epistulae 124, 5 = ed. Labourt VII (n. 29), 100–101; Justinianus, Epistula ad Menam = E. Schwartz, *Acta Conciliorum Oecumenicorum III* (Berlin 1940), 211, l. 24–27; see also SC 253, 144–146.

[61] De Princ III, 6, 9, l. 280–282 = SC 268, 254.

[62] Ibid. I, 6, 2, l. 46 = SC 252, 196; De Princ III, 6, 3, l. 78–80 = SC 268, 240.

[63] Procopius Gazaeus, Comm in Gen 3, 21 = PG 87, 1, 221AB.

[64] See especially Crouzel, "Véhicule" (n. 1), 231–233; "Mort et immortalité" (n. 1), 181–187; Hennessey, "Philosophical Issue" (n. 2), who corrects Bostock, "Quality" (n. 2), 336–337; Edwards, "Origen no Gnostic" (n. 2).

[65] See n. 53.

[66] Pascha 47, l. 36 – 48, l. 10 = O. Guérard, P. Nautin, *Origène. Sur la Pâque. Traité inédit publié d'après un papyrus de Toura* (CAnt 2; Paris 1979), 246–248.

[67] De Oratione 25, 3 = GCS 3, 359, l. 8–10.

[68] See n. 25, 41, 50, 51, 57.

evolution of the souls of the Christians, as well as the purification of the souls of the sinners, start immediately after the death of the body.[69] – Eugène de Faye and Hal Koch concluded that for Origen a concrete resurrection is out of the question, since everything will happen in a slow and progressive evolution, according to the free will of the rational creatures.[70] In our opinion this conclusion is too radical, for it cannot be denied that Origen regularly speaks about the resurrection as a future event at a precise moment. He explicitly refutes the view of those who were called Christians but deny the scriptural doctrine of resurrection.[71] In our opinion the reason why Origen adhered to the belief in the resurrection of the dead was his faithfulness and loyalty towards the Church. For basically he was a man of the Church.[72] Nevertheless it seems quite clear that his theological convictions, which were strongly marked by Platonism, might easily have done without the notion of a concrete resurrection of the dead. We should acknowledge that in his learned examination of the apostolic preaching of the Christian faith his attempt to integrate the belief in the concrete resurrection of the dead at the end of times was not fully successful. So at least in part we have to agree with de Faye and Koch, and we have to say that this aspect of Origen's approach of the resurrection has been passed over in Henri Crouzel's essays, perspicacious though they may be otherwise. As a member of the catholic Church Origen did not feel any need of denying either the concrete coming of Christ or the general resurrection of the dead, but in reality it must have been very difficult for him to consider these beliefs as events that were to be expected concretely. He was interested in the spiritual progress and ascent of each human individual, both during their earthly lives and after the death of the material bodies, so that in the end they would all together form the body of Christ. [73] We can conclude that it is not surprising that Origen's daring approach has given rise to suspicion and rejection by the Church.

---

[69] Cf. R. Roukema, "Les anges attendant les âmes des défunts: une comparaison entre Origène et quelques gnostiques", in *Origeniana Octava* (ed. L. Perrone, P. Bernardino, and D. Marchini; BEThL 164; Leuven 2003), 367–374.

[70] E. de Faye, *Origène, sa vie, son oeuvre, sa pensée* (vol. 3; Paris 1928), 249–268; H. Koch, *Pronoia und Paideusis: Studien über Origenes und sein Verhältnis zum Platonismus* (Berlin and Leipzig 1932), 89–96.

[71] Contra Celsum V, 22, l. 1–3 = SC 147, 66–68.

[72] J.W. Trigg, "Origen: Man of the Church", in *Origeniana Quinta* (ed. R.J. Daly; BEThL 105; Leuven 1992), 51–56.

[73] See the texts collected by H.U. von Balthasar, *Origenes Geist und Feuer: ein Aufbau aus seinen Schriften* (2nd ed.; Salzburg 1956), § 877–892; English translation by R.J. Daly, *Origen Spirit and Fire: A Thematic Anthology of his Writings* (Edinburgh 1984), 320–325.

Animal Resurrection in the Apocryphal Acts of the Apostles

JANET E. SPITTLER

1. Introduction

C.S. Lewis, who in his narratives casts the divine logos as the lion Aslan, writes in *The Problem of Pain* that he has been warned not even to raise the question of animal immortality or resurrection, lest he find himself "'in company with all the old maids.'"[1] If, as some have suggested,[2] we should understand the "old wives' tales" (γραώδεις μῦθοι) in 1 Tim 4:7 to be a reference to the sorts of stories contained in the apocryphal acts of the apostles, it is perhaps not surprising that these narratives do indeed address the topic. In the *Acts of Peter*, our sole extant manuscript of which is the *Actus Vercellenses*,[3] the apostle resurrects a dried, salted tuna (*sarda*) in order that the crowds might believe in Jesus;[4] in the *Acts of Andrew and Matthias in the City of the Cannibals*, when a deluge of putrid water has engulfed and drowned the wicked residents of the city, along with their cattle (κτήνη), Andrew prays and all – presumably including the animals – return to life (πάντες ἀνέζησαν).[5] In contrast, when, in the *Acts of Thomas*, the crowd laments the death of a talking ass and begs the apostle to resurrect it, Thomas refuses, saying: "I am able to raise him through the name of Jesus Christ, but this is entirely beneficial; for the one who gave speech to him so that he might talk was able to make him not die; I do not raise him not because I am unable, but because this is suitable and beneficial to him (τὸ συμβαλλόμενον αὐτῷ καὶ συμφέρον)."[6]

---

[1] C.S. Lewis, *The Problem of Pain* (New York 1944), 124. For a discussion of contemporary Christian thought on animal afterlife and resurrection, see S.H. Webb, *On God and Dogs* (New York and Oxford 1998), 174–180.

[2] See, for example, D.R. MacDonald, *The Legend and the Apostle* (Philadelphia 1983), 54–77.

[3] To avoid confusion, throughout this article I will simply cite this text as the "*Acts of Peter.*"

[4] *Acts Pet.* 13.

[5] *Acts Andr. Mat.* 32.

[6] *Acts Thom.* 41.

Photius, the 9th century patriarch of Constantinople and last person known to have read a corpus of apocryphal acts roughly comparable to the major apocryphal acts extant today, includes among the most objectionable elements of these texts the "ridiculous and childish resurrections of dead men and oxen and other beasts" (νεκρῶν δὲ ἀνθρώπων καὶ βοῶν καὶ κτηνῶν ἄλλων παραλογωτάτας καὶ μειρακιώδεις ... ἀναστάσεις).[7] Modern scholars, too, have classified these episodes as prime examples of the "teratological" or simply "popular" nature of the texts, often with the result that they are not given much consideration in the evaluation of the theological thought represented in these works. In fact, in early Christianity the question of animal resurrection was not at all the stuff of old wives' tales (though old wives undoubtedly enjoyed these fantastic narratives as much as anyone). To the contrary, these tales of animal resurrection (or the refusal to resurrect) are another instance in which the apocryphal acts take up, albeit in highly entertaining (and indeed "teratological" and "popular") narrative form, an issue that is of central importance in early Christian thought. As will be seen below, animals are ubiquitous in patristic discussions of resurrection, though they are introduced into two markedly different types of arguments. On the one hand, animals – particularly the phoenix – provide for many authors a natural-world example of resurrection and thus evidence for the feasibility of the resurrection of human beings; on the other hand, many authors' arguments in defense of resurrection are based on an anthropocentric view of the phenomenon as necessarily and exclusively human.

In the pages that follow, I will survey the references to and discussions of animal resurrection in Greco-Roman literature, beginning with the few examples from non-Christian sources; I will then turn to the patristic sources, first considering the authors that use examples of animal resurrections in arguments for the plausibility of the phenomenon, then those who argue for the plausibility of human resurrection by explicitly ruling out the resurrection of animals. Finally, I will return to the apocryphal acts in an attempt to understand the thinking behind these rather enigmatic animal resurrection episodes, setting them within the context of the Christian thinking of their day.

---

[7] Photius, *Bibl.* 114.

2. Animal Resurrection in non-Christian Greco-Roman Literature

There are relatively few references to animal resurrection or revivification in non-Christian Greco-Roman literature. Nevertheless, there are a few key instances, several of which are particularly relevant in interpreting the episodes in the apocryphal acts. One such account comes at the close of Herodotus' *Histories*. In 9:116, it is reported that Artauctes, the Persian governor of the Chersonesus, had plundered the heroon of Protesilaos at Elaious, stealing the treasure and defiling the precinct by keeping his harem in the sanctuary. In the final episode of the *Hist.* as Artauctes, now captured by the Athenians, sits in prison, a sign (τέρας) appears to one of the guards: the salt-fish (τάριχοι) that he is roasting begin to flop and gasp as if just caught (νεοάλωτοι). All present marvel at the sign, but, reassuring the chef, Artauctes himself provides the correct interpretation:

Ξεῖνε Ἀθηναῖε, μηδὲν φοβέο τὸ τέρας τοῦτο· οὐ γὰρ σοὶ πέφηνε, ἀλλ' ἐμοὶ σημαίνει ὁ ἐν Ἐλαιοῦντι Πρωτεσίλεως ὅτι καὶ τεθνεὼς καὶ τάριχος ἐὼν δύναμιν πρὸς θεῶν ἔχει τὸν ἀδικέοντα τίνεσθαι.

"Athenian stranger, don't fear this wonder, for it did not appear for you; rather, Protesilaos at Elaious is giving me a sign that, although dead and dried (lit.: 'being a τάριχος'), he has power from the gods to punish the one who has wronged him."[8]

This episode has several clear parallels to the episode in the *Acts Pet.*, which will be discussed in detail below; for now, we might make the following observations. First, it should be noted that in the first centuries C.E., this animal resurrection was not just associated with the hero's post-mortem power to punish, but with the hero's own ability to return from the dead. As Glen Bowersock has argued, Protesilaos, famously the first Greek to die in the Trojan war, becomes in the first centuries C.E. the "new representative of bodily resurrection,"[9] being invoked as such by Chariton, Petronius, Aelius Aristides and Lucian.[10] He is featured in Philostratus' early third century dialogue the *Heroicus*, where he is depicted as not only resurrected, but as the regular visitor of a vineyard worker at the sacred precinct at Elaious. Philostratus makes reference to the Artauctes episode in the *Heroicus* 9,5, where the vineyard worker, showing a Phoenician guest around the heroon, says:

[8] Herodotus, *Hist.* 9:120. See G. Nagy's discussion of this passage in "The Sign of Protesilaos," *Métis* (1987), 207–213, and *Pindar's Homer: the lyric possession of an epic past* (Baltimore 1990), 269–273.

[9] G.W. Bowersock, *Fiction as History* (Berkeley 1994), 113.

[10] See Chariton, *Chaer.* 5:10:1; Petronius, *Satyr.* 129:1; Aelius Aristides, *Orat.* 3:365; Lucian, *Dial. mort.* 28 (23), *Luct.* 5:6.

Τὸ δέ γε ἱερόν, ἐν ᾧ κατὰ τοὺς πατέρας ὁ Μῆδος ὕβριζεν, ἐφ' ᾧ καὶ τὸ τάριχος ἀναβιῶναί φασι, τοῦτο ἡγοῦ, ὦ ξένε·

"Consider this heroon, stranger, in which the Mede committed outrage in the time of our fathers, for which reason, they say, the salt-fish came back to life."

The fact that this reference is so brief – that the salt-fish resurrection can be mentioned with no explanatory detail – suggests that the story would have been well known to the early third century reader.[11]

Other reports of animal resurrections are found in ancient natural history texts (e.g. of Aelian and Pliny) which enjoyed a surge of popularity in the first centuries C.E. Aelian reports that, although flies are prone to drowning when they fall into the water, "if you pick up its dead body, sprinkle it with ash and set it out in the sun, you will bring the fly back to life" (εἰ δὲ αὐτῆς ἐξέλοις τὸν νεκρόν, καὶ τέφραν ἐμπάσειας καὶ καταθείης ἐν ἡλίου αὐγῇ, ἀναβιώσῃ τὴν μυῖαν).[12] Pliny expresses some doubt when describing a similar phenomenon with bees,[13] but gives the same report on flies: "when flies have been killed by moisture, if they are buried in ash they return to life" (*muscis umore exanimatis, si cinere condantur, redit vita*).[14]

Lucian also knows this zoological factoid and, naturally, includes it in his ironic encomium of a creature that too often does not get its proper respect:

"The greatest aspect of their nature is what I am about to tell. It does indeed seem to me that Plato overlooked this one thing in his account of the soul and its immortality. For the dead fly, if ash is sprinkled upon it, is resurrected (ἀνίσταται) and has a certain rebirth (παλιγγενεσία τις) and another life (βίος ἄλλος), begun afresh, so that all are accurately persuaded (ὡς ἀκριβῶς πεπεῖσθαι πάντας) that the soul of those creatures is immortal (κἀκείνων ἀθάνατός ἐστιν ἡ ψυχή); for at any rate, after departing, it returns again, recognizes and reanimates the body, and makes the fly take flight; indeed it confirms the story about Hermotimus of Clazomenae: that his soul often left him and would go about on its own, then, returning, would inhabit his body again and resurrect (ἀνίστα) Hermotimus."[15]

[11] Herodotus' phrase describing the salt-fishes' return to life is quoted also by Athenaeus, *Deipn.* 3:119d. See also discussion in P. Grossardt, *Einführung, Übersetzung und Kommentar zum Heroikos von Flavius Philostrat* (SBA 33; 2 vols.; Basel 2006), 2:405–406.

[12] Aelian, *Nat. an.* 2:29.

[13] Pliny writes: "There are some who think that dead [bees] (*mortuas*), if they are preserved indoors in winter then exposed to the spring sun and warmed with hot fig-wood ash, are revivified (*revivescere*)" (*Nat.* 11:22).

[14] Pliny, *Nat.* 11:43.

[15] Lucian, *Musc. Laud.* 7.

However ironic his encomium of the fly might be, Lucian clearly sees in this report the possible ramifications for human beings: if a dead fly can return to life, surely this lends credence to reports of human resurrections!

Undoubtedly the most famous example of animal resurrection in Greco-Roman literature is the report of the phoenix. While the phoenix is mentioned in Hesiod,[16] Herodotus gives the most complete and influential early account:

"Another sacred bird is the one called the phoenix. Now, I have not actually seen a phoenix, except in a painting, because they are quite infrequent visitors to the country; in fact, I was told in Heliopolis that they appear only at 500-year intervals. They say that it is the death of a phoenix's father which prompts its visit to Egypt. Anyway, if the painting is reliable, I can tell you something about the phoenix's size and qualities, namely that its feathers are partly gold but mostly red, and that in appearance and size it is most like an eagle. There is a particular feat they say the phoenix performs; I do not believe it myself, but they say that the bird sets out from its homeland in Arabia on a journey to the sanctuary of the sun, bringing its father sealed in myrrh, and buries its father there. The method it uses for carrying its father is as follows. First it forms out of myrrh as big an egg as it can manage to carry, and then it makes a trial flight to make sure it can carry the egg. When this has been tested, it hollows out the egg and puts its father inside, and then seals up with more myrrh that part of the egg which it had hollowed out to hold its father. The egg now weighs the same, with its father lying inside, as it did before it was hollowed out. So when the phoenix has sealed the egg up again, it carries its father to the sanctuary of the sun in Egypt. That is what they say the bird does."[17]

Notably, this description in Herodotus is *not* of a resurrection. The extraordinary characteristics of this bird are not its ability to return to life, but its long life span (apparently 500 years) and the filial piety shown by the offspring, carrying the myrrh-encased body of its parent from Arabia to the temple of the sun in Heliopolis for burial. Notable, too, is that, while Herodotus doubts the accuracy of the account of the bird's preparation and transportation of its parent's remains, he does not doubt that this is a *real animal*.

The first detailed natural-historical account of the phoenix in a Roman source is that of the senator Manilius, recorded by the somewhat doubtful Pliny:

"Among Romans, Manilius, that senator famed for great learning gained without a teacher, put forth the first and most detailed account about it: he stated that no one has ever existed that has seen one feeding, that in Arabia it is sacred to the Sun, that it lives 540 years, that when it grows old it constructs a nest from sprigs of cinnamon and frankincense, it fills it with aromatics and dies upon it; then, from its bones and marrow is born first a sort of worm, and this becomes a chicken, and that this first thing makes the

[16] See Plutarch, *Def. orac.* 415d.

[17] Herodotus, *Hist.* 2:73. Trans. R. Waterfield (Oxford 1998), 123–124.

funeral rites for the former bird and carries the whole nest back to the City of the Sun near Panchaia and deposits it upon an altar there."[18]

According to Pliny, Manilius also claims that the bird last appeared in the consulship of Publius Licinius and Gnaeus Cornelius (97 B.C.E.), while Cornelius Valerianus reports the appearance of the phoenix in Egypt in the consulship of Quintus Plautius and Sextus Papinius (36 C.E.); Pliny notes that a phoenix was brought to Rome and displayed in the forum in the reign of the emperor Claudius (in 47 C.E.), though this bird was generally recognized as a fake.[19] In Manilius' account we find the beginnings of the notion of resurrection, though the birth of the new phoenix from the body of the old might be interpreted rather as an instance of miraculous generation. Indeed this report is quite similar to the popular Greco-Roman notion that snakes are generated from the spines of the corpses of evil men.[20] Ovid, in any case, seems to have connected the two phenomena, describing the generation of snakes from human marrow as the last example of animals that originate from other living creatures before turning to the phoenix as the only example of an animal that "revives and reproduces itself" (*reparet seque ipsa reseminet*).[21]

The report of the Roman geographer Mela likewise emphasizes the miraculous birth of the "only one of its kind" (*semper unica*) phoenix:

"It is not truly conceived by coitus or generated through birth (*non enim coitu concipitur, partuve generatur*); rather, when it has survived a 500 year lifespan, it rests itself upon a pile heaped with various spices and disintegrates. Then, taking form from the decay of the rotting body, it conceives itself and, renewed of itself, it is born (*ipsa se concipit, atque ex se rursus enascitur*)."[22]

Mela, like Herodotus and Manilius, does not doubt that the phoenix is a real bird. Neither does Aelian, though, in his report on the phoenix, few details are given. Instead, assuming that the characteristics of the bird are well known – "the account is common knowledge," he writes (δημώδης ἐστὶν ὁ λόγος) – he cites the phoenix as evidence for the intelligence of animals: while human priests have great difficulty keeping track of the calendar, the animal "divinely guesses by signs the right time and appears (ἀποσημαίνεται δαιμονίως τὸν καιρὸν καὶ πάρεστιν)."[23] Philostratus' account of the phoenix, placed in the mouth of the sage Apollonius, is relatively brief, describing the bird's physical appearance much as Herodotus does. The only addition to the account is a detail Apollonius attributes to

---

[18] Pliny, *Nat.* 10:2.
[19] Ibid.
[20] See Aelian, *Nat. an.* 1:51.
[21] Ovid, *Met.* 15:392.
[22] Mela, *De situ orbis* 3:8.
[23] Aelian, *Nat. an.* 6:58.

the Indians, that is, that "as the phoenix is consumed in its nest, it sings funeral hymns for itself" (τὸ τὸν φοίνικα τὸν ἐν τῇ καλιᾷ τηκόμενον προπεμπτηρίους ὕμνους αὑτῷ ᾄδειν), much like the swan.[24] The reader may have noted that the descriptions of the phoenix considered thus far do not correspond well to the most well-known contemporary of the tale: i.e. that the new phoenix rises from the smoldering ash of its parent's pyre. Here in Philostratus' account we find perhaps a hint of that fire: the body is "consumed" (τηκόμενον). This could be interpreted as consumption by heat (the term often refers, for example, to smelting), though "melting" or "disintegrating" through decomposition are equally plausible. Fire is clearly present in Tacitus' account, though it is the funeral pyre of the parent phoenix, ignited only after the corpse is brought to Heliopolis by the mature new phoenix; as in the versions of Manilius, Ovid and Mela, the new phoenix is generated from the decomposing body of the parent in the prepared "nest" of spices.[25] The notion that the new phoenix is born from the ashes of its parent's cremated corpse seems to be a conflation of what were (in Manilius, Ovid and Mela) two separate functions of the spice heap: first as nest for the fledgling, then as burial encasement for the parent.

The first account of the phoenix by a pagan author in which the new bird rises from the funeral pyre of its parent is a late 4th century poem of Claudian (if indeed he *was*, as Augustine thought, a pagan and not a Christian).[26] In an extended encomiastic poem dedicated to the phoenix, Claudian details its habitat ("a leafy wood fringed by Ocean's farthest marge beyond the Indes and the East"), its appearance ("its crest shines

[24] Philostratus, *Vit. Apoll.* 3:49. Also notable is the appearance of the phoenix in Achilles Tatius' *Leuc.* 3:25; there, in addition to the standard Herodotean report concerning the appearance and behavior of the bird, its inspection and correct identification by the priests at Heliopolis is given peculiar emphasis. The description of the phoenix's willingness to submit to inspection of every body part, including its "private parts" (τὰ ἀπόρρητα) seems to prefigure the virginity inspection that the heroine Leucippe will endure later in the novel; see J.E. Spittler, *Animals in the Apocryphal Acts of the Apostles* (WUNT II; Tübingen 2008), 60–61.

[25] Tacitus, *Ann.* 6:28. Note that, while Tacitus finds at least elements of the account "doubtful and exaggerated with myth" (*incerta et fabulosis aucta*), "there can be no doubt that this bird has been seen at various times in Egypt" (*aspici aliquando in Aegypto eam volucrem non ambigitur*). Note also that Tacitus places one of these appearances during the consulship of Paulus Fabius and Lucius Vitellius, i.e. 34 C.E.

[26] There is some evidence that Aelius Aristides, though he gives few details, has in mind a version of the account in which the parent dives into its own funeral pyre, from the ashes of which the new bird rises. Note that Aelius uses the phoenix to represent the rejuvenation of ancient cities, not unlike Chicago after the fire (and hence the choice of the phoenix as symbol of the University of Chicago). See *Or.* 2:426; 17:2; 18:9 and 20:19.

with the sun's own light and shatters the darkness with its calm brilliance"), its miraculous generation ("never was this bird conceived nor springs it from any mortal seed, itself is alike its own father and son"), and its mode of death and resurrection, including the divine intervention of Apollo:

> "Now the Phoenix's bright eye grows dim and the pupil becomes palsied by the frost of years, like the moon when she is shrouded in clouds and her horn beings to vanish in the mist. Now his wings, wont to cleave the clouds of heaven, can scarce raise them from the earth. Then, realizing that his span of life is at an end and in preparation for a renewal of his splendor, he gathers dry herbs from the sun-warmed hills, and making an interwoven heap of the branches of the precious tree of Saba he builds that pyre which shall be at once his tomb and his cradle.
>
> On this he takes his seat and as he grows weaker greets the Sun with his sweet voice; offering up prayers and supplications he begs that those fires will give him renewal of strength. Phoebus, on seeing him afar, checks his reins and staying his course consoles his loving child with these words: 'Thou who art about to leave thy years behind upon yon pyre, who, by this pretence of death, art destined to rediscover life; thou whose decease means but the renewal of existence and who by self-destruction regainest thy lost youth, receive back thy life, quit the body that must die, and by a change of form come forth more beauteous than ever.'
>
> So speaks he, and shaking his head casts one of his golden hairs and smites willing Phoenix with its life-giving effulgence. Now, to ensure his rebirth, he suffers himself to be burned and in his eagerness to be born again meets death with joy. Stricken with the heavenly flame the fragrant pile catches fire and burns the aged body. The moon in amaze checks her milk-white heifers and heaven halts his revolving spheres, while the pyre conceives the new life; Nature takes care that the deathless bird perishes not, and calls upon the sun, mindful of his promise, to restore its immortal glory to the world.
>
> Straightway the life spirit surges through his scattered limbs; the renovated blood floods his veins. The ashes show signs of life; they begin to move though there is none to move them, and feathers clothe the mass of cinders. He who was but now the sire comes forth from the pyre the son and successor; between life and life lay but that brief space wherein the pyre burned."[27]

In this description, Claudian has clearly taken a turn away from the natural-historical toward the mythical. Notable additions to the story include the role of the sun-god Apollo, bringing about the death of his own sacred bird – his "devoted child" (*pium…alumnum*)[28] – and the animal's own willing role, meeting its death with joy (*iam sponte crematur ut redeat gaudetque mori*).[29]

---

[27] Claudian, *Carm. Min.* 27:36–71. Trans. M. Platnauer (Cambridge 1963).
[28] Ibid. 27:49.
[29] Ibid. 27:57–58.

3. Animal Resurrection in Patristic Authors

As has undoubtedly already become clear, the reports concerning animal resurrections offer multiple possibilities for Christian authors. The phoenix is particularly promising: here is a natural-world example of both miraculous birth (involving only one parent) and resurrection. Claudian's version (whether he was a pagan or Christian) allows the phoenix to be read not just as a representation of resurrection in the abstract but as a figure of Jesus: the devoted child of the god who goes willingly to his own death to bring about resurrection. All these elements are exploited by patristic authors. But while the phoenix is clearly the favorite example of "natural-world" resurrection cited by early Christians, the more humble fly is not completely overlooked.

The earliest Christian mention of the phoenix (or of any animal resurrection) is *1 Clem.* 25–26:

"Let us consider the paradoxical sign that takes place in the eastern parts, that is in the regions near Arabia. There is a bird called the phoenix. This [bird], the only one of its kind (μονογενής), lives 500 years; and when it comes time for its dissolution in death, it makes itself a sepulcher of frankincense and myrrh and other aromatics, and when the time is fulfilled it enters into it and dies. From the rotting of its flesh some sort of worm is born, which, nourished from the juice of the dead bird, puts forth wings. Then, when it is mature, it takes up that sepulcher, where the bones of its predecessor are, and carries them from the Arabian region as far as Egypt, into the city called Heliopolis; and when it is day, with all looking on, it flies to the altar of the Sun, places them there, then starts back home. The priests then inspect the registers of dates, and they find that [the phoenix] has come at the fulfillment of the 500th year.

Do we regard it as any great wonder, then, that the creator of the universe will bring about the resurrection of all those serving him with holiness in the conviction of good faith, when even through a bird he shows us the greatness of his promise?[30]

The phoenix appears in *1 Clem.* as the last and most detailed of several examples of "resurrection" in nature; in 24, we find that "day and night show us a resurrection" (ἡμέρα καὶ νὺξ ἀνάστασιν ἡμῖν δηλοῦσιν), and that resurrection is figured in the sprouting of plants from the decaying of seed. The example of the phoenix is an argument from the lesser to the greater, proving the plausibility of the resurrection of Christians: if God resurrects a bird, is the resurrection of a human so very astounding? Moreover, in *1 Clem.* the bird is a *sign* (σημεῖον) through which God indicates the promise of resurrection.

The next Christian author to take up the phoenix is Tertullian. In *De resurrectione carnis*, after establishing that flesh is worthy to be resur-

---

[30] *1 Clem.* 25:1–26:1. For a detailed commentary on this passage, see J.B. Lightfoot, *The Apostolic Fathers* 1.2 (London 1890), 84–89; R.M. Grant, *Early Christians and Animals* (London and New York 1999), 39–41.

rected, he turns to the question of God's ability to restore what has been "decayed and devoured and by whatever means torn apart" (*dilapsum et devoratum et quibuscumque modis ereptum*).[31] Tertullian argues, first, that the God who created the world, whether out of nothing or out of pre-existing material, is surely able to re-recreate the human body, again either out of nothing or out of its now scattered parts. Next, he turns to "specific examples of divine power" (*ipsa quoque exempla divinae potestatis*).[32] Here, Tertullian follows the pattern of *1 Clem.*, beginning with the example of day and night, agricultural cycles and "this entire scheme of the revolving of things" (*totus...hic ordo revolubilis rerum*).[33] For those who would object that the changing of seasons and renewal of crops is not resurrection – not the revivification of something that has died, but merely a reformation – Tertullian offers as a "most profound and trustworthy example" (*plenissimum atque firmissimum...specimen*) the bird "which, willingly performing its own funeral, is renewed" (*qui semetipsum libenter funerans renovat*).[34] For Tertullian, this is proof positive: "What could be clearer and more indicative in this case or for what other matter is there such proof?"[35] Moreover, the example of the phoenix is read not just in God's creation but in his words: "God even says in his own scriptures: 'And you shall flourish like the phoenix,' that is, from death, from burial, so that you might believe it is possible for the substance of the body to be claimed even from the flames."[36] Here, Tertullian takes the "phoenix" of Psalm 92:12 (δίκαιος ὡς φοῖνιξ ἀνθήσει, LXX 91.13) as the bird, not the tree (the date palm) of the same name.[37] Tertullian closes the section, again like *1 Clem.*, with an argument from the lesser to the greater, though using also a New Testament quotation: "Our Lord has stated that we are superior to the many sparrows: if not also to the phoenix, it amounts to nothing. But shall human beings be destroyed once and for all while the birds of Arabia are assured of resurrection?"[38] Notably, while Tertullian seems concerned to stress the plausibility of bodily resurrection even after cremation, his

[31] Tertullian, *Res.* 11:3.

[32] Ibid. 12:1.

[33] Ibid. 12:7.

[34] Ibid. 13:2.

[35] Ibid. 13:3.

[36] Ibid.

[37] Rabbinic sources do not see the phoenix in Psalm 92:12, but do find the bird in Job 29:18: "I shall die in my nest, and I shall multiply my days like the *chol*." For complete discussion of this and other passages read in rabbinic sources as referring to the phoenix, see M.R. Niehoff, "The Phoenix in Rabbinic Literature," *HTR* 89 (1996), 245–265. Note also that Justin reads Psalm 92:12 as referring to the date-palm, citing it along with other instances in which the wood of the cross is prefigured in the Hebrew Bible (*Dial.* 86.4).

[38] Tertullian, *Res.* 13:4.

brief account of the phoenix itself has no reference to the bird rising from the ashes of its parent's pyre. Tertullian might be unaware of this element of the phoenix account; on the other hand, he might assume it is common knowledge as he writes.

The birth from the ashes is, in any case, well known to the author of the *Physiologus*, a notoriously difficult to date Christian natural-historical collection.[39] As most entries in the *Physiologus,* the section on the phoenix begins with a quotation of scripture, here John 10:18: "I have the power to lay down my life, and I have the power to take it up again." In the *Physiologus'* account, the bird begins in India, making its way to Heliopolis by way of Lebanon, where it collects its own burial spices. When it arrives in Egypt, it finds a pyre prepared by the priest of Heliopolis on an altar; it flies onto the altar, lights the fire, and burns itself up. One day later, the priest finds in the ashes a worm, the second day a chick, and on the third day he finds the mature phoenix, which greets him then flies away "to its own place" (εἰς τὸν ἴδιον αὐτοῦ τόπον).[40] The account ends, like Clement's and Tertullian's, with an appeal from the lesser to the greater, though here it is not God's power to resurrect Christians but Jesus' power to resurrect himself: "If then this bird has the power to kill and make itself alive, how are the stupid Jews vexed by the Lord's saying, 'I have power to lay down my life and I have power to take it again'?"[41] The account closes as follows:

> "The phoenix assumes the role of our Savior, for when he came from heaven, spreading his two wings, he carried them full of sweet scent, that is of virtuous heavenly words, so that we might extend our hands in prayer and send up a spiritual smell through good lives."[42]

In the *Physiologus* we see for the first time the space of three days between the death of the old phoenix and rising of the new, which, along with the bird's willing self-sacrifice and post-resurrection return "to its own place," clearly is meant to figure Christ. Even the form of the phoenix – wings spread – for the author of the *Physiologus* represents the crucified Jesus; a reference to the *orans* prayer pose and the allegorical interpretation of the scent of the spiced pyre as heavenly words allows the connection of the phoenix also with Christians in prayer.

Cyril of Jerusalem's approach to the phoenix is perhaps more recognizably natural-historical than the "natural historian" *Physiologus.* After presenting as the argument of the "Greeks and Samaritans" the familiar list

---

[39] On date, see U. Treu, "Zur Datierung des Physiologus," *ZNW* 57 (1966), 101–104; see also Grant, *Animals* (n. 30), 52–72.

[40] *Physiologus,* 7.

[41] Ibid. Trans. Grant, *Animals* (n. 30), 55.

[42] Ibid.

of objections to bodily resurrection (i.e. that the body decomposes, that it is consumed by animals (including fish that are themselves consumed), that it is consumed by fire and its ashes dispersed), he presents a wide variety of arguments, ranging from the scale of the earth (immense to human beings, yet fitting in the palm of God's hand) to human social practice (if bodies are forever dead, why is the violation of a corpse regarded a crime?). Cyril repeats the appeal to the cycles of agriculture, then, for those who might object that plants are not truly animate, gives instances from the animal kingdom. Like Lucian, Cyril offers the example of the fly, adding that bees, too, revive after being drowned. Similarly, the dormouse lies apparently dead through the winter, only to be revived in the spring.[43] For those Greeks who might object that in these examples of revivification the animals' bodies have not been corrupted, God, foreseeing their disbelief, provided the phoenix as clear evidence. In Cyril's account, the phoenix does not rise from the ashes of its parent's pyre (no fire is mentioned), but, as in Pliny and Mela, a worm develops from the very decaying flesh itself. And for Cyril, this is not to be seen as particularly miraculous: "for you see the offspring of bees thus formed out of worms; and you have seen the wings and bones and sinews of birds formed from the most watery eggs."[44] The familiar closing argument from the lesser to the greater gets a slight twist in Cyril's account: if the irrational bird, which does not know God, is resurrected, how much more those who know God and keep his commandments?[45]

A similar tack is taken by Epiphanius, who counts among the many indicators of the resurrection both "the ring-dove among birds and the dormouse among [land] animals." [46] The dormouse, he reports, is dead for six months and the ringdove for forty days; "and after their allotted time, they come back to life again" (αὖθις ... ἀναβιοῦσι).[47] Epiphanius, after noting that the phoenix is so well known to both believers and unbelievers that it is superfluous for him to even mention it, gives the most detailed account found in a Christian author, including at least one new element: the phoenix breaths flames with which it lights its own pyre (πῦρ ἀπὸ τοῦ σώματος αὐτοῦ προφερόμενος ἐμπίπρησι τὴν ὑποκειμένην ὕλην).[48] As in the *Physiologus*, the resurrection of the phoenix is completed on the third day.

In the *Apostolic Constitutions*, the phoenix is drawn upon again as proof of the plausibility of resurrection, though the force of the argument has

---

[43] Cyril of Jerusalem, *Cat.* 18:7.
[44] Ibid., 18:8.
[45] Ibid.
[46] Epiphanius, *Anc.* 84:1.
[47] Ibid.
[48] Ibid. 84:4.

shifted slightly. Instead of an appeal based on the evidence of nature, here the point is rather that there is evidence of resurrection in the pagans' *own* literature. The example of the phoenix is introduced after a quotation regarding resurrection from the *Sibylline Oracles*, that is "[the Gentiles'] own prophetess"; the report about the phoenix is presented as what "they say."[49] After describing the phoenix's willing death in flames and resurrection from the ash, the author concludes: "if, as they themselves say, the resurrection is demonstrated in an irrational bird, why do they vainly slander us?"[50] Rufinus, too, though using the phoenix as proof of the plausibility of the virgin birth, sets this example from the natural world alongside other examples from pagan thought and literature (e.g. the birth of Minerva from Jupiter's skull).[51]

4. The Avoidance of Animal Resurrection in Patristic Sources

While it is surely hazardous to engage in argumentation from silence, guessing at why the phoenix does *not* appear in an individual patristic author's discussion of resurrection, we might note that several authors do seem intentionally to omit or gloss over the amazing bird.[52] The first of these is Theophilus of Antioch, who takes over all the analogies of the resurrection in *1 Clem.* 24–25 (including the succession of the seasons, days and nights, seeds and fruits) except for the phoenix;[53] likewise, Clement of Alexandria, though he summarizes much of the content of *1 Clem.* in *Strom.* 4:109ff., does not include the phoenix.[54] Lightfoot has suggested

---

[49] *Ap. Const.* 5:1:7.

[50] Ibid.

[51] Rufinus writes: "Does it really seem so miraculous that a virgin conceived, when everyone knows that the bird of the east, which they call the phoenix, is born in such a way without conjugal union, or born again; that there is always just one, and that it always, by being born of itself or born again, succeeds itself?" (*Symb.* 11).

[52] We might also note that, at least in the first four centuries, there is virtually no notion that this is a mythical creature. Where authors express some doubt concerning the account, it seems to be directed primarily at the journey made by the new phoenix, delivering its parent's tomb to Heliopolis. The generation of the phoenix worm from the corpse of the parent is, as Cyril of Jerusalem points out, not particularly miraculous. For the ancient scientist or laymen, this phenomenon must have fit quite easily with the observable generation of maggots from rotting flesh and flies from maggots or, again as Cyril notes, the generation of bees.

[53] Theophilus, *Autol.* 1:13.

[54] On both Theophilus' and Clement of Alexandria's omission of the phoenix, see Grant, *Animals*, 40–41. Grant takes Clement's use of the term "phoenix" (as an astrological symbol) in *Strom.* 6:35:4 as referring to the bird; it seems equally plausible that the "date palm" is meant.

that Theophilus' knowledge of Egyptian antiquities may have "saved him from the error" of including the phoenix,[55] and the same might be said of Clement of Alexandria. However, given the general acceptance in the Greco-Roman world of the phoenix as an amazing but nevertheless very *real* member of the animal kingdom, it is difficult to see how more knowledge of Egypt might have had this effect. Grant writes that "evidently [Theophilus] was trying to provide analogies of a more rational character."[56] Again, the rather scientific analysis of the phoenix's generation offered by Cyril and others indicates that phoenix is by no means an irrational example.

More might be said about Origen's avoidance of the phoenix as evidence for resurrection. The bird is introduced in the last quarter of book four of the *Contra Celsum* in which Origen replies to Celsus' critique of Christian anthropocentrism. As Origen reports, Celsus rejects the notion that "God made all things for human beings"; rather, "from the history of animals and from the sagacity (ἀγχίνοια) which is exemplified in them, he wants to show that *he created everything no more for human beings than for irrational animals.*"[57] The material included in the remainder of book four is well-known indeed to those familiar with the philosophical debate over animal rationality. Here, Celsus has taken up the pro-animal rationality position and Origen the Stoic anti-animal rationality position; the examples cited on both sides are drawn from a large body of stock material, found also in Philo, Plutarch and elsewhere.[58] Earlier in the book, Origen accepts Celsus' statement that "a snake is formed out of a dead man, as most say, generated from the marrow of the spine, and a bee from an ox, and a wasp from a horse, and a dung-beetle from an ass, and generally worms from most animals," refuting Celsus' claim that this is evidence that these animals are not created by God and associating the phenomena instead with the resurrection and Christian belief "that changes occur in the qualities of bodies."[59] The phoenix would seem to fit well here. Origen's treatment of the phoenix, however, seems driven primarily by the desire to disprove Celsus' arguments. Celsus offers the phoenix as an example of filial piety among animals, describing the bird's journey from Arabia to Heliopolis to deliver its parent's remains.[60] Origen replies first with doubt:

---

[55] Lightfoot, *Apostolic Fathers* (n. 30), 86.

[56] Grant, *Animals* (n. 30), 41.

[57] Origen, *Cels.* 4:74.

[58] See H. Chadwick, "Origen, Celsus and the Stoa," *JTS* 48 (1947), 36–37.

[59] Origen, *Cels.* 4:57.

[60] The identification of filial piety, mutual affection, and loyalty among animals is a topos in the debate over animal rationality. See, for example, Plutarch, *Soll. an.* 967d–971a. Cf. Aelian's use of the phoenix as evidence of animals correctly measuring long stretches of time, cited above.

"This is the story. But even if it is true, it is possible that this also happens by instinct."[61] It is unclear if Celsus included any reference to the new bird's generation from the corpse of the old; if so, it is not quoted. Origen does, however, seem to know the other half of the account: "And if indeed he made a 'unique' (μονογενής) creature, it was in order that he might accomplish this: not that the animal be admired but the one who made it."[62] The term μονογενής or the Latin *unica* is used of the phoenix also in *1 Clem.*, Ovid, Pliny and Claudian and can only be understood in the context of the bird's miraculous generation from its parent. Celsus' praise of the phoenix apparently rules out for Origen the possibility of including the positive valuation given it in other patristic sources. As Henry Chadwick has described Origen's basic method in the *Cels.*, "if his opponent takes one side, he will take the other."[63]

Again, it is hazardous to guess why an author might omit the phoenix or other instances of animal resurrection (such as the fly or dormouse). Nevertheless, it is very tempting to ask: where is the phoenix in Christian sources of the second century? As noted above, it appears in *1 Clem.* only to reappear again in Tertullian. Before returning to the apocryphal acts, I will briefly treat the discussions of resurrection in Tatian, Athenagoras and Irenaeus; as opposed to looking for specific reasons why the phoenix (or fly or dormouse) is absent from their arguments, I will consider the extent to which animal resurrection is compatible or incompatible with their argumentation in defense of the resurrection of human beings.

Tatian is interested in animals; he has even written a treatise on the subject (his unfortunately lost Περὶ ζῴων). His anthropology, in fact, is largely presented in contrast to his zoology. He writes:

"For man is not, as the squawkers teach, a rational animal, with the capacity of intellect and understanding; for according to them even the irrational animals are proven to have the capacity of intellect and understanding. Rather, man alone is the "image and likeness of God," and by man I mean not the one acting like animals, but the one having advanced beyond humanity towards God himself. I have written about this in greater detail in my treatise 'On animals', but the important issue now is in what sense [man] is the divine image and likeness."[64]

While the initial definition of a human provided here, that is, a "rational being capable of intelligence and understanding" (ζῷον λογικὸν νοῦ καὶ ἐπιστήμης δεκτικόν), sounds quite Stoic, the parenthetical comment ("for according to them even the irrational animals are proven to have the capac-

[61] Origen, *Cels.* 4:98. Note that Origen's doubt concerns the journey to Heliopolis and, more importantly, the notion that this represents true filial piety in an animal.

[62] Ibid.

[63] Chadwick, "Origen" (n. 58), 39.

[64] Tatian, *Or.* 15:2.

ity of intellect and understanding") must be understood to refer to the other, pro-animal rationality (and thus anti-Stoic, whether associated with Middle Platonism or another philosophical group) side of the animal rationality debate. Tatian's lost treatise likely responded to the popular essays (such as those of Plutarch[65] and Celsus, Tatian's contemporary) that collected dozens if not hundreds of examples of animals acting with apparent intelligence, perhaps countering with argumentation not unlike Origen's. Another possibility is that Tatian's apparent lumping together of the anti- and pro-animal rationality positions here is an intentional jab at both sides of the debate. It is clear in any case that for Tatian it is not simply *reason* that separates human from animal:

> "The soul is a bond of flesh, but the flesh is retentive of the soul (δεσμὸς δὲ τῆς σαρκὸς ψυχή, σχετικὴ δὲ τῆς ψυχῆς ἡ σάρξ); if such a form of constitution is as a temple, God wishes to dwell in it through the spirit as his representative; but if the dwelling (σκήνωμα) is not such as this, then man is better than the beasts in articulate speech alone; as for the rest of his way of life, it is the same as theirs, since he is not a likeness of God."[66]

Tatian virtually restricts the designation "human" to Christians, to the extent that non-Christians have rejected the very thing that sets them apart from animals, the presence of God's spirit.

Elsewhere, Tatian explicitly rules out the possibility of the resurrection of animals. In section six he writes that, when this age comes to an end, the resurrection will take "for human beings alone," for their judgment."[67] Of particular interest with reference to the account of the phoenix is Tatian's explicit criticism of the notion that, "as the Stoics teach," individuals will go through continual cycles of birth and death, with no real benefit;[68] clearly none of the analogies of resurrection offered in *1 Clem.* (all of which are recurrent cycles) would fit comfortably alongside this statement. A final note on Tatian's treatment of animals in the *Or.* concerns his use of animal metaphors. In the passage quoted above, he calls the philosophers involved in the animal rationality debate "squawkers" or more literally "raven-voiced" (κορακόφωναι), that is, they sound like irrational animals. Later he will take up the obvious insult, scolding Cynics for "emulating the dog" and, having no knowledge of God, "imitating irrational animals."[69] He criticizes the ostentatious use of foreign terms as "like a jackdaw, decking yourselves out with feathers that aren't you own."[70] In his critique of Greek mythology, he is particularly appalled by the notion that gods

[65] E.g., Plutarch, *Soll. an.*, *De esu*, and *Brut. an.*
[66] Tatian, *Or.* 15:2–3.
[67] Ibid. 6:1.
[68] Ibid.
[69] Ibid. 25:1.
[70] Ibid. 26:1.

change into animal forms: "Tell me, does god become a swan? And does he take up the form of an eagle?"[71] Although Tatian is clearly interested in animals and is familiar with contemporary literature on animals,[72] his estimation of animals is ultimately very negative. Without pressing the case too far, it seems safe to conclude that examples of resurrection among the animal kingdom would add little to his particular approach to the topic of human resurrection.

Athenagoras holds a similarly low view of animals. Whereas Tatian critiques Stoic positions at several points, in *De resurrectione* Athenagoras introduces one of the most important aspects of the Stoic assessment of animals, that is, the impossibility of doing injustice to animals. For Athenagoras, as opposed to the Stoics, the issue centers specifically around the question of whether the limitation of resurrection to human beings is in any sense unjust:

"Nor indeed [would] the nature of irrational animals nor the soulless (τῶν ἀλόγων ἡ φύσις οὐδὲ τῶν ἀψύχων) [be wronged], for they will not exist after the resurrection, and there can be no injustice in the case of what does not exist."[73]

In the second half of the treatise, Athenagoras introduces animals again, arguing (much like the Stoics)[74] that animals were created exclusively for the sake of human beings. Notably (with respect to the account of the phoenix), Athenagoras cites as evidence the short life-spans of animals:

"[God] created man ... for the sake of the life of the created themselves, a life not to be kindled for a short time then altogether extinguished. To the crawling things, I suppose, and the flying and swimming things, or indeed, to put it more generally, to all irrational creatures did He apportion such a short life; but to those who bear in themselves the image of the creator, and carry with them a mind, and have a share in rational judgment, He has allotted eternal preservation."[75]

In an earlier section of the treatise, Athenagoras confronts the common objections to resurrection, quite similar to those addressed by Cyril of Jerusalem and Epiphanius (described above). What happens if a Christian's body is devoured by beasts or cremated? What if a Christian dies in a shipwreck,

---

[71] Ibid. 10:1.

[72] Tatian was familiar with several of the animal anecdotes typically introduced as evidence for animal rationality, such as animals' knowledge of medicinal plants. In a critique of the Greeks' use of "pharmacy," including both drugs and spells, he asks: "Why do you not go to the lord of greater power, but rather heal yourself, just like the dog with grass, the deer with a snake, the pig with river-crabs and the lion with monkeys" (*Orat.* 18:2)? Cf. Plutarch, *Soll. an.* 974a ff.; Philo, *Anim.* 38–41; Sextus, *Pyr.* 1:70–71; Aelian, *Nat. an.* 5:39; 15:17.

[73] Athenagoras, *Res.* 10:2.

[74] Cf. Cicero's summary of Chrysippus' position in *Fin.* 3:67.

[75] Athenagoras, *Res.* 12:5–6.

is eaten by a fish, and that very fish is consumed by another Christian? This particular objection (that is, as Athenagoras describes it, the thesis "that the resurrection is impossible, since the same parts cannot rise again for different individuals")[76] prompts not examples of resurrection in nature but a lengthy and very technical medical discussion of digestion.[77] He argues that the nature of the human being is such that it is incapable of assimilating the flesh of another human, and so whatever elements of human flesh might accidentally be consumed would pass through the digestive tract without absorption and thus be available for re-assimilation by their original owner at the resurrection.[78] It is a scatological argument to be sure, but also ingenious. Athenagoras has in fact constructed a neat criterion for distinguishing human and animal: in its inability to assimilate the flesh of another human, the human species seems to be biologically engineered for resurrection in a way that animals are not.

The final patristic author to be considered here is Irenaeus, important particularly because he is often cited in contemporary discussions of animal afterlife as an ancient proponent of the notion.[79] According to Irenaeus, when the just are resurrected and reign, all of creation is also restored.[80] Quoting Isaiah 11:6–9 ("And the wolf shall feed with the lamb, and the leopard shall rest with the kid," etc.), Irenaeus argues strenuously against an allegorical interpretation:

> "I am aware that some try to refer these texts metaphorically to savage men who out of various nations and various occupations come to believe, and when they have believed live in harmony with the just. But though this now takes place for men who come from various nations into the one doctrine of the faith, nevertheless it will take place for these animals at the resurrection of the just, as we have said; for God is rich in all things, and when the world is re-established in its primeval state all the animals must obey and be subject to man and return to the first food given by God, as before the disobedience they were subject to Adam and ate the fruit of the earth."[81]

Irenaeus should not be understood as proposing the personal resurrection of individual creatures. Ultimately, Irenaeus' opinion of animals is as low as Tatian's or Athenagoras': they are created for the benefit of human beings, certainly incapable of receiving the spirit of God that makes human beings immortal and incorruptible in the resurrection. Nevertheless,

[76] Ibid. 4:4.

[77] As many have noted, Athenagoras seems here to be dependent on Galen's treatment of digestion. See references to Galen in W.R. Schoedel's edition and translation, *Athenagoras: Legatio and De Resurrectione* (Oxford 1972), 99.

[78] Athenagoras, *Res.* 5:1–7:4.

[79] See, for example, Webb, *On God and Dogs* (n. 1), 179–80.

[80] Irenaeus, *Haer.* 33:3. Trans. R.M. Grant, *Irenaeus of Lyons* (London and New York 1997), 179–80.

[81] Ibid.

Irenaeus' emphasis on the presence of animals in the eschatological future is a significant departure from other patristic thinking.

5. Animal Resurrection in the *Acts of Peter*, *Acts of Thomas*, and *Acts of Andrew and Matthias in the City of the Cannibals*

At the close of *Acts Pet.* 12, the apostle stands with a dead dog at his feet. In the preceding sections, this dog had, at Peter's command, acquired human voice and served as go-between in a confrontation between Peter and the arch-heretic Simon Magus. When the dog's job was finished, he lay down before the apostle and gave up the ghost. The totality of the events (which included also an exorcism and the miraculous reconstruction of a broken statue) brought many of those in the observing crowds to belief in Jesus Christ; others, however, asked Peter for "another sign" so that they might believe that Peter is a minister of the living God (*ut credamus tibi tamquam ministro dei vivi*).[82] Peter looks around and spots a salt-fish (*sarda*) hanging in a nearby window. Taking the fish, he asks: "If you will now see this, swimming in the water like a fish, will you be able to believe in him whom I preach?" They agree that they will, and Peter throws the fish into a nearby fishpond, saying: "In your name, Jesus Christ, in whom there is not yet belief, in the presence of all these people, live and swim like a fish." The fish is immediately revivified and begins to swim, not just for an hour or so – this could be some illusion (*fantasma*); that this fish has truly returned to life is proved by its continual swimming (at least long enough to attract crowds from all over to gather) and the fact that it even eats all the bread tossed at it by spectators.[83] Now, as promised, a great number follow Peter and believe in the Lord.

This episode has two key elements in common with the revivified salt-fish (τάριχος) in Herodotus, discussed above. First is the notion that this phenomenon is a sign. At the end of *Acts Pet.* 12, the crowds ask Peter for a sign (*signum*) and by resurrecting the fish Peter obliges. Similarly, the "wonder" (τέρας) reported by Herodotus is not simply a miraculous occurrence, but is specifically described as a sign: "Protesilaos is giving me a sign" (ἐμοὶ σημαίνει ὁ ἐν 'Ελαιοῦντι Πρωτεσίλεως), says Artauctes. And in his interpretation, Artauctes clearly identifies the fish with the hero: Protesilaos *is himself* in some sense a τάριχος, a notion that is taken up and emphasized in Philostratus' reference to the episode in the second century C.E. In the *Acts Pet.* the identification of Jesus with the fish is implicit but,

[82] *Acts Pet.* 13.

[83] Note the similar phrasing of the result of this miracle (*sardam piscem factum*) with that of Jesus' miracle at Cana in the Vulgate (*aquam vinum factam*).

in my opinion, clearly present.[84] In these two episodes, then, the sign functions in much the same way: in the *Histories*, just as the fish, though quite dead, have the power to leap and gasp, Protesilaos, though dead, has the even greater power to punish; in the *Acts Pet.*, just as the fish, though quite dead, has the power to live again, Jesus, though dead, has the power to live again and eternally.

We have seen that through its multiple iterations in patristic sources, the phoenix account accumulates more and more Christian themes: the process of its regeneration is spread over three days, mirroring Jesus' resurrection; the form of the bird, wings outstretched, is associated with both the form of Jesus on the cross and the *orans* posture. In the same way, the author of the salt-fish episode in the *Acts Pet.* has imbued every aspect of this short account with Christian meaning: clearly, the resurrection of the dead is represented in the resurrection of the fish, but Peter's first career as fisherman and second life as a "fisher of men" are also perhaps referenced; the bath of baptism has its counterpart in the revivifying plunge taken by the *sarda*, and, as noted, the use of the fish as a symbol of Christ is surely at play. Moreover, there are narrative elements in the salt-fish episode that evoke the gospel accounts of Jesus' resurrection appearances, particularly Luke's: just as in Luke 24:41–43 Jesus asks for and eats food (a piece of broiled fish, no less) as evidence of the physical nature of his return, in the *Acts Pet.* the fish eats bread (the body of Christ?) to the same effect. We noted that accounts of the phoenix in patristic sources were often accompanied with an argument from the lesser to the greater: if an irrational bird can be resurrected, how much more a human being? The implicit argument in the *Acts Pet.* might be read as an argument from the more difficult to the less difficult: this fish is not recently deceased; it has been dried and salted. It does not get any deader than that. If a salt-fish – the ancient equivalent of a can of tuna – returns to life, swims and eats, surely the resurrection of the human body does not stretch the imagination.

In the *Acts Thom.* act four, the apostle, while traveling on a highway, is approached by a colt of an ass, which speaks to Thomas, asking that the apostle rides on its back for the rest of his journey to the next city. The apostle initially refuses, but the ass persists, identifying himself as the descendent of Balaam's ass:

"I am of that race that served Balaam (τῆς γενεᾶς εἰμι ἐκείνης τῆς ἐξυπηρετησαμένης τῷ Βαλαάμ), and your Lord and your teacher sat upon one belonging to me by race (κατὰ γένος). And now I was sent to give you rest by sitting upon me; and that I may take faith and that portion might be added to me (προστεθῇ μοι ἡ μερὶς ἐκείνη) which I am now

---

[84] Alternatively, the fish could be identified not simply with Jesus but with all Christians, as Tertullian's reference to Christians as *pisciculi* in *Bapt.* 1 might suggest.

about to obtain through the service which I do for you; and whenever I serve you, it will be taken from me."[85]

The apostle eventually relents and rides the ass to the next city's gates, followed by crowds of people walking before and behind. When Thomas dismounts, he commands the colt: "Depart and be kept where you were" (*Acts Thom.* 41). To the great dismay of the crowds – and perhaps the reader – the ass immediately drops dead. Those present beg the apostle to "make him live" and to "raise him" (ζωοποίησον αὐτὸν καὶ ἀνέγειρον), but the apostle refuses, saying:

"I am able to raise him (ἐγὼ μὲν ἠδυνάμην ἐγεῖραι αὐτόν) through the name of Jesus Christ, but this is entirely beneficial; for the one who gave speech to him so that he might talk was able to make him not die; I do not raise him not because I am unable, but because this is suitable and beneficial to him (τὸ συμβαλλόμενον αὐτῷ καὶ συμφέρον)."[86]

At Thomas' command, the crowds then dig a trench and bury the colt's body.

This is a very strange episode to say the least, leaving the reader with multiple questions: why does not the apostle raise the colt? Why is death "suitable and beneficial to him"? Why does it die as soon as Thomas dismounts? Multiple explanations have been offered by modern scholars.[87] Following Günther Bornkamm's initial suggestion,[88] I contend that this episode must be read as a doublet, interpreted together with act eight, in which the apostle encounters another colt of an ass on the highway – now a wild ass, not a domestic one. As the apostle is on his way to exorcise demons from the wife and daughter of a captain, the four beasts of burden drawing the cart become exhausted and can go no further. Seeing a herd of wild ass colts in the field beside the highway, Thomas commands the captain to go into the group, inform the animals of the apostle's situation, and command them to come be yoked to the cart, which they immediately do. When they arrive at the home of the captain, one of the wild asses acquires voice and, like the domestic ass previously, speaks to the apostle. In the course of a fascinating episode, the wild ass takes the lead in the exorcism of the two women, delivering two lengthy speeches, including, among other topics, a warning against "false apostles" and "prophets of lawless-

---

[85] *Acts Thom.* 40.

[86] Ibid. 41.

[87] See, for example, C. Matthews, "Articulate Animals: A Multivalent Motif in the Apocryphal Acts of the Apostles," in *The Apocryphal Acts of the Apostles* (ed. F. Bovon, A. Graham Brock and C. Matthews, Boston 1999), 224; A.F.J. Klijn, *The Acts of Thomas. Introduction, Text and Commentary* (NT.S; Leiden ²2003), 112.

[88] G. Bornkamm, *Mythos und Legende in den apokryphen Thomas-Akten: Beiträge zur Geschichte der Gnosis und zur Vorgeschichte des Manichäismus* (Göttingen 1933), 35.

ness." These false apostles are described as those who "are thought to have self control (σώφρονες) and ... command others to keep away from fornication, theft and greed," but "live their lives in them, while teaching others not to do them."[89] At the close of the episode, Thomas dismisses the wild ass, much as he did the domestic ass; instead of dying at separation from the apostle, the wild ass returns to his pasture.

I have argued elsewhere that the characteristics of the wild ass, well known in the Greco-Roman natural historical literature, make the wild ass the perfect representative of this message: the adult male wild ass was thought to be the jealous keeper of a harem of female wild asses; when any of his mates gave birth to male offspring, the father would castrate its own sons with his teeth, thus preventing them from becoming rivals. The herd of wild ass colts encountered by the apostle must be understood as a group of eunuchs.[90] Other well-known characteristics of the wild ass, particularly in contrast to the domestic ass, (e.g. its simple lifestyle and self-sufficiency, its freedom from slavery in exchange for the feedbag, provided for only by Nature or God) strengthen an association with the ideal ascetic lifestyle espoused throughout the *Acts Thom.* The use of an ass as metaphor for the body is a commonplace in Greco-Roman philosophy and literature more broadly.[91] Thus, I have proposed that the two asses – one domestic, slave to its own belly, the other ascetic, wild and free – represent two different types of bodies with which the Christian might yoke his soul and spirit (represented in the narrative by the apostle). The death of the domestic ass is like the death of the non-Christian or, from the perspective of the author of the *Acts Thom.*, perhaps the non-ascetic Christian. Its resurrection will be a resurrection to judgment, therefore it is indeed to the ass' benefit that Thomas does not raise it. The wild ass, in contrast, does not taste death at all.

There are two points that are particularly significant with respect to the question of animal resurrection. First is that the refusal to resurrect the domestic ass is not an objection to animal resurrection *per se*. The apostle in fact emphasizes his ability to do so. The second point involves the author's use of evidence from nature. Just as so many patristic authors draw on the phoenix (or fly, or dormouse) as examples of resurrection, proof of Christian doctrine written into the natural world, the author of the *Acts Thom.* cites the wild ass as a natural example of his own ascetic doctrine. Animals are not simply symbols here; their natural characteristics – confirmed by natural historians – are understood as pointing to the truth of Christianity.

---

[89] *Acts Thom.* 78–79.

[90] See Spittler, *Animals* (n. 24), 209–221.

[91] See, for example, Epictetus, *Disc.* 4:1:79–80.

The final instance of animal resurrection in the apocryphal acts is the very brief reference in the *Acts of Andrew and Matthias in the City of the Cannibals.* As described above, the apostle Andrew, after rescuing his colleague Matthias from the brutal cannibals, punishes the city by bringing forth a putrid deluge that drowns the residents and their cattle (κτήνη) alike. At the close of the episode, however, the apostle prays for their resurrection and "all returned to life" (πάντες ἀνέζησαν), presumably including the animals. The role of animals, at least as presented in extant versions of the text, is so limited that extended comment here is not warranted. Nevertheless, there is perhaps an interesting parallel to the position taken by Irenaeus, discussed above. What happens in the city of the cannibals seems to be less resurrection than restoration; whether the destruction and restoration of the city is taken as a deluvian or eschatological scene, it seems that the author of the episode's view of creation, to the extent that he emphasizes the inclusion of animals, aligns nicely with Irenaeus' insistance on the presence of animals in the re-establishment of the world to its primeval state.

6. Conclusions

The notion of animal resurrection does indeed seem like the concern of a child, wondering if her dog will go to heaven. Today, it may well be a topic that is treated in popular film more often than in theological journals. But this situation is rather misleading if applied directly to our ancient sources. Animal resurrection was a serious topic of discussion in both pagan and Christian texts of the first centuries C.E., as we have seen. In the introduction I quoted Photius' evaluation of the apocryphal acts, including his derisive remarks on the "ridiculous and childish resurrections of oxen and cattle." At first blush, there is nothing surprising in this remark; we would expect nothing else. But we should not take this as a statement of the obvious – as the re-statement of a position universally held by Christians of the previous centuries. Another entry in Photius' *Bibl.* underscores the point: in his evaluation of *1 Clem.*,[92] Photius approves generally of the content, but criticizes the inclusion of the phoenix as proof of the resurrection. This is often taken as reflecting Photius' recognition of the phoenix as a mythological creature,[93] but this may not be the case. In a lengthy review of Philostratus' *Vit. Apoll.*, Photius rather painstakingly goes through much of the natural historical information included in the text; of the phoenix, he only remarks that "concerning the phoenix-bird" Philostratus

[92] Photius, *Bibl.* 126.
[93] Lightfoot, *Apostolic Fathers* (n. 30), 86.

"records the same information as everyone else" (περὶ τοῦ φοίνικος τῆς ὄρνιθος τὰ αὐτὰ καὶ οὗτος τοῖς ἄλλοις ἅπασιν ἀναγράφει), without critiquing the report as fabulous or inaccurate.[94] Photius rejects the notion of animal resurrection as symbol or evidence of Christian resurrection – this much is clear. What the preceding study has shown is that in early Christian literature, whether entertaining narrative or patristic treatise, this was not a foregone conclusion.

We began with the warning given to C.S. Lewis, that to speculate on life after death for animals is to risk being counted among the "old maids." Lewis replied: "I have no objection to the company." Nor was he "greatly moved by jocular inquiries such as 'Where will you put all the mosquitos?' – a question to be answered on its own level by pointing out that, if the worst came to the worst, a heaven for mosquitos and a hell for men could very conveniently be combined."[95] Lewis is more troubled by "the complete silence of Scripture and Christian tradition on animal immortality," though this obstacle is only insurmountable if Christian revelation were "intended as a *systeme de la nature* answering all questions," which it clearly is not.[96] He goes on to argue for a manner of immortality for certain animals, based in the very Stoic view of animals (adopted by many patristic authors):

> "Man was appointed by God to have dominion over the beasts, and everything a man does to an animal is either a lawful exercise, or a sacrilegious abuse, of an authority by divine right. The tame animal is therefore, in the deepest sense, the only 'natural' animal – the only one we see occupying the place it was made to occupy, and it is on the tame animal that we must base all our doctrine of beasts."[97]

Ultimately for Lewis, an animal might achieve some immortality through the human master of whom it has in some sense become a part. Not only is the Christian tradition *not* silent on the topic of animal immortality, many of the Christian authors discussed above go a step beyond Lewis. In the animal kingdom these authors see Christian significance which, while it may well be valuable to those that turn a contemplative eye toward nature, is woven into the natural characteristics and behavior of animals – perhaps particularly the wild animals – quite independent of human beings.

---

[94] Photius, *Bibli.* 241 (347a).

[95] Lewis, 125.

[96] Ibid.

[97] Ibid. 126–127.

Autorenverzeichnis

István Czachesz, PD Dr. habil., Helsinki Collegium for Advanced Studies, University of Helsinki, Finland

Derek S. Dodson, Ph.D., Lecturer, Department of Religion, Baylor University, Waco, Texas, USA

Jutta Dresken-Weiland, Prof. Dr., Wissenschaftliche Mitarbeiterin am Lehrstuhl für Historische Theologie (Alte Kirchengeschichte und Patrologie) an der Katholisch-Theologischen Fakultät der Universität Regensburg

Paul Foster, Dr., Senior Lecturer New Testament, School of Divinity, University of Edinburgh, United Kingdom

Christiane Furrer, Dr., Faculty of Theology and Religious Studies, University of Lausanne, Switzerland

Peter Gemeinhardt, Prof. Dr., Abteilung Kirchengeschichte an der Theologischen Fakultät der Universität Göttingen

Judith Hartenstein, PD Dr., Privatdozentin im Fach Neues Testament, Philipps-Universität Marburg

Cornelia B. Horn, Ph.D., Assistant Professor of Early Christianity and Greek and Oriental Patristics, Department of Theological Studies, Saint Louis University, USA

Thomas R. Karmann, Dr., Akademischer Rat am Lehrstuhl für Historische Theologie (Alte Kirchengeschichte und Patrologie) an der Katholisch-Theologischen Fakultät der Universität Regensburg

Petri Luomanen, ThD, Docent of New Testament Exegetics, Department of Biblical Studies, University of Helsinki, Finland

Antti Marjanen, Prof. Dr., Department of Biblical Studies, University of Helsinki, Finland

Martin Meiser, Prof. Dr., Wissenschaftlicher Mitarbeiter am Seminar für Kirchengeschichte und Territorialkirchengeschichte (Kirchengeschichte des Altertums und des Mittelalters) an der Universität des Saarlandes, Saarbrücken

Andreas Merkt, Prof. Dr., Ordinarius für Historische Theologie (Alte Kirchengeschichte und Patrologie) an der Katholisch-Theologischen Fakultät der Universität Regensburg

Patricio de Navascués, Prof. Dr., Facultad de Teología San Dámaso, Madrid, Spain

Tobias Nicklas, Prof. Dr., Ordinarius für Biblische Theologie (Exegese und Hermeneutik des Neuen Testaments) an der Katholisch-Theologischen Fakultät der Universität Regensburg

Jean-Michel Roessli, Dr., Assistant Professor an der University of Sudbury (Religious Studies), Canada

Riemer Roukema, Prof. Dr., Professor für Exegese des Neuen Testaments an der Protestantischen Theologischen Universität Kampen, Niederlande

Janet E. Spittler, Ph.D., Assistant Professor an der Texan Christian University, Fort Worth, USA

Stellenregister (in Auswahl)

1. Biblische Bücher

1.1 Altes Testament

1.2 Neues Testament

2. Qumranschriften

3. Christliche Apokryphen

4. „Gnostisches“ Schrifttum

5. Christliche Autoren/Werke

6. Nichtchristliche Autoren/Werke

Sachregister

1. Sachregister deutsch

2. Sachregister englisch

Wissenschaftliche Untersuchungen zum Neuen Testament

Alphabetische Übersicht der ersten und zweiten Reihe

Ådna, Jostein: Jesu Stellung zum Tempel. 2000. *Bd. II/119.*
Ådna, Jostein (Hrsg.): The Formation of the Early Church. 2005. *Bd. 183.*
– und *Hans Kvalbein* (Hrsg.): The Mission of the Early Church to Jews and Gentiles. 2000. *Bd. 127.*
Aland, Barbara: Was ist Gnosis? 2009. *Bd. 239.*
Alexeev, Anatoly A., Christos Karakolis und *Ulrich Luz* (Hrsg.): Einheit der Kirche im Neuen Testament. Dritte europäische orthodox-westliche Exegetenkonferenz in Sankt Petersburg, 24.–31. August 2005. 2008. *Band 218.*
Alkier, Stefan: Wunder und Wirklichkeit in den Briefen des Apostels Paulus. 2001. *Bd. 134.*
Allen, David M.: Deuteronomy and Exhortation in Hebrews. 2008. *Bd. II/238.*
Anderson, Paul N.: The Christology of the Fourth Gospel. 1996. *Bd. II/78.*
Appold, Mark L.: The Oneness Motif in the Fourth Gospel. 1976. *Bd. II/1.*
Arnold, Clinton E.: The Colossian Syncretism. 1995. *Bd. II/77.*
Ascough, Richard S.: Paul's Macedonian Associations. 2003. *Bd. II/161.*
Asiedu-Peprah, Martin: Johannine Sabbath Conflicts As Juridical Controversy. 2001. *Bd. II/132.*
Attridge, Harold W.: siehe *Zangenberg, Jürgen.*
Aune, David E.: Apocalypticism, Prophecy and Magic in Early Christianity. 2006. *Bd. 199.*
Avemarie, Friedrich: Die Tauferzählungen der Apostelgeschichte. 2002. *Bd. 139.*
Avemarie, Friedrich und *Hermann Lichtenberger* (Hrsg.): Auferstehung – Ressurection. 2001. *Bd. 135.*
– Bund und Tora. 1996. *Bd. 92.*
Baarlink, Heinrich: Verkündigtes Heil. 2004. *Bd. 168.*
Bachmann, Michael: Sünder oder Übertreter. 1992. *Bd. 59.*
Bachmann, Michael (Hrsg.): Lutherische und Neue Paulusperspektive. 2005. *Bd. 182.*
Back, Frances: Verwandlung durch Offenbarung bei Paulus. 2002. *Bd. II/153.*
Backhaus, Knut: Der sprechende Gott. 2009. *Bd. 240.*
Baker, William R.: Personal Speech-Ethics in the Epistle of James. 1995. *Bd. II/68.*
Bakke, Odd Magne: 'Concord and Peace'. 2001. *Bd. II/143.*
Balch, David L.: Roman Domestic Art and Early House Churches. 2008. *Bd. 228.*
Baldwin, Matthew C.: Whose *Acts of Peter*? 2005. *Bd. II/196.*
Balla, Peter: Challenges to New Testament Theology. 1997. *Bd. II/95.*
– The Child-Parent Relationship in the New Testament and its Environment. 2003. *Bd. 155.*
Bammel, Ernst: Judaica. Bd. I 1986. *Bd. 37.*
– Bd. II 1997. *Bd. 91.*
Barrier, Jeremy W. : The Acts of Paul and Thecla. 2009. *Bd. II/270.*
Barton, Stephen C.: siehe *Stuckenbruck, Loren T.*
Bash, Anthony: Ambassadors for Christ. 1997. *Bd. II/92.*
Bauckham, Richard: The Jewish World around the New Testament. Collected Essays Volume I. 2008. *Bd. 233.*
Bauernfeind, Otto: Kommentar und Studien zur Apostelgeschichte. 1980. *Bd. 22.*
Baum, Armin Daniel: Pseudepigraphie und literarische Fälschung im frühen Christentum. 2001. *Bd. II/138.*
Bayer, Hans Friedrich: Jesus' Predictions of Vindication and Resurrection. 1986. *Bd. II/20.*
Becker, Eve-Marie: Das Markus-Evangelium im Rahmen antiker Historiographie. 2006. *Bd. 194.*
Becker, Eve-Marie und *Peter Pilhofer* (Hrsg.): Biographie und Persönlichkeit des Paulus. 2005. *Bd. 187.*
Becker, Michael: Wunder und Wundertäter im frührabbinischen Judentum. 2002. *Bd. II/144.*
Becker, Michael und *Markus Öhler* (Hrsg.): Apokalyptik als Herausforderung neutestamentlicher Theologie. 2006. *Bd. II/214.*
Bell, Richard H.: Deliver Us from Evil. 2007. *Bd. 216.*
– The Irrevocable Call of God. 2005. *Bd. 184.*
– No One Seeks for God. 1998. *Bd. 106.*
– Provoked to Jealousy. 1994. *Bd. II/63.*
Bennema, Cornelis: The Power of Saving Wisdom. 2002. *Bd. II/148.*
Bergman, Jan: siehe *Kieffer, René*
Bergmeier, Roland: Das Gesetz im Römerbrief und andere Studien zum Neuen Testament. 2000. *Bd. 121.*

Bernett, Monika: Der Kaiserkult in Judäa unter den Herodiern und Römern. 2007. *Bd. 203.*
Betz, Otto: Jesus, der Messias Israels. 1987. *Bd. 42.*
– Jesus, der Herr der Kirche. 1990. *Bd. 52.*
Beyschlag, Karlmann: Simon Magus und die christliche Gnosis. 1974. *Bd. 16.*
Bieringer, Reimund: siehe *Koester, Craig.*
Bittner, Wolfgang J.: Jesu Zeichen im Johannesevangelium. 1987. *Bd. II/26.*
Bjerkelund, Carl J.: Tauta Egeneto. 1987. *Bd. 40.*
Blackburn, Barry Lee: Theios Aner and the Markan Miracle Traditions. 1991. *Bd. II/40.*
Blanton IV, Thomas R.: Constructing a New Covenant. 2007. *Bd. II/233.*
Bock, Darrell L.: Blasphemy and Exaltation in Judaism and the Final Examination of Jesus. 1998. *Bd. II/106.*
Bockmuehl, Markus N.A.: Revelation and Mystery in Ancient Judaism and Pauline Christianity. 1990. *Bd. II/36.*
Bøe, Sverre: Gog and Magog. 2001. *Bd. II/135.*
Böhlig, Alexander: Gnosis und Synkretismus. Teil 1 1989. *Bd. 47* – Teil 2 1989. *Bd. 48.*
Böhm, Martina: Samarien und die Samaritai bei Lukas. 1999. *Bd. II/111.*
Böttrich, Christfried: Weltweisheit – Menschheitsethik – Urkult. 1992. *Bd. II/50.*
– */ Herzer, Jens* (Hrsg.): Josephus und das Neue Testament. 2007. *Bd. 209.*
Bolyki, János: Jesu Tischgemeinschaften. 1997. *Bd. II/96.*
Bosman, Philip: Conscience in Philo and Paul. 2003. *Bd. II/166.*
Bovon, François: New Testament and Christian Apocrypha. 2009. *Bd. 237.*
– Studies in Early Christianity. 2003. *Bd. 161.*
Brändl, Martin: Der Agon bei Paulus. 2006. *Bd. II/222.*
Breytenbach, Cilliers: siehe *Frey, Jörg.*
Brocke, Christoph vom: Thessaloniki – Stadt des Kassander und Gemeinde des Paulus. 2001. *Bd. II/125.*
Brunson, Andrew: Psalm 118 in the Gospel of John. 2003. *Bd. II/158.*
Büchli, Jörg: Der Poimandres – ein paganisiertes Evangelium. 1987. *Bd. II/27.*
Bühner, Jan A.: Der Gesandte und sein Weg im 4. Evangelium. 1977. *Bd. II/2.*
Burchard, Christoph: Untersuchungen zu Joseph und Aseneth. 1965. *Bd. 8.*
– Studien zur Theologie, Sprache und Umwelt des Neuen Testaments. Hrsg. von D. Sänger. 1998. *Bd. 107.*
Burnett, Richard: Karl Barth's Theological Exegesis. 2001. *Bd. II/145.*
Byron, John: Slavery Metaphors in Early Judaism and Pauline Christianity. 2003. *Bd. II/162.*
Byrskog, Samuel: Story as History – History as Story. 2000. *Bd. 123.*
Cancik, Hubert (Hrsg.): Markus-Philologie. 1984. *Bd. 33.*
Capes, David B.: Old Testament Yaweh Texts in Paul's Christology. 1992. *Bd. II/47.*
Caragounis, Chrys C.: The Development of Greek and the New Testament. 2004. *Bd. 167.*
– The Son of Man. 1986. *Bd. 38.*
– siehe *Fridrichsen, Anton.*
Carleton Paget, James: The Epistle of Barnabas. 1994. *Bd. II/64.*
Carson, D.A., Peter T. O'Brien und *Mark Seifrid* (Hrsg.): Justification and Variegated Nomism.
Bd. 1: The Complexities of Second Temple Judaism. 2001. *Bd. II/140.*
Bd. 2: The Paradoxes of Paul. 2004. *Bd. II/181.*
Chae, Young Sam: Jesus as the Eschatological Davidic Shepherd. 2006. *Bd. II/216.*
Chapman, David W.: Ancient Jewish and Christian Perceptions of Crucifixion. 2008. *Bd. II/244.*
Chester, Andrew: Messiah and Exaltation. 2007. *Bd. 207.*
Chibici-Revneanu, Nicole: Die Herrlichkeit des Verherrlichten. 2007. *Bd. II/231.*
Ciampa, Roy E.: The Presence and Function of Scripture in Galatians 1 and 2. 1998. *Bd. II/102.*
Classen, Carl Joachim: Rhetorical Criticism of the New Testament. 2000. *Bd. 128.*
Colpe, Carsten: Griechen – Byzantiner – Semiten – Muslime. 2008. *Bd. 221.*
– Iranier – Aramäer – Hebräer – Hellenen. 2003. *Bd. 154.*
Coppins, Wayne: The Interpretation of Freedom in the Letters of Paul. 2009. *Bd. II/261.*
Crump, David: Jesus the Intercessor. 1992. *Bd. II/49.*
Dahl, Nils Alstrup: Studies in Ephesians. 2000. *Bd. 131.*
Daise, Michael A.: Feasts in John. 2007. *Bd. II/229.*
Deines, Roland: Die Gerechtigkeit der Tora im Reich des Messias. 2004. *Bd. 177.*
– Jüdische Steingefäße und pharisäische Frömmigkeit. 1993. *Bd. II/52.*
– Die Pharisäer. 1997. *Bd. 101.*
Deines, Roland und *Karl-Wilhelm Niebuhr* (Hrsg.): Philo und das Neue Testament. 2004. *Bd. 172.*
Dennis, John A.: Jesus' Death and the Gathering of True Israel. 2006. *Bd. 217.*
Dettwiler, Andreas und *Jean Zumstein* (Hrsg.): Kreuzestheologie im Neuen Testament. 2002. *Bd. 151.*

Dickson, John P.: Mission-Commitment in Ancient Judaism and in the Pauline Communities. 2003. *Bd. II/159.*
Dietzfelbinger, Christian: Der Abschied des Kommenden. 1997. *Bd. 95.*
Dimitrov, Ivan Z., James D.G. Dunn, Ulrich Luz und *Karl-Wilhelm Niebuhr* (Hrsg.): Das Alte Testament als christliche Bibel in orthodoxer und westlicher Sicht. 2004. *Bd. 174.*
Dobbeler, Axel von: Glaube als Teilhabe. 1987. *Bd. II/22.*
Docherty, Susan E.: The Use of the Old Testament in Hebrews. 2009. *Bd. II/260.*
Downs, David J.: The Offering of the Gentiles. 2008. *Bd. II/248.*
Dryden, J. de Waal: Theology and Ethics in 1 Peter. 2006. *Bd. II/209.*
Dübbers, Michael: Christologie und Existenz im Kolosserbrief. 2005. *Bd. II/191.*
Dunn, James D.G.: The New Perspective on Paul. 2005. *Bd. 185.*
Dunn , James D.G. (Hrsg.): Jews and Christians. 1992. *Bd. 66.*
– Paul and the Mosaic Law. 1996. *Bd. 89.*
– siehe *Dimitrov, Ivan Z.*
Dunn, James D.G., Hans Klein, Ulrich Luz und *Vasile Mihoc* (Hrsg.): Auslegung der Bibel in orthodoxer und westlicher Perspektive. 2000. *Bd. 130.*
Ebel, Eva: Die Attraktivität früher christlicher Gemeinden. 2004. *Bd. II/178.*
Ebertz, Michael N.: Das Charisma des Gekreuzigten. 1987. *Bd. 45.*
Eckstein, Hans-Joachim: Der Begriff Syneidesis bei Paulus. 1983. *Bd. II/10.*
– Verheißung und Gesetz. 1996. *Bd. 86.*
Ego, Beate: Im Himmel wie auf Erden. 1989. *Bd. II/34.*
Ego, Beate, Armin Lange und *Peter Pilhofer* (Hrsg.): Gemeinde ohne Tempel – Community without Temple. 1999. *Bd. 118.*
– und *Helmut Merkel* (Hrsg.): Religiöses Lernen in der biblischen, frühjüdischen und frühchristlichen Überlieferung. 2005. *Bd. 180.*
Eisen, Ute E.: siehe *Paulsen, Henning.*
Elledge, C.D.: Life after Death in Early Judaism. 2006. *Bd. II/208.*
Ellis, E. Earle: Prophecy and Hermeneutic in Early Christianity. 1978. *Bd. 18.*
– The Old Testament in Early Christianity. 1991. *Bd. 54.*
Elmer, Ian J.: Paul, Jerusalem and the Judaisers. 2009. *Bd. II/258.*
Endo, Masanobu: Creation and Christology. 2002. *Bd. 149.*
Ennulat, Andreas: Die 'Minor Agreements'. 1994. *Bd. II/62.*
Ensor, Peter W.: Jesus and His 'Works'. 1996. *Bd. II/85.*
Eskola, Timo: Messiah and the Throne. 2001. *Bd. II/142.*
– Theodicy and Predestination in Pauline Soteriology. 1998. *Bd. II/100.*
Fatehi, Mehrdad: The Spirit's Relation to the Risen Lord in Paul. 2000. *Bd. II/128.*
Feldmeier, Reinhard: Die Krisis des Gottessohnes. 1987. *Bd. II/21.*
– Die Christen als Fremde. 1992. *Bd. 64.*
Feldmeier, Reinhard und *Ulrich Heckel* (Hrsg.): Die Heiden. 1994. *Bd. 70.*
Fletcher-Louis, Crispin H.T.: Luke-Acts: Angels, Christology and Soteriology. 1997. *Bd. II/94.*
Förster, Niclas: Marcus Magus. 1999. *Bd. 114.*
Forbes, Christopher Brian: Prophecy and Inspired Speech in Early Christianity and its Hellenistic Environment. 1995. *Bd. II/75.*
Fornberg, Tord: siehe *Fridrichsen, Anton.*
Fossum, Jarl E.: The Name of God and the Angel of the Lord. 1985. *Bd. 36.*
Foster, Paul: Community, Law and Mission in Matthew's Gospel. *Bd. II/177.*
Fotopoulos, John: Food Offered to Idols in Roman Corinth. 2003. *Bd. II/151.*
Frank, Nicole: Der Kolosserbrief im Kontext des paulinischen Erbes. 2009. *Bd. II/271.*
Frenschkowski, Marco: Offenbarung und Epiphanie. Bd. 1 1995. *Bd. II/79* – Bd. 2 1997. *Bd. II/80.*
Frey, Jörg: Eugen Drewermann und die biblische Exegese. 1995. *Bd. II/71.*
– Die johanneische Eschatologie. Bd. I. 1997. *Bd. 96.* – Bd. II. 1998. *Bd. 110.*
– Bd. III. 2000. *Bd. 117.*
Frey, Jörg und *Cilliers Breytenbach* (Hrsg.): Aufgabe und Durchführung einer Theologie des Neuen Testaments. 2007. *Bd. 205.*
– *Jens Herzer, Martina Janßen* und *Clare K. Rothschild* (Hrsg.): Pseudepigraphie und Verfasserfiktion in frühchristlichen Briefen. 2009. *Bd. 246.*
– *Stefan Krauter* und *Hermann Lichtenberger* (Hrsg.): Heil und Geschichte. 2009. *Bd. 248.*
– und *Udo Schnelle* (Hrsg.): Kontexte des Johannesevangeliums. 2004. *Bd. 175.*
– und *Jens Schröter* (Hrsg.): Deutungen des Todes Jesu im Neuen Testament. 2005. *Bd. 181.*
–, *Jan G. van der Watt,* und *Ruben Zimmermann* (Hrsg.): Imagery in the Gospel of John. 2006. *Bd. 200.*
Freyne, Sean: Galilee and Gospel. 2000. *Bd. 125.*
Fridrichsen, Anton: Exegetical Writings. Hrsg. von C.C. Caragounis und T. Fornberg. 1994. *Bd. 76.*
Gadenz, Pablo T.: Called from the Jews and from the Gentiles. 2009. *Bd. II/267.*

Gäbel, Georg: Die Kulttheologie des Hebräerbriefes. 2006. *Bd. II/212.*
Gäckle, Volker: Die Starken und die Schwachen in Korinth und in Rom. 2005. *Bd. 200.*
Garlington, Don B.: 'The Obedience of Faith'. 1991. *Bd. II/38.*
– Faith, Obedience, and Perseverance. 1994. *Bd. 79.*
Garnet, Paul: Salvation and Atonement in the Qumran Scrolls. 1977. *Bd. II/3.*
Gemünden, Petra von (Hrsg.): siehe *Weissenrieder, Annette.*
Gese, Michael: Das Vermächtnis des Apostels. 1997. *Bd. II/99.*
Gheorghita, Radu: The Role of the Septuagint in Hebrews. 2003. *Bd. II/160.*
Gordley, Matthew E.: The Colossian Hymn in Context. 2007. *Bd. II/228.*
Gräbe, Petrus J.: The Power of God in Paul's Letters. 2000, [2]2008. *Bd. II/123.*
Gräßer, Erich: Der Alte Bund im Neuen. 1985. *Bd. 35.*
– Forschungen zur Apostelgeschichte. 2001. *Bd. 137.*
Grappe, Christian (Hrsg.): Le Repas de Dieu – Das Mahl Gottes. 2004. *Bd. 169.*
Gray, Timothy C.: The Temple in the Gospel of Mark. 2008. *Bd. II/242.*
Green, Joel B.: The Death of Jesus. 1988. *Bd. II/33.*
Gregg, Brian Han: The Historical Jesus and the Final Judgment Sayings in Q. 2005. *Bd. II/207.*
Gregory, Andrew: The Reception of Luke and Acts in the Period before Irenaeus. 2003. *Bd. II/169.*
Grindheim, Sigurd: The Crux of Election. 2005. *Bd. II/202.*
Gundry, Robert H.: The Old is Better. 2005. *Bd. 178.*
Gundry Volf, Judith M.: Paul and Perseverance. 1990. *Bd. II/37.*
Häußer, Detlef: Christusbekenntnis und Jesusüberlieferung bei Paulus. 2006. *Bd. 210.*
Hafemann, Scott J.: Suffering and the Spirit. 1986. *Bd. II/19.*
– Paul, Moses, and the History of Israel. 1995. *Bd. 81.*
Hahn, Ferdinand: Studien zum Neuen Testament.
Bd. I: Grundsatzfragen, Jesusforschung, Evangelien. 2006. *Bd. 191.*
Bd. II: Bekenntnisbildung und Theologie in urchristlicher Zeit. 2006. *Bd. 192.*
Hahn, Johannes (Hrsg.): Zerstörungen des Jerusalemer Tempels. 2002. *Bd. 147.*
Hamid-Khani, Saeed: Relevation and Concealment of Christ. 2000. *Bd. II/120.*
Hannah, Darrel D.: Michael and Christ. 1999. *Bd. II/109.*
Hardin, Justin K.: Galatians and the Imperial Cult? 2007. *Bd. II /237.*
Harrison; James R.: Paul's Language of Grace in Its Graeco-Roman Context. 2003. *Bd. II/172.*
Hartman, Lars: Text-Centered New Testament Studies. Hrsg. von D. Hellholm. 1997. *Bd. 102.*
Hartog, Paul: Polycarp and the New Testament. 2001. *Bd. II/134.*
Heckel, Theo K.: Der Innere Mensch. 1993. *Bd. II/53.*
– Vom Evangelium des Markus zum viergestaltigen Evangelium. 1999. *Bd. 120.*
Heckel, Ulrich: Kraft in Schwachheit. 1993. *Bd. II/56.*
– Der Segen im Neuen Testament. 2002. *Bd. 150.*
– siehe *Feldmeier, Reinhard.*
– siehe *Hengel, Martin.*
Heiligenthal, Roman: Werke als Zeichen. 1983. *Bd. II/9.*
Heliso, Desta: Pistis and the Righteous One. 2007. *Bd. II/235.*
Hellholm, D.: siehe *Hartman, Lars.*
Hemer, Colin J.: The Book of Acts in the Setting of Hellenistic History. 1989. *Bd. 49.*
Hengel, Martin: Jesus und die Evangelien. Kleine Schriften V. 2007. *Bd. 211.*
– Die johanneische Frage. 1993. *Bd. 67.*
– Judaica et Hellenistica. Kleine Schriften I. 1996. *Bd. 90.*
– Judaica, Hellenistica et Christiana. Kleine Schriften II. 1999. *Bd. 109.*
– Judentum und Hellenismus. 1969, [3]1988. *Bd. 10.*
– Paulus und Jakobus. Kleine Schriften III. 2002. *Bd. 141.*
– Studien zur Christologie. Kleine Schriften IV. 2006. *Bd. 201.*
– Studien zum Urchristentum. Kleine Schriften VI. 2008. *Bd. 234.*
– und *Anna Maria Schwemer:* Paulus zwischen Damaskus und Antiochien. 1998. *Bd. 108.*
– Der messianische Anspruch Jesu und die Anfänge der Christologie. 2001. *Bd. 138.*
– Die vier Evangelien und das eine Evangelium von Jesus Christus. 2008. *Bd. 224.*
Hengel, Martin und *Ulrich Heckel* (Hrsg.): Paulus und das antike Judentum. 1991. *Bd. 58.*
– und *Hermut Löhr* (Hrsg.): Schriftauslegung im antiken Judentum und im Urchristentum. 1994. *Bd. 73.*
– und *Anna Maria Schwemer* (Hrsg.): Königsherrschaft Gottes und himmlischer Kult. 1991. *Bd. 55.*
– Die Septuaginta. 1994. *Bd. 72.*

–, *Siegfried Mittmann* und *Anna Maria Schwemer* (Hrsg.): La Cité de Dieu / Die Stadt Gottes. 2000. *Bd. 129.*
Hentschel, Anni: Diakonia im Neuen Testament. 2007. *Bd. 226.*
Hernández Jr., Juan: Scribal Habits and Theological Influence in the Apocalypse. 2006. *Bd. II/218.*
Herrenbrück, Fritz: Jesus und die Zöllner. 1990. *Bd. II/41.*
Herzer, Jens: Paulus oder Petrus? 1998. *Bd. 103.*
– siehe *Böttrich, Christfried.*
– siehe *Frey, Jörg.*
Hill, Charles E.: From the Lost Teaching of Polycarp. 2005. *Bd. 186.*
Hoegen-Rohls, Christina: Der nachösterliche Johannes. 1996. *Bd. II/84.*
Hoffmann, Matthias Reinhard: The Destroyer and the Lamb. 2005. *Bd. II/203.*
Hofius, Otfried: Katapausis. 1970. *Bd. 11.*
– Der Vorhang vor dem Thron Gottes. 1972. *Bd. 14.*
– Der Christushymnus Philipper 2,6–11. 1976, [2]1991. *Bd. 17.*
– Paulusstudien. 1989, [2]1994. *Bd. 51.*
– Neutestamentliche Studien. 2000. *Bd. 132.*
– Paulusstudien II. 2002. *Bd. 143.*
– Exegetische Studien. 2008. *Bd. 223.*
– und *Hans-Christian Kammler:* Johannesstudien. 1996. *Bd. 88.*
Holloway, Paul A.: Coping with Prejudice. 2009. *Bd. 244.*
Holmberg, Bengt (Hrsg.): Exploring Early Christian Identity. 2008. *Bd. 226.*
– und *Mikael Winninge* (Hrsg.): Identity Formation in the New Testament. 2008. *Bd. 227.*
Holtz, Traugott: Geschichte und Theologie des Urchristentums. 1991. *Bd. 57.*
Hommel, Hildebrecht: Sebasmata.
Bd. 1 1983. *Bd. 31.*
Bd. 2 1984. *Bd. 32.*
Horbury, William: Herodian Judaism and New Testament Study. 2006. *Bd. 193.*
Horn, Friedrich Wilhelm und *Ruben Zimmermann* (Hrsg): Jenseits von Indikativ und Imperativ. Bd. 1. 2009. *Bd. 238.*
Horst, Pieter W. van der: Jews and Christians in Their Graeco-Roman Context. 2006. *Bd. 196.*
Hultgård, Anders und *Stig Norin* (Hrsg): Le Jour de Dieu / Der Tag Gottes. 2009. *Bd. 245.*
Jackson, Ryan: New Creation in Paul's Letters. 2009. *Bd. II/272.*
Hvalvik, Reidar: The Struggle for Scripture and Covenant. 1996. *Bd. II/82.*
Janßen Martina: siehe *Frey, Jörg.*
Jauhiainen, Marko: The Use of Zechariah in Revelation. 2005. *Bd. II/199.*
Jensen, Morten H.: Herod Antipas in Galilee. 2006. *Bd. II/215.*
Johns, Loren L.: The Lamb Christology of the Apocalypse of John. 2003. *Bd. II/167.*
Jossa, Giorgio: Jews or Christians? 2006. *Bd. 202.*
Joubert, Stephan: Paul as Benefactor. 2000. *Bd. II/124.*
Judge, E. A.: The First Christians in the Roman World. 2008. *Bd. 229.*
Jungbauer, Harry: „Ehre Vater und Mutter". 2002. *Bd. II/146.*
Kähler, Christoph: Jesu Gleichnisse als Poesie und Therapie. 1995. *Bd. 78.*
Kamlah, Ehrhard: Die Form der katalogischen Paränese im Neuen Testament. 1964. *Bd. 7.*
Kammler, Hans-Christian: Christologie und Eschatologie. 2000. *Bd. 126.*
– Kreuz und Weisheit. 2003. *Bd. 159.*
– siehe *Hofius, Otfried.*
Karakolis, Christos: siehe *Alexeev, Anatoly A.*
Karrer, Martin und *Wolfgang Kraus* (Hrsg.): Die Septuaginta – Texte, Kontexte, Lebenswelten. 2008. *Band 219.*
Kelhoffer, James A.: The Diet of John the Baptist. 2005. *Bd. 176.*
– Miracle and Mission. 1999. *Bd. II/112.*
Kelley, Nicole: Knowledge and Religious Authority in the Pseudo-Clementines. 2006. *Bd. II/213.*
Kennedy, Joel: The Recapitulation of Israel. 2008. *Bd. II/257.*
Kieffer, René und *Jan Bergman* (Hrsg.): La Main de Dieu / Die Hand Gottes. 1997. *Bd. 94.*
Kierspel, Lars: The Jews and the World in the Fourth Gospel. 2006. *Bd. 220.*
Kim, Seyoon: The Origin of Paul's Gospel. 1981, [2]1984. *Bd. II/4.*
– Paul and the New Perspective. 2002. *Bd. 140.*
– "The 'Son of Man'" as the Son of God. 1983. *Bd. 30.*
Klauck, Hans-Josef: Religion und Gesellschaft im frühen Christentum. 2003. *Bd. 152.*
Klein, Hans: siehe *Dunn, James D.G.*
Kleinknecht, Karl Th.: Der leidende Gerechtfertigte. 1984, [2]1988. *Bd. II/13.*
Klinghardt, Matthias: Gesetz und Volk Gottes. 1988. *Bd. II/32.*
Kloppenborg, John S.: The Tenants in the Vineyard. 2006. *Bd. 195.*
Koch, Michael: Drachenkampf und Sonnenfrau. 2004. *Bd. II/184.*
Koch, Stefan: Rechtliche Regelung von Konflikten im frühen Christentum. 2004. *Bd. II/174.*

Köhler, Wolf-Dietrich: Rezeption des Matthäusevangeliums in der Zeit vor Irenäus. 1987. *Bd. II/24.*
Köhn, Andreas: Der Neutestamentler Ernst Lohmeyer. 2004. *Bd. II/180.*
Koester, Craig und *Reimund Bieringer* (Hrsg.): The Resurrection of Jesus in the Gospel of John. 2008. *Bd. 222.*
Konradt, Matthias: Israel, Kirche und die Völker im Matthäusevangelium. 2007. *Bd. 215.*
Kooten, George H. van: Cosmic Christology in Paul and the Pauline School. 2003. *Bd. II/171.*
– Paul's Anthropology in Context. 2008. *Bd. 232.*
Korn, Manfred: Die Geschichte Jesu in veränderter Zeit. 1993. *Bd. II/51.*
Koskenniemi, Erkki: Apollonios von Tyana in der neutestamentlichen Exegese. 1994. *Bd. II/61.*
– The Old Testament Miracle-Workers in Early Judaism. 2005. *Bd. II/206.*
Kraus, Thomas J.: Sprache, Stil und historischer Ort des zweiten Petrusbriefes. 2001. *Bd. II/136.*
Kraus, Wolfgang: Das Volk Gottes. 1996. *Bd. 85.*
– siehe *Karrer, Martin.*
– siehe *Walter, Nikolaus.*
– und *Karl-Wilhelm Niebuhr* (Hrsg.): Frühjudentum und Neues Testament im Horizont Biblischer Theologie. 2003. *Bd. 162.*
Krauter, Stefan: Studien zu Röm 13,1–7. 2009. *Bd. 243.*
– siehe *Frey, Jörg.*
Kreplin, Matthias: Das Selbstverständnis Jesu. 2001. *Bd. II/141.*
Kuhn, Karl G.: Achtzehngebet und Vaterunser und der Reim. 1950. *Bd. 1.*
Kvalbein, Hans: siehe *Ådna, Jostein.*
Kwon, Yon-Gyong: Eschatology in Galatians. 2004. *Bd. II/183.*
Laansma, Jon: I Will Give You Rest. 1997. *Bd. II/98.*
Labahn, Michael: Offenbarung in Zeichen und Wort. 2000. *Bd. II/117.*
Lambers-Petry, Doris: siehe *Tomson, Peter J.*
Lange, Armin: siehe *Ego, Beate.*
Lampe, Peter: Die stadtrömischen Christen in den ersten beiden Jahrhunderten. 1987, [2]1989. *Bd. II/18.*
Landmesser, Christof: Wahrheit als Grundbegriff neutestamentlicher Wissenschaft. 1999. *Bd. 113.*
– Jüngerberufung und Zuwendung zu Gott. 2000. *Bd. 133.*
Lau, Andrew: Manifest in Flesh. 1996. *Bd. II/86.*
Lawrence, Louise: An Ethnography of the Gospel of Matthew. 2003. *Bd. II/165.*
Lee, Aquila H.I.: From Messiah to Preexistent Son. 2005. *Bd. II/192.*
Lee, Pilchan: The New Jerusalem in the Book of Relevation. 2000. *Bd. II/129.*
Lee, Simon S.: Jesus' Transfiguration and the Believers' Transformation. 2009. *Bd. II/265.*
Lichtenberger, Hermann: Das Ich Adams und das Ich der Menschheit. 2004. *Bd. 164.*
– siehe *Avemarie, Friedrich.*
– siehe *Frey, Jörg.*
Lierman, John: The New Testament Moses. 2004. *Bd. II/173.*
– (Hrsg.): Challenging Perspectives on the Gospel of John. 2006. *Bd. II/219.*
Lieu, Samuel N.C.: Manichaeism in the Later Roman Empire and Medieval China. [2]1992. *Bd. 63.*
Lindemann, Andreas: Die Evangelien und die Apostelgeschichte. 2009. *Bd. 241.*
Lindgård, Fredrik: Paul's Line of Thought in 2 Corinthians 4:16-5:10. 2004. *Bd. II/189.*
Loader, William R.G.: Jesus' Attitude Towards the Law. 1997. *Bd. II/97.*
Löhr, Gebhard: Verherrlichung Gottes durch Philosophie. 1997. *Bd. 97.*
Löhr, Hermut: Studien zum frühchristlichen und frühjüdischen Gebet. 2003. *Bd. 160.*
– siehe *Hengel, Martin.*
Löhr, Winrich Alfried: Basilides und seine Schule. 1995. *Bd. 83.*
Lorenzen, Stefanie: Das paulinische Eikon-Konzept. 2008. *Bd. II/250.*
Luomanen, Petri: Entering the Kingdom of Heaven. 1998. *Bd. II/101.*
Luz, Ulrich: siehe *Alexeev, Anatoly A.*
– siehe *Dunn, James D.G.*
Mackay, Ian D.: John's Raltionship with Mark. 2004. *Bd. II/182.*
Mackie, Scott D.: Eschatology and Exhortation in the Epistle to the Hebrews. 2006. *Bd. II/223.*
Magda, Ksenija: Paul's Territoriality and Mission Strategy. 2009. *Bd. II/266.*
Maier, Gerhard: Mensch und freier Wille. 1971. *Bd. 12.*
– Die Johannesoffenbarung und die Kirche. 1981. *Bd. 25.*
Markschies, Christoph: Valentinus Gnosticus? 1992. *Bd. 65.*
Marshall, Jonathan: Jesus, Patrons, and Benefactors. 2009. *Bd. II/259.*
Marshall, Peter: Enmity in Corinth: Social Conventions in Paul's Relations with the Corinthians. 1987. *Bd. II/23.*
Martin, Dale B.: siehe *Zangenberg, Jürgen.*
Mayer, Annemarie: Sprache der Einheit im Epheserbrief und in der Ökumene. 2002. *Bd. II/150.*
Mayordomo, Moisés: Argumentiert Paulus logisch? 2005. *Bd. 188.*

McDonough, Sean M.: YHWH at Patmos: Rev. 1:4 in its Hellenistic and Early Jewish Setting. 1999. *Bd. II/107.*
McDowell, Markus: Prayers of Jewish Women. 2006. *Bd. II/211.*
McGlynn, Moyna: Divine Judgement and Divine Benevolence in the Book of Wisdom. 2001. *Bd. II/139.*
Meade, David G.: Pseudonymity and Canon. 1986. *Bd. 39.*
Meadors, Edward P.: Jesus the Messianic Herald of Salvation. 1995. *Bd. II/72.*
Meißner, Stefan: Die Heimholung des Ketzers. 1996. *Bd. II/87.*
Mell, Ulrich: Die „anderen“ Winzer. 1994. *Bd. 77.*
– siehe *Sänger, Dieter.*
Mengel, Berthold: Studien zum Philipperbrief. 1982. *Bd. II/8.*
Merkel, Helmut: Die Widersprüche zwischen den Evangelien. 1971. *Bd. 13.*
– siehe *Ego, Beate.*
Merklein, Helmut: Studien zu Jesus und Paulus. Bd. 1 1987. *Bd. 43.* – Bd. 2 1998. *Bd. 105.*
Merkt, Andreas: siehe *Nicklas, Tobias*
Metzdorf, Christina: Die Tempelaktion Jesu. 2003. *Bd. II/168.*
Metzler, Karin: Der griechische Begriff des Verzeihens. 1991. *Bd. II/44.*
Metzner, Rainer: Die Rezeption des Matthäusevangeliums im 1. Petrusbrief. 1995. *Bd. II/74.*
– Das Verständnis der Sünde im Johannesevangelium. 2000. *Bd. 122.*
Mihoc, Vasile: siehe *Dunn, James D.G.*.
Mineshige, Kiyoshi: Besitzverzicht und Almosen bei Lukas. 2003. *Bd. II/163.*
Mittmann, Siegfried: siehe *Hengel, Martin.*
Mittmann-Richert, Ulrike: Magnifikat und Benediktus. *1996. Bd. II/90.*
– Der Sühnetod des Gottesknechts. 2008. *Bd. 220.*
Miura, Yuzuru: David in Luke-Acts. 2007. *Bd. II/232.*
Mournet, Terence C.: Oral Tradition and Literary Dependency. 2005. *Bd. II/195.*
Mußner, Franz: Jesus von Nazareth im Umfeld Israels und der Urkirche. Hrsg. von M. Theobald. 1998. *Bd. 111.*
Mutschler, Bernhard: Das Corpus Johanneum bei Irenäus von Lyon. 2005. *Bd. 189.*
Nguyen, V. Henry T.: Christian Identity in Corinth. 2008. *Bd. II/243.*
Nicklas, Tobias, Andreas Merkt und *Joseph Verheyden* (Hrsg.): Gelitten – Gestorben – Auferstanden. 2010. *Bd. II/273.*
Niebuhr, Karl-Wilhelm: Gesetz und Paränese. 1987. *Bd. II/28.*
– Heidenapostel aus Israel. 1992. *Bd. 62.*
– siehe *Deines, Roland*
– siehe *Dimitrov, Ivan Z.*
– siehe *Kraus, Wolfgang*
Nielsen, Anders E.: "Until it is Fullfilled". 2000. *Bd. II/126.*
Nielsen, Jesper Tang: Die kognitive Dimension des Kreuzes. 2009. *Bd. II/263.*
Nissen, Andreas: Gott und der Nächste im antiken Judentum. 1974. *Bd. 15.*
Noack, Christian: Gottesbewußtsein. 2000. *Bd. II/116.*
Noormann, Rolf: Irenäus als Paulusinterpret. 1994. *Bd. II/66.*
Novakovic, Lidija: Messiah, the Healer of the Sick. 2003. *Bd. II/170.*
Obermann, Andreas: Die christologische Erfüllung der Schrift im Johannesevangelium. 1996. *Bd. II/83.*
Öhler, Markus: Barnabas. 2003. *Bd. 156.*
– siehe *Becker, Michael.*
Okure, Teresa: The Johannine Approach to Mission. 1988. *Bd. II/31.*
Onuki, Takashi: Heil und Erlösung. 2004. *Bd. 165.*
Oropeza, B. J.: Paul and Apostasy. 2000. *Bd. II/115.*
Ostmeyer, Karl-Heinrich: Kommunikation mit Gott und Christus. 2006. *Bd. 197.*
– Taufe und Typos. 2000. *Bd. II/118.*
Paulsen, Henning: Studien zur Literatur und Geschichte des frühen Christentums. Hrsg. von Ute E. Eisen. 1997. *Bd. 99.*
Pao, David W.: Acts and the Isaianic New Exodus. 2000. *Bd. II/130.*
Park, Eung Chun: The Mission Discourse in Matthew's Interpretation. 1995. *Bd. II/81.*
Park, Joseph S.: Conceptions of Afterlife in Jewish Insriptions. 2000. *Bd. II/121.*
Pate, C. Marvin: The Reverse of the Curse. 2000. *Bd. II/114.*
Pearce, Sarah J.K.: The Land of the Body. 2007. *Bd. 208.*
Peres, Imre: Griechische Grabinschriften und neutestamentliche Eschatologie. 2003. *Bd. 157.*
Perry, Peter S.: The Rhetoric of Digressions. 2009. *Bd. II/268.*
Philip, Finny: The Origins of Pauline Pneumatology. 2005. *Bd. II/194.*
Philonenko, Marc (Hrsg.): Le Trône de Dieu. 1993. *Bd. 69.*
Pilhofer, Peter: Presbyteron Kreitton. 1990. *Bd. II/39.*
– Philippi. Bd. 1 1995. *Bd. 87.* – Bd. 2 [2]2009. *Bd. 119.*
– Die frühen Christen und ihre Welt. 2002. *Bd. 145.*
– siehe *Becker, Eve-Marie.*
– siehe *Ego, Beate.*
Pitre, Brant: Jesus, the Tribulation, and the End of the Exile. 2005. *Bd. II/204.*

Plümacher, Eckhard: Geschichte und Geschichten. 2004. *Bd. 170.*
Pöhlmann, Wolfgang: Der Verlorene Sohn und das Haus. 1993. *Bd. 68.*
Pokorný, Petr und *Josef B. Souček:* Bibelauslegung als Theologie. 1997. *Bd. 100.*
Pokorný, Petr und *Jan Roskovec* (Hrsg.): Philosophical Hermeneutics and Biblical Exegesis. 2002. *Bd. 153.*
Popkes, Enno Edzard: Das Menschenbild des Thomasevangeliums. 2007. *Band 206.*
– Die Theologie der Liebe Gottes in den johanneischen Schriften. 2005. *Bd. II/197.*
Porter, Stanley E.: The Paul of Acts. 1999. *Bd. 115.*
Prieur, Alexander: Die Verkündigung der Gottesherrschaft. 1996. *Bd. II/89.*
Probst, Hermann: Paulus und der Brief. 1991. *Bd. II/45.*
Räisänen, Heikki: Paul and the Law. 1983, [2]1987. *Bd. 29.*
Rehkopf, Friedrich: Die lukanische Sonderquelle. 1959. *Bd. 5.*
Rein, Matthias: Die Heilung des Blindgeborenen (Joh 9). 1995. *Bd. II/73.*
Reinmuth, Eckart: Pseudo-Philo und Lukas. 1994. *Bd. 74.*
Reiser, Marius: Bibelkritik und Auslegung der Heiligen Schrift. 2007. *Bd. 217.*
– Syntax und Stil des Markusevangeliums. 1984. *Bd. II/11.*
Reynolds, Benjamin E.: The Apocalyptic Son of Man in the Gospel of John. 2008. *Bd. II/249.*
Rhodes, James N.: The Epistle of Barnabas and the Deuteronomic Tradition. 2004. *Bd. II/188.*
Richards, E. Randolph: The Secretary in the Letters of Paul. 1991. *Bd. II/42.*
Riesner, Rainer: Jesus als Lehrer. 1981, [3]1988. *Bd. II/7.*
– Die Frühzeit des Apostels Paulus. 1994. *Bd. 71.*
Rissi, Mathias: Die Theologie des Hebräerbriefs. 1987. *Bd. 41.*
Röcker, Fritz W.: Belial und Katechon. 2009. *Bd. II/262.*
Röhser, Günter: Metaphorik und Personifikation der Sünde. 1987. *Bd. II/25.*
Rose, Christian: Theologie als Erzählung im Markusevangelium. 2007. *Bd. II/236.*
– Die Wolke der Zeugen. 1994. *Bd. II/60.*
Roskovec, Jan: siehe *Pokorný, Petr.*
Rothschild, Clare K.: Baptist Traditions and Q. 2005. *Bd. 190.*
– Hebrews as Pseudepigraphon. 2009. *Band 235.*
– Luke Acts and the Rhetoric of History. 2004. *Bd. II/175.*
– siehe *Frey, Jörg.*
Rüegger, Hans-Ulrich: Verstehen, was Markus erzählt. 2002. *Bd. II/155.*
Rüger, Hans Peter: Die Weisheitsschrift aus der Kairoer Geniza. 1991. *Bd. 53.*
Sänger, Dieter: Antikes Judentum und die Mysterien. 1980. *Bd. II/5.*
– Die Verkündigung des Gekreuzigten und Israel. 1994. *Bd. 75.*
– siehe *Burchard, Christoph.*
– und *Ulrich Mell* (Hrsg.): Paulus und Johannes. 2006. *Bd. 198.*
Salier, Willis Hedley: The Rhetorical Impact of the Se-meia in the Gospel of John. 2004. *Bd. II/186.*
Salzmann, Jorg Christian: Lehren und Ermahnen. 1994. *Bd. II/59.*
Sandnes, Karl Olav: Paul – One of the Prophets? 1991. *Bd. II/43.*
Sato, Migaku: Q und Prophetie. 1988. *Bd. II/29.*
Schäfer, Ruth: Paulus bis zum Apostelkonzil. 2004. *Bd. II/179.*
Schaper, Joachim: Eschatology in the Greek Psalter. 1995. *Bd. II/76.*
Schimanowski, Gottfried: Die himmlische Liturgie in der Apokalypse des Johannes. 2002. *Bd. II/154.*
– Weisheit und Messias. 1985. *Bd. II/17.*
Schlichting, Günter: Ein jüdisches Leben Jesu. 1982. *Bd. 24.*
Schließer, Benjamin: Abraham's Faith in Romans 4. 2007. *Band II/224.*
Schnabel, Eckhard J.: Law and Wisdom from Ben Sira to Paul. 1985. *Bd. II/16.*
Schnelle, Udo: siehe *Frey, Jörg.*
Schröter, Jens: Von Jesus zum Neuen Testament. 2007. *Band 204.*
– siehe *Frey, Jörg.*
Schutter, William L.: Hermeneutic and Composition in I Peter. 1989. *Bd. II/30.*
Schwartz, Daniel R.: Studies in the Jewish Background of Christianity. 1992. *Bd. 60.*
Schwemer, Anna Maria: siehe *Hengel, Martin*
Schwindt, Rainer: Das Weltbild des Epheserbriefes. 2002. *Bd. 148.*
Scott, Ian W.: Implicit Epistemology in the Letters of Paul. 2005. *Bd. II/*205.
Scott, James M.: Adoption as Sons of God. 1992. *Bd. II/48.*
– Paul and the Nations. 1995. *Bd. 84.*
Shi, Wenhua: Paul's Message of the Cross as Body Language. 2008. *Bd. II/254.*
Shum, Shiu-Lun: Paul's Use of Isaiah in Romans. 2002. *Bd. II/156.*
Siegert, Folker: Drei hellenistisch-jüdische Predigten. Teil I 1980. *Bd. 20* – Teil II 1992. *Bd. 61.*
– Nag-Hammadi-Register. 1982. *Bd. 26.*
– Argumentation bei Paulus. 1985. *Bd. 34.*
– Philon von Alexandrien. 1988. *Bd. 46.*

Simon, Marcel: Le christianisme antique et son contexte religieux I/II. 1981. *Bd. 23.*
Smit, Peter-Ben: Fellowship and Food in the Kingdom. 2008. *Bd. II/234.*
Snodgrass, Klyne: The Parable of the Wicked Tenants. 1983. *Bd. 27.*
Söding, Thomas: Das Wort vom Kreuz. 1997. *Bd. 93.*
– siehe *Thüsing, Wilhelm.*
Sommer, Urs: Die Passionsgeschichte des Markusevangeliums. 1993. *Bd. II/58.*
Sorensen, Eric: Possession and Exorcism in the New Testament and Early Christianity. 2002. *Band II/157.*
Souček, Josef B.: siehe *Pokorný, Petr.*
Southall, David J.: Rediscovering Righteousness in Romans. 2008. *Bd. 240.*
Spangenberg, Volker: Herrlichkeit des Neuen Bundes. 1993. *Bd. II/55.*
Spanje, T.E. van: Inconsistency in Paul? 1999. *Bd. II/110.*
Speyer, Wolfgang: Frühes Christentum im antiken Strahlungsfeld. Bd. I: 1989. *Bd. 50.*
– Bd. II: 1999. *Bd. 116.*
– Bd. III: 2007. *Bd. 213.*
Spittler, Janet E.: Animals in the Apocryphal Acts of the Apostles. 2008. *Bd. II/247.*
Sprinkle, Preston: Law and Life. 2008. *Bd. II/241.*
Stadelmann, Helge: Ben Sira als Schriftgelehrter. 1980. *Bd. II/6.*
Stein, Hans Joachim: Frühchristliche Mahlfeiern. 2008. *Bd. II/255.*
Stenschke, Christoph W.: Luke's Portrait of Gentiles Prior to Their Coming to Faith. *Bd. II/108.*
Sterck-Degueldre, Jean-Pierre: Eine Frau namens Lydia. 2004. *Bd. II/176.*
Stettler, Christian: Der Kolosserhymnus. 2000. *Bd. II/131.*
Stettler, Hanna: Die Christologie der Pastoralbriefe. 1998. *Bd. II/105.*
Stökl Ben Ezra, Daniel: The Impact of Yom Kippur on Early Christianity. 2003. *Bd. 163.*
Strobel, August: Die Stunde der Wahrheit. 1980. *Bd. 21.*
Stroumsa, Guy G.: Barbarian Philosophy. 1999. *Bd. 112.*
Stuckenbruck, Loren T.: Angel Veneration and Christology. 1995. *Bd. II/70.*
–, *Stephen C. Barton* und *Benjamin G. Wold* (Hrsg.): Memory in the Bible and Antiquity. 2007. *Vol. 212.*
Stuhlmacher, Peter (Hrsg.): Das Evangelium und die Evangelien. 1983. *Bd. 28.*
– Biblische Theologie und Evangelium. 2002. *Bd. 146.*
Sung, Chong-Hyon: Vergebung der Sünden. 1993. *Bd. II/57.*
Svendsen, Stefan N.: Allegory Transformed. 2009. *Bd. II/269*
Tajra, Harry W.: The Trial of St. Paul. 1989. *Bd. II/35.*
– The Martyrdom of St.Paul. 1994. *Bd. II/67.*
Tellbe, Mikael: Christ-Believers in Ephesus. 2009. *Bd. 242.*
Theißen, Gerd: Studien zur Soziologie des Urchristentums. 1979, [3]1989. *Bd. 19.*
Theobald, Michael: Studien zum Römerbrief. 2001. *Bd. 136.*
Theobald, Michael: siehe *Mußner, Franz.*
Thornton, Claus-Jürgen: Der Zeuge des Zeugen. 1991. *Bd. 56.*
Thüsing, Wilhelm: Studien zur neutestamentlichen Theologie. Hrsg. von Thomas Söding. 1995. *Bd. 82.*
Thurén, Lauri: Derhethorizing Paul. 2000. *Bd. 124.*
Thyen, Hartwig: Studien zum Corpus Iohanneum. 2007. *Bd. 214.*
Tibbs, Clint: Religious Experience of the Pneuma. 2007. *Bd. II/230.*
Toit, David S. du: Theios Anthropos. 1997. *Bd. II/91.*
Tomson, Peter J. und *Doris Lambers-Petry* (Hrsg.): The Image of the Judaeo-Christians in Ancient Jewish and Christian Literature. 2003. *Bd. 158.*
Tolmie, D. Francois: Persuading the Galatians. 2005. *Bd. II/190.*
Toney, Carl N.: Paul's Inclusive Ethic. 2008. *Bd. II/252.*
Trebilco, Paul: The Early Christians in Ephesus from Paul to Ignatius. 2004. *Bd. 166.*
Treloar, Geoffrey R.: Lightfoot the Historian. 1998. *Bd. II/103.*
Tsuji, Manabu: Glaube zwischen Vollkommenheit und Verweltlichung. 1997. *Bd. II/93*
Twelftree, Graham H.: Jesus the Exorcist. 1993. *Bd. II/54.*
Ulrichs, Karl Friedrich: Christusglaube. 2007. *Bd. II/227.*
Urban, Christina: Das Menschenbild nach dem Johannesevangelium. 2001. *Bd. II/137.*
Vahrenhorst, Martin: Kultische Sprache in den Paulusbriefen. 2008. *Bd. 230.*
Vegge, Ivar: 2 Corinthians – a Letter about Reconciliation. 2008. *Bd. II/239.*
Verheyden, Josef: siehe *Nicklas, Tobias*
Visotzky, Burton L.: Fathers of the World. 1995. *Bd. 80.*
Vollenweider, Samuel: Horizonte neutestamentlicher Christologie. 2002. *Bd. 144.*
Vos, Johan S.: Die Kunst der Argumentation bei Paulus. 2002. *Bd. 149.*
Waaler, Erik: The *Shema* and The First Commandment in First Corinthians. 2008. *Bd. II/253.*

Wagener, Ulrike: Die Ordnung des „Hauses Gottes". 1994. *Bd. II/65.*
Wahlen, Clinton: Jesus and the Impurity of Spirits in the Synoptic Gospels. 2004. *Bd. II/185.*
Walker, Donald D.: Paul's Offer of Leniency (2 Cor 10:1). 2002. *Bd. II/152.*
Walter, Nikolaus: Praeparatio Evangelica. Hrsg. von Wolfgang Kraus und Florian Wilk. 1997. *Bd. 98.*
Wander, Bernd: Gottesfürchtige und Sympathisanten. 1998. *Bd. 104.*
Wasserman, Emma: The Death of the Soul in Romans 7. 2008. *Bd. 256.*
Waters, Guy: The End of Deuteronomy in the Epistles of Paul. 2006. *Bd. 221.*
Watt, Jan G. van der: siehe *Frey, Jörg.*
Watts, Rikki: Isaiah's New Exodus and Mark. 1997. *Bd. II/88.*
Wedderburn, A.J.M.: Baptism and Resurrection. 1987. *Bd. 44.*
Wegner, Uwe: Der Hauptmann von Kafarnaum. 1985. *Bd. II/14.*
Weiß, Hans-Friedrich: Frühes Christentum und Gnosis. 2008. *Bd. 225.*
Weissenrieder, Annette: Images of Illness in the Gospel of Luke. 2003. *Bd. II/164.*
–, *Friederike Wendt* und *Petra von Gemünden* (Hrsg.): Picturing the New Testament. 2005. *Bd. II/193.*
Welck, Christian: Erzählte ‚Zeichen'. 1994. *Bd. II/69.*
Wendt, Friederike (Hrsg.): siehe *Weissenrieder, Annette.*
Wiarda, Timothy: Peter in the Gospels. 2000. *Bd. II/127.*
Wifstrand, Albert: Epochs and Styles. 2005. *Bd. 179.*
Wilk, Florian: siehe *Walter, Nikolaus.*
Williams, Catrin H.: I am He. 2000. *Bd. II/113.*
Winninge, Mikael: siehe *Holmberg, Bengt.*
Wilson, Todd A.: The Curse of the Law and the Crisis in Galatia. 2007. *Bd. II/225.*
Wilson, Walter T.: Love without Pretense. 1991. *Bd. II/46.*
Winn, Adam: The Purpose of Mark's Gospel. 2008. *Bd. II/245.*
Wischmeyer, Oda: Von Ben Sira zu Paulus. 2004. *Bd. 173.*
Wisdom, Jeffrey: Blessing for the Nations and the Curse of the Law. 2001. *Bd. II/133.*
Witmer, Stephen E.: Divine Instruction in Early Christianity. 2008. *Bd. II/246.*
Wold, Benjamin G.: Women, Men, and Angels. 2005. *Bd. II/2001.*
– siehe *Stuckenbruck, Loren T.*
Wolter, Michael: Theologie und Ethos im frühen Christentum. 2009. *Band 236.*
Wright, Archie T.: The Origin of Evil Spirits. 2005. *Bd. II/198.*
Wucherpfennig, Ansgar: Heracleon Philologus. 2002. *Bd. 142.*
Yates, John W.: The Spirit and Creation in Paul. 2008. *Vol. II/251.*
Yeung, Maureen: Faith in Jesus and Paul. 2002. *Bd. II/147.*
Zangenberg, Jürgen, Harold W. Attridge und *Dale B. Martin* (Hrsg.): Religion, Ethnicity and Identity in Ancient Galilee. 2007. *Bd. 210.*
Zimmermann, Alfred E.: Die urchristlichen Lehrer. 1984, ^{2}1988. *Bd. II/12.*
Zimmermann, Johannes: Messianische Texte aus Qumran. 1998. *Bd. II/104.*
Zimmermann, Ruben: Christologie der Bilder im Johannesevangelium. 2004. *Bd. 171.*
– Geschlechtermetaphorik und Gottesverhältnis. 2001. *Bd. II/122.*
– (Hrsg.): Hermeneutik der Gleichnisse Jesu. 2008. *Bd. 231.*
– siehe *Frey, Jörg.*
– siehe *Horn, Friedrich Wilhelm.*
Zugmann, Michael: „Hellenisten" in der Apostelgeschichte. 2009. *Bd. II/264.*
Zumstein, Jean: siehe *Dettwiler, Andreas*
Zwiep, Arie W.: Judas and the Choice of Matthias. 2004. *Bd. II/187.*